MATERIAL DREAMS

AMERICANS AND THE CALIFORNIA DREAM

Americans and the California Dream, 1850–1915

Inventing the Dream
California Through the Progressive Era

Material Dreams
Southern California Through the 1920s

MATERIAL DREAMS

Southern California Through the 1920s

KEVIN STARR

New York   Oxford
OXFORD UNIVERSITY PRESS
1990

Oxford University Press

Oxford   New York   Toronto
Delhi   Bombay   Calcutta   Madras   Karachi
Petaling Jaya   Singapore   Hong Kong   Tokyo
Nairobi   Dar es Salaam   Cape Town
Melbourne   Auckland

and associated companies in
Berlin   Ibadan

Copyright © 1990 by Kevin Starr

Published by Oxford University Press, Inc.,
200 Madison Avenue, New York, New York 10016

Oxford is a registered trademark of Oxford University Press

Library of Congress Cataloging-in-Publication Data
Starr, Kevin.
Material dreams : Southern California through the 1920s /
Kevin Starr.
p.   cm.   Bibliography: p.   ISBN 0–19–504487-8
1. California, Southern—History.
2. Los Angeles (Calif.)—History.
I. Title.
F867.S82   1990 979.4'9—dc20   89-16122   CIP

2 4 6 8 9 7 5 3 1
Printed in the United States of America
on acid-free paper

For Dorothea and John Stein

Preface

In the first volume of this series, *Americans and the California Dream, 1850–1915*, I set myself the task of suggesting certain aspects of the moral and imaginative drama of California in the nineteenth and the early twentieth century. In the second volume, *Inventing the Dream: California Through the Progressive Era*, I returned to the nineteenth century in order to set forth the related but distinct story of the rise of Southern California into the early 1920s. In each of these volumes I was concerned with the process whereby California was encountered and settled in imagination and symbol as well as social fact. From this perspective California emerges as a fascinating colony of nineteenth- and early twentieth-century America—just as it is today an equally intriguing colony of the planet. In *Material Dreams: California Through the 1920s*, I am focusing on the making of Southern California, its design and material construction in the early and mid-twentieth century, with special reference to the visions and metaphors underlying such a process. This is a book about design, construction, and identity, whether in aqueducts, architecture, gardens, city-plans, transportation systems, hotels, studio sets, symphony orchestras, or hydroelectric grids. I am concerned with the process through which Americans in Southern California materialized or acted out in material forms their individual and collective aspirations. The result of such materialization was the physical fabric of Southern California.. Since matter is a form of energy, the fabrications thus achieved pulsate with suggestions for their own interpretation. One can follow the process of materialization forward from vision or metaphor to physical fact or decode a physical object backwards to its originating metaphor. In each case, my emphasis remains on the social and symbolic context of the dreams which were materialized.

As with *Inventing the Dream*, this installment in the *Americans and the*

California Dream series returns to the nineteenth century when it becomes necessary and moves forward into the twentieth century in a crabwise fashion. The emphasis upon the Southern California story also continues, for this region experienced the most dramatic growth, hence the most fabrication, during this era. Although the narrative of *Material Dreams* enters the 1930s, it does not deal with the Great Depression at any length as a social or political event. That important story is reserved for the forthcoming *The Dream Endures: California Through the Great Depression*, the fourth installment in the *Americans and the California Dream* series. *Material Dreams*, rather, deals with developments which have their origins in the boom times before the crash of October 1929. It is a story energized by exuberance, prosperity, growth, and heightened prospects in the creation of California.

Material Dreams begins with a consideration of the water engineering proposals through which the increasingly sub/urban society of twentieth-century Southern California was first envisioned, then made possible. The enthusiastic embracing of this sub/urban identity by Los Angeles and its equally deliberate rejection by Santa Barbara offer case studies of how two contrasting visions of Southern California, nineteenth- and twentieth-century in inspiration, continued to compete as formulas. Having sketched out the story of these foundations in water, the narrative proceeds to examine various aspects of life in the premier hydropolis of the Southland, Los Angeles. The rise of the City of the Angels constitutes a strong secondary theme in this narrative. Nearly every chapter is concerned in one way or another with this very important American city. In many cases the terms Los Angeles, greater Los Angeles, the Southland, or even Southern California are used with an interchangeability I found impossible to avoid, so dominant was Los Angeles in the developments of this era.

The underlying theme in my treatment of Los Angeles is its deliberately fashioned identity in this era as an Anglo-American colony on the Pacific Rim. Although the Los Angeles of today is a polyglot, polycultural world city, its controlling oligarchy in the early twentieth century had an entirely different outcome in mind. It considered Los Angeles the latest and most promising English-speaking city on the planet and placed special emphasis on its Anglo-American heritage. While this attitude represented a legitimate assertion of Anglo-American identity, it also possessed its repressive, even sinister aspects. In the long run, however, the other peoples of Los Angeles and Southern California refused to be colonized. Even as the Anglo-American ideology reigned triumphant, other peoples and other points of view destined to assert themselves powerfully in the postwar period were gathering numbers and strength.

Part Three of *Material Dreams* deals with history and the employment of historical myths and identities. With their region growing so rapidly, Southern Californians of this period used history as an arsenal of ready-made metaphors for self-definition. These metaphors filtered into design and they guided the emergence of cultural institutions as well. In the case of Santa Barbara, an entire city was constructed around a historical myth. Bohemia and the literary life, finally, conceived broadly over a range of activities—reading, writing, book selling and collecting—occupy the fourth portion of the narrative. Eagerly, Southern Californians sought to boost themselves into traditional print culture with the same headlong exuberance with which they had appropriated water and spread a sub/urban megalopolis across the Los Angeles plain. Much has been written regarding the expatriate Hollywood literary culture of Southern California in this period, American, British, and European. Part Four, however, seeks to suggest the indigenous aspects of literary life and local literary institutions, focusing on them primarily in terms of psychological and social experience.

Again, as in the case of two previous installments in the *Americans and the California Dream* series, *Material Dreams* focuses frequently upon individual Californians as they came into creative response to the social challenges and possibilities of their era. Artist, architect, engineer, entrepreneur—each pursued his or her calling on its own terms as work to be done in the world. At the same time these projects also offered opportunities for the externalization of internal visions and the fulfillment of psychological needs. Because such needs and dreams were acted upon, private experience shaped the social and material environment; hence the drama of inner life constituted an energy source along with socio-economic factors for the materialization of Southern California. It is perhaps quixotic to pursue the notion that men and women as individuals can make history along with the masses and their accompanying data bases. To assert this, however, is not to deny the shaping realities of all the other explanations historians are so willing to give these days for individual and social conduct. It is, rather, to assert the parallel truth that individuals also make history.

The Bibliographical Essay suggests that I have made every effort to decode and present the symbolic drama of social experience with extensive dependence upon and reference to the facts and interpretations established by others. Frequently another scholar has been there before me, as is not surprising amidst such a profusion of topics and personalities, and I had only to read, write, and cite with gratitude. In the case of water, for instance, the story has already been extensively told by the authors whom I cite in my bibliographical essay. And yet, it was necessary for me to re-present and reinterpret certain aspects of the water epic which are applicable to my larger theme of dreams and their materialization. A general reader, furthermore, needs to have these foundations of Southern California in water clearly in mind before proceeding to the story of growth through the 1920s. In some cases I wandered into terra incognita, guided personally by survivors of this era such as Oscar Lewis, Ward Ritchie, Lawrence Clark Powell, and the late Jacob Israel Zeitlin. Librarianship, my chosen if interrupted calling, is enamored of order and interconnection amidst variety, of diversity assuming pattern. However much they differed, all these lines of activity, all these individual responses, did manage to converge into the physical design and construction of Southern California in the early twentieth century. As Southern California was being designed and materialized, it was being simultaneously interpreted. As it was being interpreted, it was also being designed and materialized. *Material Dreams* is concerned with each aspect, physical and symbolic, of this epoch of optimistic growth, development, and interpretation on the southern portion of the Pacific shores of the United States.

San Francisco and Los Angeles   K.S.
September 1989

Contents

the Channel City: dreams of monasteries and cathedrals, of Spanish-Yankee dynasties, recovered health and sunny seaside days in Arcadia. At the end of the nineteenth century, wealth staked out Santa Barbara for its own. Along the Channel, especially at Montecito, wealth sought an idyll realized through architecture. The city that took its mission church as a controlling metaphor also became the Newport of the Pacific.

Given the choice, the Santa Barbara oligarchy rejected the big-city option being pursued by Los Angeles. A tightly controlled community, Santa Barbara turned its back on glitter and razzmatazz in favor of aesthetic historicizing and other preoccupations of the genteel tradition. The city became a stage set for Spanish romance. Even within the parameters of its elite circumstances, however, the Santa Barbara alternative, with its persistent strain of naturalism and aesthetic value, sustained a suitable message for the urbanizing Southland.

IV LIFE AND LETTERS IN THE SOUTHLAND

Seeking a vehicle to express their collective belief that they and their city had at long last arrived, the intellectuals of Los Angeles decided upon a magazine called Opinion. In an embarrassingly short time, it folded. There were just too many opinions for a single publication. As briefly as it lasted, Opinion dramatized the presence of an urban intelligentsia in the City of the Angels. Consolidating itself around the bookseller Jake Zeitlin, this intelligentsia explored, expanded, and further defined the aesthetic and imaginative possibilities of its region.

Even as Southern California sent out its aqueduct lifelines, it was also making itself a bibliographical center of national importance. Decades before the emergence of Los Angeles as an art and museum capital, book collecting on an international scale emerged as a powerful local pursuit. Into Southern California poured an array of international library treasures that established the region as a developing center of humanistic research. Book culture ran the gamut from exclusive circles in the oligarchy to raffish bohemias in Hollywood. Fine printing emerged as a strong local art form. New or antiquarian, the book helped a brash but aspiring region orient itself in the direction of humanistic culture.

In the early 1930s a group of young Southern Californians, each of them formed by the spirit of Pasadena, discovered France. Three of them spent important time at the University of Dijon in Burgundy. There they learned how people, places, ideas, food, drink, books, and other things fit together in pattern and memory. Learning this, they became better prepared for their Southern California-based writing careers. The Blue Train through Dijon led back to a better understanding of Southern California.

EPILOGUE

*Thus an inner Southern California externalized itself as dreams were given local habi-
tation and a name. For all such materializations, however, did these Southern California dreams remain airy nothings, or had an American place of significance been achieved?
No sooner had the question presented itself than the Great Depression hit with full force.
The prosperous optimism of the previous decade yielded to a different condition and mood
entirely. Yet the material fabric created in the 1920s persisted and was expanded upon.
Not even the Great Depression could undermine what had been achieved.*

I

FOUNDATIONS
IN WATER

Water lies at the basis of the modern prosperity of California,
and the history of the state is in large part the history of water
development.

WILLIAM L. KAHRL
The California Water Atlas (1979)

1

Prophesying Through Water

Hydraulic Visions and Historical Metaphors

The water engineering projects that created modern Southern California had first to be envisioned before they were planned and built. The envisioning of these projects was in and of itself a bold imaginative act. Working in their special medium, imagined public works, the early water engineers of California were artists and prophets of social and moral development. Prophesying the bringing of water to the desert and to the cities on the plain, they saw themselves embarked upon a work of social redemption Biblical in metaphor and suggestion. Over the course of a century, virtually all these early visions attained the solid reality of public works. Whether in the final outcome they fostered life on the land for the many, as was their original intention, was another matter. Prophets can sense but not control the future.

Water is life, and in its northern reaches the pioneers found California blessed with life abundantly. Extending north and south for 400 miles, the Sierra Nevada seals California off from the arid regions that begin west of the one-hundredth meridian and make the search for water the central obsession of the Far West. Rising to heights of 14,495 feet, the Sierra Nevada captures and holds the winter snow, releasing it in the spring to the plains below. An acre-foot of water fills 43,560 cubic feet. Some 200 million acre-feet fall on California each year as rain or snow. Before the great water projects were constructed, nearly 65 percent of this yearly precipitation was either immediately evaporated by the sun or ran uselessly to the sea. Two-thirds of all precipitation fell in the northern third of the state. Only 11 percent of the rainfall fell south of the Tehachapis. Given the 65 percent loss rate, Southern California was left with a small percent of the state's natural water supply, and even this was endangered by frequent bouts of drought, such as the great drought that began in 1863 and destroyed the cattle economy. There were no major rivers in the

Southland littoral. Those which existed—the Los Angeles, the Santa Ana, the San Diego, the San Luís Rey—were intermittent and untrustworthy as sources.

In terms of human settlement, the essential water problem of Southern California was getting water to where it could be used, for agriculture, industry, or household use. The Spanish Franciscans solved the problem at Mission San Diego de Alcalá, the first European settlement in upper California, by damming the San Diego River at Mission Gorge and bringing water down to the Mission by six miles of tile-lined conduit. Begun in 1773 and completed over a period of years, Old Mission Dam was the first irrigation and domestic water system ever built by Europeans in the Far West. Together with the other water systems subsequently created by the padres for their twenty-one missions extending up the California coast, Old Mission Dam and its tiled aqueduct stood as a precursor to all who saw it of that day when larger and larger water systems would make possible an increasingly diversified and socially complex Southern California.

Sixty miles east of Los Angeles, the Mormons of San Bernardino offered the prophetic paradigm of an irrigation cooperative held together by a common identity. The Mormons arrived at the Rancho San Bernardino in June 1851, sent overland from Salt Lake City by Brigham Young to establish an outpost for the Mormon Church. Young intended the San Bernardino colony as an agricultural supply center for Salt Lake and as a Pacific Coast entrepôt for Mormon migrants from Europe who were scheduled to sail to Southern California from New York, then proceed inland via San Bernardino to Salt Lake. Purchasing eight square leagues from the Lugo family for a promise of $77,500 to be paid by cash earnings from future grain crops, 800 Mormons led by Amasa Lyman and Charles Rich subdivided the property among themselves and got to work. Three thousand acres of grain were immediately planted for harvesting in the spring. Working together, the Mormons dug an open ditch to turn their gristmill. Another ditch system was dug to bring in water from Lytle Creek and the other creeks debouching on the north side of the San Bernardino plain. While the local Native Americans remained hostile, the Mormons gathered each evening in a defensive stockade where each family lived in separate apartments. In 1853 the city of San Bernardino was laid out and home building began in earnest with lumber cut from a sawmill in the nearby mountains. While the Mormons kept their family life separate and private, with each family maintaining its own acreage, they did cooperate with each other on all large-scale projects, especially in maintaining the colony's growing irrigation system. In 1857 a defensive Brigham Young, embattled by the presence of federal troops in Utah dispatched there to enforce the installation of his federally appointed replacement as governor, ordered all outlying Mormon colonists to return to Salt Lake. Out of a population of 2000, all but forty or so Mormon families in San Bernardino complied, selling in 1858 for $18,000 what they had purchased in 1851 for three times that amount and had substantially improved through irrigation. For all the brevity of their sojourn, the Mormons had created the state's first cooperative irrigation colony, bound together by water and religion. With its individual homes and plots, its cooperative roads, mills, and irrigation systems, the Mormon colony of San Bernardino stood as a prophetic type of the good life in Southern California made possible by water.

Appropriately, the leading citizen of San Bernardino in the 1860s, Oliver M. Wozencraft, was California's first important prophet of water. By 1859, a year after the Mormon wagon train had headed back to Utah by way of Cajon Pass, Wozencraft was busy proposing no less than the irrigation of the vast southeastern desert with the waters of the Colorado. A physician by training, Wozencraft had first seen what he described as the "Rhadamanthine region" of the desert Southwest in 1849 while en route from New Orleans to California across the arid Apache country of northern Mexico. It was then that he beheld the Colorado River for the first time, encountering it at its juncture with the Gila near Yuma in southwestern Arizona. Whether there and then or somewhat later, Wozencraft conceived the idea of bringing water from the Colorado by gravity canal westward into the Colorado Desert of southeastern California. An energetic graduate of St. Joseph's College in Bardstown, Kentucky, Wozencraft played an important role in California from the time of his arrival. Settling in Sonora in Tuolumne County in the central Sierra foothills, he was elected a delegate to the first Constitutional Convention meeting later that year in Monterey. When statehood was voted, President Millard Fillmore appointed Wozencraft one of three federal Indian commissioners in California. From 19 March 1851 to 7 January 1852 Wozencraft and his fellow commissioners traveled throughout the interior of California, north and south, meeting with 402 chiefs or head men and concluding eighteen treaties. During this period, as he experienced first-hand the climatological variations of California, from the watery Shasta County in the north where Wozencraft met with the Indians of Reading's Ranch to the parched southern Central Valley where he spent most of his time as commissioner, Wozencraft's irrigation scheme took further hold of his imagination. For the meanwhile he had an even more pressing concern on his mind, a transcontinental railroad. In an oration he delivered on 12 December 1854 at the invitation of the Mechanics' Institute in San Francisco at a mass rally held at Musical Hall—at the time the largest mass meeting ever held in California—Wozencraft extolled the railroad as an agent of civilizing change, the impending transformer of California into a settled, prosperous society linked by culture and rapid travel and communication to the older states of the East. Emphasizing public works as a civilizing agent, Wozencraft called upon the federal government to take an ever more active role in the railroad development of California and the West.

The very next year, 1855, in the fifth volume of the *Pacific Railroad Reports*, Dr. William P. Blake reinforced both of Wozencraft's interests, railroads and the irrigation of the Colorado Desert. Blake had first surveyed the Colorado Desert in 1853 as a staff geologist with the Railroad Survey under the command of Lieutenant R.S. Williamson of the United States Topographical Engineers. The Survey traced out a possible transcontinental rail route through the San Gorgonio Pass. In his report, Blake suggested that the Colorado Desert could be irrigated from the river of the same name. Blake thus predates Wozencraft in print as the first to propose the irrigation of the Colorado Desert with water from the Colorado River. It is part of the prodigality of the *Pacific Railroad Reports* that such a dazzling proposal was made so offhandedly on two pages in the fifth volume. It could very well be that Wozencraft got his idea entirely from Blake or that Blake's suggestion might have given the quasi-official sanction of a government report to Wozencraft's earlier intuition. In any event, Wozencraft continued to devote his energies to both the transcontinental railroad and the irrigation of the Colorado Desert. In 1859 the California legislature voted formal approval of Wozencraft's irrigation proposal. He accompanied railroad visionary Theodore Judah to Washington that year to lobby on behalf of both projects. Judah's scheme for a transcontinental railroad eventually prevailed, although Judah died in 1863, six years before the railroad was completed; but Wozencraft's irrigation proposal languished in the more pressing business of subduing the insurgent South. Moving to San Bernardino, Wozencraft stayed close to his dream physically and psychologically. He became an ardent irrigationist, if only in his imagination. Too intelligent and successful as a physician to degenerate into pamphleteering crankdom as was so often the case with baffled visionaries in the nineteenth century, he nevertheless kept the faith that one day the Southern California portions of the Colorado Desert would bloom and that cities and towns of Southern California would be nurtured by Colorado River water.

2

By the late 1870s a comprehensive water plan encompassing both irrigation and flood control had clearly emerged as a necessity for California. Ever since the 1850s there had been intermittent gestures in the direction of a systematic water policy and program, usually in the form of suggestions from the state surveyor-general or the state geologist briefly mentioned in an annual report. Some of these suggestions attained the half-reality of drafted but abandoned legislation. In 1865 the legislature went so far as to appropriate a small sum to study the feasibility of digging a drainage channel along the western edge of the Sacramento Valley. Not until 1878 did the legislature pass the Drainage Act which created the position of state engineer and appropriated $100,000 for irrigation, drainage, and navigation studies of the Sacramento and San Joaquin rivers.

William Hammond Hall, whom Governor Will Irwin appointed state engineer (the post paid $6,000 a year, the same as a governor's salary), went far beyond this limited mandate. Working patiently over the years, William Hammond Hall imagined the California that was realizable through hydraulic engineering. Like so many prophets, Hall had more than his share of faults. Initially intended for West Point, where he might have studied engineering formally, Hall was forced upon a course of self-education when his plans for the Academy fell through with the outbreak of the Civil War. Although raised in Stockton, Hall was born in Maryland, and out of respect for his mother's ardent Southern sympathies he abandoned his West Point plans in favor of practical training in the field and private study. In 1865 at age 21, after three years in the field as a surveyor's assistant, Hall joined the Board of Military Engineers in San Francisco as a lowly rodman, gradually rising in responsibilities. He next worked for the city surveyor of San Francisco and as a mining engineer in Nevada. By August 1870, the year Hall returned to San Francisco on contract to survey, map, and prepare a comprehensive plan for Golden Gate Park, he had made himself an engineer of first-rate local reputation. Work as a rodman and a leveler throughout California, Oregon, and Nevada, private tutorials, and constant study had been Hall's West Point.

This effort at self-education, this steady rise from unschooled obscurity, left Hall more than a little stiff-necked and defensively arrogant and, with equal defensiveness, more than slightly superior in his dealings with others. Early obscurity had left Hall a little greedy as well, ever on the alert for the money and the career that a lack of formal education had initially denied him. Smallish in stature, a self-centered, defensive, but superior man in a trim beard and well-tailored tweeds, William Hammond Hall could be and often was difficult to work with. He was also a formidable scholar and an engineering visionary. Somehow in the course of his apprenticeship in purely frontier circumstances, William Hammond Hall had assimilated engineering as a mode of high humanistic intent. He had read widely in engineering history, irrigation law, and the comparative study of engineering and public works across differing social structures and had evolved for himself a philosophy of engineering and public works as shaping agents in social development. He had also made himself the wielder of a graceful, virile late Victorian prose style, compact and informative, with a suggestion of moral force in even the most instrumental of his sentences.

For five years, until his resignation in 1876 to go into private practice, Hall served as engineer and superintendent of Golden Gate Park. A disciple of the English park theorist Charles Sprague Sergeant and the American landscape architect Frederick Law Olmsted, creator of Central Park in New York City, Hall guided San Francisco's developing park towards the romantic English rustic ideal Sergeant and Olmsted each advocated. Hall envisioned Golden Gate Park as a romantic woodland in total contrast to its surrounding urban environment. All landscaping and planting was keyed to recreate natural environments; even park furnishings—benches, picnic shelters, refreshment sheds, toilets—were kept as rustic as possible. And yet Golden Gate Park, a thousand acres of irrigated woodland set artificially on previously bare and shifting sand dunes, was purely the creation of engineering art.

Golden Gate Park afforded Hall the opportunity to envision, if not to complete, a micro-California garden shaped by imaginative ideals and enacted through water engineering. The park theory and practice Hall absorbed from Sergeant, Olmsted, and the other landscape theorists encountered in his omnivorous reading stressed the need to enliven the land through water engineering while doing as little damage to the natural landscape as possible. This philosophy also underscored water systems as the key principles of environmental unity. A region was, first and foremost, what its water system enabled it to be.

Showing how Golden Gate Park might be wrested from the sand dunes, how nature might be rendered even more serviceable and aesthetic through engineering, Hall graduated to the task of imagining California as irrigated parkland ready for productive use.

The opportunity for such envisionings came in May 1879, when Governor William Irwin appointed Hall, then serving as chief engineer of the Central Irrigation District centered upon Fresno in the central San Joaquin Valley, to be California's first state engineer. Never the instinctive diplomat in even the most serene of circumstances, Hall assumed office at a time when his own worst traits—his contempt for compromise and the political process, the inevitable didacticism of the auto-didact, his tendency, even in the midst of heroic public service, to be ever on the lookout for personal investment opportunities—rendered him especially vulnerable to attack from both flanks of a deeply divided water community. The hydraulic have-nots of Southern California and the southern San Joaquin Valley suspected Hall of being an agent of the water barons of the north, which Hall's frequently stated preference for private development of water resources might seem to corroborate. On the other hand, Hall opposed the doctrine of prior appropriation which was keeping water, locally and statewide, from flowing downstream to where others wanted it as well. This opposition to riparian rights (whoever owns the riverbanks owns the water) earned Hall the suspicion of vested interests wherever they were. In general, the water-parched southern part of the state favored the creation of a statewide distribution system and had introduced scores of doomed bills on its behalf, while the north was willing to go along only insofar as the water thus distributed remained a private salable resource like any other mined mineral. Theoretically, both Northern and Southern California might be expected to favor flood control, an important part of Hall's mandate, yet even here divisions emerged, the north being interested exclusively in runoff, the south in runoff storage and redistribution.

Research-oriented, Hall began his tenure as state engineer with a survey, convinced that once the proper information was assembled and presented, consensus and plan would follow. Taking up the task inaugurated in 1873 by Colonel B.S. Alexander, the Army engineer under whom he had learned his engineering in the mid-1860s, Hall and his staff embarked upon nothing less than an hydraulic survey of California itself: rainfall, snowfall, stream flow, drainage, ground and surface storage, flooding, aridity, all of it measured and recorded in notebooks which were sent back to Sacramento to be extracted and cross-referenced. As long as his budget lasted, Hall kept his survey in the field and this data flow in motion. Each measurement of a remote stream or a grandly flowing river was of use to his overall plan. Having established this foundation in fact, Hall sought in 1880 to address himself to two perennial problems: debris from hydraulic mining and the flooding of the Sacramento River. George H. Mendell, an Army engineer, and James B. Eads, a nationally recognized engineer seconded to Hall's staff by newly elected governor George C. Perkins (perhaps as an early warning to Hall that he could be replaced), joined Hall in designing two woven-brush debris screens on the Yuba and Bear rivers along with an attendant levee system. At the same time Hall prepared and published a memorandum to Eads and Mendell regarding drainage, flood, and debris control on the Sacramento River.

The debris screens designed by Hall were highly criticized. Too much debris managed to get by, Hall's critics claimed, and the project was overly expensive. Hall's Sacramento River memorandum, by contrast, offered solid solutions—the removal of channel bars, the protection and alignment of banks, the straightening of channels, the closure of crevasses and other outlets, leveeing, the construction of high-flood overflow channels—towards containing California's premier flood problem, the Sacramento River. A pattern was emerging which grew in intensity throughout the decade as Hall's difficulties increased: the greater the resistance and criticism Hall encountered, the more he took refuge in prophetic planning. The more narrow became his possibilities or capacities for action, the larger and more powerful grew his reports. In the long run, as far as an overall state water system was concerned, prophecy and imagination became Hall's most important form of public action.

By 1881, the year Hall completed his first full annual report to the legislature, it was becoming obvious that his plan to overhaul and systematize water in California involved too many forfeitures and sacrifices for the established water interests of the state. The very fact that Hall was using his office to propose the reform of water policy rather than spend his time clearing rivers of debris offended many legislators. Rather than commence his report with data or an appeal, Hall began with a sweeping assertion of the irrigation principles that should shape state policy, including the role of the state government as protector, mediator, and overall guardian of water resources and rights in California. Hall, it was soon charged, wanted to create a state water bureaucracy with himself as czar. He could not be trusted.

In the midst of this mistrust, on 31 December 1884, his budget cut to a bare
minimum, his effectiveness as state engineer at a low ebb (it would soon ebb
even further), attacked in the press as a do-nothing official, Hall again returned
to pattern. Through the state printer he issued a thirty-two-page prospectus
address to Governor George Stoneman announcing nothing less than a seven-
volume publication project that would trace the rise of irrigation historically,
inventory the existing water resources of California, describe all present irrigation works of the state (a volume each for north and south), then proceed in
the remaining volumes to recommend water law reforms and propose a statewide water system. Was this delusion—or a peculiar form of reverse compen-
sation? A state engineer with but one public work to his credit, the flawed
debris dams of 1880, with an under-staffed and under-funded office and no
discernible power base of his own, proposed to accomplish as scholarship, as
prophetic vision, what was rapidly eluding him in fact, the proper foundation
of California in water. Two years later, with Hall's situation even more tenuous, the state printer issued the first two volumes of Hall's projected series
under the titles *Physical Data and Statistics of California* and *Irrigation Development.* The first volume presented the tabulated research and measurements
gathered over seven years in the field by Hall's survey teams, or, as the subtitle
more completely expressed:

> TABLES AND MEMORANDA
> relating to
> Rainfall, Temperature, Winds, Evaporation, and other Atmospheric
> Phenomena; Drainage Areas and Basins, Flows of Streams,
> Descriptions and Flows of Artesian Wells,
> AND OTHER FACTORS OF WATER SUPPLY;
> Mountain, Valley, Desert, and Swamp-land Areas, Topography
> Topographical Features.

This, at least, was useful solid fact. The subtitle of the six hundred-page *Irrigation Development,* by contrast,

> History, Customs, Laws, and Administrative Systems
> Relating to Irrigation, Water-Courses, and Waters
> in France, Italy, and Spain

suggested that the beleaguered state engineer, who had already twice tried and
failed to establish a scholarly irrigation journal, was taking refuge from correc-
tive action at the taxpayers' expense in self-indulgent academic study.

Was this the case? Yes and no. Halfway into his tenure as state engineer,
Hall realized that he was in a no-win situation. In a fiercely competitive free-
market economy dominated by large landholders and their privately held irrigation districts, Hall was preaching the regulation of water by the state on
behalf of fairness and the public interest. He was also fighting the water-

hogging of exclusive riparian rights and the doctrine of prior appropriation which backed this practice with references to English common law. Hall favored the formation of irrigation districts which would ensure fair distribution of waters to their membership regardless of riparian relationships. The present unregulated system, Hall argued, far from serving private interests, was actually impeding capital investment. Merely as a proposal, Hall's pre-Progressive program, with its commitment to doctrines of regulation and fair use, threatened the vested interests who controlled the political party leaders who controlled the politicians. At the same time, the more radical water groups distrusted Hall because of his stout defense of regulated private ownership and his close personal connections (too close, they argued) with the investment community. Hall was thus seen by one side as a wild-eyed radical and by the other side as a crook.

Hall also seemed overly fond of research and reluctant to take action. Yet what action save the action of his pen could Hall take on a budget that barely met his office expenses? California was clearly not ready for the actions Hall wanted taken, and so he turned to writing as his best form of defense. When the *San Francisco Chronicle* attacked Hall on 16 August 1886 as a deliberately do-nothing state engineer, he replied with *The Irrigation Questions*, a brilliant memorandum to the governor and the legislature. Point by point in a series of pithy aphorisms which left behind the language of bureaucracy in favor of a prophetic utterance, the embattled state engineer flung to the elected officials of California the essential premises—public ownership and control of natural water courses, modification of riparian rights based on strict common law, irrigation associations and districts which raised their own capital and owned and operated their own waterworks—which they must assent to and act upon if there were ever to be water progress in California. If these assertions (there were 95 of them) seemed overly schematic, Hall argued, dogmatic even, he was confirmed in them by a review of the irrigation experience of England, France, Italy, Spain, and several other countries where differing experiences had yielded results of relevance to the situation in California.

Thus Hall justified the relevance of the monumental scholarship of *Irrigation Development*, his historical prolegomena nine years in preparation, which his critics considered such a waste of public time and money, to the entire irrigation question in California. Nothing less than an encompassing comparative study of irrigation technology, law, and custom would have sufficient force to confer on Californians the depth of knowledge and insight necessary for the creation of their own irrigation culture. Believing this, Hall proudly sent his unprecedented study forward to Governor George Stoneman, the third governor under whom he had served. Through nine busy years, Hall, the self-instructed scholar, had made himself the American master of irrigation history—nay, more, the international master, as he suggested in his Introduction, citing the lack of precedent for a work of this sort. Beginning *Irrigation Devel-*

opment with a study of Roman water law, Hall spent the ensuing twenty-two chapters shifting through the history, theory, law, practice, and comparative results of irrigation in France, Italy, and Spain.

Aside from the wealth of information he made available, information he hoped would constitute the data base for effective action, Hall also advanced in and through each densely packed chapter an implicit yet subliminally powerful cultural argument: the challenge to California to transform itself through irrigation into a comparably civilized neo-Mediterranean commonwealth. Brought properly into mutual usefulness, water and land underlay the civilizations of Southern Europe, irrigated societies, which in their complexity and richness suggested the irrigated future of California. Because they are even more intensely the results of deliberate value, choice, and concerted social action, Hall argued, irrigated societies are even more intensely nurturing of civilization than societies that merely exploit an available abundance. As in the case of the societies of Southern Europe, California had only to make its history happen by transforming itself into another Valley of the Po.

The next year, tired of legislative delay in drafting new water rights laws, Hall recommended the creation of a special commission to revise and systematize the water laws of California. The state senate rejected the proposal. Hall's career thereupon ran a rapid downward course until his resignation in January 1889. In March 1888 Hall was formally investigated—and acquitted— for unauthorized spending of state funds. Fully aware of the precariousness of his support in the legislature, Hall had disbursed $20,000 against future costs rather than have the money revert to the general fund. He was cleared of personal dishonesty, but the end of his tenure loomed even more clearly in sight. That year, 1888, the second and final volume of Hall's announced seven-volume study appeared, *Irrigation in California [Southern]*, a descriptive inventory of irrigation in San Diego, San Bernardino, and Los Angeles counties. Since the legislature of 1887 had cut Hall's budget to $3600, he had partially financed the field surveys for *Irrigation in California [Southern]* out of his own pocket.

Bitterness over the shabby way he was being treated perhaps eased Hall's conscience as he continued to speculate in land that would increase in value a hundredfold once water arrived, basing his investments on information acquired while in the field on public service. Hall hinted at his bitterness in the Preface to his Southern California study, announcing that the manuscript for the third volume of the series, a descriptive inventory of the San Joaquin Valley, had been completed and was awaiting public funds for publication. It never appeared. In January 1889 William Hammond Hall, tiring of the battle, resigned to join the United States Geological Survey. Between 1893 and 1906 the state government virtually ceased all water planning whatsoever.

William Hammond Hall's tenure as state engineer had resulted in no statewide plan and no significant public works, only the reports. And yet in these densely packed pages, virtually all of which he had personally written, rewritten, or revised, Hall accomplished in his thirties an epic of research and imaginative prophecy. Through Hall, California imagined itself as an irrigated society. Hall's work suggested a framework, a plan, for one hundred years of public works. A pre-Progressive reformer, he correctly argued for public regulation of water resources. An ardent capitalist, he wanted as much as possible of the apparatus and administration of irrigation kept under private ownership and control.

Defeated when the tenuous balance of power between Northern and Southern California collapsed, Hall stayed on in public service for a year as supervising engineer, Far Western region, in the United States Irrigation Investigation. He then returned to consulting in Central and Southern California, where he worked for private irrigation districts. He later consulted for Cecil Rhodes in South Africa and for the Russian government in the Transcaucasus region of Central Asia as well as advising the Czar on the irrigation of the imperial estates. Perhaps the imperial mode of Cecil Rhodes and the Czar was more to Hall's taste after his bitter experience with the California legislature. There was less arguing and things got done. At once an academic with a faith in the long-range relevance of basic research and an entrepreneur ever on the lookout for the main chance, Hall trod a narrow line, and not always to his personal credit. A complex man, divided in motivation, neither a pure public servant nor a pure entrepreneur, William Hammond Hall nevertheless achieved the first consistent act of foundational thinking regarding the future California might have through water. In this act of water prophecy, Hall made an enduring contribution.

In 1877, the year before Hall became the first state engineer, the San Joaquin Valley land barons Henry Miller and Charles Lux, joined by other ranchers, filed suit against the Kern County Land and Water Company, controlled by James B. Haggin. Miller and Lux accused Haggin of diverting waters that were theirs by riparian right. Given the vastness of each party's resources, it is not surprising that *Lux v. Haggin* dragged on for nine years before the California Supreme Court upheld the Miller-Lux claim to riparian rights. The lawsuit focused attention on the appropriation/riparian issue in manner infinitely more dramatic than Hall's historical and theoretical discussions. Under the pressure of the lawsuit itself and the subsequent public scrutiny, not to mention the millions each side spent legally and illegally lobbying against each other in Sacramento, the search for a compromise began. On 28 July 1888 an agreement was signed allowing Miller, Lux, and the other riparian plaintiffs exclusive use of the Kern River from September to February. The Kern County Land Company and its affiliates in the suit, thirty-one ditch companies in all, could appropriate water between March and August. Each side would share the costs of building and maintaining dams, canals, and levees.

Based on a split theory of riparian rights and appropriated use, which integrated into one system the needs of large landowners, irrigation companies, cooperatives, and individuals, this 1888 pact, ratified even as Hall's *Irrigation in California [Southern]* was being published, proved on a practical level that the powerful and opposing water interests of California could be forced into creative compromise. The Wright Act of 1887, meanwhile, the brainchild of state Senator C.C. Wright of Modesto, empowered local communities to form irrigation districts that could tax, issue revenue bonds, acquire land by *eminent domain*, and divert river water to dry lands for irrigation and/or flood control. Thus by the time William Hammond Hall was leaving office, California, while it had not yet agreed to a statewide waterplan, had on a practical level established a model of compromise in the judicial resolution of *Lux v. Haggin* and had created through the Wright Act a legislative framework for creating cooperative irrigation projects that stood up under constant legal challenge until the U.S. Supreme Court upheld its legality once and for all in 1896.

3

In 1880, the year William Hammond Hall, two years into his tenure as state engineer, issued his first proposals for flood control on the Sacramento, a young Canadian engineer, George Chaffey of the province of Ontario, was visiting his father and brother in the newly founded citrus colony of Riverside in Southern California. Self-taught like Hammond, Chaffey had studied maritime engineering as a purser on one of his father's ships. Returning to land, he worked briefly in the insurance business in Toronto before turning in 1875 at age 27 to the design of steamers for the Great Lakes. Drawing upon the engineering study he had pursued since leaving the sea, Chaffey designed a series of Great Lakes steamers, *The Geneva, The Sunbeam, The Zinfandel*, that set new standards for their era. In the winter of 1880 Chaffey traveled to Riverside, where his retired father and older brother William had already joined the growing Anglo-Canadian community. In Riverside another self-instucted engineer, Matthew Gage, a former jeweler from Kingston, Ontario, conducted Chaffey on a tour of the High Line Canal Gage had designed to bring artesian water up from the valley floor to the citrus groves on Arlington Heights. Overwhelmed by what Gage had accomplished, Chaffey determined to leave shipbuilding and design in Canada for irrigation development in Southern California.

On Thanksgiving Day, 1881, while walking after dinner with their host Captain J. S. Garcia, George and his brother, by then organized as Chaffey Brothers, a land-development partnership, made a $1.50-an-acre offer to their host for a thousand acres of the Garcia Ranch plus water rights. Situated on the Cucamonga Plain near the intersection of the old Santa Fe Trail and El Camino Real, fourteen miles west of the onetime Mormon colony of San Bernardino, the Garcia property was watered by three streams flowing down from the nearby San Gabriel canyons. A retired seaman of Portuguese descent, Garcia had understood the irrigation possibilities of the property, having himself planted orange trees, vines, and alfalfa in a leisurely manner; but the elderly rancher had no desire whatsoever to become an active developer. He sold Chaffey Brothers the thousand acres and water rights there on the spot, with a handshake. All in all, the Chaffeys consolidated 2500 acres of contiguous Cucamonga property, which they subdivided into ten-acre parcels. To the highest point of each parcel they brought in water by cement pipe.

At this point, the Chaffeys and their associate, the visionary journalist L.M. Holt, onetime editor of the *Southern California Horticulturalist*, advanced the water practice of Southern California by a quantum leap. Assigning to each lot a proportionate share of incoming water, the Chaffeys organized the Mutual Water Company, responsible for getting the water onto the property. To each acre of property, there was permanently assigned one share of stock in the company. These mutual shares were then reassigned to the company in exchange for permanent water rights pro-rated according to acreage. Thus each purchaser received land, water, and an irrigation system. The Chaffeys received the profits from the land sale and the ongoing profits from the water company, incorporated on 9 May 1882 as the Etiwanda Water Company. Planning to market his project in Canada, George Chaffey chose the name Etiwanda, a Lake Michigan area Indian chief, as the name of the new colony because of its strong Canadian associations. Within eight months the Chaffeys sold 1400 irrigated acres to Canadian colonists, who planted vineyards as an initial investment, followed up by more slowly yielding citrus trees.

At the time, 1882, Etiwanda was the most innovative agricultural colony in the Far West, not only because of its irrigation system, innovative in both its cement pipes and cooperative stock structure, but because of its telephones and electric light. With swift and simple acumen, George Chaffey discerned that the water descending from the San Gabriels to the Cucamonga Plain could become, in the form of the electricity it could generate, another cash crop. Installing a small hydroelectric generator at the irrigation head works, Chaffey ran a wire down to the Garcia ranch house in which he was living. With this hydroelectricity, Chaffey lighted his home with the first incandescent lamps ever used in Southern California and also placed a powerful arc light atop his roof. The arc light could be seen as far away as Riverside. The Garcia ranch house thus became the first electrified home west of the Rockies and a harbinger of those vast seas and flowing rivers of light which today make a nighttime descent by airplane over Southern California such a dramatic experience. An avid believer in the telephone since he had personally seen Alexander Graham Bell demonstrate his invention at the Centennial Exposition in Philadelphia six years earlier, Chaffey also installed a telephone line between Etiwanda and San Bernardino, extending it later to include the second Canadian-named colony he founded, Ontario. Hydroelectricity, electric light, the telephone, a workable irrigation system—George Chaffey endowed his infant colony with the technology and symbols of the future. In 1884 Chaffey organized the Los Angeles Electric Company, having as his goal nothing less than transforming Los Angeles into the first electrically lit city in the United States, which it eventually became.

George Chaffey also sought to create in his second enterprise, Ontario, a model colony that would demonstrate the full possibilities of a Southern California life-style based on irrigation, technology, and middle-class cultural values. Walking to a high mesa one sunny morning in the fall of 1882, Chaffey looked out over the Cucamonga and Kincaid ranchos extending to the base of the San Gabriels. Here was a property even more energized by development possibilities than the rapidly expanding Etiwanda: more than six thousand acres, watered by the San Antonio Canyon and Cucamonga Creek. There and then, Chaffey later reported, he resolved to acquire the property and development it as a model colony—which he did, paying $60,000 for the land and coming to an agreement with the nearby colony of Pomona regarding water rights. Ontario, as Chaffey named the development, was based on four principles: water rights, urban planning, an agricultural college, and the prohibition of alcohol.

Using the mutual model pioneered at Etiwanda, Chaffey Brothers organized the San Antonio Water Company and began to lay down forty miles of conduits. Tunneling into San Antonio Canyon, Chaffey discovered a strong underground stream, which he tapped with the first underground water tunnel in Southern California. Ontario's hydroelectric system, empowering its telephones and electric lights, was also organized on a cooperative basis. Chaffey then laid out Euclid Avenue (he studied surveying as a hobby), a two-hundred-foot-wide central thoroughfare, which he lined with double rows of trees, a center double row of pepper and palm, and outer rows of grevillea and eucalyptus. At the center of town Chaffey placed smaller lots, 33 by 150 feet, bordered by a belt of two-and-a-half-acre villa sites. Chaffey thus created an agricultural colony that incorporated within itself an urban/rural interplay deliberately orchestrated to preserve for middle-class horticulturalists the feel and amenities of an urban community. Chaffey offered free lots to churches and assigned twenty acres for an agricultural college, begun in March 1883 and later named in his honor.

These provisions, together with the prohibition of saloons, were intended to attract a better class of settlers, whom Chaffey brought in by railroad from Los Angeles for inspection tours. He also installed a large water fountain near the railroad crossing, which sprayed forth a conspicuous jet of precious water as passenger trains passed through so as to advertise Ontario's fully functioning irrigation system.

In 1903 U.S. government engineers erected a scale panaorama of Ontario at the St. Louis World's Fair as a model irrigation colony, a reputation Ontario already possessed as early as January 1885 when an Australian delegation headed by Alfred Deakin, a future prime minister, arrived on a tour of inspection.

Believing that the western United States offered the only parallel to the irrigation challenge facing Australia, Deakin was bringing a commission of inquiry to study irrigation colonies in the American West. At Ontario the commission encountered not only an irrigation and hydroelectric system but schools, churches, a library, a spacious town plan, and an evolving social structure that suggested to Deakin, already a convinced irrigationist, that Australians as well might create comparable colonies in northern Victoria and South Australia. Upon returning to Australia, a journalist member of the commission, J. L. Dow, wrote a glowing article for the Melbourne *Age* of 2 May 1885 describing Ontario as a model for what Australia could accomplish and singling out the Chaffey brothers for special praise. George Chaffey and his brother allowed themselves to become convinced that with the sponsorship of Alfred Deakin and other irrigation-minded public men they could accomplish even more in Australia then they had in Southern California. Deciding upon a personal investigation, George Chaffey sailed for Sydney from San Francisco on the R.M.S. *Mavaros* on 17 January 1886, leaving his brother in charge of their Ontario interests.

Altogether, George Chaffey spent eleven years in Australia. The two pioneering colonies he and his brother established there—Mildura in the State of Victoria, the first irrigation colony in all Australia, and Renmark in the State of South Australia—proved that the arid regions of the Murray Valley could be irrigated from the Murray River and settled. Hastily selling their Ontario interests before emigrating, the Chaffeys staked everything on the Australian venture. Although Mildura and Renmark were brilliant as engineering feats (the direct-drive, shaft-driven pumps Chaffey designed were named in his honor and won him election to the Institution of Mechanical Engineers of London), the incipiently socialist attitude towards resource development in Australia, the belief that irrigation should be carried on by government as a public interest venture, thwarted Chaffey's entrepreneurial instincts. The state governments of Australia played participatory roles in both the Mildura and the Renmark enterprises, which meant governmental interference and unfortunate political infighting that eventually brought the brothers up before a Royal Commission of Inquiry. Had the Chaffeys remained in Southern California, Ontario would have continued to prosper while they embarked upon other money-making ventures. In Australia they lost money. By 1897 the Chaffeys were no longer in the business of developing irrigation colonies. While not formally convicting them of malfeasance, the government inquiry put them under a cloud. In contrast to the early success of Etiwanda and Ontario, Mildura continued to struggle against great difficulties throughout its early years. Virtually broke, George Chaffey decided to return to Southern California. He sailed from Sydney in June 1897. His brother and one of George Chaffey's three sons remained behind as ranchers in the Murray Valley outback.

While a bitter financial disappointment, the Australian venture did teach George Chaffey that European peoples could survive, and even thrive, in hot arid regions if they were provided with the benefits of irrigation: a lesson Chaffey would soon act upon in the hottest, most arid region of Southern California. The beginnings of a continuing irrigation dialogue between Australia and California, moreover, had been established with the arrival of the Deakin commission in late 1885 and with the work of the Chaffey brothers Down Under. In this dialogue, Australia helped California escape the dead end of exclusive riparian rights. Australia also altered California to the creative role government could play in initiating and regulating irrigation projects. California, on the other hand, as Prime Minister Stanley Melbourne Bruce was to point out in 1928, showed Australia how private land ownership could be successfully combined with public water management.

Both George Chaffey and William Hammond Hall epitomized the Californian as empire builder. Motivated by profit, Hall and the Chaffeys were public-spirited dreamers as well, capable of envisioning the future that water would make available if proper action were taken. Committed to a philosophy and practice of individual settlement, Hall and Chaffey wanted irrigation to bring as many Americans to the land as possible. The subsequent acquisition of irrigated lands by large agribusiness corporations doomed their dreams to ironic reversal.

Empires built on water might inevitably tend towards centralized ownership and management, as George Marsh had argued in his pioneering *Man and Nature* (1864). Yet in their time and place, moving towards irrigation as an imaginative goal, Hall and Chaffey glimpsed only the positive possibilities of irrigation, not its ironic results. Hall, in fact, felt it necessary explicitly to refute Marsh in the preface to *Irrigation in California [Southern]*. While it may be true, Hall argued, that irrigation in the Valley of the Po in northern Italy concentrated land ownership in the hands of the nobility who controlled water rights, such concentration did not occur in Spain where water rights were fixed to land rights according to ancient Moorish law. In California, irrigation made it financially feasible to subdivide large tracts and settle more people on the land, who, thanks to irrigation and attached water rights, could make a living through intensive agriculture. In Fresno and San Bernardino counties, Hall pointed out, it was not uncommon for agriculturalists to make a living off twenty- to forty-acre tracts. An irrigated San Joaquin Valley, Hall speculated, might support up to two hundred settlers per square mile, some ten to twelve million Californians in all, each of them enjoying the benefits of life on the land.

History had other results in store, but for the time being the dream of bringing people to the land endured. What Hall surveyed and historicized, a civilization based on water, Chaffey created and demonstrated. The very years that Chaffey was bringing Etiwanda and Ontario into operation, Hall was plunging himself into his future-oriented surveys and his historical scholarship. Each activity sustained a high level of prophetic intent. Across a hundred years of pioneering effort, the Franciscans of San Diego, the Mormons of San Bernardino, Oliver Wozencraft, William Hammond Hall, and George Chaffey, among others, showed California how it might invent itself through water.

2

Imperial Ironies

The Dreams and Realities of Social Irrigation

As a highly speculative real-estate development based on water, the Imperial Valley stands as a prototype of the entire development of Southern California. On a deeper level, the Biblical metaphors attached to the project are found throughout the beginnings of numerous Southern California townships and developments. The very flooding of the Imperial Valley by a rampaging Colorado River offers a paradigm of nature and technology in conflict that also asserts itself elsewhere in the Southern California story. Without the resources of the Colorado River, there would be no modern Southern California. Its appropriation, however, was an arrogant act for which a number of southern Californians paid dearly. Rising at the Continental Divide, the Colorado River flows southwesterly for 1400 miles towards the Gulf of California. In everything save navigability, it is the Mississippi of the Far West. A great river, draining more than 260,000 square miles extending south from lower Wyoming, the Colorado links seven states—Wyoming, Colorado, Utah, Nevada, New Mexico, Arizona, and California—into one unified drainage and watershed region, just as the Mississippi unifies the Midwest.

In ancient times, the Gulf of California extended all the way to San Gorgonio Pass, ninety miles east of present-day Los Angeles; but over the eons the mighty Colorado created a delta-plain of sediment that cut the Gulf of California into two parts. Augmented by some 160 million tons of sand, gravel, clay, and silt each year (including the titanic excavations of the Grand Canyon), this delta-plain extended itself over the ages across a shallow depression or basin from the intersection of the Colorado and the Gila at present-day Yuma, Arizona, northwest to San Gorgonio, where the Gulf of California had once reached. Diverted by this alluvial plain, the Colorado River turned in a southeast direction and discharged itself into the lower Gulf of California, which it continued to do in modern times. Over the centuries, however, the Colorado occasionally defied the geological levee it had created against itself and resought its ancient discharge point to the northwest. Each of these incursions created a freshwater lake extending north to the Coachella Valley near present-day Indio in Riverside County. Each of these lakes would in time recede, leaving behind yet another ring of freshwater marine fossil shells and even richer deposits of alluvial soil, in certain places up to a thousand feet in depth. Lake Cahuilla, the most recent of these intermittent freshwater lakes created by the time-dance of the Colorado, extended as recently as ten thousand years ago for a hundred miles across the inland sink. Ten thousand Native Americans supported themselves on its shores as fisher folk, hunter-gatherers, and agriculturalists. By the time the Spanish explorer Melchior Diaz, in search of the mythical Seven Cities of Cibola, reached the region in 1540 the Cahuilla Basin had reverted to an arid desert.

In 1884 the agronomist E. W. Hilgard of the University of California argued in a report of the United States Department of Agriculture that since aridity and fertility went hand in hand, a common assumption at the time, there could be no more fertile area than the Salton Sink area of the Colorado Desert, once it was irrigated. Why, then, did George Chaffey initially reject an aging Dr. Wozencraft's suggestion, made in 1885 when they met in San Bernardino, that having established Etiwanda and Ontario, Chaffey should now turn his attention to the Colorado Desert? The answer was heat. A Canadian in love with the salubrious climate of coastal Southern California, George Chaffey did not believe that white men could tolerate living permanently in the harsh heat of the inland desert, which reached well over 100 degrees Farenheit many months of the year. Eleven years in Australia changed Chaffey's mind. There in the outback he had witnessed British immigrants living day by day in climates as harsh as any offered by the deserts of Southern California. While Dr. Wozencraft was a decade deceased by the time of Chaffey's return to California in 1897, the dream of irrigating the Colorado Desert had not died with its most persistent protagonist. In May 1899 at a meeting in Los Angeles, George Chaffey sat down with another visionary entrepreneur, Charles Robinson Rockwood, and once again discussed the irrigation of the Colorado delta.

Just turning forty, Charles Robinson Rockwood had spent twenty years as a survey and irrigation engineer in the Far West. Hired in the summer of 1892 by John C. Beatty of the Arizona and Sonora Land and Irrigation Company to investigate the feasibility of bringing Colorado River water into Sonora, in northwestern Mexico, where the company claimed 1.5 million acres, Rockwood based himself out of Yuma, Arizona, and commenced his survey. Unable to locate a proper canal route to Sonora, Rockwood reported negatively on the Sonora proposal. The Salton Sink, however, was another matter. It lay lower in altitude than the Colorado River, Robinson reported; hence a gravity canal no more than sixty miles long would suffice to bring Colorado River water east-northeast through Mexico into the Sink with no pumping necessary. Joined by his associate engineer Charles N. Perry, Rockwood spent the winter of 1892 in further surveys of the Salton Sink before going to Denver to present a new proposal to Beatty and his fellow investors: the irrigation of the Salton Sink via a Mexican canal. Thereupon ensued a decade-long saga of organization, reorganization, promotion, and frustrated efforts at capitalization involving three trips to Europe.

Rockwood first worked with John C. Beatty under the sponsorship of the Colorado River Land and Irrigation Company, which raised and spent $175,000 before going bankrupt in the Panic of 1893, leaving Rockwood stranded in the field with an unpaid survey party. Rockwood next associated himself with Charles Perry, his field colleague, and Samuel W. Ferguson, manager of the Kern River Land Company and formerly a land agent with the Southern Pacific. Borrowing $5000 from a fourth associate, W. T. Heffernan, an Army physician stationed in Yuma, the partners obtained an option on the Mexican lands owned by Guillermo Andrade, Consul General of Mexico in Los Angeles. In order to hold the property after the Mexican government refused to allow American companies to hold title to Mexican lands, the group organized a subsidiary, *La Sociedad de Terrenos y Irrigacion de la Baja California*, which increased their overhead considerably. The partners also obtained options on certain properties on the American side necessary for the planned diversion.

Anthony H. Heber, a Chicago promoter, entered the partnership, which was incorporated under the laws of New Jersey on 26 April 1896 as the California Development Company (referred to hereafter as CDC) with Heber as president. In the spring of 1899 Mrs. Heber pawned her personal jewelry to send Rockwood on another futile fund-raising expedition, this time to Detroit. Stranded in Detroit, Rockwood accepted a $250 advance on a job in Puerto Rico while Heber resigned and returned with Chicago with nothing to show for the four years he had spent as the itinerant president of the CDC. As of March 1900, CDC owned its options, its filing on ten thousand cubic feet per second of Colorado River water, some battered camp and survey equipment, and its even more battered dream of liberating the fertility of the Salton Sink of the Colorado Desert through irrigation. On the debit side CDC owed $1,365,000 to investors to whom it had sold stock and land scrip, ten cents on the dollar, over the past four years to raise enough operating capital to stay in business. Payments on the crucial land options fell into default. When CDC failed to pay its annual corporate tax, the Attorney General of New Jersey initiated a suit to cancel its charter.

Contacted by his former associate, the publicist L. M. Holt of Riverside, about Rockwood's tenuously surviving Colorado Desert project, George Chaffey informed Holt that he might be interested. Holt notified Samuel W. Ferguson, who still owned stock in the venture, regarding Chaffey's positive response, and Ferguson telegraphed Rockwood in New York. The prospect of associating George Chaffey with the Colorado project, with all of Chaffey's engineering expertise and all his financial contacts, was enough to bring Rockwood out to California for a buckboard survey with Chaffey, Holt, Ferguson, and Heffernan of the proposed canal route. The party spent more than two months in the field examining the site specifics of Rockwood's proposal. Chaffey emerged from the desert with two major reservations. What would be the true costs of constructing the canal along the route selected by Rockwood, and once it was constructed could CDC promote enough settlement into the Salton Sink to enable the project to pay for itself? Bitterly disappointed by Chaffey's reservations, Rockwood returned to New York to face increasingly bleaker prospects for 1900.

Then, mysteriously, George Chaffey returned to the Colorado Desert on his own, leaving Yuma with a Native American guide for a second look at the terrain. Rockwood's route might be faulty and his engineering expertise not fully up to Chaffey's standards, but for all his faults Rockwood did have the courage to tackle the project that its longtime advocate Oliver Wozencraft (just before his death, as if in apostolic succession) had personally urged upon Chaffey. Was Chaffey now to walk away, leaving it to others to reclaim a million acres of Colorado desert? Australia had proved to Chaffey's satisfaction that Europeans could stand temperatures soaring as high as 125 degrees Farenheit. Chaffey's financial and political defeats at Mildura and Renmark had also left him at age 52 with an obsession to repair his damaged reputation with what was undoubtedly the most major irrigation project ever to offer itself on the North American continent. Rockwood's route was too expensive. It involved too much cutting and excavation. Let the river itself suggest the best path for the gravity flow of the canal. Assisted by his Indian guide, Chaffey searched for routes whereby the Colorado River had in ancient times reached the Salton Sink. In one *barranca* (dry watercourse) called the Alamo, Chaffey found the efficient west-by-northwest route that could, millennia after it had dried up, be revived as an active canal into the Salton Sink at one-tenth the cost of Rockwood's route. The Alamo had briefly carried Colorado River overflow into the Salton Sink as recently as 1891, but for all practical purposes it was an inert, gravity-flowing watercourse. Another *barranca*, New River, branched out from the Alamo at the Mexican-American border. It also could be used as a readymade channel through the western side of the valley.

Pushing himself for three weeks through some of the most ferocious desert badlands in North America, Chaffey returned to Yuma exhausted (it was later claimed that he suffered the beginnings of his eventual hearing loss during this forced trek) but exhilarated as well by a new sense of mission. When George Chaffey met with Rockwood, Heber, Heffernan, and other CDC investors in Los Angeles in March 1900, he sat down on his own terms, a Daniel come to judgement. Without the assistance of an attorney, Chaffey had himself drawn up the contract. Under its terms Chaffey was to control the company for five years as president, chief financial officer with power of attorney, and chief engineer, and was also to assume full responsibility for the construction of the canal, assisted by Charles N. Perry, the engineer who had been with Rockwood throughout the entire enterprise. The canal was to cost no more than $150,000, which Chaffey himself promised to raise. In payment for these efforts Chaffey would receive one-quarter of all capital stock and a combined payment of $60,000 in cash, water rights, and other securities when revenue commenced from water sales.

Rockwood later claimed that he considered Chaffey's demands excessive, but having nowhere to turn he signed CDC over to Chaffey as of 3 April 1900. For some reason Chaffey signed the agreement without examining CDC's books, which were in New Jersey; nor did Rockwood and his associates volunteer any information on the company's true condition. There is a strong possibility, in fact, that they actively deceived Chaffey with misleading statements. Had Chaffey pressed the matter, he would have discovered, first of all, that CDC's books were being held because of unpaid legal fees. He would have also discovered the true financial condition of the company. Some form of messianic arrogance, a blinding obsession with the engineering and entrepreneurial challenge he had glimpsed during his three-week sojourn in the desert, drove Chaffey headlong into a hasty, careless contract.

In June, after construction of the canal had already commenced, Chaffey, the principal stockholder, president, chief financial officer, and chief engineer, belatedly opened CDC's books, which Rockwood had at long last produced. Among other things, Chaffey discovered that CDC did not own the capital stock of the Mexican subsidiary as the contract had suggested. Its payments on the Mexican option were in default. Nor had CDC secured ownership of critical property on the American side at Hanlon Heading. Hall Hanlon, owner of the crucially necessary American property, had been paid only $1,000 on a promised $20,000 and thus considered CDC's option to have expired. Nor was General Guillermo Andrade under any binding obligation to sell his Mexican properties to the *Sociedad*. Furthermore, CDC owed the State of New Jersey $1,000 in back taxes and was in imminent danger of losing its charter.

At this point the defrauded George Chaffey could have walked away from CDC and organized his own enterprise; but because construction had already started, Chaffey determined upon another strategy so the project would not become bogged down in legal controversy. Organizing the Delta Investment Company, Chaffey invested his own money and raised other funds in Los Angeles to pay Andrade and Hanlon on behalf of CDC and to meet the company's tax and legal fee obligations in New Jersey. Delta Investment also redeemed at face value $350,000 in land script CDC had issued for ten cents on the dollar during its frantic efforts to raise capital. In control of Delta Investment, which controlled CDC, George Chaffey demoted Charles Robinson Rockwood, the man who had kept the dream of irrigating the Colorado Desert alive for a decade but who had also deceived him, to an assistant engineer on a feeder canal with no duties or responsibilities for construction of the main canal. Silent, bitter, Rockwood kept his counsel—and hired a lawyer to search for flaws in Chaffey's original contract.

Constructing a diversion headgate at Pilot Knob on the Colorado River opposite Yuma, Chaffey and Perry ran their canal parallel to the river for 600 feet until it crossed the Mexican border. Then they dug south for four miles until the canal reached the ancient *barranca* Alamo. It then became a matter of clearing or enlarging this existing westerly waterway created by the Colorado in ancient times. Not only did Chaffey supervise the digging, plowing, scraping, and surveying, he personally negotiated the purchase of equipment, materials, food, and water for the workmen. Day in, day out, he oversaw every detail of the project through long days spent scraping westward in the blazing heat of the Colorado Desert, a man possessed, a sunburned, bearded Scot in pursuit of personal vindication and empire. At the suggestion of L.M. Holt, Chaffey renamed the Salton Sink to which he was bringing the empowering waters of the Colorado. The Sink would henceforth be called the Imperial Valley: imperial as in empire, for the million acres of arable land seized from the desert by irrigation were linked in Chaffey's Anglo-Canadian imagination to the march of empire in Canada and Australia in which he had played a part through his engineering and entrepreneurial skills. Imperial: not a kingdom inherited, but an empire seized from inhospitable nature through engineering and water.

Forty miles west of the Colorado, Chaffey and Perry left the Alamo and dug northwards across the border into Southern California until their canal connected with three feeder canals which Rockwood and others had simultaneously been constructing. After five months of construction and a mere $100,000 in costs, the canal, so long the dream of Wozencraft and his successors, had almost anticlimatically been brought to completion. In the late morning of 14 May 1901 Chaffey ordered the headgate at Pilot Knob lifted. After ten thousand years of denial the mighty Colorado River once again enjoyed access to its ancient seabed.

2

Chaffey, Rockwood, and the other investors connected with the California Development Company were businessmen out to make money from the Imperial Valley as Chaffey had made money with Etiwanda and Ontario. They were selling water, however, not land. The land came free from the government. Under the provisions of the Homestead Act of 1862 a settler could acquire up to 160 acres of surveyed public domain through either five years' residence or the payment of $1.50 an acre after six months. The Desert Land Act of 1877 authorized the federal government to sell up to 320 acres of desert land to settlers at $1.25 an acre. In turn, settlers were obliged to irrigate their properties within three years. The Carey Land Act of 1894 authorized the federal government to turn over to each state up to one million acres of desert lands to be disposed of under the provisions of the Desert Land Act of 1877. Organized by George Chaffey as a sales and settlement agency, the Imperial Land Company took settlers through the process of filing all necessary claims in the United States Land Office in Los Angeles to land available to them in Imperial Valley under either the Homestead Act or the Desert Land Act, or a combination thereof. Each settler purchased $7900 worth of water stock from Imperial Land in a mutual water company assigned and fixed to their claim. Water shares in one of thirteen mutual water companies had to be purchased for every acre of a claim. There could be no partial or phrased irrigation. Settlers were obligated to assign their mortgages to Imperial Land as security on a 6 percent note for this water stock or to assign the stock itself back to Imperial Land as security. Settlers also were required to deed rights-of-way to Imperial Land across their claims for railroads, canals, telegraph, and telephone lines.

It was an exacting and severe scheme, fraught with the possibilities of abuse and conflict. It also represented a massive use of public resources for private profit. Without the privately financed irrigation system completed by Chaffey, the lands of Imperial were worthless—true, but the waters of the Colorado River, the ultimate source of profit, acquired at no cost, were in the public domain to begin with. By scraping a downhill ditch for little more than fifty miles, Chaffey and his associates had acquired control of the productivity, hence the ultimate value if not the formal ownership of a million public acres. Not only did the Chaffey syndicate acquire its water at no cost, it also avoided the rate-fixing authority of California by assigning ownership of the water to its Mexican subsidiary while the water passed across Baja California. Colorado River water thus re-entered the United States as the property of a foreign corporation, hence exempt from American rates as it was transferred by secondary canals to the thirteen mutual water companies that would take it to the individual properties. The settlers on these properties, some two thousand of them by 1903, were at once brought to the land by the Imperial Land Company as well as bonded to the company in a ferociously feudal relationship. Only the Imperial Land Company had the water, and without this water their properties were but so much alkaline dust.

Appointed by Chaffey as advertising manager of the Imperial Land Company, publicist L.M. Holt threw himself into the challenge of creating a positive image for vast empty stretches of flatland desert, eventually a million acres in extent, whose resident population had hovered around a dozen before water arrived. In promoting San Bernardino and Riverside counties a decade and a half earlier, Holt had used the Mediterranean metaphor to package the emergent citrus belt as a healthful sanitarium where the bourgeoisie might find a neo-Mediterranean life of outdoor work beneath orange, lemon, and olive trees. The Imperial Valley, however, was no sunny neo-Mediterranean littoral. Even irrigated, it was hot, dusty, forbidding. Its dry, flat landscape suggested no easy metaphors. While the press followed Chaffey's engineering feat with interest, the very evocation of the harsh environment encountered by Chaffey's construction crews worked negatively as promotional imagery. On 8 April 1901 Hold brought in a trainload of Southern California newspaper editors organized as the Southern California Editorial Association for a five-day tour of Imperial. During this tour, the needed metaphor emerged.

The Imperial Valley was the Egyptian Delta of America, and the Colorado River was its Nile. Returning to their newspapers, the editorialists, perhaps only half-aware that they had been innoculated by Holt with a favorable metaphor, opened a floodgate of Egyptian comparisons. The linkage of the Imperial Valley to the ancient lands of the Bible through envisioning the Imperial as the Nile Valley of America, a new Egypt growing Egyptian corn and Egyptian cotton, endowed the area with an advantageous association. The Imperial Valley was alien to Southern California, true, as had been Egypt to the Israelites; but like Egypt it was fertile as well from the ancient floods that had layered the valley with rich deposits of alluvial soil. Going down to Imperial, Southern Californians re-enacted the going down into Egypt of Joseph and his brethren, called by the Lord into an environment at once exotic and threatening but affording as well the chance for a better life. In the early 1900s enough religiosity survived in the first generation of Imperial settlers to render this promotional metaphor not so far-fetched. By the time histories of Imperial were appearing a decade and more later, the Biblical comparison had become a fixed element of social identity and had been extended further to include a whole range of attendant metaphors: the sacramental nature of water, the redemptive work of irrigation, the righteousness of making the desert bloom. No historians or publicists pointed out, however, that the Children of Abraham, having gone down to Egypt to seek a better life, within a short time found themselves in bondage.

Pharaoh of this neo-Nile domain, George Chaffey laid out the urban settlements that were initially only lines on a map but as properties belonging to Imperial Land represented the control California Development had exercised on all growth in the region. Where the Imperial Canal re-entered Southern California from Mexico, there were to be two towns, Mexicali on the Baja California side of the border, Calexico on the American side where CDC set up its headquarters. The town of Imperial was placed in the center of the valley, with the town of Brawley to its north. Other investors later established Holtville to the east of Imperial on the once-again flowing Alamo Barranca and El Centro just south of Imperial. By 1902 Imperial had itself a temporary hotel, a First National Bank with a deposits of over $30,000, a post office, several stores, a newspaper, the *Imperial Press*, and telephone service to Cal-exico. A branch line of the Southern Pacific reached Imperial in February 1903.

Even before the water arrived, three Arizona families—William Van Horn, his wife, and six children; Lawrence Van Horn, a widower, and his four children; and the Frank Giletts and their seven offspring—discouraged by their unsuccessful efforts to farm in the water-scarce Salt River Valley, decided to join up with CDC in the Imperial venture. Loading the smallest of their seventeen children into three wagons, together with two Fresno scraper plows, their household goods, and several crates of chickens, the five adults set out towards Yuma, driving five cows and a bull before them in a twentieth-century recapitulation of two centuries of westward treks. Reaching the Colorado River, they rafted their possessions across its muddy waters on platforms consisting of lashed floating debris. Meeting up with Chaffey's crew in the field, the migrants went to work. The men ran plows and scrapers. The two women, in the midst of caring for their collective seventeen children (the vanguard of the 300 children in the valley by 1902), managed the commissary and did the cooking for the thirty-two-man construction crew.

After 1903 the train made migration easier than the arduous journey endured by the Van Horn clan in 1900. Some 500 new settlers arrived by train in 1903; but even they, once alighted from the relative comfort of their railroad cars, faced what the pioneers of 1900, 1901, and 1902 had faced and were, for that matter, still facing. Temperatures soared to as high as 125 degrees Fahrenheit in the shade. Severe sandstorms blew away tents, threatened eyesight, remained annoyingly as grit in the mouth or on the skin. Rattlesnakes and scorpions made the very land itself seem poisonous. It took backbreaking labor to plow crusted soil resting atop caliche that had solidified over thousands of years of dry heat and was further impacted by greasewood bushes that sank their ferocious roots into the stone-like silt, defying extraction. It was often necessary to use dynamite to breech the resistant earth. Then came the incessant labor with hoe and hook over fragile rows of barley, sorghum, wheat, oats, alfalfa, melons, grapes, and vegetables. The irrigated defiance of these crops seemed at times, for all the water flowing in from the Colorado, a puny, doomed challenge to the implacable immensity of the desert.

Bearing the grand name Imperial, the central city of the valley, as O.B. Tout and his wife encountered it in 1901, consisted of a dozen tent houses, one frame church, two large tents linked together into a hotel dormitory, a light frame building where the newspaper was published and the editor's family lived, and a frame general merchandise store supporting a lean-to on one side where Mr. Leroy Holt presided over the town bank. One Sunday the dust was so thick that Mrs. Holt could not cook. She kept the children in bed all day, reading to them and telling stories, hoping all the while that the sandstorm would not blow away their ominously flapping tent shelter. Yet the Holts stayed on and others arrived, attracted by this one last chance to take up homestead land in California. When lumber became available, they built brave little cottages on their treeless properties and calculated projected crop income against what they owed for water. By January 1904, 10,000 settlers and townspeople were farming 150,000 acres watered by 780 miles of uncemented canals and ditches.

By this time George Chaffey had been ousted from control of the enterprise he had saved in 1900. Throughout 1900 and 1901, as the canal was dug and, once water arrived, as settlers began to trickle into the newly irrigated Imperial acres, Charles Robinson Rockwood, humiliated at having been displaced by Chaffey, who had demoted him to the subsidiary role of engineer for one water district, patiently plotted a coup d'état. Rockwood's vehicle for revenge was the thirteen mutual water distribution companies. Busy in the field and arrogantly continuing to function without legal advice, Chaffey neglected to insure his control over the proxy votes of the thirteen water companies by putting the stock certificates in escrow at the time he assumed nominal control of the proxies. As the valley filled up, the stock certificates became valuable and were sold by their owners. Once they were sold, Chaffey lost control of the proxies. Quietly, Rockwood began to obtain control of the increasing number of proxy votes slipping away from Chaffey's influence. By early 1902 Chaffey was realizing that Rockwood, not he, had control of the thirteen mutual water companies and hence the entire company. By April 1902 Rockwood was demanding that Chaffey resign as president of CDC or confine himself exclusively to canal operations, and leave control of the valley to Rockwood. Stunned by this turn of events in which he had lost control not only for himself but for the investors he had brought into the Delta Investment Corporation, Chaffey resigned. Disastrously, he sold out his interests to the Rockwood group for $300,000 in securities, on which he realized only $100,000 in cash when he refused to press for full face value and thus drive CDC into bankruptcy. A few years later, when the Imperial Valley was flourishing, Chaffey's stock would have made him a millionaire many times over. As it was, he realized $100,000 on a scheme destined to gross millions.

And so at age 55 George Chaffey walked away from the one last great big thing he wanted to do with his life. In place of the expected decline, however—the brooding, the bitterness over stolen possibilities or, worse, over his own negligence—Chaffey spent another fifteen years in the field building water systems for the expanding suburban cities of Los Angeles. By bringing water to the East Whittier La Habra Valley, for instance, Chaffey increased property values there from $50 to $9,000 an acre. Working closely with his banker son Andrew, Chaffey avoided any further financial reversals such as he had experienced in the Imperial. After the death of his wife in 1917, Chaffey went into semi-retirement in Balboa on the Orange County coast, moving later to a seaside cottage at Pacific Beach near San Diego, where he lived on until 1932.

Anthony H. Heber, meanwhile, an indoor promoter given to winged collars and a pince-nez, assumed the presidency of CDC on behalf of the Rockwood syndicate. Heber was not destined to have an easy time of it.

3

First of all, many deplored the exploitation of the Homestead and Desert Land acts by private entrepreneurs, no matter how good they were as water engineers. One such critic, William Ellsworth Smythe, whom Charles Fletcher Lummis later described as the Peter the Hermit of the Irrigation Crusade, possessed superior credentials as a water prophet. Born in 1861 in Worcester, Massachusetts, Smythe was working as a reporter in his home town when he came under the influence of James Parton's biography of Horace Greeley, and he decided to go West and grow up with the country. Moving to Kearney, Nebraska, in 1888, Smythe edited a small newspaper before being hired in 1890 as an editorial writer on the Omaha *Bee*. At the time Nebraska was in the midst of a terrible drought. As the rainless prairies dried up, farmers began shooting their livestock to prevent them from dying of thirst and starvation. That summer, Smythe vacationed on the Vermejo River in New Mexico. Contrasting the New Mexican farmers, secure in their use of irrigation waters from the Vermejo, with their drought-destroyed counterparts in Nebraska, Smythe experienced an insight that he would over the next thirty years elaborate into a fully explicated gospel and call to missionary action.

Aridity, Smythe intuited, was a blessing not a curse. Aridity necessitated irrigation, and irrigation conferred system and predictability. It was unscientific to depend upon the vagaries of rainfall for crop water; better a system of predictable source, steady storage, continuous distribution and availability. Aridity also testified to fertility. Arid soil had not been washed clean of its valuable minerals and nutrients. Irrigation was by definition a cooperative, hence socializing, enterprise. Civilization itself began in the irrigated lands of the Tigris-Euphrates delta; and in the United States, civilization, by which Smythe meant social democracy, would advance through irrigation projects as it had among the Sumerians, Egyptians, Israelites, Arabs, Aztecs, and Incas. Returning from New Mexico to his editorial post in Omaha, Smythe urged Nebraskans to stop praying for rain and to start digging irrigation ditches. To reinforce his point and to stave off criticism that he was being anti-religious, Smythe argued from Genesis 2:10 that Eden itself had been an irrigated garden. Meeting with a positive response in Nebraska, Smythe founded the magazine *Irrigation Age* in 1891. Also that year he organized the first of many irrigation congresses.

In *The Conquest of Arid America* (1900), which Smythe was seeing through the press at the very same time George Chaffey was determining upon the irrigation of the Imperial, Smythe presented the full implications of his irrigationist vision. If William Hammond Hall offered historical analogies and an engineering blueprint and George Chaffey was even then offering bold examples of field engineering, William Ellsworth Smythe, a non-engineer publicist, offered an apologia that touched the deepest dimensions of the persistent American longing for life on the land in a just and prophetic commonwealth. In its arid regions west of the ninety-seventh meridian, Smythe predicted that the United States awaited the fulfillment of its home-making, civilizing destiny. The West had superior fertility and a healthier climate. Because it demanded irrigation, the West also demanded a higher practice of cooperative citizenship and that would lead to social democracy. The arid regions offered Americans a unique partnership with the Almighty Himself in finishing the unfinished work of creation. In its most important level of existence, Smythe expostulated, irrigation was a religious rite, a prayer for rain involving intelligence and science as well as faith, an active partnership with the divine instead of passive dependence and rote superstition.

In this grand and grandiloquent scheme, destined very soon to encounter the counter-realities of the Imperial Valley, Smythe envisioned a special role for California, which he considered America's Empire State on the Pacific, the counterpart of New York. Smythe traveled to Los Angeles in 1893 as presiding officer for the first International Irrigation Congress, which he organized. Visiting the irrigated holdings of the Kern County Land Company, he rejected the polity of corporate ownership but confessed himself thrilled by the paradigm of how irrigation released the latent fertility of arid acres out to the horizon as far as the eye could see.

Writing in *Century* for December 1896, Smythe reported that a new civilization was in the offing in Southern California, localized and made participatory through such tested American institutions as the joint stock company and the New England town meeting, and agriculture based on irrigation would be its foundation. As in the case of Holland, this evolving Ultimate California would be a culture in which each square foot of the land would be cherished and crafted as either irrigated agriculture, landscaped garden, or fallow soil resting for future productivity. Even now the feudal estates, tended by Chinese labor, were being subdivided into irrigated family holdings. "Progress towards this end," Smythe asserted, "is already well begun. It must go on until the last great estate is dismembered and the last alien serf is returned to the Orient. Upon the ruins of the old system a better civilization will arise. It will be the glory of the common people, to whose labor and genius it will owe its existence. Its outreaching and beneficent influence will be felt throughout the world."[1]

In *The Conquest of Arid America* Smythe expanded his *Century* observations to include case studies of Anaheim and Riverside, two Southern California irrigation colonies which, along with Salt Lake City and Greeley, Colorado, Smythe considered paradigms of the higher values brought on by irrigation. A visitor, Smythe eulogized, had only to note the comfortable homes of Anaheim and Riverside, their broad verandas awash in vines and flowers, the tree-planted streets, the plenteous vineyards and orange groves, the churches, schools, meeting halls, the absence of saloons, to realize the positive social effects of irrigation.

By this time Smythe was himself a Southern Californian, having settled in San Diego, where he began to write for the development-oriented magazine *Land of Sunshine* in July 1901 just as the sales office of the Imperial Land Company was opening in Los Angeles. Why editor Lummis, a Republican with strong ties to the local oligarchy, hired Smythe to conduct the Twentieth Century West department of the magazine is an open question; for Smythe lost no time in arguing an irrigation development model diametrically opposed to what was occurring in the Imperial Valley. New Zealand, Smythe argued, where government built the water works and supervised the distribution of water, offered the fairest, most efficient mode of irrigation development. Water rights should be attached to the land itself, not vested in private stock in mutual water companies. If and when water was brought in by private entrepreneurs, rates should be fixed by a state commission. In the long run (and here Smythe advanced his most startling point), it would be better for Americans to follow the New Zealand model altogether by allowing government to irrigate and improve the public domain, then lease homesteads to settlers and thereby preclude the exploitative development techniques of private enterprise.

To spread his socialistic ideas further and perhaps to translate some of them into action, Smythe founded the California Constructive League in February 1902 and ran unsuccessfully for Congress as a Democrat. Although the League lasted only a year, and Smythe left the *Land of Sunshine* shortly after, his presence as an impassioned publicist in the critical years 1901–1903 when Imperial Valley was emerging circulated vigorously dissenting notions as to who exactly owned the water flowing into the Imperial and even who owned the land itself. The Imperial land scheme had for all practical purposes turned water rights into land rights and thereby created a way for private investors to seize ownership of publicly granted lands when heavily mortgaged and leveraged settlers could no longer pay their water bills.

Smythe's key argument, that government could bring system and fairness to irrigation, built upon the ideas of no less than John Wesley Powell, explorer of the Colorado and author of the *Report on the Lands of the Arid Region* (1878), the single most important statement regarding the inhabitability of the rainless lands west of the hundredth meridian. Powell believed that only the federal government had the final authority, much less the ability, to devise a comprehensive irrigation plan for the western arid regions. At Powell's urging, Congress authorized the Secretary of the Interior in March 1888 to commence a comprehensive survey of the water resources of the West. As director of the Irrigation Survey, Powell found his efforts limited by lack of funds, which expressed the divided mind of Congress as to exactly how much responsibility the federal government should assume in a matter so extensively involving the individual states. With his budget cut to a paltry $162,500 Powell resigned, and what had seemed so possible in 1888, a comprehensive survey, mapping, and inventory of the water sources and reservoir sites of the Arid West, collapsed into another piece of unfinished national business.

To opponents of federal involvement, the Irrigation Survey represented the first step towards the active management by the federal government of water in the West. With the passage of the Newlands Reclamation Act, signed by President Theodore Roosevelt on 17 June 1902, federal involvement in western water became a fait accompli. Named in honor of its sponsor, Nevada Congressman Francis Griffith Newlands, an ardent irrigationist, the Act created a Reclamation service reporting to the U.S. Geological Survey until it became a separate agency of the Interior in 1907, empowered to use funds from the sale of lands for the construction of irrigation projects. The federal government was now formally and officially in the irrigation development business. As such it could not help but be affronted by the use of public water and lands in the Imperial Valley as a source of private profit. Almost immediately the Reclamation Service declared war on the California Development Company. A number of offensive weapons were already available. In January 1902 two soils analysts from the Department of Agriculture, J. Garnett Holmes and Thomas H. Means, had reported in the U.S. *Department of Agriculture Bureau of Soils Circular No. 9* that much of the 125,000 acres already claimed by prospective settlers contained too much alkali ever to become productive farmland. The prevalence of gullies and sand dunes, moreover, would make prohibitive the cost of leveling some 27 percent of the prospective farmland. "The land may produce a crop for a year, or even two years," the federal soils analysts claimed of the acres upon which so many investors and even more settlers had staked their hopes, "and then, having become thoroughly saturated, the alkali will rise and kill the crops." Not content with merely publishing the circular, the Department of Agriculture vigorously circulated it throughout the rest of the country, actively warning prospective claimants to avoid the Imperial.

Needless to say, settlers on these claims panicked. Sales fell off in the Los Angeles office and bankers grew reluctant to extend further credit. One school of interpretation, seeking the motivation for Chaffey's abrupt withdrawal, cites *Circular No. 9* as the real cause of his self-punishing departure. Since publisher Harrison Gray Otis was himself buying up large tracts of property adjacent to Imperial extending into Baja California and since these lands were being irrigated by CDC from its canal at next to no cost, the Los Angeles *Times* thundered against the conclusions of the circular and questioned Holmes's and Means's motivation. Other papers, by contrast, began to attack the entire Imperial scheme as a vast fraud. Taking to the defense, Heber and Rockwood derisively asked how two soils analysts, in the field only forty days, could make testing valid for 169 square miles, which came to their testing an

average of 2700 acres a day? As president of the company Anthony Heber
traveled to Washington and argued his case before the Secretary of the Interior,
who ordered a reinvestigation. A conciliatory second opinion from Agriculture
allowed the matter to die down; but Reclamation had disclosed the vulnerabil-
ity of CDC's fragile hold on the Imperial: its slender operation capital and
shaky credit, first of all, but also, as the Director of Reclamation Service reported to the Secretary of the Interior, the fact that its canal system was already
showing a dangerous buildup of silt.

By then, Reclamation had formulated and announced its counterproposal,
the Yuma Project, which called for the damming of the Colorado just below
the Laguna Weir, then bringing the water into Arizona east of Yuma and
southwest into the Imperial. This. obviously, involved getting CDC out of the
picture. Under the guidance of William Ellsworth Smythe, a number of Imperial settlers formed a Water Users' Association to raise the necessary capital
and enter into negotiations with CDC for the cooperative purchase of its system, which would then be connected to the Yuma Project canal with its abundance of low-cost federally sponsored Colorado River water.

As this line of action unfolded, the Reclamation Service advanced on another axis of attack, the navigability of the Colorado River. If the Colorado
were to be declared navigable, it would revert to federal jurisdiction; hence
CDC would have to request permission to divert its waters, which would of
course be denied.

Reclamation eventually did extract from Justice in early 1903 a memorandum agreeing that, since the lower Colorado was potentially navigable, it did
fall under federal jurisdiction. Without explicit federal permission, the continuing diversion of water by CDC was arguably illegal. The most damaging charge
that Reclamation and the Water Users' Association were making against CDC,
however, a charge reiterated by the Justice Department in its report of early
1903, was not that the company was illegal but that its engineering was dangerously inefficient. Finishing construction in six months on a less-than-
adequate budget, George Chaffey had moved too fast and cut too many corners. Already, silt was building up to dangerous levels in the hastily scraped
main canal and distribution network. Others began to question the soundness
of the diversion works at Pilot Knob. Had the mighty Colorado River, surging
southward with a force that had cut out the Grand Canyon itself, been so easily
tamed and appropriated? Many doubted it. The specter of flood lingered.

Anthony Heber, meanwhile, the embattled president of CDC, fought back
with the weaseline fury of inverted arrogance stung to desperate action. There
was in Heber an anger, a zeal for confrontation that drove him towards the
offensive and to gratuitous offensiveness. When Reclamation announced its
Yuma Project in August 1903 with plans for four dams, each with its own
hydroelectric capacity, and canals serving 1.2 million acres, Heber taunted its

chief engineer for the Southwest, J. B. Lippincott, with the assertion that CDC, for all practical purposes, controlled the lower Colorado with its original 20,000 acre-feet claim, a boast he later repeated at Lippincott's request to Reclamation district director Frederick H. Newell. In his precarious personal and professional situation, Heber did not need the resulting bad publicity in the press over his arrogant statement, nor the increased iron his remarks injected into Reclamation's bureaucratic will.

Undaunted, Heber took his case to Washington itself, persuading U.S. Senator George Perkins and Congressman Milton Daniels of the Eighth District to introduce a bill declaring the Colorado an irrigation stream beyond federal jurisdiction and not a navigable river. Heber gained nothing from this ploy. First of all, Smythe used his allotted testimony to discredit CDC as inefficient, parasitical, and dishonest: a company wanting a 400 percent return from settlers but giving water away free to Mexican property owned by Harrison Gray Otis and other members of a Los Angeles syndicate, a company led by a president arrogant enough to lay claim to a great river and even the melting snows of the Rocky Mountains. Heber testified in that taunting vein he had first used against Lippincott. When one congressman asked him if he would accept any limitations on private profit made from public water, Heber said he opposed any limitations whatsoever. When it became apparent that the Daniels bill would never make it out of committee, Heber angrily threatened: "It is my earnest desire to worship at our own altar and to receive the blessing from the shrine of our own government, but if such permission is not given, of necessity I will be compelled to worship elsewhere."[2]

Heber meant Mexico. Even as he testified, he was opening negotiations with President Porfirio Díaz for the right to cut a canal from the Colorado River to the Imperial Valley completely on Mexican territory, thereby bypassing all American jurisdiction. The idea of irrigating American acres with Mexican water fed Heber's sense of revenge against an interfering Reclamation Service. On 10 June 1904 Heber signed a contract with Mexico which the Mexican Congress had ratified three days earlier. Fifty percent of the water to be carried by the proposed Mexican canal would go to Mexican properties. The Mexican canal was necessary not only to allow CDC to escape federal jurisdiction, but because Chaffey's canal was becoming increasingly silted, especially in its first four miles, where an insufficient grade resulted in a flow too sluggish to clear away the daily silt deposits. Rockwood had tried as chief engineer to clear this silt by bringing a bypass channel from the river around the headgate and into the main canal. This extra water increased the rate of flow and carried off the silt. Rockwood, however, left the bypass channel open too long. When the river receded, the silt came in via the bypass channel and once more filled up the main canal. When Rockwood found himself reduced to trolling logs along the bottom of the canal from a tiny river steamer in hopes of dislodging the accumulated silt, Heber came to the conclusion that a second canal, cut four miles south of the border and running exclusively through Baja California, was the only solution.

Heber pressured Rockwood to cut the lower canal as soon as possible, despite the fact that Mexico had not given permission for a permanent headgate. Even were such permission granted, CDC lacked the $200,000 necessary for construction, so the point was moot. In October 1904 Rockwood made a direct cut into the western bank of the Colorado River, fifty feet wide, six to eight feet deep. At the time the Colorado was so low that additional dredging became necessary to get the water into gravity flow through this new new feeder channel into the Imperial Canal. For the meanwhile, the lack of a permanent concrete headgate (it took a year for Mexico to approve its construction) seemed a risk worth taking.

The Mexican cut and the new 3300-foot canal put Heber to advantage in CDC's battle against Reclamation. Humiliated in Washington that April by Smythe and by Reclamation, Heber found himself in a commanding position by the first week of October 1904 when he mounted the platform at a farmers' meeting in Brawley to debate Paul Van Dimas, a local resident who had worked closely with Smythe in organizing the pro-Reclamation Water Users' Association. Reclamation had known all along that CDC was negotiating with Mexico, Heber charged, but kept quiet about it so as to further the Water Users' Association's plans to buy the company. But CDC was no longer for sale. Thanks to the Mexican canal, CDC had the water, and Reclamation had only promises and red tape. If the farmers continued to negotiate with the federal government, Heber threatened, CDC would cut the valley dry. What would it be, CDC water or Reclamation promises? Whipped to fear and fury by Heber's rhetoric, a group of farmers stormed the stage and seized Van Dimas as he tried to speak. Dragging him outside, they tarred and feathered him (the tar and feathers were available by prearrangement) and ran him out of town on a rail. Afterwards, the farmers enjoyed a festive barbecue and fireworks display courtesy of CDC. It was a barbaric moment, prophetic of similar clashes in Imperial during the Great Depression.

4

Even as Paul Van Dimas was recovering from his ordeal and an angry President Theodore Roosevelt was ordering an investigation into this vigilante action against the federal government, the Colorado River, in one of its semi-millennial shifts, was turning westward to reseek its ancient resting place in the Salton Sink. Two forces were at work: flooding and the redirection of the river. Twice before in recent memory, in 1861 and 1891, the Colorado had feinted westward, temporarily filling portions of the Salton Sink; but the redirection of the spring of 1905, intensified by five floods between February and March, was no

mere gesture in the direction of an ancient destination. It was, rather, a shift of titanic proportions, a westward wrenching of a major American river that at its height would pour 360 million cubic feet of water per hour into the Imperial Valley. Had Rockwood and Heber been able to predict this shift in the summer of 1904 as they dug their Mexican canal (had, for that matter, they been capable of thinking systematically of what they were doing), they would have strengthened, not weakened, the western bank of the Colorado River as they did by cutting into it without a headgate at Intake Number Three. But they wanted water and they wanted it as quickly and cheaply as possible. And so the spring-gorged Colorado River now ran at a level from 25 to 200 feet above the rim of the Imperial Valley, a gaping wound on its mud-soft western flank.

After three floods in the spring of 1905, Rockwood admitted that his unprotected cut was courting catastrophe. In March 1905 Rockwood attempted to close the Mexican cut with a dam of piles, brush, and sandbags. The river swept this dam away on 25 March. A second dam was immediately built. It too was swept away. By mid-June 1905 the Colorado was running westward into the Imperial at the rate of 90,000 cubic feet of water per second, having dug for itself a 160-foot-wide channel. Assisted by engineers Charles N. Perry and Tom Beach, Rockwood next sought to build a dam between the west bank and a large sandbar called Disaster Island in the middle of the river. Such a dam, if successfully completed, would be capable of diverting the river back into its channel. By 1 September 1905 the CDC engineers had completed a 2800-foot dam of pilings linked by brush and barbed wire behind which some 30,000 sacks of sand were laid down. Renewed flooding, however, carved a 125-foot break in this barrier and it continued to widen. By the end of September this third attempt to check the flooding of the Colorado River into the Imperial Valley was also abandoned.

Having exhausted its available cash on the three dams, CDC turned to the Southern Pacific for financial support. In June 1905 SP president E. H. Harriman authorized a loan of $200,000 for the purpose of containing the Colorado River if CDC would put two-thirds of its stock in trust as collateral. Harriman also demanded three seats on the CDC board, together with the presidency. Naturally, Anthony Heber bitterly resisted this offer ending his direction of the company. Having nothing but debt and a titanic flood in its portfolio, however, Rockwood's group of investors agreed to the SP's terms. In June 1905 the SP assumed control of CDC. Epes Randolph of the SP became the new president, Rockwood remained on as assistant general manager, Anthony Heber was sent into exile, and the Colorado River continued to pour westward into the Imperial Valley. While Rockwood turned his attention to management, F. S. Edigner, superintendent of bridges for the SP, launched in October 1905 the fourth attempt to redirect the Colorado back into its proper channel. Edigner tried two variations of the barrier dam concept, the first (it was rapidly abandoned) involving a complex gate mechanism, the second a simple affair of pilings,

brush, and fascines repeating Rockwoods' attempt of the previous August. On 29 November 1905 this fourth dam was swept away in a flood. After four attempts at a dam at a cost of approximately $100,000, some 80 percent of the Colorado River was still flowing into the Salton Sink and the recently reclaimed Imperial Valley. When the New Liverpool Salt Company, located since 1883 on the margin of the Salton Sink, sank submerged by the newly forming Salton Sea, the farmers of Imperial Valley wondered how long it would take for the rapidly rising inland sea to reach their newly settled acres as well.

Desperately, on 15 December 1905 the SP-controlled CDC authorized Charles Rockwood, whose ill-conceived Mexican cut had caused the disaster in the first place, to make a fifth attempt at taming the rebellious Colorado. Rockwood placed his hopes on the emplacement of a concrete and iron headgate constructed by the Llewellyn Iron Works Company of Los Angeles. This heavy headgate would replace a temporary wooden structure ironically named in Rockwood's honor. The headgate would be centered in a causeway across the opened western bank constructed with rocks from a nearby quarry. An SP spur line would bring the rocks out to the site, then dump them into the river until the causeway built itself up to sufficient height and strength to redivert the river into its proper channel. Once that occurred, the preconstructed steel and concrete headgate could be lowered into place.

Empowered by a $250,000 loan from the SP, Robinson began work on 7 January 1906 on this fifth attempt to contain the runaway Colorado. To build the levee causeway, Robinson proposed to drive a colonnade of ninety-foot piles across the opening. Huge mattresses of woven brush, woven by Native American labor, would then be emplaced atop barges anchored to the piles. These brush mattresses would be linked to each other and secured to the piles with steel cables. When the barges were towed away, the brush mattresses would sink against the piles and create the spaces that would then be filled with rock from the nearby quarry. Eventually, the trestle causeway from which the rock was dumped would be built into a permanent dam. The heavy headgate could then be dropped into its center. Some four hundred Native Americans from nearby tribes and from Arizona and Mexico—Pimas, Papagoes, Maricopas, Yumas, Cocopahs, and Dieguenos—worked on the brush mattresses or helped white workers move and dump tons of rock. In the midst of the fifth attempt, on 18 April 1906, an earthquake destroyed San Francisco, including major SP properties in that city. Discouraged by his deteriorating relationship to the SP, Rockwood resigned as chief engineer a day later. Tied down by the San Francisco disaster and fearing that the Colorado River closure was proving a bottomless financial pit, E.H. Harriman placed his top engineer, Henry Thomas Cory, in charge of the closure operation.

Cory had come to the SP as Harriman's personal assistant after an academic career at the University of Cincinnati, where he served as professor and dean

of civil engineering. An assured scholar and outdoorsman, Cory, then 36, brought to the Colorado River enterprise a wide range of personal and engineering skills. In his best-selling Imperial Valley novel *The Winning of Barbara Worth* (1911) Harold Bell Wright would later fictionalize Cory as Willard Holmes, a New York engineer epitomizing the best qualities of the Gibson Man: strength, virility, intelligence, caste—a great big white engineer in boots and khaki drill. Not so easily impressed, however, was the Colorado River; for despite Cory's energetic direction—the work of hundreds of men pouring tons of rock from boxcars which ran right up to the river itself via a trestle causeway—the Colorado remained unsecured throughout the summer of 1906. The fifth attempt seemed successful by the fall, but on the afternoon of 11 October 1906, the temporary wooden headgate broke from its anchorage and floated down river. Part of the levee pulled away with it. Cory decided to continue the damming without using a headgate or brush mattresses. Just rock and fill and more rock and fill against the raging Colorado.

So began the sixth attempt at closure, a brute race of rock and fill against titanic water. On 4 November 1906 the Colorado turned from its westward course into the Salton Sea and regained its normal channel. Elated, Cory left a work force of seventy-five men on watch before returning to CDC headquarters in Calexico to assess the financial and administrative situation of the sorely strained SP subsidiary. On 5 December 1906 the Gila River, suddenly rising, poured its torrent into the Colorado, which now regained its westerly force. Cory's levee, so painfully closed over a year of effort, developed leaks. Within twenty-four hours the levee gave way entirely. Once again, as it had for the past year and a half, the Colorado seethed westward into the Salton Sea.

Surveying the destruction of this sixth effort to control the Colorado, Cory advised Harriman that it was beyond the ability of the SP to mount a seventh attempt at its own expense. The federal government would have to offer assistance. A rising Salton Sea, meanwhile, expanded southwards towards the settlements of the Imperial Valley. It seemed to settlers that, within the year, the Imperial, won from the desert a mere half-decade earlier, would soon lie at the bottom of a vast flood-created sea. Throughout mid- and late December 1906 a flurry of telegrams passed between Theodore Roosevelt, President of the United States, and E. H. Harriman, president of the SP.

"I assume you are planning to continue work immediately," TR telegraphed Harriman on 15 December. Having already spent $2 million, Harriman telegraphed TR on the 19th, the SP could not be expected to continue on its own. The Reclamation Service must help. CDC, not the federal government, had caused the problem with its Mexican cut of October 1904, TR wired back on the 20th. Replying the same day, Harriman both fibbed and capitulated. The SP, he lied, did not control CDC. "However, in view of your message, I am giving authority for the Southern Pacific officers in the west to proceed at once with efforts to repair the break, trusting that the Government, as soon as you can procure the necessary Congressional action, will assist us with the burden."[3]

Harriman was referring to a bill introduced by Senator Frank P. Flint from California to provide $2 million to reimburse the SP and to expand Reclamation Service projects and jurisdiction into the Imperial Valley. On 21 January 1907, keeping his side of the bargain, Roosevelt sent a special message to Congress urging the passage of the Flint bill. The very day of the last exchange of telegrams, 20 December 1906, Harriman had wired Epes Randolph, the president of CDC, "Close that break at all cost!" Randolph personally brought the telegram to Cory, his general manager and chief engineer. The seventh, final, and successful effort to contain the runaway Colorado began that very same day. With all available SP rolling stock at his disposal, together with a 1500-strong army of Indian and white laborers, H.T. Cory went on campaign against the Colorado. His strategy was simple: close the breech with rock, gravel, and clay, some 2500 carloads in all, blasted from nearby quarries then brought out onto the levee by railroad car and dumped, again and again, every hour of each day from morning until midnight from 27 January to 10 February 1907, until an eight-foot-high levee stretched for fifteen miles on both sides of the original break and held, held, held—as it did finally at eleven in the evening of 10 February 1907 when the Colorado turned southwards towards the Gulf of California and remained flowing in that direction. Fifteen hundred men and a thousand flatcars had been pressed into service. Rock had been quarried and hauled in from hundreds of miles in every direction, some 80,000 cubic yards of rock handled over fifteen days: the fastest such handling of that much rock in engineering history up to that era. Another 900,000 cubic yards of earth had been packed onto the embankments then blanketed by 5,285 carloads of gravel. This seventh closure had cost the SP precisely $1,663,136.40 by its own reckoning, for a total of $3.1 million spent overall since the SP had assumed control of CDC in June 1905. Not a penny of this sum was ever regained from the federal government. Keeping his word to his fellow New York clubman E.H. Harriman, Roosevelt argued vigorously for compensation. Two bills were introduced to this effect. One languished in committee; the other failed in vote.

Assaulted by damage claims (half a million to the New Liverpool Salt Company now submerged beneath the Salton Sea, $900,000 in gold to the Mexican government), the California Development Company declared bankruptcy in December 1909 with liabilities of more than $2 million. As Epes Randolph discovered, the principal stockholders had already begun to gut the company of its resources even before the SP took over. Sued for the return of an alleged $900,000 in fraudulently diverted assets, CDC investors Heber, Heffernan, Blaidsdell, and Rockwood returned all their outstanding stock to the SP in an out-of-court settlement. Only when Cory reversed his initial opinion that the

Mexican cut was criminally negligent did Rockwood and his associates escape prosecution for the calamity they had caused in their attempt to make an end-run to the Imperial Valley through Baja California. All in all, it was a shabby end for a company that, for all its ambiguities, had brought into being a new Southern California place.

5

As large-scale irrigated desert subculture, the Imperial Valley by 1910 nurtured its distinct version of the Southern California experience. The inland desert now supported cities, towns, urban institutions, farmlands, and local worthies. The Imperial even had its own inland ocean, 45 miles long, 17 miles across, 83 feet deep, for a total of 410 square miles and six million acre feet. The Salton Sea was now the largest inland body of water in the State of California. It was also an exact recreation of Lake Cahuilla of ancient times, likewise created by a westering Colorado. Ironically, had the Salton Sea not been brought into being by the rampaging Colorado, it would have had to be developed in some form or other as an inland sump for excess flows and normal irrigation runoff. The heroic floods of 1905–1907 had accidentally brought the Imperial Valley into ecological balance. The Salton Sea also reinforced the Biblical metaphors implicit in the redemption of the Imperial by providing an analogy to the Dead Sea of the Holy Land. Vast, smooth, saline, beginning abruptly at the edge of the desert in an assertion of water against aridity, the Salton Sea offered the deepest possible metaphor of the region. In time stocked fish would bring life to these waters; but no amount of stocking, however successful, could fully transform the Salton Sea into a purely natural body of water. A sump for diverted Colorado River waters that had finished their course through the head-gates and canals through the very earth itself and now rested, still, exhausted, saline from soil leachings, after having given life to the valley, the Salton Sea asserted on a macro-ecological scale William Ellsworth Smythe's notion that irrigation offered human beings the opportunity to cocreate with divinity itself.

This, as a deeply humanistic enterprise with theological overtones, was how Harold Bell Wright, a Disciples of Christ minister turned novelist, depicted the creation of the Imperial Valley in his 1911 best-selling novel, *The Winning of Barbara Worth*. A combination of ill health and dissatisfaction with the restrictions of his calling led Wright in 1908 to settle on the Tecolote Ranch near the city of Imperial, in an effort to regain his strength through an outdoor life which would also leave him time to write. A year later, Wright produced the first of his successful novels, *The Calling of Dan Matthews*, based on his own search for role and vocation. He then turned his attention to the epic of reclamation in the Imperial. Appearing in 1911, *The Winning of Barbara Worth* sold 175,000 copies in its first two years of publication. Wright's novel tapped that amalgam of progressivism, profit, and religiosity so deeply lodged in the mainstream American identity of this era. The novel also offered a gloss on the Imperial experience which Wright, a populist preacher ever in touch with his audience, knew from observation that Imperial residents believed of themselves. Like the best-selling novel *Ramona* in the previous generation, *The Winning of Barbara Worth* functioned as a vehicle of self-identification through an explicit parable reinforced by underlying cultural and religious metaphors.

The heroine of Wright's novel, Barbara Worth, is literally born of the desert, having been rescued from *La Palma de la Mano de Dios* (the palm of God's hand) at the age of four by banker Jefferson Worth when her settler parents lose their way in the desert and die of thirst and exposure. Barbara is thus raised as the foster daughter of the leading citizen of the Imperial. Now in her early twenties, she is in every respect the imperial daughter of the Imperial Valley: a tall, outdoorsy Girl of the Golden West who speaks fluent Spanish and spends much of her time riding the desert on horseback. Barbara, who symbolizes the desert, has four men in her life, each of them embodying one aspect of Wright's parable: her foster-father Jefferson Worth, a banker committed to the saving work of private capital applied to reclamation (Wright considered his novel, among other things, a sermon on "the ministry of capital"); the Seer, a mystical Smythesque reclamation advocate ever dreaming of desert utopias and a new moral order created by irrigation; Abe Lee, a local surveyor in love with Barbara; and Willard Holmes, a New York engineer based on Henry T. Cory, scouting possible reclamation projects for eastern interests. In the course of the novel, Jefferson Worth manages to keep the financing of the Imperial under local control. The Seer manages to convince eastern bankers that reclamation is more than a risky investment; it is the cutting edge of civilization itself. New York engineer Willard Holmes, after first coming under the spell of the desert, manages to turn back the flooding Colorado, assisted by local resident Abe Lee. Barbara, in turn, chooses the educated New Yorker Holmes over local boy Lee to be her husband and the father of her children. Wright's parable is obvious. Reclamation needs eastern money, technology, and brains; but it also needs local control and commitment. The desert cannot be merely invested in or even watered. The desert must be lived in imaginatively with a transcendental vision of place. Reclamation was once a communion and a conquest. "The desert waited," so ran the inscription over the main entrance to the Barbara Worth Hotel in El Centro, quoting Wright's novel, "silent, hot, and fierce—its desolation holding its treasures under the seal of death against the coming of the strong ones."[4]

One such strong one was W. F. Holt, the prototype of Jefferson Worth and the friend to whom Wright dedicated his novel. In making Worth the paragon of responsible local control, Wright was ignoring the irony that it was the locally based CDC that had perpetrated the disastrous Mexican cut, plundered its own assets, and endangered land titles through falsifications that later came to light. No matter: the impressive W. F. Holt, the founding entrepreneur of Imperial other than George Chaffey and the original CDC investment group, was the logical choice to stand in as Barbara Worth's foster father. Born in Missouri, Holt had migrated to Colorado and southwestern Arizona. Visiting Imperial out of curiosity in 1901, the young banker saw his opportunity. Let CDC control the water, Holt decided, he would develop the infrastructure—the gas, electricity, and telephones, the banks, stores, hotels, newspapers, ice machines, and local railroad tracks—all of which Holt and his brother Leroy proceeded to do. By 1910, when Wright was writing, the Imperial Valley was Holt country: the Holt Power Company, the city of Holtville itself, Holt this, Holt that. From this perspective *The Winning of Barbara Worth* represented Wright's effort to baptize and make holy his friend W. F. Holt's overt or silent participation in so many aspects of the valley's economy. Holt, after all, was the supreme practitioner of what Wright described as the ministry of capital.

Things had turned out well for W. F. Holt, and for others as well, through all the perturbations of clogged canals, flooding, and title disputes. During the go-go years of growth, the Imperial Valley functioned as the truck garden of Los Angeles, a source for food equivalent to the Owens Valley as a source for water. Such a large-scale operation, the feeding of millions from a million irrigated acres, tended inevitably towards an equally large-scale, increasingly centralized form of agriculture later described as agribusiness.

Environmental historian Donald Worster finds in the Imperial Valley clear proof that in ages past and present irrigation by its very nature produces not Smythe's localized land-holding yeomanry but bureaucratic centralism and vast estates. The peculiar financial structure of the Imperial, moreover, in which water stocks equaled water equaled land, allowed speculation rapidly to consolidate large holdings through the acquisition of water stock from settlers unable to go the distance. It did not take long for the Imperial Valley, eventually subsidized by the Reclamation-built All American Canal as well, to become dominated by the same landowner class already present in 1900 when Harrison Gray Otis and his partner Moses H. Sherman purchased a 700,000-acre ranch adjacent to the Imperial Valley and extending into Mexico.

Below the Mexican border, Otis and Sherman's California-Mexican Land and Cattle Company drew its water gratis, no water stock needed, from the Imperial Canal. Rockwood and other CDC directors likewise availed themselves of this Mexican privilege. By 1904 land below the Mexican border, much of it American-owned, was consuming free of charge seven times as much Colorado River water from the Imperial Canal as was being used in the valley itself.

By 1966 eight hundred individuals or corporations owned 90 percent of all Imperial acreage. A significant percentage of individual owners, moreover, was leasing its land back to corporations, thus even further consolidating the management of a valley that had been made even more profitable by further tax-supported Reclamation projects. Thus public water ironically continued to enrich an increasingly smaller circle of private investors. The CDC model, not Smythe's vision, prevailed. As its name suggested, the Imperial seemed destined to remain the empire of the few.

3

Aqueduct Cities

Foundations of Urban Empire

By 1900 the sub/urban destiny of California had asserted itself. Some 40 percent of the 1.5 million population of the state lived either in the San Francisco Bay Area or in greater Los Angeles. Of all the cities and towns of California, only San Francisco and Los Angeles proper showed signs of soon becoming major metropolitan regions. Accelerated into urbanism by the Gold Rush, San Francisco had become the tenth largest city in the United States by 1870. Essentially a maritime colony in its first decades of growth, San Francisco displayed the ability of a maritime colony to replicate, even if on a smaller scale, the high urban forms of the originating culture. Thus San Francisco sustained a complex civic life and range of institutions when it was the only urban settlement of any size west of the Rocky Mountains. Los Angeles grew more slowly, but by 1900 the City of the Angels possessed a civic ambition comparable to the high provincial security of San Francisco, destined to remain for another fifty years the financial and social capital of the Far West.

Each city needed more water if it were to continue to grow. As in the case of agriculture, the sub/urban destiny of coastal California around San Francisco Bay and the Los Angeles basin depended upon the location of new water sources, followed by the construction of dams, reservoirs, and distribution systems. In ages past, before the formation of the bay, the Russian River (as it came to be called) ran across a great plain through the Golden Gate into the Pacific. In prehistoric times a geological catastrophe, most likely a major earthquake, caused the littoral to subside massively. There survived in local Indian memory a recollection of this event through folklore, thereby dating it to within the last 30,000 years. As the plain collapsed, the sea rushed in to form the present San Francisco Bay, and the outlet of the Russian River was shoved northwards to its present site at Jenner by the Sea. The newly formed bay pushed itself eastwards until it encountered the downward freshwater flow of the Sacramento and San Joaquin rivers converging in a delta region of linked marshes. The salinity of the bay penetrated the delta region, and so these river waters proved unfit for human consumption. San Francisco would have to look elsewhere for its water.

During the Gold Rush, as San Francisco grew to rapid maturity, water had to be shipped across the bay from Marin County in casks and hawked on the streets, or it was brought in from Mountain Lake on the northwest edge of the peninsula by donkey and sold by the bucketful. By 1858 water from Lobos Creek and Mountain Lake, two freshwater sources on the San Francisco peninsula itself, was being shipped for 5.3 miles into the city by a tunnel and redwood flume system ending at Black Point on the northern edge of the peninsula. From there the water was pumped to two reservoirs on Hyde Street, one at Greenwich, the other at Francisco, which to this day are still in use. The dominant water company of San Francisco, the Spring Valley Water Works, ably directed by Herman Schussler, a German-born engineer trained at Karlsruhe and Zurich, turned south for its water supply to San Mateo County, where under Schussler's direction a series of reservoirs was created at Lake Pilarcitos, Lake San Andreas, and Crystal Springs Lake, augmented by another reservoir across the bay at Sunol in Alameda County. From 1862 to 1929, when it was at last acquired by the city, Spring Valley exercised a monopoly on the water supply of San Francisco. The company and the city quarreled constantly. At one time the city owed Spring Valley $400,000 in disputed back payments for the irrigation of Golden Gate Park. In 1898 San Franciscans voted approval of a reform charter that theoretically authorized the city to acquire the Spring Valley system. It took another thirty-one years for this to happen.

By that time, 1929, Los Angeles had already municipalized its water supply and completed a major aqueduct sixteen years earlier in 1913. Unlike San Francisco in the water-abundant north, Los Angeles in the semi-arid Southland had no doubts whatsoever that water controlled its destiny. So uncertain a source was the Los Angeles River, even the frontier cattle town felt threatened. With almost a sigh of gratitude, the city council in 1868 turned over the water franchise to the Los Angeles City Water Company, which constructed a system of reservoirs and open ditches clearly obsolete by the boom-era expansion of the 1880s. The driving force behind the Los Angeles City Water Company was Fred Eaton, a native-born Los Angeleno who served as superintending engineer of the system from 1877 to 1886. As city engineer of Los Angeles from 1886 to 1890, Eaton pushed for municipalization. As in the case of the Spring Valley Water Works in San Francisco, the owners of the Los Angeles Water Company held on to their franchise by placing on it too high a price. Eaton nevertheless continued to argue for public ownership after leaving the city engineer's office and returning to private practice. When Fred Eaton was elected mayor of Los Angeles in 1898, he pushed even more vigorously for the municipalization of the company he had once directed.

When the State Supreme Court ruled that Los Angeles held jurisdiction over the Los Angeles River watershed, which had also been claimed by the Los Angeles City Water Company, the case for municipalization gained further momentum. Fred Eaton had left office by the time the company backed off its $3 million asking price and agreed to accept $2 million instead. A bond issue was passed on 28 August 1901; by 13 February 1902 the City of the Angels, having bought out the Los Angeles City Water Company, held in its municipal hands the ability to create its urban future through water. In the first phase of this process, the translation of water into a public enterprise, Los Angeles edged out San Francisco by a quarter-century. Although the two cities employed parallel strategies and engineering solutions to gain the water necessary for their growth, Los Angeles never lost this initial momentum, and completed its aqueduct twenty-one years before San Francisco.

Each city, first of all, established a special administrative structure to handle water matters. San Francisco's reform charter of 1898 established a three-member Board of Public Works, appointed by the mayor, responsible for the selection of the city architect and the city engineer and for all engineering and public works in the city. After experimenting with a popularly elected Board of Water Commissioners, Los Angeles created in January 1903 a five-member board appointed by the mayor. This second board exercised an extraordinary degree of autonomy. In San Francisco the mayor and the county board of supervisors held tight controls on the Board of Public Works. Its finances were part of the general fund of the city. In Los Angeles the Board of Water Commissioners reported to the City Council only in the matter of rates and maintained jurisdiction over all its own monies. The Los Angeles board was soon to become a government within the government or, as many believed, the real government of Los Angeles. It was as if the city, out of a mixture of ambition and Progressive reform, wanted its water future structured and empowered beyond the vagaries of electoral sentiment as the one abiding doctrine, water and growth, to which all Los Angeles must give its assent.

Each city, secondly, surveyed possible sources for its future water supply. As far back as 1871 Lieutenant Colonel B.S. Alexander of the Army Corps of Engineers and Professor George Davidson of the State Geological Survey recommended Lake Tahoe and Clear Lake in Northern California as possible sources for San Francisco. Water engineer T.R. Scowden recommended in 1874 that a dam be built across Calaveras Valley in the Sierra Nevada Mother Lode, thereby creating a reservoir out of Calaveras Creek from which a downhill aqueduct could be constructed to San Francisco. Another engineer, J.P. Dart, employed by the highly speculative, briefly existing Tuolumne and San Francisco Water Company, advocated that San Francisco dam the Hetch Hetchy, a valley in the northwest Yosemite through which the Tuolumne River flowed, and build an aqueduct. William Hammond Hall, then heading the California division of the U.S. Geological Survey, recommended the Hetch Hetchy site in 1891 and, characteristically untroubled by conflict of interest, proceeded to buy up property in the region as an investment. In 1901 San Francisco city engineer C.E. Grunsky cited Hall's 1891 report and made the same Hetch Hetchy recommendation after considering fourteen other sites. The Board of Public Works accepted Grunsky's recommendation, citing the purity of the Tuolumne River water, the reservoir sites available at nearby Lake Eleanor and the Hetch Hetchy itself, once dammed, and the potential for hydroelectrical generation by water descending from the Sierra Nevada to San Francisco.

While San Francisco was orienting itself to the Tuolumne River and the Hetch Hetchy as its future water source, Los Angeles, in the person of its former city engineer and mayor Fred Eaton, was looking to the Owens Valley 200 miles to the north on the eastern side of the southern Sierra Nevada. A long narrow graben or depressed fault, the Owens Valley runs for a hundred miles between the Inyo-White Mountains to the east and the Sierra Nevada to the west. Through this narrow valley, five to twelve miles wide, ran the Owens River which emptied into Owens Lake at the southern terminus.

Camping there in the early 1890s, Eaton noted how the fresh, pure water of the Owens River served no purpose other than to empty into the brackish and stagnant Owens Lake. How much more serviceable, Eaton thought, to bring the Owens River into water-starved Los Angeles by aqueduct. Ceaselessly throughout the 1890s—as manager of the City Water Company, as city engineer, as mayor, and as a former mayor—Eaton advocated the Owens Valley and its river as the logical source for water for the City of the Angels.

The two rivers, interestingly enough—the Tuolumne desired by San Francisco and the Owens coveted by Los Angeles—each had their origins only fifteen miles apart from each other in a living glacier atop the 13,000-foot Mount Lyell in Mono County. Whereas the Hetch Hetchy was remote and unsettled, however (not until 1961 would the Hetch Hetchy be linked to the outside world by a fully modern road), the Owens Valley was equally remote but settled. Throughout the 1890s, as Eaton dreamed of diverting Owens River water to Los Angeles, settlers attracted by the excellent soil and abundant water of the valley had brought some 41,000 acres under cultivation in cereals and fruit. In 1903 the Reclamation Service was targeting the Owens Valley as a logical site for a major irrigation project.

In the third phase of water development, San Francisco and Los Angeles, having located their sources, each staked their claims. In the case of San Francisco, this process began simply and then bogged down into thirteen years of paralyzing complexity and delay. Los Angeles's effort, by contrast, began in a labyrinth of conflicting loyalties and ambitions, public and private, honorable and otherwise, that conferred on the city's modern foundations in water an ambiguity, an unease, that would very soon become part of the essential personality of the City of the Angels in fact and metaphorical suggestion.

At first it appeared that the Owens Valley might become the site of an early and very successful Reclamation project, a prophetic example of what federally sponsored irrigation could accomplish. On 29 April 1903 Frederick Haynes Newell, the director of the newly established Reclamation Service, commissioned his chief of operations in California, Joseph B. Lippincott, to survey the Owens Valley for a possible Reclamation project. Lippincott sent a young engineer by the name of Jacob C. Clausen into the field to investigate. Noting the abundant stream flows, the possible dam and reservoir sites, the already existing agricultural settlements, the availability of land in the public domain, Clausen took only a few weeks to report back enthusiastically to Lippincott by telegram. Joining his junior colleague in the field, Lippincott helped complete the survey. On 20 July 1903 Lippincott reported with equal enthusiasm to his boss Newell: the Owens Valley was the ideal place for Reclamation to prove itself as an agency. By December 1903 over half a million Owens Valley acres in the public domain were withdrawn from settlement and reserved for Reclamation. Lippincott, meanwhile, remained in the field, surveying and mapping the proposed project. He selected Long Valley just north of Bishop, where Inyo, Fresno, and Madera counties intersect, as the best possible dam and reservoir site. The Owens Valley proposal was mentioned prominently in Reclamation's annual report for 1903 and was also touted by Lippincott in the April 1904 issue of *Forestry and Irrigation* magazine. Thus far the entire situation appeared a certain triumph for irrigation, land settlement, and the rural vision in California. One hundred sixty miles from the coast, on the far side of the Sierra Nevada, the already prosperous Owens Valley bespoke California as a land of farms and homes enhanced by irrigation. The urban alternative, it would seem, had little if anything to do with Owens Valley and all that it stood for.

In addition to his superiors at Reclamation, however, Lippincott was also in contact with his former boss Fred Eaton. Settling in Los Angeles in 1891, Lippincott, a University of Kansas-trained engineer, had spent the 1890s as an engineering consultant in the Los Angeles area, including direct work for Eaton when Eaton was mayor. Since leaving office, Eaton had devoted himself to the municipalization of Los Angeles water, which was accomplished in February 1902. Municipalization enabled the people of Los Angeles to raise large sums of money through bond issues. Eaton hoped to promote the public financing of an aqueduct from Owens Valley to Los Angeles in which he would have vested rights. Half the water would go to Los Angeles for domestic use; the other half would be distributed by Eaton to irrigation districts and other clients on the south coast. It was a public/private scheme of dual motivation: water and growth for Los Angeles, profit for Eaton.

Lippincott himself had spent his career at such public/private intersection points, and so it was with mixed motivation that the Reclamation engineer took the former mayor turned water entrepreneur on a tour of Long Valley in the upper Owens Valley in August 1904. Lippincott would later swear that he had no idea of Eaton's interest in the Owens Valley on behalf of Los Angeles until November. This makes no sense whatsoever. It was clear that Lippincott, in taking Eaton whom he had known and worked for, whose investments and ambitions for the Owens Valley he can be expected to have been aware of, on this Reclamation-sponsored tour, and talking openly about Reclamation's plans to his young assistant Clausen within hearing range of Eaton, was clearly signaling the former mayor that he had better move quickly.

Eaton, for his part, got the message. Returning to Los Angeles, he persuaded William Mulholland, the chief engineer of the municipalized water company, to travel by buckboard with him back to the Owens Valley, which Eaton was telling Mulholland was the best possible source of water for Los Angeles.

A classical poet writing the history of Los Angeles in the style of Virgil's *Aeneid* might very well see in this buckboard journey across the desert a symbolic journey into Los Angeles's future, two founders of the city in search of destiny. A comic poet would note the trail of empty liquor bottles left behind and see in this ribbon of glass the first mapping of the aqueduct route. In any event, city engineer William Mulholland was thus being introduced by the former mayor to the source and the route of the aqueduct he would soon be building. The success of the aqueduct would transform Mulholland, an obscure self-taught Irish immigrant, into the one universally acknowledged Founder of Los Angeles.

Born in Dublin in 1855, Mulholland arrived in the United States in 1874 as a merchant seaman. He spent the next three years, variously, as a Great Lakes sailor, a lumberjack in Michigan, an itinerant mechanic, and a drygoods clerk in Pittsburgh, where he read Charles Nordhoff's *California for Health, Wealth and Residence* (1872) and determined to see for himself. At the age of 21 Mulholland and his brother sailed for Colon, Panama, then walked across the isthmus to save the $25 railroad fare. Working their way to San Francisco as sailors, the brothers rode by horseback down the San Joaquin Valley to Los Angeles, which they reached in the summer of 1877. There, in a small settlement of less than five thousand people, William Mulholland found the place, Los Angeles, and the calling, water engineering, that would occupy him for a lifetime. Taking a job as a *zanjero* or ditch tender with the Los Angeles City Water Company at a time of severe drought, the young Irishman learned in a simple but effective way how dependent Los Angeles was on its solitary water source, the Los Angeles River. The river and the City Water Company, augmented by bouts of study and wide reading in his rooming house near the Plaza, constituted Mulholland's engineering education.

The City of the Angels proved to be the only place he exercised his calling throughout his long lifetime. In later life Mulholland suggested an almost mystical affinity between himself and the uncertain but friendly willow-lined Los Angeles River where he took long walks after a day of keeping the *zanja madre* free of weeds and debris before returning to his room for a night of study. Active, physical, lean, tan, and fit into his old age, William Mulholland also studied hydraulics, botany, and history with the strong memory of the Irish.

When it came time for him to play the Founder, he was ready for the role. As he studied and achieved promotion, becoming superintendent of the entire system in 1886, a post he retained when the company was acquired by the city, Mulholland also made an exhaustive inventory of ways to maximize the resources of the Los Angeles River. As supervising engineer he put most of them into practice—the Elysian Reservoir, the Solano Reservoir, the Buena Vista pumping plant, a tunnel in the bedrock beneath the river itself for the collection of groundwater; but by 1904 when Fred Eaton invited him up to the Owens Valley, William Mulholland was on record that the City of Los Angeles needed a dramatic new water source if it were to continue its development.

No record of Eaton and Mulholland's campfire conversations over whiskey are available, but it is not difficult to imagine the two men talking by the firelight in the midst of a vast and empty Mojave Desert night: talking about the Los Angeles which had so profoundly shaped each of them and sustained their careers in politics and engineering, talking about the water that Los Angeles needed if it were ever to become more than just another south coast urban settlement, talking, in Eaton's case, of the Owens River wasting itself into the useless sump of Owens Lake when it could be bringing into being a great American city. Made aware by Lippincott of Reclamation's designs on Owens Valley, Eaton swore Mulholland to secrecy. One wonders how reticent Eaton was in those whiskeyish talks regarding his hopes to cut himself in for a percentage of future water rates. Already, the water destiny of Los Angeles was unfolding as a conspiracy in which public ambition and private self-interest mingled murkily.

Shown the Owens Valley by Eaton—the river, the reservoir site at Long Valley—Mulholland was convinced. Here was water enough for two million people, ten times the population of Los Angeles in 1904. Here was a future worth struggling for. Returning to Los Angeles, Mulholland met secretly with the Board of Water Commissioners, whose support he won for what was now his and Eaton's grand scheme. From this meeting, the word went out among Los Angeles's tightly knit oligarchy. Everyone was pledged to secrecy, including the newspapers, so as to allow room for maneuver on both sides and to prevent either protest or speculation in the Owens Valley. Eaton's plan now enveloped the inner circle of Los Angeles. Surprisingly, no one broke the silence.

Lippincott, meanwhile, continued to play a double game as he carried on the Owens Valley surveys ostensibly on behalf of Reclamation while aware that other plans were afoot, which he himself had initially stimulated by contacting

Eaton. Cagily, Lippincott played both sides against a possible middle. On 17 September 1904 he dutifully and confidentially notified Reclamation chief Frederick Newell in Washington that Los Angeles was giving consideration to Owens Valley as a water source. With this one stroke, Lippincott at once eased his conscience and protected himself from charges of duplicity should such charges ever surface, which they eventually did. Even more cunningly, he was providing Reclamation with the option of retiring gracefully from Owens Valley should it choose not to come into conflict with Los Angeles. Such withdrawal on the part of Reclamation would have won Lippincott the instant gratitude of the Los Angeles establishment. As it was, he had successfully positioned himself as the man in the middle. A meeting was held in Los Angeles on 22 November 1904 among Newell, Lippincott, Eaton, Mulholland, and W.B. Mathews, the city attorney. The Los Angeles representatives said they were interested in the Owens Valley but needed more information. Lippincott volunteered to turn over all Reclamation studies. Reclamation stated that if it withdrew, it would be only on the condition that the proposed Owens Valley/ Los Angeles Aqueduct be publicly financed, owned, and managed. Reclamation would step aside only for another public project.

And this, step aside, is what Reclamation proceeded to do in the months that followed. Work on the Owens Valley project ceased at Reclamation by September 1904. By the end of that year Owens Valley had even disappeared from Reclamation's annual report. Despite his status as a Reclamation engineer, Lippincott went on the payroll of the Los Angeles Water Commission in March 1905 as a consultant to Mulholland at more than half his salary at Reclamation. When Newell upbraided him for this, Lippincott brazenly replied that he had the support of the senior United States Senator from California, George C. Perkins, who had told him, Lippincott claimed, that Reclamation as a publicly supported agency owed its consulting services to state and local government. Even more brazenly, Lippincott provided Fred Eaton, a private citizen, with a letter of introduction which Eaton used to acquire Reclamation maps and surveys of strategic Owens Valley sites. Thwarted in his desire to participate directly in the financing and revenues of the proposed aqueduct, Eaton now had another strategy: to buy up options on critical land sites in the Owens Valley for later resale to Los Angeles. Aside from helping him gain access to the invaluable Reclamation maps and surveys, Lippincott's letter left the impression which Fred Eaton encouraged (or at least never dispelled) that he was in the valley buying property on behalf of a public project.

Ironically, this was in part true. As of yet the Water Commission of Los Angeles had no funds authorized for the purchase of Owens Valley property. The entire Owens Valley gambit, in fact, remained a secret known only to the oligarchy. In an unofficial, ambiguous, but totally effective way, the former mayor—to his own great profit—was operating on behalf of a Los Angeles government which had not been as of yet empowered by the voters to act on its own behalf. The oligarchy went so far as to raise $300,000 from private sources for an indemnity bond to cover Los Angeles's payments to Eaton, should the projected bond issue fail to win the voters' approval. Eaton acquired options on Owens Valley property which he sold to Los Angeles for $450,000. He made another $100,000 on commission as agent for the sale of other Owens Valley properties to the city. He also retained control of the fully stocked 23,000-acre Rickey Ranch. The Ranch included the crucial Long Valley reservoir site, over which Eaton maintained exclusive rights. All this from an initial cash outlay of $15,000! Rarely has public service been so richly rewarded.

Once the water commissioners found themselves paying out these sums from the city treasury in June 1905, they knew they had to go public with their secret program. Most immediately, Reclamation would have to cede its Owens Valley claims to Los Angeles. Second, a bond issue would have to be passed raising the money to cover the sums already paid Eaton and to make necessary further purchase in the Owens Valley. Third, the aqueduct had to be planned and designed. Fourth, a second bond issue would have to be passed to cover construction costs. Astonishingly, all this was made to happen within the two years between June 1905 and June 1907.

When a specially appointed Reclamation panel decided on 28 July 1905 to suspend its activities in the Owens Valley, the Los Angeles *Times* went public the next day with the entire story. In the Owens Valley at the time of this unexpected disclosure, Fred Eaton fled at once to San Francisco rather than confront angry ranchers who now felt betrayed by Reclamation, or, worse, who now knew themselves to have been deceived by Eaton, who had been passing himself off as some kind of government agent. A few days later, the *Times* called for a $1.5 million bond issue to be put on the ballot in September to cover the cost of land and water rights. Two weeks later, the water commissioners complied, setting the election for 7 September. Mulholland went to work immediately as a volunteer publicist for the bond issue. Unfortunately, there existed at the time no detailed studies, drawings, or plans, which did not stop Mulholland from saying the project would cost $25 million (he was only $2 million off) and would take four years to build (it took six). Backed by all but one Los Angeles newspaper, the Hearst-owned *Examiner*, Mulholland also evoked the specter of Los Angeles's dwindling water resources, making reference to a drought which was supposed to have lasted for the previous ten years but which up to that time only Mulholland seems to have noticed. Without new water sources, Mulholland exaggerated, Los Angeles's population was destined to hover indefinitely at the quarter-million mark.

The Los Angeles *Examiner* disputed Mulholland's claims and offered counterarguments and statistics against the bond issue. *Examiner* publisher William Randolph Hearst, an outsider in an insiders' city, resented the power of the oligarchy, specifically the pre-eminence of *Times* publisher Harrison Gray Otis. As a newspaperman Hearst was seething over the *Times*'s unilateral breaking of the water story in late July. On 25 August, less than two weeks before the election, the *Examiner* turned over what Hearst considered a particularly nasty rock. Otis of the *Times* and Edwin T. Earl, publisher of the *Express*, the *Examiner* revealed, were part of a syndicate, the San Fernando Mission Land Company (other members included Henry Huntington of the Pacific Electric Railroad, E.H. Harriman of the Southern Pacific, and Joseph Sartori of Security Trust and Savings), which was quietly buying up land in the San Fernando Valley which would soar in value once water arrived. Water commissioner Moses Sherman later joined the syndicate, a defiance of conflict of interest notable for its chutzpah even in the elastic ethos of that era. The papers were promoting a project that would enrich the publishers.

For a few days, even the accommodating oligarchy was shocked. There was talk of a taxpayers' inquiry, of calling in the Army Corps of Engineers for an independent review. The Chamber of Commerce sent an investigative team out to Owens Valley. But then the oligarchy grew weary of virtue and began to rally to its own defense. Hearst himself, then a congressman from New York seeking the Democratic party nomination to the presidency, was personally invited out to Los Angeles for a meeting with the business leadership on 3 September 1905. At this meeting the oligarchy stressed to Hearst the public nature of the proposed aqueduct. Hearst had long since been advocating the public ownership of municipal utilities. The leadership also agreed to submit Mulholland's plan to an independent outside board of review, as suggested the day before by the Chamber of Commerce, before expending any further funds. Whatever else was said at this meeting, there was most likely some subtle linking of the aqueduct with Hearst's own desire for a larger role in the public affairs of Los Angeles. In any event, Hearst emerged from the meeting with a changed mind. Going over to the offices of the *Examiner*, he personally wrote out an editorial that, while repeating a key *Examiner* objection to the project (funds had been spent without proper authorization), gave the bond issue his endorsement.

2

The $1.5 million authorized by the voters on 7 September 1905 (fourteen to one in favor) put the Board of Water Commissioners and Mulholland in the welcomed position of being at last capable of planning for the aqueduct openly and officially. It took less than two years to work out a design program and to secure the necessary approvals. Credit for the Los Angeles Aqueduct belongs to the Los Angeles oligarchy. Failing to fight the entry of Los Angeles into the Owens Valley, Reclamation had created an expectation of impending public works which Los Angeles was able to exploit. It was this sense that the government was about to do something in the way of an irrigation project which Eaton used to shield his purchases.

As the matter of the aqueduct reached Washington it was strengthened by the Progressive preference for public works projects offering the greatest good for the greatest number of citizens. Public projects such as the proposed Los Angeles Aqueduct spoke directly to the Progressive desire to bring efficiency and prudent use to American life. Progressives wished to bend the power and resources of America to the public good in a way that transcended the short-term goals of pragmatic politics. Thus when the residents of Owens Valley, led locally by Stafford W. Austin, Registrar of the United States Land Office in Owens Valley, and represented in Washington by Congressman Sylvester C. Smith, a former Bakersfield newspaperman, attempted merely to qualify the aqueduct in Washington, arguing that Los Angeles should be allowed to use the Owens River for domestic purposes but not for the irrigation of the San Fernando Valley, they ran head on into the formidable opposition of the most energetic of the ever-energetic Progressives, President Theodore Roosevelt. When Congressman Smith attached a no-irrigation amendment to a bill introduced by California Senator Frank Flint, a prominent Los Angeles attorney, author-izing the passage of the aqueduct across federal lands, Roosevelt personally intervened to have the restricting rider removed from Flint's bill, which passed both houses on 27 June 1906.

A month later, Reclamation formally abandoned all claims to the Owens Valley. At the recommendation of Gifford Pinchot, chief of the Forestry Bu-reau, Roosevelt also declared some treeless acres in the Owens Valley a federal forest reserve, thereby precluding any further homesteading, private filings, or claims in this area. Roosevelt personally drew the new boundaries extending the eastern limits of the Sierra Forest Reserve so as to protect the aqueduct. Congressman Smith was pointedly not invited to White House meetings re-viewing the situation and was arrogantly admonished by Roosevelt when he politely asked for a discussion. "I should like to talk with you further before you act," Smith requested. "You don't need to talk," TR snapped. "I am doing the talking." Sent by Los Angeles to lobby the Flint bill through Congress, city engineer Mulholland and city attorney W.B. Mathews returned to a welcom-ing crowd at the Los Angeles train depot in early July. "We got what we went after," Mulholland told the crowd.[1]

In late 1906 a specially convened panel of consulting engineers, meeting in Los Angeles, reviewed Mulholland's proposal, as was promised before the 1905 bond issue. Seven years later, the panel's most eminent member, John R. Freeman, past president of the American Society of Mechanical Engineers and consultant to the Panama Canal and to the water systems of Boston and New York, would play a similar role in helping San Francisco refine its proposal. In an effort to contain costs the panel eliminated all three reservoir sites—one at Long Valley in the Owens Valley, the other two in San Fernando Valley— whose storage capacity Mulholland considered crucial to the maintenance of the system year to year, whatever the fluctuations of annual rainfall. Without the three reservoirs, Mulholland pointed out, the Los Angeles Aqueduct merely siphoned the Owens Valley directly. However grand, it was little more than a diversionary ditch.

The panel also eliminated Mulholland's elegant distribution system, based on his lifetime study of the Los Angeles River watershed, and also scratched plans for a municipally sponsored railroad to run parallel to the aqueduct, initially for construction purposes, later to link the Owens Valley and Los Angeles together economically and thereby benefit the settlers, who would then be able to sell and ship their harvests directly to the Los Angeles market. In order to generate revenues from hydroelectricity, the panel rerouted the aqueduct into the San Fernando Valley via the San Francisquito Canyon, creating three major drops from which could be generated enough electricity to service Los Angeles, Long Beach, Pasadena, and Santa Monica.

With this hydroelectrical option, the second government of Los Angeles, the Department of Water and Power, insulated from the direct control of the voters, responsive to and staffed by the Progressive oligarchy, was assured of a dominance that would soon become the central continuity of politics in the City of the Angels. Naturally resenting this municipalization of electricity as well as water, the private power companies fought the $23 million bond issue set for 12 June 1907. Securing control of the failing Los Angeles *Evening News*, the power companies fought the bond issue through Samuel T. Clover, a onetime Chicago newsman who adamantly denied being on the power companies' payroll. This futile resistance only caused the *Evening News* to lose advertising. On election day, 12 June 1907, nine out of ten voters authorized the City of Los Angeles to issue the bonds to raise the money for William Mulholland to go out to the desert and build the longest aqueduct in the Western Hemisphere. It was as if Boston had decided to draw its water from the St. Lawrence River, or Washington, D.C., were reaching out to the Ohio, or St. Louis were reaching across the State of Illinois to Lake Michigan.

Formal responsibility for overseeing the construction of the aqueduct resided in the Los Angeles Board of Public Works, whose chairman was no less than the former Chief of Staff of the United States Army, Lieutenant General Adna R. Chaffee. A veteran of the Civil War, the Indian campaigns of the Southwest, the Spanish American War, and the Boxer Rebellion, Chaffee, a cavalryman, had worked his way up from the enlisted ranks to the Army's top position without benefit of a West Point ring. In 1906 he retired to Los Angeles and two years later was appointed to the Board of Public Works. While Mulholland supervised in the field, Chaffee brought his military experience to bear on providing the field crews with staff and logistical support.

Another important staff member, project attorney William Burgess Mathews, formerly the city attorney of Los Angeles, oversaw financial and legal matters and handled labor negotiations. In the field, where he spent most of his time, Mulholland depended heavily upon the former Reclamation engineer J.B. Lippincott, now officially on Los Angeles's payroll as assistant chief engineer, and E.F. Scattergood, who maintained a high degree of autonomy as chief engineer for hydroelectrical construction and operations. Early on in the project, Scattergood built two hydroelectric plants on creeks falling into the Owens River. The electricity thus generated, carried out along 169 miles of transmission lines, made the project energy self-sufficient.

Forecasting the eventual need for 1.2 million barrels of cement, Mulholland put Los Angeles in the cement business at Monolith on the Tehachapi plateau, where 250 workers were kept busy at a city-owned plant preparing a special cement formula which Mulholland had himself devised. The Southern Pacific, meanwhile, constructed a railroad out from Mojave across the desert along the aqueduct route to Lone Pine, where it connected with a narrow-gauge line railway serving Owens Valley. Two hundred and forty miles of telephone lines, 500 miles of roads and trails, and 2300 buildings and tent houses rounded out the supporting infrastructure of the enterprise.

Non-unionized day laborers built the aqueduct, transient men for the most part, in whom the West abounded, men without families who worked from ten-day bonus period to ten-day bonus period, then drifted down the line. One foreman reported that he had one crew drunk, one crew sobering up, and one crew working. However disreputable, the aqueduct laborers at least expressed one aspect of the Progressive agenda: they were, so it was boasted, 100 percent American, which is to say, Mexicans, blacks, Asians, or conspicuously ethnic immigrants were rarely in evidence on the line. Like so much else in Los Angeles, the aqueduct was the prerogative of white America. Under the bonus system, specially devised for tunneling the fifty miles of tunnels which had to be dug, frequently blasted out of solid rock, a base rate was set for so many feet of advance per ten-day period per tunnel; for every foot completed after that, tunnelers received a forty-cent bonus. The better crews were soon earning the bulk of their pay in bonuses. One aqueduct crew set a new world's record for hard-rock tunneling, 604 feet in the month of August 1910.

Not only was the aqueduct publicly owned and financed, it was publicly built by the Board of Public Works operating through Mulholland and his supervisory staff of civil service engineers. Intuitive, self-educated, hating paperwork, Mulholland came into his own in the field riding horseback up and down the line like a general on campaign, supervising the construction of the aqueduct which he himself had designed. For nearly six years Mulholland—tanned, leathery lean, military in his mustachios—stayed in the field, supervising, exhorting, devising ad hoc design solutions when necessary, leaving the paperwork to others. As in the case of any good general, Mulholland was at once admired and feared by his men. When a tunnel worker, submerged in a cave-in, was kept alive by hard-boiled eggs rolled down to him through an open conduit, Mulholland dryly suggested that the trapped worker be charged board for the time of his involuntary stay. Since the worker was rescued shortly after,

Mulholland's remark made a good story. It also underscored his obsession with keeping the project on schedule and on budget.

In February 1910, with the aqueduct two-thirds complete, Mulholland ran out of money when the New York syndicate financing the project refused to accelerate its rate of purchase of bonds. In pushing the aqueduct ahead of schedule, Mulholland had also pushed it ahead of its scheduled cash flow. By refusing to buy bonds ahead of schedule, Wall Street was also punishing Los Angeles for its decision to municipalize the hydroelectrical plants attached to the aqueduct. Offered immediate financing if it would back off from its commitment to public power, Los Angeles refused. Thereupon ensued a year of delay and political infighting, including a full-scale investigation by a specially appointed Aqueduct Investigation Board which asked a lot of questions, many of them excruciatingly repetitive, but which reconfirmed the original scope and operation of the project, including its commitment to publicly owned electricity. Sensing Los Angeles's determination, the New York syndicate headed by A.E. Leach and Company and Kountze Brothers resumed its bond purchase, and Mulholland headed back into the field. By the fall of 1913 the Los Angeles Aqueduct—235 miles of canals, conduits, tunnels, flumes, penstocks, tailraces, and siphons—was nearing completion. Commencing at its intake point twelve miles above the town of Independence, the aqueduct moved southwest past Owens Lake before arching across the Mojave Desert to the west end of the Antelope Valley, where it headed south through the Coast Range via the five-mile Elizabeth Tunnel, then pushed into the San Fernando Valley via the San Francisquito Canyon.

Although there were a number of reservoirs en route—at Haiwee, Fairmont, Bouquet Canyon, Dry Canyon, and two in San Fernando from which the water entered the Los Angeles distribution system—these reservoirs functioned essentially as catchment devices in the downward flow. There was no long-term storage facility where it should have been at Long Valley, a twenty-square-mile meadow, hence a natural reservoir. Why was such an essential component not constructed? The Board of Public Works, first of all, had eliminated it in its overall downscaling of Mulholland's original scheme to save on expenses; but even had the board reversed itself and decided upon a permanent reservoir at the Long Valley site, it would have been stymied by the fact that Fred Eaton was asking a million dollars for 12,000 strategically placed acres in southern Mono County.

Mulholland denounced Eaton's price as excessive. Had Los Angeles acquired the property, even during the construction phase when Eaton made his offer (Mulholland's refusal shattered their friendship), Mulholland might have been able to persuade Los Angeles to return to the proposal he had made in his 1907 report: a simple dam across Long Valley, 165 feet high, 525 feet across, creating a reservoir of 260,000 acre feet that would arm Los Angeles against the dry years. It made no sense whatsoever to build an aqueduct with-

out a storage facility at the source. To make matters worse, the intake point of
the aqueduct was located at the upper reaches of the Owens River so as to
avoid any traces of alkali. Like a vampire, Los Angeles had affixed itself to the
primal source point for the Owens River and the valley it watered.

On the morning of Wednesday, 5 November 1913, a crowd of between
30,000 and 40,000, many of them carrying tin cups to take their first drink,
gathered outside the city of San Fernando at the base of the last spillway in the
Los Angeles aqueduct system. A distracted Mulholland, his wife gravely ill in
the hospital, ascended a bunting-bedraped stand alongside Mayor H.H. Rose,
Congressman William D. Stephens, the president of the Los Angeles Chamber
of Commerce, and other dignitaries. Mulholland and Lippincott were each
presented with silver loving cups. Fred Eaton, the third in the triumvirate who
had set in motion the aqueduct program a decade earlier, should also have
been on hand but he was still quarreling with Mulholland and Los Angeles
over the price of his ranch in Long Valley and had decided to boycott the
ceremony. After a brief speech, Mulholland unfurled an American flag, an
Army cannon boomed, the spillway gates were raised, and the water of the
Owens River cascaded down a long spillway. Abandoning the formal program,
the crowd rushed to taste the waters. "There it is. Take it," Mulholland remarked to the mayor with characteristic understatement.[2] Informed that his
wife had taken a turn for the better and was now out of danger, a reinvigorated
Mulholland walked over to taste the waters of the Los Angeles future.

3

Thus in the early years of the twentieth century, the two dominant metropolitan regions of California, greater Los Angeles and greater San Francisco, envisioned and materialized their futures by water brought in from great distances. By the latter years of the twentieth century, these two metropolitan
regions would rank second and fourth in population in the entire nation. Like
the ancient Romans to whom it frequently compared itself, the Los Angeles
oligarchy employed two essentials to human life, land and water, to transform
the City of the Angels within three decades into an imperial American metropolis. As early as 1911 it was admitted that the Owens Valley aqueduct would
bring into Los Angeles eight times as much water as was needed and four times
as much as Los Angeles could ever use within its geographical boundaries. This
surplus constituted an irresistible force for expansion. In 1913, the year the
water arrived, Mayor Rose appointed an Annexation Commission to oversee
the expansion of Los Angeles through water. By making Owens Valley water
available to the San Fernando Valley, the Los Angeles oligarchy not only en-
riched those of its members who had acquired land in this adjacent area, it
also acquired its own agricultural region: 200 square miles of adjacent backcountry transformed by irrigation into productive acreage rendering Los Ange-

les a self-subsistent citystate on classical lines. Even an opponent of the oligarchy such as William Ellsworth Smythe welcomed the aqueduct because, thanks
to inexpensive public water, hundreds of thousands of Americans, so he believed, might soon be making their homes and livelihoods as intensive agriculturalists in the San Fernando Valley. Not only would Owens River water be
available to the San Fernando, but part of the drainage, percolating back into
the natural underground reservoirs of the watershed, was also available for reuse.
Los Angeles not only had eight times as much water as it needed, it could also
use some of what it did have twice over.

Los Angeles initially found its aqueduct expensive to maintain. By 1915 the
city was servicing its bond debt at the rate of $4000 a day for water it did not
need and refused to sell. Mulholland, among others, successfully opposed the
selling of aqueduct water wholesale to any community unless it was a candidate
for annexation. A community might have all the water it needed—provided
that it become part of Los Angeles. Between 1913 and 1927 Los Angeles expanded itself through annexation into the largest metropolitan territory under a
single government in the United States. Aside from legitimizing the use of
Owens River water there, the annexation of the San Fernando Valley in 1915
alone doubled the size of Los Angeles to 284.81 square miles. It would take
time for the full drama of growth to play itself out, but the structure and infrastructure of a major American city had become materialized through engineering, vision, greed, and ferocious force of will.

San Francisco, by contrast, did not display the same territorial ambition as
Los Angeles. The Hetch Hetchy had the capacity to service four million Bay
Area residents, especially after the O'Shaughnessy Dam at Hetch Hetchy was
raised 86 feet in height in 1938, but Bay Area communities were not forced to
become absorbed into San Francisco if they wished to enjoy its water. In 1923,
the cities on the eastern edge of San Francisco formed their own water district
and began building an aqueduct down from the Mokelumne River in the Sierra,
completed in 1929.

While Los Angeles controlled and sold its hydroelectricity through the all-
powerful semi-autonomous Department of Water and Power, San Francisco
was expressly forbidden by the Raker Act of 1913 to compete with private utilities, and so it sold its power wholesale to Pacific Gas & Electric, with the
exception of the electricity it used for its Municipal Railway System. While
San Francisco remained confined to the tip of the San Francisco Peninsula,
however, the Bay Area as a whole could now grow because of Hetch Hetchy
water, not according to the imperial pattern of Los Angeles but into a mosaic
of interdependent communities from San Jose northward to San Francisco.
The San Francisco project, furthermore, lacked the murky ambiguity of the
Los Angeles venture, the sinister suggestions of conspiracy filmed so persua-
sively by Roman Polanski in *Chinatown* (1974). With the exception of William
Hammond Hall, comfortably ensconced in his leather chair in the Pacific Union
Club atop Nob Hill, living on until 1934, the year the waters arrived, no one

got really rich from the Hetch Hetchy the way people got very, very rich from the Los Angeles Aqueduct. The real estate syndicate realized millions in profits on their San Fernando subdivisions irrigated by the Los Angeles taxpayers with the blessings of the federal government. Ironically, Fred Eaton, who had held out for a million dollars for his Long Valley property, was finally forced to sell to Los Angeles in 1932 when the Pacific Southwest Trust and Savings Bank of Los Angeles foreclosed on the property. In the end, Los Angeles acquired the strategic Owens Valley property for $100,000 less than it had offered Eaton in 1913.

In assessing gains and losses for both projects, the loss of the Hetch Hetchy Valley was the most immediate. As soon as the O'Shaughnessy Dam was put into operation, the Hetch Hetchy Valley, the Little Yosemite—like its name-sake a glacier-carved primeval pageant of cliffs, valley meadows, forest, and stream—disappeared beneath the impassive surface of the reservoir. Weakened by the long struggle to save the Hetch Hetchy and suffering as well from an infected right lung, John Muir died on Christmas Eve, 1914, being spared the actual trauma of the disappearance of the Hetch Hetchy. It took a little longer for the Los Angeles Aqueduct to destroy the Owens Valley.

The symbology in both cases was clear and unambiguous. Two natural environments were sacrificed so that two urban regions might be materialized. Either the destructions were worth it or they were not. Whether one valued California primarily as wilderness, as irrigated farmlands, or as sub/urban metropolises determined the judgment. Out of mixed motivations of public-spiritedness and private gain, the oligarchies of San Francisco and Los Angeles believed the Hetch Hetchy and the Owens Valley to be fair exchanges for great cities. For others, such as John Muir, growth did not constitute in and of itself the greatest good for the greatest possible number as the Progressives were promising through their ambitious public works programs, especially when such growth came at such great cost to the environment. Was not the environment, they asked, everyone's legacy as well? In the case of the Hetch Hetchy, the loss was inevitable once the site was selected. In the case of the Owens Valley, the farmlands might have been saved had the Long Valley reservoir been constructed along with the aqueduct. Without the aqueduct, however, albeit in its flawed form, Los Angeles would not have been able to materialize itself in the 1920s with such astonishing fullness and rapidity—as it now proceeded to do. Securing its water from the Owens Valley, the City of Los Angeles asserted itself as a corporate entity that virtually constituted an autonomous state within the Southern California region. Los Angeles resembled a Swiss canton: possessed, that is, of a city-state identity second only to the national allegiance and an oligarchy thoroughly identified with the corporate/civic polity which was the source of its own continuing prosperity. It soon became difficult to distinguish Los Angeles, greater Los Angeles, Los Angeles County, and Southern California, so pervasive was the hold of the city of Los Angeles on the region.

II

THE CITY ON THE PLAIN

Still, whatever its faults, Los Angeles is to my mind the most
"American" city, within a certain restricted meaning of that ad-
jective, the meaning, indeed, that an alien would have in asking
us to name the town least influenced by European and Asiatic
sources. It, not New England, is the most recent extension of
our Puritan forefathers, a point seemingly so obvious I shall not
labor it.

JOSEPHY LILLY,
"Metropolis of the West,"
North American Review (September 1931)

4

From Oz to Oildorado

The Rise of Los Angeles in the 1920s

In February 1904 the famous children's writer Lyman Frank Baum, author of *The Wonderful Wizard of Oz* (1900), made a winter visit with his wife Maud to Southern California. Escaping the subzero temperatures of Chicago, the couple sojourned at Coronado in the early part of the month before proceeding northwards from San Diego to Pasadena and Santa Barbara. Enchanted by the sunshine, the blue of the Pacific, the magical landscape of fruits and flowers, the rambling Hotel del Coronado, itself a kind of self-contained enchanted city by the sea, the Baums returned to Coronado for the next six winters, with the exception of the winter of 1906, which they spent in Egypt and on the Continent. In 1910 the Baums and their four sons settled permanently in Hollywood. While staying at the Hotel del Coronado in 1904, Baum resumed, somewhat reluctantly, the Oz narrative which had met with such success four years earlier. *The Marvelous Land of Oz* (1904) was the second of the fourteen Oz stories Baum would produce before his death in 1919, an Oz book plus one for each year Baum spent wholly or in part in Southern California. All in all, every Oz book save the first was written at either Coronado or Hollywood.

Like the million or more other Midwesterners who poured into Southern California, greater Los Angeles especially, in the first three decades of the twentieth century, L. Frank Baum, as he signed himself, sought and to a certain extent discovered a new life, an American Oz, in the Southland. Coronado, first of all, made of him a beloved celebrity, and Baum returned the affection. Even after the Baums rented a house in Coronado so that their youngest son might accompany them, they continued to frequent the Hotel del Coronado, whose amiable manager Morgan Ross, a Wizard of Oz of hostelry, became a close personal friend. For the spacious main dining room of the Hotel del Coronado, Baum designed crown-shaped light fixtures which are still in use. After a morning of writing, he would spend his afternoons at archery or golf or lazing by the sea. In the evening there was entertainment at the hotel or parties in town, or Baum would frequently give a benefit reading at a private home. A photograph from the period shows him sitting beneath an oak tree with a little boy and three Dorothy lookalikes, resplendent in the oversized headbows and frilly frocks of the period, telling them Oz stories.

Bits and pieces of California began to find their way into Baum's writing. The *San Diego Union* for 13 January 1905 described *The Marvelous Land of Oz* as being "brim full of the sunshine of California." There are descriptions or suggestions of California in *Dorothy and the Wizard of Oz* (1908), in which Dorothy returns to Oz via the San Francisco earthquake of April 1906, as well as in *Aunt Jane's Nieces and Uncle John* (1911), *The Sea Fairies* (1911), *Sky Island* (1912), and *Aunt Jane's Nieces Out West* (1914). In the short story "Nelebel's Fairyland" (1905), which Baum graciously wrote for the student publication of Russ High School in San Diego, Coronado itself is recast as a fairyland. Banished from the forests of Burzee, Nelebel finds happiness in a lovely seaside place called Coronado.

As a Southern Californian Baum was thoroughly enjoying himself in his newly earned prosperity after a lifetime of struggle as an actor, playwright, chicken farmer, small-town newspaper editor in the Dakota Territory, traveling salesman (china and glassware), department store window-dresser, and, finally, as an author of children's books, beginning with *Mother Goose in Prose* (1897), illustrated by Maxfield Parrish. Diversely energetic as a writer, with comic plays, verse, journalism, newspaper humor, a treatise on raising Hamburg chickens, and a treatise on decorating and dressing windows and interiors in retail stores to his credit, Baum found his métier at age 41 as a children's writer. Over the next twenty-two years he produced some one hundred juvenile titles under his own name and half a dozen pseudonyms. The income from these children's books returned him to the comfortable upper-middle-class life-style he had known in his youth in upstate New York.

Admittedly, Baum wrote *The Wonderful Wizard of Oz* five years before he first visited Coronado and twelve years before he settled in Southern California permanently; yet the essential storyline of this first Oz book functions as a prophetic probe into the inner imaginative texture of the mass migration of Midwesterners to Oz/Southern California and the Emerald City of Los Angeles down through the 1920s. Los Angeles, in other words, was Oz come true; Southern California as a whole was Baum's Oz dream materialized.

Writing under the influence of Hamlin Garland, another Midwesterner who eventually formed a Southern California connection, Baum depicts Dorothy as living on a gray, depressing Kansas farm. Baum mentions the word *gray* nine times in four paragraphs. From there she is swept by cyclone to "a country of marvelous beauty. There were lovely patches of green sward all about, with stately trees bearing rich and luscious fruits. Banks of gorgeous flowers were on every hand, and birds with rare and brilliant plumage sang and fluttered in the trees and bushes. A little way off was a small brook, rushing and sparkling along between green banks, and murmuring in a voice very grateful to a little girl who had lived so long on the dry, gray prairies."[1] Oz is the Garden of the West, so long struggled for on the prairies of the Midwest and frequently so elusive. This garden might be found anywhere, even in Kansas, but Baum and a million and more others were to seek it in Southern California.

Rising from the plain, the Emerald City can also be seen as Chicago, the great white city which subsumed unto itself and transformed so much creative Midwestern aspiration, Baum's included, in the 1890s; but by the 1910s much of Chicago was relocating to Los Angeles, another city rising on a plain. Oz might have begun as Chicago, but when Chicago in turn envisioned its own Oz it was the City of the Angels.

One line of inquiry considers the Oz stories an allegory of Midwest populism, with a greenback Emerald City, a William Jennings Bryan Cowardly Lion, and silver-standard shoes to fly Dorothy back to Kansas. The fact is, this revolt extended to many of the newly or temporarily prosperous as well. Many Midwesterners—farmers or small-town businessmen who had managed to sell out, professionals looking for new opportunities, together with a perhaps equal number who were tiring of the struggle against the weather and the banks—did not want to stay in Kansas or anywhere else in the Midwest for that matter if they had the choice. In later books, written in California, Dorothy returns to Oz from Kansas, as did an entire Midwest generation, including Los Angeles real-estate developer Harry Culver, who like the Wizard himself hailed from Omaha, Nebraska, and Edgar Rice Burroughs and L. Frank Baum of Chicago.

Oz was ordinary America transformed, made magic, and so for Baum was Southern California. Oz was beautiful; it was also a tidy, prosperous utopia, recognizably mid-American in its benevolent technology and bourgeois prosperity. Its rulers, the Wizard succeeded by Princess Ozma, governed Oz as Progressive autocrats, doing what was best for the people. Unbothered by poverty, served by proper machines in lovely gardens, cared for by a benevolent political order, the citizens of Oz were able to concentrate on the business of living, which for them was the life of emotion and imagination—and having adventures.

By 1911 L. Frank and Maud Baum and their four sons and, eventually, a red cocker spaniel named Toto were snugly ensconced in Hollywood at Ozcot, the spacious two-story home they built for themselves in 1910 a block north of Hollywood Boulevard, which Maud later remembered as being still lined with orange trees. Maud Baum's inheritance from her mother financed the venture; for her husband was living beyond his means in his private life and was professionally overextended in a road show "radio-play" venture (film presentations of Oz characters, with Baum himself, backed by a full orchestra, telling the stories at a podium to the side of the screen). He eventually slid into bankruptcy, which he declared on 3 June 1911 in the Los Angeles Federal District Court. In an effort to settle his accounts, Baum relinquished his existing royalties and secured new income by bringing Oz back from behind the Barrier of Invisibility with which he had tried to end the series in 1910.

With Oz and a steady stream of other children's titles paying the bills, Baum was able to rise from the ashes of bankruptcy and enjoy a Hollywood/Los Angeles version of the good life for his remaining years. Ozcot, at 1749 Cherokee Avenue, Hollywood, was a spacious, tastefully furnished upper-middle-class home of the period. There was a great fireplace in the parlor which Baum kept crackling on chilly days, and an equally spacious sun porch. Baum's library study was snug with books, Morris chairs, a desk lamp of his own design, and his file cabinets, including the drawer labeled O-Z which had first inspired the name of his fairyland. Measuring 100 by 183 feet, Baum's lot left plenty of room for a spacious backyard, large enough for archery practice in fact. Baum built a small open-air cottage on one end, where he wrote on summer days, and put in a large gold fish pond and aviary housing over forty birds. Enclosing his backyard with a six-foot-high fence, Baum made of it a *hortus conclusus*, an Oz within Ozcot, where he would repair each morning to tend the dahlias and chrysanthemums that soon won him twenty-one prize cups and a region-wide reputation among horticulturists.

His friends were many, and he dedicated *The Scarecrow of Oz* (1915) to his fellow members of the Uplifters Club of Los Angeles, an organization he particularly enjoyed along with the Los Angeles Athletic Club. When the movies came to Hollywood, Baum, an inveterate showman, formed the Oz Film Manufacturing Company in the summer of 1914 with other Uplifters, including his friend the composer Louis F. Gottschalk. The Oz studio made ten delightfully acted and costumed, technically superior films, including three Oz stories, before Baum and his fellow investors, unable to establish national distribution, sold the company to Universal.

Movies and chrysanthemums: all in all a very representative Hollywood/Los Angeles sort of life, made more intriguing by being led by the Wizard of Oz himself, transformed into a Southern Californian. Life in Southern California as well as life in Oz was largely a matter of how one looked at it. The Emerald City was emerald only because the Wizard insisted that everyone wear emerald-tinted glasses. The Tin Woodman, the Scarecrow, the Cowardly Lion found their dreams—a heart, a brain, courage—in the very act of envisioning them as needs. Perhaps the Wizard was himself wearing emerald-tinted glasses, but when the end came he was writing yet another Oz story, *Glinda of Oz* (1920), a story about goodness and happiness triumphant.

2

Water made imperial Los Angeles possible; but it was real-estate development and a phantasmagoria of attendant activities—buying, subdividing, building, selling, and finance—which within the decade of the 1920s propelled greater Los Angeles past the million mark, making it the fifth largest city in the United States. An oil boom fueled this emergent economy, together with a tourist industry energized by Hollywood. The port of Los Angeles, meanwhile, wrestled from a resistant topography in the years before the war, emerged from a condition of underdevelopment and became, so local boosters claimed, the second busiest deep-water port in the United States. Surprisingly, the financing of Los Angeles's exfoliating real-estate, construction, oil, port, manufacturing, entertainment, and aviation industries remained largely in local hands, and so Los Angeles emerged as a banking center as well. When it was over, when the stock market crashed in October 1929, an important new American city had been materialized: a City of Dreams, its boosters called it; for onto and into its very physical presence—its idiosyncratic, occasionally fantastic *fàbbrica della città* functioning as an oversized screen—was being projected at fast-forward speed a dream of romance and enhanced circumstances testifying in a very American way to the notion that imagination and even illusion not only are the premise and primal stuff of art, they play a role in history as well.

Dreams have a way of struggling towards materialization. Los Angeles did not just happen or arise out of existing circumstances, a harbor, a river, a railroad terminus. Los Angeles envisioned itself, then materialized that vision through sheer force of will. Los Angeles sprung from a Platonic conception of itself, the Great Gatsby of American cities. Los Angeles demanded and received its railroads almost before it was certain that there would be either adequate passengers or freight. Los Angeles demanded and built its deep-water harbor and with equal vision and arrogance appropriated its water. Now in the 1920s, with equal assertiveness, Los Angeles invited Americans from elsewhere to resettle there, which they did in heroic numbers. Los Angeles at once benefited from and helped to cause a major internal mass immigration in the United States. Between 1920 and 1930 two million Americans migrated to California. Three-quarters of these, or 1.5 million, settled in Southern California. Of these, some 1.2 million settled in Los Angeles County alone; and of these approximately half, or 661,375, settled in the City of the Angels, arriving at a peak rate of 100,000 a year between 1920 and 1924. Los Angeles began the decade with 576,673 citizens. In 1920 it surpassed San Francisco (population 506,676) as the largest city in California, and also became the tenth largest city in the United States. By 1930 Los Angeles had a population of 1,470,516, which represented a tripling of its population over ten years. It was now the fifth largest city in the nation.

New construction at once met the needs of this self-tripling population and maintained its momentum. Only 6000 new building permits were issued in Los Angeles in the war year 1918. The annual figure jumped to 13,000 in 1919. But by 1921 it had climbed to 37,000; by 1922 to 47,000. In 1923, the peak year of the boom, an astonishing 62,548 building permits for some $200 million in building projects were being issued. Only New York and Chicago,

with five and three times the population, were exceeding Los Angeles in total
construction between 1921 and 1923. Even in the manic market of a frenzied
land rush, subdivision outran need, and by the end of 1924 the boom hovered
on the edge of collapse. It was estimated that Los Angeles had some 600,000
subdivided lots standing vacant by 1925, or to put it another way, Los Angeles
had subdivided itself into a city of seven million people half a century before
the realities of population caught up with the speculations of real-estate investors. Even so, despite the bankruptcies, foreclosures, and unbought subdivisions returning to agriculture, the city issued 51,134 building permits in 1924.
The figure dropped to 37,478 in 1926 but then reversed itself and climbed
steadily for the remaining four years of the decade. Even with its boom arrested, Los Angeles continued to grow and to build with unprecedented energy.
The city was, as real-estate usage put it, a white spot, white suggesting heat
and light, on the map of the United States.

Such massive development required comparably gargantuan amounts of capital. Not only was Los Angeles being colonized at an unprecedented rate by
Americans from elsewhere, journalist Albert Atwood observed in May 1923,
these colonists, so many of them prosperously retired or otherwise endowed
with assets, were bringing unprecedented amounts of money with them. These
accumulated savings from their elsewhere lives, these profits from sold-out elsewhere businesses, were eventually but invariably reinvested in Los Angeles real
estate. "One hardly registered at a hotel," Atwood observed, "before the telephone and a little later the mail brings offers of real estate opportunities."[2] In
many instances such investments worked out. Tour guides peppered these commentaries with specific examples of soaring land values, especially in the Hollywood area. "This steady, speedy growth is the one most important thing to
understand about Los Angeles," Bruce Bliven was noting in the New Republic
by July 1927. "It creates an easy optimism, a lazy prosperity which dominates
people's lives. Anything seems possible; the future is yours, and the past?—
there isn't any."[3]

If real estate was bought and subdivided, it also had to be quickly sold for
the self-actualizing boom to continue. Thus the real-estate salesman, whether
corporate entrepreneurs such as Frank Meline and Harry Culver, who controlled the entire cycle of development from subdivision to sales, or the indi-
vidually employed pitchman, emerges as an archetypal Los Angeleno of the
1920s. A figure of folkloric significance, a Wizard of Oz, part preacher, part
confidence man, the real-estate salesman pitched the Southern California dream
at its most fundamental and most powerful level, an Ozcot gospel of homes
and happiness in greater Los Angeles, of redemption in the Emerald City through
home ownership. Throughout the decade local realtors made much of the high
percentage of home ownership and occupancy in Los Angeles. Fully one-third
of the Los Angeles population owned and occupied its own home, as opposed
to an 87.3 percent rental rate (in 1920) in New York, an 81.5 percent rental

rate in Boston, and a 72.6 percent rental rate in San Francisco. In 1923 alone some 25,000 homes were built and sold to one-family owners, according to *Los Angeles Realtor* magazine. By the late 1920s Los Angeles had 398,805 residences, a third of them owner-owned and -occupied. Home ownership, the *Los Angeles Realtor* editorialized in September 1922, was rapidly stabilizing the in-migrating Los Angeles populace and establishing the moral and psychological conditions of committed citizenship, a concern for schools, parks, playgrounds, and good government that reflected a higher and finer sense of purpose than possible to mere renters.

The selling of these homes, all 300,000-plus of them, involved flamboyance, gross exaggeration occasionally, and sometimes deliberate deception. One tract was promoted as being fourteen minutes from downtown Los Angeles by a subway system that seventy years later remains a daydream. Perhaps the most fantastic of all subdivision concepts and sales pitches involved Girard in the western San Fernando Valley, a Potemkin village of false fronts held up by rear braces so as to suggest the city that would soon rise there. A platoon of salesmen, warmed earlier to their task by group calisthenics, met prospects arriving by bus. A numbered nametag affixed to his or her lapel, each prospective buyer was then led by a single salesman, drawn by lottery, through a rehearsed sequence of lunch followed by a walking tour of the subdivision. At the right moment the salesman brought the client to specially placed closing booths, where a senior sales specialist, the closer, cinched the sale.

Despite the occasional frauds, the ever-present hoopla, the bus rides out to new tracts, the free lunch, the stemwinding spiels by salesman standing in empty fields marked off by fluttering pennants where soon, very soon, communities called Gardena, Compton, Lynwood, El Sereno, Roscoe, Sepulveda, Canoga Park, or Culver City would be given local habitation and a name, despite the perils and temptations of the boom, a million Americans were in the course of a brief decade placed in homes and recycled into new lives in some two dozen or more constituent communities of greater Los Angeles. From this perspective, the real-estate salesmen of the Southland, for all their brass bands, aviation stunts, free lunches, lottery prizes, promised subway systems, and other exaggerated claims, were not hucksters at all but were rather shamans of a new and, it was hoped, better identity and circumstances. Like wizards of Oz behind green curtains, they spoke to that dream of a better life that was bringing a million and a half Americans into Southern California, a dream symbolized so vividly in a bungalow still under construction, adjacent to hundreds more like it, in a recently graded bean field.

The roll call of modern Los Angeles realtors, or, more correctly its Burke's Peerage, commences with William May Garland, the Prince of Realtors as he was known, who subdivided and sold off Westlake, Ocean Park, Hermosa Beach, and Beverly Hills in the 1890s and early 1900s. Next in line of succession comes Frank Meline, a former department store window dresser from Illinois who in 1912 formed his own Los Angeles construction company, which he expanded in 1919 to a full-service real-estate development and sales operation with (by 1924) eighteen branch offices throughout the Los Angeles basin. As a broker, Meline sold half the homes purchased in Beverly Hills before 1930. As a developer in partnership with Alphonzo E. Bell, the creator of Bel-Air, Meline materialized a string of coastal communities, together with parts of Brentwood. Each of Meline's homes were beautifully situated on two-acre graded lots. Most of them had magnificent views of the sea. Meline brought into being a Southern California Riviera running south from Malibu along the Santa Monica Mountains, a succession of architecturally distinctive villas, lavishly landscaped (the gardens of Meline's own Brentwood Heights home were used as a locale for an early film version of *The Count of Monte Cristo*) and reinforcing in their cumulative effect, their cypress and ilex and lawns, their tile roofs, creamy walls, and Mediterranean designs, the Côte d'Azur/Costa Brava metaphor that so enlivened coastal development in Southern California from Montecito and Santa Barbara south to San Clemente throughout the 1920s.

When the recently rich arrived in Southern California, Frank Meline saw to it that they were properly housed. Harry Culver, by contrast, sought a wider market, hard-working younger couples of middle income anxious to establish themselves in home ownership. Himself a representative Midwesterner turned Californian, a bespectacled bantam rooster of a man fully capable of standing in for the film comedian Harry Langdon whom he uncannily resembled, the Nebraska-born Culver arrived in Los Angeles from Omaha in 1910 just as he was turning thirty. After a period of apprenticeship under I.N. Van Nuys, then in the process of subdividing his holdings in the San Fernando Valley, Culver struck out on his own as a developer. By 1913 Harry Culver had formed the Culver Investment Company and was announcing at a banquet held on 25 July 1913 at the exclusive California Club in downtown Los Angeles the forthcoming creation of Culver City on Rancho La Ballona property he had acquired on land between Los Angeles and Venice on the sea. Setting up a ready-made community infrastructure—two churches, a newspaper, a grocery store and a hardware shop, seven miles of sidewalks, and a real-estate office, the first building to be constructed—Culver recruited a corps of 150 salesmen and over the course of the next ten years proceeded literally to put Culver City on the map. When film producer Thomas H. Ince located his film studios at Culver City in 1915, the forerunner of the Metro-Goldwyn-Mayer studios established there in 1924, Culver City achieved, as far as the tastes of Harry Culver's targeted middle-class market were concerned, the most compelling identity of all, an actual connection with the dream-producing film industry that was motivating the movement of so many migrants into Southern California in the first place.

As developer Harry Culver mastered the art of using other people's money to finance his projects. Culver City, for instance, was financed by local landowners eager to attain a higher yield on their property than possible through agriculture; by the Pacific Electric Railway Company, anxious to disperse the population of Los Angeles out into the suburbs; and by a group of bankers mesmerized by Culver's evocation of the inevitability of the westward expansion of Los Angeles to the sea. Culver himself brought a mere $3000 in personal funds to the table. He liked, Culver said, "the subdivider who is short on cash but long on courage—the man who jumps to his feet before the banker counts nine."[4] By the late 1920s Culver was announcing the formation of a $100 million national real-estate investment trust targeted at even further Southern California development. Unfortunately, the stock market had other plans.

As skilled as Culver was as a fundraiser, it was as a salesman that he excelled. Harry Culver was the super supersalesman of a supersalesman era, *primus inter pares* at a time of flourishing skills in real-estate promotion and acknowledged as such by his election to the presidencies of the California Real Estate Association in 1926, the Los Angeles Realty Board in 1927, and the National Association of Realty Boards in 1929. "Did you ever hear of the Salesman's Cocktail?" Culver once asked. "Take one ounce of determination, mix with another ounce of stick-to-it-iveness, add plenty of confidence, two dashes of conceit, fill the glass with pep and drink while standing."[5] Culver's own salesmanship proceeded on a number of levels simultaneously. Most obviously, Culver was the master of the stunt, the pitch, the flamboyant gesture. Atop his Culver City sales office, he mounted a searchlight, the second largest in the West, which by night sent a shaft of light into the sky visible for thirty miles. He sponsored baby beauty contests, boys' boxcar races, and marathons between the runners of Culver City and Los Angeles. He raffled off world cruises for the best name submitted for a new subdivision. He organized a polo game between players mounted on the running boards of Model T Fords. Most of Culver's promotions, the honorary Culver City constable's badges presented to celebrities, the monthly Chamber of Commerce booster parades, were harmless enough and attracted the desired attention.

Culver operated on a deeper level as well, one keyed to the psychological needs of his middle-income clientele. In weekly training sessions Culver's salesmen, 250 of them by 1924, were drilled to base their pitches on an awareness that the majority of their customers were taking a major step up in the world in buying their own homes, most of them for the first time.

A small-town boy from Nebraska who had spent his restless twenties in a variety of indeterminate pursuits—a minor civil servant in the Philippines, a special agent in the Treasury, a traveling salesman—Culver had found and consolidated himself through Southern California real estate, and he knew that this process was being constantly repeated, if on a lesser scale, in every first-time home-buyer who followed the searchlight beam out to Culver City. Yes indeed, Harry Culver had prospered: the California Club and Los Angeles Country Club memberships, the many directorships of banks and loan associations, the vice presidency of the Los Angeles Realty Board and the Los Angeles Grand Opera Association, a socially prominent wife and picture-perfect daughter, summers in Paris, the private airplane which was also a fully equipped office; but Culver also kept vibrant a salesman's empathy for the equally compelling if less flamboyant hopes of clients. Knowing them, for instance, to be uprooted, from elsewhere as he was and unsure of their tastes as he had been, he fully furnished many of his homes—furniture, dishes, cutlery (down to the potato masher, he boasted), linen and bedding, a Victrola, pictures on the walls, a cuckoo clock, a Ford in the garage—all for $500 down and $80 a month on a 7 percent loan compounded semi-annually.

What Culver's Hollywood contemporary Cecil B. De Mille was doing through film, instructing the expanded middle-class world of the 1920s in taste, Culver was providing in the actuality of a furnished home and ready-made identity. The subdividers of Southern California and their salesmen, Culver argued, were embarked upon a noble work in service of high ideals. "Whenever you can take a family out of an apartment house," Culver urged his salesmen, "out of the dust, dirt and smoke of a crowded city where it is throwing its rental money out of the window each month and its health with it, and place that family in a fresh, pure, health-giving district in a home of its own, I want to say to you that you are not only starting that family out on the road to success, but you are rendering a service to the community and a service to humanity." [6]

You could also enrich yourself in the process, which is what Edgar Rice Burroughs, the creator of Tarzan and the founder of the subdivision of Tarzana, wanted very much to do in the San Fernando Valley to the northwest of Culver City. A Chicagoan (Oak Park, more correctly) who had resettled in Los Angeles in the take-off year 1919, Burroughs in many ways typified the wave of affluent Midwestern migrants who were then in the process of transforming the Southland. Like so many of them, Burroughs had first come to Southern California as a tourist, seeking relief in San Diego from the Chicago winter of 1913 after a particularly painful attack of neuritis. Like so many, Burroughs was middle-aged and had money, being some seven years into his success as a writer of popular fiction. Like Jack London, whom Burroughs consciously modeled himself upon when he began to write and whom he resembled in so many ways—an adventurous youth, the daily stint of writing, a sure sense of audience—Edgar Rice Burroughs sustained within himself a complexity of ambivalent impulses regarding nature and civilization, escape and involvement, that rendered him at age 44 a ready-made Southern Californian.

Raised in solid upper-middle-class respectability in Oak Park, Burroughs was supposed to follow his three older brothers to Yale but went West instead, spending his twenties as a U.S. Cavalry trooper in Arizona, a cowboy and gold prospector in Idaho, a railroad policeman in Utah. Paradoxically, Burroughs also had a heart condition, which he more or less defied during these Roose-veltian years of the strenuous life. Married and a father, Burroughs returned to

Chicago to spend his early thirties in diametrically opposite circumstances as
an executive with Sears Roebuck. Like Jack London (or Theodore Roosevelt,
for that matter, or Owen Wister, Frank Norris, and an entire generation of
young men of the late nineteenth century, enamored simultaneously of the
frontier and the establishment), Burroughs wanted money, power, and status
as well as release into an imagined edenic frontier. He had, after all, prospected
for gold and dreamed while working as a railroad patrolman of one day joining
the corporate bigwigs who swept by in their private cars. Leaving the security
of Sears Roebuck, Burroughs failed at a number of get-rich schemes and was,
at the age of 35, selling pencil sharpeners when he wrote his first successful
story, A Princess of Mars, which was followed within the year by Tarzan of the
Apes. He also began a series of tales centered on John Carter, an inventive
investor and efficiency expert given to interplanetary adventures. The essential
formula of both the John Carter and the Tarzan stories was that of an upper-
class hero confronting a challenging, radically exotic environment, a lush jungle eden or an eden of extra-planetary technology, without loss of caste or cash
resources. Back on Earth, John Carter had his portfolios, and Tarzan could
always draw upon the treasure vaults of Opar.

Edgar Rice Burroughs thus arrived in Los Angeles as did L. Frank Baum
and the Western writer Zane Grey, possessed, that is, of an inner world externalized into an oeuvre that functioned as a guide and prophetic gloss to the
Southern California experience. On the immediate level, Burroughs came to
escape the winters of Chicago now that he was making money, $100,000 an-
nually, and to be near Hollywood, a most promising source of even further
income from his Tarzan stories. Eventually, there would be some forty films
starring the Ape Man. Southern California also offered a pastoral alternative,
an imagined outre mer, sunny and edenic, like the savannahs and rain forests
of Africa he could describe for millions of readers but would never personally
visit. Like Jack London on his Beauty Ranch in the Valley of the Moon in
Sonoma, Burroughs chose ranch life, exurban but not severely rural, as his
best personal formula for the good life in California. Shortly after his removal
to the Southland, Burroughs purchased from the estate of Harrison Gray Otis
of the Times 550 acres in the San Fernando Valley contiguous to the Santa
Monica Mountains. The impressive property, which Burroughs named Tarzana Ranch in honor of the fictive figure who had made him a wealthy man,
also contained a mansion-like ranch house, to which Burroughs moved his
family. Like London, Burroughs fully intended to pursue a career as a rancher-
writer, producing his daily stint each morning, followed by afternoons in the
outdoors. His letters from his first months on Tarzana Ranch teemed with
enthusiastic details of hogs, sheep, Angora kids, barley, alfalfa, lima beans, and
apricots.

As in the case of Jack London in Sonoma, however, paradoxes surfaced
immediately. Ostensibly, Burroughs wanted the simple, Tarzanesque life in

Tarzana, far from the madding crowd. Yet as soon as he had taken possession of his estate, he expanded it to include a swimming pool, a ballroom, and a theater for private screenings. He began to give elaborate weekend parties for the Hollywood crowd whom, in another side of his nature, he professed to despise. In the 1923 novel *The Girl From Hollywood*, Burroughs searingly indicts the drug and sex-crazed film colony. The novel contrasts the efforts of an old-fashioned Virginia family to re-establish itself as ranchers in the San Fernando Valley with the cocaine and morphine-ridden world of nearby Hollywood, which seduces and addicts at least one ranch girl, for whom the California dream becomes a nightmare of enslavement. Graphic in its depictions of drug addiction (Burroughs's dope-crazed lesbian film star Gaza De Lure is a tour de force of high camp) and ominously suggestive of the Svengali seductions of the young by predatory producers, *The Girl From Hollywood* must be considered among the most powerful of the chorus of anti-Hollywood jeremiads to appear just before and in the aftermath of the murder of Desmond Taylor, the Fatty Arbuckle case, and the death of Wallace Reid from drug addiction. Yet Hollywood paid Burroughs's bills. The 1918 film version of *Tarzan of the Apes* starring Elmo Lincoln grossed $6 million, putting it among the top box-office hits of the emergent industry. Burroughs's bills, however, were also increasing as his life-style expanded and the Tarzana Ranch, a gentlemanly preoccupation, began to lose money.

In coming to California, Edgar Rice Burroughs had transformed Tarzan into a Southern Californian as well. On Tarzana Ranch all wildlife was zealously protected, as if by the great Ape Man himself, whose imagined presence as a presiding spirit, a mythic shade on the verge of materialization, Burroughs encouraged in so many direct and indirect ways. Tarzan was among the first figures to be given life by the newly emergent popular culture based in mass media—in Tarzan's case, pulp fiction, movies, radio, comic strips—and this life was proving itself very real indeed, at once mythopoetic and palpably present, as it became energized by constant repetition in the media. Tarzan spoke to that hunger for escape, for release into the joyously physical, that characterized the Southern California experience and energized the entire California myth. So much of the art and thought of the state—the animal stories of Jack London, the naturalism of Frank Norris, the wildlife sculptures of Arthur Putnam, the bio-ethical thought of Joseph Le Conte and David Starr Jordan, the tide-pool metaphors of John Steinbeck—revolved around the very same biologism Burroughs had tapped and drawn upon in the figure of Tarzan, who returned Americans to their physical selves without loss of ethics or caste.

As Los Angeles was approaching its take-off era, a massive cache of prehistoric animal skeletons was discovered in some asphaltum bogs on Rancho La Brea property soon to be enveloped by an expanding Los Angeles. By the mid-1920s an area of twelve square city blocks, the La Brea Tar Pits, the largest discovered fossil depository in North America, had been set aside as a county park. From it over the years hundreds of skeletons were being recovered under the supervision of the Los Angeles County Museum of Natural History, established at Exposition Park in 1913. Los Angeles might not have much in the way of Old Masters to display in its museum, but it did have a ferocious array of skeletal survivors of the Pleistocene as icons of local identity: mammoths, mastodons, saber-toothed cats, the giant ground sloth and dire wolf, the California lion, weighing over a thousand pounds, the ground stork, the golden eagle (800 of these) and one solitary human, a female named the La Brea Woman. That many of these creatures had met their end sinking into the sulphurous ooze as they pounced upon other animals already mired in the muck might have offered a subconscious metaphor to competitive, go-ahead, boostering Los Angeles; in any event, even as the urban future was being achieved, the prehistoric past reasserted itself on Wilshire Boulevard, and this assertion struck a chord in the collective consciousness of the city, which was intensified with the imagined arrival of Tarzan the Ape Man in San Fernando Valley. The urban ethos contained within itself the principle of its own repudiation. From La Brea ancient animals arose from tar pits that were still dangerous and once again stalked the savannahs of the imagination, and out in the San Fernando the call of Tarzan, animal-inspired, yet for all that, haunting and hierophantic, rolled out against the encroaching subdivisions. "I, Tarzan of the Apes, have left my jungle and gone to the cities built by men," Burroughs's hero states in *Tarzan and the Golden Lion* (1923), written on Tarzana Ranch, "but always I have been disgusted and been glad to return to my jungle—to the noble beasts that are honest in their loves and in their hates—to the freedom and genuineness of nature."[7]

The author of these words, meanwhile, was subdividing. A mysterious stranger had called upon him in late 1919 or early 1920, Burroughs later claimed, with plans for the City of Tarzana—then vanished, never to be heard from again, like the messenger from civilization who informs Tarzan of his real identity. He also claimed, weakly, that what he had in mind was an artists' colony, not your run-of-the-mill subdivision. In 1921 Burroughs began to auction off his livestock and farming equipment. By 1922, after a failed attempt to start his own movie studio on the property, he began to subdivide 63 commercial and 139 residential sites on 50 acres. In 1924 his mansion ranch house and adjacent 120 acres were developed as El Caballero Country Club. (Could Tarzan adjust to golf?) By 1926 Edgar Rice Burroughs was living in a rented home in downtown Los Angeles.

The mysterious stranger was obviously a projection of the other side of Burroughs himself, the Tarzan antitype Jimmy Torrance in Burroughs's novel *The Efficiency Expert* (1921), the systems manager entrepreneur, the consultant, and the investor possessed of a technocratic cunning that paralleled Tarzan's mastery of the jungle. Jimmy Torrance was also the Spirit of Los Angeles, summoning the creator of Tarzan from his dreams of edenic release to more realistic and profitable alternatives. Banished from the canyons and rolling hills of Tarzana, the Ape Man re-emerged as an intense local Southern Californian cult. Numerous foods and products bore the Tarzan logo. A chain of stations sold Tarzan gasoline.

3

Fueled with Tarzan or Gilmore Red Lion gasoline, the automobile determined the cityscape of Los Angeles as it emerged in the 1920s. Because of the automobile, Burroughs achieved an innovative urban model that left behind thousands of years of urban archetypes in favor of an expanding network of communities linked by roadways. It was as if cell colony after cell colony were replicating itself, each remaining linked to the other via macadamic and hydroelectric lifelines. For all its vaunted modernity, the interurban Pacific Electric system that linked the communities of the Los Angeles basin via Big Red Cars whizzing along at fifty miles an hour did not defy the established urban archetype. Downtown Los Angeles remained the actual and symbolic center of the city. Speedy, efficient, unhampered by competing automobile traffic, the interurban cars allowed Los Angelenos to live in 45 communities scattered over a 35-mile radius while working downtown or in the adjacent industrial areas. Like the roads leading to Rome, the entire system converged in a nine-story central downtown terminal at Sixth and Main built in 1905 at a cost of three-quarters of a million dollars, the Charing Cross of Los Angeles, where the ambience of departing and arriving streetcars, newsstands, coffee shops, and rushing passengers gave Los Angeles the feel of big cities such as London, New York, and Chicago. Thus even as Los Angeles began to expand in the early 1920s, its downtown identity and real estate values sustained themselves.

It is simply a myth to state that twentieth-century Los Angeles had no downtown. Year by year through the 1920s, Los Angeles investors and architects expanded and embellished a traditional downtown. To leaf through the pages of the *Los Angeles Realtor* magazine for these years is to encounter a fast-forward video of downtown Los Angeles asserting itself. Half a dozen banks and a stock exchange went up in 1921. A Bank of Italy building, a new headquarters for the Southern California Telephone Company, and the magisterial Biltmore Hotel facing Pershing Square were announced in 1922. The year 1924 witnessed the completion of 22 major downtown office buildings, including new headquarters for the Chamber of Commerce, together with impressive facilities for the Jonathan Club and a new downtown central library. Some $87 million in downtown high-rise construction was either being planned or under way in 1925. Completed that year were more banks (another Bank of Italy at Seventh and Olive), the Pacific Finance Building down one block at Sixth, and the elegant United Artists Theater Building on Broadway between Ninth and Tenth. Two major structures, the new City Hall, at 200 North Spring

Street, the tallest building in Los Angeles, and the Richfield Building, at the corner of Sixth and Flower, climaxed a decade of downtown development. Designed by the Los Angeles firm of Morgan, Walls and Clements as a statement of skyscraper Gothic in transition to Art Deco, the Richfield Building, which opened in 1929, asserted in its vertically soaring recessed fenestration, its black, blue, and gold ornamentation, and its pioneering use of air conditioning the continuing vitality of downtown Los Angeles as a locale of intensified civic identity.

On the other hand, the Richfield Building also featured a sophisticated underground garage that connected directly to five high-speed elevators. Visitors to the building and the rest of downtown were increasingly expected to arrive by automobile, which was how thousands of "flivver emigrants" as they were called, a "flivver" being the nickname of the Model T, had been arriving each year since 1918, the year Aimee Semple McPherson and thousands of others arrived by flivver at Los Angeles, looking for a second or third start. The expected comparison of the flivver as the covered wagon of 1920 immediately surfaced. In the concern that too many riffraff were arriving by flivver, there surfaced as well a prophetic gesture forward to the fears and resentments of the Great Depression. By 1927 Los Angeles County had one car for every 3.2 people, for a total of 560,136 passenger cars and 76,000 trucks, served by 450 gasoline stations. Los Angeles County was also pioneering public transportation by motor bus (or motor stage as they were then called), especially out to the San Fernando Valley from downtown Los Angeles. Between 1917 and 1927 Los Angeles County spent $24 million grading and paving 1300 miles of roads and further sums building 14 reinforced concrete bridges. In 1928 the county allocated $5.2 million for some 126 miles of roadway construction.

The yellow cars of the urban Los Angeles Railway, meanwhile, and the red cars of the interurban Pacific Electric found themselves in increasingly disadvantageous competition. In the 1910s, the very time other American and European cities were building subways and elevateds to bring mass transit into and out of the central city above or below street traffic, Los Angeles was rejecting such alternatives in the belief that Los Angeles County would peak with 100,000 automobiles by 1919. By 1924 there were four times that number, not including the automobiles of tourists. Even when downtown Los Angeles became embroiled in traffic jams by the mid-1920s no major action was taken to save the mass transit system with subway tunnels or elevated overpasses.

As private companies, subsidized by the Southern Pacific in the case of Pacific Electric, the streetcars did not have the lobby they might have had were they publicly owned. The interurbans were expected to pay their own way. And besides: as late as 1924 Pacific Electric was experiencing a peak year, with 110 million passenger trips.

Traffic, meanwhile, was becoming a way of life for Los Angeles. Approximately 310,000 automobiles, more than the total registered in the State of New

York, were daily entering Los Angeles by the end of 1924. With 69,797 cars passing daily, the corner of Adams and Figueroa was the heaviest traveled intersection in the United States, with more than double the traffic of its nearest competitor, the corner of Forty-second Street and Fifth Avenue in New York. Stalled in this traffic, which they could not avoid, streetcars lost their competitive edge. The average running speed of the Santa Monica interurban dropped to thirteen miles an hour. Interurban routes also slowed down as developments sprung up between destination points. As the highway system was extended, motorbuses successfully entered the interurban competition. By 1933 streetcar usage had halved since the peak year of 1924. By 1935 it had halved again.

One of the hardest hit sectors of interurban business was Sunday travel, although this business was somewhat regained during the Depression with the sale of special all-day Sunday passes. By the late 1920s Sunday had become motor car touring day in metropolitan Los Angeles. Founded in 1900, the Automobile Club of Southern California both expressed and served this intense relationship to the automobile as a source of pleasure. Not only did this organization provide practical assistance to its member motorists—some 124,000 by 1927—it also advanced a philosophy of the good life in which the automobile stood at ground zero, a radiant source of freedom and pleasure. Since 1923 the club was headquartered in a spacious Hispanic Revival building at the corner of West Adams and Figueroa. Its directors were recruited from the heart of the oligarchy. Its magazine *Touring Topics* (later *Westways*) was the best general magazine in the Southland. A serious, well-edited journal of travel, history, cultural commentary, and informed promotionalism, *Touring Topics* was the *Overland Monthly*, the *Atlantic Monthly* even, of Southern California: a fact which expressed and reinforced the awareness that Southern California had structured its very cultural identity as well as its diffuse, distended suburbia upon the automobile as artifact, ennobler, first premise, and source of delight.

Los Angeles, Bruce Bliven observed in 1927, "is now a completely motorized civilization. Nowhere else in the world have human beings so thoroughly adapted themselves to the automobile. The advertisers' ideal, two cars to a family, has very nearly been attained, not merely among the rich, but on the average. The number of licensed drivers is just about equal to the adult population, and all the children above the age of ten are bootleg chauffeurs. Any Angeleno without his automobile is marooned, like a cowboy without his horse, and cannot stir from the spot until it has been restored to him. The highest form of popular art is found in the decoration of filling stations; one tours them as one does the chateau country of France."[8]

What other city, Bliven might have asked, with the exception of Detroit, would have adopted as its local hero a Packard dealer, Earle C. Anthony, the Harry Culver of the automobile? A graduate (1903) of the University of California at Berkeley, where he founded *The Pelican*, the campus humor magazine, Anthony sold Packards to Los Angeles as a total way of life, just as Culver sold furnished houses. When aspiring Los Angelenos purchased a Packard from Earle C. Anthony, they bought into a club, an identity, as well as a franchised service system. Anthony established a chain of gasoline stations, which he lighted at night with a pioneering use of neon so that his clients might gas up or have their Packards serviced in uniformly identifiable surroundings. Through KFI, his equally pioneering radio station, Anthony strengthened even further the ties that bound him to his clients. Like Helena Rubenstein or Ralph Lauren in the years to come, Anthony understood that in conditions of emergent taste and identity a brand, a label, a neighborhood, a specific make of car anchored identity on premises at once materialistic and symbolic. Nowhere was this reanchoring more necessary than in Los Angeles of the 1920s, and nothing, with the exception of a home, could do it more dramatically than an automobile, especially a shiny new black Packard.

Whether Packard or Ford, the automobile also intensified the value of outlying real estate and hence stimulated Los Angeles to expand, expand, expand. Since 1907, reported William C. Garner in the *Los Angeles Realtor* for July 1927, land values in downtown Los Angeles had increased by 800 percent. Thanks to the automobile, however, property values in the outlying districts of Los Angeles had increased twice as much in the last ten years as downtown values had increased over the past twenty. By tying up downtown Los Angeles in impossible traffic, the automobile encouraged the growth of satellite commercial centers in the outlying districts. Just as Manhattan ascended vertically over a subway system, Garner noted, Los Angeles was expanding horizontally from district to district along its auto routes. Banks, theaters, and department stores were also decentralizing their presence through branch operations.

Wilshire Boulevard epitomized this trend. The Champs Élysées of Los Angeles was designed not for pedestrians but for the automobile. One morning in 1921 developer A.W. Ross sat looking at a map of Los Angeles. As he mused, Ross made two judgments. Los Angeles, first of all, would not grow southwards as had been predicted, not yet anyway, but would head westwards toward Santa Monica on the sea. Second, the motorized citizenry of Los Angeles would be willing to drive up to four miles to shop. Drawing a circle around the four most prosperous residential districts of the city—Hollywood, Beverly Hills, West Adams Heights, and Wilshire—Ross saw that his circle centered on the narrow east-west roadway called Wilshire at a point halfway between Los Angeles and the sea. There, Ross decided, in the bean fields fronting Wilshire between La Brea and Fairfax avenues, he would create a shopping district, Wilshire Boulevard Center, that would capitalize on the automobile and the westward thrust of the city.

The fact that Wilshire Boulevard crossed the La Brea Tar Pits only underscored the geographical appropriateness of this roadway as an important new thoroughfare. The axis of approach so calculatingly decided upon by Ross had been a natural path since prehistoric times. Down along it in the Pleistocene came the great animals whose bones were only then being extracted, cleaned, and assembled for display at the County Museum. In pre-European times the Shoshonean residents of Yang-na in the Los Angeles Plain traveled the trail to fetch tar for caulking and sealing. From there, the trail continued west to the seaside villages of the fishing tribes, who traveled inland to the tar pits as well. The Spanish used the trail in 1769 when they first explored the region, and by the end of the Hispanic era it had long since become El Camino Viejo, the Old Road. Five major ranchos abutted or crossed the trail. Three of these—La Brea, Las Cienegas, Rodeo de las Aguas—became important components of Los Angeles and Beverly Hills. In 1860 the Hancock family purchased Rancho La Brea and in the teens and twenties a second generation subdivided it into Hancock Park, Windsor Square, and New Windsor Square. The Rodeo Land and Water Company purchased Rancho Rodeo de las Aquas in 1906, subdividing it as Beverly Hills, whose Rodeo Drive recalled its origins. In the 1920s and '30s Rancho Las Cienegas spun off half a dozen major districts and another important boulevard, La Cienega. In 1895 the millionaire socialist H. Gaylord Wilshire, among the first to glimpse the possibilities of this region, named both the subdivision he planned there and the roadway after himself. To his credit Wilshire also predicted the westward expansion of Los Angeles, although not, in 1895, the dominance of the automobile. Having more Fabian preoccupations, Wilshire never capitalized on either his insight or his ownership of the Wilshire Tract, as it was first called.

The recycling of El Camino Viejo, the Old Road, into the future of Los Angeles was to be the work of A.W. Ross. Buying eighteen well-sited acres on the south side of Wilshire Boulevard between Fairfax and La Brea avenues (the $54,000 he paid scandalized his contemporaries), Ross began the subdivision of Wilshire Boulevard Center. It worked. Shoppers drove in from the nearby districts, parked their cars, and made their purchases. Within the decade Los Angeles was developing a west-side identity. For the first time in urban history a city was building itself around the automobile. Wary of repeating downtown traffic jams, Ross secured a prohibition against street parking. To the rear of each building he built spacious parking lots. In 1924 Wilshire Boulevard was widened to create a major traffic artery out to the ocean. Ross and his merchants also pioneered the use of synchronized traffic signals and landscaped traffic islands to facilitate turns.

At the suggestion of a fellow developer, Foster Stewart, Ross's original tract was renamed the Miracle Mile in 1928. By that time the Wilshire merchants, renamed the Miracle Mile Association, had developed themselves into an effective lobbying organization. Most of Wilshire was zoned for residential use. Unnerved by the success of the Wilshire commercial district, downtown merchants, joined by Wilshire district homeowners, vigorously opposed any and all requests by the Miracle Mile Association to expand the commercial zoning of the original Wilshire district. The Wilshire merchants and developers, however, successfully fought for the expansion of the Miracle Mile block by block, variance by variance. The resistance encountered by the Miracle Mile Association underscored that even Los Angeles itself could not believe in, much less accept, the full implications of the auto-retail paradigm A.W. Ross was offering the city.

By 1934, however, the success of Wilshire Boulevard and its implementation of the future was beyond dispute. A cut was made through Westlake (now MacArthur) Park joining Wilshire to Grand Avenue in the downtown. A sixteen-mile boulevard, itself a new form of horizontal downtown, now connected downtown Los Angeles to the sea. Wilshire Boulevard had become the central thoroughfare of the City of the Angels.

Even before this 1934 capitulation, downtown Los Angeles was replicating itself like a cell colony along this emergent western axis. The Ambassador, the first important hotel of the 1920s boom era, opened on Wilshire Boulevard in 1921. The decade ended with the opening of one of the most architecturally distinguished buildings ever to grace Los Angeles, Bullock's Wilshire, a branch of a major downtown department store and an Art Deco masterpiece designed by architects John and Donald Parkinson, with a number of other designers and artists responsible for the interior. As in the case of the Richfield Building downtown, Bullock's Wilshire celebrated and climaxed the expansion of a decade. Each feature and detail of the building bespoke the confidence and optimism of Los Angeles in 1929: its sculpted mass rising ten stories from a base of five, reflective of the new City Hall downtown; the green copper siding against beige cast stone, as if the building were an oversized art object half-encased in metal; the frosted glass and dark tropical wood of the interior; the disc and torch branch chandeliers ready to light an Art Deco *Meistersinger* with festival radiance.

From one perspective, the Bullock's Wilshire department store was itself a temple to the automobile. The grander of two main entrances faced not Wilshire Boulevard but the rear parking lot, where automobiles arrayed themselves in reverent formation like giant black mantises praying before a copper-green altar. The oversized windows facing Wilshire were especially designed to display merchandise to passing motorists. To offer instruction as to what gods were being celebrated, Herman Sachs's ceiling mural on the porte cochere of the south entrance celebrated images of transportation, from the god Mercury to the *Graf Zeppelin* which had visited Los Angeles in August 1929. Here and throughout the store, like icons in an Orthodox cathedral, were repeated depictions of the automobiles which had created a new type of American city.

And so Los Angeles grew and grew and subdivided itself and grew some more, an urban plasm clustering and reclustering and extending itself like an organic being. Annexations expanded the square mileage of the city from 337 in 1916, making it the largest single incorporated urban area in the United States, to 392 square miles in 1923, to 450 square miles by the end of the decade. As of June 1921 Los Angeles had 91,973 acres available for development. Photographs from the 1920s constitute a fast-forward film of these acres filling up like mushroom fields after a spring rain. Visiting Los Angeles in 1927, Bruce Bliven was shown two photographs of the downtown Los Angeles skyline. They seemed to depict two different cities, Vienna and Chicago, perhaps, despite the fact that they were taken only four years apart. The separately incorporated streetcar suburbs of Los Angeles—Pasadena, San Marino, Glendale, Alhambra, San Gabriel, Long Beach, Santa Monica—continued the growth already under way in the previous era, while the newly energized automotive districts of both metropolitan Los Angeles and the independent suburbs added their spreading subdivisions to the emerging cityscape.

Because of the automobile, Frank A. Vanderlip, formerly president of the National City Bank of New York, felt confident in reaching out as far as the Palos Verdes Peninsula itself, 25 miles from downtown Los Angeles. Acquiring 3200 acres on a promontory between Redondo Beach and Los Angeles Harbor with more than fourteen miles of ocean frontage, Vanderlip retained the famous architect-planners Frederick L. Olmsted, Jr., and Charles Cheney to lay out a garden suburb maximizing the site and the views. The resulting subdivision, Palos Verdes Estates, gave Los Angeles a suburb comparable to Hillsborough/Burlingame south of San Francisco or the elegant Long Island suburbs of New York. Huntington Palisades in the ocean-fronting foothills north of Santa Monica and Bel-Air near Westwood between Beverly Hills and Pacific Palisades were also intricately platted landscaped developments which took maximum advantage of sweeping montane views. Even in less expensive developments—Playa del Rey near Venice by the sea, Highland Park and Eagle Rock on the eastern edge fronting the San Rafael Hills, Burbank adjacent to the still agricultural San Fernando Valley, Van Nuys and Canoga Park in the Valley itself, Culver City southwest of the urban center—there were surprising elements of care in the deliberate curving of a road, the emplacement of homes in a landscaped declivity, the care given even a mass-produced design. Los Angeles might have become, as a witticism put it as early as the early 1920s, six suburbs in search of a city; yet each of these suburbs, even the least pretentious, was touched by the materialized dream of a better life. By 1930 Los Angeles, with a population of 1,261,231, was the fifth largest city in the United States. In ten years it had more than doubled its population. Many of the cities of Los Angeles County—Long Beach, Pasadena, Glendale, Santa Monica, Alhambra, Huntington Park—had likewise doubled, tripled, or even quadrupled their populations. The sub/urban destiny of Southern California stood materialized, and the United States possessed a seemingly instant metropolis destined within the ensuing decades to take its place beside New York and Chicago as an imperial city.

4

The economy sustaining this population boom and thereby bringing into being this new and unique American city was based on oil, maritime trade and shipping, industrial manufacture, agriculture, banking, movie-making, and tourism. Petroleum had been a mainstay of the Los Angeles basin economy ever since the oil rush of the 1890s and early 1900s had forested residential neighborhoods with thousands of derricks which served the tree-scarce city in partnership with equally recent palms. Outside the city, rows of derricks competed with rows of orange trees as totems of prosperity. "Yes it's oil, oil, oil / that makes LA boil!" L. Frank Baum and his fellow members of the Uplifters Club would sing in their official drinking song.

While the oil boom within the city limits of Los Angeles peaked in the prewar period, the automobilization of Southern California that began with the armistice necessitated the search for new fields. Like everything else in Los Angeles, oil suburbanized itself in the 1920s. The oil boom of the 1920s began at Huntington Beach forty-one miles southeast of Los Angeles in Orange County. On 13 November 1920 the Standard Oil Company brought on line a major well, Bolsa Chica No. 1, yielding 2000 barrels a day. Within a few years, the derrick over Bolsa Chica No. 1 had hundreds of counterparts as half a dozen other companies joined Standard in tapping the four major pools that lay beneath the beachfront. Since Huntington Beach was already subdivided into town lots, property owners prospered with the pumping of each backyard derrick. Bathers swam or lazed on the sand against a forest line of derricks that crowded the beach itself. Wells were drilled at steep angles so as to slant beneath the beachline and tap the oil pools extending beneath the sea.

In April 1920, upon the recommendation of its staff geologists, the Shell Oil Company leased 240 acres of Signal Hill, a promontory twenty miles south of Los Angeles within the city limits of Long Beach. Eleven months later the first well, Alamitos No. 1, was sunk. By May workers on the rig were hearing "a growl below like waves roaring through a sea cave," and on 23 June 1921 at 9:30 p.m. Alamitos No. 1 erupted in a geyser that roared and soared 114 feet into the nightime sky before the wellhead capped itself with sand falling back into the opening. As workers cleaned the wellhead and prepared to begin pumping, word of the discovery spread throughout Los Angeles. Two days later some five hundred spectators were on hand at four in the morning as Alamitos No. 1 began to pump. As in the case of Huntington Beach, hundreds of derricks (steel now, replacing the previous wooden structures) soon transformed Signal Hill and environs into an industrial forest where each day by 1925 some 244,000 barrels of oil were being sucked from the earth.

Oil from Signal Hill alone caused ship traffic through the Panama Canal to double in 1923 as tankers hurried this petroleum harvest to the East and other world markets. Hissing with escaping steam and noisy with the pumping of

machines, the clanging of metal, the cries of roughnecks and roustabouts, Signal Hill was by day an industrial landscape, sown with derricked dragons' teeth. By night, when accumulations of natural gas burning with a muffled roar illumed the sky, Signal Hill became a Dantesque landscape of flares and shadows and moving machinery bent upon its obstreperous work. Thousands of men poured in, looking for jobs; and in their wake arrived the prostitutes competing for scarce bungalows, together with speakeasy operators and their bootleg suppliers. Once again it was the frontier, with its society of rugged men working themselves to exhaustion, then taking their unambiguous evening pleasures in places like the Old Baker Winery Barn, where music blared, girls danced, and there was whiskey, pool tables for billiards, or dice, roulette, slot machines, blackjack, and poker. A garish volatility pervaded such scenes. Fistfights broke out, the psychological equivalent among the roughnecks and roustabouts of the explosions and blowouts caused by hazardous natural gas in the drilling fields. One such fire, at Mesa No. 1, burned two days before it could be brought under control. Another well erupted in a torrent of mud, oil, and rocks which rained down on a bungalow and family car two hundred feet from the offending derrick. Early in the boom the oil came naturally, almost gushing to the surface on its own momentum. Later it had to be pumped. By 1927 wells at Signal Hill were reaching five to seven thousand feet beneath the surface of the earth.

George Franklin Getty, meanwhile, was growing rich from the wells that covered the property he had leased on Telegraph Hill at Santa Fe Springs between Los Angeles and Anaheim. By 1923 Telegraph Hill was producing 70 million barrels a year. Trained as a lawyer at the University of Michigan, Getty had first become interested in oil while practicing law in Minneapolis, as an investment opportunity for himself and his legal clients. In 1903 he organized the Minnehoma Oil Company, with operations in Oklahoma. By 1906, when Getty moved with his wife Sarah and his son Jean Paul to Los Angeles, he was already a very wealthy man. California oil made him a multimillionaire and in time skyrocketed his son to perhaps the greatest personal fortune of the twentieth century. Raised and educated in the Midwest, a Mason and a Christian Scientist of middle-class life-style and middlebrow tastes, George Getty fit in comfortably with the earnest bourgeois tone of early twentieth-century Los Angeles. He joined the Brentwood Country Club and was active in the Chamber of Commerce and the Automobile Club of Southern California. As a boon to loyal employees, Getty organized the Loyal Petroleum Company in 1917, assigning a portion of its stock to his work force as a reward and incentive. When he died in 1930 after refusing conventional medical treatment according to his faith, George Getty was hailed as the best possible representative of the oil industry. It comforted his eulogizers that he was also among the richest men in Los Angeles.

Huntington Beach, Signal Hill, Telegraph Hill—to the names of these oil

fields were added others as the 1920s unfolded: Torrance 1922, Dominguez 1923, Inglewood 1924, Seal Beach 1926. In 1924 oil surpassed agriculture as the leading industry of the State. The Los Angeles basin alone that year produced 230 million barrels of crude oil and 300 billion cubic feet of natural gas. A front of oil derricks ran down along the coast from Los Angeles south towards San Diego. At Long Beach, an autonomous city adjacent to the Los Angeles port at Wilmington-San Pedro, two major regional ambitions, oil and homeownership, coalesced with the promotion of subdivided lots as combined housing and drilling sites. Prospective customers were bused into Long Beach, where they were heartily lunched in the sort of modified circus tent used for a religious revival. After lunch a skilled pitchman spieled either oil leases or housing sites or a combination thereof. One developer, Frank P. Cross, called his subdivision near the Santa Fe Springs oil fields Petroleum Gardens. "Get your lots AT ONCE," a flyer for Petroleum Gardens urged. "Don't wait until tomorrow. Buy where BIG DEVELOPMENTS are coming. Buy where land values are increasing. Buy where BIG PROFITS loom GREAT. All OIL and MINERAL RIGHTS go with each lot." By way of caution, the flyer also noted: "Purchasers of these Lots are restricted to the Caucasian or White Race."

In his novel *Oil!* (1927) Upton Sinclair described the transformation of Paradise (Long Beach), so recently, as another observer put it, "a quiet little seaside village where retired Iowa farmers pitched horseshoes," into a bustling boom town porcupined with derricks. The road into Long Beach, Sinclair wrote, was "lined with placards big and little, oil lands for sale or lease, and shacks and tents in which the selling and leasing was done. Presently you saw derricks—one right alongside Eli's new church, and another by that holier of holies, the First National Bank. Somebody would buy a lot and build a house and move in, and the following week they would sell the house, and the purchaser would move it away, and start an oil derrick. A great many never got any farther than the derrick—for subdividers of real estate had made the discovery that all the advertising in the world was not equal to the presence of one such structure on the tract."[9]

As with the gold rush, the wheat rush, and the citrus rush, the oil rush (Oildorado it was waggishly called) produced some winners and even more losers. "Scores of poor people," noted Bruce Bliven, "who, by years of effort, had managed to get legal title to a bungalow and a twenty-five foot lot, found on Tuesday that their income, beginning Monday, was a hundred dollars a day—or three thousand, or any other incredible figure. Shall Ali Baba count the pearls he finds in the robbers' cave? A duck-hunting club in the marshes discovered that its memberships were worth $125,000 each."[10] One group of New England investors in Huntington Beach lots became rich by accident. They had previously purchased encyclopedias which had as a bonus titles to lots in Huntington Beach out in Southern California. Those who had paid taxes on the lots and thus kept their titles found them worth hundreds of thousands of dollars in leasing fees when their property turned out to be directly over a major oil field.

Investors in the Julian Petroleum Corporation, by contrast, found themselves victims of the biggest swindle in the 1920s oil boom. Himself a former Texas and California oil field roustabout, Chauncey C. Julian raised $11 million in four months in 1922 from 40,000 investors eager to participate in the profits the flamboyant promoter (spats, derby, cane, nattily tailored double-breasted suit, manicure, and Pierce Arrow to hasten him from meeting to meeting) promised to bring in from drillings in Santa Fe Springs. "You'll never make a thin dime just lookin' on!" Julian exhorted small investors, promising to pay $30 on the dollar when his wells came in. When Julian's Santa Fe Springs well actually began to generate some small profits, he raised even more capital and at the same time began to water his stock and juggle his books. It took Harry Chandler of the *Times* and the FBI some three-plus years to make it convenient for Julian to remove himself to Oklahoma, from whence he fled a federal warrant on a second scam to Shanghai, where he committed suicide in 1934. After excusing himself from a banquet he arranged at his hotel as a farewell gesture but did not pay for, Julian went upstairs to his room and took poison.

Julian's successors, S. C. Lewis (he had arrived in Los Angeles in 1924 with all his belongings in a single suitcase) and Jake Berman, acquired Julian's company using company funds and pyramided Julian's chicaneries even further by means of a pooling scheme until some $150 million of worthless oil stock had soaked up some $40 million in real money. When it was over, Lewis and Berman were in federal prison, former District Attorney Asa Keyes was in San Quentin for throwing the first trial, and innumerable Los Angeles investors, great and small, were out of pocket. Stretching across the 1920s, the entire saga of Julian Pete, the name of the first company, and its successor, California Eastern, epitomized in its admixture of sophisticated stock swindle and Damon Runyonesque scam the socio-economic polarities of the oil rush itself. Whereas C. C. Julian took in the small investor, the Midwestern retiree, "the Folks," as Louis Adamic described the average Southern Californian of this era, Lewis and Berman soaked $40 million from the establishment itself in its downtown California Club variety and from among the emergent plutocracy of Hollywood and even suborned District Attorney Keyes.

In the nineteenth century, Southern California had missed El Dorado, the gold rush, with its intensities of profit and loss, strike and swindle. In Oildorado this imbalance was redressed. As early as August 1926 geologist Joseph Jensen was predicting the inevitable decline of the Southern California oil boom in the Chamber of Commerce magazine *Southern California Business*. By the Great Depression Oildorado had vanished like a dream. Its legacy, however, its wild hope of sudden transformations and better days, melded easily into the larger myth of the region, which it accelerated and intensified.

An amalgam of dream and material reality, material power and subliminal aspiration, nurtured the Oz metaphor. The Emerald City was, as Dorothy and her friends discovered, a rather ordinary place that was made to seem emerald-like because it was viewed through emerald-tinted glasses. The Wizard, a Mid-westerner from Nebraska, fully realized that vision transforms the ordinary. Los Angeles from one perspective was a place of shipping, real estate, tire manu-facturing, and plain folk. And yet this solid and very real American place was touched by magic as well. Like the Emerald City, this other Los Angeles rose from a shimmering plain, by day ablaze in sunlight and by night sparkling with electricity. This second Los Angeles, this dream city, interpenetrated the first. It was always there, even in moments of crass commercialism. Sheer economic ambition energized and sustained the amazing growth of the 1920s; but even before the first suburb was set out, the first palm trees planted, the golf courses enlarged, or the new temples of commerce, industry, and governance erected, a Los Angeles of the imagination, an Emerald City rising from a plain carpeted in orange-gold poppies, like the logo on the end of an orange crate, guided material ambitions of every sort. And thus the Emerald City, the City of Dreams, became as material as it could possibly be.

Boosting Babylon

Planning, Development, and Ballyhoo
in Jazz-Age Los Angeles

Just as gold transformed San Francisco into an important American seaport, oil boomed the Port of Los Angeles into international significance. Tankers from around the world steamed to Los Angeles to take on oil in as swiftly as five hours, thanks to first-rate facilities. In 1923, the year it became the second busiest port in intercoastal tonnage after New York, oil from the Port of Los Angeles doubled traffic through the Panama Canal, which had been fully reopened in 1921 following wartime restrictions. The next year one hundred million barrels of petroleum products left the port. By 1925 70 percent of the traffic coming or going through the Panama Canal was bound for or leaving the Port of Los Angeles. By 1926, 150 regularly scheduled passenger and freight lines were using the port for a total of 13,000 entries and departures that year. Locally, the resident fishing fleet numbered more than a thousand large and small vessels. In 1930 the Port of Los Angeles and the adjacent Port of Long Beach were handling a billion dollars plus in products. As oil went out, lumber for the building boom poured in. More than 1.3 billion board feet of lumber was unloaded in the peak construction year of 1924, brought to Los Angeles by 45 coastwise lumber lines plying between Oregon, Washington, Canada, and the port, together with cargoes of exotic hardwoods coming in from the Philippines and Central America. It was not uncommon for dozens of lumber schooners to be lined up in the harbor awaiting their turn to unload.

Despite the port at Wilmington-San Pedro to which it was connected by a gerrymandered umbilical cord sixteen miles in length, Los Angeles remained inland in ambience. The City of the Angels was too far away to hear the call of steamers entering the harbor or to smell the salt on the air. A Midwestern colony near the Southern California coast, Los Angeles could often seem strangely indifferent to the sea to which it had so determinedly obtained access. In the detective fiction of the next decade, the port existed in autonomous surreality, another city, another place, touched by Los Angeles, true, but unlike the parent city touched as well by the deeper tonalities and mysteries known only to cities by the sea.

Led by U.S. Senator Stephen Mallory White, to whom it raised a statue in thanksgiving after his premature death, the turn-of-the-century elite of Los Angeles willed the port as being as essential to the Progressive imperial formula as was water; and when the oligarchy at last obtained the port, it ran it according to the strictest Progressive doctrine—which is to say, efficiently and for the greatest public good. In 1921, stimulated by the reopening of the Panama Canal, the Los Angeles Chamber of Commerce urged the city to make the development of its port a priority for the 1920s comparable to what water had been in the early years of the century. At the urging of the Chamber, a Greater Harbor Committee of 200 was formed in 1922. Each member of the committee contributed $1000 to finance a comprehensive plan for port development. Over the next eight years the essential features of the plan were carried out by a five-member Harbor Commission established in 1925, whose autonomy from political interference paralleled the independence of the Department of Water and Power. Empowered by a $15 million obligation bond passed by voters in 1923, the Harbor Commission doubled wharf space in two years and in 1925 widened the main channel to 1000 feet. By 1927, 58 miles of railroad track and 23 miles of paved highways had been added and dynamiting begun on Deadman's Island, a navigational hazard at the harbor entrance, loathed by sailors since the Spanish era. After the disinterment and reburial of those found there—two Spanish soldiers, two sea captains, a Native American, six Marine casualties from the War of Conquest of 1846, a female with blond hair, and an indeterminate skeleton with an arrow protruding from its skull—two years were spent dynamiting Deadman's Island into the history it had witnessed and obstructed. Used as fill, the debris added 62 acres of useable space to Terminal Island, where a 410-acre commercial airport with seaplane ramp was completed in 1928.

As inland as Los Angeles might be by site and Midwestern temperament, it could not escape completely the festival pageantry of the sea. In August 1919 the newly authorized Pacific Fleet of the United States Navy, thirty-two ships in all, dropped anchor at Los Angeles and Long Beach, preparatory to its dispersal up and down the Pacific Coast. The two cities spent $100,000 entertaining the officers and men of the fleet. Thousands flocked to the port in specially scheduled trolleys to enjoy the spectacle of colorfully pennanted battleships, cruisers, and destroyers, symbolizing by their presence the emergence of the United States as a Pacific power and the emergence of Los Angeles as a strategic port, guarded by two massive fourteen-inch guns which the Army fired once, in 1926, frightening local residents and shattering windows.

The battleships *New Mexico* and *Mississippi*, the cruiser *Birmingham*, and six destroyers were home-ported at the San Pedro facilities of the Port of Los Angeles, with the rest of the fleet assigned to Long Beach, San Diego, and Pearl Harbor. Los Angeles and Long Beach became anchorage for the major U.S. naval force on the Pacific Coast. Thousands of naval families settled in Long Beach, prompting the magazine *Los Angeles Saturday Night* to add a special department covering the teas, balls, receptions, weddings, change of command ceremonies, and athletic competitions which constituted such an important aspect of naval life in peacetime. It could never be just parties, however, officers splendid in whites, wives in light frocks pressed against them by sea breezes. In early 1924 an explosion aboard the *Mississippi* during gunnery practice off Catalina Island killed 56 men. Their coffins, solemnly arrayed on the pier during the services that followed, testified to the fact that naval service involved more than glittering receptions and ceremonial cruises.

The Navy brought éclat to greater Los Angeles, together with celebrities such as Commander Richard Byrd, who sailed from Los Angeles harbor on 6 December 1928 on the whaler ice-breaker *C. A. Larsen* bound for Antarctica. President-elect and Mrs. Herbert Hoover arrived six weeks later, en route to Latin America aboard the dreadnought *Maryland*. "As the mighty dreadnought passed out of the harbor around the lighthouse, headed for southern waters," reported *Saturday Night* in February 1929, "hundreds of small craft that had been grouped around the battleship, burst forth in a bedlam of whistles and sirens. Mr. and Mrs. Hoover, from the quarter deck of the *Maryland*, and within the shadow of the Stars and Stripes, waved farewell to the hundreds aboard the small craft and several additional hundreds on the government breakwater." Scenes such as this did much to promote the self-esteem of an arriviste city. Smaller in scale, the daily departures of the *Harvard* and the *Yale*, coastal passenger ships plying overnight between Los Angeles and San Francisco, or the *Catalina*, which left twice a day for the island resort of Catalina, were comparably festive. Swift, semi-luxurious and fun—a jazz band playing each night for dancing, with Lawrence Clark Powell, the future librarian of UCLA, sitting in on piano and saxophone for the summer season of 1928—the *Harvard* and the *Yale* made an overnight party of the trip between San Francisco and Los Angeles.

Festive as well was the Pacific Southwest Exposition of August 1928, a Tunisian fantasy city spread across a sixty-acre site fronting the harbors of Los Angeles and Long Beach like a studio set from *The Thief of Baghdad*, *The Sheik*, *The Garden of Allah*, or *Sinbad the Sailor*. Encompassing twelve immense Hollywood/Tunisian exhibition palaces, the exposition celebrated a successful decade of expansion and improvement for the two adjacent ports. In the very week before the exposition opened, 166 vessels, including 59 passenger ships, were anchored at Los Angeles or Long Beach—a new record, according to the Marine Exchange. As far as the sponsoring Chambers of Commerce of Los Angeles and Long Beach were concerned, the domes, towers, minarets, and palm trees fronting the Pacific Ocean were totally appropriate. Sinbad the Sailor had come home to his favorite port.

The exhibits of the Palace of Varied Industry of the Pacific Southwest Exposition reminded Sinbad that he was arriving at an industrializing metropolis. The boosters of the early 1920s took Chicago, not Tunis or Baghdad, as the model for what Los Angeles might become. The Chicago metaphor, minus the brutal winters, served as a transitional image in the early 1920s as Los Angeles businessmen sought to bring manufacturing to the Southland. A group of Los Angeles investors led by J. A. McNaughton traveled to Chicago in early 1921 to study the stock and railroad yards and the central manufacturing district of the Windy City. A year later Arthur G. Leonard, president of the Union Stock Yards and Transit Company of Chicago, visited Los Angeles to advise on the location of the livestock market then being planned. By November 1922 the pens of the Los Angeles Union Stock Yards were filling with cattle, and the Central Manufacturing District of Los Angeles, Inc., a group of Chicagoizing businessmen, were announcing the development of a Chicago-style industrial center in the southeastern section of the city. "Our vision of the future Los Angeles," stated H. E. Poronto, president of the company, "is a gigantic city— the third in population and a mecca for progressive business as well as for work-worn individuals seeking rest and pleasure under the setting sun." [1]

Unlike Santa Barbara to the north, Los Angeles was never interested in becoming a resort city, although, as Poronto noted, retirees were welcomed. The vision of Los Angeles as an industrial city was implicit in the hydroelectrical component of the aqueduct system and, once water and power were available, was vigorously promoted by the Los Angeles Chamber of Commerce from 1914 onwards. As an industrial center, the Chamber pointed out, Los Angeles had nine major advantages. It was situated where the United States, Latin America, and the Asia Pacific Basin met. It was both a major railroad center and an important port. It had a good climate and an abundant local supply of petroleum. Water and electricity were plentiful and inexpensive. Development capital was abundant and locally controlled. Bankers, moreover, were not afraid of entrepreneurs. And, labor was abundant and labor unions weak.

Of all these factors, the last, the open shop, a fixed dogma since the bombing of the *Los Angeles Times* in 1910, was perhaps the most compelling attraction. Union activists found it herculean, if not impossible, to organize the ever-growing, ever-shifting, highly skilled Los Angeles labor pool. Something in the very nature of Los Angeles, something beyond the anti-unionizing skills of the ownership and managerial class and the bad taste left by the *Times* bombing, something to do with the persistent autonomy, the isolation and loneliness even, of a city peopled in such great measure by strangers from elsewhere, worked against the perception of class or craft solidarity upon which union membership depended. In San Francisco, which had developed in the nineteenth century along classic urban patterns of the East and Midwest, workers perceived a consolidating identity—a job, a common adversary, an ethnic group, an ideology—and organized. In Los Angeles the worker, having left these things behind in the very act of relocating, was reluctant to take them up again. The open shop remained the dominant practice not only because business wanted it and knew full well how to enforce its demands, but because enough workers from elsewhere wanted the open shop as well.

Throughout the 1920s Los Angeles industrialized. The $900 million industrial output of 1921 became the billion-dollar-plus industrial output of 1927. By then over one hundred factories were located in the Central Manufacturing District, developed a few years earlier. With the exceptions of sunshine and motion pictures, the Chicago metaphor was being rapidly realized. In meat-packing, a quintessentially Chicagoan activity, Los Angeles ranked fourth in the nation. Ford and Willys-Overland were making automobiles. Iron and steel had become a $120 million industry employing 20,000 workers.

Of all its manufacturing industries—glass, garments, furniture, metals, cars, canned fruit, motion pictures—the tire industry, like Hollywood, oil, and the port, possessed strong regional significance. Appropriately, the most automo-bilized city in the nation became by 1920 the second largest tire manufacturer in the world after Akron. Goodyear built a smartly designed tire factory in Los Angeles in 1919, followed in short order by Goodrich, Firestone, U.S. Rubber, and, later, Samson Tire, a local company seeking to take advantage of the low freight rates of the newly opened Panama Canal to achieve an eastern distri-bution. By 1928, when the tire industry employed 8000 workers for an annual payroll of $15 million, it had become necessary to expand each of these plants to meet the daily production quotas of 30,000 tires and 40,000 inner tubes. Samson Tire announced a new administration building as well, splendidly neo-Babylonian in motif. Located in the City of Commerce just south of downtown Los Angeles, this Babylonian pile still dominates its surroundings with its stage-set evocation of the Biblical era when the company's namesake Samson ground grain at the millstone, eyeless in Gaza. Each of the big four, moreover—Good-year (for whom the tire manufacturing district was named), Firestone, U.S. Rubber, and Samson—proudly stressed their Los Angeles identities in their advertising, as had Goodyear in 1919 when it housed this emergent industry in one of the most distinguished industrial buildings in the city. Tires lacked the glamour of Hollywood, the bigness of oil, the drama of the port, and the vi-sionary futurist aspects of aviation. The Los Angeles economy, however, did run smoothly and exuberantly throughout the 1920s on locally molded rubber.

The Los Angeles economy also tended to be financed from local capital. "Our banks," noted Joseph F. Sartori, president of Security Trust in December 1926, "are meeting the legitimate demands of industry almost entirely from their own resources."[2] A billion-dollar-plus economy, Sartori claimed, was matched by comparable funds on deposit in local banks. Sartori's own bank, headquartered in an elegant building at the corner of Fifth and Spring, was the seventh largest bank in the country, with forty branches throughout metropolitan Los Angeles and resources totaling more than $253 million. In many ways Sartori played a role in the rise of Southern California comparable to A. P. Giannini's in the north as guru of local finance, his loans empowering a myriad of local projects. Unlike Giannini, however, who sought to create a statewide, even national branch banking system, Sartori confined the expansion of Security Trust to metropolitan Los Angeles. For a number of years he skillfully thwarted through his influence with the state superintendent of banks Giannini's efforts to extend the Bank of Italy to the Southland.

In many ways Sartori was typical of the generation of the 1880s which had put Los Angeles into the first boom period of growth, which in turn had created the governmental, public utility, and financial capabilities supporting the expansion of the 1920s. Born in 1858 in Cedar Falls, Iowa, to prosperous Italian-German parents, Sartori was educated at the University of Freiberg in Germany, where he became a skilled fencer, and the Law School of the University of Michigan. He was already flourishing as an attorney when he emigrated to Southern California in 1887. He founded a bank in Monrovia the very same year, followed by a second bank, Security Trust of Los Angeles, in 1888. Better educated than Giannini, although without Giannini's streak of genius, Sartori mastered banking through meticulous study, like a lawyer preparing a brief. Few if any Southern Californians of his generation and prominence possessed his scholarly knowledge of the economic structures of the region, much less his merchant-banker's desire to participate positively in the rise of the Southland. Small in stature, quiet and reserved, with golf at the Los Angeles Country Club his only distraction, Sartori personally supervised the Southern California-oriented research department of his bank, using its findings to convince eastern investors to put more capital into developments backed by Security Trust. By the 1920s, with a billion-plus dollars on deposit, Sartori and his colleagues at other Los Angeles banks no longer had to go east for funds. Los Angeles controlled its own investment capital.

Among the many projects backed by Sartori was the Biltmore Hotel on Pershing Square. By 1925, in fact, $250 million had been invested in hotels, rooming houses, or other forms of short-term residence in greater Los Angeles, testimony to the half-million-plus visitors the region was by then receiving. Tourism, in other words, was emerging in the 1920s along with oil, the port, and tires as a major Los Angeles industry. At the urging of Frank Wiggins, secretary of the Chamber of Commerce, and *Times* publisher Harry Chandler, the hotel owners of Los Angeles, frustrated by plummeting winter occupancy rates, raised $46,000 in late 1920 to promote Southern California as a year-round tourist destination. Formally organized in 1921 as the All-Year Club of Southern California, the organization spent $5 million during the 1920s successfully booming the region as a tourist resort.

The program worked. By the end of 1923 Los Angeles was enjoying nearly a million and a half visitors a year. Sixty conventions were booked for 1928. By 1930 tourism and conventions accounted for 10 percent of the Los Angeles economy. Although tourists arrived by train and passenger steamer, it was the automobile that made the tourist industry possible on a mass basis. In 1924 it was estimated that 350 tourist cars were arriving in Los Angeles each day, bringing in thousands of visitors. By 1927 the Automobile Club of Southern California was claiming that 250,000 tourists visited the region in 1926 in 125,000 motor cars. A new institution, the municipal auto camp, sprung up to service this influx—a publicly owned campsite offering sanitary and cooking facilities that foreshadowed the evolution of the motel in the next decade. Tenting together by night, moving in picturesque caravans by day down the excellent roads of Southern California, the automotive tourist drove in the vanguard of an era of mass leisure and recreation that would become increasingly characteristic of the twentieth-century United States.

For both tourist and resident alike, the favorite destination was the beach, where, on Sundays especially, thousands of parked cars lined the coastal frontage like beached sea mammals lazing in the sun. If these were the Mediterranean shores of America, as had been claimed for nearly half a century, then an Isle of Capri was needed to counterpoint the Naples of Los Angeles. Twenty-six miles off the Palos Verdes Peninsula, the island of Santa Catalina exquisitely served this purpose. Twenty-one miles long, no more than eight miles at its widest point, Santa Catalina included bays as blue as any celebrated by the Roman poets of Capri and mountains rising two thousand feet from the sea into an equally Mediterranean clarity of light. William Wrigley, Jr., a Chicago chewing-gum magnate turned Pasadenan, purchased Santa Catalina in 1919 from the Banning family and spent the last years of the 1920s developing the settlement of Avalon on the southeastern end of the island into a mini Monte Carlo, complete with a $2 million casino in the Moorish/modern style rising on the shores of Avalon Bay like a fantasy from the Arabian Nights. Two steamers, the *Catalina* and the *Avalon*, made the two-hour voyage alternately, with a ticket costing $5 for a round trip. Aside from two hotels, the St. Catherine and the Atwater, Santa Catalina tourist facilities included 1250 one-room bungalettes, as they were called, containing a dresser and a double bed. By day there was sea-bathing, golf, tennis, horseback riding, mountain walks, tours of the fish-rich kelp fields in glass-bottomed boats, or visits to a seven-and-a-half-acre aviary featuring hundreds of rare birds. At night a full orchestra played for dancing at the casino, where gambling was not allowed.

Other Los Angeles-based tours included sightseeing bus tours of Hollywood and Beverly Hills with stopovers at the Bernheimer Japanese Gardens and the Hollywood Bowl; an excursion to Mount Lowe with a side tour of the Famous Players-Lasky Ranch near Glendale, where movies were being filmed; and a beach-oriented tour that included Santa Monica, Ocean Park, Venice, Playa del Rey, and Manhattan, Hermosa, and Redondo beaches.

Prominent tourists to Los Angeles—General John Pershing, who came in 1920 and 1923; Major General George Washington Goethals of Panama Canal fame, another 1923 visitor; the Crown Prince and Princess of Sweden, 1926; Colonel Charles A. Lindbergh, 1927; Winston Churchill, 1929—had along with other affluent visitors their pick of Los Angeles's major hotels, another materialized dream of the decade. The Ambassador on Wilshire Boulevard and the Biltmore on Pershing Square downtown each epitomized how hotels expressed and fulfilled the aspirations of an emergent city.

Organized and financed in 1919 by a group of local investors, the Ambassador was intended to serve affluent locals as well as tourists. To that end architect Myron Hunt designed a nine-hundred-room resort hotel and urban social center complete with theater, ballroom, nightclub (the famous Cocoanut Grove), meeting rooms, and other civic amenities. Its golf course and grounds planted in thousands of shrubs, trees, and flowering plants served the Wilshire district as a park available to the well-behaved portion of the pedestrian public. Vast and sumptuous, its lobby the largest in North America, its dining room covering half an acre of uninterrupted floor space, the Ambassador evoked and helped define Los Angeles as a major new American city, which was why the oligarchy, its ladies especially—Mrs. William McAdoo, daughter of President Woodrow Wilson and wife of the Secretary of the Treasury, Mrs. Edward Laurence Doheny, the oil heiress, and Mrs. I. N. Van Nuys among them— flocked to its opening dinner ball held on the evening of 18 January 1921 with all the considerable splendor of velvet, taffeta, satin, chiffon, brocade, ostrich fans, jewelry, tiaras, and furs they could muster.

Opening on 1 October 1923 with an equally sumptuous ball, the Los Angeles Biltmore at Fifth and Olive facing Pershing Square in the downtown, the largest hotel west of Chicago, was also a locally organized civic enterprise. Bond broker S. W. Straus spearheaded the development of the Ambassador. Banker Joseph Sartori organized the six-hundred-stockholder syndicate behind the Biltmore whose leadership—Harry Chandler, Marco Hellman, Henry M. Robinson, Lee Phillips—proceeded from the same social groupings which had secured water from Owens Valley in 1913 and were about to improve the port. Designed in opulent Italian and Spanish Revival motifs by the firm of Schultze and Weaver, the Biltmore, like the Ambassador, was an exuberantly public performance whose oversized ballroom and banquet hall were intended primarily for Los Angeles itself. With the opening of the Ambassador and the Biltmore, augmented by the Beverly Hills Hotel, the Hotel Maryland (later Huntington) in Pasadena, the Hotel Virginia in Long Beach, the Mission Inn in Riverside, and by 1927 some 740 other city establishments, Los Angeles possessed one more major component of its economy.

Another crucial economic factor, Hollywood, functioned as both a tourist attraction and a source of local employment. Few ordinary tourists or prominent visitors to Los Angeles, including Winston Churchill, who enthusiasti-

cally lunched at Metro-Goldwyn-Mayer on 28 September 1929, failed to include Hollywood or the stars' homes in Beverly Hills on their itineraries. What
they encountered in the Hollywood of the 1920s was at once a representative
district of Los Angeles, a suburban city annexed in 1910 (41 banks, an athletic
club, a Chamber of Commerce building, 16 movie houses, two daily newspapers, a population of 150,000 by 1927), and a place energized by dreams.
Hollywood was also an important industrial center. As early as 1920, filmmak-
ing had become the biggest industry in Los Angeles. The local payroll of 1922,
$30 million, doubled in 1923. By 1926, the year motion pictures became the
fourth largest industry in the world and the first of California's 35 top industries, some 35,000 Los Angeles area residents were earning $1.25 million a
week from the film industry, not including extras on call. In 1927 an heroic
$103 million was spent making movies, up 25 percent from the previous year.
Conversions to sound studios after 1928 poured another $247 million into the
regional economy. Little wonder that the praising of Hollywood as Los Angeles's leading industry, with 90 percent of all films being made somewhere in
greater Los Angeles by 1922, became a staple of local promotional rhetoric,
begrudgingly voiced even by some who maintained the anti-Hollywood social
attitudes of the pre-World War I era.

Producer Cecil B. De Mille, an Episcopalian of Anglo-Dutch descent in an
industry dominated by Eastern European Jewish immigrants, came as close as
anybody to bridging WASP Los Angeles and Jewish Hollywood. Movie people,
De Mille admitted in December 1923, had not been warmly received in Los
Angeles during the early years of the film industry. It was partly Los Angeles's
fault for looking down on film folk as socially disreputable, but it was partly
the fault of the film people as well. Transient in culture, used to living out of
a trunk as members of road companies, actors and actresses established few
social connections outside their own circle. But now in 1923, with films as the
leading industry in the region, De Mille argued, the movie colony was becoming integrated into local socio-economic landscape.

Proof positive of this Los Angelesation: movie people were investing in real
estate. De Mille himself belonged to a major real-estate syndicate and served
as a director of Giannini's Bank of Italy and as vice president of a local savings
and trust. Other film figures such as Ruth Roland, Mary Pickford, Harold
Lloyd, Jackie Coogan, Sid Grauman, Agnes Ayres, Noah Berry, Thomas Ince,
and Charles Christie were also important real-estate investors. "When you old
residents with a wide forward vision and a belief in the future of Los Angeles
came to us," De Mille told Los Angeles realtors, "and suggested sub-division
of bare acreage, then miles from the center of things, you found in the motion
picture colony not scoffers but friends."[3] Flattered by praise which acknowl-
edge simultaneously Hollywood as a source of investment capital and the social
superiority of pre-movie Los Angeles, the oligarchy allowed De Mille through
the barriers that had kept (and were still keeping) other Hollywood magnates

from social acceptance. His daughter Cecilia, an ardent equestrienne, became prominent in the Junior League of Los Angeles, and De Mille received invitations to the better clubs.

Just as the tourist industry stimulated the materialization of hotels rich with local metaphor, the film industry inspired an equally evocative public place, the film palace, through which Los Angeles might further define and boost itself. Even in the pre-film era theaters such as the Majestic (1909) and the Orpheum (1911) provided Los Angeles with its earliest celebratory spaces. Encased within Broadway office buildings, these two early theaters also constituted pioneering engineering and architectural additions to the city.

When film began to replace vaudeville, showman Sidney Grauman set about to create on Broadway, Los Angeles, the movie palace counterpart of the legitimate theater district of New York. Born to vaudeville, the impresario son of an impresario father, Grauman understood intuitively that the new medium of film had a power to engage the subliminal consciousness of audiences even more powerfully than live entertainment on the vaudeville stage. Beginning with the New Grauman Theater at Third and Broadway, which opened in 1918, the pixieish exhibitor (Grauman reminded Anita Loos of the Mad Hatter) created progressively elaborate environments that pushed archeological exactitude to the point of fantastic pageant. One contemporary critic described the New Grauman Theater as "a dream worth building," which succinctly expressed the sophisticated subliminal statements Grauman had his team of architects and designers, led by William Lee Woollett of San Francisco, carefully implant into the murals, statues, decorative carvings, carpets, and furnishings of the new facility. "I never dreamed it possible for one person to feel so many different kinds of ways at one and the same time," said one early visitor, enchanted by the color, lighting, and decorative profusion of Grauman's masterfully erudite film palace. Even as the subliminal self was being touched by the architectural dream that framed the dream on the screen, there was also, as this critic noticed, a sense of dignity, of a compliment being paid the audience, in the scholarly content of the decorative motifs.[4]

In the Grauman's Metropolitan Theater which Woollett designed in the early 1920s (it opened in Los Angeles in 1923) and the Grauman Egyptian Theater in Hollywood (another 1923 opening), archeological reference in the service of subliminal suggestion reached even greater levels of intensity. Architect Bernard Maybeck hailed the Metropolitan Theater as an important new art form. "There is a sense of spaciousness, of order, of color, of grandeur that is indescribable," Maybeck noted of the mezzanine foyer, praising it as a distinctly Southern Californian public space, at once suggestive of the semi-arid coastlands and the European tradition.[5] In bringing painting and sculpture into dynamic unity with architectural design, noted another critic, the Metropolitan Theater struck an almost liturgical chord. "All the great buildings," he argued, "have votive elements in their character. There is something votive in the Metropolitan Theater. It is built for and dedicated to the American public, millions strong, who find in the color and rhythm of gorgeous spectacles and syncopated music a satisfaction that is a national characteristic."[6] The cathedral comparison implicit in this description, a cathedral of color and fantasy with jazz as liturgical music, emerged explicitly in the didacticism of the great asbestos curtain, which playfully re-presented the theory of evolution according to H. G. Wells.

Grauman's Egyptian Theater in Hollywood was designed as an archeologically exact "film temple," in which each detail—the courtyard and lobby ablaze in brightly colored murals and hieroglyphics, the statuary and sarcophagi, the profusely decorated proscenium hovering over the screen like a baldachino above a baroque altar—was intended to create an overall effect of mystic reverence, as one might feel in an ancient Egyptian temple. Sid Grauman and his architects and artists, William Woollett especially, created public spaces that satisfied through secular entertainment the votive urge, the need to congregate and be impressed and instructed, to feel awe and offer reverent assent to something mysterious without and within. All great cities must have their places of worship. Opening on Broadway near Ninth in December 1927, the United Artists Theaters, a Spanish cathedral designed by the firm of Walker and Eisen working with C. Howard Crane, pushed this cathedral parallel even further. The dome of the theater exploded in a giant golden sunburst, intended to suggest the energy of creation itself, while throughout the murals below numerous Hollywood stars, explicitly depicted and recognizable—Norma Talmadge, Douglas Fairbanks, Charles Chaplin, John Barrymore, Rudolph Valentino, Gloria Swanson, D. W. Griffith, and many others—played various parts in tableaux depicting the conquest of ignorance and superstition by the film industry, a sturdy female using film for reins, riding like a goddess around the globe.

2

Hotels and theaters functioned as booster statements idealizing the Los Angeles locale. From the first seventeenth-century plantations, boosterism has been a perennial American trait, a natural corollary of sustained development and willful self-invention; but in the Los Angeles of the 1920s boosterism constituted a fixed creed, a local rite, sweeping away in its inexorable rush of rhetoric any doubts whatsoever that at this particular time and place in history Los Angeles, California, was on the cutting edge of American experience. In Los Angeles everyone, or nearly everyone, high or low, felt at least once the urge to come forth and testify to the faith delivered to the saints. Los Angeles, railroader Henry Huntington testified in the early 1900s, was destined to become the most important city in the country, if not the world. Los Angeles, the mystical aesthete Edgar Saltus testified in 1909, was destined to become the artistic capital of the United States, the Florence of America.

Founded in 1873 and refounded in 1888 after the collapse of its first effort, the Los Angeles Chamber of Commerce functioned along with the All Year Club, the Automobile Club of Southern California, and the Los Angeles Realty Board as a principal propagandist of the 1920s. In Chamber of Commerce secretary Frank Wiggins, a tall, thin, droopy-mustachioed Quaker, more parson than publicist in his demeanor, Los Angeles enjoyed the services of one of the master promoters of the early twentieth century. Arriving in Los Angeles in 1886 after selling out his harness and saddlery business in Richmond, Indiana, Wiggins joined the Los Angeles Chamber of Commerce in 1890 as superintendent of exhibits and became secretary in 1897, a position he held until his death in October 1924.

Like so many converted Midwesterners, Frank Wiggins believed in Southern California with an ardor that drew much of its energy from an even deeper Quaker faith, with its emphasis upon community rooted to place and kept together by powerful invisible bonds. Surprisingly, Wiggins also turned out to be a skilled showman. In 1893 he dazzled visitors to the Columbian Exposition at Chicago with a theatrically organized exhibit of pyramided citrus—a Hanging Gardens juggernaut of oranges, other fruits, and flowers, pre-Hollywood in dimension and spectacle. Repeating this feat successively at other exhibitions and fairs for the following two decades, Wiggins used the orange to promote Southern California, Los Angeles County especially (the leading agricultural region in California until the 1940s), as a region of sunny healthfulness. For a while the Chamber maintained a special exhibit train, "California on Wheels," that toured the nation promoting the Southland. Not only did Wiggins sell Los Angeles County products, he sold Los Angeles County as well, especially after the Sunkist Cooperative he helped organize used a series of innovative advertising and packaging techniques to make orange-eating a near declaration of intent to migrate to Southern California. The only way to stop the growth of Los Angeles, William Mulholland was supposed to have joked in the teens, was to do away with Frank Wiggins.

By the time of Wiggins's death in 1924, a new message, the City of Los Angeles itself, and a new medium, photography, had begun to replace the orange as a promotional vehicle at the Chamber of Commerce. Inaugurated in 1923, the photo files of the Chamber grew to an estimated 50,000 images before the series was discontinued in the war years. Working through the 1920s, Chamber photographer Arch Dunning, succeeded by Newton Berlin in 1928, assembled thousands of images of an ideal Los Angeles that, like the orange pyramids of the prewar era, went forth to the world and recruited.

In 1928 alone the Chamber placed nearly 17,000 prints in publications across the country. Eschewing all signs of urban ugliness or social stress, the Chamber images communicated an utopian ideality comparable to the orange-crate labels of the same period. Fords sit prosperously before bungalows or garden-court apartments. Industrial areas shimmer in the sunshine. Oil fields run gracefully into orange groves. Families enjoy the beach. A teacher brings her students, all of them in bathing suits, to an outdoor class on the seaside sand. By night the Los Angeles basin becomes a fairyland of electric light. Obvious propaganda, devoid of tenements, skid rows, or any other signs of impoverishment, these Chamber of Commerce photographs nevertheless convinced thousands to join the hegira to the Southland.

Los Angeles *Times* editor and publisher Harry Chandler, son-in-law and successor of Harrison Gray Otis, was the biggest booster of them all. A New Hampshire native, Chandler dropped out of Dartmouth with hemorrhaging lungs and pneumonia and came to Los Angeles in 1883, a dispirited victim of tuberculosis living in a boarding house on the Plaza, not expecting to last the year. Fortunately, Chandler met a physician, also tubercular, who was struggling to regain his health as a fruit rancher near Cahuenga Pass at the edge of the San Fernando Valley. The physician offered Chandler a job. Going to work on the fruit ranch, Chandler went shirtless by day to absorb the sun, acquiring a deep mahogany tan unusual for that era. (Can it be said, among other things, that Harry Chandler pioneered the Southern California suntan?) By night he slept in a tent pitched beneath the fruit trees. He also began to peddle fruit to Mexican workers on the nearby 60,000-acre Van Nuys Ranch. With money earned from this enterprise, Chandler, who by now had recovered his health (after suffering a relapse during a brief effort to return to Dartmouth), began to buy up and subcontract newspaper circulation routes throughout Los Angeles. He soon netted $500 a month, a princely salary for the 1880s. Shortly thereafter, publisher Harrison Gray Otis appointed Chandler circulation manager of the *Times* followed by an appointment to business manager, and, later, the post of son-in-law.

For Chandler, Horatio Alger married to the boss's daughter, the *Times* which he took over from his father-in-law in 1917 was a source of power and profit; but, more important, the newspaper served the assembling of a real estate empire that eventually encompassed two million acres in Southern California and Mexico. Unlike his arch-rival William Randolph Hearst, who for all his wealth threw himself enthusiastically in his early years into the ink-stained camaraderie of the city room, Chandler came to journalism exclusively via circulation and management. Personally untouched by the *Front Page* obsessions that were forever gripping Hearst or by Hearst's obsession with national power through a newspaper chain and press syndicate, Chandler considered the *Times* a source of regional power and the lead element in a portfolio whose real depth was in real estate. A businessman anxious to foster the development of his property, Chandler used the *Times* to boost the specific applications of water, hydroelectricity, bond issues, and zoning that would simultaneously boost Los Angeles and Southern California—and enhance his holdings. Reserved and flinty in the manner of upstate New Hampshire, fully aware that his arch-conservative policies rendered him anathema to portions of the population, Chandler had the self-awareness and the good sense to remain as private as possible in both his personal and his business life. His name rarely appeared in his own newspaper. The philosophy and specific practice of the *Times*, however, perfectly expressed Chandler's boosterism as a mode of enlightened self-interest.

Throughout the 1920s the *Times* preached the doctrines of growth and subdivision in which its owner-publisher was such an active protagonist. Meanwhile, the booster/anti-booster, Babbitt/anti-Babbitt dialectic, so characteristic of the United States at large during the decade of the 1920s, continued locally with special intensity, given the massive growth and boostering that was occurring. While Burton Smith, state editor of the *Times*, might write a stirring defense of Babbittry, Southern California-style ("No section of the country is better located than Southern California to witness at first hand the accomplishments of Babbitt and to profit by his untiring endeavors"), others felt at odds with the prevailing ethos. "The whole coast wearies me," noted Hamlin Garland in his diary for 14 April 1923, "with its incessant and self-conscious advertising, its eternal boom, its monotonous note of optimism."[7] The booster culture of Los Angeles, admitted maverick journalist Louis Adamic, was infectious. "As a matter of fact, I must put restraint upon myself in order not to join the great horde of Los Angeles boomers and boosters and shouters; for I have now been living in or near Los Angeles for several years and there are moments when I have real difficulty resisting the spirit of the place (which may be saying less for myself than for the spirit)."[8]

An even more ironic reversal characterizes Mark Lee Luther's novel *The Boosters* (1924). Himself the offspring of old American stock and the son of a forty-niner, Mark Lee Luther, an easterner, lived in Los Angeles in the early 1920s for the expressed purpose of writing a novel about the emergent city. Through his hero, architect George Hammond, Luther suggested his own experience as an easterner with a latent California heritage. Trained at MIT and the Ecole des Beaux-Arts in Paris, Hammond is a scholarly patrician Boston architect wearing a Van Dyke beard and nearing fifty. With a practice devoted mainly to Colonial Revival in affluent Boston suburbs, Hammond collects books, writes scholarly articles for journals, enjoys his club and the symphony, and in the depression following the war goes broke. His wife Harriet, fortunately, inherits a legacy of $50,000 from the estate of her forty-niner father, who ended his days in Los Angeles. After learning that Harriet's brother Spencer Ward, a Los Angeles real-estate developer, has increased his $50,000 inheritance tenfold, the middle-aged couple remove to the City of the Angels with their college-aged son and daughter. On the train, the Hammonds encounter a Los Angeles booster operating in verbal overdrive. "Our people are the salt of the

earth," the booster tells the Hammonds. "You betcha. You'll find no starch in
their manners. They're first of all Americans; second, Californians; third, Angelenos; and, fourth, boosters every minute they're awake. Want me to tell you
why they're boosters? It's because Los Angeles delivers the goods. You betcha.
She's happy, healthy and handsome. Our water supply comes sparkling from
the mountains through the longest aqueduct ever built. Absolutely. You've
read history. You know that one of Rome's chief glories was her aqueducts.
Well, they weren't a patch on ours. Ever heard its capacity? It's ten times that
of all the aqueducts that Rome could boast."[9]

Into this harangue Luther has distilled the essence of innumerable sales pitches,
luncheon speeches, Chamber of Commerce brochures, and magazine articles
from the Los Angeles of the 1920s. Ironically, as the novel unfolds, Hammond
discovers that much of this boosterism contains a strong element of truth. Introduced to prospective clients by his brother-in-law ("Don't be modest," Spencer tells him. "It doesn't pay. We're all boosters in Los Angeles. We boost the
city. We boost ourselves"), Hammond experiences a sea change in his standoff-
ish attitude. Establishing himself as an architect/developer, he devotes himself
to the creation of elegant suburbs characterized by good landscaping and architecture that respect the environment and traditions of the region. No longer
dependent upon his wife's money, Hammond recovers from chronic indiges-
tion. In the final scene he sits surrounded by his books in the study of his
highland home as nighttime descends and Los Angeles becomes a carpet of
light extending to the sea. "It seemed his city at last," the novel concludes.
"He thought of what it had done for him and his and what he hoped to do for
it in return. He felt superbly fit. This climate they bragged about—well, it was
a climate. And this land—well, it was a land to love. Then, with the humor
which seldom deserted him, he saw himself from the outside and laughed. 'By
all that's ironical,' he said aloud, 'I've gone and done it!' The fact was inescap-
able. George himself had become a booster."[10]

Considered in its debased aspects, boosterism could be so much hot air.
Boosterism could also be a way of envisioning the future as the three classes of
Los Angeles, Oligarchs, Babbitts, and Folks, struggled to make the future happen. A city so dramatically dependent upon self-invention—no Gold Rush, no
railroads, no harbor in its first one hundred years—needed the adrenaline of
boosterism to make the future seem plausible. After all, the city had been
boosted before, in the 1880s, and it had collapsed. In so many instances—the
aqueduct most dramatically, with eight times the capacity of what was needed
in 1913, but also in the port and the long-range, even excessive subdivision of
properties unsellable for another forty years—Los Angeles was lashing itself into
futurity. It is not surprising that a passion for growth also discovered, hesitantly,
a dawning sense of limits. A taste for exuberant exurbanism led paradoxically
to the circumscriptions of a cityplan.

3

To boost the future is a far easier task than to plan for proper growth and, more important, to bring such planning to fruition. For all its headlong exuberance Los Angeles did plan; and although the needs of developers, together with an early fixation on the automobile, prevented the most imaginative plans from being brought to reality, major disasters were forestalled, which was an accomplishment in a city growing at such a ferocious rate. Planning in Los Angeles centered itself around three axes: growth, zoning, and the automobile. In 1908 the city had been zoned into residential and industrial districts; but by 1913, when the City Council established the first citywide planning commission, a more sophisticated pattern had become necessary. Even this simple division between industrial and non-industrial zones was fought unsuccessfully all the way to the State Supreme Court by aggrieved Los Angeles property owners. In an era of assured growth, zoning emerged as a simple solution to the planning problem. Zoning directed an assured energy into equally assured solutions, residential or industrial.

But could Los Angeles zone for vision as well? What kind of a city, finally, did Los Angeles wish to become? Even as zoning emerged, there also emerged the vision of Los Angeles as the City Beautiful. To the north, a group of private citizens led by former mayor James D. Phelan had in 1904 commissioned the famed architect and city planner Daniel Hudson Burnham to do a master plan for San Francisco, completed in 1906. In the same year Los Angeles enacted its first zoning ordinance, the Municipal Art Commission sponsored a similar plan from another City Beautiful advocate, Charles Mulford Robinson. While not as elaborately prepared as the Burnham Plan for San Francisco, Robinson's recommendations eloquently suggested the development of Los Angeles into a City Beautiful of distinguished public buildings, plazas, parks, boulevards, monuments and statuary, greenbelts and landscaped residential zones. The Beaux Arts neoclassicism of the City Beautiful, however, even in Robinson's modified version, failed to take into account growth, growth, growth—and the automobile. In the Robinson plan pedestrians strolled through plazas and promenades. By the early 1920s, Robinson's imagined walkers were driving by automobile through a distended cityscape.

In 1923 a pamphlet appeared entitled *Why Los Angeles Will Become the World's Greatest City*. The essential dynamic behind this predicted rise to greatness was and remained growth. Down through the 1920s scores of speeches, magazine articles, and other modes of prophesy repeated the assertion that Los Angeles was becoming great because it was becoming big. It was, in the terminology of the day, a white spot. "The spaces of yesterday," exulted Ernest McGaffey, a publicist for the Automobile Club of Southern California, in October 1922, "are the fetters of today, and the figures of a last year's progress sink into insignificance compared with the result of the succeeding twelve-month."[11] Population predictions ran from two million by 1942 to four million by 1950. If suburbs are included, neither of these figures was far from the mark. "Four million people," predicted Chamber official Clarence H. Matson in September 1924, "will not only fill up most of the space 'from the mountains to the sea,' but beautiful homes also will cover the hills of Hollywood and the Santa Monica mountains, and the San Fernando Valley will be thickly populated—a condition which seemed impossible a generation ago when the San Fernando Valley was only a gigantic ranch given over to dry farming."[12]

As evidence of this growth obsession, William Mulholland, a mere ten years after the aqueduct came on line, called for its extension one hundred miles northwest to Mono Basin, and, even more ambitious, he advocated the construction of yet another aqueduct across the desert from the Colorado River to a reservoir in Riverside County for distribution throughout the Los Angeles basin. Los Angeles, the city and the county, got behind both projects. In 1928 a Metropolitan Water District was formed to administer the Colorado River project, and a series of bond issues were passed for both the Colorado aqueduct and the Mono Basin extension, each project being completed within the next decade. Once again, the future, perceived as growth, was being made possible through water. Even the 150-foot height limit of Los Angeles, which prevented the rise of a Chicago- or New York style skyline, was enacted not for aesthetic reasons but because it promoted the spreading of the city.

Along with unquestioned growth, an obsession with sheer size, the automobile which made such diffusion possible naturally emerged as the major planning consideration as Los Angeles entered the 1920s. Downtown Los Angeles, noted city traffic consultant Miller McClintock in September 1924, was receiving 200,000 vehicles a day, half the automobiles registered in Los Angeles County, a figure ten times that of 1914. Both steady movement and parking had become impossible. McClintock's solution was not to limit or to reroute traffic so as to liberate the streetcar system, slowly dying from the congestion, but to "eliminate the use of streets for purposes which are private and have nothing to do with transportation upon the streets." By this he meant not only cars double-parked to disembark passengers, but also street vendors and even parades. The streets of downtown Los Angeles, McClintock argued, must be reserved for automobile traffic first and foremost. Without such a priority, the downtown would lose its attractiveness as a retail and commercial center to the outlying satellite cities.[13] Thus McClintock and his thinkalikes—the vast majority of the business establishment—threw themselves behind a vision of Los Angeles that implicitly, even explicitly, rejected the rich pedestrian culture, the daily spectacle of human life—the strolling, shopping, lounging of humanity—that since time immemorial had characterized successful urban cultures. Of course, they could never succeed in such an effort. Downtown Los Angeles refused, finally, to become completely automobilized; yet this vision of the city as, in its spatial essence, a free-flowing traffic artery underscored an important, indeed dominant civic self-image and premise.

The voters of Los Angeles agreed with McClintock. In 1924 they overwhelmingly authorized a Major Traffic Street Plan that facilitated the automobilization of downtown Los Angeles through an ambitious program of street widening and traffic enhancement. Nor was this attitude confined to the city itself. When the Los Angeles County Board of Supervisors established a Regional Planning Commission in 1923, the first such body in the nation (it encompassed forty cities and fifty unincorporated towns), it specifically charged the agency to make a countywide highway system a major priority. Such an integrated highway system, it was argued, would soon mold Los Angeles County into one great metropolis. Over the next twenty years, the county spent some $150 million building eight thousand miles of highways. Another ten thousand miles of highway were on the drawing boards.

Thus the automobile became both the planning problem and the planning solution. Enlarged streets and a more efficient feeder system brought more automobiles into the city, which in turn necessitated further accommodations to the automobile. A better county highway system further encouraged the development of satellite communities dependent upon the automobile. Subdividers and developers keyed their efforts to the necessities of automobile traffic. A compulsive gridiron arrangement of streets at ninety-degree angles, for instance, might defy possible harmonies of streetplan and landscape, but it made automobile traffic easier. Only the wealthy and politically independent suburbs such as Palos Verdes and Beverly Hills were capable of planning with the landscape, not the automobile, as the primary consideration.

Rejecting elevated streetcar tracks at the ballot box in 1926, Los Angeles wedded itself even more firmly to the automobile, rather than to the form of public transportation that had fostered the first era of sub/urban growth. Ironically, this decision also involved an affirmation of another transportation form, the railroad, that had also contributed to the rise of the region. Three transcontinental railroads, the Southern Pacific, the Union Pacific, and the Sante Fe, served Los Angeles. Each possessed its own station. As Los Angeles expanded and its streets began to intersect with pre-existing railroad tracks, arriving and departing trains—the SP especially, which approached its Central Station via Alameda Street—began to constitute a traffic problem. In 1915 Los Angeles filed a plea with the California Railroad Commission in Sacramento that the SP, UP, and Santa Fe be required to build a Union Station at a suitable location so as to consolidate entrance and egress from the city. In the pre-Progressive era, when the SP wielded major political influence, such a demand, had it dared be made, would have languished in the derision of smoke-filled rooms. As it was, the decision of the Railroad Commission, favorable to Los Angeles's request, was fought back and forth through the courts for nearly

two decades. By 1926, in the penultimate phase of the struggle, the City of the
Angels sought to strengthen its position by taking its case to the people in the
May election. By that time the fate of mass transit by streetcar to and through
downtown Los Angeles had become inextricably bound up with the question
of the location of the proposed Union Station.

The previous year, 1925, the Pacific Electric Railway had brought to Los
Angeles a brief one-mile suggestion of what so many had been advocating since
the war—a subway. Tunneling for a mere mile through Bunker Hill in downtown Los Angeles, Pacific Electric turned its Glendale, Burbank, and Hollywood runs into rapid transit defiant of the automotive congestion that was gradually bringing streetcar transportation in downtown Los Angeles to a halt.
Gratified by the overwhelmingly favorable response, the interurban announced
its next proposal: not more subways, which were prohibitively expensive for a
private company, but an elevated system that would swiftly shunt high-speed
streetcars in and out of the city above automotive traffic. Pacific Electric made
its proposal in conjunction with the SP, which was anxious to get its trains off
Alameda Street; the Santa Fe; and the UP. The four railroads agreed to construct a Union Station at Fourth and Central, and, more important, to build
(at the cost of $25 million) an elevated railway that utilized the already cleared,
privately owned SP and UP rail lines. Both the Pacific Electric and the SP
agreed to share the same elevated railway as their trains entered or departed the
city across the Los Angeles River. Most of Los Angeles—four newspapers, the
Chamber of Commerce, suburban interests—endorsed the proposal enthusiastically, gratified by the vision of some 1200 streetcars speeding each day to and
from the city via the Pacific Electric terminal at Sixth and Main, the Union
Station at Fourth and Central, and the Los Angeles River approach, all without
touching the ground. An estimated 18,000 daily grade crossings between streetcars and automobiles would thus be avoided.

Harry Chandler of the *Times*, however, was not pleased. Chandler favored
locating the proposed Union Station near the Plaza where Los Angeles had
been centered since the late eighteenth century and where, some claimed but
could never prove, Chandler himself was reputed to own real-estate holdings
destined to soar in value once the area, then shabby and rundown, was revitalized. The Plaza location also precluded the elevated plan since no railroad
owned established rights of way into this area. In the months prior to the May
1926 election, the Los Angeles *Times* pounded away at the elevated proposal.
Elevateds were dangerous and unsightly. Worse: they smacked of the crowded
eastern and Midwestern cities so many citizens of Los Angeles had fled from
in the first place. Elevateds, the *Times* argued, were alien to the spirit of Los
Angeles. Although the proposition favoring the Plaza location for the central
terminal narrowly won in May by 4000 votes, the proposition favoring the
elevated went down in defeat by a margin of two to one. Los Angeles had

envisioned itself crisscrossed by elevated railways, even the elegant ones promised by Pacific Electric, and rejected the image.

Unfortunately, this rejection did not go hand in hand with a willingness to
undertake a subway program at public expense. Whatever its problems, the
privately owned automobile remained the preferred transportation alternative
and hence the dominant factor in the planning or non-planning of Los Angeles. Ironically, the interurban streetcar system was at the very apex of its service
level when it was being banished from the inner city. As the 1920s opened,
some 6000 cars a day whizzed along five trunk lines that radiated from downtown Los Angeles in all directions of the basin, linking Los Angeles, Orange,
San Bernardino, and Riverside counties. While the system had another thirty-
five years of service left before fading away completely, after the May 1926 vote
it was no longer a major element in the functioning of Southern California.
The streetcar had been vanquished by the automobile. Like the Mission Inn at
Riverside, the big red cars belonged to the Progressive era, which had brought
Robinson's City Beautiful to Los Angeles in 1908 and had put its faith in
zoning as the solution to planning difficulties.

Basing itself in a philosophy of public interest that sought to soar above self
and special interests, the Progressive philosophy of zoning—which in 1913
had differentiated the initial residential/industrial zones of 1908 into business,
single-family, multiple-family, light industrial, and heavy industrial zones—
envisioned zoning officials as arbitrators above the fray. The businessmen and
developers of Los Angeles, however, saw zoning as just another procedure to
be manipulated by the political process. While Los Angeles pioneered the use
of zoning to guide growth, it also pioneered another strategy born of the Progressive passion for fair play: the exemption of zoning decisions through appeal
and variances. Wilshire Boulevard, for example, was initially zoned as a lushly
landscaped parkway lined with single-family residences. Appeal after appeal
transformed it into a traffic corridor lined with large-scale commercial buildings
and apartment houses. By the late 1920s the private sector dominated the zoning process through political influence. Ironically, this conferred even greater
power on developers, who now had official approval for their ventures. If the
zones made available by government were overly schematic, developers liked it
that way. Provided they were ultimately under private control, zones stabilized
and protected investments. A developer wanting residential or commercial zones,
for instance, was now capable of using the zoning process to insure the stable
nature of his investment. He could also bring increasingly larger portions of
the city under bloc control.

Shaped by the monodromic forces of the automobile and the restrictive zone,
each of them demanding and receiving a clarity and completeness of response,
Los Angeles had difficulty evolving the mixed, in-between spaces which give
each city its humanity and character: the Roman *via* where apartments rise

above shops, and where churches crowd against cafes and movie theaters; the London square, at once a traffic circle, park, residential block and subway stop; or Greenwich Village in New York or North Beach in San Francisco, villages within the city, challenging the abstractions of the metropolis with a thousand details of local life. Rigidly zoned Los Angeles, by contrast, with the conspicuous exception of the bohemian Bunker Hill area downtown, began to take on an abstract character of clarified zone succeeding clarified zone, which because of automotive distances could under certain circumstances be perceived as anonymous and sinister, as the detective story writers of the 1930s knew full well. Zoned for clarity and bloc development, attenuated by highways, Los Angeles threatened to dilate its centrality into a mosaic of abstract spaces through which only automobiles might hurry.

4

In 1922 city planning secretary G. Fordon Whitnall suggested that Los Angeles, since it was beginning with a relatively clean slate, had the opportunity to become a model metropolis, exempt from the mistakes of older American cities. Crucial to this goal were successful public buildings and spaces such as the Coliseum under construction in Exposition Park. Financed under a lease agreement with the county by a private syndicate calling itself the Community Development Association, the Coliseum, like the great hotels, prefigured and boosted the very growth it promised to serve. In 1921 not one but two major stadia, the Rose Bowl in Pasadena and the Coliseum, were launched in deliberate anticipation of the emergence of greater Los Angeles as a world center of athletic competition. The Coliseum was directly linked to a bid made by Los Angeles to the Olympic Committee meeting at Antwerp in 1919 to be the site of the 1932 Olympiad. Such an invitation, formally accepted in 1920, constituted a bold act of futurity by Los Angeles, as did the 73,000-seat Coliseum completed in October 1923. When sprinter Charles Paddock broke the world's record for the 100-yard dash in 1927 at the Coliseum, running it in 9.5 seconds, that future—envisioned as sport, as public spectacle, as the Olympics— seemed even further assured.

Nothing symbolized the unfinished planning business of greater Los Angeles better than the question of its parks. In 1927 a Citizen's Committee on Parks, Playgrounds and Beaches was formed under the sponsorship of the Chamber of Commerce to take up the issue. The committee included E. L. Doheny and George Getty from oil; Samuel Goldwyn, Cecil B. De Mille, Mary Pickford, Joseph Schenck, and Carl Laemmle from the film industry; developers Alphonzo Bell and J. B. Van Nuys; architect David Allison; bankers Irving and Marco Hellman and A. P. Giannini; water engineer J. B. Lippincott; and figures such as Samuel Kress, John and Stuart O'Melveny, Lena Pepperdine, and Harvey Mudd from deep within the oligarchy. An executive committee that included Hellman, Lippincott, O'Melveny, and Pickford was secondarily selected to represent the various constituencies of Los Angeles County. The prestige of this committee testifies to the importance of the task as perceived by the regional leadership. The City of Los Angeles alone possessed more than 5000 acres of parkland, some of it (Elysian Park, Westlake Park) adequately developed but most of it, some 3000 acres in Griffith Park alone, woefully underdeveloped and hence under-utilized.

Colonel Griffith J. Griffith had himself castigated Los Angeles for this neglect. In 1896 the fiery Griffith, a portly, paranoid Welshman, given to strong language and drink, deeded 3000 acres of the Rancho Los Feliz to the city. His enemies, of whom the egomanical self-made millionaire (mining investments) had many, claimed that he was merely tired of paying taxes on the property. In 1903 Griffith disgraced himself. In the course of a drunken evening, having accused his wife, an ardent Catholic, of conspiring with the Pope to divert his money to the Church, Griffith shot the hapless woman with a pistol. Serving two years in San Quentin for attempted murder, Griffith tried to donate an observatory for the park upon his release. This time, his enemies had a field day. Los Angeles, the newspapers editorialized, needed no gifts from a disgraced felon wanting to win his way back to respectability.

In the time-honored tradition of pamphleteering Welshmen, Griffith took to his own defense in *Public Parks and Playgrounds* (1910), which for all its self-servingness made a forceful plea that Los Angeles develop the resource Griffith had made available in 1896. Griffith Park was, in fact, the largest single park tract in the possession of an American city and was to grow even larger after Griffith's death in 1919 when he left the contemptuous city another $700,000 (this time accepted) for an observatory and outdoor amphitheater.

Throughout the 1920s the City of Los Angeles as well as many Los Angeles County suburbs missed opportunity after opportunity to exact parkland donations from private developers. After the decline of Progressivism, neither local government nor a shared conviction of public interest was strong enough to encourage much less enforce such donations or tax appropriations. Much of the southern coast, meanwhile, was being subdivided and developed up to the very beachline, as in the case of Santa Monica, where expensive beachfront homes walled residents off from what should have been accessible public space. Should this process have continued, the entire Los Angeles and Orange county coastline might have developed as a strip suburb, a ribbon of house backs blocking scenic vistas and keeping the general public from the beach.

Park, Playgrounds and Beaches for the Los Angeles Region, the report issued by the Citizens' Committee in 1930, expressed a compelling vision of greater Los Angeles's coming of age through the creation of a unified park and shoreline program over the next fifty years. The very ability of this citizens' group to propose in detail half a century of projected effort—the acquisition of parks, playgrounds, athletic fields, and thirty-two miles of coastline; the transformation of highways to parkways; the upgrading of Griffith Park; the enhancement of desert and mountain forest reserves—underscored the process of envisioning the future that was such a favorable aspect of boosterism in this era. In its rush to grow, the report argued, greater Los Angeles had neglected to acquire and develop sufficient public space. It was fortunate that the population density— more than two million living in forty cities spread across 1500 square miles— had not yet reached a crisis point. Even within city limits there was still much open space that could be acquired. The detailed recommendations of the re- port—$47 million for parks and athletic fields, $27 million for beaches, $145 million for parkways, the entirety projected out over a fifty-year time frame— were never exactly implemented as recommended. Such plans rarely are. As telesis, however, as a statement on behalf of the future, modified and restated, hammered out and compromised but kept alive through the political process, the report worked its influence across the half-century to follow. While many opportunities were lost, greater Los Angeles and Orange County did possess by the 1970s a regional park, beach, and recreational system such as that argued for so testily and so pertinently by Colonel Griffith J. Griffith in 1910.

If Los Angeles was to be a great city, it would also require a civic center where significant public buildings could be grouped and something of Los Angeles's consciousness of itself as a polity might be symbolized. The search for a civic center site began in 1918. A 1922 referendum endorsed the recom- mendation of the Planning Commission that the city reserve a site bounded by Main, Broadway, First, and Temple for the Civic Center. The voters also au- thorized a $7.5 million bond issue for the construction of a new City Hall.

Designed by the local firm of Parkinson, Martin and Austin, the new City Hall opened in 1928, symbolically concluding a decade of astonishing growth. The previous City Hall, a graceful Romanesque structure built in 1888 and torn down in 1929, bespoke Los Angeles as a romantic City of the South, the Rome or Naples of the American Italy. The new City Hall, a buttressed sky- scraper tower atop a square colonnaded base, unambiguously bespoke civic power and ambition. There was something deliberately Babylonian, an echo of the set built a decade earlier by D. W. Griffith for *Intolerance* on the corner of Sunset and Hollywood boulevards, in the way that the City Hall tower, at 464 feet the tallest structure in the city, tapered into an Halicarnassan ziggurat at its apex. The Romanesque City Hall of 1888 asserted neo-Mediterranean romance. The City Beautiful proposal advocated by Robinson in 1909 would have suggested the historicity and orderly grandeur of the American Renais- sance. By the 1920s, however, Los Angeles was preferring an evocation, at once historical and abstract in its design elements, of power—the power of money and technology, of growth and civic will—to symbolize the collective identity and shared consciousness of the new metropolis. Raising the ancient ziggurat symbol of power and wealth above its skyline, Los Angeles declared its material dream.

Had the plan unveiled by the Allied Architects Association in February 1925 been adopted, Los Angeles would have been able to express in its civic center the full spectrum of its identity, not just its neo-Babylonian love of money and power. Formed in 1921 as a way of organizing private architects on behalf of public projects, the association brought the talents of some seventy Los Angeles architects to bear on a voluntary eleven-month charette throughout 1924 dealing with the whole question of public buildings and spaces in downtown Los Angeles. The resulting Los Angeles City and County Administration Center Plan was, as might be expected, boldly visionary and historically encompassing. The Allied Architects proposed that a nearly square-mile site running on an east-west axis bounded by the Plaza on the east and Bunker Hill on the west be integrated and developed as public space. At the eastern end, the Plaza, the surviving central space of eighteenth-century Los Angeles, would be restored with low-rise Hispanic Revival buildings in conformity to the mission-era church. Spanish as well would be the ambience and names—El Prado, La Rambla, Las Alturas, El Paseo, La Alameda—of the linked public squares extending westward to Bunker Hill and including the Main and Broadway site already chosen for the new City Hall. At the western edge of the civic center a special boulevard connection would provide swift entry and egress to the complex. In devising this scheme, the Allied Architects worked closely with the Traffic Commission, devising among other automotive amenities a network of depressed boulevards and convenient parking lots so that even this grandiose Spanish Revival conception might function in harmony with the automobile.

It would be Santa Barbara, however, and not Los Angeles which would reorder its downtown in Spanish Revival, albeit on a much smaller scale, a choice that loudly proclaimed the differing identities of the two communities. Critics of the Allied Architects scheme correctly pointed out the impossibility of securing so much property for the public domain. The architects, in turn, countered with the argument that, if predictions regarding the inevitable size of Los Angeles proved true, the city would need such a public space at its center if it were to preserve its civic identity in spatial and architectural terms. Flattered perhaps by the grand historicity and futurity of the Allied Architects scheme, its Washingtonian grandeur, the Board of Supervisors of Los Angeles County voted to approve the plan, then promptly proceeded to implement the City Hall proposals of a less ambitious program simultaneously advanced by the Los Angeles firm of Cook and Hall.

Los Angeles was forced to compromise. Civic Center would be bounded by Hill, Main, First, and Ord streets. It would not include a revitalized Plaza nor a park on Bunker Hill, nor would it encompass an ambitious series of public squares and depressed boulevards. It would, rather, be crisscrossed by automotive traffic in the preferred Los Angeles manner, and its City Hall would testify to modernity and power, not Spanish romance.

The Allied Architects plan was not a complete failure, however, despite its non-implementation after formal acceptance. The plan itself, first of all, envisioned and prophesied a glorious future calling for the boldest sort of public buildings and spaces. It also encouraged the city, so recently arriving at metropolitan status, to think in aesthetic and in historical terms. The very year City Hall opened in all its neo-Bablylonian futurity, restoration began on the surviving Hispanic structures on the Plaza and along Olvera Street. In two very important buildings, furthermore, the Public Library and the Union Station, each of them grand Spanish Revival structures, the intent of the Allied Architects plan was realized.

Ever since assuming office in 1911, city librarian Everett Robbins Perry had been agitating for a new central facility. A Harvard graduate with extensive experience as a bibliographer in the Astor Collection at the New York Public Library, Perry worked closely with the director Dr. John Shaw Billings when that institution moved into its splendid McKim, Mead and White building on Fifth Avenue. Becoming city librarian of Los Angeles, Perry determined to build a similar facility. Meanwhile, he concentrated upon expanding programs (by 1926 Los Angeles enjoyed the highest per capita circulation of books after Cleveland), expanding and deepening the central collection and gearing his reference department to serve with special efficiency the needs of the business and motion-picture communities. Under Perry and his successor Althea Warren, the Los Angeles Public Library developed a first-rate patents collection keyed to local industries and a motion picture research and reference service (What did the death warrant for Mary Queen of Scots look like? Were lamb chops eaten in ancient Chaldea? What was the field uniform of the Bengal Lancers?) that glamorized the library and strengthened its position as a competing public service. Within ten years of his arrival, Perry had his chance to build. A series of bond issues in 1921, 1923, and 1925 provided a total of $3.5 million for the purchase in 1922 of a site on Normal Hill on Fifth Street between Flower and Grand, behind the Biltmore Hotel and adjacent to the California Club.

Desiring a Hispanic Revival building fully in conformity with the mood of the times and the recommendations of the Allied Architects plan, the Library Board secured the services of New York City architect Bertram Grosvenor Goodhue, the master of the Hispanic idiom whose scheme for the Panama-California Exposition, held in San Diego in 1915, had helped fix Spanish Revival as the predominant public style of the Southland through the 1930s. Assisted by architect Carleton Monroe Winslow of Los Angeles, Goodhue initially experimented with a structure surmounted by a massive tiled dome similar to his design for the California Building in San Diego. When this alternative proved too expensive, Goodhue simplified his conception to a design paralleling his Nebraska State Capitol. Employing a calm and orderly massing of reinforced concrete surfaces, Goodhue pitched his design midway between the Hispanic pageantry of the California Quadrangle in Balboa Park, San Diego, and the impending modernity of the Los Angeles City Hall. When Goodhue died suddenly in April 1924, the design was far enough along for Winslow to complete it according to the master's wishes. Opened to the public in July 1926, the Central Library provided Los Angeles with its most distinguished public building to date.

It took another thirteen years to build the Union Station, which had also been part of the Allied Architects plan of 1924. Opened in May 1939, Union Station came from the drawing boards of a design team of Southern Pacific, Union Pacific, and Sante Fe architects headed by F.W. Markus, with outside consultation by Donald B. Parkinson and John Parkinson, who were responsible for the triumph of Bullock's Wilshire. Expressive of Spanish Revival at its most graceful and purified, hauntingly appropriate to its Plaza site, ground zero of the Los Angeles experience, Union Station welcomed passengers to a spacious $16 million terminal powerfully Hispanic-Californian in ambience, a soaring cathedral within and without, landscaped in orange and palm trees. Disembarking from the Los Angeles Limited or the City of Los Angeles, passengers from elsewhere could finally experience the City of the Angels for the first time in a drama of public space fully equal to the expectations of 1924.

5

Other travelers might choose to arrive by airplane, since Los Angeles was the aviation capital of the United States. Of all its local industries, aviation offered Los Angeles its most compelling symbol of the future. Aviation bespoke technology, modernity, Los Angeles as a crossroads of world civilization. In its relationship to Southern California aviation parallels the film industry. Each industry began in the East but soon migrated to Southern California and consolidated. Like film, aviation emanated a sense of futurity linked to the possibilities of place. Curtiss, Martin, Lockheed, Northrop, Douglas, Ryan, Vultee—the names of Southern Californians active in aviation in its founding era, like the names of Griffith, De Mille, Sennett, Ince, Goldwyn, and Lasky, their contemporaries in Hollywood, underwent the transformation into product designation that is reserved for founders and inventors. Their names became the names of the airplanes they created.

At the very time, January 1910, that D.W. Griffith was first taking his troupe of Biograph players out to Mission San Gabriel to film the story of Ramona and thus graft the film industry literally and symbolically onto Southern Californian root stock, thousands of spectators were converging at Dominguez Field at the Rancho San Pedro near Wilmington and Long Beach to watch demonstrations of the seven-year-old phenomenon of manned heavier-than-air flight.

Deliberately orchestrated by the Los Angeles Chamber of Commerce to dramatize the aviationability of Southern California, its clear skies and open spaces, the Dominguez Air Meet more than achieved its purpose. The star

American aviator at the meet, Glenn Curtiss, was already building his own airplanes, as was another aviator, Glenn Martin, who had transformed an abandoned church in Santa Ana into an airplane assembly site. Curtiss and Martin also flew as stunt pilots for the movies, reinforcing the parallel development of the two industries. After World War I the Lockheed Aircraft Company moved its operations to Hollywood-Burbank, thereby putting the two emergent industries into close physical proximity.

Associated with Glenn Martin and Jack Northrup were two other pioneers, T. Claude Ryan and Donald Douglas. Like early film, early aviation was a movable feast, with the now legendary figures, then young men in their twenties and early thirties, combining and recombining with each other as opportunities presented themselves. Graduating from MIT in 1914 with the first degree in aeronautical engineering granted by that institution, Donald Douglas joined Glenn Martin in 1915 as chief engineer. By then Martin had moved his plant from the former church in Santa Ana to an assembly building near the site of the present-day Los Angeles International Airport. After service during the war as chief civilian aeronautical engineer for the Aviation Section of the U.S. Army Signal Corps, Douglas rejoined Martin, who by then had moved his operation to Cleveland, Ohio. Urged by his wife, who wanted to return to Southern California, and himself believing that Los Angeles, not Cleveland, possessed better possibilities as an aviation center, Douglas returned to Los Angeles in 1920, part of the great migration of that year, and set up his company in the back room of a barbershop on Pico Boulevard. Assisted by Harry Chandler of the *Times*, Douglas raised $15,000 from a group of Los Angeles businessmen and began delivery on three torpedo planes for the Navy. By the fall of 1922 Douglas was manufacturing an airplane a week out of a former movie studio on Wilshire Boulevard in Santa Monica.

Jack Northrop joined him there in 1923. Northrop remained with Douglas until 1926, when he joined Allan Lockheed for two years before forming his own company in 1928 in Burbank. In 1926 Northrop, still working for Douglas, began helping his friend T. Claude Ryan refine the M-1, a pioneering monoplane which Ryan had designed. Turned down for a job by Glenn Martin for lack of experience, Ryan won his wings with the Army in 1920, then left the service to go into design, manufacturing, and airline operations as Ryan Airlines of San Diego, a mail and passenger carrier. The M-1 was Ryan's first production venture. Northrop and his associate Art Mankey redesigned the wing of the M-1 and reduced its overall weight by two hundred pounds. As the M-2 Ryan's monoplane became a successful long-distance mail carrier. In February 1927 pilot Charles Lindbergh, backed by a group of St. Louis investors anxious to win the $25,000 prize offered by New Yorker Raymond Orteig for the first New York to Paris nonstop flight, chose the Ryan M-2, the first production monoplane in the nation, as the plane having the best chance to fly across the Atlantic. Modified as the N-X-22 Ryan NYP, Ryan's monoplane, improved by an apostolic succession of aviation pioneers, left Roosevelt Field on Long Island at 7:52 a.m., 20 May 1927, with Lindbergh at the throttle. Thirty-three and a half hours later, Lindbergh landed at Orly field in Paris, and the era of modern aviation began.

When Colonel Lindbergh, the Lone Eagle himself, returned to Los Angeles in 1928 for a triumphal visit, he found a beacon commemorative of his flight affixed to the pinnacle of City Hall. By the late twenties, Los Angeles was unquestionably the aviation capital of the United States. More than twenty-five airplane and aviation motor manufacturers were active in the region, accounting for a billion-dollar industry. The roll call of companies included long-term survivors such as the Lockheed Company of Burbank and the Douglas Aircraft Company of Santa Monica, as well as now forgotten manufacturers such as the Joseph Kreutzer Corporation, which made tri-motors, and Bach Aircraft of Van Nuys, a pioneer in developing passenger planes. Fully a third of the aviation traffic in the United States operated from the fifty private landing fields in greater Los Angeles, where there were some 3000 licensed pilots. Four passenger lines—Western Air Express, Maddux Air Lines, Pacific Air Transport, and Standard Air Lines—were offering regularly scheduled service to Salt Lake, San Francisco, Seattle, and the Southwest.

Established as a mail carrier, Western Air Express began passenger operations between Los Angeles and Salt Lake City in 1926. Some 209 passengers flew the first year. In 1929 Western announced plans for service to Kansas City, connecting to New York, in Fokker DP-32 passenger planes to be manufactured near the Western terminal in Alhambra. Flying Ford Tri-Motors, Maddux Air Lines inaugurated passenger flights between Los Angeles and San Diego in late July 1927. Charles Lindbergh flew the inaugural run as pilot, and Cecil B. De Mille was an early investor. By early 1929 Maddux was serving Central and Northern California (Bakersfield, Fresno, San Francisco), Southern California (San Diego, and Agua Caliente in Mexico), eastern Southern California, and the Southwest (San Bernardino, Riverside, Palm Springs, Imperial, Calexico, Phoenix) on a regularly scheduled basis. Controlled by Oregon interests, Pacific Air Transport handled the Los Angeles-Seattle run. Businessmen, meanwhile, were discovering the convenience of scheduled and chartered flights; in a number of cases, companies began to maintain their own aircraft. Harry Culver, for example, began maintaining his own pilot and aircraft in the late 1920s.

Flight provided promoters such as Culver a convenient, legitimate means of envisioning the future. "American airports in the future," Culver predicted in August 1929, "will resemble railroad terminals, with passengers streaming in and out, baggage being loaded, freight and mail weighed, time tables being scrutinized, gongs ringing, and babies crying. Hotels, restaurants, and shops will rise on the edge of flying fields to accommodate the passengers of the air; industries will clamor for adjacent factory sites and will run switch tracks to the

hangars to expedite the rapid transportation of their products through the sky."[14]
All this implied more growth and further subdivisions for the likes of Harry
Culver. Yet it also suggested the emergence in the not-too-distant future of a
brave new world of transcontinental, even intercontinental, aviation that would
link Los Angeles to the great cities of the world as an equal partner.

Culver's remarks coincided with the arrival on 26 August 1929 at Mines
Field, site of the present day Los Angeles International Airport, of the *Graf
Zeppelin*, the gigantic (776 feet in length) German passenger dirigible which
was at the time the world's largest airship. Commanded by Hugo Eckener, the
Magellan of the Air, the *Graf Zeppelin* was arriving from Tokyo, having left
Lakehurst, New Jersey, eighteen days earlier on a record-setting flight around
the world via Germany and Japan. An estimated 150,000 visitors flocked to the
airport by automobile and streetcar to catch a glimpse of the beached behemoth
as, guarded by sailors and marines, it was being refitted and refueled for the
third leg, across the United States, of its circumaviation of the globe.

During the brief stay of the *Graf Zeppelin* Los Angeles found itself in the
throes of zeppelin fever. First of all, there was the craft itself, so expressive of
the modernity and technology of flight. As a lighter-than-air vessel carrying
fifty-four passengers and crew, the *Graf Zeppelin* bridged the worlds of trans-
oceanic liners and commercial airline passenger traffic, only then developing.
The speeches and articles surrounding the arrival of the *Graf Zeppelin*—Commander Eckener's speeches at the airport and at a civic banquet that evening
at the Ambassador Hotel, the remarks of Major John Porter at the airport reception, the live radio-telephone broadcasts by Herbert Hoover, Jr., the President's son, from a Fokker tri-motor following the dirigible into the city, the
editorials in the *Times*—all evoked that impending day when airships such as
the *Graf Zeppelin* would be regularly arriving and departing from Los Angeles,
linking it to the other great cities of the world by the glamorous miracle of
passenger flight.

Glamour aplenty the *Graf Zeppellin* possessed. Among its passengers were
Sir Hubert Wilkins, the famed Australian aviator and explorer of the Antarctic,
and Lady Drummond Hay, the super-chic British journalist whom Louella
Parsons interviewed on a live coast-to-coast hookup the minute she disem-
barked from the dirigible, Condé Nast-commanding in a dark suit and yellow
blouse, a great diamond brooch accentuating her black turban like one of the
Graf Zeppelin's searchlights. Flying in over Los Angeles, Lady Hay told Miss
Parsons, resembled the flight over Barcelona (once again, the Spanish metaphor for Southern California asserted itself from this unexpected quarter), but
for the time being, having just crossed the Pacific, sleeping a mere three hours
a night what with all the excitement, she needed a manicure, a bath, and some
sleep.

Sped to the Ambassador Hotel under motorcycle escort, Commander Eckener, Lady Hay, Sir Hubert, and the other passengers had time to rest before

that evening's grand civic banquet. Attended by Governor Clement Young, Mayor John Porter, Eckener and his two chief officers, the *Graf Zeppelin* passengers, and hundreds of the oligarchy, together with William Randolph Hearst, Marion Davies, Douglas Fairbanks, Mary Pickford, and a host of film celebrities, the banquet long remained in Los Angeles's memory as the single most glittering event to date. (There would be others.) In his after-dinner remarks Commander Eckener spoke directly to Los Angeles's sense of futurity through aviation in his evocation of the forthcoming LZ-129, a passenger dirigible in the planning stages twice the size of the *Graf Zeppelin* and twice as safe. In the near future, Eckener suggested, the LZ-129 would be making its calls in the City of the Angels.

Safety was very much on Eckener's mind later that evening as the *Graf Zeppelin* cleared electric power lines by a mere 15 feet on take-off, thanks only to some brilliant last-minute maneuvering by Eckener, together with a rushed jettisoning of cargo over the runway of Mines Field, including a large shipment of hors d'oeuvres sent along from the Hotel Biltmore to fortify the passengers and crew on their flight across the Rockies. No matter: the *Graf Zeppelin* cleared the wires, just barely, and arrived in Lakehurst three days later, having circumaviated the globe in twenty-one days. The Los Angeles it left behind, a Barcelona at night to Lady Hay's way of thinking, would continue to boost itself into futurity through the aviation metaphor. No sooner had the *Graf Zeppelin* left the city than artist Herman Sachs was painting the dirigible on the ceiling of the porte cochere at Bullock's Wilshire. "The *Graf Zeppelin* is a ship with a soul," noted Lady Hay. "You have only to fly in it to know that it's a living, vibrant, sensitive, and magnificent thing."[15] She might as well have been talking about the City of the Angels itself.

6

The People of the City

Oligarchs, Babbitts, and Folks

The Los Angeles of 1926 was a predominantly white city. Of a population of 1.3 million the census for that year revealed 45,000 Hispanics, 33,000 blacks, and 30,000 Asians. Everyone else, more than nine-tenths of the people, was of European descent. Most of these were either Americans of British or Celtic origin or immigrants from Great Britain, Central and Western Europe, or Canada. With the exception of a surprisingly vigorous Jewish community estimated to be between 50,000 and 100,000, Los Angeles did not support a very significant Southern or Eastern European population.

Within the white population, Protestants predominated over a Roman Catholic community of approximately 300,000. White Protestants of Anglo-American stock, or WASPs as they were later called, held the clear majority. Los Angeles, as one contemporary observer succinctly put it, constituted "an interesting experiment for the Anglo-Saxon in America."[1]

Like Caesar's Gaul, White Anglo-Saxon Protestant Los Angeles divided itself into three discernible sub-groups: Oligarchs, Babbitts, and Folks. The Oligarchs tended to be a generation, even two, into their Los Angeles residency, although a figure such as attorney William Gibbs McAdoo, ex-Secretary of the Treasury and son-in-law to Woodrow Wilson, might arrive as late as 1922 and be brought instantly into the inner circle. Bred to power by Wall Street and the Treasury, and well-connected through marriage, McAdoo was a Democrat of patrician stripe. In 1924 he became Los Angeles's first serious contender for the presidency and later (1933–38) represented California in the United States Senate. Another former office holder, Ole Hanson, erstwhile mayor of Seattle, also arrived in the early 1920s, and was taken up and prospered in a second career as the developer of San Clemente on the coast between Los Angeles and San Diego. More typical of the establishment, however, were longtime residents such as George Smith Patton, Jackson A. Graves, Senator Frank Putnam Flint, and the Right Reverend Robert Burton Gooden, Protestant Episcopal Bishop of Los Angeles and longtime headmaster of the Harvard School.

George Smith Patton enjoyed connections with the Confederacy, the land-grant era, and successful real-estate investment, each of them diversely flattering to the Los Angeles identity. His father, a Virginian, fell for the South at Fredericksburg as a colonel of infantry. Brought to Los Angeles as a boy of ten in 1866 by his widowed mother, who was joining her brother, Patton returned to his native Virginia in the mid-1870s to complete his education at the Virginia Military Institute, where he later sent his son, George, Jr., who later transferred to West Point and pursued a career in the regular Army. Upon his return to Southern California, George Senior read for the bar and in 1888 was elected District Attorney of Los Angeles County. A Democrat of the conservative southern type so prominent in Los Angeles through the First World War, Patton also ran unsuccessfully for the House and the Senate. In 1884 Patton married the daughter of Benjamin Davis Wilson, a pioneer settler of Los Angeles and a landowner. Wilson's first wife, whom he married in 1844, was Ramona Yorba, daughter of one of the great landowners of the Mexican era. Patton thus joined his Southern heritage with that of Old California in a manner doubly reinforcing his identity as a squire on the local scene. To his landed connections by marriage—Rancho Jurupa, Rancho Santa Ana—Patton added important holdings accumulated by his own enterprise while serving Henry Huntington as legal advisor and manager of the Huntington Land and Improvement Company.

Dying in 1927, George Smith Patton took into the postwar boom era a living connection with the antebellum ambience of old Los Angeles, rescued from genteel antiquarianism by a vigorous legal and business career. In a world of the newly arrived, frequently uncertain of its taste, George Patton—trustee of the Huntington Library and Art Gallery, trustee of the California Institute of Technology, director of the Union Oil Company, member of the vestry of the Church of Our Saviour in San Gabriel, member of the California Club of Los Angeles, the Sunset Club, the Flintridge Riding Club, the Midwick Country Club, father of an up-and-coming polo-playing major of cavalry—emanated a mood of lineage, of caste achieved, around which the expanding oligarchy could construct its new identity. Prosperity had happened all too rapidly to so many so uncertain of their position. George Smith Patton suggested that it could be properly consolidated.

Jackson Alpheus Graves and Frank Putnam Flint suggested that new men as well were rising in the Southland. In 1928 Graves, president since 1920 of the Farmers and Merchants National Bank, where he succeeded Los Angeles pioneer I.W. Hellman, issued his autobiography *My Seventy Years in California, 1857–1927*, a richly detailed Horatio Alger tale of how the son of Kentucky refugees fleeing the Civil War arrived in Northern California via Iowa, mastered Latin through his mother's home instruction, followed by Greek at St. Mary's College then located in San Mateo County, where he graduated in 1872 and remained on as a classics instructor while completing his master's degree and reading for the bar. In 1875 the young attorney migrated to Los Angeles, where in partnership with Henry O'Melveny, another establishment pillar, he became one of the leading real-estate and banking attorneys of his busy generation. A trained scholar endowed with a phenomenal memory and more than his share of gregariousness, the legal intelligence at the center of innumerable land and financial deals across half a century of practice, Graves wrote an autobiography second only to Harris Newmark's *Sixty Years in Southern California* (1916) as a guide to the people, events, and institutions of late nineteenth- and early twentieth-century Los Angeles. If George Patton stood for heritage inherited or married into, Graves embodied the deliberate creation of the self as upper-class gentleman in Los Angeles circumstances. One could, in other words, be intensely part of the Los Angeles commercial scene and at the same time evolve into a full-fledged American squire with a ranch in Alhambra. To Jackson Graves's great satisfaction he wound up resembling, in some respects at least, George Smith Patton.

When the Los Angeles oligarchy, operating through the state legislature, selected Frank Putnam Flint, U.S. Attorney for the Southern District of California, for the United States Senate in 1905, it found the right man in the right place at the right time to handle the appropriation of the Owens River. Of seventeenth-century Massachusetts stock, the San Francisco-raised Flint arrived in Los Angeles in 1887 at the age of 24 and began reading for the bar. After a succession of subordinate appointments in the office of the U.S. Attorney, Flint practiced privately for a few years before being appointed U.S. Attorney in his own right in 1897. A Republican of the Progressive Theodore Roosevelt mold, Flint served only one term in the Senate by his own choice, 1905 to 1911, before returning to Los Angeles for the compelling pursuits of banking and real estate. While in the Senate, he backed Roosevelt on reform and defense and worked closely with his friend and ally as the President smoothed Los Angeles's path to the Owens River. Flint also secured federal assistance to expand the Port of Los Angeles and to gain tariff benefits for Southern California citrus. Like his predecessor Stephen Mallory White, Flint was in every way the United States Senator from Los Angeles.

Returning in triumph in 1911, Flint proceeded to prove that he was no mere spokesman but an equal among equals in an age of entrepreneurs. In the remaining eighteen years of his life, Flint rescued the Los Angeles Investment Company from near-bankruptcy, transforming it into one of the most dynamic housing developers of the era. He built his own suburb, Flintridge, and involved himself in lumber, drydocking, hotels, newspaper publishing, and banking. His public service included the National Boulder Dam Association, which sought to tap the Colorado River for Los Angeles, the All-Year Club of Southern California, the Los Angeles Chamber of Commerce, the Pasadena Tournament of Roses Association, Occidental College, Stanford University, the Republican Party, and the First Presbyterian Church of Pasadena. He belonged to all major clubs (the California, the University, the Jonathan, the Sunset, the Annandale Golf, the San Gabriel Valley Country), the Masons, the Shriners, and was frequently called upon to speak at public occasions. When Flint died in early 1929 while on a world cruise, his body was returned to Los Angeles to lie in state in the new City Hall. The crowd at the memorial service spilled out onto the street and had to listen by loudspeaker as Governor C.C. Young, Mayor George E. Cryer, and publisher William Randolph Hearst, among others, extolled the virtues of the deceased. In Flint, one of the most important players in the drama of making Los Angeles happen, the oligarchy had a comforting symbol of public and private ambitions working together in creative synergy. It was the oligarchy, after all, which along with Flint had effected the arc of development so powerfully expressed in this soaring new City Hall. As much as any member of his generation, Flint embodied the values and successes of the Los Angeles establishment, its perhaps doomed hope that one might get rich and still stay good.

The sons of the oligarchy had to be properly educated, which was the task of the polished and erudite Rt. Rev. Robert Burton Gooden, D.D., Suffragan Bishop of Los Angeles and the Headmaster of the Harvard School. English-born, a graduate of Trinity College, Connecticut, and the Berkeley Divinity School at Yale, Gooden assumed the headmastership of the Harvard School in 1912 after holding pulpits in Ventura, Escondido, and Long Beach. Founded in 1900 by Grenville Emery, a Harvard-trained master from the Boston Latin School, the Harvard School was explicitly approved at its foundation by President Charles Eliot. In 1911 the school passed to the sponsorship of the Episcopal Church and began under Gooden's headmastership a phase of steady expansion on its twenty-five-acre campus on Sepulveda Canyon Road west of what would eventually become the new campus of the University of California at Los Angeles. In the previous generation, the oligarchy sent its children to Los Angeles High School along with everyone else, but as prosperity increased, the power of private schools to reinforce a sense of caste asserted itself.

Founded in 1888 in Pasadena by Mary S. Caswell, a widow from Maine, the Marlborough School provided a comparable educational experience—at once deepening (Latin, French, mathematics) but narrowing as well in its message of caste identity—for the daughters of the emergent oligarchy who in a previous generation had recited, played, and on beach holidays swam beside the boys at Los Angeles High. Moved to the Hancock Park district of Los Angeles in 1916, the Marlborough School continued to emphasize a Pasadena-serious program of education, sports, good manners, and even better marriages. Mary Caswell, who lived on until 1924, personally compiled a long list of what she called Marlborough Don'ts. Among them: "Don't talk about yourself or your family affairs. It is a sign of verdancy. Don't be inquisitive with either tongue or fingers. Curiosity is wholly vulgar and common. . . . Don't take soup noisily, and don't, even once, allow yourself to put celery, Saratoga potatoes, toast, biscuit, or any other crisp eatable into your mouth without closing your lips upon it before you bite it and your teeth upon it before you chew it."[2] As the private school option gained ground among the affluent, the Marlborough School grew in social prestige. In 1926 the girls were put into English-style uniforms.

Not every member of the establishment came from real estate, banking, or attendant activities. Cecil B. De Mille, for instance, entered it from pictures, albeit with the refining attendant activities of real estate and aviation; and Zane Grey, very much the grand seigneur on his Altadena estate, entered it from the avenues of successful myth-making and sport. Grey arrived in Southern California in 1918, lured there from the East by a lucrative contract from Jesse Lasky of Famous Players. At forty-six Grey was making more than a hundred thousand dollars a year from the sales of his novels and from movie rights, appreciably more than he was bringing in a few years earlier as a dentist in New York City. Initially established in Hollywood, Grey moved his family to a Spanish-style mansion in Altadena in 1920, and in the summer months to a pueblo-style home atop a hill overlooking Avalon Bay on Santa Catalina Island. Grey and his wife had first seen Altadena on their honeymoon in 1905. They had remembered it as an enchanted savanna ablaze in orange-gold poppies and planned to return there permanently. The Avalon home perfectly served Grey's passion for deep-sea fishing. As Berkeley professor T.K. Whipple was noting as early as the 1920s, Zane Grey was the epic storyteller, the skaldsman par excellence, of Anglo-Saxon America. Grey's innumerable Westerns— the classic *The Heritage of the Desert* (1910), *Riders of the Purple Sage* (1912), and *The Rainbow Trail* (1915) above all—projected a world in which Protestant rectitude depicted as cowboy manliness triumphed over evil.

At the conclusion to *Riders of the Purple Sage*, the hero Lassiter seals himself, his wife, and child in a hidden valley by creating an avalanche against pursuing Mormons. This conjunction of rectitude and withdrawal, moralism and disdain, came increasingly to characterize Zane Grey's life. Believing that society was sliding downhill, Grey withdrew increasingly into bouts of solitary writing, filling innumerable pencil-written pages with starker and starker confrontations of good and evil in an imagined Western frontier. When he died in 1939, twenty unpublished books lay stockpiled at the publisher's. Grey relieved this marathon writing with bouts of hunting and deep-sea fishing. In Grey's proto-Hemingwayesque stance, only the moments between him, the bear, or the big fish were honest, good moments. The rest were lies. Grey also retreated further into wide reading of the classics (at Pennsylvania he had taken a master's degree in literature as well as a dental degree), which reinforced his conviction that literature was going downhill along with everything else. Thus

Zane Grey explored a sensibility parallel to, but distinct from, the country-club entrenchment that gripped major sectors of the Southern California squirearchy. In his life more than his writings, which became rushed and repetitive as he wrote ceaselessly to pay for his lifestyle, Grey expressed a right-of-center view of the world that would become increasingly characteristic of affluent white Southern California and the Southwest as the century wore on: a conviction, that is, that they had come into God's country only to have it come under threat.

A sense of threat was very much what Edward Laurence Doheny and his wife Estelle were experiencing during the mid- to late 1920s as the prominent oilman came under indictment during the Teapot Dome scandal. Irish, German, and Roman Catholic, the Dohenys constituted their own separate branch of the oligarchy, too different to be assimilated, too wealthy to be ignored. Arriving in Los Angeles in 1892 at the age of 36 after spending nearly twenty years on the frontier as a prospector and mining developer, Edward Laurence Doheny and his partner Charles Canfield had the good sense to discover oil near the corner of Second and Glendale Boulevard. By 1900 each partner was realizing half a million dollars a year from his investment. This initial discovery sparked an oil rush that sunk more than 2300 wells within the city. Eventually more than 75 million barrels of crude would be pumped from this urban Oildorado.

Not content with such modest rewards, Canfield and Doheny went prospecting in Mexico in May 1900. In contrast to their previous prospecting treks together through the Far West in their younger days (one night Doheny had been mauled by a mountain lion), the partners traveled this time in a private railroad car, attended to by a porter and a chef. Near Tampico, they left their car and roughed it inland into the jungle to investigate reports of *brea*, oily tar seeping from the ground, the same reports they had so successfully pursued on Glendale Boulevard in 1892. Sure enough, they discovered a large crater filled with thick tar and hissing with escaping gas. Returning to civilization, Canfield and Doheny bought up the surrounding 400,000 acres, a jungle kingdom unto itself. They then spent millions in setting up drilling rigs and building a pipeline into Tampico. Over the next nine years, operating as the Mexican Petroleum Company, the partners took some 80 million barrels of oil from their Mexican domain.

Money, in other words, was not a problem for Edward Laurence Doheny and his second wife. He met her in 1900 just as he was launching the Mexican enterprise: he, a 44-year-old widower with a seven-year-old son; she, Carrie Estelle Betzold, a 25-year-old telephone operator (so one report has it) whose voice had captivated him over the wire. She was a handsome German girl, blessed with an hourglass figure and large brown eyes. Whether or not she was working as a telephone operator at the time, the metaphor behind the story rings true, for it was a Cinderella story: she was from the family cottage on

South Alvarado Street via Marshalltown, Iowa, and he was en route to becoming one of the richest men in the United States. Married on 22 August 1900, just after he had returned from his first trip to Mexico, the Dohenys soon asserted themselves as the premier couple of an as of yet embryonic wing of the oligarchy, for Catholics of great wealth and social position were few and far between in the City of the Angels in that era. Purchasing a rambling Spanish Gothic mansion at 8 Chester Place near Adams Boulevard and Figueroa, they expanded it over the next few years to include a dining room seating more than a hundred, supported by columns of Siena marble and covered by a dome of Tiffany glass; a deer park; a swimming pool; tennis courts; and an enormous glass-and-steel conservatory where Edward Doheny grew palm trees and other exotic plants brought up from Mexico and Venezuela and Estelle grew orchids, ten thousand of them, imported from around the world—the first such major orchid collection of its kind in Southern California. The Dohenys supplemented the American Renaissance lushness of Chester Place with a four-hundred-acre ranch in Beverly Hills, which they purchased in 1912; four other ranches in Ventura County; the *Casiana*, a steam yacht berthed at San Pedro; and a home in midtown Manhattan.

Naturally, such conspicuous wealth attracted the attention of the Roman Catholic Church. From the point of view of the Church, the Dohenys offered dazzling prospects for patronage and a conspicuous presence in the oligarchy to assert the interests of the Catholic community. Both expectations were grandly confirmed. Among their many charities, the Dohenys financed an entire church, St. Vincent de Paul's at the corner of West Adams and Figueroa, a magnificent Spanish Renaissance structure designed by Albert C. Martin. Even today, nearly seventy years after it was dedicated, St. Vincent de Paul's Church dazzles bypassers (which in Los Angeles means motorists) with the drama of its proportions and the Moorish elegance of its multicolored oversized tile dome. The Dohenys were devoted to the historic St. Vincent de Paul, a seventeenth-century French priest, and to the two orders he founded, the Daughters of Charity, a congregation of nursing sisters, and the Congregation of the Mission, also known as the Vincentian Fathers, missionaries and educators with a strong Southern Californian presence. Thus they gave generously to the Los Angeles Orphanage and St. Vincent's Hospital, two institutions conducted by the Daughters of Charity, and sponsored the education of Vincentian seminarians for the priesthood.

The Church, in turn, rewarded the Dohenys with the solaces of religion, which they would shortly need in full measure, and with something equally important and necessary, the assurance of caste. Both the Dohenys were new people, first generation in their wealth, not formally educated at the great universities of the East as were so many of the upper classes of West Adams, Pasadena, and San Marino. In exchange for their patronage, the Church rewarded the Dohenys with the prerogatives and titles of the Catholic nobility of

Europe. The Archbishop became a confidant, a family friend and counselor, available in times of great stress or grief, especially the horrible family tragedy of February 1929, or for a quiet dinner *en famille* on Chester Place, just His Excellency and the two of them (and the servants of course), like a parish priest stopping by for a quiet Sunday supper. The Archbishop allowed the Dohenys the privilege of a private chapel in their various homes, with permission to have mass said there and the consecrated eucharist reserved on the altar for veneration. They became Knight and Lady of the Equestrian Order of the Holy Sepulchre in 1925, and in 1939 His Holiness Pope Pius XII raised Estelle Doheny, onetime telephone operator, to the rank of Papal Countess.

Through its legacy of European culture, its titles and its tutelage, the Roman Catholic Church, in this instance the Archdiocese of Los Angeles, the Most Reverend John J. Cantwell Archbishop, helped the ever-generous Dohenys in the vital matter of taste and social self-confidence. A psychological reserve of self-esteem became very much necessary for both Dohenys in August 1924 when E.L. Doheny was charged in the Federal District Court of Los Angeles with bribing Secretary of Interior Albert B. Fall in November 1921 (a loan of $100,000 in cash, carried to Fall in a satchel by Edward Doheny, Jr.) so as to obtain favorable leases on naval oil reserves at Elk Hills in Kern County. President Harding had previously transferred the administration of the two reserves at Elk Hills and Teapot Dome in Wyoming to Fall in May 1921, itself a dubious action. Fall, in turn, had signed favorable leases with Doheny and oilman Harry F. Sinclair. The Teapot Dome scandal dragged on for six long years of investigation and trial. In 1927 the government canceled the leases, and in 1929 Fall was convicted of taking a bribe from Doheny and went to jail. Doheny, however, got off on technicalities after two trials, thanks to his brilliant lawyer, Frank J. Hogan of Washington, D.C., who once observed that the ideal client was a rich man who was scared. Doheny was both rich and scared, and between 1924 and his acquittal in 1930, Edward and Estelle regarded Hogan with a species of awe, dependency, and a thirst for deliverance that surpassed the intensity of their relationship to the Archbishop. While His Excellency might hold the keys of the kingdom, Mr. Hogan bore an equally compelling relationship to the keys to the slammer.

Then an even worse tragedy struck. Edward Doheny adored his only son Edward, Jr., more commonly known as Ned. In 1914 Ned married Lucy Smith of Pasadena, and in time Doheny Senior adored her and his five grandchildren, four boys and a girl, with equal ardor. In the early 1920s E. L. Doheny commissioned architect Gordon Kaufmann to design for his son and family a grand mansion for the Beverly Hills property, Greystone, forty-six thousand square feet within, various modes of English Revival without, set amidst four hundred acres of formal Italian gardens and Shakespearean forests. There, on 16 February 1929 Edward Laurence Doheny, Jr., age 36, and his valet were found shot to death under what has then and now been described as mysterious circumstances. Grief-stricken, the Dohenys buried Ned at Forest Lawn beneath an elaborate replica of a Roman temple and in the months that followed searched for a further memorial as a way of coping with their anguish.

2

Dancing in attendance to the oligarchy, linked to it by a web of economic relationships and dependencies, reading Zane Grey's books, were the bourgeois newcomers, the Babbitts, the boosters, the middlemen in sales, marketing, and construction who were making the boom times happen on the frontline level. Characteristic of much of urban America in the 1920s, Babbitt found a special home in Los Angeles, where middlebrow values had triumphed. "The type," noted Bruce Bliven, "is the big, beaming man, with clipped military moustaches, whose golf is in the nineties, motor speed in the sixties, waistline in the forties, wife in the thirties, and sweetheart in the (early) twenties. . . . Mr. Babbitt, the New American, in Los Angeles as elsewhere, is noisy, cheerful, pleased with himself. He makes plenty of money, spends most of it, drives a snappy car, dressed in snappy clothes."[3]

If there was one pastime most favored by both the oligarchy and by Babbitt, it was golf. "There are fifty golf courses within an hour's run of the city," noted Bliven of mid-twenties Los Angeles, "and heaven knows how many beach clubs. These latter are so snobbishly reserved that they sometimes take advertisements four newspaper pages in length to ask for new members—'if you feel you can pass our rigid tests, clip the coupon.' "[4] The Los Angeles Country Club, the Annandale, Midwick, Brentwood, Wilshire, Sunset Canyon, San Gabriel, Hollywood: Los Angeles abounded in country clubs whose rolling green golf courses offered eloquent testimony to the power of Owens River water. Here a newly expanded elite reconsolidated itself over rituals of golf and tennis and social gatherings at the clubhouse. With its attendant mentality, the country club became in the 1920s a dominant mode of Southern California social expression among the arrived and the aspiring. Women took to golf with special energy, producing fine players such as Doren Kavanagh, the women's state champion, and Mary Brown, the Southern California champion. In 1922 four hundred Los Angeles area women made the handicap list issued by the Southern California Gold Association. The women's list included four scratch players; the men's list, only one.

Among the most affluent, polo and yachting also gained in popularity. By the 1920s there were yacht clubs at Santa Barbara, San Pedro, Santa Catalina, Newport, and San Diego. Beginning in 1921, the year the Southern California Yachting Association was founded, a biennial San Pedro-to-Honolulu race was held. An estimated five hundred sailing boats saw the six entries off in 1926, filling the offshore with a dazzling spectacle of sail. By May 1928, Sunday polo games, open to the public at a dollar a person or car, were being regularly played by Santa Barbara, Burlingame, and Los Angeles teams at the Uplifters Club field on Beverly Boulevard. Screen star Will Rogers, who built a polo field on his Pacific Palisades ranch in the Santa Monica Mountains, played for the team captained by polo champion Eric Pedley of the Midwick Country Club, as did director Hal Roach and screenwriter Frank Dazey. Polo provided film folk a way of bonding with established Los Angelenos such as Pedley, Snowy Baker, Charles Wrightman, C.B. Brunson, and Dr. Harry H. Wilson.

Such a burgeoning town and country life required a town and country magazine, which duly appeared in the form of *Saturday Night*, a weekly of impressive content and editorial format. Founded in 1922 by Samuel Travers Clover, *Saturday Night* covered the Los Angeles of the 1920s as *Land of Sunshine* and *Out West* had covered the 1890-1915 period and as *Touring Topics* (later *Westways*) would later cover the 1930s era. Born in London in 1859, Clover emigrated to the United States in the early 1880s after traveling the world in the style of adventurous young Englishmen of his generation. He spent a decade on the frontier as a journalist, covering for the Chicago *Herald* the settlement of the Dakotas, the Cheyenne Indian uprising of 1890, and the 1891 uprising of the Sioux. After a stint as managing editor of the Chicago *Evening Post*, Clover followed the yellow brick road from Chicago to Los Angeles in search of better opportunities.

As editor of the Los Angeles *Evening News*, Clover was on the losing side of the aqueduct debate; yet his championing (for a price, it was alleged) of the existing private utilities against municipal takeover, while doomed to defeat, solidly entrenched him among a portion of the establishment. Like Phil Townsend Hanna in the 1930s, Clover, a member of the California Club, had an honorary membership in the establishment he covered as a journalist. The author of a number of books on travel, book collecting, and the frontier, Clover brought high standards of literacy to the editing of *Saturday Night*. His literary column, "Browsings in an Old Book Shop," erudite and enthusiastic, helped consolidate Los Angeles as a center of the antiquarian book trade. At a time when the *Overland Monthly* of San Francisco was in steep decline, *Saturday Night* covered the music, theater, cinema, golf, tennis, polo, real-estate, architecture, and social life of Los Angeles with style and skill. Clover himself, later assisted by a young USC law student by the name of Carey McWilliams, handled book reviewing and the literary life. Today the oversized, densely printed, highly illustrated pages of *Saturday Night* reveal not show business or the eccentric LaLaLand obsessively belittled to this day by eastern observers but town and country Los Angeles: suburban, affluent, upper-middle-class, Republican, rather assured in its taste—Gatsby's Long Island on the Southern Californian coast.

Not everyone was impressed. "Not long since," noted Louis Adamic in 1927, "I spent an evening in a new beach club, one of those gaudy architectural affairs lately invented by Los Angeles go-getters to give the well-to-do immigrants from Iowa and Illinois and Nebraska some place to go and spend their money. Walking through the building I saw prosperous-looking people, men wearing knickers and striped sweaters, women in sport costumes, sitting in those deep arm-chairs, looking blankly at the weird dragon figures on the Chinese rugs at their feet, or staring at the cold fireplace, or playing checkers or dominoes; eating dinner in a sumptuously appointed dining-room, their water poured for them by dusky-faced Filipino boys in tight-fitting green suits with gilt buttons, and their hot rolls brought to them by doll-like Chinese girls in mauve and lavender pajamas; not an animated conversation anywhere, indeed hardly any talk at all: their chins moved masticating lobster a la Newburg, their hands reached for the hot roll offered by the dainty Chinese girl, but in their eyes one read embarrassment: they were out of place, worse than bored."[5]

Despite such dissenting opinions, Los Angeles listed some two hundred flourishing clubs by 1927, including more than fifteen beach clubs between Malibu and Venice. The more established clubs—the Los Angeles Athletic, the California, the Jonathan, the University, the Los Angeles Country Club, the Wilshire Country Club—had nineteenth- or turn-of-the-century origins. During the 1920s these older clubs experienced an intensification of identity and, in most cases, a major upgrading of physical facilities. The Jonathan, for example, founded in 1895, moved in 1925 to an impressive building on South Figueroa designed by Schultze and Weaver, architects of the Biltmore Hotel. Its walls and ceilings were decorated by Giovanni Smeraldi, the artist responsible for many of the murals and decorations at Grand Central Station in New York. In 1929 the California Club completed a grand Renaissance palazzo on Flower Street adjacent to the new Central Library. Designed by Robert Farquhar, a graduate of the Ecole des Beaux-Arts, the California Club featured a skylit dining room soon judged one of the most impressive interior spaces in the country. Also headquartered in the new California Club building was the Sunset Club, a dining and discussion society founded in 1895.

As such clubs become more elite, they also become severely restrictive, another characteristic of 1920s America. In 1887 the charter members of the California Club included a diverse grouping of surviving Californios (Reginaldo Del Valle, Francisco Estudillo), American pioneers of Christian and Jewish heritage (Joseph Banning, Fred Bixby, George Patton, Isias Hellman, Leon Loeb, Maurice Newmark, Jacob Loew), young men on the rise (Jackson Graves, Henry O'Melveny), and unclassifiables such as publicist Benjamin Truman, entrepreneur Abbot Kinney and Fabian socialist fruit rancher and real-estate developer H. Gaylord Wilshire. This founding group was later augmented by more Hellmans, Van Nuyses, banker Joseph F. Sartori, and Packard dealer Earle C. Anthony. By the late 1920s lines began to be drawn reflecting a less inclusive spirit—even in Los Angeles, a city that had so recently welcomed everyone. As anti-Semitism swept the country, establishment Los Angeles, so eager to distance itself from what it considered the vulgarity of Hollywood, experienced an especially intense temptation to which it frequently succumbed.

The Cocoanut Grove of the Ambassador Hotel, by contrast, remained open to anyone who could afford the prices, and in the flush 1920s many could. Dinner at the Cocoanut Grove, the premier nightclub of Los Angeles in the 1920s, cost $2.50, with a cover charge of 75 cents for an evening of dancing to Abe Lyman's Ambassador All-Star Orchestra. Opening the evening of 26 January 1922 with a floor show featuring ballroom dancers Maurice and Leonora Hughes and mental telepathist Sidar Ramma Setti, the Cocoanut Grove featured an exotic Moorish North African decor, complete with tents, an oasis waterfall, and massed palm trees secured from the set of *The Sheik* at the suggestion of Ambassador resident Rudolph Valentino. Throughout the 1920s Hollywood and establishment Los Angeles, frequently suspicious of each other, achieved a rapprochment at the Cocoanut Grove in the pursuit of nighttime pleasure. The nightclub catered to each clientele equally with Hollywood-oriented shows such as Stars' Night and dancing competitions for aspiring starlets (Lucille LeSueur, later Joan Crawford, was an easy winner) alternating with such Los Angeles-oriented events as College Nights on the eve of USC football games and an annual Champagne Ball.

A frequent habitué of the Cocoanut Grove was the young oil heir and playboy Jean Paul Getty. Getty had returned to Los Angeles from Oxford University in 1920 and was spending the decade in pursuit of wine, women (he married three times within the decade), and song. In his off-hours, Getty boxed, sparring on one occasion with champion Jack Dempsey in a friendly match, and more or less assisted his father George in the oil business. Getty also spent part of each year in Europe, which as the Depression unfolded would become increasingly the center of his activities, commercial and domestic. When in Los Angeles, he frequently enjoyed himself at the Cocoanut Grove; a smallish, agile man, he was an athlete and a good dancer. Throughout the 1920s the Cocoanut Grove provided the music—Art Hickman, Abe Lyman, Gus Arnheim, and their orchestras, the Rhythm Boys, featuring Harry Barris, Al Rinker, and Bing Crosby—to which Jean Paul Getty and other affluent citizens of Los Angeles and Hollywood danced away the riotous and magic evenings of the Jazz Age.

3

The Folks, by contrast, could be found of an evening dining, very early, at another unique Los Angeles institution, the cafeteria. Pioneered in downtown Los Angeles in 1905 by Helen Mosher and rapidly expanded throughout the city in the 1920s by the Boos brothers—Horace, Cyrus, Henry, and John, who operated six clean and efficient Boos Brothers Cafeterias in the city by the mid-

1920s—the cafeteria (a Mexican word, taken from early Los Angeles) met the unembellished nutritional and social needs of the largely Midwestern middle classes. Like their clientele, cafeterias were earnest and unpretentious, although certain upscale cafeterias offered chamber music during dinner. Cafeterias also provided a meeting hall for clubs and associations, useful in a city still needing to catch up in its infrastructure of socially supportive institutions and gathering places. Los Angeles impressed H.L. Mencken as a Double Dubuque. For Irvin Cobb, it was the Corn Belt in a Maxfield Parrish setting. Local writer Louis Adamic coined the term "folks" to describe the hordes of Midwestern migrants, many of them of retirement age, who flocked to Los Angeles after the First World War. Visiting Los Angeles in early 1929, Hamlin Garland found himself "greatly interested in the floods of Middle Westerners filling the streets. The throngs of women shopping, and the cords of men in the park, were all American, of familiar form and coloring."[6]

Ever since the 1880s Southern Californians had been forming state associations as a means of reassociating and stabilizing themselves amidst the dislocations of their new circumstances. Under the auspices of umbrella organizations such as the Federation of State Societies of Los Angeles and the All States Society of Long Beach, annual picnics were held near Long Beach and Ontario on the opposite edges of Los Angeles County, to which thousands flocked for a day of speeches, games, picnicking, entertainment, and reunions. The Midwestern picnics, especially those of the Iowa Society, attracted the most visitors. "A gathering of the Iowa Society," noted Bruce Bliven, "is a sight to think about. A huge park, or other open space, is taken over, and the map of Iowa laid out upon it, each county in its proper place, being marked by a flagpole and pennant. When the erstwhile Iowans arrive in their Dodges and Chevrolets—and 125,000 is not an uncommon figure for the attendance—each family rallies round its own flag amid its former neighbors, and holds high carnival, with reunion, reminiscence, fried chicken and hard-boiled eggs."[7] A sympathetic Midwesterner such as Hamlin Garland might find in the folks of Los Angeles a certain American Gothic dignity. "They were in truth," he noted of an Iowa Society dinner, "incredibly unaesthetic and yet they were worthy, fine serious folk who do not believe in drinking, smoking, or philandering."[8] Other observers were not so kind. "No matter where one goes and what one does," noted Louis Adamic, "one cannot get away from The Folks in Los Angeles. They are everywhere and their influence is felt in well-nigh every phase of city life. They are simple, credulous souls; their bodies are afflicted with all sorts of aches and pains, real and imaginery; they are unimaginative and their cultural horizons are sadly limited—and as such they are perfect soil to sprout and nourish all kinds of medical, religious and cultural quackery."[9]

This note of physical decrepitude, of being worn down by a lifetime of farm toil, received frequent mention. Bruce Bliven linked it to a special form of poverty born, ironically, from longevity. "Too often," he observed, "the farmer and his wife who have reached the age of sixty, gnarled and weather-worn, exhausted by the long struggle against cyclones, blizzards, drought, locusts and low prices, sell the farm and come to California with the proceeds, expecting that they will only survive a few years, and that by spending their capital a little at a time, they can keep going in the interim. In that salubrious climate, of course, no one ever dies; and so, not infrequently, their calculation goes astray and they are left facing the world penniless at seventy-five or eighty." [10] Many observers noted a lost, pathetic quality to the Folks as they lived out their American Gothic lives in the sunshine, as if the move to Southern California could never fully meet the hungers of the Midwestern heart. "The people, the ideas, the hopes," observed journalist Victor Walkers, "are all transplanted, and, as such, struggle for a pale and sickly life under the glaring sun of the south." [11] Los Angeles *Times* literary editor Paul Jordan-Smith blamed the Folks for overwhelming the once robust Yankee-Latin ambience of Los Angeles and thereby disappointing visiting writers. Expecting to find Los Angeles "an American Port Said, reeking with wine and the hootcheekootchee," the ambivalent journalist encounters instead "a population of Iowa farmers and sun-burned old maids in an endless chain of cafeterias, movie palaces and state picnics." [12]

The mass migrations of the 1920s expanded and pushed to the edge a religious fundamentalism that was already evident in the prewar period. In 1913 Willard Huntington Wright, a former Southern Californian then serving as editor of the *Smart Set* in New York, pulled off in "Los Angeles—The Chemically Pure" one of the most outrageous diatribes ever to be launched against an American city. Educated locally (St. Vincent's and Pomona) before going on to study music at Rochester and anthropology and ethnology at Harvard, Wright spent a number of years in further studies at Munich and Paris without ever once taking a degree. In 1910 he returned to Los Angeles ("perhaps," as Carey McWilliams later described him, "the first intellectual to flourish south of the Tehachapis") and went to work as literary editor of the *Times*. Fortunately, Wright left work early with a headache the night the *Times* was obliterated by dynamite. The reporter at the adjacent desk lost his life. In 1912 Wright's friend H.L. Mencken recommended him for the editorship of the *Smart Set* and the young journalist shook the dust of his native city from his feet. A year later Wright (who later turned to detective fiction under the name S.S. Van Dine in an effort to reinvigorate a writing career devastated by alcohol, drugs, and a nervous breakdown) gave a scathing assessment of his home town.

Los Angeles, Wright claimed, had adopted Puritanism as its inflexible doctrine. Fun-loving and robust in its earlier era, Los Angeles now teemed with " 'leading citizens' from Wichita; honorary pallbearers from Emmetsburg; Good Templars from Sedalia; honest spinsters from Grundy Center—all commonplace people, many of them with small competencies made from the sale of farm lands or from the lifelong savings of small mercantile businesses. These good folks brought with them a complete stock of rural beliefs, pieties, superstitions and habits—the Middle West bed hours, the Middle West love of corned beef, church bells, *Munsey's Magazine*, union suits and missionary societies. They brought also a complacent intransigent aversion to late dinners, malt liquor, grand opera and hussies. They are a sober and phlegmatic people, with a passion for marching in parades and wearing badges. They are victims of the sonorous platitude; at concerts they applaud the high notes, and they vote for their pastor's choice of candidate." [13]

Wright was exaggerating, but not completely. Los Angeles was an openly Christian community, including its public entertainment. In December 1915, for example, some 3500 citizens attended an outdoor evening Christmas pageant at Exposition Park accompanied by orchestra and chorus. One of the Magi, the King of the South, made his entrance on a live elephant. In 1919 a wealthy patron, Christine Wetherill Stevenson, established another tradition, a twelve-part Pilgrimage Play depicting the life and death of Jesus Christ. Elaborately staged at night in a picturesque canyon in the Hollywood hills, later developed as the Hollywood Bowl, the Pilgrimage Play employed the actual language of the Scriptures to present an Oberammergau-like pageant that enlisted both local citizens and professional actors in the production. In 1927 Lady Diana Manners played the Madonna. Other performers included Sir George Alexander, Lily Langtry, Maude Adams, and John Drew. Actors performed from various parts of the canyon, their positions illumed by two dozen floodlights and dimmers. The Samaria scene alone put forty thousand watts into service. The Pilgrimage Play in part inspired Cecil B. De Mille to bring *The King of Kings* to the screen in 1927, premiering it at Grauman's Chinese Theater. Each year, *Saturday Night* gave the Pilgrimage Play extensive coverage, and it gave *The King of Kings* an enthusiastic review as well; for these productions testified, it was believed, to the fundamental Christian culture of the city at a time when Hollywood and, by extension, Los Angeles were under attack as dens of immortality.

The fundamentalists of Los Angeles, Wright complained in 1913, had no reservations about imposing their standards on others. "Hence, the recent illumination and guarding of all public parks lest spooning, that lewd pastime, become prevalent. Hence, the Quakerish regulation of public dance halls. Hence, the stupid censorship of the theaters by professional moralists, a censorship so incredibly puerile that even Boston will have to take second place." [14] Thirteen years later, Wright might still have cause for complaint. On 18 February 1926 the police broke up a performance at the Orange Grove Theater of Eugene O'Neill's *Desire Under the Elms*. Seventeen actors and actresses were hauled off to Central Station, fingerprinted, and kept in the vice squad holding area until 4:30 the next morning. When the defense demanded a jury trial that April, the judge allowed the jury ("housewives, salesmen, retired farmers," one reporter described them) to witness a special performance of O'Neill's play by the seventeen actors and actresses standing trial. An impressive array of experts, including the chairwoman of the drama committee of the Friday Morning Club, also testified on the play's behalf. When it was over, however—despite the performance and all the supportive testimony, despite defense attorney Frank McGlynn's citations of equally controversial scenes of Sophocles, Euripides, Aeschylus, Racine, Schiller, and Shakespeare—eight of the twelve jurors still held out for conviction. In Los Angeles, they believed, most people did not appreciate plays about wayward stepmothers.

Nor did the citizens of Long Beach appreciate lewd behavior on the seashore. In 1920 the citizens of Long Beach adopted an ordinance drawn up by one William Peek, a mortician serving as commissioner of public safety. "No person," the ordinance read, "over the age of six shall appear on any highway or public place or on sand or beach or in the Pacific Ocean in Long Beach clothed in a bathing suit which does not completely conceal from view all that portion of the trunk of the body of such person below a line around the body even with the upper part of the armpits except a circular arm hole for each arm with the maximum diameter no longer than twice the distance from the upper part of the armpit to the top of the shoulder and which does not completely conceal from view each leg from the hip joint to a line around the leg one-third of the way to the knee, and without such bathing suit having a skirt made of opaque material surrounding the person and hanging loosely from the waistline to the bottom of such suit." [15] Another Long Beach ordinance forbade "caresses, hugging, fondling, embracing, spooning, kissing or wrestling with any person or persons of the opposite sex in or upon or near any public park, avenue, street, court, way alley or place, or on the beach, or any other public place. . . . And no person shall sit or lie with his or her head, or any other portion of his or her person upon any portion of a person or persons of the opposite sex upon or near any of the said public places." [16] Violators of this draconian measure faced a $500 fine or up to six months in prison.

Louis Adamic claimed that Los Angeles counted a mere 142,000 souls on the active rolls of its Protestant churches in the mid-1920s, roughly a tenth of the population. These were scattered, however, through some 300 active congregations, giving the impression, as another observer put it, that Christianity ranked as the city's leading industry after real estate and motion pictures. Bridging two local industries, a Los Angeles preacher invited Rin Tin Tin to sit on the rostrum during his sermon. Announcements of forthcoming sermons testified to a folkloric interpenetration of sacred and secular concerns. "What would Jesus do if he controlled the street railways of Los Angeles?" one announcement asked. "If Jesus Christ were on earth today," claimed another, "he would be a Shriner."

As early as 1913 Willard Huntington Wright noted a tendency to cults and religious quackery in the Los Angeles temperament: a taste "for faddists and mountebanks—spiritualists, mediums, astrologists, phrenologists, palmists and all other breeds of esoteric wind-jammers. . . . Whole buildings are devoted to occult and outlandish orders—mazdaznan clubs, yogi sects, homes of truth, cults of cosmic fluidists, astral planers, Emmanuel movers, Rosicrucians and other boozy transcendentalists." [17] Thirteen years later, Paul Jordan-Smith described even more of the same. The cults of Los Angeles, he argued, organizations such as the Children of the Sun Church or the Pre-Astral Fraternity of Love and Nature-Way Medical College for Drugless Healing, were "the sick survivors of New England transcendentalism" coming from Boston via Chicago. "The milder climate enables them to keep the illusion that they have conquered disease through spiritual power." [18]

By the mid-1920s two preachers, Bob Shuler of Trinity Methodist in the downtown and Aimee Semple McPherson of the Angelus Temple in the Echo Park district, dominated the evangelical scene. Taken together, in comparison and in contrast, Shuler and McPherson theatrically expressed the psychology of fervid hopes and palpable resentments characteristic of lower-middle-class white Protestant America in the Los Angeles area.

4

Fierce, patriarchal, bigoted, Bob Shuler personified the Bible Belt in all its relish for hellfire and damnation and its capacity for Cromwellian counterattack. Of poor white stock, raised in a log cabin in the hardscrabble hills of Tennessee, Shuler first rose to prominence as a Methodist preacher in Texas, where his ad hominem style of pulpit denunciation earned him a major libel suit and a number of fistfights. Having used up his welcome in rural Texas, Shuler moved to Los Angeles in 1920 as pastor of Trinity Methodist, an embattled downtown church with a dwindling membership and huge debt. Within the decade Shuler increased his congregation from 900 to 42,000, largely paid off the debt, and made himself, as one journalist put it, the Methodist Savanarola of Los Angeles. Shuler knew his audience, the Folks, and had the genius for publicity. From the start his preaching had a prosecutorial bent. Fighting Bob, as he came to be known, was out to get the wicked and, as it turned out, to put himself in charge. In 1922 Shuler commenced *Bob Shuler's Magazine*, which he mostly wrote himself, keeping up a ferocious torrent of invective until he folded the publication in 1933 at the depth of the Depression.

Bob Shuler loved certain people and things, the Bible and William Jennings Bryan especially ("the mantle of the Prophets was upon him"); but he hated with an even greater relish. Among other people and things, the Reverend Bob Shuler hated Jews, Catholics, movies, evolution, jazz, and dancing. When he beheld that stream of girls pouring into Los Angeles's dance halls, he closed his eyes and said a little prayer for the unborn: "God have mercy upon the little sons and daughters of those who are now being taught to 'just jazz around.' " Shuler's virulent anti-Catholicism was standard Whore of Babylon fare, with a special emphasis upon Governor Al Smith of New York as agent of a papal

takeover. In an early issue of his magazine, Shuler ran a spirited defense of the
Ku Klux Klan against its Catholic and Jewish opponents. "The Ku Klux Klan,"
Shuler inveighed, "is the result of conditions, whatever that organization may
be the cause of. They have found the Jew gradually taking over the nation
financially and the Roman Catholic Church as surely taking over the nation
politically. So they are here."[19] Fighting Bob's campaign against motion pictures combined attacks on Jewish producers with a local emphasis upon the
damage Hollywood was doing to Los Angeles by making the city a font of
national corruption. "There are poisons here," Shuler fulminated against Hollywood in March 1922, "that shall destroy the home, besmirch the virtue of
womanhood and sully every whitened principle of social intercourse unless a
mighty cleansing be wrought." The Hollywood producers, Shuler charged,
"apostles of looseness that aim their arrows of death at the Christian Sabbath,
at the American home, and at the very program of sane and safe Americanism"
were giving Los Angeles a bad name.[20] When comedian Roscoe "Fatty" Arbuckle won acquittal in San Francisco on charges of causing the death of starlet
Virginia Rappe through forced and violent intercourse, Shuler blamed the producers of Hollywood for getting Arbuckle acquitted. When Postmaster General
Will Hays arrived in Hollywood to clean it up, Shuler pilloried him as a
suborned tool of Jewish producers.

Shuler considered himself at the center of nothing less than a battle for the
soul of the City of the Angels, the last purely American city in the nation.
"Los Angeles," he argued, "is the only Anglo-Saxon city of a million popula-
tion left in America. It is the only such city that is not dominated by foreigners.
It remains in a class to itself as the one city of the nation in which the white,
American, Christian idealism still predominates."[21] This City of Saints and
Angeles, however, stood in grave danger of corruption from within—from for-
eign-born movie producers, from local Catholic politicians, from the slack
Protestant establishment itself. Living in theatrical simplicity on a small exurban spread, where he and his wife grew crops and butchered hogs, Shuler
loathed the WASP oligarchy of the city, with special loathing extended to Harry
Chandler, the Los Angeles *Times*, and rah-rah USC fraternity boys. A paranoid
populist of a distinctly American caste of mind, Shuler believed that the establishment ran Los Angeles as a conspiracy and private club and was out to get
him as well. The fact that Shuler was partly correct in these assessments only
reinforces Delmore Schwartz's contention that even paranoids have enemies.

In the Christmas season of 1926 Elizabeth Glide, a devout Methodist oil
heiress, presented Shuler with the gift of a private radio station, KGEF. With
an audience of 200,000 listeners, increasing by an estimated 100,000 new listeners a year in the late 1920s, Bob Shuler now had the wherewithal to become
the Savanarola of the Southland. Like Savanarola, Shuler exhorted, scolded,
named names, and quite soon became a political power in his own right. He
became, in fact, along with Aimee Semple McPherson, whom he detested, the

prototypical radio evangelist, the first of many media preachers to rise to power in the United States. KGEF broadcasted Shuler's sermons and services from Trinity Church, together with an ambitious programming of church music, children's hours, and guest addresses.

Most pertinent to greater Los Angeles were Shuler's Monday evening sessions in which the fiery preacher preached, prayed, answered questions, and assailed the local establishment, especially politicians, with withering scorn. If this were not enough, Shuler followed up these Monday night sessions with equally Savanarolan Civic Talks, occasions for even more sustained castigation. On the night of 31 October 1927, for example, Shuler criticized Christian Scientists for not teaching the doctrine of atonement and discussed the possibilities of salvation for upright non-believers. The bulk of the program, however, to judge from its transcript, dealt with local personalities and issues. Among others, Shuler attacked Los Angeles *Examiner* publisher William Randolph Hearst ("one of the most menacing individuals that has come the way of America within a generation"), Los Angeles Mayor Charles Cryer ("there ought to be some tangible explanation for the sudden riches of our honorable Mayor"), and police captain Bert Wallis, who had reportedly vowed "to get Shuler if it took the rest of his life." Over the years, a number of his enemies had hired private detectives to catch him in a compromising position, Shuler replied, either with women or money, but he had no fears on that score. His life was an open book. In the same broadcast, Shuler also took on city officials for not closing down the "the lewd, vile, and debasing performances" in theaters on Main Street and blasted the juvenile court for sending Protestant children to Catholic boarding schools and orphanages. "It is amazing how much attention government has in the Bible," Shuler argued. "The trouble today is that too many people want to preach a part of the Bible but not all." [22]

Shuler's questioning of Mayor Cryer's real-estate investments on Western Avenue earned him a libel suit, as did his attacks on the Knights of Columbus in the pamphlet *The Rise of Beastism*. Only when Shuler directly attacked the Superior Court, however, did he suffer any real consequences. When millionaire theater-owner Alexander Pantages and his wife came up for separate trials in 1929, he for rape, she for drunk driving and manslaughter, Shuler stated openly on the radio that the juries would be fixed by the millionaire's money. After Mrs. Pantages was convicted, the Los Angeles Bar association, another of Shuler's bêtes noires (he hated lawyers), successfully pressed contempt of court charges, and Shuler was given thirty days. He served fifteen, making each day a triumph of personal publicity. Comparing himself to St. Paul and John Bunyan, Shuler was followed about his daily routine by reporters and photographers as he ate, made up his bunk, wrote in his cell (a pamphlet entitled *Jailed* appeared soon after his release), conferred with a sympathetic chaplain, or ministered to the other prisoners.

When Shuler's candidate John Porter, a church-going used-automobile-parts dealer from Iowa and a former Klan member, was elected Mayor of Los Angeles in 1928, taking office in 1929, Shuler's influence reached its peak. Like Shuler himself, like the congregation of Trinity Methodist and the listening audience of KGEF, Porter was a nobody: an anonymous, teetotaling, clumsily mannered, poorly educated evangelical Midwesterner typical of the million or so who had poured into greater Los Angeles since the war seeking an upgrading of life which they both wanted and feared but which also eluded them. Now he, Porter, and they, Shuler and his flock, had reached a position of strength enabling them to win the mayor's office. Even with Savanarola directly connected to city hall, however, the resentment lingered. "I have been an underdog all my life," Shuler told Edmund Wilson, "and my sympathies will always be on the side of the common people."[23]

Aimee Semple McPherson, by contrast, while she pursued an even more flamboyant ministry than Shuler, preached a more encompassing message. Where Shuler slashed and attacked, McPherson exalted and encouraged. Shuler's patriarchal Christianity, rigidly sectarian in its concepts of sin and atonement, stood in complete contrast to McPherson's Foursquare Gospel, with its broadly conceived interdenominational emphasis upon a personalized encounter with conversion, healing, the second coming, and redemption. Chunky, open-faced, drawling, Shuler played the rural American as crafty good old boy. McPherson, by contrast—female, Canadian, never losing the instinctive civility of the Canadian temperament, a handsome women with thick strawberry blond hair, strong features, and an actress's voice—played, variously, the beloved sister in Jesus; Mary Magdalene, redeemed yet still possessed of erotic power; Hawthorne's Hester Prynne, whose scarlet A bespoke both angelism and adultery; or an Isadora Duncan in the pulpit, the preacher as leading lady, her name up in lights.

As a farm girl growing up in Ontario, Canada, where she was born in 1890, Aimee Kennedy gravitated away from the strict Methodism of her father, with its emphasis upon excluding categories of salvation and non-salvation, in favor of the salvationalist theology of her mother, the daughter of a Salvation Army captain. The Salvation Army taught that everyone was ultimately redeemed. Religion became a discovery of just exactly how one had been saved as opposed to worrying whether or not salvation had occurred. Like Mary Baker Eddy, whose emphasis on healing she would later appropriate, Aimee Kennedy experienced a crisis of faith in late adolescence. A handsome Scotch-Irish Pentecostal evangelist by the name of Robert James Semple reconverted her to Christianity, and the young couple were married in 1908 when Aimee was still seventeen.

A photo exists depicting the Semples at the time of their marriage. Aimee wears a high-necked gown, bridal white, of the period. Her glorious hair is rolled into a severe chignon. She is very much the minister's wife, the comforting support of her husband who encouraged her to preach at his side as the couple traveled eastern Canada and the United States conducting revivals. Again like Mary Baker Eddy, the young Irish-Canadian minister's wife showed an early capacity for vivid extempore discourse. Mrs. Semple could preach, that was certain from the start.

In 1910 the young couple left for China as missionaries. Robert Semple died of typhoid fever as they awaited their entry visas in Hong Kong. Returning to New York with her infant daughter Roberta, Aimee Semple went to work for the Salvation Army and recommenced her preaching career, this time as a solo evangelist. Marrying a second time in 1912, to Harold McPherson, a Providence, Rhode Island, grocery salesman, she tried to settle down as a housewife. She had another child, a son, whom she named Rolf; but the lure of the road, the call to Macedonia, soon came back upon her.

Aimee Semple McPherson, as she now styled herself, loved automobiles as well as Jesus Christ—big, open touring cars which she could emblazon with evangelistic slogans and take to the road, preaching an amalgam of Pentecostalism, Holy Rollerism (with its emphasis upon popular music, theatrics, and audience participation), and the Foursquare Gospel she herself devised. Appropriately, she drove to Los Angeles in 1918 with her mother and two children after her divorce from McPherson, already a preacher of some reputation, stopping en route to preach to subscribers to her *Foursquare Monthly* but looking for a new life as well along with thousands of others similarly motivated, heading west in flivvers. Before setting out on her trek, McPherson promised her two children a bungalow and a pet canary when they reached Southern California. When the children grew tired or cranky on the long journey, she comforted them with stories of the bungalows, canaries, gardens, and rosebushes of Los Angeles, of the happiness they would all enjoy together in that magical little house. In later years she remembered this automotive hegira (she claimed she put four thousand miles on the speedometer) as a Biblical journey, a spiritual quest for the promised City of the Angels.

Approaching Los Angeles via the Needles route, which insured a steady, downhill, gas-saving glide into San Bernardino, McPherson felt the promised city draw nigh as she drove through the aromatic orange, lemon, and grapefruit groves of eastern Los Angeles County. Throughout the afternoon she drove, and then as daylight faded, there it was: the city on the plain to which the Lord had beckoned her! "It was just growing dusk when we caught our first glimpse of Los Angeles," she later wrote. "The sun, after leading us ever westward since early morning, had laid itself like a scarlet sacrifice upon an altar of cradled clouds. Rapidly there spread across the sky a mantle of ever deep blue, darkening to purple. . . . Upon terraced lawns, rows of palms became feathered sentinels against the dusk—gigantic, grotesque—their fronds gently astir. The hum of heavy traffic resounded faintly from downtown streets, above which already hung the calcined glare of a million lesser glares. It was twilight when we entered Los Angeles. Twilight in the Southwest; a delight in the antechamber of Heaven. An eternity of beauty packed into the space of half an hour."[24]

The words of Joshua 6:16 came to her: "Shout, for the Lord hath given you the city," which the Lord seemed very much willing to do. As in the case of Jericho, the walls of Los Angeles all but tumbled down as she drove into the city with her mother and two children, $100 to her name and a tambourine with "Jesus Is Coming Soon—Get Ready" emblazoned across the side of her touring car. Two nights later she preached in a rented upper room. Shortly thereafter she signed a lease on a small church. She was soon preaching to standing-room crowds at the Philharmonic Auditorium, the largest assembly space in the city, with ushers struggling to keep the aisles free in conformity to fire laws. When she shared her bungalow story with her audience, men stood up volunteering land, lumber, and labor, and built her a bungalow near Culver City.

Los Angeles, however, was a material city. Or was it that America, as well as possessing a strong evangelistic strain, was also a material place? In any event, Aimee Semple McPherson soon became a very material woman. She wanted her own temple, not a rented hall, and by January 1923 she had one— the $1.5 million Angelus Temple at the northwest edge of Echo Park. Seating 4300, Angelus Temple was claimed as the largest class A church building in the United States. McPherson had herself raised most of the money for it through revival tours throughout California, the Midwest, and Australia. She and her mother, and not the congregation, held the deed to the property. Adjacent to the Temple she built a Bible school and administration building from which she administered the Foursquare Gospel program, which eventually enrolled some 240 affiliated churches throughout Southern California and the Southwest. Skilled as a preacher, McPherson was a gifted organizer as well, among the first to establish a ministry of affiliated individuals and congregations brought together through the written word and through the power of Angelus Temple radio station KFSG (Kall Four Square Gospel), the third radio station to be established in Los Angeles. Flamboyant on the stage as a preacher, McPherson—Sister Aimee to her congregation—nevertheless ran an organizationally sophisticated ministry, complete with choir and orchestra, rescue mission, home visitors' organization, and publishing house. From her Salvation Army background she promoted the use of uniforms for herself and for a phalanx of female attendants who escorted her to the stage and stood guard as she preached. With success came money ("Sister has a headache tonight," she would say at collection time, "just quiet money please") and a mansion to replace the bungalow near Culver City, a shiny new car, expensive coiffures, and elegant clothes. Now when she preached on the road she traveled by train and stayed at first-class hotels.

Today, Aimee Semple McPherson is remembered, if at all, for her eccentric, histrionic preaching and for the faked kidnapping and sex scandal of 1926.

Each of these tend to be recounted from a comic point of view, as if she were of no other significance. The comedy, however is understandable. It derives easily from the material. Take her preaching, for example. Knowing her audience, their limited background, their credulity, their love of movies and make-believe, McPherson evolved a technique of costumed sermonizing linked to a theme. Dressed as a USC football player, she preached on carrying the ball for Christ. Entering the Temple on a motorcycle in a policeman's uniform, she placed sin under arrest and urged her audience not to speed to ruin. Prodding with a pitchfork, she chased the devil from the stage. Dressed as a nurse, she prayed over the sick. Other appearances included one as an admiral in the Salvation Navy or as George Washington at Valley Forge. When she traveled she collected costumes, which she added to her already impressive dressing-room press for later pulpit appearances. As Sister Aimee acted, preached, and prayed, the mighty Temple organ thundered in accompaniment, joined by a brass band and a well-rehearsed female choir in the Salvation Army-like uniforms. In architecture and usage the Angelus Temple was more motion-picture theater than church. It even had an electric marquee over its entrance, announcing Sister Aimee's latest sermon.

Once widowed, once divorced, Sister Aimee was in her mid-thirties, vital in every aspect of life, at the height of her fame. The object of one aspect of her vitality was Kenneth G. Ormiston, employed at the Temple as station engineer for KFSG, but unfortunately a married man. The ensuing farce survives today as Aimee Semple McPherson's enduring claim to notoriety. On the afternoon of 18 May 1926 McPherson was last seen at Ocean Park, a swimming area near Venice. She was presumed to have drowned, but a massive search by police and Temple members failed to discover any body. In the search two people, a diver and a Temple member, were themselves drowned. A little more than a month later, three days after an all-day memorial service at Angelus Temple, McPherson resurfaced on 23 June in the small Sonoran town of Agua Prieta, claiming to have been kidnapped and to have escaped from a shack in the Sonoran desert where she was being held captive. Researchers with a taste for American-style grande guignol have patiently unraveled the entire episode. It is all but certain that Sister Aimee took a month's vacation in the company of Kenneth Ormiston, spending part of this time in a honeymoon cottage in Carmel. District Attorney Asa Keyes produced a grocery list from the Carmel cottage in what was unmistakenly McPherson's handwriting. For nearly half a year, Keyes gathered evidence preparatory to taking McPherson to trial on charges of conspiracy to produce false testimony. The embattled minister defended herself vociferously all the while against the storm of scandal and innuendo that swept Los Angeles. The Reverend Bob Shuler took to his desk to produce a sixty-four-page pamphlet on the affair which, even if one grants the venom running through every line, reduced McPherson's kidnapping story to total absurdity while at the same time ridiculing her on dozens of other points of theology and behavior.

McPherson escaped going to trial when the District Attorney, fearing that his case fell short of the total conclusiveness needed to convict a person of McPherson's popularity, withdrew charges at the last possible moment. Her disappearance and feigned kidnapping, however, spiced by the motive of sexual adventure, rendered her a laughingstock. After a year and more of press scrutiny and legal investigation, Aimee Semple McPherson became that from which no public figure can ever recover momentum—an object of public ridicule. The faithful held on, joyously mobbing her in a Temple celebration on the evening charges were dropped; but any larger influence she might have once possessed disappeared. She continued to preach until her death in 1944 from an overdose of Seconal (ruled accidental), but the scandal and the need to refute it proved a distracting burden.

As comic as was her exit from civic influence, Aimee Semple McPherson cannot be dismissed as a mere fool. For more than half a dozen years, until the scandal increasingly restricted her influence to the International Church of the Foursquare Gospel, she preached a message that assisted the thousands who heard her at the Temple or over the airwaves in their new lives in Southern California. They were, by and large, the inconspicuous, the frequently damaged rural nobodies from the eccentric borderlands of evangelical American Protestantism. She helped them become somebodies in Los Angeles.

Her healing ministry, so intense in the first three years of her Los Angeles career, represented a vigorous response to the invalidism noted by so many contemporary journalists. The Folks had come to Southern California in the hopes of getting better, and she encouraged them to rise from their pallets and walk, which some of them did, leaving their canes, crutches, and braces behind in a special display area at the Temple. They had come to the Southland seeking betterment, and she preached not sin but salvation in the here-and-now material dream called Los Angeles.

Bob Shuler castigated her for her Holy Roller beginnings, but were his poor white origins any more aristocratic? With the Temple built, she downplayed the extreme aspects of Holy Rollerism (a padded room was, however, provided for discreet writhings) and began the transition from Pentecostal to Baptist. Part of the redemption Los Angeles offered was the chance to become middle-class—the glory road led to a bungalow.

Her published sermons and hymns (she composed 180 of them, together with a number of musical pageants) pulsate with this sense of spiritual and material well-being, of belonging, of having at last found a new identity and a new home. Taken at its best, her pulpit presence—feminine, healing, radiant with her special magnetism and physical energy—warmed and reconciled but rarely divided. It is difficult to find any adverse judgments against others in any of her published writings. She was histrionic and sensual and at least once deceitful, but she was also tolerant and kind. "Here in this 'city of angels,' " she later wrote of her ministry, "where the power had so wonderfully fallen years ago, we learned that divers doctrinal differences had gotten the eyes of many off the Lord, and that there was a dearth in the land. Hungry hearts were praying earnestly, however, and the Lord answered prayer in a wonderful way." [25]

5

Non-Protestant Los Angeles, meanwhile, was also seeking its place in the sun. Jewish Los Angeles, for one thing, paralleled the dominant Protestant society in being primarily lower-middle-class and upwardly mobile. Jewish labor migrated to Los Angeles in the late teens and early 1920s to find employment in the city's garment industry. By 1920 an estimated two-thirds of the city's Jewish population worked in garment manufacturing, clerical positions, or blue-collar jobs in the film industry. Whatever strength the labor movement possessed after 1910 in the open-shop city belonged to Jewish-dominated unions such as the International Ladies' Garment Workers Union and the Amalgamated Clothing Workers. As opposed to the haut bourgeois tone of German-Jewish San Francisco, the dominant tone of Jewish Los Angeles (destined to be the second largest Jewish city after New York in the United States by 1969) was secular, socialistic, and Yiddish—Hester Street in the sunshine. Politics tended to center around the Russian Revolution, dividing Yiddish Los Angeles into pro- or anti-Bolshevik camps. In the 1920s Los Angeles had a Yiddish newspaper, two brief-lived Yiddish literary magazines, and a circle of Yiddish writers which included the poets Lune Mattes and Henry Rosenblatt, the playwright Maurice Roger, and the short-story writer S. Miller. The most representative Yiddish writer of Los Angeles, W. Lossman, had already died from tuberculosis in 1918 at age 32. Lossman's themes, however—memories of Europe played off against the almost surreal contrasts of Southern California, this presented in laconic, poetic intuitions—proved a staple of Yiddish writing in the next decade.

The Jewish establishment had two camps, downtown and Hollywood. Downtown had significant origins in the German-Jewish frontier which had played such a major role in the creation of San Francisco. Its most conspicuous nineteenth-century families were the Hellmans and the Newmarks.

Towards the end of his life, merchant philanthropist Harris Newmark, assisted by researcher Perry Worden, produced *Sixty Years in Southern California, 1853–1913* (1916), the single most valuable memoir to deal with the rise of the Southland in the nineteenth century, an informed, gossipy Pepys's Diary of Southern California, as Lawrence Clark Powell later described it, and, according to another source, one of the great autobiographies of the American Jewish experience. In 1915, a year before Newmark's death, Rabbi Edgar Magnin, a 25-year-old graduate of Hebrew Union College, assumed direction of the Wilshire Boulevard Temple and, thus positioned in what was to become the wealthiest temple congregation in the United States, succeeded Newmark as spokesman for the Jewish establishment.

Despite these resources, traditional Hebrew learning, with the exception of the Mishnah studies of Rabbi Isaac Werne and the literary/philosophical studies of Russian immigrant physician Louis G. Reynolds, in no way matched the vitality of Yiddish culture. Nor did the Hollywood establishment make much of a connection with the world of the Wilshire Temple, at least in this period. Jesse Lasky, Samuel Goldwyn, Marcus Loew, Adolph Zukor, William Fox, Louis Mayer, Carl Laemmle, Lewis Selznick, and the others had their own world, attuned to the financial center in New York and to American popular taste. Largely Eastern European in origin (with the exception of Zukor, who came from Hungarian rabbinical stock), the producers had closer affinities with the Jewish-owned and -operated garment and furniture industries of Los Angeles, also geared to mass production, distribution, and popular taste, than they did with the German-Jewish establishment.

This establishment, meanwhile, as the 1920s unfolded and anti-Semitism emerged as a factor in American life, was experiencing for the first time in its collective experience rejections and exclusions based upon its Jewishness, in some cases in the very clubs which members of their community had helped found. There had been early warning signs. When Progressive activist Meyer Lissner, a founder of the Lincoln-Roosevelt League, ran afoul of Harrison Gray Otis, publisher of the *Los Angeles Times*, he found himself pilloried as "Three Ball Lissnerski" in reference to the three globes above a pawn shop, "true to the traditions and precepts of his race."[26] As painful as all this might be, establishment Jews remained active in civic life, especially on the library and education commissions; for the time had long since passed that Jewish Los Angeles could be bullied out of its identity and influence. In time, the Yiddish life of Los Angeles, as it Americanized, evolved into a point of connection with New York, conferring on Los Angeles a vitality in education, the arts, and intellectual life that came to fruition after the Second World War.

As Yiddish Los Angeles developed, Chinese Los Angeles declined. Through the World War I period Los Angeles nurtured a vigorous Chinese quarter to the north of the Plaza. Chinatown Los Angeles had emerged from the frontier and it atmospherically sustained frontier institutions such as gambling, prostitution, and, a specialty, opium dens. Pre-1920s Chinatown had its own Chinese language theater, weekly newspaper, telephone exchange, three temples or joss houses, and a flourishing red-light life. Disputes over prostitutes and gambling motivated a series of tong wars, the last of them in the early 1920s. But even as the Hop Sing shot it out with the Bing Kong in narrow alleyways adjacent to the Plaza for one last time, the Chinese population of Los Angeles had dropped from 7500 in 1900 to 2000 by 1923.

A ban on immigration stopped the flow of single Chinese men into California, and so the traffic in prostitutes waned. While Chinatown remained Los Angeles's red-light and gambling district through the 1920s, supervised by the ambiguously functioning Chinatown Detail of the Los Angeles Police Department, a group notoriously amenable to payoffs, vice dens tended to be replaced by chop-suey houses.

The Japanese community, by contrast, steadily increased and prospered. By 1930 there were 35,000 Japanese in Los Angeles County, all but a few thousand of them living within a three-mile radius of First and San Pedro streets in the city. Fully half were *Nisei*, American-born, but of these only 4000 were over 21. Japanese Los Angeles was a young community, propelled into its growth by the immigration boom of 1907, when some 30,000 *Issei* immigrants came to the United States, and a baby boom in the late 1920s, when thousands of *Nisei* children were born to *Issei* parents. The Japanese began as shopkeepers (dry goods, confections, bamboo for landscaping and furniture), restaurant operators, and road crewmen for the Pacific Electric Railway, but their full consolidation as an economic force came from the produce business, which they soon dominated. By the teens Japanese producers and wholesalers operating out of the City Market at Ninth and San Pedro were supplying Los Angeles with 75 percent of its fresh vegetables.

The more the *Issei* prospered, the more they became the objects of discrimination and envy. As early as 1897 a Japanese Association of Los Angeles was formed as a self-protecting and mediating organization. This and similar organizations had their hands full as anti-Japanese feeling mounted in California in the prewar years, fanned by Progressive politicians Hiram Johnson and James Duval Phelan and publishers William Randolph Hearst and V.S. McClatchy, all of them pushing their Yellow Peril propaganda. Matters grew particularly ugly in the early 1920s both statewide and locally. After years of lobbying, the Asiatic Exclusion League of California, having secured legislation in 1913 outlawing the ownership of land in California by the non-citizen *Issei*, persuaded Congress in 1924 to forbid Japanese immigration to the United States altogether. Locally, as in the case of nearly everything else in Los Angeles, it came down to a matter of real estate. Despite their increasing prosperity, *Issei* and *Nisei* alike were kept from buying homes they could afford outside the confines of the Little Tokyo area. Resistance in Hollywood, spearheaded by the Hollywood Protective Association, was especially vitriolic. JAPS KEEP MOVING, blared a sign over one Hollywood bungalow, THIS IS A WHITE MAN'S NEIGHBORHOOD.

Ironically, Japanese Los Angeles reflected Anglo-American Los Angeles with remarkable fidelity. There was nothing strange or removed about Japanese-American Los Angeles. It was, on the contrary, a mirror image of the larger culture, middle-class, church-going, success-oriented, and boosterish, albeit with a Japanese accent and cultural orientation. Since 1903 the community enjoyed a Japanese language newspaper *Rafu Shimpo*. In 1914 an orphanage was established; in 1918, a hospital. Initially, Japanese women were in short supply, but between 1910 and 1924 more than 30,000 immigrated to the United States, most of them with marriages already arranged to *Issei* from their local regions according to ancient Japanese custom. Others came as "picture brides," their marriages arranged through private agencies. As family life took hold, Japanese Los Angeles, like Anglo-American Los Angeles, showed itself as home-owning and church-oriented, with a number of flourishing Christian, Buddhist, and Shinto congregations. In 1924 the Nishi Hongwanji congregation built the largest Buddhist temple in North America. The Buddhists also ran Little Tokyo's Boy Scout program. *Nisei* boys enjoyed a flourishing baseball league. Girls were instructed in traditional dance and flower arrangement but they also roller-skated and took piano lessons. Sixty percent of the *Nisei* graduated from high school during the 1924–1942 period; an astonishing 33 percent went on to college.

Did Anglo-American Los Angeles have its Iowa and Kansas associations? The *Issei* formed forty *kenjinkai* based around Japanese prefectures which sponsored lavish summer reunion picnics and New Year's celebrations, while also acting as credit unions and benevolent societies. The Hiroshima, Kumamato, Yamaguchi, Fukuoka, Wakayama, Nagasaki, and Okayama *kenjinkai* were the most prominent. Did the Folks flock en masse to picnics and the beach? Little Tokyo was filled on Saturday nights with Model Ts bringing *Issei* and *Nisei* in for a night of shopping and silent films imported from Japan. There were sumo wrestling tournaments, judged by Mrs. Mitsuye Suzuki, whose word was law; and over at the Tokyo Club, operated since 1927 by Yasutaro Yasuda (gunned down, alas, in 1931 by a rival operator) *Issei* and *Nisei*, after climbing three flights of stairs, might enjoy such demimondaine pleasures as gambling *(fan-tan, hanafuda, bakappe)*, bootleg liquor, including *sake*, and the attentions of beautiful hostesses. The Japanese-American oligarchy, meanwhile, might turn out resplendent in long gown and white tie as it did in 1931 to welcome the Prince and Princess Takamatsu at an elaborate banquet. Three years later, the oligarchy, hit hard by the Depression, organized its own promotional event, *Nisei* Week, paralleling similar booster festivals throughout Southern California.

Like *Nisei* Los Angeles, Mexican-American Los Angeles was also growing. Between 1920 and 1930, the Mexican-American population of Los Angeles tripled, from 33,644 to 97,116, surpassing San Antonio, Texas, as the leading Mexican-American population in the United States. Los Angeles County had a Mexican-American population of 167,000. Only a few large cities in Mexico surpassed this figure. Most of this growth came from children born in the United States. In 1929, for example, the birth-over-death ratio in Los Angeles was 241 for Anglos; for Mexican-Americans it was 4,070. Nearly half the Los Angeles-area Mexican-American families surveyed during this period had more than five children. The average per household was 4.3. Initially, Mexican-

American life had centered quite naturally in the downtown Plaza area, the site of pre-conquest Los Angeles, but with this tripling of population, Mexican-Americans migrated to Elysian Park, then east across the Los Angeles River to Boyle Heights near Lincoln Park and into Belvedere, which by the late 1920s had some 30,000 Mexican-American residents.

The streetcar, then beginning to be abandoned by Anglos, enabled Mexican-Americans to disperse themselves to these outlying districts while remaining in contact with their older neighborhoods and with their previous places of employment. Because of the streetcar, even Pasadena had a Mexican-American community, which commuted to manufacturing or service jobs in the inner city or to agricultural work in the outlying districts. The tire industry employed many Mexican-Americans, the Samson Tire Company especially, which deliberately located its major new plant near the Mexican-American labor pool. Meat packing, steel, and auto assembly operations also employed large numbers of Mexican-American workers.

Working-class Los Angeles of the 1920s, then, possessed a distinctly Mexican-American coloration. Racial animosity made upward mobility difficult, except for film stars such as Ramon Navarro and Dolores del Rio, each of them from already established backgrounds, and wealthy expatriates of the pre-Revolutionary elite who were accepted in upper-class Anglo-American circles. Excluded from many communities by restrictive purchase contracts, Mexican-American life tended to be barrio-centered and strongly inward in focus. Associations such as the Alianza Hispano-Americana, an insurance and financial services organization, El Club Anachuac and La Sociedad Montezuma for young men and women respectively, and La Sociedad Mutualista Mexicana, an inter-barrio, inter-organizational coordinating agency, reinforced this inwardness of cultural focus and civic life. Kept from active participation in mainstream Los Angeles, Mexican-Americans learned the immigrant lessons of waiting, patience, and survival. Religion, family, and work kept them strong. Anglos might consider them a transient people, which was the exact opposite of the truth. They were stable, rooted to place, and as they survived and waited, they gained strength. By the late 1920s they were already the largest single minority group in the city.

Black Los Angeles doubled itself in the 1920s, although in its case the figures remained small, growing from 15,579 to 38,894, or 3.1 percent of the city's population. In contrast to Mexican-Americans, blacks increased more by migration from the South than by birthrate. To judge by the declining illiteracy rate among Los Angeles blacks, down from 16 percent in 1900 to 4.3 percent in 1920, both those born in Los Angeles and those migrating there were becoming progressively more middle-class. By the mid-1920s, one study noted, it was becoming increasingly rare to see black men sit out on their porches on Sundays wearing overalls.

As in the case of Mexican-Americans, black Los Angelenos were kept to certain districts by economics and through restrictive trust deed clauses from homes that might otherwise be available to upwardly mobile members of the black community. Originally centered in Boyle Heights, Western Avenue, Temple Street, and the Furlong Tract, the black community, again like the Mexican-American, moved eastward in the 1920s. Blacks passing as whites in many cases would break onto a block initially and others would follow, or in many instances whites would willingly sell to prosperous blacks, often at better than average prices. "Many whites secretly welcomed the coming of the blacks," remembered an attorney active in the black community of this period, "for they desired to rid themselves of their property. The Negro from the South provided the opportunity. Many had come to Los Angeles with ready cash; and even though many of the residential sections then occupied by the whites were nothing to brag about, these communities were veritable Edens to some of the Negroes." [27] During this period, the Watts subdivision in the southeast emerged as a primary point of black settlement. Low, damp, and sandy, Watts functioned as a water basin for the rest of the city. Few trees grew in the sandy soil. Blacks flocked there in such numbers, however, that it became apparent to the remaining whites that Watts would soon have a black mayor, which the oligarchy found disquieting. In 1926 the embattled white community orchestrated the annexation of Watts to Los Angeles.

Whatever the difficulties, however—housing restrictions and hence de facto segregation in schools, Jim Crow laws in public swimming pools which allowed blacks to swim there only on the day before the pool was to be drained—the black people of Los Angeles continued to consolidate themselves in what was for the majority of them a welcomed prosperity. As an undergraduate at the Southern Campus of the University of California (later UCLA) in the mid-1920s, Ralph Bunche told the story of a Southern black who spent some time in Los Angeles. Returning to the South, he was offered hog-jobs by his white employer. Declining the offer, the gentleman informed his employer that, no thanks, hog jobs would not do. In Los Angeles he had learned to eat high on the hog. The product of middle-class black Los Angeles and its de facto segregated public schools, Ralph Bunche excelled at the university as a debater, although one society rejected his membership on the basis of his race. In one speech to the black community Bunche recommended that it raise a million dollars from its own resources to fight segregated swimming pools: hardly an appeal to a financially desperate community. "We have youth," said Bunche of his generation of young black people, "we have racial pride; we have indomitable will and boundless optimism for the future. We can't help but come out on top of the heap!" [28] In Bunche's case, this prediction rang true. Going on to Harvard for his doctorate, Bunche taught at Howard University before entering government service. In 1950 he won the Nobel Peace Prize for his work as principal secretary to the United Nations Palestine Commission. He later served as U.N. Under Secretary. High-minded, impeccably middle- (later upper-middle-) class, Ralph Bunche epitomized the prevailing prosperity of black Los Angeles in the 1920s, a community which, as Bunche himself noted as an undergraduate, seemed in the 1920s to be still voting Republican.

Thus the minority groups of 1920s Los Angeles, Asian, Hispanic, and black, struggled to materialize their dreams alongside the Folks. Not surprisingly, minority Los Angeles produced a number of Babbitts and Oligarchs as well. History must record the prejudice and discrimination on the part of white Los Angeles; but history must report shared aspirations between white and non-white centered on the desire for better employment, better schools, a better quality of life, sunshine, a bungalow and garden of one's own. The material dreams nurtured by Los Angeles fixed themselves in minority Americans with a conditioned, even constricted, intensity born of external rejection based on color—but it was an intensity nevertheless. Within the half-century, these communities, once rejected, would look around to discover that they were now the dominant people of the city.

USC, Electricity, Music, and Cops

The Emergence of Institutional Los Angeles

Ralph Bunche chose to attend the Southern Branch of the University of California, then still an extension of the main Berkeley campus in Northern California. Had he enrolled at the University of Southern California (USC) he would have encountered white Los Angeles in its most triumphant mode, probably to his personal distress. In the institutional life of the emerging city, two institutions, USC and the Department of Water and Power (DWP), fully expressed and served the ambitions of Anglo-American Los Angeles in its expansionist exuberance. Two other institutions, the Philharmonic Orchestra and the Los Angeles Police Department, expressed the high-minded aspirations and social realities of the burgeoning city. Each of these institutions attained a high level of autonomous power and authority as they emerged as arbiters and brokers of the Los Angeles identity.

Founded in 1880 as a Methodist institution, the Los Angeles-based University of Southern California developed through the 1920s with the rapidity of the city it served. The architect and demiurge behind this growth, the man who inextricably melded the fortunes of USC to the rise of Los Angeles, was its energetic president Rufus Bernhard von KleinSmid. Like Los Angeles itself, von KleinSmid was a Midwesterner who came up the hard way as a product of self-invention. Born in small-town Illinois in 1875, von KleinSmid graduated from the Academy of Oberlin College in Ohio in 1897 and became a certified country school teacher and superintendent for several years after graduation. Von KleinSmid read intensely during these obscure years and practiced his oratory on small-town audiences. In 1901 he traveled and studied in Europe. In 1905 at the age of 30 he finally completed a bachelor's degree at Northwestern, where he took an M.A. the next year. All his other degrees, including the doctorate which became a fixed component of his name (he was always Doctor, even if only Doctor K to USC undergraduates), were honorary.

Ten more obscure years followed, teaching education and psychology and working as a criminology consultant at De Pauw University in Greencastle, Indiana. In 1914, at age 39, Rufus B. von KleinSmid got his first big chance, an appointment to the presidency of the University of Arizona. Aside from giving him an honorary doctorate, Arizona offered von KleinSmid an opportunity to make a difference in an emerging environment. Admitted to statehood only in 1912, Arizona might be undeveloped and provincial, its university having only 203 regularly enrolled students, but von KleinSmid courted their parents and within a short time he had become the primary spokesman for the Arizona future and the dominant member of numerous public and private boards and associations. Skillfully, von KleinSmid keyed the rise of the provincial university he led to the rise of Arizona, making the two one in the minds of his constituency. By 1921 he found himself contemplating three offers of more important presidencies. He chose USC, where he was the second choice after a Methodist minister who refused the appointment because of its heavy obligations of public relations and fund raising, tasks which von KleinSmid relished. At USC the onetime country school superintendent, now forty-seven, at long last found an arena adequate to his ambitious and talents, as well as an official residence and an annual salary of $8500. A new American region was rising in Southern California, centered in an exuberant new American city. Serving this emergence, USC and von KleinSmid might prosper as well.

Only marginally a scholar by either instinct or practice, von KleinSmid understood growth primarily in terms of buildings and service programs keyed to the requirements of the developing infrastructure of Los Angeles and Southern California. The region needed businessmen, teachers, architects, engineers, doctors, dentists, lawyers, social workers, and civil servants, and USC geared up to provide them. Pure research, in which von KleinSmid had little interest, could wait. Looking back on the rise of USC in this era, USC graduate Carey McWilliams clearly isolated the obstacles von KleinSmid faced. There was little, if any, old money in Southern California and virtually no tradition of philanthropy. Having no endowment, von KleinSmid would have to support USC largely through tuition income, especially from the professional schools, while he sought major gifts. He would thus be forced to squeeze his faculty with heavy teaching loads and to de-emphasize research, which was of no immediate financial benefit. Such a program might create a physical plant and even an effective service organization, but could it create a distinguished university?

These, however, were long-range questions, to be asked, answered, and re-asked over the next half-century; in the interim von KleinSmid rolled up his sleeves and got to work. For his inauguration in April 1922, he arranged a pageant—a parade of robed academic delegates from the Pan-American Conference being held in Los Angeles, the granting of eight honorary degrees followed by his own ambitious address, "A World View of Education"—whose color and rhetoric glossed over the fact that USC had three permanent buildings, 4000 students, a disorganized array of affiliated but autonomous professional schools, and no money. Von KleinSmid's first drive, a $10 million community-wide campaign, flopped almost as soon as it began, despite the unprecedented prosperity of the Southland. After more than forty years as an inwardly focused Methodist institution, USC found it difficult to connect with a wider audience. Von KleinSmid thereupon turned to the cultivation of individual donors and football as sources of revenue.

Between 1921 and 1931 USC erected nine major buildings. The first professional school von KleinSmid turned his attention to was the College of Commerce and Business Administration, which he placed under the direction of Rockwell Hunt, a Johns Hopkins-trained professor of government and history with a gift for administration. Founded in 1920, the USC business school was already pioneering research and instruction in real estate. Business, Rockwell Hunt argued soon after taking the helm, was emerging as a profession alongside law, medicine, and engineering. Business education was therefore obligated to be at once practical and principled. The leaders of Los Angeles in the year 1940, Hunt predicted, would be graduates of the USC business school.

Along with business, von KleinSmid turned his attention to the law school, then virtually autonomous. Bringing it into the administrative structure of the university in 1923, von KleinSmid erected a new law school building in 1925. Three years later the school of engineering was reorganized and upgraded. To serve the huge educational enterprise of Los Angeles County—7,678 teachers teaching 246,897 students in 137 districts as of 1925—he reorganized the school of education in 1928, which soon became the largest professional school at USC.

That same year, 1928, USC opened a school of medicine in conjunction with the Los Angeles County General Hospital. By the 1930s the USC professional schools in law, education, medicine, and dentistry dominated their fields in Southern California. Only engineering, outdistanced by the California Institute of Technology in Pasadena, failed to achieve such dominance. Thus USC became the vehicle whereby an entire generation of Southern Californians realized its career aspirations. The payoffs to USC in loyalty and extended influence were enormous as the institution became increasingly identified among alumni and the general public with upward mobility and service to Los Angeles and the region.

As professional school-oriented as he was, von KleinSmid did not completely neglect more purely academic programs. He fostered the organization of a School of Religion, a Graduate School of Arts and Sciences, which brought the Ph.D. to the Southland, a School of Social Work, and a School of Architecture, the first in Southern California, created in conjunction with the Allied Architects

Association of Los Angeles. During this era USC pioneered instruction in cinematography, radio broadcasting, and print journalism. The cinematography program commenced in 1927 in conjunction with the newly organized Academy of Motion Picture Arts and Sciences. USC courses in film technology, scenario writing, and set design pioneered academic instruction in these subjects in the United States. Douglas Fairbanks, writer/publicist Frank Woods, producer Irving Thalberg, writer/director William C. de Mille, and others served as guest lecturers. On the level of a more traditional, even rarefied, academic pursuit, USC established a separate School of Philosophy, which in December 1929 moved into the newly completed Seeley Wintersmith Mudd Hall of Philosophy, an elegant Romanesque structure on University Avenue at Exposition Boulevard, across from the Los Angeles County Museum. Donated by the widow and son of Colonel Seeley Mudd in his honor, the school housed the James Harmon Hoose Library of Philosophy, endowed in honor of a longtime USC philosophy professor. That year, Dr. H. Wildon Carr of the University of London, an authority on the thought of Benedetto Croce and Henri Bergson, and Dr. F.C.S. Schiller of Corpus Christi College, Oxford, each accepted appointments to the school, the vanguard of innumerable British academics who would find employment in Southern California over the next five decades. Dean Ralph Tyler Flewelling, meanwhile, was editing *The Personalist*, a journal of philosophy and literature, while Carr planned a series of English translations of important European texts, to be called *The Southern California Classics*.

Despite this impressive record of activity—the buildings, the improved professional schools, even a separately established School of Philosophy—USC could still earn the contempt of such as journalist Victor Walkers, who observed of USC in the mid-1920s: "It is the darling of patriotic Angeleanos, and is exactly what the darling of such a race might be expected to be: large, sprawling, noisy and vulgar, and if it has any intellectual significance, that fact has not as yet become generally known, even to people living near it."[1] USC, Walkers was brutally suggesting, was a brainless, rah-rah sort of a place, a mere football school. He was being snobbish, of course, in the time-honored manner of intellectuals. But was he being fair? USC was not Harvard, to be sure, but was it as sprawling, noisy, and vulgar as Walkers charged?

The problem lay with football, in which von KleinSmid had found the solution to USC's financial problems. Supported by tuition, possessed of virtually no endowment (hardly more than $1 million by 1926) with which to finance its expansion, USC needed money. Football offered a solution. In 1919 USC hired a new coach, Elmer C. Henderson, and sought admission to the Pacific Coast Conference. USC football began to develop a following. A thirty-piece USC student band played on the docks in the fall of 1921 as the *Yale* set sail for San Francisco, packed with USC rooters heading north to Berkeley for the big game with California. Twenty-five thousand attended this UC-USC contest. In 1921 USC gained admission to the Pacific Coast Conference. When the USC Trojans went to the Rose Bowl in 1922, defeating Penn State, von KleinSmid authorized a $1000 bonus to Coach Henderson. Overnight, USC had developed a Los Angeles constituency of football fans willing to flock to USC games.

The collegiate culture of USC became increasingly more football-oriented. With no money to build dormitories, von KleinSmid encouraged the presence of Greek letter fraternities and sororities as a housing alternative. These organizations soon dominated undergraduate life, creating at USC a rah-rah atmosphere energized by crosscurrents of restrictive Babbittry and contempt for people and values outside the WASP mainstream. Unfortunately, admission and academic standards for football players fell in direct proportion to USC's rise as a football power.

In 1924 USC suffered the humiliation of being asked to leave the Pacific Coast Conference because of its lax scholastic standards, a disinvitation made infinitely more humiliating by the fact that it was first announced before 60,000 fans at the 1924 UC-USC game in Berkeley, which USC lost 7-0. An angered von KleinSmid retaliated by seeking games with the biggest drawing football team in the United States, Notre Dame, another upwardly mobile, religiously affiliated school for whom football was proving a cash cow. Significantly, Notre Dame had also been excluded from its football conference. Under a new coach, Howard Jones, one of the greatest coaches in American football history, USC began playing Notre Dame in 1926. The first game sold out the Coliseum. The 1927 game, held in Soldier Field, Chicago, attracted 120,000, the largest single crowd thus far to gather for an intercollegiate football game.

Throughout Jones's tenure at USC, 1925 to 1940, gigantic crowds gathered to cheer on the Thundering Herd, as the team became known. In 1929, 123,000 attended the USC game with Notre Dame. When USC defeated Notre Dame with a last-minute field goal in 1931, a crowd of 300,000, one-third the population of Los Angeles, greeted the returning USC team at the train station.

Thus von KleinSmid secured money for his buildings. USC acquired its plant. Academic excellence, for both USC and its arch-rival Notre Dame, would have to come later. In the meanwhile Los Angeles possessed in the Thundering Herd of the USC Trojans a perfect reflection of its own brassy ambition thrusting itself onto the national scene: a little noisy and vulgar perhaps, as USC critic Victor Walkers had charged; but, then again, fastidious intellectuals could not expect to feel at home in the demotic spectacle of self-assertion that was USC football.

2

Like USC, the Department of Water and Power (DWP) grew by serving the rise of the region. Political power in Los Angeles ran in two streams, elective and appointive. Throughout the 1920s, from 1921 to 1929, George E. Cryer, a Woodrow Wilson lookalike, served as mayor. Cryer's administration was orchestrated by former USC football star Kent Kane Parrot, a USC-trained lawyer who established a USC old boys' network that constituted the basic political machine of Los Angeles in the 1920s. Survivors of the prewar Progressive movement, meanwhile, men such as Dr. John R. Haynes, Meyer Lissner, and Marshall Stimson, reconsolidated themselves around DWP, which the charter reforms of 1924 established as a powerful force in local government, presided over by a largely autonomous commission. As DWP commissioners, the Progressives could continue to wield influence at one or two levels of removal from the day to day dealings and compromises at City Hall. Mayor Cryer and his USC lawyers held one kind of power; the commissioners of the DWP, another. The Los Angeles business establishment as symbolized in the Chamber of Commerce, the Merchants and Manufacturers Association, and the Associated Jobbers joined this DWP alliance, although DWP's efforts to displace altogether the privately owned Los Angeles Gas and Electric Corporation, which was holding on to its franchises, caused rifts between DWP supporters such as William Randolph Hearst, a longtime advocate of public power, and Harry Chandler, who favored public water but competitive private electricity. The fact is, DWP was delivering what Los Angeles needed, water and electricity, and from this service it derived enormous political power. Within DWP, moreover, there flourished an influential employees' organization which campaigned effectively along with police, fire, and other municipal departments for a series of bond issues throughout the 1920s and could field thousands of precinct workers on behalf of candidates it favored.

If political power in Los Angeles ran in a divided stream, elective and appointive, power within DWP also ran in two streams, water and hydroelectricity, each of them directed by a powerful civil servant. The legendary William Mulholland, not yet broken by the St. Francis Dam disaster of 1928, ran water affairs, while Ezra F. Scattergood presided over hydroelectricity. Trained at Rutgers and Cornell in mechanical and electrical engineering, Scattergood migrated to Los Angeles in the early 1900s after resigning a professorship at the University of Georgia in search of a better climate for his precarious health. He began his Los Angeles career as an outdoor construction worker. After regaining his strength, Scattergood went into private practice. In 1909 he became chief electrical engineer on the aqueduct under Mulholland. Over the next decade and a half, Scattergood worked to build the Los Angeles Municipal Bureau of Power and Light into the dominant source of electricity for Los Angeles.

Initially, hydroelectricity was an afterthought, a byproduct, in comparison with water. Not until 1916 did hydroelectricity from the Owens Valley aqueduct reach Los Angeles, and then only a few thousand customers were served. By 1925, however, Scattergood was presiding over a 3000-employee organiza-

tion serving 200,000 individual consumers and most major Los Angeles industries via the largest municipally owned electrical generation and distribution
system in the world. In 1925 Power and Light produced $2.6 million in surplus
earnings on gross revenues of $9.9 million, more than enough to serve bonded
indebtedness and to enlarge the system. What the Bureau of Power and Light
could not provide Los Angeles was subcontracted to Southern California Edison. So rapid was expansion in the mid-1920s, it took three organizations working together—the Bureau of Power and Light, Southern California Edison, and
the Los Angeles Gas and Electric Corporation—to meet the electrical needs of
the Los Angeles basin. Southern California Edison sank $55 million into the
new power plants between 1923 and 1925. Los Angeles Gas and Electric spent
$14 million on a new steam generating plant at Seal Beach and on other im-
provements. In all this expansion the Bureau of Power and Light led the way.
Like the Lindbergh Light atop the newly dedicated City Hall, claimed a 1928
advertisement, Power and Light had illumed the progress of Los Angeles to its
future. "The Municipal Bureau of Power and Light is the beacon light of the
long established plan of Los Angeles people," the advertisement stated. "There
shall be no jeopardizing this factor of prosperity. Anything less than full support
of the City's water and electric investment by any citizen is disloyalty to the
deliberately established policy and purpose of Los Angeles."[2] Public power thus
asserted itself as more than a voter preference. It was a dogma demanding
assent. Anything less constituted heresy.

The magical power of hydroelectricity made such quasi-religious language
plausible. Nighttime Los Angeles had become a wonderland of light. From
atop Mount Lowe one beheld Los Angeles, Pasadena, and fifty-six contiguous
cities and suburbs spread out in a vast sea of illumination. In sheer extent, the
horizontal equivalent of vertical New York, there was no other spectacle like it
in the United States. "There was, at that distance," recalled Louis Adamic of
the view from the Hollywood Hills, where he served on fire watch, "something
vaguely fascinating, beautiful almost, in that confusion of lights, in those flash-
ing signs and advertisements, in those streams and rivulets of motor headlights
on the boulevards; a rhythm in the distant roar of the city as it reached my
ears; and down at San Pedro harbor, the battleships had frequent searchlight
drills, making the sky to the south gay and fantastic with long slender shafts of
white light."[3]

All this growth, so beautiful by night, required increasing amounts of water
and power. This meant more dams, aqueducts, and hydroelectric stations. With
the limitations of the Owens Valley aqueduct already asserting themselves by
the mid-1920s, the water interests of Los Angeles turned increasingly in the
direction of the river giant of the Southwest, the mighty Colorado. In 1919 a
Southern California-dominated delegation headed by Imperial Irrigation District counsel Phil Swing, formerly district attorney of Imperial County, successfully persuaded the Bureau of Reclamation to look into the matter of flood

control on the Colorado and the construction of a major canal on American territory. Issued in 1922, the Reclamation report recommended the construction of a 550-foot-high dam across the Colorado River at Boulder Canyon between Nevada and Arizona, together with the construction of a new irrigation canal into the Imperial and Coachella valleys entirely on United States territory. The dam at Boulder Canyon would exercise flood control on the lower Colorado River and would create reservoirs capable of irrigating 1.24 million presently arid acres in Southern California and the Southwest. It would also provide a million horsepower of hydroelectricity, which Reclamation could sell to public and private power companies as a means of financing the project.

The bill making Boulder Dam possible was first introduced into Congress in April 1922, and originated in the California delegation, cosponsored by Representative Phil Swing, representing Imperial Valley, and Hiram Johnson in the Senate. Six years of setbacks and maneuverings lay ahead, but Swing and Johnson, and hence Southern California, never lost control of the bill.

William Mulholland, meanwhile, chief engineer of the Municipal Water Bureau of Los Angeles, was seizing the initiative on the home front. As soon as the Reclamation proposal for Boulder Dam had been made in 1922, Mulholland and his allies among the water interests began organizing a bond issue to finance a feasibility study as to how Los Angeles could obtain water and hydroelectricity from the Colorado. When the bond issue passed, Mulholland, then nearing seventy, set forth on an expedition with a small party of engineers down the lower Colorado by rowboat and made a rapid survey of the terrain in late October and November of 1923, a recapitulation of that buckboard-and-whiskey journey out to Owens Valley with Fred Eaton in August 1904. This time, the scale of what was being envisioned had increased by fourfold. Flowing at 400 second-feet, the Owens River served two million people. With a 1500 second-feet capacity, the Colorado River could provide water for 7.5 million. Over the next four years Mulholland sent sixteen survey parties into the rugged desert and mountain region bounded by Boulder Canyon, the Colorado River, lower California, and the Southern California coast seeking the best route for an aqueduct. Survey studies and route alternatives were posted on a huge topographical map at Water and Power headquarters at 207 South Broadway. When these surveys were complete, one route had emerged as superior. From a downstream storage site at Parker, Arizona, the 242-mile aqueduct would cross the desert, then proceed via tunnels through the San Jacinto Mountains to a storage basin in Riverside County. From this point, gravity would distribute the water to Los Angeles and other Southern California cities. Remarkably, this route recapitulated the one sketched out by Mulholland when he returned from his preliminary survey in November 1923.

Even as Los Angeles planned this massive appropriation of the Colorado, its Owens Valley aqueduct, in service for a decade, was running into serious difficulties. Since Los Angeles, meaning William Mulholland, had refused to pay Fred Eaton $1 million for his Long Valley Property, there was no reservoir in the Owens Valley; hence water could not be stored for local needs. The Los Angeles Aqueduct merely transferred the Owens River from the Owens Valley to the San Fernando Valley 255 miles away. By the summer of 1923, after a long dry spell, the voracious needs of San Fernando Valley farmers used up the aqueduct's resources. A mere ten years into its existence—an existence that began with an eightfold surplus—the aqueduct could no longer serve, simultaneously, urban Los Angeles and the agricultural empire that had been annexed in San Fernando Valley. And so Mulholland, temporarily halting irrigation of the San Fernando, went to work expanding the water sources of Los Angeles in the Owens Valley. Wells were dug and water rights purchased from farmers upriver from the Intake Point.

When farmers in the Big Pine area sold the water rights of their upriver Big Pine Canal to Los Angeles for $1.1 million, other farmers, anxious for a comparable windfall, began to divert Owens River water heading towards the Intake Point into their own canals so as to force Los Angeles into another major purchase. When a delegation of San Fernando Valley farmers, their acres parched, their livelihoods disappearing, met with the Owens Valley leadership, they were startled by a frank offer: Los Angeles could buy the entire upper Owens Valley for $8 million. As tempting as it is to cast this conflict in chiaroscuro shadings of imperial Los Angeles versus yeoman farmers, most Owens Valley farmers, led by the banker brothers Wilfred and Mark Watterson, preferred a windfall over a lifetime of toil. Long since out-maneuvered by Los Angeles and the pro-Los Angeles policies of Washington, they understandably wanted out on favorable terms.

When Los Angeles resisted these demands for a buyout, California's so-called Little Civil War ensued. An hour after midnight on 21 May 1924, forty or more Owens Valley residents dynamited the aqueduct a few miles north of Lone Pine. When a buy-out offer was still not forthcoming from Los Angeles, an automobile caravan of one hundred Owens Valley farmers and townspeople, led by banker Mark Watterson, seized the aqueduct at the Alabama Gates near Lone Pine on 16 November and with the help of a renegade employee shut off the aqueduct and diverted the water back into the parched bed of the long-dry Owens River. In the four days that followed, the crowd grew to 1500 and the occasion became a mixture of folk festival, social protest, and Cataline conspiracy. A tent city sprung up. By day there were speeches; by night, hymns and songfests around the campfire. Cowboy star Tom Mix, on location in the area, sent over a mariachi band. Hastily printed signs sprung up at various worksites: "If I am not on the job, you can find me at the Aqueduct." Banker Wilfred Watterson went down to Los Angeles to promote the sale of the entire Owens Valley irrigation district. When the talks proved tentatively successful, the occupation was called off on the fourth day, and the diversion gates were lowered, returning the Owens River into the aqueduct. A giant barbecue was held in celebration. Even the sheriff attended.

At first, it looked as if Los Angeles would be willing to pay $2.5 million to purchase all water rights held by the district. When negotiations broke down six months later over the matter of reparation payments, the dynamiting resumed and Los Angeles moved a hundred armed men into the valley to patrol the aqueduct. The guards also placed the Owens Valley under a species of informal and illegal martial law. Despite these precautions—armed patrols, searches of suspicious vehicles, monitoring of local leadership—dynamiters successfully struck the aqueduct ten times within the next two months. What Los Angeles could not suppress in the field, it could checkmate through the more sophisticated means of arranging an audit of the Wattersons' books by the state banking commissioner on charges that bank funds were being used to finance the dynamiting. When the audit revealed an $800,000 shortage, the residents of the Owens Valley, led so long in their resistance by the banker brothers, became stunned and confused. When the five Inyo County banks owned by the Wattersons failed, ruining many Owens Valley residents, and the brothers were themselves convicted of embezzlement and sent to San Quentin for six years, effective resistance to Los Angeles collapsed.

The following year, Los Angeles voters authorized a $12 million bond issue to buy out the Owens Valley once and for all. At long last, Los Angeles was able to purchase the Long Valley site from Fred Eaton, who had been bankrupted by the bank failures brought on by the embezzlements of the Wattersons. In 1941 Long Valley was successfully dammed and the reservoir thus created was named in honor of Father John Crowley, a local Roman Catholic priest who had played an important role in the revitalization of the valley as a tourist and recreation center for Los Angeles. Had the Long Valley reservoir come on line in 1913 when it could have, the Owens Valley might have survived as an agricultural community.

The dynamiting of the aqueduct and the diversion at the Alabama Gates reinforced the determination of the public water and power lobby of Los Angeles not only to stabilize its interests in Owens Valley but to push forward as well on the Colorado River project. The troubles at Owens Valley, compounded by a shortfall in Sierra runoff, caused a severe shortage of electricity in Los Angeles in the summer of 1924. Industrial, agricultural, streetcar, and public lighting uses had to be curtailed by 25 percent. Only hydroelectricity from Boulder Dam, Ezra Scattergood of Power and Light announced, could answer the present and long-term needs of the expanding city. As if to confirm Scattergood's assessment, the next year the Department of the Interior increased the hydroelectric component of the 1922 Boulder Dam proposal as a way of helping the project pay for itself. At the height of the Owens Valley crisis, on 28 July 1924, William Mulholland dramatically filed on behalf of Los Angeles a request with the state Bureau of Water Rights asking permission to divert 1500 second-feet of Colorado River water into Southern California.

Throughout the 1920s public and private Los Angeles power interests battled among themselves as to who should control Boulder Dam water and hydro-electricity if and when it arrived. Each group had applications on file in Washington. Public water and power advocates—the Progressive commissioners, Mulholland, Scattergood, the bureaucracies each controlled, and Mayor George E. Cryer—organized themselves as the Public Power League. Private power advocates—Southern California Edison, Los Angeles Gas and Electric, bankers and corporate attorneys such as Marco and Maurice Hellman and H.W. O'Melveny, developer J.B. Van Nuys, the controlling group at the Chamber of Commerce—joined the battle as the People's Economy League. Harry Chandler and his syndicate of San Fernando Valley investors held vast tracts across the border in Lower California, planted in cotton and conveniently irrigated by the Imperial Canal running through Mexico. Since the proposed All-American Canal north of the border posed a direct threat to these interests, Chandler resisted the Boulder project altogether, engaging in constant warfare with Hearst's *Examiner* on this issue. After some early defeats, public power advocates won a majority of positions, including mayor, in the municipal election of 1924. In January 1925 Los Angeles state senators A.B. Johnson and Ralph E. Swing, Phil Swing's brother, introduced a bill in the legislature authorizing the creation of a Metropolitan Water District (MWD) among Los Angeles, Beverly Hills, Burbank, Glendale, Pasadena, Santa Monica, San Marino, San Bernardino, Colton, Anaheim, and Santa Ana, which would be responsible for the financing and construction of the Colorado Aqueduct. The bill failed in the legislature but was overwhelmingly passed in referendums held in these cities. In 1927 a second bill passed. Southern California now possessed the super-agency necessary to embark upon the construction of a Colorado Aqueduct, once Congress approved the Swing-Johnson bill and the Bureau of Reclamation could build the Boulder Dam. The MWD eventually became one of the largest non-federal governmental agencies in the United States.

William Mulholland had by this time made a number of trips to Washington to testify on behalf of the second Swing-Johnson bill. In his testimony, Mulholland emphasized the hydroelectric potential of the Colorado River, once it was harnessed at Boulder. "The Colorado River," he stated, "is wasting more power today than the greatest oil field in California is producing."[4] Reaching seventy in September 1925, Mulholland had begun to dream that perhaps he, already past retirement age, might be called upon to direct, or at least guide through its preliminary stages, this final great water project on behalf of Los Angeles. Throughout 1925, 1926, and 1927 he continued to testify on behalf of the Boulder Dam project as it wended its way tortuously through the Congress. Tragically, Mulholland was not on hand on 21 December 1928 when President Coolidge signed the bill. By then, the chief had retired from his position and from his hopes, a shattered man.

In 1926, very discreetly, so as not to provoke another Owens Valley controversy, the Los Angeles Department of Water and Power built a dam and reservoir in the remote San Francisquito Canyon north of Los Angeles. Sited and designed by William Mulholland, the St. Francis Dam, as it was called, was intended as a backup reservoir for the hydroelectrical power houses of the aqueduct system and as further protection against a recurrence of the drought years that had driven Mulholland further and further up the Owens River in the early 1920s. The St. Francis reservoir, in short, was a substitute for the reservoir that should have been built at Long Valley. Unfortunately, the dam, as subsequent investigations determined, was located on unstable geological foundations. On 12 March 1928, three minutes before midnight, its reservoir filled to capacity, the St. Francis Dam experienced a sudden, total, catastrophic collapse. Within minutes, a wall of water sixty to a hundred feet high was roaring down the Santa Clara Valley in Ventura County towards the Pacific Ocean. It took five and a half hours for the torrent created by 38,000 acre-feet of water leaving the reservoir in less than 70 minutes to travel its 55-mile course to the sea. As the flood cascaded westward through Castaic Junction, Camulos, Piru, Fillmore—smashing power houses and towns, uprooting orchards and citrus groves, absorbing into its mass tons of topsoil and debris—it raged like a surreal monster down across the fertile fields of the Santa Clara Valley of the south. By dawn, when the horror was over, between 400 and 450 Southern Californians lay dead from drowning, suffocation, or traumatic injury. It took weeks to recover 319 bodies (over a hundred of the reported missing were never found), and it took months for a work force of 2000 men hired by Los Angeles to clean up the devastation left behind.

On the very day of the disaster, Mulholland had been summoned to the dam to examine some leakage, which he determined to be routine. In less than 24 hours, he was there again, standing in shock before the twisted concrete fragments that forlornly fronted an empty reservoir. It did not take much imagination to see in the still-standing central portion of the dam a gravestone on the floor of a mud-strewn valley. Buried beneath it were as many as 450 men, women, and children, together with what remained of Mulholland's life. Founder of the city, hailed as the Goethals of the West, doctor of engineering (honoris causa) from the University of California, builder of the aqueduct, designer of thirteen successful dams and one that had proved less than successful, Mulholland said that, as of that moment, he envied the dead.

While it resisted the settlers of the Owens Valley, Los Angeles accepted full responsibility for the St. Francis Dam disaster. The city spent $13.5 million removing debris, rebuilding homes, barns, fences, roads, bridges, and power houses, restringing telephone wires, laying new railroad tracks, refurbishing schools and libraries. Another $5 million was paid out in death and disability claims. The fact that virtually all these reparations were accepted voluntarily by Los Angeles and were adjudicated and administered outside the court system by a Joint Restoration Committee of delegates from Los Angeles and Ventura County testified to the level of Los Angeles's acceptance of its responsibility.

Just as the glory of the aqueduct had settled on Mulholland in 1913, its shame now settled with equal force on his 72-year-old shoulders. Tears came into his eyes as he testified before the coroner's jury. Privately, Mulholland suspected sabotage by Owens Valley diehards. Publicly, he assumed all responsibility. He had selected the site and designed the dam. The jury agreed: Mulholland was responsible. Ignoring warnings regarding the possible instability of the site, the chief had succumbed to the worst traits of the auto-didact: a self-assertion edging into arrogance, a hostility to experts approaching culpable negligence. And yet, the coroner's jury did not recommend criminal proceedings against the founder. Los Angeles had also profited from these very same traits in the chief. Los Angeles had granted Mulholland the very power that had resulted in the disaster. In selecting the site of the St. Francis Dam, Mulholland might have been acting alone, but he had long since come to think of himself as equal to the city he served, and Los Angeles had long since come to think of itself in terms of Mulholland. "The construction and operation of a great dam," the coroner's verdict stated laconically, "should never be left to the sole judgment of one man, no matter how eminent."[5]

3

Slightly before 3:30 on the afternoon of Friday, 24 October 1919, a gong sounded and ninety musicians in white tie seated themselves on the stage of the Trinity Auditorium in Los Angeles before a capacity audience of 2400. After a hasty summer of organization and rehearsal, the newly founded Philharmonic Orchestra of Los Angeles was giving its first concert under the direction of Maestro Walter Henry Rothwell. The program selected by Rothwell for this first concert—Dvořák's *New World Symphony*, Weber's Overture to *Oberon*, *Les Preludes* of Liszt, the *España Rhapsody* of Chabrier—did not tax the musical capacities of his audience; but the London-born, Vienna-educated conductor had correctly judged both the occasion of this ceremonial inauguration and the capacities of his audience. Rothwell further protected himself with the policy that this and following concerts should never exceed an hour and forty-five minutes. At the conclusion of the program, the audience thundered its applause, at once for the music and for the fact that Los Angeles now possessed a fully endowed and staffed orchestra, a Minerva sprung to life full-grown, the *Examiner* reported, organized, staffed, and rehearsed in four short months. As the audience applauded endlessly, ushers banked the stage with floral tributes, including a gigantic horseshoe sent jointly by the orchestras of Boston, Philadelphia, New York, Cincinnati, St. Louis, Minneapolis, and San Francisco, into whose symphonic company Los Angeles now entered. Maestro Rothwell seemed especially pleased by this tribute from other orchestras.

In the audience that afternoon sat the founder himself, William Andrews Clark, Jr., the Montana-born mining heir, bibliophile, and patron of the arts who had endowed the orchestra that June with an initial gift of $200,000 and the guarantee of $150,000 annually for the first five years of its existence. By 1924 Clark would have spent a million dollars on behalf of the Los Angeles Philharmonic. Educated in law at the University of Virginia, Clark studied violin in Paris at the turn of the century before returning to Montana where he joined his father, a copper baron and United States senator, in expanding and consolidating even further the extensive Clark family interests. Already, however, the young heir was envisioning another career for himself as collector and patron. He also chose another place to live, Los Angeles. Arriving there in 1908 at age 31, William Andrews Clark, Jr., joined Henry and Arabella Huntington in bringing to the still provincial city the full spirit of the American Renaissance: that combination of means, connoisseurship, and patronage which in the 1890 to 1915 era established or consolidated the major cultural and philanthropic institutions of the United States. At his mansion on West Adams Boulevard, a de facto library building designed by Robert Farquhar with a storage capacity for forty thousand volumes, Clark assembled a major collection of British literary books and manuscripts, with an emphasis upon the works of the poet John Dryden. In this effort he was assisted by the bibliophile and bibliographer Robert Ernest Cowan, whom Clark installed in a nearby home as his personal advisor and librarian. A man of many interests—manuscripts, books, wine, cooking, boxing, sumo wrestling—Clark determined in early 1919, which was in so many other respects as well a take-off year for Los Angeles, to establish a philharmonic orchestra.

As conductor, Clark chose Walter Henry Rothwell, an Anglo-Austrian teacher and freelance conductor based in New York. Then forty-eight, Rothwell had trained in piano and conducting at the Royal Academy of Music in Vienna, then pursued a career as a concert pianist before devoting his full energies to conducting as a protégé of Gustav Mahler. Active with the operas of Amsterdam and Frankfurt, Rothwell made his first tour of the United States in 1905. A few years later he accepted a position at St. Paul. When the war forced the St. Paul Symphony to suspend concerts, Rothwell moved to New York where he was flourishing as a teacher and guest conductor when Clark first interviewed him for Los Angeles.

Rothwell spent the summer of 1919 in New York interviewing and recruiting musicians. The war had displaced a number of fine musicians from Europe, and Rothwell had little trouble recruiting. As concertmaster, he selected Sylvain Noack of the Boston Symphony. By 13 October, Rothwell was holding his first full rehearsal in Los Angeles. In later rehearsals William Andrews

Clark, Jr., sat in occasionally as second violin. Delighted with the energy and resourcefulness of his maestro, Clark presented Rothwell with an autographed manuscript of a Mozart mass and later, at the completion of the first season, a jeweled ebony and ivory baton in a gold case.

As impressive as all this might be, it did not represent the arrival of serious music in Los Angeles. At the very time Rothwell was organizing, Los Angeles already had a symphony orchestra, the financially strapped Los Angeles Symphony, two-thirds the size of the Philharmonic, staffed by part-time musicians who made their livings as teachers and providers of background music at local hotels and restaurants. In the late 1880s amateur orchestras had been formed under the sponsorship of the YMCA, the First Congregational Church, and the Philharmonics, a musical society whose honorary chair was none other than retired Major General John Charles Frémont. A Women's Symphony Orchestra was organized in 1893 and began to offer public programs. A local musician, A.J. Stamm, assembled a small private orchestra in the mid-1890s and began a series of concerts that emphasized light classics and occasionally more ambitious music. In 1898 Stamm's former concertmaster, Harley Hamilton, established the Los Angeles Symphony, with the painter/violinist J. Bond Francisco serving as concertmaster. Only New York, St. Louis, Boston, Chicago, and Cincinnati preceded Los Angeles in the establishment of such an orchestra. Lurching financially from season to season, six to eight programs a year, the Los Angeles Symphony brought symphonic music to Southern California at a credible level of performance, given the fact that musicians were paid from event to event and enjoyed only a minimum of rehearsal time. When Clark announced his endowment in June 1919, Adolph Tandler, director of the Los Angeles Symphony, offered to merge his organization with the new Philharmonic, but Clark preferred to proceed with an entirely new structure. When the Los Angeles Symphony folded the next year, the Philharmonic acquired some of its best musicians.

Clark also acquired the services of Lynden Ellsworth Behymer, the longtime Los Angeles Symphony business agent, as general manager. In linking Behymer to the new symphony orchestra, Clark was grafting his organization onto the impresarial rootstock of the region. For nearly thirty years, L.E. Behymer had functioned as the first demiurge and impresario of the performing arts in the Southland. Driven from the Dakota Territory to Los Angeles in 1886 when a cyclone destroyed his general store, Behymer, a native Ohioan of Dutch descent, went to work as a bookseller at Stoll & Thayer, book dealers and stationers. In the evenings he read the books in his store or scalped tickets at the Grand Opera House. He later went to work for the opera house as a sales agent and for the *Herald* as an unpaid book reviewer. By the mid-1890s Behymer was beginning, tentatively, to book acts as impresario, a career he continued to expand after becoming manager of both the Women's Symphony and the Los Angeles Symphony in 1900.

It is improbable that a self-educated country boy, a Midwestern storekeeper turned Southern Californian promoter, possessed of no musical education or experience of Europe or New York, should make the transition from ticket scalper to serious impresario; but that is exactly what Behymer accomplished. As an example of self-instructed, self-invented aspiration, of limitations seeking release through the performing arts, Behymer perfectly reflected the city he served. In securing Behymer's services in 1919 for the newly established Los Angeles Philharmonic, William Andrews Clark acquired Behymer's experience and European connections, but he also wanted the impresario's commitment to developing a local audience.

From the start serious music in Los Angeles had a populist bent which it never lost. The day after the Philharmonic made its debut at Trinity Auditorium, Clark and Behymer offered a Sunday afternoon concert of even more accessible music at ticket prices beginning at twenty-five cents. A month later, the orchestra inaugurated a series of special concerts for school children and began performing at Los Angeles high schools. Clark later sponsored a series of outdoor concerts with tickets priced at ten, twenty-five, and fifty cents. For Easter 1920, at the request of the Hollywood Bowl Association, Clark underwrote a performance of the orchestra at a sunrise service held on Olive Hill in Barnsdall Park, Hollywood. Ten thousand people gathered to hear the orchestra greet the sunrise with the decidedly non-Christian but nevertheless stirring "Entrance of the Gods into Valhalla," followed by a concert of sacred music with a massed community choir. For Easter 1921 the orchestra was on hand in the Hollywood Bowl itself, greeting the dawn this time with the more appropriate Grail music from "Parisfal," Sibelius's "Finlandia," and a choral concert of religious music with the Hollywood Community Chorus.

As an institution, the Hollywood Bowl underscored the popular, pageantesque direction serious music was taking in Los Angeles: the result, in part, of fine weather and a dramatic outdoor setting, but arising as well from the role music was playing in the creation of community feeling and identity. In a city and region of people from elsewhere, with few highly developed civic institutions, music and music-related pageantry, including the continuing vitality of choral music in the churches, provided an important bond among people struggling to reassert themselves in new surroundings. Nowhere was this more true than at the Hollywood Bowl.

In May 1916 Shakespeare's *Julius Caesar* was successfully staged in Beachwood Canyon in the Hollywood Hills to commemorate the tercentenary of the Bard's death. A cast of three thousand, which included Tyrone Power, Sr., Douglas Fairbanks, Jr., and the student bodies of Hollywood and Fairfax high schools as opposing armies, played before a crowd estimated at forty thousand. Two years later the Theosophical Society successfully performed Sir Edwin Arnold's *Light of Asia* pageant in a similar setting.

Stimulated by the success of these outdoor performances, including the sense of community they fostered, a group of civic activists formally organized itself as the Theater Arts Alliance in May 1919 and began to promote the idea of a permanently established outdoor theater and arts center in the Hollywood Hills. Christine Wetherill Stevenson, one of the organizers of the *Light of Asia* event, was elected president. Charged by the Alliance with scouting a suitable site, actor H. Ellis Reed, another *Light of Asia* veteran, roamed the Hollywood Hills until he discovered Daisy Dell, a sage- and chaparral-covered natural amphitheater with excellent acoustics west of Highland Avenue. With the help of C.E. Toberman, a theatrically minded land developer who for some time had been promoting the idea of an Oberammergau-style religious pageant in the Hollywood Hills, options were secured on the Daisy Dell site, which was owned by Myra Hershey, proprietress of the Hollywood Hotel, and two adjacent properties, for a total of sixty acres. Christine Stevenson and another wealthy patron, Mrs. Chauncey D. Clarke, donated $21,000 each towards the $47,500 purchase price. The Theater Arts Alliance then fell apart on the issue of how exactly to employ the property. Mrs. Stevenson and her clique wanted an emphasis upon religious plays; the others, an emphasis upon cultural programs. As a result of the dispute, the Alliance was dissolved and reorganized in October 1920 as the Community Park and Art Association. Reimbursed for her portion of the purchase price, Stevenson purchased the twenty-nine-acre Cahuenga Canyon east of Daisy Dell, terrain she believed closely resembled the Holy Land. There, beginning in 1920, she sponsored an annual Pilgrimage Play based on the life of Christ, employing clothing and props which she personally selected and imported from Palestine.

Ironically, given the dispute that had broken up the first organization, it was a religious event, the Los Angeles Philharmonic's Easter sunrise service of 1921, which first fully dramatized the possibilities of Daisy Dell as a site for community gatherings energized by music. Mrs. Artie Mason Carter, president of the Community Sing of Hollywood, a choral group organized in 1917 as a wartime morale-builder, spearheaded this inaugural event. Its success led the young music teacher and physician's wife, who had herself studied music in Vienna before her marriage, to promote a series of summertime concerts at the Hollywood Bowl Park by the Los Angeles Philharmonic, which William Andrews Clark, Jr., agreed to sponsor. Mrs. Carter showed further strength as a fundraiser. Under her leadership, enough money was raised from private sources to prepare the amphitheater with staging, lighting, and benches. On the evening of 11 July 1922 bewhiskered guest conductor Alfred Hertz stepped before the Los Angeles Philharmonic Orchestra, and, with Wagner's overture to "Rienzi," the Symphonies Under the Stars series was launched. In 1924 the Hollywood Bowl Association, with Mrs. Carter as president, replaced the earlier Community Park and Art Association.

The Bowl site, by then completely paid for, was donated to the County of Los Angeles. More than 250,000 people attended Bowl concerts in the summer of 1924, paying as little as twenty-five cents a ticket. In 1925 the County Board of Supervisors voted $100,000 to the Bowl Association for improvements. Allied Architects of Los Angeles prepared an extensive series of architectural and site enhancements, which were capped in 1929 when the new Bowl president Allan C. Balch (Mrs. Carter resigned in 1926 when the board of directors refused her sole authority over programming) donated a soaring white all-steel performance shell designed by Lloyd Wright. It soon became the most prominent landmark in Southern California.

By that time, musical luminaries such as Bruno Walter of Berlin, Pierre Monteux of Amsterdam, Sir Henry Wood of London, and Walter Henry Rothwell of Los Angeles (before his much too early death in 1927) had each conducted the Los Angeles Philharmonic under the stars before mass audiences, which were themselves a new phenomenon in serious music. The success of the Hollywood Bowl concerts expressed an experiment in the democratization of taste that went beyond the low ticket price. Festive, persistently evangelical in its links to religion (a massed choir of a thousand sang a requiem for Woodrow Wilson in 1924), vigorously popularizing, the Hollywood Bowl perfectly reflected the city and region it served. Even at twenty-five cents a ticket, the Bowl attracted crowds large enough to cover its operating expenses. With the donation of the Bowl to Los Angeles County and the ensuing allocation of public funds for its improvement, the Bowl became an established component of the popular culture of the region.

The Los Angeles Philharmonic, by contrast, depended solely upon William Andrews Clark, Jr., its sole guarantor until Clark's death in 1934; nor was the support of the ninety-musician orchestra, by agreement one of the best in the nation, all that overwhelming. In 1920 Clark secured a long-term lease at the spacious Clune Auditorium at the corner of Fifth and Olive streets, which he improved considerably. By 1926 Clark had spent $1.7 million on the orchestra. The Philharmonic Auditorium, however, was a difficult house to fill. By 1926 many of the Philharmonic's eighty-one season concerts were taking place before an embarrassing array of empty seats, despite the subsidized tickets and the universally recognized excellence of the performances. By November 1927 fourteen hundred season tickets for the Thursday evening concerts, with prices starting as low as $6 for a season ticket, remained unsold. Boosters found this lack of support disturbing. The Philharmonic, argued the *Los Angeles Realtor*, brought people of wealth and refinement to Los Angeles, which was good for the real estate industry; "yet hundreds of seats remain vacant at each concert, because the support Mr. Clark is entitled to from our citizens is denied him, while indifference and apathy reign."[6] Clark's orchestra thus ran ahead of Los Angeles's taste and capacity for support. No matter: the Los Angeles Philharmonic was organized and functioning. Within a few short decades, it would achieve the status of a fully supported world-class orchestra—just about the time Los Angeles became a world-class city.

4

Like USC, the Department of Water and Power, and the Los Angeles Philharmonic Orchestra, the Los Angeles Police Department also enjoyed a lively and locally relevant institutional identity. It was, after all, the bootlegger era. The intricate Southern California coast provided innumerable hidden coves for ships from Canada, allegedly en route to Mexico, to offload their cargoes of whiskey and gin stealthily by night for shipment by truck to the city. By 1926 the Los Angeles *Times* was estimating that smuggling of liquor from Canada had become one of California's leading industries. Hijacking of smuggled cargoes became in itself a subsidiary industry. One fabled cargo was hijacked en route from San Pedro to Los Angeles, then rehijacked by its original owners as the truck reached the city. Another smuggling route led from Tecate to Tijuana to San Diego County, the so-called Bootleg Highway. Of all the Los Angeles-centered bootleggers of this era, and there were many, Tony Cornero and his brother Frank dominated the field. Known for their well-maintained trucks and smooth distribution system, the Cornero brothers brought their merchandise down from Canada in a lumber schooner, at 7000 cases a trip. Handsome, dapper, well-dressed, Tony could also play it tough, as he did on the evening of 30 May 1924 when surprised in a sting operation by Los Angeles police. Despite the gunfire, Tony got off easy: two flesh wounds and a $300 fine. Caught on his yacht with a thousand cases of whiskey, Tony received two years at the federal penitentiary at McNeil Island, Washington. He escaped en route and spent the years 1925 to 1929 as a fugitive before turning himself in. Released from prison, Cornero went into the business of offshore gambling ships during the Depression.

Like everything else, crime in Los Angeles had its distinct patterns. The leading bootleggers, for instance—entrepreneurs such as Tony and Frank Cornero, Melvin Schouweiler, Tony Paragini, Bill Nard, Ralph Shelton, Dominic Di Ciolla, Dick Scout, and Walter South—distributed their product across a wide territory. With no more than an estimated dozen important speakeasies operating in the city, the bootleggers had to market their product directly to country clubs, restaurants, and individuals. The Southern California bootlegger paid more attention to supply, sales, distribution, and service than to territorial protection, a major concern of organized crime in the Midwest and East. Hence the prohibition era in Southern California did not sustain the levels of organized violence so prominent in other parts of the country. Statistics from the 1920s showed Los Angeles to be competitive with Detroit, Cleveland, Chicago, New York, and Philadelphia in crime, but not in crimes resulting from gangland warfare. Although there were spectacular exceptions—the murder of oil heir E.L. Doheny, Jr., for instance, on 16 February 1929 by his secretary Hugh Plunkitt, who then committed suicide—the crimes of Los Angeles tended to be the less spectacular ones of drunkenness, minor meyhem, petty theft—

the vagrancy crimes of a dislocated, not yet fully urbanized population. "I wonder which disconcerts Los Angeles most," asked a visiting journalist, "the number of crimes or the ruralness of their character?"[7]

The woefully overcrowded Central City Jail of Los Angeles, an airless dungeon near the newly rising City Hall, was processing some 50,000 annual bookings by the mid-1920s, a significant number of them for drunkenness or other violations related to prohibition. This high ratio of arrests for a city only just passing the million population mark expressed the pressure placed on Los Angeles police and magistrates by the temperance-oriented evangelical community to enforce the Wright Act, California's ratification of the Volstead Act passed by Congress. In Los Angeles, with its strong temperance community, prohibition had widespread support. Thus the enforcement of visible compliance, including vagrancy laws, became a high priority for the police department and municipal courts—hence the heavy traffic and revolving door at the Central City Jail. By 1927 it was becoming rather easy to find oneself busted in Los Angeles, as a party from Hollywood discovered to its dismay early in the a.m. in May of that very year. Fortunately, a night reporter was on hand at the Central City Jail to observe and chronicle the comedy:

> At 2:30 a.m. one hears in the upper reaches of the Jail House a sudden outburst of screams and oaths and decides that a cargo of bedlam has arrived from Patagonia. Going down to the print room to observe, one finds that a bevy of movie queens have been pinched on charges of drunk-driving (112 C.V.A.), drunk, resisting an officer, etc., and are in a fair way to being finger-printed. (Women are still printed at Central although quartered elsewhere.) There is much ado. Gin, temperament, *lese majeste*, a fear of publicity, general cussedness and a certain knowledge that they soon will be out again all combine to make for a general melee and an interesting close-up. In the group are a star of world-wide fame, the sister of another famous celebrity, near stars, maids in waiting, and a bevy of attending sheiks and bull fighters, everybody more or less cock-eyed drunk. Seeing the ladies about to be printed like ordinary folk the male attendants feel that something is expected of them. One leads a right to an officer's jaw. The officer counters three times and three bull fighters bite the dust—only it is a cement floor. "Come along, sister, and give me a hand," the cop addresses the star, "I'm going to print you." "Not by a damn sight. Let go my arm—take yer paw off'n me, you mammal," she replies indignantly and without that pause between each and every word Belasco is said to love. "You'll hear from this outrage." One is distinctly disappointed in not observing that poise, that *haute monde* one is educated to expect from a screenland favorite. The officer puts a brawny arm of enforcement around a classic waist. This is too much. He is kicked efficiently amidship. Another cop comes to the rescue of his mate. He is assaulted by the remainder of the bevy. The aforesaid sheiks and bull fighters begin to revive and engage to the death. Business of general melee. Much swearing, screeching, kicking, pulling of hair, and everything. The cops work methodically and effectively. The sheiks and bull fighters again hear the sound as of little

birds singing. The best way of quieting a temperamental and irate movie queen, it has been found, is to sit on her. More cops enter and each places a damsel prone on the floor and sits on her, protecting his eyes from French heels, whilst the printing goes forward. But before this printing process is completed there is a great scurrying down the corridor and a whole brigade of bondsmen, wire-pullers and fixers come charging upon the scene. The climax is quickly past. The records are inspected to see that aliases are used, warnings issued against giving anything to the paper, and the guests prepare to depart. The star, now somewhat sobered, feels that the parting shot is expected of her—an exit is after all an exit—and drawing herself up to her full five feet and six inches she withers with a single glance the offending officer who has printed her and declares so that all may hear. "You damn big bum, I'll let you know that I'm a lady."[8]

The police of Los Angeles, so strenuously performing in this Damon Runyonesque scenario, did not, as in the case of eastern cities, grow up in the precincts they policed. How could they when so many of these precincts had only recently been lima bean fields? Law enforcement in 1920s Los Angeles tended to be abstracted: not the patrolman on the beat, at one with the strengths and the weaknesses of his community, but strangers in blue uniforms patrolling in police cars an extended cityscape peopled by other strangers. The plainclothes detectives of the Los Angeles Police Department, an inner elite, were accused by their critics of being a corrupted law unto themselves, a shadowy autonomous bureau similar to Water and Power, unaccountable and on the take. Perhaps this is why reform Mayor George Cryer, elected in 1921, had such difficulties in finding a chief who could keep the department under control. His first candidate, Charles A. Jones, quit after a few months, brought to his knees by the inner hierarchy. Cryer then appointed a war hero with no previous police experience, Colonel W. Everington, who made the mistake of cracking down on property owners with excellent ties to the oligarchy who owned hotels that were being used for prostitution. Then Cryer turned to Louis D. Oakes, a flamboyant member of the bureau of detectives, whom the Reverend Bob Shuler suspected of being an immoral man. Chief Oakes did not help matters by being observed emerging from one of these same hotels, a demimondaine on either arm, or, one night in San Bernardino, being arrested in flagrante delicto in his official chief's car, a half-consumed bottle of whiskey on the floorboard.

Already, a group calling itself the Citizens' Anti-Crime Commission of Los Angeles was in conversation with August Vollmer, the reforming police chief of Berkeley and a pioneer in modern police administration, concerning Vollmer's serving as consultant in an effort to clean up and modernize the LAPD. With Oakes's disgraced departure, Mayor Cryer prevailed on the nationally respected Vollmer to become chief for one year. Arriving in August 1923 and departing in September 1924, Vollmer threw himself into reforming the department with the strengths and the limitations of his self-limited tenure. He put an honest captain in at the vice division and, empowered by $100,000 in private funds, set up an intelligence network that very soon resulted in raids on gambling and liquor operations. He organized a special bank surveillance squad, and bank robberies declined. Vollmer established a police academy and took major steps towards reforming the internal administration of the department, including the keeping of statistics and a modus operandi file on repeat criminals. The satraps of the department resented the Berkeley reformer, as might be expected, yet few dared confront such a nationally respected figure in the open. They preferred to wait him out.

Not until the appointment of the 37-year-old James Edgar Davis in 1926 did Cryer find a chief capable of lasting for more than a year. Davis lasted for three. Texas-born, Davis joined the force in 1912 and rose through the ranks, his bravery under fire and crack pistol marksmanship earning him the sobriquet Two Gun Davis. As chief, Davis put on a superb show. A dandy, vain of his good looks, Davis seemed sent from central casting in his freshly pressed tailored uniform and polished Sam Browne belt. The Reverend Bob Shuler, however, was not impressed. "I can't get it into my head," said Fighting Bob, "that a man with a pink complexion who looks like he had a massage every morning and his fingernails manicured is a good chief of police."[9] The fact was, Davis knew exactly what he was doing. Coming up through the ranks, he knew how power was apportioned in the LAPD. Making a rapproachment with the satraps of the department, Davis played chief to the general public, who responded to his personal style and gift for public relations. The oligarchy, meanwhile, appreciated Davis's red-baiting, ultra-right-of-center approach to police administration. Constitutional rights, Davis once stated, were "of no benefit to anybody but crooks and criminals."[10]

When Shuler's candidate John R. Porter, a godfearing teetotaling onetime auto-parts dealer, became mayor in 1929, Davis was demoted to the traffic bureau on charges of incompetence and neglect. Porter lasted only one term, and in 1933 the new mayor, Frank Shaw, reappointed Davis chief of police. Shaw himself was recalled in 1938 amidst charges of corruption, and the reform mayor, Judge Fletcher Bowron, fired Davis for the second time. Davis went on to become chief of security at Douglas Aircraft. A red-baiting spit-and-polish professional, a terror to radicals, drunks, vagrants, petty criminals, and others who offended the prevailing ethos of evangelical Los Angeles, James Edgar Davis could be tolerant when necessary of arrangements that cut to the core of local power. Davis knew when to push and when to leave well enough alone. When demoted in 1929, Davis claimed that he was being punished for keeping the mob out of Los Angeles; indeed, the eastern and Midwestern syndicates never did establish themselves in the city to any significant degree in this era. When it came to the rackets, Los Angeles preferred to make its own arrangements.

5

With the emergence of the Southern California detective story in the 1930s, this murky underworld of hidden arrangements became the central theme of an important literary genre. For the 1920s, however, detective work of a scholarly kind yields no neglected masterpieces. From this perspective, Edgar Rice Burroughs's *The Girl From Hollywood*, Mark Lee Luther's *The Boosters*, and Upton Sinclair's *Oil!* are fictional standouts from this era. In 1927 Willard Huntington Wright returned to the fictional career he had begun so auspiciously with *The Man of Promise* (1916), perhaps the sole Los Angeles novel of note from this earlier decade. Since castigating Los Angeles so ferociously in 1913 in the *Smart Set*, Wright had been forced into a humiliating return from New York during the war. Supporting himself as a writer for movie magazines, the would-be linguist, composer, and aesthete, so proud of being expelled from Harvard for sipping absinthe during a lecture, drifted into drugs and drink and in 1923 suffered a nervous breakdown. Reading detective novels during his recovery, Wright decided to try the genre himself under the pseudonym S.S. Van Dine. The success of the Philo Vance series got Wright off the payroll of the pulp movie magazines. Once more shaking the dust of Los Angeles from his feet, Wright made his Philo Vance stories defiantly East Coast in orientation. Los Angeles would have to await the debut of Raymond Chandler's Philip Marlowe before it secured the services of a private detective capable of probing the ambiguous arrangements of the establishment and the plainclothesmen at LAPD.

In 1927 a former newspaperman by the name of Don Ryan, working in Hollywood as a title and scenario writer, published *Angel's Flight* with Boni & Liveright, and with this "kaleidoscopic, dithyrambic, cinematic book" (so Lawrence Clark Powell later described it) pushed the Los Angeles novel to a new plateau. Born in 1889 in Lawrence County, Ohio, Ryan attended West Virginia University before going to work on some fourteen different newspapers. He interrupted this journalism with stints as an actor in vaudeville, a dancer, and a first lieutenant of infantry during the war. Failing to secure a job in New York after being mustered out, Ryan left for Los Angeles, where he landed a daily column on the Los Angeles *Record*, which he later took to the *Evening Herald*. Entitled "The Merry-Go-Round," Ryan's column dealt with the places, people, scenes, and gossip of the city. Amidst the boosters, Ryan dared to be satirical, to catch the frequently grotesque edges of life in America's newest city. After seven years of street life and deadlines, Ryan conceived of a jazzy panoramic novel, *Angel's Flight*. He finished it while working in Hollywood as a minor screen actor with a specialty in villains and, later, as a writer of screen titles.

Ryan centered his novel on Angel's Flight, a funicular railway built in 1901 to connect Third and Hill streets to Third and Olive streets atop Bunker Hill in downtown Los Angeles. Moving up and down the steep grade, the black and orange funicular cars, like the cable cars of San Francisco, defined an urban area and gave it atmosphere. By the late 1920s when Ryan wrote, Bunker Hill, an established residential and business community in 1901, had become bohemian in atmosphere, the neighborhood of choice for the aspiring artist and for the offbeat and the eccentric. Ryan's protagonist William Ashley Spencer lives on Bunker Hill with his dancer girlfriend. Like Don Ryan, Spencer is an anti-booster newspaper columnist on the lookout for the gritty side of the city. *Angel's Flight* abounds in settings and cityscapes, as if for the first time the mood and measure of a new idiosyncratic city were being taken: Bunker Hill itself and the funicular Angel's Flight which takes Spencer to and from his daily encounters with reality; Pershing Square, with its street preachers, missions, soda fountains, dairy lunches, and cafeterias; the city by night, winking its innumerable yellow eyes. Ryan takes us to Hollywood, where Chaplin is being fawned over in a restaurant and a character based on Erich von Stroheim is fired for running over budget. A scene at the Cocoanut Grove is vital with the dance-prose rhythmns of the Jazz Age. Impressionistically, cinematically, Ryan pans rapidly from scene to scene, place to place, advancing his story line of a failed writer turned forty, burnt out and trying not to be fatally cynical. Anticipating the work of Nathaniel West in the next decade, Ryan depicts lonely Los Angeles filled with solitary people desperate to connect but not knowing how or to whom. He anticipates Raymond Chandler as well in a hijacking and machine-gun murder. As a courtroom-based columnist, Spencer encounters an establishment frenetically concerned with keeping a lid on the city it created but profoundly mistrusts.

"Los Angeles," Spencer exults from atop Bunker Hill, "city with aspirations for the Los Angelicizing of the world! City engaged in puffing down its own windpipe to inflate itself to a degree that it shall be reckoned the largest city in the world! City of oranges, ostriches, lemons, alligators, olives, missions, sardines, aqueducts, harbors, tunas, bungalows, abalones, loquats, casabas, horned toads, snowy peaks, burrows, eucalyptus, pepper trees, Thanksgiving celery and Christmas strawberries—Los Angeles the optimistic, the positive, the vociferous—Jazz Baby of the Golden West, I greet you."[11]

Spencer might very well have greeted the arrival of the Los Angeles novel as well, for *Angel's Flight*, whatever its faults, attempted the biggest bite thus far taken out of the Big Orange, as Los Angeles would someday be designated in affectionate response to the Big Apple of New York. Others as well made attempts to define Los Angeles, albeit few with the dithyrambic cataloging of *Angel's Flight*. Definitions ranged from booster rhetoric to fierce rejections. Sometimes one definition encompassed violent mood swings from one point of view to another, as if the observer were enmeshed in ambivalence.

Definitions frequently encompassed an economic argument. Los Angeles, noted Garet Garrett in the *Saturday Evening Post* for 18 October 1930, reversed the normal process of urban development. Most cities happen. Los Angeles willed itself into being. What economic activity it did possess as the center of an agricultural and citrus region might have made Los Angeles an important farm town but not a major city. Money first came to Los Angeles as Americans chose to move there for the climate. Money then began to diversify and express itself through the building of a city. A farm-town resort was transformed into a metropolis. "There was no need for anything to be produced here," Garrett argued, "more than was convenient for the needs of a sensory paradise. Yet it is as if they imagined necessity, only in order to meet it; as if they fabricated difficulties, only in order to be obliged to overcome them." Self-invented, Los Angeles functioned behind or ahead of traditional urban forms and loyalties. Its founding premise was the question and the quest. "What brought you here?" Los Angelenos were constantly asking each other. And next: "How do you like it?" [12]

Created by the raw power of money, Carey McWilliams argued in 1927, Los Angeles groaned under the yoke of its parvenu plutocracy, the people who flattered themselves in *Saturday Night*, the country clubbers, the boosters. "Once your middlewestern banker or farmer has made his 'pile,' " McWilliams claimed, "he invariably longs for distant social fields to conquer, and moved by the urge of a gigantic inferiority complex he migrates to Los Angeles. Seeking to escape the barrenness of their own intellectual incompetence, they throng to Los Angeles and join beach clubs, attend the movies religiously, sport golf knickers and take chiropractic treatments for diversion." [13] Faced with this onslaught of newcomers, McWilliams continued, the previous generation wrapped itself up in a myth of Old California, of padres and tinkling guitars and legends of old families exaggerated beyond their true importance. Like so many others, McWilliams blamed this element of pose, if not outright fakery, on Hollywood and the movies. Like Hollywood itself, J.B. Priestley noted, Los Angeles was a stage set, strangely surreal in the sunshine, as brittle and impermanent as a reel of film. It was a Puritan city in transition to paganism, Bruce Bliven believed. It was a pagan city, countered Louis Adamic, only temporarily dominated by Puritans. It was both, Carey McWilliams argued, at once a harlot and a Comstock prude. Los Angeles was "mob-mad, unimaginably democratic—hopelessly vulgar . . . a democratic brothel!" [14]

Los Angeles, the English artist Maxwell Armfield wrote in the *Christian Science Monitor* in 1925, was an irrigated city, hence curiously insecure and impermanent. Were the population to take a month's holiday en masse, it might return to find that the city had returned itself to desert wilderness. Los Angeles was an irrigated city, Marrow Mayo agreed, albeit with a different conclusion. Irrigation had made the City of the Angels greedy and imperialistic. Los Angeles based its prosperity on the rape of the Owens Valley, an act of chicanery that made the Teapot Dome fade into insignificance. Los Angeles,

John Lilly asserted, was a Midwest city in transition. Midwesterners might go to New York to escape the Midwest. In Los Angeles they brought their Midwestern values with them, and now these values were slowly being transformed by the sunny possibilities of Southern California. Los Angeles "does not stir and provoke and set at unrest. It is softening, because life is easy and pleasant, utterly without hardship—to its inhabitants a cloudy day is a relief from monotony—and within its easy contours it is basically the same existence that is led, half actually, half imaginatively, in Shelbyville, Indiana." [15] Los Angeles, Sarah Comstock informed *Harper's* readers in May 1928, was like the rest of the United States, only more so. Others agreed. The face of Los Angeles, wrote Garet Garrett in the *Saturday Evening Post*, was "the truest conceivable representation of the whole American face, urban, rural, big town, little town, all together." [16] Comstock and Garrett meant their references to American paradigms as compliments. Victor Walkers offered the same argument as a criticism. "Los Angeles," he asserted, "carries to the final degree of caricature the various traits of American society which have been more or less under universal condemnation ever since they became powerful enough to make their influence felt. It is a fit study for a social psychiatrist." [17] Los Angeles, noted British philosopher Bertrand Russell in a similar vein, represented the ultimate segregation of the unfit.

Los Angeles, others argued, constituted the most recent English-speaking Anglo-Saxon city to be achieved across three centuries of Anglo-American expansion. It was the final arc of Anglo-American empire set strategically at the intersection of the Pacific Southwest and the Pacific Rim. "Facing Eastward on the Western sea dwells half the human race," noted the veteran Progressive journalist activist Chester Rowell in 1929. "Until now it has been to us a world apart, as if on another planet. Henceforward, forever, it is to be the other half of our world and a participant in our life." [18] Set at the very point where the resources and emergent energies of the developing Sunbelt, as this region eventually came to be called, encountered the impending era of the Pacific, Los Angeles, its boosters prophesied, had the makings of a world city. *Saturday Night* called Los Angeles the new New York.

Such positive assessments were expected from boosters, but even non-boosters offered encomiums as well, frequently tagged on as repentant codas to otherwise unfavorable judgments. D.H. Lawrence visited Los Angeles from Taos, New Mexico, in early September 1923. Ensconced in the Hotel Miramar in Santa Monica, Lawrence spent long hours walking the beach or trying to arrange a charter cruise to Mexico from private boats docked at Wilmington–San Pedro. He later moved to a rooming house on Bunker Hill. In the company of his hosts, Los Angeles-based artists whom he had met in Taos, Lawrence picnicked in Topanga Canyon and traveled up to Lompoc to witness a total eclipse of the sun. One night, Lawrence and his pals all went out to a dance hall. The prophet of erotic delight was horrified by the dance girls. At another time they visited the Hollywood Bowl, where Lawrence annoyed those sitting near him with his jokes during the performance. In his letters Lawrence described Los Angeles as queer, silly, loose, easy, foolish, selfish, and self-absorbed; yet the city had its own crazy-sensible logic as well. "A great deal of falseness is also left out," Lawrence admitted, and that constituted a tepid plus.[19]

"There is a bright side to Los Angeles," Louis Adamic admitted; "only to see it, one must have good eyesight."[20] Many had good eyes and used them. Even a harlot city, Carey McWilliams admitted, had her points. "There is something about the surging life of Los Angeles, its very crowds, that is impressive. Its plain of lights at night—jewels on the breast of the harlot—and its jauntily designed houses and terraced foothills, go far towards supplying the lack of culture. The very showiness of the place attracts like an enormous scarlet beetle or the huge amethyst ring of a bishop."[21] Rage as he might, Paul Jordan Smith confessed, "the bug of optimism seizes me; I succumb. It is now my firm conviction, Mencken notwithstanding, that out of this motley throng of goose-steppers and propagandists there will grow the most splendid center of genuine culture and enlightenment on this continent. For, with all its uncouthness, the place is alive with illusions, and illusions are the stuff of art."[22] Exulted Bruce Bliven: "Speaking for myself, I adore it. I am aware, of course, that such an attitude is most unusual. Nearly everyone I know who comes from the East, or from Europe, to visit Los Angeles, goes away declaring that it is embodied nightmare; but I can only say that those who hold this view seem to me amazingly short-sighted. For this city is a social laboratory *in excelsis*. It offers a melting-pot in which the civilization of the future may be seen, bubbling darkly up in a foreshadowing brew."[23]

By 1930 Los Angeles had fully asserted itself as an idiosyncratic city in an emergent American region. In the 1920s the California Dream became the Southern Californian Dream in terms of intensity; and Los Angeles, in turn, was materializing the Southern California Dream with a mid-American flamboyance special to itself. Ambiguities abounded, but for those who delighted in the California Dream, in Southern California and in cities, the decade-swift rise of Los Angeles as an assertive American city constituted an achievement of vision, energy, and will fascinating to boosters and critics alike.

III

MATERIALIZING HISTORY

I had the foretaste of what I was presently to feel in California—
when the general aspect of that wondrous realm kept suggesting
to me a sort of prepared but unconscious and inexperienced Italy,
the primitive plate, in perfect condition, but with the impression
of History all yet to be made.

HENRY JAMES,
The American Scene (1907)

8

Designs for Living

Architecture in Southern California,
from the Bradbury Building to the Watts Towers

Like the Los Angeles it prefigured, the Bradbury Building came out of nowhere. In other aspects as well, this *sui generis* structure, among the most innovative interior spaces in North America, arose out of distinctly Southern California circumstances. Once completed—once in motion, rather, for the Bradbury Building did not merely open for business; it came alive one day in the sunlight—this orchestration of steel and light announced the city that was to be.

The story of the origins of the Bradbury Building reads like a parable of the Southern Californian experience. Born in Dayton, Ohio, in the heartland of Southern Californian migration, George Herbert Wyman came to Los Angeles in 1891 at the age of 31 because he was weakened by pneumonia and wanted to get better in the sunlight. Already, Wyman had apprenticed himself to his uncle, an architect in Dayton, and this brief exposure constituted his only architectural education. In Los Angeles, his health recovered, Wyman obtained a position with Sumner P. Hunt, an established late nineteenth-century architect with a practice in downtown office buildings. Hunt was in the process of designing an office building for Louis Bradbury, a millionaire investor in Mexican mines, anxious to see his name memorialized in a downtown office block at Third and Broadway. With an eye for talent, Bradbury detected a special creativity in Hunt's young draftsman, George Wyman; and when Hunt presented Bradbury with a conventional design, the mining speculator, accustomed to taking chances, rebelled. Rejecting Hunt's proposal, Bradbury offered the commission to Wyman. Wyman was both flattered and appalled. A self-taught draftsman does not steal a contract from his established employer without weighing the consequences. If he accepted Bradbury's offer, Wyman realized, he would be forced to go out on his own sans degree and with minimal experience. Bradbury persisted. Whether or not Wyman accepted the commission, he told the young draftsman, Hunt would not get the contract.

Thus the recovered health-seeker from the Midwest and the adamant mining investor, two representative men, played out the beginnings of a representative drama that would soon result in an intensely symbolic building. At this point two more prototypical factors, nationalism and spiritualism, came into play. In 1888 New York journalist Edward Bellamy wrote an utopian novel, *Looking Backward: 2000–1887*, set in the socialist future. Inspired by Bellamy's vision of a cooperative economic order, Nationalist Clubs devoted to discussing and promulgating the pre-Fabian socialist program of *Looking Backward* sprang up across the United States. Los Angeles alone had thirty-three Nationalist Clubs by the time of Wyman's arrival. Bellamy's program included a reformed architecture. In *Looking Backward* he described the commercial office building of the future as "a vast hall full of light, received not alone from the windows on all sides but from the dome, the point of which was a hundred feet above. . . . The walls were frescoed in mellow tints, to soften without absorbing the light which flooded the interior."[1] Since Bellamyism, utopian and futurist, was so much in the Los Angeles air, Wyman quite naturally became intrigued by this brief description of an office building built to and from the light. He might even have discussed it at a Nationalist Club meeting. Bradbury's offer of the Third and Broadway commission pushed utopian dreaming to the edges of reality.

But first, the other world must be heard from. If Los Angeles were utopian, it was also characterized by a special receptivity to swamis, seances, spiritualist movements, and parapsychology. George Wyman and his wife were fond of the game of planchette, in which a vertical pencil was suspended over a small board mounted on casters. When one rested one's fingers lightly on the board, the pencil moved across the paper mounted on the board, leaving trace lines which could sometimes be seen as letters or words or even messages from beyond. According to Wyman's daughter, who later told the story to architectural critic Esther McCoy, the planchette game played a role in the creation of the Bradbury Building. Concerned over whether or not to take the contract, George Wyman used the planchette to contact his brother Mark who had died six years earlier at the age of twelve. "Take the Bradbury Building," Mark is said to have channeled back via the planchette pencil. "It will make you famous."[2]

It did, and it continues to do so; for the Bradbury Building, constructed in 1893, was not only great architecture, it was comparably great as art and social statement. As a prophetic metaphor of Southern California, the Bradbury Building yielded clues to regional identity like oranges from a Southland tree. In the years to come, for example, Chicago would populate Los Angeles, which in turn used the Chicago metaphor to envision and promote its astonishing growth. In one dimension of its design—its steel-frame construction, its central light court, its suggestions of the Romanesque in its façade and fenestration—the Bradbury Building brought the early Chicago School to Los Angeles in architectural anticipation of the mass Midwestern migration of the next decades. The Bradbury Building thus challenged Los Angeles, then passing the 55,000 mark in population, to begin thinking of itself as a big city, a Chicago on the Pacific. Chicagoan as well was the exuberant industrialism of the building—its Art Nouveau cast-iron elevators rising and falling on externalized tracks over the open interior courtyard, like a Jules Verne fantasy of flight, and its steel and iron interior, futuristically functional and streamlined in its staircases and bridge-like crossings, traditionally sculptural in their Corinthian columns and organic imagery—as if to suggest, in all this steel, in its integration of functional forms and asethetic memories, the poetic possibilities of the industrial technology that would soon transform the economy and cityscape of Los Angeles into a new kind of American city.

Yet nature, not technology, had played a strong part in George Wyman's recovery from the effects of pneumonia, specifically the healing warmth of the sun, and so, following the suggestions of *Looking Backward*, Wyman flooded the Bradbury Building with Southern California sunlight from an oversized skylight which Esther McCoy calls a fairy tale of mathematics. Light from above was augmented by a series of rhythmically descending clerestory windows. The movement of the light met the movement and rhythms of the interior steel, and the Bradbury Building leapt into motion, into being, energized equally by technology and the sun. This futurist reconciliation of nature and technology, the machine and sunlight, contained within itself a utopian parable easy to construe in terms of Southern California. Mysteriously, an aspiring architect had dreamed and designed himself into a materialized utopian metaphor far superior to the slender suggestions found in *Looking Backward*. In an architecture of steel and glass, marble, tile, and movement, George Wyman envisioned and presented the material dream of Southern California as a technology flooded by sunlight.

His work done, Wyman left Hunt's office and set out on his own. The first thing he did, this neophyte designer who had arguably created the most innovative interior space yet realized in the country, was to enroll in a correspondence course in architecture! None of Wyman's subsequent buildings pursued the implications of the Bradbury, which remained, as Esther McCoy phrased it, a student's dream which had somehow crossed the borderlands of fantasy into materialized reality. In later years Wyman, whose buildings had by then become progressively more heavy and dark, grew increasingly intrigued by the possibilities of intelligent life in outer space. He drew innumerable cartoons of space creatures for his grandson. In 1982 filmmaker Ridley Scott chose the Bradbury Building as a key locale for the dystopian science-fiction film *Blade Runner*. Set in the late twenty-first century, *Blade Runner* depicted Los Angeles as a city in which runaway technology had all but blocked out the sun. In this dystopia only the Bradbury Building seemed still capable of receiving the light.

2

From sunlight grew gardens, and from gardening and landscape arrangements as well as from the steel and technology of the Bradbury Building arose compelling design metaphors for Los Angeles and the rest of Southern California. By the early 1900s the gardens of Southern California had asserted themselves as vivid icons of local identity. Southern California, after all, had itself been most dramatically planted as a regional civilization: imposed, that is, on a landscape which the Franciscan missionaries found treeless save for the few willows and sycamores managing to thrive in damp stream beds and canyons, the live oaks which intermittently established themselves on the seaside hills, and the running stand of native palms at what later was named Palm Springs. The padres planted pepper trees for shade and fruit and olive trees for horticulture. American ranchers brought in walnut, almond, and chestnut trees, then planted citrus trees as far as the eye could see.

In the case of the Australiam gum tree or eucalyptus, an entire species was transplanted up from the Southern Hemisphere through the promotional efforts, initially, of Santa Barbara rancher and college president Ellwood Cooper. Alarmed by George Marsh's warning in *Man and Nature* (1864) that the United States was dangerously depleting its forest resources, Cooper saw in the eucalyptus the answer to the problem. At his Santa Barbara ranch alone, he planted some fifty thousand of them, representing dozens of varieties. By the 1880s the planting of eucalyptus had become a California crusade, cheered on by Cooper, the Los Angeles-based Forest Grove Association, and Abbot Kinney, the state forester. In 1904 the United States Forest Service predicted an impending shortage of eastern hardwoods, and the eucalyptus crusade took on renewed intensity. Green eucalyptus, however, proved a poor substitute for oak, hickory, ash, maple, and mahogany, and so the boom went bust, but not before the eucalyptus had been established alongside the redwood and the live oak as an accepted feature of the landscape.

Since Southern California had been previously so treeless, its eucalyptization had an even more dramatic effect in the south than it did in the forested northern portion of the state. Whether lining rural roadways and railroads (the Southern Pacific and Santa Fe planted them alongside their tracks so as to have them available for railroad ties), running at right angles against the prevailing winds as stately windbreakers, their silver-green leathery leaves sparkling in constant motion, or ceremoniously standing sentry at the entrances to hundreds of communities, the eucalyptus conferred a powerful suggestion of design, of park-like emplacement, on the landscape of the Southland.

Next ensued the landscaping emplacement of palm trees, especially along urban streets and boulevards. More than a thousand species were introduced to augment the single species indigenous to the region. Palms brought to Southern California the ambience of the Mediterranean, North Africa, and the Middle East. Just as the eucalyptus helped organize the open vistas of the Southland by defining roadways and declivities, the palm helped organized urban spaces. By the 1920s the cityscapes of the Southland, Los Angeles most dramatically, exfoliated in palm trees, giraffes nodding wisely, many of them rising more than seventy feet against the blue sky. Palms also created oasis environments in countless private courtyards and patios and lent Biblical dignity (the eighteenth-century Swedish botanist Carlus Linnaeus called them the Queens of Sheba of the tree world) to the frontages of churches, schools, libraries, and hospitals, associating these new California institutions with the distant dignity of the Holy Land.

Thus did Waldron Gillespie of Montecito first encounter the palm, in illustrations of the garden of Eden in a book he read as a boy in Sunday school. Shortly thereafter, the boy Gillespie stood before an actual palm planted in an exhibition garden at the Centennial Exposition at Philadelphia in 1876. It was a magical moment as the Sunday school depiction of the lost Garden of Eden came alive for the boy in the presence of this Biblical tree. Forty and more years later, in designing, building, and landscaping El Fureidis, his Montecito estate, Gillespie made every effort to recapture the palm-crowded luxuriance of the picture in his boyhood book. In the opinion of then director of the Arnold Arboretum at Harvard, El Fureidis, which was designed by Bertram Goodhue as a classical Mediterranean villa surrounded by formal gardens, contained the most extensive palm garden in the United States in terms of size and the number of species planted. The palm, Waldron Gillespie believed, offered an organizing principle for landscaping that was totally appropriate to Southern California. While the English garden could be achieved in the Southland, Gillespie argued—conifers in the background, lawns and flowering shrubs in the foreground, an overall impression of intimacy and moist, picturesque coziness—such gardens seemed as out of place as the Gothic architecture he had seen in British India. On the same latitude as Morocco, Southern California demanded a dryer garden, characterized by rhythms of unplanted spaces, water symbolically displayed ceremoniously in pools and fountains, and stately palms providing background and topographical definition.

Into such a scheme the cactus fit perfectly. The cactus, after all, was by genesis and long habitation a survivor amidst semi-aridity. The cactus entered the Southern California garden as a hardy local asserting itself amidst the exotic imports. Requiring next to no care, cacti organized the dry Southern California garden like soldiers on parade, bearing on their persons water sufficient for the long march and armed with spiny weapons, colorful in their uniforms of red, purple, lemon yellow, or cream flowers laced with carmine, depending upon the species. With their frank evocations of the deserts to the east, cacti asserted Southern California as habitable drylands, open, treeless, resistant to the traditional Eastern American or Northern European predilection for intimate and watered spaces. Properly grouped, cacti could be civilized to garden purposes. Interest in their cultivation and garden use soared in the early twentieth century. The Henry E. Huntington Library and Art Gallery in San Marino developed a two-hundred-acre botanical garden specializing in cacti and other succulents, which helped further enhance their value as a regional symbol. Thus one school of Southern California garden theorists, Mediterraneanizers inspired by Edith Wharton's *Italian Villas and Their Gardens* (1904), with its sumptuous illustrations by Maxfield Parrish, brought the dry formal garden to Southern California (and to the campus of Stanford University in the north), with its emphasis on dry spaces and pools; Mediterranean, North African, and Levantine trees and flora; and classically inspired statuary and architecture.

The English garden, meanwhile, flourished in Pasadena and in the moist regions around the San Francisco Bay, although even here, in Peninsula estates such as Filoli, designed by Willis Polk in 1915 for Empire Mine heir William Bourn, the dry formal garden kept its ascendancy. In fact, Californians had innumerable options from which to choose. Everything grew and the growing season continued throughout the year. Without snow, the winter in California consisted of periods of rain followed by sunshine and riotous blossoms. Even amidst the rains, the garden cycle continued as summer-planted flora—portulaca, oxalis, anemones, freesias, gaillardias, marigolds, verbena, poinsettias, violets, birds of paradise planted against backgrounds of wild laurel and holly—were tricked into blooming out of season. Not only did everything grow and the growing season continue throughout the year, everything grew so quickly. "There is much to be said for a climate," noted one garden writer, "where one can sit under one's own vine and fig tree and pick the fruit too—apricots, peaches, nectarines, persimmons, and avocados as well, in less than three years from the day they were planted as little whips of green. In this short length of time the pepper, acacia, sycamore, have attained such height and such spread of branches as are incredible."[3]

Gardening, then, easily attained the status of a common symbol of regional identity. "Everybody in California has a garden," noted a garden writer in 1915. "It is a bond of sympathy that establishes friendly relations between capitalists and socialists, meat packers and vegetarians."[4] Even the film industry participated in this garden orientation, as another observer noted in 1920: "The educational opportunity of the film folk in the matter of gardens is unlimited. Their sets put them in intimate contact with vivid bits of all the known world; the vegetation of Australia, of India, of Brazil, of Japan, become part of their daily living. Familiarity with such a wide range of horticultural material and California's hospitality to nearly all forms of plant life afford unprecedented gardening opportunities, which the stars and lesser movie lights have been quick to take advantage of, as their many gardens testify."[5]

The implications of all this garden theory and practice upon the emerging architecture of the early 1900s is self-apparent. The garden soon became a controlling factor in Southern California domestic design. Moorish Spain, it was pointed out, had developed the landscaped inner courtyard, which had come to New Spain as the interior patio. Together with the walled garden, another Spanish legacy, the patio or in larger buildings the courtyard garden unified landscape and architecture into a single household space. In 1915 architect Irving Gill, taking the patio metaphor one step further, designed a home for a San Diego client, Mrs. George T. Fulford, with a garden set squarely in the center of the structure. All rooms of the house opened upon and were entered through this interior garden-room courtyard, which was surrounded by an arcade tiled in oversized floor brick and lightly screened overhead. "A wall fountain tinkles from one side," noted the *Craftsman* magazine of this garden room. "This is the main living room of the house. Meals are sometimes served here and afternoon teas. Swinging couches and hammocks, some across a corner, some under the arcade, are often used for the rest at night as well as the afternoon siesta. A screen or more in front of the arches, sometimes converts a portion of the arcade into impromptu bedrooms when week-end guests are numerous. Potted plants are set all about, other plants are grown in the corners where the earth was left uncovered for them. Vines trail from the trusses. Rugs, chairs and tables with books, magazines and writing materials offer attractive comfort."[6]

3

Thus the machine, as symbolized in the exquisite light-drenched Jules Verne art nouveau technology of the Bradbury Building, and the garden, as in the garden room of Gill's Fulford house, exercised their influences on the design vocabulary of Southern California. Not until the late 1920s and early 1930s, however, would the technology metaphor emerge with any true force in the designs of Rudolph Schindler, Richard Neutra, and the other regional proponents of the International Style. In the meanwhile, the garden metaphor, aside from its obvious effects on architecture, also underscored another regional characteristic. Just as everything grew in the Southern California garden, so too did every architectural tradition take hold as well. In the 1920s, under the influence of Hollywood, this eclecticism reached a special intensity, with frequently ridiculous results. Up and through the 1850s architecture in Southern California had evolved within the simple design vocabulary of the Hispanic frontier. The Southern California of the mid- and late nineteenth century was by and large designed and constructed according to prevailing American standards of style and taste. Neither the downtown office blocks of this era nor the private homes or ranch houses would, with the exception of their exuberant gardens, be in any way recognizably regional in appearance. In the 1890s, however, a concern for regionalism asserted itself in Southern California as it was also doing elsewhere in the United States. This aspiration towards regionalism expressed itself architecturally in three directions: Craftsman Bungalow, Mediterranean, and the various evolutions of Spanish Revival.

Whatever its origins, the Southern California bungalow, as it flourished in the early 1900s, constituted a dramatically successful solution to the challenge of creating moderately priced, regionally suitable domestic architecture. Named after the cottage tradition of Bengali, which also served as a distant archetype, the bungalow featured a patio and a covered porch in response to the climate and an open floorplan that avoided dark hallways. Inexpensively constructed in wood and frequently shingled, the bungalow achieved a new level of tasteful functionalism in affordable housing. In the hands of master architects such as Bernard Maybeck of Berkeley and the Greene brothers of Pasadena, the redwood-shingled bungalow evolved into a major expression of Craftsman value and style adapted to California circumstances. Throughout the early 1900s Maybeck was kept busy filling the Berkeley hills with exquisitely sited bungalows which blended into their tree-planted sites like natural constructions and glowed within in harmonies of polished wood. Charles Sumner Greene and Henry Mather Greene, meanwhile, were functioning with equal success and along parallel lines in Pasadena. In 1908 the Greenes achieved the best known of their many masterpieces, a winter home in Pasadena for David Gamble of the Procter & Gamble Company of Cincinnati. Studying surviving masterpieces such as the Gamble House and Maybeck's Church of Christ Scientist in Berkeley (1910), critics have decoded from the Maybeck and Greene and Greene vocabulary a diverse melding of Queen Anne, Stick and Shingle, Arts and Crafts, Swiss, Bavarian, Scandinavian, Tibetan, Bhutanese, Sikkimese, and Japanese influences.

What held these all together, blending them into a regionally appropriate response, was an Arts and Crafts passion for wood and a mastery of the subtleties of site. Every influence scholars have detected in Maybeck and the Greenes derives from a wood-building tradition. In once treeless but now tree-planted Southern California, wood, like garden displays of water amidst semi-aridity, possessed an especially symbolic value as an image of scarcity transcended. A successful bungalow, whether a Greene and Greene masterpiece or a modest middle-class home, emplaced wood on the landscape in pleasing configurations that suggested the previously absent but longed for and willfully recovered garden forests that had been dreamed of, then materialized through planting. In a sense, the Craftsman bungalows were themselves planted on the landscape as arboreal forms. The Greene brothers, for instance, took great care to echo surrounding hill forms in their roof lines and to stain their exteriors, not paint them, so as to blend their wood tones into the grays, greens, and browns of the surrounding environment. If landscaping was also successful, as it so often was in the case of Greene and Greene creations in general and in so many other Craftsman bungalows built in this period, then the trees, shrubs, and hedges surrounding the wood art of the bungalows further added to the effect of an imagined forest given local habitation and a name.

Actress Helena Modjeska named her Anaheim hideaway Arden in reference to the enchanted forest of Shakespeare's *As You Like It*. Coastal Southern California, from this perspective, abounded in Arden-like developments—Pasadena, San Marino, Palos Verdes, Beverly Hills, Bel-Air, Brentwood, Montecito—where trees had been planted and gardens emplaced so as to effect both a mood and a reality of a time and a place away, spent in an Arden forest of enchantment.

Of all the influences operating on Greene and Greene, the Japanese influence most expressively linked the architecture of wood and the garden metaphor. Enroute to Pasadena, the Greenes found themselves delighted by the Japanese pavilion at the Columbian Exposition in Chicago. In 1894 they traveled north to San Francisco to see its recreation as the Japanese Tea Garden of the Midwinter Exposition then being held in Golden Gate Park. They also began to collect and study books on Japanese architecture and garden theory. In these interests, the Greenes were paralleling the inquiries of other Americans such as John La Farge, Percival Lowell, Henry Adams, Ernest Fenollosa, and Lafcadio Hearn into Japanese culture and aesthetics. In matters of woodblock printing, painting, screens, vases, fabrics, flower arrangements, and interior design, the *fin de siècle* in both Europe and the United States was enamored of *japonaiserie*. In California, however, geography and an admixture of admiration and threat conferred special intensity to questions of Japanese influence on local design. Racial feeling against Japanese immigrants ran high in California. American presidents were twice forced to intervene in local affairs when anti-Japanese legislation proved diplomatically embarrassing to the United States. While a few prominent Californians, notably David Starr Jordan, the founding president of Stanford University, were Japanophiles, the majority of the early twentieth-century Progressive leadership of the state feared the Japanese as a domestic and strategic threat.

Aesthetic currents, meanwhile, were running in the opposite direction. San Francisco painter Theodore Wores spent two extensive sojourns in Japan in the mid-1880s and the late 1890s, returning each time with a pioneering series of canvases depicting Japanese landscape, architecture, and scenes from daily life. The wildly popular Japanese Tea Garden exhibition at the Midwinter Fair of 1894 was continued as a permanent feature of the Golden Gate Park in San Francisco. Japanese screens, vases, and other decorative objects became widespread elements in interior design, favored for the elegant ease with which they could be introduced against polished redwood surfaces. Hostesses presiding over such interiors, both in real life and in the novels of the period, frequently entertained wearing Japanese kimonos. Japanese garden design, together with the ubiquitous Japanese lanterns for outdoor lighting, became increasingly characteristic of domestic landscaping. A generation of Japanese gardeners, meanwhile, especially in Southern California where the Japanese gained preeminence in such employment, was slowly coaxing the garden landscapes of the Southland into arrangements inspired by the Land of the Rising Sun. Under the influence and labor of Japanese landscapers whose work calls for further study, the gardens and public landscapes of Southern California became increasingly more painterly, more picturesque and serene.

The Japanese gardeners tended to organize their efforts around a dominant element, a tree, pool, hill, or rock outcropping, which in turn was used as the lead feature in a unified scene. Unlike their formalist counterparts, who were much more engineering oriented and tended to move earth, rocks, and trees to conform to an ideal design, Japanese gardeners preferred to work inexpensively and with great aesthetic effect with what was before them, conforming as much as possible to the existing landscape. Their skilled use of stones linked them to other dry-garden traditions of Southern California, moreover, as did their use of falling rivulets leading to the water-lily-covered carp and goldfish ponds which, thanks to their influence, became increasingly popular. In the locally important matter of trees, the Japanese introduced blossoming cherry, plum, and peach trees into their compositions with great regard for the yearly pageant of falling blossoms. They also used pines, which they considered emblems of good luck, for boundaries and background definition. Through outdoor lanterns skillfully emplaced in the style of Japan, the Southern California garden became further integrated into the day-to-evening cycle. By night the garden became a subtly lit magical environment, suitable for seated conversations or shared silence that further extended the garden into the domestic interior and vice versa.

Picturesque, intimate, environmentally unobstrusive, eclectic in everything save its avoidance of roses (their beauty being considered too splashy, too overpowering), the Japanese garden wielded its steady influence on Southern California landscaping even as white California meditated legal restrictions on the Japanese people. Early coverage of Greene and Greene bungalows, interestingly enough, frequently stressed the Japanese nature of their design and woodcraft (the avoidance of nails, say, in favor of dowels or wrought-iron bands) and the obviously Japanese influence on siting and landscaping arrangements; yet this very analogy, however complimentarily intended, also weakened the acceptance of the Greene and Greene redwood bungalow as a full-blown prototype for the region.

Not only were Greene and Greene houses exquisitely crafted and hence expensive to build, they also contained within themselves the temporarily unassimilable metaphor of Japan as a conscious model for imitation and usage by white California. As of the early 1900s, the assimilation of Asian metaphors into California lay far into the future. And besides: the Craftsman intricacies of Greene and Greene or of Maybeck in the north did not translate easily into the production of mass housing for exploding cities and suburbs. Already by 1915 on the lower end of the market, the redwood bungalow, while it managed to hold on as middle-class housing in pockets of Los Angeles and elsewhere in the region, was being increasingly replaced by a more mass-produceable stucco version that substituted inexpensiveness and rapidity of construction for Crafts-man value. Up in Berkeley, Bernard Maybeck was kept busy with commissions both before and after the great fire of September 1923 which destroyed much of his early work; in Southern California, by contrast, then in the throes of a massive in-migration, the golden age of Greene and Greene was over by the time the First World War ended and the hordes of new Southern Californians poured into the region.

4

Mediterranean and Spanish Revival, by contrast, gained in ascendancy as Craftsman waned or lost its integrity. Here were two styles supported by the regional myth of California as the Mediterranean shores of America and even, in the case of Spanish Revival, supported by a slight degree of historical justi-fication. They were also styles which were applicable at either end of the cost spectrum, whether the Mediterranean mansions of Montecito or the Spanish-style stucco homes in the expanding suburbs. Each style had its origins in the 1890s: Spanish in the Mission Revival ushered in by the California Building designed by A. Page Brown, Bernard Maybeck, and A.C. Schweinfurth for the Chicago World's Fair of 1893; Mediterranean during this same period with the work of Beaux Arts-trained architects such as Albert Pissis in San Francisco, followed by the younger group—Maybeck, Schweinfurth, Willis Polk—gath-ered in A. Page Brown's San Francisco office. In 1894 Brown brought Mission Revival to the Southland, doing a row of vacation cottages in this style in Santa Barbara for his patrons, the Crocker family of San Francisco. In the years that followed the Santa Barbara suburb of Montecito witnessed the construction of dozens of distinguished mansion villas in the Mediterranean style.

In the years before and after World War I, architect Myron Hunt emerged as the leading Mediterraneanizer of Southern California. Moving to Los An-geles in 1903 because of his wife's tuberculosis, Myron Hunt brought Boston, Chicago, and Florence with him to the Southland. Never before, in fact, had such a well-trained, well-traveled architect moved to Southern California as a permanent resident. (One does not wish to push the health-seeking metaphor too strongly; but it should be noted that an entire generation of talented archi-tects—among them Irving Gill, the Greene brothers, Gordon Kaufmann, whose wife, like Harriet Hunt, had lung problems—came to Southern California for tuberculosis or other respiratory difficulties.) Born in Massachusetts, where his father was a prominent nurseryman, serving as the national president of the Society of American Nurserymen when Hunt was a boy, Hunt finished his high school and college years in Chicago. He attended Northwestern for two years before going on to MIT to study architecture. After a year as a draftsman in the Boston firm established by H.H. Richardson, Hunt married, then moved to Europe for two years, spending most of this time in Florence studying the architecture of the Renaissance. Returning to Chicago in 1896, Myron Hunt joined the regional office of Shepley, Rutan and Coolidge, the Boston firm which had inherited much of Richardson's commissions, including Stanford University, when Richardson died unexpectedly in 1886. Hunt also joined the Steinway Hall circle of progressive architects, soon to emerge as the Prairie School.

By the time Harriet Hunt's lungs forced a move to Southern California, Myron Hunt, aged 35, had assimilated at MIT the best architectural instruction then available in the United States, two apprenticeships associated with the master himself, H.H. Richardson, two years of European study, and membership in a circle of architects even then in the process of making Chicago the cutting edge of architecture in the United States. Hunt's own practice in Evanston had taught him the possibilities of suburban architecture as a high form, something which H.H. Richardson had understood and put into practice in the suburbs around Boston. From the Richardson legacy as carried on by Shepley, Rutan and Coolidge, Hunt had acquired the habit of thinking through and planning each project as thoroughly as possible. From the Richardson legacy as well, augmented by his private study in Florence, Hunt had learned to assimilate historical forms not superficially as decorative motifs but through a solid and adaptive grasp of their underlying principles and tectonics. An American architect did not merely translate a historical idiom to the United States; he or she grasped what was essential and translatable, re-envisioning a tradition in American terms, just as Richardson had re-envisioned the Romanesque.

In the Los Angeles of 1903 Hunt encountered some Romanesque (the City Hall, the County Courthouse, Los Angeles High School) and much Second Empire in the downtown, but little else. With its population of 100,000, its paucity of school-trained or well-traveled architects, Los Angeles must have seemed to Hunt a poor exchange, in everything save weather, for Chicago.

It is thus not surprising that Hunt gravitated northwards to San Francisco, attracted there by his first major California commission, the Livingston Jenks house on the eastern side of Russian Hill, and the congenial circle of architects, among them Willis Polk, already at work in the Bay Area. What Bernard Maybeck was to the Greene brothers, the Northern California counterpart, Willis Polk was to Myron Hunt. A self-taught but profoundly learned historicist, Polk grasped the essence of classical, Italian Renaissance, and French

Classical Revival forms—then proceeded to translate them into Northern Cal-
ifornian terms, just as Myron Hunt would soon be doing with the restrained
Mediterraneanism of his comparably appropriate Southern California style. But
first the Livingston Jenks commission. Hunt designed it as a Viennese Seces-
sionist hillside eyrie about to take flight over San Francisco Bay. Like Frank
Lloyd Wright and the other young architects of the Steinway Hall group in
Chicago, Hunt had poured over published photographs and plans of Viennese
Secessionist designs in the late 1890s, finding in them the basis for a new
American architecture. As a gesture to California Hunt gave his first West
Coast creation an Italian courtyard. He also used a concrete foundation and
stucco surfaces and thereby suggested an alternative to the predominant wood-
and-shingle style of Maybeck. Stucco, moreover, provided a point of departure
from the Craftsman style towards the Mediterraneanism that would soon become Hunt's predominant mode. In any event, the Livingston Jenks house
announced in no uncertain terms that an important new architectural talent,
in touch with the most vital European and American developments, was at
work in California.

As congenial as Myron Hunt found San Francisco, his wife Harriet required
a Southern Californian climate. Just as the Frank Lloyd Wrights chose the
Chicago suburb of Oak Park for its ambience of Progressive high-minded New
Englandism, the Hunts chose to settle in Pasadena, the Oak Park of Southern
California. The Hunts moved there just as its late nineteenth-century generation of New Englandish haute bougeoisie was being supplemented by an even
more affluent class of Tory Progressives. During these years, two Pasadenas
were in the process of defining themselves. The Arroyo Seco crowd (the Native
American ethnologist and Southwest desert enthusiast George Wharton James
can be seen as a representative type) tended to be artists, intellectuals, bohemians, and Progressives of various persuasions. As their designation indicates,
these intellectuals preferred to live in Craftsman homes perched on hillsides of
the great arroyo which cut into the otherwise staid city, bringing with it a
powerful suggestion of the rugged terrain of the desert Southwest. Indeed it was
the metaphor of Southern California as Spanish Southwest that the Arroyo
Seco dwellers most vividly internalized into their lifestyles: Craftsman homes,
Indian blankets and baskets within as decorative motifs, bookshelves lined with
the ethnological and environmental writings, copies of *Land of Sunshine/Out
West* on reading tables lit softly by California Decorative lamps. The Valley
Hunt Club crowd, by contrast—which is to say, newly arriving Midwestern
and Eastern wealth—preferred grand residences on Orange Grove Avenue and
riding to hounds at the Valley Hunt Club founded by sportsman Charles Frederick Holder in the late 1880s.

In questions of taste and in other matters as well, Arroyo Seco Pasadena and
Valley Hunt Pasadena never completely sorted themselves out from each other.
A fundamental tension between Pasadena as Southwest Craftsman and Pasa-

dena as Montecito, Burlingame, Brookline, or Sewickley, continued through
the early decades of the century. Cross-references were everywhere. The Gamble House by Greene and Greene, for example, brought Craftsman values to
Orange Grove Avenue (4 Westmoreland Place, actually, a spur outcropping of
millionaires' row), and a number of the Valley Hunt crowd collected Indian
memorabilia, hung their homes with paintings by Frederic Remington and
Charles Russell, and worked with Charles Fletcher Lummis for the establishment of a Southwestern Museum.

Moving into this dichotomous situation, with each side representing a distinct vision of what Southern California promised, Myron Hunt initially split
the difference. In 1905 he designed for himself a two-story shingle house at
200 North Grand Avenue, but its stucco first floor and its progressive Midwestern idiom recalled the Hunts' just-left home in Evanston, Illinois. Inside,
however, Hunt used exposed redwood beams and earth-tone tile in the best
manner of the Arroyo Seco; yet the wall and ceiling spaces between the redwood beams and the tile were plastered and painted white, adding a Mediterranean rather than the usual English effect to Craftsman wood and tile.

In the landscaping and garden designs of his home, Hunt signaled an already
emergent Southern California Mediterraneanism. As a design for living, after
all, the garden constituted the central Southern Californian connection. The
son of a distinguished nurseryman, Myron Hunt loved and understood trees,
shrubs, flowering plants. He also knew and loved the garden and landscaping
traditions of Italy. Hunt's very first Southland commission had been the redesign of the gardens of the Hotel Maryland in Pasadena. Among other amenities, Hunt designed a plastered masonry pergola translated romantically from
the Amalfi coast. Soon overgrown with vines, the Hotel Maryland pergola became a local landmark, reproduced on postcards as a popular image of Southern California as the Mediterranean shore of America. For his own home Hunt
created a formal Mediterranean pergola and garden graced by a circular pool.
He considered such welled gardens as directly linked to the gardens of the
Mission era and back beyond that to the gardens of Moorish Spain, Rome,
Mesopotamia, and the Biblical imagery of Eden itself: gardens that combined
watered luxuriance with surrounding scarcity, domestic planting with a constant awareness of the desert beyond. "The real California garden is on the
border of the desert," Hunt told the Los Angeles *Evening News* for 7 October
1907. The *News* was interviewing Hunt regarding the garden and pergola he
had designed for the home of Mrs. John D. Hooker on West Adams Boulevard
in Los Angeles. "We must accept the wilderness and use it as the background
for our picture, the setting for our jewel."[7] As an Italian garden for an ardent
Italophile, the Hooker garden, together with the gardens Hunt designed for the
Hotel Maryland and his own home, pointed in the scholarly romantic direction
that Hunt's highly schooled talent would take amidst the eclectic opportunities
of Southern California.

And indeed, opportunities abounded. Hunt might live in Pasadena but he kept his office in downtown Los Angeles, a city that would grow from 100,000 to 1.25 million between Hunt's arrival and 1930. The south coast, meanwhile, from Santa Barbara to Laguna Beach, was growing at an even faster rate. There was plenty of business and Myron Hunt soon secured more than his share: apartment houses in Los Angeles at Main and Sixteenth and Hope and Fifth, bungalows for the Hotel Maryland, private homes in Pasadena and Los Angeles. Within the year, Hunt was on the lookout for a partner. He found one in Elmer Grey, whom he met while horseback riding on weekends between Pasadena and Monrovia.

Trained as a draftsman in Milwaukee, Grey had studied briefly in Europe on special scholarship as an apprentice and had made several other study trips there while working in Milwaukee. Rising to architect's status, Grey suffered a nervous collapse in the course of working on the First Church of Christ Scientist of Milwaukee and had moved to Southern California, where he was working as a ranch hand to regain his health when he and Hunt met. Aside from their both being equestrians, Hunt and Grey resembled and differed from each other in ways conducive to partnership. Hunt was educated at MIT. Grey had risen from an apprentice draftsman. A Valley Hunt Club member, a party-giver and -goer highly socialized from his Steinway Hall days in Chicago, Myron Hunt liked people and social life and the process of securing business through social contacts. Diffident, reclusive, frequently insecure, Grey had already suffered one nervous collapse and would experience another before the decade was out. Without peace and quiet, he later said of himself, he just could not cope. Each architect, however, possessed a scholarly streak. Grey's pen-and-ink sketches of European architecture were superb, as were all his sketches and renderings, an activity in which he far surpassed Hunt. Like Hunt, Grey prized simplicity and hated fake historical ornament. Like Hunt, he also loved gardens.

Gardens, in fact, provided the common characteristic of the diversely styled homes Hunt and Grey designed in the early years of their partnership. While most of their homes were in the Craftsman bungalow mode, Hunt and Grey also designed in Spanish, Italian, and even American Colonial Revival which, as in the cases of the J.E. Speer house in Pasadena (1905) and the E.M. Taylor home in Altadena (1910), they modified into a variant later designated California Colonial, a mode they first used in 1907 for the Valley Hunt Club. Whatever their style, however, Hunt and Grey reversed the usual arrangement of rooms so as to achieve a rear-garden orientation. The kitchen was brought from the back of the house to the street side. The street became a mere entrance point. The rear of the house, by contrast, looked out through oversized windows to the gardens, which were immediately accessible to the rear living room.

In a Hunt and Grey home designed for Robert C. Gillis of Santa Monica, one approached the dining room through an open-air loggia leading out from the rear living room in much the same manner that Irving Gill had devised for the Fulford house in San Diego. For the Hollywood estate of G.W. Wattles, Hunt and Grey combined Pueblo, Mission, and Italian motifs in a structure roofed in red tile and covered with pebbledash grey cement as a gesture to Southwestern adobe. At one end of the home they established a cloister garden planted in orange, lemon, grapefruit, tangerine, almond, walnut, plum, peach, apricot, pomegranate, and fig trees; and behind the home, sweeping up the hillside, they emplaced an ascending orchestration of terraces, balustrades, and stairways, landscaped in palms, cypress, ilex, shrubbery, and flowering plants. Reviewing and publishing photographs of these garden homes of Hunt and Grey, *The Craftsman* magazine praised the Southern California team for evolving a new style of indoor/outdoor American architecture.

Towards the end of their association, which terminated in 1910, Hunt and Grey turned increasingly to the Mediterranean idiom, Italian and Spanish. As supervising architects for Cram, Goodhue and Ferguson of New York, Hunt and Grey in 1906 worked on El Fureidis, the Montecito mansion of James Waldron Gillespie which served as a prototype for an era of Mediterraneanizing. El Fureidis, house and gardens, evoked a transforming vision of Southern California as Mediterranean dream which Hunt referred to frequently in the course of his career. In 1908 Hunt and Grey achieved their own prototype, a home and gardens in Hollywood for the Southern Californianized Omaha banker G.W. Wattles. Having lived in Mexico, Wattles wanted a Spanish-style hacienda. Hunt and Grey forthwith designed perhaps the first truly Spanish Revival, as opposed to Mission Revival, home of importance in Southern California, a two-story masterpiece of restrained historicism set serenely against a ninety-acre Hollywood hillside.

For railroad magnate Henry Huntington, Hunt and Grey achieved another masterpiece of Mediterranean chaparral, in this case a grand palazzo on Huntington's San Marino Ranch, which the inveterate art and book collector was already developing with cactus and Japanese gardens. Set against the background of the swiftly ascending San Gabriel Mountains, the Huntington mansion, completed in 1910, unfolded itself in isolated grandeur on the as-of-yet undeveloped ranchlands. Within time, gardens would grow up to enhance the architecture and priceless paintings, and books would pour in from England to be installed like hot-house plants of a different sort amidst the vanquished chaparral. All in all, the Huntington estate provided a compelling paradigm of Southern California as the product of acquisition and self-invention, a garden palace rising in the wilderness.

Eventually, the Huntington estate was to be opened to visitors as a library, art gallery, and public garden. It was in their public designs, perhaps, that Hunt and Grey most conspicuously expressed their vision of Southern California as an American Mediterranean. Three developing institutions of higher education—the Throop (later California) Institute of Technology in Pasadena, Pomona College in Claremont, and Occidental College in northeast Los Angeles—turned to Hunt and Grey for campus plans, just as the Stanfords had turned to H.H. Richardson, and the University of California regents had turned to John Galen Howard for architectural interpretation. From Jefferson's University of Virginia onward, campus plans by definition offer strong opportunities for utopian statements. Although they fell out with each other on the specifics of the Throop plan, Hunt and Grey masterplanned all three campuses as neo-Mediterranean versions of Jefferson's integrated scheme.

Through Grey's skillful renderings, Throop/Cal Tech, Pomona, and Occidental took shape in imagination as what they were later, with adjustments, materialized to be—utopian evocations of Southern California as linked in architecture and general culture to Spain and Italy. To this day, these three campuses still possess the capacity to enchant visitors with their integrated orchestrations of Italian and Spanish motifs, their arcaded walkways and courtyard gardens, their harmonized arrangements and stately open spaces. Here indeed is still preserved the pre-1930 dream of Southern California as recovered Mediterranean, as sunny garden of the South. Unfortunately, Grey favored a central building and rotunda for Throop, which Hunt felt was dishonest. Rejecting Hunt's alternative proposal, the trustees sided with Grey, and the partnership dissolved.

In the years that followed, Elmer Grey pursued a quiet, slowly paced career more suitable to his fragile temperament. For himself he designed a Prairie/ Italian hybrid in Pasadena, surrounded by oak and orange trees. In 1912 he designed the Beverly Hills Hotel, a retardataire Mission Revival complex, destined to become smothered in an exotic tropical garden that like the hotel itself pushed the resort metaphor to its lush outer limits. To overlook the gardens of the Wattells estate in Hollywood, which he and Hunt had designed together, Grey created an Italian cloister home for Mrs. M.C. Russell and her daughter. It was perhaps the most scholarly Italian design to emerge in that era in all Southern California, an exquisite arrangement of a villa and an adjoining tea house bridged by cloistered courts through whose gardens one might expect to catch a glimpse of Renaissance humanist philosophers strolling and discussing Plotinus.

In contrast to his erstwhile partner's more leisurely pace, Myron Hunt, working alone until 1920, then after that in partnership with Harold Coulson Chambers, embarked upon an epic period of design and construction. Between 1910 and 1929 Hunt completed some five hundred projects in Southern California, an outpouring which included homes, churches, hotels, including the fabled Mission Inn in Riverside, the Rose Bowl Stadium, the Huntington Library, country clubs, a school for pre-delinquent boys, and the continuing construction programs of Cal Tech, Pomona, and Occidental colleges. If any single architect can be said to have played a major role in establishing the pervasive appearance, the design environment, of pre-Depression Southern California, it was Myron Hunt, signature architect of the Southland.

Obviously no one architect could dominate the private housing sector. As opposed to the splendid isolation of his pre-1915 work as a domestic architect, during which he shared honors with no more than three or four comparable talents, Hunt's domestic designs occurred in the increasingly crowded field of post-1915 architectural creativity. Yet he still managed to distinguish himself. For philanthropist Margaret Fowler, who lived in Chino in southwestern San Bernardino County near Ontario, Hunt designed a home in 1915 modeled on the architecture of the fishing villages of southern Italy—tiled roof, a Successionist chimney extruding abruptly, bold unadorned white surfaces, oversized grilled windows, an outside staircase to the second story—which the *American Architect* hailed as distinctly Southern Californian in idiom. For the Peshines of Santa Barbara, a pioneering Hispanic-Yankee family humorously rumored to pray daily for the return of Spanish rule to Santa Barbara, Hunt designed in 1918 a residence and private chapel that helped convert Santa Barbara to Spanish Revival as its official style. In his other Spanish Revival houses—the house of Huntington librarian George Watson Cole in Pasadena, for example, or the home Hunt designed in Palos Verdes for Frederick Law Olmsted, Jr.—Hunt employed hollow-walled concrete which, aside from its coolness, created surfaces that recalled the adobe of the Spanish era while remaining assertively modern.

In an era of hotel building, Hunt designed more than his share, among them the Huntington Hotel in Pasadena (1913), designed initially in 1906 by Charles F. Whittlesey, another Chicagoan, but left half-built for a number of years before Henry Huntington acquired the property. Locating the entrance off a large landscaped parking lot, Hunt completed the Huntington as the first major hotel in Southern California to orient itself primarily to guests arriving and departing by automobile. At the time, Hunt was himself living in the Hotel Maryland in Pasadena, having moved there when his wife Harriet succumbed to the tuberculosis that had brought them both to Southern California a decade earlier. The next year Hunt filled in the pergola he had designed for the Maryland in the year of his arrival with small retail shops and ran a roof garden across its upper level. Within ten short years of his arrival, Hunt's Southern California work was already beginning to recycle itself. The Ambassador Hotel of Los Angeles (1921) represented Hunt's triumph of hotel design—unless one compared it with the stunning Hispanic modernity of the Hotel Flintridge in the suburb of the same name, or the scholarly tour de force of the Mission Inn at Riverside.

Hunt came to the immediate attention of Frank Miller, owner of the Glenwood Mission Inn, when Hunt and Grey were chosen to design a new structure for the First Congregational Church of Riverside, where Frank Miller worshipped. When the partnership broke up, Hunt finished the Spanish Renaissance design on his own and the church, completed in 1912 as a basilica with Churrigueresque tower, played a major role in promoting the Spanish Revival through Southern California. Three years before the success of Bertram Goodhue's California Building at the Panama-California Exposition at San Diego, Myron Hunt demonstrated to Southern California through this Congregational Churrigueresque basilica the appropriateness of authentic Spanish Revival, as opposed to the purely imaginary Mission Revival, to the public life of the Southland. In Southern California, even Congregationalists felt at home in Spain.

Thus impressed, hotelier Frank Miller commissioned Hunt to design a north wing for his idiosyncratic Mission Revival hotel, originally designed by Arthur Benton a decade earlier. Just as he had upgraded Mission Revival to authentic Spanish Revival at First Congregational, Hunt now produced for Miller a visual tone poem, Spanish Venetian in inspiration. In the center of his U-shaped confection of rising arches and towers, completed in 1914, Hunt placed the most successful public courtyard space thus far achieved in Southern California. Protected by a retractable multicolored awning at roofline, the Spanish Patio, as it was called, became the most charming outdoor dining area in the Southland. Not only could Southern Californians now worship in Spanish Renaissance splendor at First Congregational, thanks again to the scholarship of Myron Hunt, they might dine as well in a setting worthy of Tintoretto and Velasquez.

At the Flintridge, which Hunt designed for Senator Frank Flint in 1926, Southern Californians were dazzled by an integrated hillside village suggestive of the Greek islands, southern Italy, the Côte d'Azur, and Costa Brava. By allowing the hollow concrete walls of the Flintridge to bulge out slightly or to recede at irregular intervals, Hunt reinforced the effect of a habitat arising naturally from its hilltop site as the patient work of ages. In the Mediterranean, the accretions of such architectural environments took centuries. On behalf of Southern California, a region in a hurry, Myron Hunt materialized these Mediterranean dreams on an overnight basis.

Did the oligarchs and Babbitts of the Southland require headquarters for their clubs and associations? Hunt designed for them the Elks Club in Pasadena (1911), in stiff and formal American Colonial, as if to suggest that the Elks of the area, still uncertain of the propriety of their circumstances, felt the need to assert themselves as uncompromisingly Yankee. For the country club crowd, Hunt designed the Los Palos Verdes Country Club (1914), the Bolsa Chica Gun Club at Huntington Beach (1915), the third Valley Hunt Club at Pasadena (1920), the Rancho Golf Club at San Marino (1921), the Flintridge Golf Club (1922), and the Surf and Sand Club at Hermosa Beach (1925), where an entire generation of Southern Californians pursued the good life.

Did Southern California require a multiplicity of commercial structures? Myron

Hunt complied, as in the case of the County National Bank and Trust Company of Santa Barbara (1920), for which he adapted the nave of Santa Maria Maggiore in Rome, or the light-drenched Spanish Revival show rooms he designed for I. Magnin and Company in Hollywood and Palm Springs.

Hunt conferred equal scholarship on the many hospitals and sanitaria he designed for the region, most notably the Huntington Memorial Hospital in Pasadena (1922), and upon the many other institutional structures, from Throop Polytechnic (1907) to Los Angeles's Hamburger Home for Jewish Working Girls (1928), which he, working alone or with either Grey or Chambers, produced in the pre-1930 era.

Hunt designed elegant public libraries for Pasadena, Palos Verdes, and other communities, and in 1919 he provided Henry Huntington with designs for a grand neoclassical structure at San Marino to house Huntington's world-class collection of art, books, and manuscripts.

At the same time, the late teens and early twenties, Hunt was busy on what was from an engineering and planning standpoint his most heroic project, the Rose Bowl Stadium in Pasadena. After mediating by moonlight on the new stadium at Harvard, Henry James noted in *The American Scene* (1907) that imperial America was now building appropriately classical forums for its Greco-Roman games. Harvard, Yale, Princeton, Ohio State, Stanford—one by one the universities of the early twentieth century erected stadia which like the great urban railroad stations modeled on Roman architecture or the world cruise of the Great White Fleet expressed the new American ascendancy. An eager participant in Tournament of Roses festivities (the float he designed for the Maryland Hotel in 1910 won first prize), Hunt, an ardent Pasadenan and civic activist, welcomed the stadium project as the first step in a program that would transform a portion of the Arroyo Seco into a public park on the scale of Golden Gate Park in San Francisco.

Commissioned to design the new stadium, Hunt prepared himself with the thoroughness of an architect trained in the tradition of H.H. Richardson and Shepley, Rutan and Coolidge. With scholarly thoroughness, he made a study of ancient and modern stadia before deciding that the Yale Bowl, an ellipse sunk into the site itself, as opposed to the Harvard model, an above-the-surface structure modeled on the Roman Colosseum, best suited the Arroyo Seco. He studied aerial photographs of American stadia during football games to determine patterns of seating preference. He also scrutinized lines of sight before determining the final shape of the stadium and its seating arrangements. As in the case of the Huntington Hotel, Hunt planned thoroughly for the automobile, both in terms of establishing suitable parking areas and using eleven natural canyons as lines of entry and exit. Cost considerations prevented the complete implementation of all of Hunt's recommendations. Among the dropped proposals was a monumental arched façade, its portals guarded by great granite buffaloes. Nevertheless the Rose bowl—ready by 1922, expanded in 1928, 1932, and 1949 until it seated 101,000 spectators—established Pasadena as the site of an important American annual ritual, a New Year's Day college football game which boasted the Southern California climate and the emergence of the Southland as an important academic and athletic center.

It was in his ongoing academic planning and design that Myron Hunt most closely and effectively connected with the vision of Southern California as a neo-Mediterranean region. In part through his continuing efforts, Cal Tech, Pomona, and Occidental emerged in the 1920s and 1930s as among the best planned and regionally appropriate college campuses in the country. Hunt devised the initial Throop/Cal Tech plan in collaboration with Grey. He inherited the Pomona project when the partnership dissolved and secured the Occidental commission on his own in 1911. In each scheme, especially Pomona, Hunt sought Jeffersonian arrangements of buildings and enclosed landscaped space. For Cal Tech, Hunt designed a headquarters building for the Mount Wilson Observatory; for Pomona, he designed six structures, including an open-air Greek theater. As in the case of the First Congregational Church at Riverside, Hunt's Bridges Hall of Music at Pomona provided Southern California with another important adaptation of the basilica, in this case an auditorium dominated by soaring organ pipes. For Occidental College, Hunt designed a total of twenty-one buildings by 1944, including a beautifully arranged athletic field and bleachers and another outdoor Greek theater.

In all this work at Cal Tech, Pomona, and Occidental as well as in the hundreds of other designs that continued to issue from his office, Myron Hunt continued to exercise that blend of Mediterranean romanticism and instinctive restraint which some have attributed to his New England temperament. Critics have noted a certain severity, a dryness even, to the Hunt oeuvre (the First Congregational Church and the north wing of the Glenwood Mission Inn at Riverside constitute obvious exceptions), as if Hunt were holding himself back, consciously or subconsciously, from the luxuriant directions his Spanish and Italian designs might take. Hunt's reserve proved fortunate; for he, more than any other architect of his era, established the visual standards and symbols of Southern California in the making. Myron Hunt found a neo-Mediterranean mean between Churrigueresque exuberance and the drive towards stark simplicity which propelled California Spanish in the direction of the International Style. A New Englander and a Chicagoan before his arrival, Myron Hunt—a Harold Lloyd of a man, in tweed suits and owlish framed glasses, an Ivy League professor in exile—functioned as court architect to the Anglo-American Midwest Protestant ascendancy of Southern California in the years of its most complete control. Hunt provided this ascendancy with a blend of romance and serious purpose which successfully expressed its own fundamental conviction about what it was doing in Southern California: following the sun to the Mediterranean shores of America but remembering the Mayflower and Plymouth Rock as well.

5

Of the two Mediterranean styles Hunt favored, Spanish Revival and Italian, Spanish Revival struck the most pervasive chord of popular acceptance. By the 1930s California Spanish, as it came to be known, had emerged as Southern California's most popular design for living. Some communities, in fact—Santa Barbara, Ojai, Palos Verdes, San Clemente, Rancho Santa Fe—went so far as to declare other styles illegal, although the constitutionality of such sweeping restrictions remains an interesting question. As David Gebhard has shown, California Spanish possessed a dichotomous inner dynamic propelling it to romantic historical luxuriance on the one hand and geometric simplicity on the other. From one perspective, this widely accepted style represented a romantic grafting of a largely imaginary past onto the physical fabric of the American present. Its first phase, Mission Revival, the style of innumerable hotels and train depots in Southern California in the pre-World War I era, paralleled the neoclassical American Renaissance style as practiced by McKim, Mead and White in the East and was, indeed, inspired by the same event, the Columbian Exposition of 1893. Even in Mission Revival, however, there was a connection to the Craftsman movement in decoration and furnishings and a link to Secessionism in the handling of elemental forms such as the cube, the rectangle, and the arch. In the case of Irving Gill of San Diego, a short-cut to the International Style of the 1930s was already developing by the early 1900s.

The second phase of the Spanish Revival, the Spanish Colonial or Churrigueresque phase, was anticipated in 1912 by Myron Hunt's First Congregational Church at Riverside and officially ushered in by Bertram Goodhue's California Building at the Panama-California Exposition of 1915 held in San Diego. Following the Exposition, innumerable homes, churches, schools, and automobile showrooms exfoliated in Churrigueresque exuberance across the sub/urban cityscapes of the Southland. Was there ever built a more luxuriantly Churrigueresque structure in the Southland, for example, than St. Vincent de Paul's Roman Catholic church in Los Angeles, designed in 1922 by Albert C. Martin? Even today it rises gorgeously in massed ornament and multicolored tile, a vice-regal Mexican daydream oblivious to the prosaic car lots surrounding its splendor. Even Churrigueresque, however, showed a continuing proclivity for elemental forms—in the case of St. Vincent's the dome being added to the cube, the rectangle, and the arch—and for stark simplicity playing off against ornament, carrying on the ongoing dialogue of Spanish Revival with the avant-garde.

Another, if subsequently neglected, factor in this dynamic of restraint and incipient modernity in Spanish Revival was the influence of the Southwest Museum itself. Designed by Sumner Hunt and S.R. Burns in 1915–16, the Southwest Museum brought the austere grandeur of the Pueblo or Santa Fe style to a conspicuous eminence overlooking Los Angeles. Like adobe, the reinforced concrete of the museum lent itself to sweepingly simple surfaces. The Southwest Museum rose from its site like the desert dream of Archbishop Jean Baptiste Lamy—a castle, a cathedral, a pueblo of learning at once aboriginal and European like New Mexico itself. Not only did the Southwest Museum establish greater Los Angeles as headquarters for the study and display of the geology, flora, fauna, and ethnology of the Southwest, it also insured in its architecture that the Native American simplicities that were also such an historically authentic part of the Southern California tradition would not be forgotten.

In the third phase of Spanish Revival, inspired in the early and mid-1920s by the elemental forms of Mexico and provincial Spain, Andalusia especially, the drive towards simplicity in architects such as James Osborne and Mary Craig, Lutah Maria Riggs and George Washington Smith of Santa Barbara; Wallace Neff of Pasadena; Reginald Johnson, Gordon Kaufmann, and Carleton Monroe Winslow of Los Angeles; and others in the San Diego area propelled Spanish Revival to a convergence point with the International Style. As in the case of so many other sectors of activity in Southern California during this period, to unravel this skein of design influences is to encounter the Midwest and Chicago. With so many Progressive Midwesterners commissioning homes in Southern California from so many architects who were themselves from the Midwest and either Chicago-trained or -influenced, it is not surprising that even within the parameters of Spanish Revival a connection with the Progressive designs of Louis Sullivan, Frank Lloyd Wright, the Prairie School, and the Viennese Secessionism that was in turn such a strong influence on the Chicago School should continue to assert itself in the Southland. While it possessed its stagy, historically exaggerated, even regressive aspects, Spanish Revival, especially in its 1920s phases, also advanced a strong regional case for Progressive architecture.

Not everyone was impressed. While Spanish Revival could be handled tastefully by individual architects, especially in Santa Barbara, noted Los Angeles journalist Victor E. Walkers in a widely distributed 1927 guidebook, when used indiscriminately in mass housing Spanish Revival lost its integrity and became a fantastic perversion. "Using the cheap stucco and frame-work of slight boards, in preference to the native adobe and massive timbers of the first builders," Walkers reproved, "painting the walls in every imaginable tint, and covering it all with everything from thrushes, shakes, shingles, imitation tile, to paper, covered with tar and either painted or covered in turn with scattered, colored rock, the results are bewildering to the eye, and, when the full enormity and significance of the thing penetrates, a bit offensive."[8]

As affluent communities controlled either by developers or by elites, Santa Barbara, Ojai, Palos Verdes, San Clemente, and Rancho Santa Fe by and large avoided such excesses born of mass production. San Clemente was developed as a de facto proprietary colony, with developer Ole Hanson, the former mayor of Seattle, functioning as an Orange County William Penn, decreeing happiness and prosperity in Spanish homes on the shores of the sundown sea. After wintering for years in Southern California, Hanson moved permanently to the Southland in the early 1920s. In 1925 he and his partners acquired a five-mile strip of Rancho Santa Margarita, nestled between the seashore and Saddleback Mountain midway between Los Angeles and San Diego. Here, Hanson decided, he would develop a Spanish Village in which the good life, Southern California-style, might be lived to paradigmatic perfection. An experienced municipal official, Hanson structured all real-estate sales and covenants so as to insure that only Spanish Revival architecture could be locally employed. He also built, again in the Spanish style, a completely equipped beach club and outdoor swimming pool, tennis courts, children's playgrounds, bridle paths and parks, an eighteen-hole golf course, a Spanish-style public plaza, a school, a social center, and a civic auditorium as part of the amenity package he was offering prospective residents.

By 1928 Hanson had sold more than $7 million in lots and some 1400 residents were pursuing the Southern California dream in a seaside environment exclusively Spanish in design. In San Clemente, moreover—white, affluent, beach-oriented, a socially controlled daydream of sun, surf, sand, Spain, and safety—the eventual culture of coastal Orange County was dramatically anticipated.

Throughout the 1920s national magazines began increasingly to showcase the Spanish Revival architecture of Southern California, beginning with an extensively illustrated article in *House and Garden* for November 1921 which cited the work of Myron Hunt, Elmer Grey, and Richard S. Requa. By January 1922 when *House Beautiful* ran a similar article, the list had grown to include homes designed by George Washington Smith, Reginald Johnson, and the team of Sylvanus B. Marston and Garrett Van Pelt. Within five years, Spanish Revival had emerged as the style considered most representatively Southern Californian by the national press and by a growing number of local residents.

In restoring the century-old Casa Flores Adobe of Pasadena as a private residence in 1920, architect Carleton Monroe Winslow connected Spanish Revival with preservationism. Incorporating the original adobe walls into his design, Winslow extended the venerable structure via a new wing and the restoration of the original patio. An ancient confessional, built into one wall, was left intact. Over in Los Angeles, preservationism arrived in full force in 1928 when Mrs. Christine Sterling, one of those forceful, single-minded women who are so frequently found at the center of public service movements, discovered to her dismay that the oldest surviving private home in the city, the Avila Adobe (1818) on Olvera Street near the Plaza north of the new City Hall, was scheduled for demolition.

All of Olvera Street, in fact, with its other surviving adobes, had degenerated over the years into rubbish-strewn neglect. Raising money with the help of Harry Chandler, who extracted $39,000 at one luncheon meeting, Sterling purchased and restored the Avila Adobe, refurnishing it with furniture and paintings from the 1820s. Raising further funds, she purchased or leased other nearby adobes through an association which soon controlled the entire street. Blocked off from traffic, its adobes refurbished and transformed into art galleries, restaurants, and retail shops, its streets lively with tourists, food stalls, Spanish music, and conversation, Olvera Street helped pioneer the concept of restoration and preservation through adaptive re-use. Olvera Street might not be authentic Old California or even authentic Mexico, but it was better than the bulldozer.

Adaptive adjustment, the recycling forward of historical precedents, characterized the designs for living which the grand eclectics Robert Farquhar, Sylvanus B. Marston, Reginald Johnson, Gordon Kaufmann, and Wallace Neff devised for Southern California in this emergent era. Eclecticism was necessary, for despite the pre-eminence of the Mediterranean mode, Southern Californians had other preferences as well. For physician, real-estate developer, and millionaire socialist John R. Haynes of Los Angeles, for example, Robert Farquhar created a French chateau—stately, serene, cerebral—similar to those Willis Polk was designing for the San Francisco peninsula.

As can be expected from a community priding itself on its Anglo-Saxon ancestry, English architecture remained a continuing preference. For client R.A. Rowan, Farquhar devised a grand Stuart pile that made a corner of Pasadena a bit of England. English also were the timbered Jacobean home created for William Hespeler by Sylvanus B. Marston and the Regency mansion Marston devised for W.D. Petersen, each of them in Pasadena. For George S. Hunt of Linda Vista, Marston designed a Gaelic country cottage, surrounding it with stone fences. Had sheep been present the day *Architect and Engineer* photographed the Hunt residence, Linda Vista might easily have passed for Kilkenny or the Highlands.

Gordon Kaufmann, another Anglicizing architect of this era, was himself London-born and -trained (at London Polytechnic and the Royal College of Art) and had served an architectural apprenticeship there under the skilled historicist A.W.S. Cross. Migrating to Southern California in 1914 via Canada because of his wife's lung problems, Kaufmann worked himself into a partnership with Reginald Johnson and Roland Coate. Before that, however, unable to find work as an architect, he supported himself and his wife as a gardener, thus earning by the sweat of his brow an honest relationship to the garden metaphor.

As designers, Johnson and Kaufmann felt at home in a variety of traditions. Each, for instance, would later be responsible for two Mediterranean masterpieces, Johnson's Biltmore Hotel in Santa Barbara and Kaufmann's Atheneum Faculty Club at Cal Tech; but each showed a proclivity for English styles as well, as evidenced in Johnson's residence for H. Page Warren in Pasadena, a commanding re-creation of a Jacobean country house. Working together in the early 1920s, Johnson, Kaufmann, and Coate produced a number of fine English houses, together with All Saints' Episcopal Church in Pasadena and the Episcopal Cathedral of St. Paul in Los Angeles, two major monuments to the Anglican tradition as translated to the Southland.

In Greystone, the massive Gothic Revival mansion Kaufmann designed for oil magnate Edward Laurence Doheny in the late 1920s for presentation to his son, English architecture reached a showy climax, Rising on a height overlooking its 428-acre estate in Beverly Hills, Greystone (1928) seems a dream materialized from the imagination of Sir Walter Scott. Is it real or a Hollywood set, this fifty-five-room extravaganza covering 46,000 square feet of living space, with its gables and seven chimneys soaring aloft like the roofline of an Oxford college? Only an Irishman such as Doheny was capable of desiring such English grandeur for his offspring. Greystone was energized by hundreds of years of suppressed longing to live in the style of the race which the Irish loved, hated, admired, and envied. Gordon Kaufmann, an assimilated English Jew turned Southern Californian, understood his Irish-American client perfectly.

Among these grand eclectics, Wallace Neff distinguished himself as the most imaginative and playful: not as correct perhaps as the others but displaying an inventiveness, a storybook theatricality that in some ways made his work seem the most appropriately Southern Californian. Neff, first of all, was a native son born in 1895 in La Mirada, a subdivision near Altadena (itself near Pasadena), which Neff's grandfather, the multimillionaire Chicago map and gazeteer publisher Andrew McNally (as in Rand McNally), was developing as a community of country estates. McNally's chief assistant in the La Mirada scheme was his son-in-law Edwin Dorland Neff, a Chicago stockbroker of Swiss-Dutch descent. Moving permanently to La Mirada from Chicago, Neff proceeded to pursue a life of sports-related leisure—riding, hunting, some ranching—as described in the brochure *The Country Gentleman in California* (1897) which he wrote to sell the La Mirada estates. When the Neff children reached school age, the family moved to a home in Altadena which Andrew McNally had presented to the couple at the time of their marriage.

A scion of the same Southern Californianized Midwestern wealth which constituted the most appreciative clientele for architecture, Wallace Neff grew up with a strong sense of personal caste and regional identity. Southern California was for Neff not a locale adopted in later life for reasons of health or economic opportunity, but the internalized landscape of his earliest and most fundamental self. He understood the place instinctively—its climate, landforms, fauna, and flora, its capacity to speak directly to dreams. Wallace Neff's father, after all, empowered by wealth, had come to Southern California to lead a storybook life as a country squire, which he proceeded to do. In later life, Wallace Neff would show an instinctive understanding of the life-style and subliminal aspirations of his clients: why, that is, they had come to Southern California in the first place; and this rapport accounted in some measure for the storybook aspects, the mood of dreams come true, that characterized so much of his work.

Between 1909 and 1914 the Neffs lived in Europe, based initially in Switzerland where they had gone to seek medical treatment for Wallace's sister Marie, who had been born with a congenital heart condition. The Neffs later moved to Bavaria, where Wallace was sent to the German-American School in Munich. Marie Neff, unfortunately, succumbed to her heart condition in late 1912, and the entire Neff family relocated to Munich until the outbreak of war drove them back to the United State. For five impressionable years, from age 14 to 19, Wallace Neff experienced Europe—Switzerland, South Germany, France, and Italy—as a student and an ardent traveler. Instructed in drawing at Munich by the landscape painter Peter Paul Muller, Neff filled his sketchbooks with depictions of picturesque rural architecture (a castle rising from rock formations, a country church emerging from a copse of trees) that could already pass as illustrations for a book of fairy tales set in the Bavarian forest.

At MIT, where Neff studied architecture from 1915 to 1917, Dean Ralph Adams Cram encouraged his propensity towards a strong narrative line based on historical precedents. Himself the master of Gothic Revival (St. John the Divine in New York, the monastery of the Cowley Fathers in Cambridge, the Graduate School and Chapel at Princeton, the United States Military Academy at West Point), Cram rejected the Beaux Arts tradition of drawing and redrawing from classical models in favor of a more experimental approach based on travel, observation, and sketching in the field. Neff's drawings from Europe had encouraged Cram to overlook the young Southern Californian's spotty preparation (Neff had already been rejected by Throop College in Pasadena) and admit him to the program. Aside from honing his technical skills, the MIT of Ralph Adams Cram encouraged Wallace Neff to continue in that course of narrational eclecticism based on observed precedents upon which he had already embarked as a student and unpaid architectural apprentice in Munich. As an architect Wallace Neff possessed a highly developed ability to set scenes and tell stories through domestic design (throughout his long career, he would rarely do other than homes) in a manner appropriate to an emerging region desirous of identity through historical metaphors: of dreams materialized as architectural fairytales.

Entering the profession in the take-off year 1919, Neff immediately displayed his eclecticism with an exquisite Craftsman cottage for his mother in Santa Barbara (1919), a courtyard stable for Edward Drummond Libbey at Ojai based on French precedents (1923), and a country club at Ojai, again for Libbey, inspired by the low-lying horizontal haciendas of Spanish California (1923–1924). Neff thus began his career with a salute to the Craftsman era just ending, a perfect performance in the Spanish Revival era just beginning (the Ojai Country Club won an Honor Award from the Southern California chapter of the AIA), and a gesture via the Libbey stable to the rural French vernaculars Neff would begin adapting in the early 1930s for the film colony. The commission from Libbey, moreover, a multimillionaire Ohioan who wintered at Ojai, underscored another emergent pattern, Neff's ability to design for Southern Californianizing wealth—King Gillette of safety razor fame, cereal mogul Carol Post, brewer extraordinaire Adolphus Busch, Mary Pickford and Douglas Fairbanks—in such a way as to corroborate for them their newly elected identity as Southern Californians through homes that bore a signature, a trademark, almost as strong as the brand names Gillette, Post, and Busch. Through such homes, Wallace Neff told his clients the story of their new lives in Southern California.

Neff's homes were widely copied by other architects and were, many of them, passed off by realtors as authentic Neff houses thirty or forty years later when they reappeared on the market. Designers of tract homes were especially wont to borrow from Neff, and he himself was not above designing for tract developers such as Frank Meline—so that the Neff imprint on domestic design, like the Myron Hunt imprint on public and commercial structures, emerged as a visual norm throughout the Southland.

When clients wanted Italian, Wallace Neff gave them Italian: the poised Tuscan perfection of the Wilbur Collins House in Pasadena (1928), for example; or the splendiferous theatricality of the Bel-Air hilltop villa Neff designed for film mogul Sol Wurtzel in 1931, modeled on the Villa Giulia designed by Giacomo da Vignola for Pope Julius III. (A Hollywood producer and a Renaissance pope, after all, have much in common.) In the bulk of his 1920s designs, however, Neff adhered to Spanish Revival, which he chose for his own home in Altadena (1923). Throughout the 1920s, in Pasadena, San Marino, Beverly Hills, Bel-Air, Santa Barbara, and Los Angeles itself, Wallace Neff designed a series of notable Spanish Revival homes which today, sixty and more years later, preserve and epitomize—the Singer House (1925) and the Bourne House (1927) in San Marino being most conspicuous in this regard—the mood of poetic taste wedded to a regional identity itself fabricated through metaphors of Italy, Spain, Algiers, or Tripoli, which constituted such an important design for living in the Southern California of the 1920s.

When it came time in 1928 for Harry Culver, who had himself housed hundreds of thousands of Southern Californians, to house his own family on a four-acre lot across from the California Country Club in Cheviot Hills, Culver chose Wallace Neff to be his architect. Neff dissuaded Culver from his original preference for American Colonial in favor of a Spanish Revival creation with some Italian, even Secessionist (the chimney) overtones in the façade and fenestration. Within, Neff provided the Culvers with a soaring two-story living room with a carved and gilded beamed ceiling and a gallery to one side fenced off in wrought iron, served by a circular stairway surmounted by a dome. Ensconced in a setting worthy of the Escorial or a Cecil B. De Mille movie set in Spain, Harry Culver might easily persuade himself that he had indeed come a long way from Omaha.

While most of Neff's prominent clients went along with the Spanish Revival preferences of the 1920s, Douglas Fairbanks and Mary Pickford chose an English Regency motif for the redesign and adaptation of Pickfair, the Buckingham Palace of Hollywood. Neff tried in vain to persuade the first couple of Hollywood to tear down their already existing Beverly Hills home and build anew. Had they done so, Neff would no doubt have led them to a Spanish Revival or Italian Revival solution; but Fairbanks and Pickford were well aware that they were acting out in their marriage and in Pickfair a drama of national significance. By keeping their design for living English, they kept Pickfair assimilable to most regions of the United States, not to mention Canada (Mary Pickford's birthplace), the United Kingdom, and the dominions of the British Empire. Built in Spanish Revival, Pickfair would have bespoken the highly localized identity of Southern California. Remodeled by Neff in English Regency, Pickfair flatteringly corroborated the general taste of the film-going public for whom the home had become a shrine of English-speaking taste. As if to authenticate the choice by Fairbanks and Pickford of English Regency, Lord and Lady Louis Mountbatten honeymooned at Pickfair in October 1922.

Already a connection between Hollywood and architecture had asserted itself. Initially, filmmakers used the existing architecture of Southern California, the Mediterranean mansions especially, as readily available locations. But then in 1915 D.W. Griffith, inspired by the Tower of Jewels at the Panama Pacific International Exposition in San Francisco, hired English stage designer Walter Hall to recreate Babylon at the corner of Sunset and Hollywood boulevards for the spectacle *Intolerance*. Surviving until 1919 before it was dismantled, the *Intolerance* set not only provided Hollywood and Los Angeles with one of its most important metaphors, the Babylonian ziggurat atop Los Angeles City Hall, it also introduced an element of theatricality into Los Angeles/Hollywood architecture itself. When the Goldwyn Studios constructed a cathedral 240 feet long and 90 feet wide dominated by an equally impressive crucifix for its 1920 production of *Earthbound*, Hollywood balanced off the Babylon of *Intolerance* with an expressive Christian metaphor.

The more sets Hollywood created, including numerous back lots built as towns, cities, or fantasies of every description (the domed minarets of Baghdad, for instance, constructed for the 1924 Douglas Fairbanks epic), the more expressively scenic became the popular architecture of the Southland. If Hollywood, working through set designers and architects, could build a perfect replica of a thatched Scottish cottage, a Montenegran villa, or Dublin townhouse from the Grattan Ascendency for use as locations, then it is not surprising that citizens of the nearby area, influenced by both the movies and the sets themselves, should also be increasingly desirous of stage-set values in their domestic architecture. In 1923, for instance, two brothers, Adolph and Eugene Bern-heimer, built a full-scale, historically accurate sixteenth-century Japanese es-tate, Yama Shiro (the Castle on the Hill), on the crest of the highest foothill in the Santa Monica Mountains overlooking Hollywood. Fronted by a pagoda, a lake, and extensive gardens, Yama Shiro featured a fully accurate interior as well, with any Western-style furnishings specially adapted to the Asian decor. Once completed, the Bernheimer estate became available as a location for films set in the Far East, thus rechanneling the stage-set values of private architec-ture back into the films that had inspired such eclecticism in the first place.

In the hands of a master such as Wallace Neff, who became by the late 1920s and early 1930s the architect of choice for Hollywood, such narrational eclecticism, properly employed, could and did result in much fine architec-ture. The homes Neff designed for Hollywood clients such as Joan Bennett, King Vidor, Darryl Zanuck, and Charles Chaplin and Paulette Goddard during their brief marriage each bore the Neff imprint of skilled siting, proportioning, and storytelling through historical motifs.

A case could be made for the urban folk art inspired by Hollywood as well, the first hat-shaped Brown Derby Restaurant (1926) on Wilshire Boulevard across from the Ambassador Hotel being the most famous example. Why, after all, should not orange juice stands be shaped like giant oranges or hot dog stands like dachshund pups? Highbrow critics might cavil, but such folk creations became instantly accepted as signature features of the Los Angeles/Hollywood cityscape, their good-humored fantasy universally enjoyed as sly fun by mid-America.

What disturbed eastern observers such as Edmund Wilson, however, was the fact that Hollywood eclecticism seemed by the early 1930s to have run amok across vast stretches of greater Los Angeles, resulting in a phantasmagoria of unassimilated, unintegrated, spurious styles which an eastern-seaboard high-brow such as Wilson might see as final evidence for his preconception that Southern California lacked depth and was merely eccentric. "The residential people of Los Angeles," Wilson observed caustically in 1932, "are cultivated enervated people, lovers of mixturesque beauty—and they like to express their emotivation in homes that symphonize their favorite historical films, their best-beloved movie actresses, their luckiest numerological combinations or their previous incarnations in old Greece, romantic Egypt, quaint Sussex or among the priestesses of love of old India. Here you will see a Pekinese pagoda made of fresh and crackly peanut brittle—there a snow-white marshmallow igloo—there a toothsome pink nougat in the Florentine manner, rich and delicious with embedded nuts. Yonder rears a clean pocket-size replica of heraldic War-wick Castle—yonder drowses a nausey old nance. A wee wonderful Swiss shilly-shally snuggles up beneath a bountiful bougainvillea which is by no means artificially colored. And there a hot little hacienda, a regular *enchilada con queso* with a roof made of rich red tomato sauce, barely lifts her long-lashed lavender shades on the soul of old Spanish days."[9]

So much for historical eclecticism! Even the revered and contemporarily appreciated Spanish Revival falls before the Atlantic gale of Wilson's eastern-seaboard scorn. As in the case of most of his California observations, Wilson is at once correct and wrong-headed. No tradition, even that of New York, deserves to be defined exclusively by its excesses or abuses. Wilson's sense that Los Angeles had emerged as an idiosyncratic cityscape challenging to eastern eyes, however, drove directly to the point. In the last analysis, it would be by Los Angeles that the civilization of Southern California, architecturally and otherwise, would be defined and judged.

6

Two contradictory judgments ran parallel, sometimes in the same critic. Edmund Wilson's dismissal had its local counterpart in Louis Adamic's indictment of the "almost unimaginable combinations of old Spanish, Bulgarian, Swiss Alpine, Italian, Slovak, French and other peasant houses and silly battlemented castles with a tower on each corner and flying banners on each tower" which characterized the newer suburbs. Yet he admitted that "there are in Los Angeles a good many fine-looking and sensible houses and attractive streets".[10]

The *Architectural Forum* for March 1923 praised Southern California for having found for itself a viable architectural tradition, which the East had yet to do, a judgment repeated by Thomas Tallmadge in his *The Story of Architecture in America* (1927). Reviewing the architecture of Los Angeles in May 1927, Harris Allen, editor of *Pacific Coast Architect*, attributed the design weakness of Los Angeles to its lack of a cityplan and its strengths to the prominent role good architects were playing in helping the city interpret itself to itself and the world. In Los Angeles, Bruce Bliven noted, good architects were asserting themselves with their clients, "and many an oil millionaire finds himself living in an Italian or Spanish house far more beautiful than he probably wanted."[11] A trickle-down effect was at work, Harris Allen claimed, as well-designed homes and larger structures "have been used as models, and thousands of more or less slightly varied copies are scattered broadcast. Reprehensible as this may seem to the originator, it is of real benefit to the community."[12]

This process of instruction by example extended itself to public and commercial buildings as well. Two important partnerships, Walker & Eisen and Allison & Allison, joined Hunt & Chambers in the challenging task of helping greater Los Angeles establish its visual identity through successful public and commercial structures. As a million and a half people poured into greater Los Angeles between 1920 and 1930, innumerable office buildings, department stores, churches, schools, hospitals, clubs, theaters, hotels, apartment buildings, and similar structures were suddenly necessary. In 1923 alone permits for new construction totaling $185 million were issued, a record which held until 1945. In 1925 the Los Angeles business community spent $25 million on new downtown office buildings. At the height of the boom, 1923 and 1924, Walker & Eisen kept fifty draftsmen busy. Like Wallace Neff, Albert Walker and Percy Eisen were native sons. Eisen, in fact, was a creature of even more exotic plumage, a native Los Angeleno, being born there in 1885, the boom year his architect father moved from San Francisco to work on the new Los Angeles County Court House. The Allison brothers, James and David (joined in 1930 by their nephew George), were native Pennsylvanians who moved their firm from Pittsburgh to Los Angeles in 1910.

What Allison & Allison and Walker & Eisen had in common, aside from their flourishing practices in the same region, was a strong tradition of Beaux Arts architecture. James Edward Allison, the senior brother, had worked as a draftsman for Adler & Sullivan of Chicago in the 1890s when that firm was playing a major role in the creation of downtown Chicago along grand lines fully in the spirit of the Beaux Arts. David Clark Allison came by the Beaux Arts tradition directly, having studied for a year at the Atelier Duquesne of the Ecole des Beaux-Arts in 1908–1909 after earlier studies at the University of Pennsylvania. Austin C. Whittlesey, a distinguished designer in his own right who joined Allison & Allison in 1927, had worked closely with Beaux Arts masters such as Bertram Grosvenor Goodhue, most recently on the Nebraska State Capitol project, and Lewis P. Hobart in the design of Grace Cathedral in San Francisco.

Founded in Paris in 1793, the School of Architecture of the Ecole Nationale et Speciale des Beaux-Arts (itself founded in 1648) emphasized the exhaustive study of historical models, the classical above all else, as the basis of architectural education and practice. The Beaux Arts spirit favored grandeur and academic correctness in public buildings, as if (this hope remained, however, discretely understated) the cities of the world might all one day look like Paris. In 1894 the Beaux Arts philosophy came formally to the United States with the founding of the Beaux Arts Institute of Design in New York.

As a young architect, Albert Walker had formed a partnership with John Terrell Vawter, a graduate of the Umbenstock Atelier affiliated with the Ecole des Beaux-Arts. From Vawter, Walker absorbed the Beaux Arts spirit, as was fully evident in the Italian Renaissance elegance of the Bible Institute on South Hope Street the pair designed in 1913, one of the most ambitious Los Angeles buildings of its era. After Walker and Eisen formed their partnership in 1919, they recruited Beaux Arts-trained designers such as Haldane Douglas, Rube Ransford, and Carl Jules Weyl, together with a number of other designers and draftsmen trained at the Beaux Arts Institute of New York. In the case of both Allison & Allison and Walker & Eisen, then, the stage was set as a matter of lineage, preference, and opportunity (the creation, in fact, of an entire urban civilization) for an outpouring of ambitious and correct Beaux Arts-inspired design.

Each firm lived up to its opportunity. A significant percentage of three generations of Southern Californians have attended grammar school, high school, college, and university in Allison & Allison buildings, including twelve buildings on the UCLA campus alone; or worshipped in Allison & Allison creations such as First Baptist, First Congregational, Wilshire Methodist, and Temple B'nai B'rith; or attended the Women's Athletic Club, the Friday Morning Club, or the University Club in the city; or shopped at Allison & Allison department stores, read in Allison & Allison libraries, posted their letters at Allison & Allison post offices, sending their utility bills to the Southern California Edison Building in downtown Los Angeles, designed by Allison & Allison, or worked in Allison & Allison factories and warehouses, banked in Allison & Allison banks, were admitted to Allison & Allison hospitals; and, finally, were laid to rest at Allison & Allison creations such as the Kerckhoff Mausoleum or the Mausoleum and Chapels of Forest Lawn Memorial Park in Glendale. They did all this, moreover, in buildings which each bore the Allison & Allison imprint of solidity, scholarly reference, and appropriately assertive public presence.

As in the case of Myron Hunt's work, the architecture of Allison & Allison, most of it Beaux Arts/Mediterranean in impulse, sought and achieved a basic dignity and appropriateness that helped restrain the underlying festivity, the stage-set nature, of Southern California architecture which could, and so often did, edge into the merely flamboyant or superficial. The Lombard Romanesque buildings the firm designed for the new University of California campus in Westwood, for example, especially Royce Hall, the centerpiece of the ensemble, conferred immediate credibility to the expansion of the University to Southern California. As president of the Southern California Chapter of the American Institute of Architects and after 1926 as a fellow of the Institute, David Clark Allison served as the semi-official spokesman for the architectural establishment of Los Angeles in the interwar period. It was David Allison, a gifted writer as well, who first recognized in print the critical role played by Myron Hunt in the emergence of the architectural vocabulary of Southern California.

As in the case of Hunt & Chambers and Allison & Allison, Walker & Eisen pursued a similar course of scholarly Beaux Arts dignity. More than any others, this partnership set the standards for downtown Los Angeles. Their contribution commenced in 1924 with the Fine Arts Building on West Seventh Street, an adaptation of Spanish Romanesque which perfectly expressed the resurgent mood, at once Mediterranean and go-getting, of the new American city, and continued through landmark structures such as the Edwards and Wildey and the Bank of America buildings. Walker prized Spanish Romanesque in commercial structures because it was at once appropriate to the overall Mediterranean ambience of Los Angeles while at the same time recalling the Bowery National Bank of New York, designed by York & Sawyer (1923), which Walker considered the most successful commercial structure in the United States. As far as Walker was concerned, New York as well as Chicago had its contribution to make to Los Angeles.

In the late 1920s Walker & Eisen turned to Gothic for its downtown structures, most conspicuously in headquarters buildings for Texaco, South Basin Oil, and Shell. Here again they were following established patterns from New York, then in its golden age as America's signature city.

In an era of theater building, Walker & Eisen created the United Artist Theater in the Texaco Building (1927), a Spanish Romanesque cathedral to film intended to rival the Roxy and the Paramount in New York. In an era of hotel construction, Walker & Eisen designed scores of hotels—among them, the Breakers at Long Beach (1925), the Beverly Wilshire in Beverly Hills (1926), the Mar Monte in Santa Barbara (1927), the El Mirador in Palm Springs (1927)— which remain today important signatures in their respective skylines, overshadowed perhaps by newer structures (Los Angeles lifted its 150-foot height limit in 1957) but still evocative of the dreamy materialism, the mingled mood of elegance and physical well-being, so characteristic of F. Scott Fitzgerald's America. In this regard, the Beverly Wilshire Hotel on Wilshire opposite Rodeo Drive in Beverly Hills, a monumental classical and Churrigueresque pile, Beaux Arts in its splendid domination of its site, still speaks effectively to that mood of glamour and chic, for comings and goings through lobbies, and piano music over twilight cocktails, and a line of lemon and robin's-egg blue taxicabs at the door, which Fitzgerald experienced in the 1920s and through his fiction made of it a locale, an expectation of elegance, bespeaking the promise of urban America.

When it became time in the 1930s to streamline their Beaux Arts vocabulary, following precedents set earlier by Goodhue and Winslow in the Los Angeles Public Library (1926) and by Austin, Parkinson and Martin in City Hall (1928), Walker & Eisen simplified with equal success, as evidenced in the Sunkist Building on West Fifth Street (1936), a Beaux Arts/Moderne edifice which, like the orange shipments being orchestrated within, took the mood and message of Los Angeles to the rest of the country.

High on the list of Walker & Eisen's commissions were apartment complexes such as the Ardmore (1924) and the Arcady and Gaylord (1926) in Los Angeles and the Havenhurst in Hollywood (1924). As with other signs of urbanism, apartment-house living was arriving in full force in Los Angeles. Throughout the 1920s hundreds of apartment-house structures were constructed on the east side of the Los Angeles River between Alhambra Avenue and Washington Street, in the Wilshire district, and in Hollywood. As late as August 1929, just two months before the crash, some fifty-one apartment buildings were under construction in greater Los Angeles, eleven of them on or near Wilshire, ten in

Hollywood. Another fifty-two permits for apartment house construction were issued in the month of the crash itself.

Apartment living was ideally suited to a city filling up with so many people seeking new identities and easily available arrangements for living. In 1913 Los Angeles developer F.O. Engstrum, sensing an impending influx of affluent renters, built three major apartment-house complexes, the Rex Arms, the Bryson, and the Westonia, which offered a full spectrum of urban amenities and, by implication, a fully materialized urban identity. The Rex Arms at 745 Orange Street was marketed by Engstrum as the most completely equipped apartment house on the Pacific Coast. In recognition of the automobile, there was a parking garage adjacent to the building for the use of residents. A grocery store operated off the first-floor lobby. Rental fees included daily bed-making and cleaning, including dish washing, together with laundry, dry cleaning, and linen services. Common facilities included a ballroom, a banquet room capable of serving up to four hundred guests on apartment-owned china and silver, a reading room stocked with well-selected books, a smoking parlor where gentlemen might enjoy their cigars away from the ladies, a men's billard room, a ladies' reading room and lounge, and a roof garden furnished in weather-proof outdoor furniture. As with a hotel, residents of the Rex Arms might move in immediately, whatever their previous situation; for each apartment came fully furnished and equipped with hundreds of household items down to linen, towels, six champagne glasses, an egg beater, a chopping bowl, and a dustpan.

Such an operation was obviously keyed to a distinct type of urban resident (Engstrum developed some four hundred fully furnished units), affluent but detached from the family-oriented, suburbanized life-style otherwise so prevalent. Yet the shared amenities of the Engstrum and the other apartment buildings being erected in the 1920s—the Arcady on Wilshire, with its full-service dining room, the Cassandra on South Alexandria, the Chateau Marmont on Sunset Boulevard—served a need for community and human association persistent among otherwise detached urbanites.

So did the bungalow court and the courtyard apartment, two other popular alternatives. Enclosed patios, walled gardens, and courtyards flourished in Southern California for a number of reasons. As watered landscapes, patios and courtyards defied the expansive semi-aridity of the environment. While the prototype of the eastern states, the house in the park, placed the home amidst a congenial setting, the patio/courtyard prototype created the garden/park within, surrounding and protecting it from harm. As private spaces, patios and court-yards allowed for a reconsolidation of personal and family identity in a social and cultural environment frequently deprived of the normal reference points of more developed cities. Patios and courtyards also spoke to the home as the center of entertainment and social life. Extended beyond the private home to the bungalow or to the apartment complex, the landscaped court helped create community out of discrete dwellings, providing a spatial expression of common identity for residents recently arrived from elsewhere. The very first bungalow court, St. Francisco Court in Pasadena—eleven units clustered around a central court, designed by Sylvanus Marston in 1909—was intended for winter visitors from the East and came fully furnished with Stickley furniture and household utensils. Many bungalow courts had common recreational facilities (playgrounds, tennis courts) and a common laundry room. Integrating garages into their designs, the automobile-friendly bungalow courts created islands of traffic-less privacy in their enclosed spaces while remaining connected to important roadways. It took only a decade for the bungalow court to evolve into the motel, which telescoped into an overnight stay the bungalow-court metaphor of instant community amidst rapidity of movement.

The Spanish Revival of the 1920s intensified this preference for courtyard architecture. Traveling through Andalusia, aspiring architects such as Austin Whittlesey, author of the pervasively influential study and source book *The Minor Ecclesiastical, Domestic, and Garden Architecture of Southern Spain* (1923), noted with delight the rich courtyard types and structures—the urban patio house, the fortified urban palace or *alcazar* (many of them later recycled as apartment dwellings), the snug courtyard inns (such as that where Don Quixote de la Mancha first beheld the fair Dulcinea del Toboso), the open marketplaces and monastery cloisters, the farmhouses combining living quarters and workspaces around a central courtyard—which comprised the harmonized architectural legacy of Andalusia's Greek, Roman, Arabic, and Christian cultures. As Santa Barbara and San Clemente showed, many of these forms were directly applicable to Southern California, albeit the courtyard format was now being used for city halls and courthouses, public high schools, hotels, restaurants, and, in the case of the Garden of Allah on Sunset Boulevard in Hollywood, bungalow courts.

There were hundreds of bungalow courts built throughout greater Los Angeles, many of them in Hollywood near the studios. They provided accessible housing to the myriads of technicians, production assistants, aspiring starlets, and the like flocking to Los Angeles during the studio boom; but the Garden of Allah subsumed and perfected the type, becoming in both fact and memory (it was bulldozed in August 1959) the distilled essence of all those Spanish-style hostelries where the aspiring, the decent, the depraved, the desperate lived by the week, the month, the year, awaiting that one big break.

The Allah of the Garden was initially not the Deity but Alla Nazimova, a Russian-born actress from Yalta in the Crimea. Exotic, dark-haired, among the first of many such European imports to filmdom, Nazimova arrived in Hollywood in 1918 and was for a while one of the highest paid film stars of the early 1920s. For her personal residence, she paid $50,000 for a ninety-nine-year lease on a Spanish Revival house at 8150 Sunset Boulevard near the termination of the Los Angeles/Hollywood streetcar run. The house abutted some orange groves and vineyards suggestive of the very recent past of Hollywood as a country village grown to market town, and sat on the edge of three acres planted in an exotic array of ferns, citrus, bamboo, banana, and cedar trees. Nazimova moved into the villa along with her live-in companion, the English actor Charles Bryant (to whom she pretended to be married before he unexpectedly married someone else) and proceeded to live and entertain there in the lavish manner of Hollywood in the 1920s. Rudolph Valentino, Nazimova's fellow European import, was a frequent guest, meeting both a wife, the set designer Natacha Rambova (real name: Winifred Shaughnessy), and a lover, the actress Pola Negri, at Nazimova soirées.

All this cost money, and although Nazimova was making plenty, she also possessed an immigrant's realization that the bottom had fallen out once before in Europe and could also fall out in the United States. A woman needed more than her looks to get by on. At the suggestion of her manager, Nazimova decided to extend the ongoing socializing at her home into more formal and, it was hoped, profitable arrangements. Forming a development and operating company, she secured a bank loan for the construction of twenty-five free-standing bungalow villas arranged around a swimming pool, the largest in Hollywood, shaped like an eight on its side to remind Nazimova of the Black Sea of her homeland. An "h," meanwhile, was added to Alla's first name, thereby associating her garden hostelry with Robert Hichens's novel of sacred and profane love in the casbahs and oases of North Africa, *The Garden of Allah* (1904), which had been staged in London in 1919, filmed by Rex Ingram in the mid-1920s, and would be refilmed by David Selznick in 1936, starring Charles Boyer and Marlene Dietrich.

Opulent and suggestive of escape into sensuous delight, the Garden of Allah was a perfect name for a bungalow-court hotel/apartment complex in Hollywood. It opened on 9 January 1927. Clara Bow, Gilbert Roland, John Barrymore, H.B. Warner (the Christ of Cecil B. De Mille's *King of Kings*), Marlene Dietrich, Francis X. Bushman, and boxer Jack Dempsey dropped by for various segments of the eighteen-hour party that launched the enterprise. "In the thirty-two-year span of its life," observed gossip columnist Sheilah Graham of the place where F. Scott Fitzgerald would in the late 1930s be struggling with her help for a second start, "the Garden would witness robbery, murder, drunkenness, despair, divorce, marriage, orgies, pranks, fights, suicides, frustration, and hope." [13] For one of the few times in her life, Sheilah Graham was guilty of an understatement.

7

Like so many other aspects of Hollywood, the Garden of Allah merely extended a good idea, the bungalow court, to its logical limits. The dramas suggested by Sheilah Graham, while legendary, only reflected and intensified the dramas of ordinary life; and it was the drama of ordinary life, albeit in extraordinary cir-

cumstances, to which Southern Californians were devoting themselves with
democratic appetite.

Doing the ordinary in an extraordinary way had long since become a recognizable signature of Southern California in both life-style and architecture. A
number of architects—among them Irving Gill, Frank Lloyd Wright, and his
son Lloyd Wright—made it their personal and very private challenge to re-
envision and transform the ordinary, the everyday American, in Southern California, as if the ordinary were being seen for the first time and from a fresh
perspective. Historical precedent in architecture had its purposes, they believed, and could help confer identity, but so too could a direct return to
nature and geometry. A direct relationship to form and structure constituted a
design for living as valid as historical reference. In the case of folk artist Simon
Rodia of Watts, history was transcended altogether in favor of constructivist
towers of filigree steel and gathered glass which like the Bradbury Building
achieved the intensity of pure symbol.

Irving Gill heads the list of innovators seeking an expression that bypassed
historical metaphor. Significantly enough in terms of the Southern California
experience, Gill commenced his quest at that persistent point of regional reference, the architecture of the mission era. Like Frank Lloyd Wright, Irving
Gill was a product of Adler and Sullivan in Chicago, where he worked as a
draftsman in the early 1890s after finishing high school. Dreamy, poetical,
intensely Celtic in his intuitive nature and Spencer Tracy good looks, the young
draftsman made of the Adler and Sullivan office his Harvard and Yale. From
Louis Sullivan young Gill absorbed a philosophy of returning to elemental
forms devoid of historical reference, unless one made reference to the geometric simplicities of North Africa, the land of cubes, arches, geometric towers,
and unadorned walks.

Moving to San Diego in 1893 both for his health and for expanded career
opportunities, Gill fell in love with what another indweller, Mary Austin of
the Owens Valley, called the Spirit of Place: the elegant austerity of the semi-
arid southern littoral as it ran westward from the desert to the Pacific. To Gill's
way of thinking, the surviving Hispanic structures of the region—Mission San
Diego itself, the first of the mission churches in Alta California; the adobe
hacienda reputed to be the place where Ramona and her Native American
lover were married, Helen Hunt Jackson's novel having already solidified into
history—emanated in their architecture the geometric forms of the earth, suggesting the possibilities of a comparable response in contemporary materials.

Other architects, coming under a similar spell, followed the missions and
the haciendas backwards in time to their more fully developed Spanish Colonial or Spanish Renaissance precedents. Gill, by contrast, decoded the structures in terms of their trans-historical geometric forms. At the same time, however, Gill was sustained in the course of this pilgrimage by a sense of history

that went beyond the merely decorative. The forms and materials he was evolving paralleled the response of the Spanish pioneers in a way that returned Gill to the very same premises of site, climate, topography, and building materials that had determined their creativity one hundred years earlier. A return to nature represented a return to history as well.

All this took some time. Gill's first work commissions—the San Diego Normal School (1895), the Pickwick Theatre (1904), First Methodist, San Diego (1906), together with the homes he did in Newport, Rhode Island, and Coronado for clients he met at the Hotel Del Coronado (Gill loved parties and dancing and secured a number of clients through his socializing)—show him working conventionally in a variety of revival or borrowed styles. Most successful among such borrowings were the Prairie homes Gill brought to the San Diego area, for these expressed a connection to basic principles of line, shape, and mass which even then he was boldly exploring in theory and tentatively experimenting with in practice.

While with Adler and Sullivan, Gill had become intensely aware, as had everyone in that circle, including Myron Hunt and Frank Lloyd Wright, of the Vienna Secessionists with their drive towards first principles of design. What, Gill was already asking himself, would such a return to first principles involve in Southern California? Even as he cranked out his competent but derivative work, Gill was preparing for the breakthrough he achieved in 1907. That year Gill turned to hollow tile and concrete as his primary building materials in two houses. In doing this, he broke through to an innovative simplicity that made possible an avant-garde regional style that remained historically suggestive via its Hispanic/North African parallelisms. Poured over an inner structure of hollow tile, concrete enabled Gill to push past ornament to uninterrupted presentations of line, form, and volume. Following the completion of these homes in San Diego and Los Angeles for Melville Klauber and Homer Laughlin, Gill pushed further and further in the direction of efficiency and simplicity. In projects designed the following two years, 1908 and 1909—the Holly Sefton Memorial Hospital for Children at San Diego, the Scripps Institution of Oceanography at La Jolla, Scripps Hall at Bishop's School in La Jolla and the Bishop's Day School in San Diego—Gill achieved a new genre of institutional expression in Southern California: buildings that were at once geometric in their massive concrete surfaces, yet suggestive in their tile and ornaments of the southern Mediterranean.

What was driving Gill forward during these innovative years leaps from the pages of a manifesto he published in *The Craftsman* in May 1916, after nearly a decade of ceaseless *sui generis* design. Gill took for his motto the adage that an artist is known rather by what he omits. "If we, the architects of the West," Gill perorated, "wish to do great and lasting work we must dare to be simple, must have the courage to fling aside every device that distracts the eye from structural beauty, must break through convention and get down to fundamental truths. . . . We must boldly throw aside every accepted structural belief and standard of beauty and get back to the source of all architectural strength—the straight line, the arch, the cube and the circle—and drink from these fountains of Art that gave life to the great men of old."[14] Gill believed in cleanliness and efficiency with an equal passion. In Southern California, he informed his *Craftsman* audience, he had been designing homes devoid of dust-gathering moldings, with steel frames for his oversized windows (Gill could never get enough light into his homes), with built-in ice boxes capable of being supplied with ice from the outside, with garbage disposal systems leading directly to basement incinerators and built-in vacuum cleaner outlets in each room leading via built-in pipelines to the incinerator as well. Bathrooms and kitchens, moreover, had concrete floors angled ever so subtly towards built-in drain pipes allowing for easy scrubbing and mopping up. In some houses Gill installed an automatic car-washing sprinkler and drainage system in the garage.

Designed in 1914 for businessman Walter Luther Dodge, maker of Tiz, a powder for tired feet, the Dodge House in West Hollywood, completed in 1916, is frequently considered Gill's most representative accomplishment. Unfortunately demolished in 1965 after a protracted but doomed preservationist struggle, the Dodge House was photographed and described to a degree sufficient to confirm its reputation. So was the home Gill designed around the same time for Mary Banning of Los Angeles, a structure touted in the press as the first Cubist house in Southern California. Architectural historian Henry-Russell Hitchcock considered the Dodge House a prophetic paradigm of modernism in America. The Dodge House led Lewis Mumford to consider Gill an equal to Louis Sullivan, Frank Lloyd Wright, and Bernard Maybeck as a pioneer of the modernist movement.

Bold and innovative, the Dodge and the Banning houses made statements about Gill's clients as well as about Gill. A home by Irving Gill proclaimed that its owner possessed a clear-headed proclivity for simplicity, efficiency, and, most important, a taste for reform. Significantly, Irving Gill flourished during the Progressive era. His take-off year, 1907, coincided with the formation of the Lincoln-Roosevelt League. He did his most important work even as the members of the league gained control of and reformed state and local government, cleaning the dust and vermin out of California politics, cutting away the useless moldings and needless ornament of machine politics. From this perspective, the Progressives were bent upon the transformation of political California into a home by Irving Gill—intelligent, efficient, upright. When Progressivism spent its energies around the time of the First World War, Gill's career went into decline.

As much as he relished concrete and simplicity, Gill also sustained a Southern California passion for gardens. He was the master of the pergola and mixed his concrete with warm earth colors or implanted it with colored tile to harmonize with the surrounding vegetation. He especially loved the slow patient work of ivy as it encompassed and transformed his initially abstract walls.

In 1910 Gill fused three features—concrete construction, the bungalow court, and the garden environment—to create Lewis Court in Sierra Madre, a small suburb at the foot of the San Gabriel Mountains near Pasadena, which made available all the amenities of Southern California living—light, air, cleanliness, the garden—to a renting, blue-collar clientele, In addition to a well-landscaped common area, each home in this garden-apartment complex opened directly onto its own adjacent garden and featured Gill's list of sanitary amenities. Few other rental properties for workers and their families anywhere else in the country could in the year 1910 show a comparable concern for the dignity and aesthetic needs of a low-income population.

Three years later Gill designed another set of low-cost garden-apartment cottages for the Echo Park area of Los Angeles. Gill dreamed of providing Southern California with an entire suburb of garden apartments for working people based on these Lewis Court and Echo Park Court prototypes. When a consortium of companies retained him as chief architect for the proposed model industrial city of Torrance in Los Angeles County, he thought that at long last he would get the chance. Moving to Los Angeles from San Diego, Gill got to work. Paradoxically, the unions objected to Gill's simplified designs and construction techniques because they cut down on the necessary work force. The workers went so far as to rally against the architect who wanted them to have walled gardens and skylights in their bathrooms. As a result of these protests, only ten experimental cottages were built. Personally and financially, Gill never recovered from the collapse of these hopes.

Even more serious problems lay ahead in the 1920s as the rage for historical revivals swept aside Gill's experiments in modernism. By the time modernism re-emerged in Southern California in the 1930s in such figures as Richard Neutra and Rudolph Schindler, whom Gill had anticipated, he was in bad health and in precarious financial circumstances, although until his death from heart failure in 1936, he was still dreaming and designing: a Christian Science Church for Coronado, fire and police stations and a city hall for Oceanside, cottages for a Native American resettlement center in Lakeside, schemes for low-cost housing in Ensenada in Baja California, and housing for the unemployed in Santa Barbara County. In his 1916 article for *The Craftsman*, Gill called the West in general, Southern California in particular, "that newest white page turned for registration." Gill filled his version of that page with designs proclaiming the brave new world he envisioned for the Southland, a society characterized by sanity, efficiency, order, aesthetics, and social justice.

In contrast to the latent pastoralism, hence escapism, of Arts and Crafts or the aristocratic aspirations implicit in so much of the Spanish Revival, Gill's schemes for wealthy clients and renters alike were functional, engaged, unpretentious, and democratic. Had the Torrance project not collapsed so ironically, the workers themselves rejecting Gill's proposals, he might have accomplished a Levittown, Southern California-style, thirty years ahead of schedule. In any event, what he did accomplish earned him an enduring reputation as a designer and social activist. Thanks to Irving Gill, the design for living in Southern California reconnected with underlying imperatives of taste and the good life for as many as possible. Capable of functioning at differing socio-economic levels, the Gill style delineated a Progressive preference for a closing of extremes among the classes. Why should workers not enjoy gardens and efficient kitchens and bathroom skylights? From this perspective, Irving Gill prefigured the mass culture of post-World War II California, with its achievements in housing, highways, parks, playgrounds, and educational facilities. His designs for Torrance might be rejected and the Dodge House demolished, but the aspiration towards democratic excellence so powerfully expressed by Irving Gill was an imperative that went beyond the survival of any one building.

As a draftsman with Adler and Sullivan in Chicago in the early 1890s, Irving Gill worked side by side with another aspiring designer, Frank Lloyd Wright, two years his senior. Nearly twenty years later, in 1911, Frank Lloyd Wright's son Lloyd Wright, a landscape architect in his early twenties, moved to San Diego to work for Olmsted and Olmsted, the partner sons of Frederick Law Olmsted, on planning the Panama-California International Exposition scheduled to open in San Diego in 1915. It was initially assumed that Irving Gill would be chosen to be exposition architect. Had this happened, Balboa Park might have blossomed in a series of powerful modernist structures, and the course of Southern California architecture might have been profoundly affected, with important residuals for Gill's career. As it turned out, cautious exposition officials chose a safer alternative, Bertram Grosvenor Goodhue of New York City, a master of Spanish Renaissance and Spanish Colonial architecture. Goodhue's California Quadrangle, dominated by the cathedral-like California State Building, set in motion the Spanish Revival of the 1920s which helped send Irving Gill into obscurity. Since it was Gill who had brought Olmsted and Olmsted into the San Diego project in the first place, the brothers withdrew when Goodhue was appointed, which left Lloyd Wright looking for new opportunities. Wright joined Gill's office shortly after the loss of the exposition commission. Irving Gill treated young Lloyd Wright like a son, providing him with work and a cottage. Gill's kindness contrasted with the harsh, hectoring, dismissive treatment Lloyd Wright was accustomed to receive from his own father, an egomaniacal genius foraging through a wasteland of devasted personal relationships. When Gill opened his Los Angeles office, Wright moved there as well.

During this apprenticeship, Lloyd Wright absorbed from Gill the theory, practice, and mystique of concrete. He learned to think like Gill in terms of walls and ascending geometric forms, so intrinsic to the capacities of concrete as a building material. He watched as Gill polished and stained his interior concrete floors until they gleamed like mahogany or Spanish leather. He noted as Gill implanted decorative devices, colored Arab tile, for example, into clear, creamy-white surfaces. Watching Gill struggle with the difficulties of tilt-up slab construction, Lloyd Wright became a fervid convert to reinforced concrete block as a primary construction material. Possessed of many of the same capacities as poured concrete, concrete blocks were far less expensive, and, in contrast to the intricacies of poured concrete, they were easy for construction workers to handle. They were also intrinsically suitable to the Cubist proportioning which Lloyd Wright was absorbing from Gill before he launched himself in 1915 as an architect, landscaper, and urban planner in partnership with Paul Thiene.

In early 1922 Father appeared, self-absorbed, dominating, recriminating as usual: the great Frank Lloyd Wright, back from his work in Tokyo on the just-completed Imperial Hotel. For the son, Southern California was a real place, a region where he had matured as a designer and found his own place and stream of commissions. For Father, Southern California was an occasion, a five-house occasion in point of fact, sandwiched between Japan and Wright's return to Taliesin in Wisconsin. Already in 1917 Frank Lloyd Wright had created one previous Los Angeles home, Hollyhock House, for Aline Barnsdall, a wealthy bohemian with an interest in the theater and performing arts. Like three of the four houses Wright would design in Los Angeles in the early and mid-1920s, Hollyhock House dominated its Olive Hill site with an arrogant contempt directly expressive of Wright's basic attitude towards the region. Four out of five of Wright's early Los Angeles-area homes, in fact, Hollyhock House itself together with the Storer, Ennis, and Freeman houses, show this same imperious imposition of house upon site. The other, La Miniatura (1923), the Pasadena home Wright designed for rare book and antique dealer Alice Millard, sits idiosyncratically at the bottom of an arroyo (flash floods quickly filled its basement with water and mud) as if to hide itself from the surrounding city. There is in all five of these houses, in fact, an obsession with privacy expressing itself in fortress-like neo-Mayan designs. The Storer house did not even have a front door, entrance being offered through a rear door only, as if to finalize the metaphor of privacy and retrenchment.

Wright's choice of Mayan motifs further reinforces this mood of withdrawal. Mayan represented a journey back past European culture altogether to the pre-Columbian era, seeking to connect the obscure indigenous heart of Mesoamerica, whose northernmost extension was Los Angeles. Restless in his personal life, tired of Secessionist forms, tired even of Midwestern Prairie, Wright used his Los Angeles occasion to make an aboriginal-modernist connection which, had his homes served as prototypes, would have acted out the fantasy of Southern California as Maya Land revived, the Native American culture that might have evolved, had not Europe interrupted its development. A fantasy, this exotic style came quickly to be confined to Hollywood office buildings and movie theaters.

The greatness of Wright made the neo-Mayan moment momentarily plausible, especially in La Miniatura, which, taken in and of itself and not as a prototype, was (and remains) a near perfect work of art. Its perfection lies in Wright's use of the concrete block, which Wright studied carefully in conjunction with (or perhaps under the tutelage of) his supervising architect, his son Lloyd.

Thus Frank Lloyd Wright became reunited with Irving Gill, his draftsman companion from Adler and Sullivan days, through the person and concrete preoccupations of young Lloyd Wright, a son to them both. The Wrights took Gill's insights into both geometry and concrete and, under the influence of Cubism and its pre-Columbian counterpart, Mayan Revival, pushed them towards a design for living based as closely as possible upon pure aesthetics. Concrete blocks were molded with cut-through designs admitting air and light. Others were cast with intricate designs to create surfaces analogous to sculptured stone. Lloyd Wright worked out a technique of internally reinforcing the blocks with vertical and horizontal rods of steel, thus allowing for a reinforced ascension of Cubist forms multiplying upwards along a vertical plane like growing crystals or numbers in a Pythagorean progression.

Throughout it all, the father hectored the son, mainly by letter and telegram from Wisconsin, as each Los Angeles house experienced the usual Wrightian amalgam of cost overruns and delay; and the son bore it with a patience that in later years created in him an aura encouraging a surge of sympathy from all those who met him and remembered, perhaps, a comparable terror of parental intimidation in their own lives.

No matter: Father went back to Wisconsin, and the son remained, not just to see Father's four homes to completion, but to continue his own career through Cubist/modernist/Mayan masterpieces such as the Taggart, Sowden, and Samuels residences in Los Angeles, together with the studio residence he designed for himself in 1927, also in the city. In 1923 Lloyd Wright prefigured his father's later involvement with the Arizona Biltmore with his design for the Oasis Hotel in Palm Springs, an ascending accretion of foot-high horizontal levels of poured Portland cement banded with interlinear levels of steel: an oversized Native American basket pueblo, as it were, woven of industrial materials, perfectly suited to the desert environment. Within, great logs blazed by night in oversized braziers and firelight played against the concrete walls to which Lloyd Wright, using rough twelve-inch redwood slipforms, gave the texture of layered adobe. The rise of Palm Springs as a major desert resort dates from the opening of the Oasis Hotel.

8

In 1925 Lloyd Wright along with Allied Architects and others submitted a proposal for a Civic Center for Los Angeles. Wright's scheme envisioned the architectural center of Los Angeles as a modernist/Mayan temple palace rising in hierophantic glory. For obvious reasons, Wright's proposal, together with his dazzling 1931 suggestion for a skyscraper Roman Catholic cathedral constructed of gigantic sculptured concrete blocks, remained just that, a vision, a dream. Lloyd Wright was forced to content himself with the commission for the second shell at the Hollywood Bowl, completed in 1928. And yet, if Los Angeles were not to have a unified civic center or a towering cathedral to assert its collective identify, what might finally stand for the city as an achieved whole? What one act of architecture could be taken to symbolize Los Angeles?

It is difficult to know whether or not Sebastiano Rodia set out deliberately to answer that question, although art, such as the Watts Towers created by Rodia between 1921 and 1954, has a way of answering questions which even artists do not know they are asking. Born in Rome in 1873 and brought to the United States at the age of ten, Sebastiano Rodia, known more commonly as Simon or Sam, worked throughout his life as a mason and tile setter. In the manner of immigrants of his generation, Rodia worked hard and saved his money. By 1921 he was living on his own property at 1727 107th Street in Watts, a small village south of downtown Los Angeles. Rodia's pie slice-shaped lot, his piece of the California dream, stood adjacent to the Pacific Electric tracks linking Watts to the city. Not much is known about Simon Rodia. He was typical of millions of immigrants who came and worked and took one step up the ladder of America. The date he arrived in Southern California is uncertain. He may or may not have been a widower. On nice evenings he drank jug red wine in a gazebo on his property and smoked cigarettes. He must have possessed some means. Both the property and his leisure testified to that, not to mention the Chevrolet he bought from a local bootlegger, a car he later replaced with a sleek black 1927 Hudson. Simon Rodia was an immigrant, smallish and sinewy with an oversized nose dominating his shrewd Trasteverine face. He spoke with an accent and was known to the rest of Watts as "El Italiano." Yet he was Folk as well. Like the Folks he had come to Southern California with some means in search of a better life. He even had an affinity for the Folks' religion, making his property available to the Pentecostal Church on Wilmington Avenue for evening baptisms and hymn-singing; and when the newly baptized emerged from the tub, Simon Rodia himself provided the clean white sheets for the dripping wet Christians to wrap themselves in.

How well Simon Rodia could read English remains an open question. He owned an eleventh edition of the Encyclopedia Britannica which he revered with the passion of the autodidact, and he read and reread in it biographies— Alexander the Great, Julius Caesar, Joan of Arc, Marco Polo, Christopher

Columbus, Amerigo Vespucci, Buffalo Bill—of people who had done something big and made a difference. "A man has to be good good or bad bad to
be remembered" was Rodia's verdict on history.[15] Few have put this truth more
succinctly. Simon Rodia wanted to do something big, something that was good
good, and by 1921, just as Los Angeles itself was booming, he determined what
it would be: a sculpture garden in honor of Marco Polo, Christopher Columbus, and the other heroes he so admired. Over the next thirty-three years, from
1921 to 1954, he worked continuously on his project: three constructivist towers resembling upside-down ice cream cones, the Niña, the Pinta, the Santa
Maria, rising 55, 97, and 99 feet respectively (which is to say, ten stories) over
a Cactus Garden, the gazebo where he drank his wine, a Ship of Marco Polo,
a Hall of Mirrors at the entrance to his house, loggias, walkways, fountains,
and various holding pools in which the Pentecostals held their baptisms. Working without scaffolding, Rodia built from the ground up. By 1923 he had attained sufficient height to emplace a cement plaque in which he impressed his
initials SR together with representations of a hammer, a tile cutter, and other
tools of his craft.

Rodia worked exclusively in cast-off materials. Over an inner structure of
steel rods, he affixed a covering of steel mesh, onto which he cemented seashells, broken tile and crockery, glass bottles, corncobs, old shoes, and other
found objects. He paid neighborhood children a penny a piece for broken plates,
a practice he ceased when parents complained that their children were deliberately smashing crockery to earn money. Running out of material, Rodia walked
the Pacific Electric tracks looking for objects, which he stored in a gunnysack.
He combed local beaches searching for seashells. All in all, over more than
thirty years, Rodia used some 7000 sacks of cement, 75,000 seashells, and tons
of broken dishes, bottles, mirrors, shoes, corncobs, cookie jars, bathroom tile,
and other cast-off material in his creation. Day by day, year by year, he worked
alone, mixing cement, carrying it bucketful by bucketful up each tower, secured to his growing structures by a window-washer's belt from which he hung
a bucket of wet cement and a burlap bag filled with objects.

Like Los Angeles itself, which reached out to incorporate Watts in 1926,
Rodia's towers and sculpture garden can be decoded from a number of perspectives. The Watts Towers are, most basically, folk art, as in the Folks of Los
Angeles: spontaneous, intuitive, self-instructed. As such, the towers express an
immigrant's testimony to his adopted country. "I wanted to do something in
the United States because I was raised here, you understand?" Rodia later told
a reporter. "I wanted to do something for the United States because there are
nice people in the country."[16] From this perspective, the Watts Towers represent a commemorative externalization by Rodia of an inner memory of Italy:
its grace and beauty, its capacity for joy and art, an Italian immigrant's daydream over thirty years through the effluvia and bric-a-brac of modern American life, presented as a gift to his adopted country. Such an interpretation links

the Watts Towers to the Mediterraneanism of Southern California architecture during the same period. Another interpretation sees Rodia's creation as folk art, true, but touched as well by a surrealist ambition akin to formal art: a Southern Californian counterpart to the Dream Palace constructed by the French postman/artist Joseph Ferdinand Cheval between 1879 and 1912. There is also the obvious resemblance to the creations of Spanish architect Antonio Gaudi, who also worked with rubble, brick, and polychrome tiles within an Art Nouveau/surreal scheme. Whether Rodia knew of Gaudi's work is highly improbable, given Rodia's limited education and reading habits. The Watts Towers thus constitute a spontaneous parallelism to the work of the Spanish master.

Such interpretations raise the Watts Towers into the realm of formal art. The Watts Towers are also sustained by the logic of constructivism. Working with no formal plan and without scaffolding, Rodia was forced to pursue the logic of his structure according to his intuitive understanding of the laws of physics and the capacities of his materials. The towers thus grew according to an organic logic of development as structural necessity determined each phase of growth. From this perspective, the towers constitute immense constructivist sculptures: pure statements of interactive material and form which point to Irving Gill and the Wrights as well as the Russian constructivists; for in his own way Rodia was following out the logic of his materials in a manner parallel to that advocated by these architects. As amateur architect and engineer, Simon Rodia took even more humble materials than concrete and transformed them into structures which played orderliness against random variety, haphazardness against design, so as to offer satisfaction on the deepest levels of aesthetic perception. Should one seek a conceptualist tinge to the Watts Towers, there is that too; for sometime in the late 1930s Rodia dismantled his beloved 1927 Hudson touring car, incorporating its gears, springs, wheels, seats, lights, fenders, and ornamentation into the fabric of the towers and burying the stripped carcass in his backyard by the railroad tracks. The most ferocious conceptualist could not have come up with a better, more pertinently Los Angeles statement. Rodia sacrificed his Hudson to the gods of the city like an ox in an ancient temple.

Los Angeles itself, however, especially its building inspectors, remained skeptical. By the 1940s Rodia's relationship with his community had gone sour. He had already built a wall around the towers to keep out vandals and curiosity seekers. The children who in an earlier, simpler age had brought their broken plates to him to sell for a penny now amused themselves by throwing trash over the walls into the sculpture garden or stealing fruit from Rodia's orchard, the very same fruit he had given away free to his neighbors in years past. Once a known and respected member of the Watts community, a friend to one and all, Rodia became by 1948, the year in which the towers were essentially completed, a despised and badgered old man, the scapegoat of the neighborhood. Various building inspectors, meanwhile, were gathering evidence—at a distance, through binoculars—for possible condemnation proceedings. The inspectors were convinced that the Watts Towers constituted a menace to public safety. One day, they argued, the towers would come collapsing to the ground with a probable loss of life. Misunderstood, harassed by a new generation of Watts residents, bedeviled by officialdom, Rodia grew disenchanted, then bitter.

In 1954, entering his eighties, he put an end to his life's work with the same mysterious abruptness with which he had initiated the towers in the early 1920s. Deeding his property to Louis Sauceda, a young man who had grown up with the towers in the neighborhood, and giving away his furniture and household effects to the very same neighbors who had driven him away, Simon Rodia walked away from his property and moved to Martinez in Northern California. For the following five years, the Watts Towers and sculpture garden stood abandoned and vandalized, treated by neighborhood residents as little more than an eccentric curiosity for daring children to climb and vandals to pilfer, or, by night, a place for neighborhood lotharios to exercise their charms. In 1959 building officials initiated formal condemnation proceedings. Had not two preservationists, William Cartwright and Nicholas King, become interested in the towers that very same year, the Watts Towers would have met an assured rendezvous with the wrecker's ball. As it was, the towers were submitted to a test pull which applied some 10,000 pounds of pressure to the structures. They stood, just as Simon Rodia always said they would.

The towers stood because they were a powerful symbol as well as sound engineering. As he shook the dust of Los Angeles from his feet and headed north to Martinez, did Simon Rodia realize that he had provided his repudiating and repudiated city with an architectural symbol equal in mystery and power to the Bradbury Building of 1893? Since the conscious perceptions of a folk artist are even more impenetrable than those of trained artists working self-consciously within a framework of tradition or revolt, it will always be impossible to tell. But then again, George Wyman provided little evidence in his subsequent career that he considered the Bradbury Building an enduring achievement. Wyman's subsequent work, in fact, grew denser and darker, as if he considered the crystalline steel and the dazzling light of the Bradbury a *jeu d'esprit* devoid of lineage or further significance. We will never fully know what Rodia thought of his work as he left it behind. Whether self taught folk artists or academy-trained MIT or Beaux-Arts graduates, all architects must finally leave their work to speak for itself, which is what both Wyman and Rodia did in their differing ways. And speak each building has: the Bradbury prophesying Los Angeles as a Bellamyite utopia, a brave new world of technology and sunlight; the Watts Towers suggesting Los Angeles as its own *sui generis* achievement, a city of one to be construed in terms of itself.

Los Angeles *Times* columnist Jack Smith has compared the Watts Towers, unique and improbable, to the boojun tree of Baja California, a strange and fantastic plant that exists in that one place and nowhere else. When one looked at the wall of broken mirrors outside the entrance to Rodia's house, its pieces fitted together into a mosaic, one saw innumerable refractions of the same image. Dispersed as many, the reflection reduced itself to the one: the one city, the one immigrant self amidst the city's strangely unified variety. Comparisons to the Eiffel Tower have been constant. But what an idiosyncratic symbol, folkloric, informal and funky, the Watts Towers are in comparison to the formal design, engineering, and intentions of the Eiffel Tower—but then again, how appropriate! A city of Folks, of grandma and grandpa in from Iowa; of identities assumed or repudiated; of eccentrics, castoffs, and drifters; cafeterias and flivvers; Sister Aimee, Fighting Bob, and Holy Rollers; of a thousand species of fantasy and make-believe, is memorialized by a construction that is itself comparably demotic and constructed from comparably discarded and compromised materials.

Into his sculptures and towers Simon Rodia enfolded the ecologies of Los Angeles: cactus from the desert, shells from the seashore, the litter and cast-off objects—bottles, plates, mirrors, car parts, tools—of human habitation. Enigmatically, he combined natural and man-made objects as if to suggest the interaction of each in the materializing of urban culture. Thus in the towers, as in Los Angeles, compromised materials are restructured and re-emerge in achievement. The broken plate, the colored bottle, the old shoe assert their beauty as part of a transformed and transforming whole. Their very incompleteness, the very fact that they were discarded in the first place, adds to their newly emergent power as material objects transformed by a larger identity. As in the case of the medieval myth of alchemy, junk materials went into the towers and by so doing were rematerialized as art. So too had the Folks come west and made a city. Just as Los Angeles architect Frank Gehry would do in a later era, Rodia saw the beauty inherent in industrial materials and compounded that beauty by bringing it into direct dialogue with the organic: a fitting emblem for a city that had so artificially imposed itself on its natural setting and would always remain in its imaginative meaning an assertion of industrial forms against the wilderness.

Los Angelenos were always struggling against a sense of emptiness, of void even, in their psychological encounter with the city: an inability to center themselves in the cityscape, aggravated by an underlying uneasiness as to whether or not Los Angeles was truly there in the first place. The City of the Angels had made itself happen through will and water; but even when it had happened, Los Angeles remained in some eerie way an emptiness, a void, the Nowhere City as Alison Lurie called it in her novel, difficult to find and fix oneself in.

Simon Rodia filled in this void with an architectural creation that defined space and the structures within space in the purest possible terms. In successfully doing this, he paralleled the achievement of George Wyman in the Bradbury Building. As Los Angeles advanced outward towards Watts, filling in its landscape with materialized ambitions (on a clear day you can see the Coliseum from atop the tallest of the towers), Rodia was also filling in the emptiness with spontaneous design and engineering. Like his fellow architects and landscapers, Rodia was busy about the task of creating a somewhere, a place fixed and defined by materialized ambitions. He was preparing for Los Angeles one of its more intriguing architectural symbols, a constructivist cathedral of discarded material made beautiful. He never asked the proper permission to do this, but neither had Los Angeles asked the proper permission as it materialized its urban dreams through a process of growth which had its own idiosyncratic and elusive logic.

Like Rodia reading the Encyclopedia Britannica and dreaming of doing heroic things, Los Angeles asserted itself as a major American city with equal directness. In each instance, an archetype—a city, a cathedral—had been seen and subsequently kept in mind, but also departed from with effrontery. Los Angeles was no ordinary American city. Its cathedral in Watts entombed a 1927 Hudson.

9

Anacapa and Arcadia

The Santa Barbara Heritage

The citizens of Santa Barbara did not want another Los Angeles. In the teens and twenties, Santa Barbara, the city and the county, emerged as a clear-cut alternative to the Los Angeles model. If Los Angeles embodied growth, industry, an eclectic urbanism, and most important, the future, Santa Barbara represented refinement, self-imposed limits, the past. Los Angeles was sprawling, brassy, democratically inclusive. Santa Barbara was selective and genteel. Possessed of political cohesiveness and significant wealth, Santa Barbara created for itself in architecture, life-style, civic value, and pageantry an alternative version of what California offered in the matter of better living. This alternative integrated agricultural and resort elements. It also embraced a distinct, sometimes paradoxical affinity for healthfulness, spirituality, education, the arts, and, most vigorously, the Hispanic metaphor. Consolidated in the mid-1920s in the rebuilding of the city after the earthquake of June 1925, this identity was built out of the elements of a 125-year-old Hispanic and American presence, itself affixed to a Native American culture that extended backwards into prehistory.

North of the Santa Monica Bay the coast of Southern California veers westward towards Point Conception. At present-day Santa Barbara the coast forms a channel between the mountainous shore and three major offshore islands. Into this region, before the Bronze Age developed in Europe, arrived an Asiatic people who for several centuries occupied the crested slopes overlooking the channel. These Oak Grove people, as they came to be called, were displaced at the dawn of the Christian era by a more vigorous Hunting People, who settled on the lowland littoral where they remained for nearly a thousand years as hunters and shellfish-gatherers, but not yet taking to the channel itself. Sometime between A.D. 800 and A.D. 1000, a third wave arrived, mixing its stock with the Hunting People. This last people, the Chumash, called the

Canalinos or the Channel People by the Spanish, took to the sea in graceful canoes up to 25 feet in length, guiding themselves at night by beacon fires atop the coastal heights. Evolving a culture reminiscent of Polynesia, the Chumash lived together in communal long houses, fed themselves from the sea, and evolved a society notably more advanced than most other Native Americans of the region.

In October 1542 Juan Rodríguez Cabrillo, a Portuguese mariner sailing under the flag of Spain, anchored his two ships *San Salvador* and *La Victoria* off the channel islands. Canoeloads of Chumash welcomed the Spanish vessels as they sailed into the channel. While exploring one of the islands, San Miguel, Cabrillo fell and broke his arm. Continuing northwards to Cape Mendocino, Cabrillo was forced south by bad weather. He returned his ships to the protected channel islands where he had anchored that fall. There, on 3 January 1543, Cabrillo died from an infection in his injured arm and was buried on the same island where he had the eventually fatal accident.

Sixty years later, in 1602, Sebastián Vizcaíno sailed north from Acapulco with two small ships in search of a harbor for the Manila galleons which since 1566 had been crossing the Pacific from the Philippines. Vizcaíno sailed into the channel on 4 December 1602, the Feast of Saint Barbara, an early Christian martyr. In her honor, Antonio de la Ascención, a Carmelite friar aboard one of the ships, named the channel and the shore Santa Barbara, and the name held. It took another 167 years for the Spanish to return to this favored portion of the Alta California they claimed but could not settle; and it was another thirteen years after that before the Royal Presidio of Santa Barbara was established near a friendly Chumash village presided over by the amiable chief Yanonalit, who had also been on hand to greet the Spanish when they passed through in 1769. An aged and frail Junipero Serra, Father President of the Missions, celebrated the mass dedicating the Presidio on 21 April 1782; but it took another four years for a Mission proper to be established at Santa Barbara by Serra's successor, Fermín Francisco Lasuén.

Between 1782 and 1820, four Mission churches, each an improvement over its predecessor, occupied the magnificent site chosen by the Franciscans on an eminence of 250 feet with a sweeping view of the channel three miles in the distance. The first church was little more than a log palisade, although it was improved within the year by adobe and tile. A more solid adobe church followed in 1789. It in turn was replaced with an even more ambitious adobe structure in 1794. This third structure continued to be expanded and enhanced (an elegant Moorish fountain *lavanderia* was installed in 1798) until it was severely damaged by earthquake on 21 December 1812. In planning the fourth mission church in 1815, pastor Antonio Ripoll guided himself by designs of the Roman architect M. Vitruvius Polion of the Augustan age, whose illustrated treatise on architecture was in Father Ripoll's possession in a Spanish translation published in Madrid in 1787.

Thus the fourth Mission Santa Barbara, based as it was on Vitruvius's Greek temple with Ionic columns, brought a note of neoclassical distinction to the scarcely settled California coast. The Mission, moreover, was not built in perishable adobe but in more permanent sandstone blocks fixed together with limestone cement. Completed in 1820, a mere two years before the end of the royal Spanish rule in California, Mission Santa Barbara, together with its adjacent monastery and gardens, its orchard of apple, pear, cherry, and banana trees, set new architectural and landscaping standards for design and construction on the California coast. Known as the Queen of the Mission for its elegance, solidity, and site, Santa Barbara constituted Ripoll's last testimony to the Spanish Catholic royalist presence which the Franciscans had been nurturing in Alta California since 1769. Through his refraction of Vitruvius's design, a Spanish priest summed up and eulogized the mission system itself, whose origins can be traced to ancient Roman methods of colonization. The fourth Mission Santa Barbara represented the European twilight of Spanish California. In 1822 Mexico broke from Spain; and on 23 January 1828 Father Ripoll, refusing to take an oath of allegiance to the Mexican Republic, fled Santa Barbara on an American vessel.

Mission Santa Barbara, then, began its fourth and major phase as an imaginative gesture in limestone to a royalist mission era only then vanishing. So too in the last years of Mexican California did another imaginative ideal, that of Santa Barbara as a socially and culturally developed episcopal city, affix itself to the Mission church. On 27 April 1840 Pope Gregory XVI, responding to a request by Don Anastasio Bustamente, President of the Republic of Mexico, authorized the upgrading of Upper and Lower California from a missionary territory dependent upon the Franciscan Order to an independent diocese with its own bishop. The Pope chose San Diego as the seat of the diocese, being midway between Alta and Baja California, and as the first bishop His Holiness selected President Bustamente's nominee, Francisco García Diego y Moreno, a Franciscan.

Born in Lagos in Jalisco, Mexico, in 1785 to prosperous parents, the future bishop began his studies in the Franciscan Order as a boy of twelve and was ordained priest in 1798. Father García Diego spent his early career as a master of novices and a professor of philosophy in the Franciscan College of Our Lady of Guadalupe at Zacatecas, appointments commensurate with his highly developed intellectual culture and ardent spirituality. Rising in his order, he became a consultor of his college, a fellow, that is, with strong advisory authority, followed by an appointment as commissary prefect for the Indian missions.

As such, Father García Diego traveled to Alta California in 1833 and worked at Mission Santa Clara at the southern edge of San Francisco Bay for two years. That year, 1833, the Mexican government set in motion a process of secularization whereby the California missions would emerge from the control of the Franciscans and become regular parish churches under the jurisdiction of diocesan priests. A bishop would replace the Franciscan Father President as senior prelate in charge of California. Theoretically, such an evolution into diocesan status had from the start been the intended outcome of the Franciscan missionary system. By this time, however, the population of Mexican California violently resented the land wealth of the missions and the protected status of the Native Americans as an intolerable legacy of Spanish royalist rule; and so the Franciscans resisted secularization, seeing in it, correctly, an anti-Native American land grab.

Wisely, the Mexican president recommended the Franciscan priest and former California missionary, Francisco García Diego y Moreno, to preside over this transition as the first Bishop of California. Consecrated at the Basilica of Guadalupe on 4 October 1840, Bishop García Diego recruited priests and seminarians for his new diocese. In late 1841 he sailed for San Diego on an English brig, arriving there in early December. Accompanying him was an entourage appropriate to his episcopal status: two Franciscan friars, six diocesan seminarians, a tailor, a gardener, his niece, Doña Josefita Gómez, and Doña Soledad, his niece's elderly duenna. Disappointed with San Diego, Bishop García Diego removed his household to Santa Barbara in early January.

The brief reign of Bishop García Diego at Santa Barbara had its most vivid existence on the level of pageantry and imaginative gesture. Disembarking at eleven in the morning on 11 January 1842, the Bishop was greeted by soldiers on parade and artillery salutes as he proceeded through a specially fashioned ornamental arch. A grand midday meal followed at the home of Don José Antonio Aguirre and his newly married bride Rosario Estudillo, who had brought the Bishop and his household to Santa Barbara on their ship. When the Bishop proceeded by carriage to the Mission, the people detached the horses and pulled the carriage themselves, stopping once to allow the Bishop to step into a small roadside bower to don his pontifical regalia. A splendid ceremony followed at the Mission. When the leading citizens of Santa Barbara petitioned the bishop on 15 April 1842 to transfer his seat permanently to Santa Barbara from San Diego, he was easily persuaded. By April 30 Bishop García Diego was announcing plans for a cathedral, a bishop's residence, a seminary, and a school for girls. Stones were gathered in anticipation of construction that would transform Santa Barbara into an episcopal city of architectural distinction. Meanwhile, the Bishop established himself in a small apartment at Mission Santa Barbara, where he made every effort to maintain the proper dignity of his state. Visiting the Mission in January 1842, Captain George Simpson, General Superintendent of the Hudson Bay Company, was received by the Bishop in a handsomely appointed room dominated by an episcopal throne hung in crimson velvet. Brandy, wines, fruit, and cigars were provided, served by Concepción Argüello, the daughter of a former governor of California who had taken the veil as a tertiary nun some thirty-five years earlier when her fiancée, Count Nikolai Rezanov of the Russian-American Company, died in Siberia. As bishop,

García Diego ordained seminarian Miguel Gómez to the priesthood on 29 June 1842, the first such ordination held in California, followed by two further ordinations in October 1843. He assigned two of these secular priests to replace Franciscan pastors at Mission San Luis Obispo and Mission San Buenaventura, which then became the first canonically established parishes in the new diocesan organization. In 1846 Bishop García Diego ordained three more diocesan priests.

Behind this surface scenario of episcopal authority and elegance, however—the splendid pontifical ceremonies at the Mission accompanied by a well-trained Chumash choir and orchestra, the episcopal throne, the ordinations, the talk of a cathedral and other ecclesiastical institutions—the underlying realities of Bishop García Diego's episcopate proved disappointing. He had hoped to have 17,000 pesos a year from the Pious Fund endowment for the support of missionary activity in California, but President Santa Anna seized the fund for the government. In such a thinly settled, socially undeveloped diocese, tithing proved an impossibility.

The Bishop thus had no means to support his ambitions for the development of Santa Barbara as an episcopal see. With income from the Pious Fund unavailable, the stones which had been gathered towards construction of a cathedral remained in scattered piles, testimony to a city that existed solely in the Bishop's imagination. He, meanwhile, lacking an official residence, which also remained a pile of gathered stones, lived in cramped quarters in the Mission which had only been begrudgingly granted him by his fellow Franciscans, who resented the displacement of the missionary system by the diocese. For his bedroom, the friars assigned the Bishop, so he himself complained, to one of the most cramped rooms in the monastery. He compared this room (it had one narrow inside window, opening on a corridor) to a cage, saying that he had trouble breathing in it.

Secularization had driven many of the Franciscans into a mood of *après moi le deluge*. They began to slaughter their cattle for hides and tallow, to neglect their orchards and gardens, and in petty ways, such as the narrow room, to resist their bishop. The Chumash, meanwhile, began to leave the missions and to resume their roving ways. Drunkenness became a problem. The choir and orchestra at Mission Santa Barbara still performed with angelic elegance, but outside the cloister an era was winding down with reports of rape, drunkenness, and cattle theft.

The Hispanic *paisanos*, moreover, wanted the mission era to end; indeed, the ordinary Santa Barbareños feared that Bishop García Diego planned to reinstitute the mission order, with its theocratic monopoly over land and cattle, its protection of the Native Americans over Mexican colonists as favored wards of the state. The upper classes of Santa Barbara might welcome the Bishop with pomp and circumstance—the presence of a prelate among them, after all, added a note of distinction to their remote presidio—but the lower orders saw in pontifical pomp the imagery of their own continued suppression. One day, as the Bishop rode by in his mule-drawn carriage, a crowd of *paisanos* drove an enraged bull directly into his path. The bull eviscerated the mule and over-turned the carriage, trapping the Bishop underneath. For the longest time (one account says four hours) no one stepped forward to help. Pinned to the earth, the Bishop wept in frustration. At another time, when the Bishop announced special services at which he would preach, the *paisanos* deliberately staged a noisy horse race near the church.

On Thursday, 30 April 1846, around midnight, the Most Reverend Francisco García Diego y Moreno, aged 60, and for some time ill and dispirited, died in his narrow room at Mission Santa Barbara after four frustrating years as the first Bishop of California. Just before he expired, the Bishop blessed the presidio city of Santa Barbara, which in a few short months would pass over to the jurisdiction of the United States.

In the realm of external accomplishment, García Diego y Moreno's episcopacy had yielded little: some splendid ceremonies, soon forgotten; the ordination of local diocesan clergy, of more lasting value; a round of episcopal visitation, well intended but accomplishing little. As a presence, however, embodying the full spiritual power of Roman Catholicism, the Bishop had brought distinction to Santa Barbara, making it, at least symbolically for four short years, the religious and cultural capital of California. Merely to plan for a cathedral, a seminary, and a girls' school as the Bishop did was to invoke the future of Santa Barbara as a city of civility and cultural importance. Envisioning Santa Barbara as an episcopal city on a hill, as a northern outpost of Hispanic civilization, Francisco García Diego y Moreno inadvertantly anticipated—and perhaps even helped to form—the dreams of a later generation. With his coffin sealed into a wall near the altar of Mission Santa Barbara, the Bishop, by explicit direction in his final instructions, added himself to the stones of the church which had so inspired his imagination. His burial there intensified the power of Mission Santa Barbara as a symbol. Someday, the stones which he had gathered would be further assembled. The Bishop's Santa Barbara, a Spanish city on the heights overlooking the channel, was a dream that history would eventually materialize.

2

Meanwhile, the Franciscans themselves remained on as a living link to the Hispanic past amidst an unfolding American era. Five young Spaniards joined the Order in 1854, followed by a number of Irishmen. In 1856 Bishop Thaddeus Amat of Monterey, under whose jurisdiction Santa Barbara now fell, transferred the Mission to the perpetual care of the Franciscans. The religious life of Mission Santa Barbara, a church historian later observed, vied with the most regulated friary of Spain in its daily round of prayer, study, and manual labor. Dressed in coarse gray robes (changed to brown in 1885), the priests and brothers went discalced (sandals with no stockings) and shaved the crown of their heads in tonsure, the ancient sign of monastic commitment. On 4 August 1860 an Irish-born San Franciscan, aged 17, by the name of Jeremiah Joseph O'Keefe, was invested in the Franciscan habit. Father O'Keefe spent his entire priestly career at Mission Santa Barbara. In 1886 he published a pioneering guide and through the 1890s served as Mission administrator. Father O'Keefe's career at the Mission spanned its unfolding existence as a monastery, a novitiate and theologate, a college and a parish.

Established in 1868 in the second story of the front wing of the Mission, the Franciscan college helped pioneer higher education in California. A faculty of Franciscan and secular priests, together with some Franciscan brothers, offered instruction on the primary, secondary, and collegiate levels. By 1877 when the college closed for lack of enrollment, some 300 young men, Hispanics and Yankees alike, had received instruction as either day or boarding students. Father Jeremiah Joseph O'Keefe served as president and professor in the 1870s of the Colegio Franciscano, as the institution was called. His duties included formal classroom instruction as well as prefecting duties in the dormitory. Another Franciscan, Brother John Cullinan, formerly a violinist in the orchestra of the California Theater in San Francisco, taught violin, using a restored instrument from the Spanish era which he claimed was the best violin he had ever encountered.

On holidays, O'Keefe and other professors would take groups of young men to the seashore for picnic lunches and games. After lunch, the amiable O'Keefe, relaxing with the students under an oak tree, would light up his Meerschaum with a twenty-four-inch stem, passing it around to the lads like an Indian peace pipe. Despite the cumbersomeness of his sandals and robes, another instructor, Father Pacificus Wade, astonished the students on these excursions with his ability to clear twenty-two feet in the broad jump.

At the Colegio Franciscano of Mission Santa Barbara, an entire generation of young Hispanic Californians—boys bearing names such as De la Guerra, Pico, Pacheco, Noriega, Gutiérrez, Olivera, Cota, Cordero—were educated side by side with the sons of the American ascendancy—the Hopes, Hills, Packards, and Freemans—in an alembic that reflected the persistence of Hispanic society in mid-Victorian Santa Barbara. By contemporary standards, the Colegio Franciscano, a secondary school with an attached primary school and junior college, hardly qualifies as higher education; yet when Father J.M. Romo, a Mexican friar associated with the ill-fated Emperor Maximilian (the Emperor wanted him to establish a hospice for Mexicans in the Holy Land) took his students by night to the belfry of the Mission tower, instructing them on the telescope beneath a sky filled with stars, or when botany lessons were given in the ancient Mission garden, education in the Franciscan spirit—instruction, that is, touched by both science and by a reverence for the beauty of nature—added its presence to the Santa Barbara identity.

Aside from his teaching duties, Father Romo served as religious superior under the title Father Guardian, a designation granted by Rome only to Franciscan communities of the first class. In late 1871 Romo had traveled from Paris to Santa Barbara to take up his assignment. Romo hoped to recruit Franciscans from Mexico to keep up the Hispanic nature of the Franciscan Order in California; but when this hope proved futile Romo successfully petitioned Rome in 1884 that Mission Santa Barbara, the only California mission to remain staffed by Franciscans, be attached to the Midwestern Province of the Sacred Heart. When this occurred in 1885, a number of German priests and brothers traveled west to supplement the efforts of their aging Hispanic colleagues and the handful of Irish recruits. With German-American energy, the Father Guardian who replaced Romo, Ferdinand Bergmeyer, began a sequence of physical improvements and expansions on the Mission and monastery, now approaching its centenary. In August 1894 Father Bergmeyer, then serving his second term as Guardian, was shot to death after breakfast by an indigent to whom he had given shelter in the Mission. Already under discussion by the time of Bergmeyer's death was a plan first broached by Bishop García Diego fifty years earlier: a seminary. The seminary College of St. Anthony, which began instruction in September 1896 and five years later moved to a gracious Spanish Renaissance building near the Mission, further defined Santa Barbara as an ecclesiastical center such as Bishop García Diego envisioned when he began gathering stones in 1842.

Through this first era of Americanization, Santa Barbara remained strongly Hispanic, more so, in fact, than any comparable coastal region in the state. The Hispanic names of so many students at the Colegio Franciscano asserted the strength of the Hispanic presence in Santa Barbara and the continuing Hispanic-Yankee dialogue that characterized the region. If Bishop García Diego embodied in an ecclesiastical idiom the dream of Santa Barbara as Spain or Old Mexico, his Santa Barbara contemporary and supporter, Alfred Robinson, acted out the successes and ambiguities of the Hispanicizing Yankee. Santa Barbara, it must be remembered, began its existence in 1782, four years before the founding of the Mission, as one of the four royal presidios on the Alta California coast, the others being at San Diego, San Francisco, and Monterey. The *commandante* of the Santa Barbara presidio, a Spanish army officer, governed civil and military affairs alike. Santa Barbara, in other words, was linked directly in the imagination of its military leadership to the Crown and culture of Spain.

By the time of the Mexican revolution of 1822, the presidio had spawned an army town of sorts, which like all such Hispanic colonial settlements sustained a discernible social stratification among a military and religious elite,

European in origin; a mestizo population of soldier and ex-soldier colonists; and, at the bottom, the Mission Indians. The secularization of the Mission replaced the ecclesiastical elite with two new figures, the *ranchero* on his land grant and the civil official now sharing political authority with the army officers of the garrison. The middle-ranked mestizo population expanded itself to include a growing population of local artisans, small farmers, and graziers, and foremen of various sorts on the large *ranchos*. The Native Americans, their population dwindling rapidly after secularization, lingered on as an exploited work force.

Strengthening the community and softening its social and racial stratifications was a *compadrazgo* network of godparental ties in which the more affluent and powerful protected a network of relatives and clients linked formally to them by baptismal ties or through an informal system of affiliation. No Santa Barbaran better exemplified the patriarchy than José-Antonio Julián De la Guerra y Noriega (1779–1858). Born in the Spanish province of Santander, De la Guerra immigrated to Mexico City as a young man to enter the mercantile house of his uncle. Chosing a military career a few years later, he joined the Spanish Army as a cadet in 1798, and in 1800 was posted to Monterey in Alta California as an ensign. In 1804 he married Maria Antonia Carrillo, the daughter of Don Raimundo Carrillo, Commandante of the Presidio of Santa Barbara and a veteran of the Sacred Expedition of 1769 which first brought the Spanish to Alta California. In 1806 De la Guerra was promoted to lieutenant and posted to Santa Barbara. After further service in Baja California and San Diego, he returned to Santa Barbara in 1817 as captain and commandante of the garrison.

When Mexico broke from Spain, Captain De la Guerra offered his resignation, which was refused by the new government. Already, however, De la Guerra's interests had broadened beyond the narrow concerns of garrison life in a remote province, broken occasionally by assignments in Mexico. Drawing upon his early experience in his uncle's trading house and upon existing family connections, De la Guerra began to enter the commercial life of the California coast. By 1819 he was prosperous enough to begin construction of a magnificent hacienda in Santa Barbara, which took some seven years to complete.

In 1829 he returned from official business in Mexico City in his own vessel laden with cargo for sale in California. Retiring from active army service, De la Guerra installed his large family in La Casa Grande, three wings surrounding a patio, now complete, and for the remaining thirty years of his life prospered as the premier merchant patriarch of Santa Barbara. Some ninety persons worked variously for Captain De la Guerra, either as household servants, vaqueros on his (eventually) 200,000 acres of property, or in connection with his merchandizing activities. Passing the adobe, workers and other Santa Barbarans would bow out of respect for De la Guerra's standing in the community. Richly furnished with imports from Boston and Mexico and featuring a wine cellar and a library, La Casa Grande teemed with an exuberant familial life of sons, daughters, sons-in-law, daughters-in-law, offspring, friends, and retainers. When De la Guerra died in 1858, he left behind more than one hundred lineal descendants.

One welcomed guest at Casa De la Guerra throughout the early 1830s was Alfred Robinson, agent in Santa Barbara for the Boston trading firm of Bryant, Sturgis and Company. Born in Boston in 1807 to Scots stock represented at Lexington Bridge and Bunker Hill, Robinson entered the trading business as a young man and made three voyages to the West Indies before he was twenty-one. In 1828 he sailed for California as clerk of the *Brookline*, a Bryant, Sturgis and Company vessel in the hide and tallow trade. After trading up and down the California coast, the *Brookline* landed at Santa Barbara in the late spring of 1829 and the young clerk, age 22, sat for the first time at the long dining table of the De la Guerra household. Captain De la Guerra's daughter Anita (a shortened usage, her full baptismal name being Ana María de Altagracia Antonia Leonarda Severa) was at the time a child of eight going on nine. For the next six years, Alfred Robinson worked energetically on behalf of Bryant, Sturgis and Company, based primarily out of the company warehouse at the foot of Chapala Street but traveling up and down the coast as well in search of hides and tallow for shipment to Boston.

Ever since Daniel Martin Call had jumped his China-bound ship in 1816 to work as a carpenter for Father Antonio Ripoll during the construction of the fourth edition of the Mission, a growing number of Americans were finding Santa Barbara a congenial place. Call set the pattern for accommodation. He learned Spanish, received baptism as a Catholic, married a local woman, and in general became Hispanicized. José De la Guerra personally admired Americans, including the young Bryant and Sturgis agent who eventually proposed marriage to his sixth child Anita when she turned thirteen. The proposal was accepted but the marriage was delayed for another two years until Anita was fully matured. Robinson, meanwhile, was baptized a Catholic on 4 May 1833 at the presidio chapel in Monterey by none other than Father García Diego, the future bishop. His sponsor was William Edward Hartnell, an Englishman who had been in California since 1822 as a trader in hides and mission produce. In 1825 Hartnell had married De la Guerra's other daughter, Teresa. The couple would eventually produce twenty sons and five daughters.

On 24 January 1836 Alfred Robinson married Anita De la Guerra at Mission Santa Barbara, Father Narcisco Durán presiding. Father Antonio Jimerro performed the pre-nuptial presentation and blessing of the bridal veil, and Anita's parents and sister Teresa stood as witnesses. A wedding reception lasting three days followed at La Casa Grande. Present at the reception was Richard Henry Dana, Jr., a young crewman from the *Alert*, a Bryant and Sturgis vessel anchored in the channel. Dana's later description of the festivities in *Two Years Before the Mast* (1840), although pervaded by Yankee ambivalence for Hispanic Californians in general and for Alfred Robinson in particular as a Protestant Bostonian willing to become an Hispanicized Catholic, teems with eyewitness detail. Three days before the wedding, Dana reported, the ship's steward went ashore with supplies to help prepare the pastry and cake for the reception. On the day of the wedding the *Alert* ran up its flags and fired a twenty-three-gun salute on its four guns as Robinson and his bride emerged from the Mission. Attending the reception that evening, Dana found a large tent capable of handling several hundred guests set up in the central patio court of La Casa Grande. Hours of dancing, Spanish dances as well as the waltz, were followed by a late supper, more dancing, and the breaking of eggshells filled with cologne over the heads of unsuspecting dancers. Alfred Robinson, Dana noted with characteristic ambivalence towards the agent, wore "a tight, black, swallow-tailed coat, just imported from Boston, a high stiff cravat, looking as if he had been pinned and skewered, with only his feet and hands left free."[1] In such Yankee attire, Robinson took to the dance floor, a total contrast to another guest, Don Juan Bandini, attired in white pantaloons, a short silk embroidered jacket, white stockings, and morocco slippers.

Robinson's Boston coat suggested, correctly, that despite his formal conversion to Catholicism and his Santa Barbara bride, he had not become completely Hispanicized. Already, in fact, Robinson was growing discontented with his limited agent's role in California, especially after 1834 when Bryant, Sturgis and Company reduced his rate of commission. On 8 October 1837 Robinson and his wife set sail on the *California* for Boston, where Robinson planned to enter more actively in the California trade as an investor. With the exception of a business trip to California between 1840 and 1842, Robinson spent the next decade and a half in Boston and New York affiliated as a co-investor with Bryant, Sturgis and Company and its successor firm (after 1842), William Appleton and Company, and his own dry-goods export house in New York. That their move was only temporary was attested to by the fact that the couple left behind their daughter Celestita with her grandparents, the dangers of a voyage around the Horn being considered too formidable for a small child.

In the midst of this busy life, Alfred Robinson found time to write—letters, first of all, to his father-in-law Don José De la Guerra, followed by a book, *Life in California During a Residence of Several Years in That Territory*, issued anonymously in 1846, the year California came under American occupation. A classic account of Hispanic California in its twilight years, *Life in California* is a descriptive panegyric to the life Robinson remembered. Filled with descriptions of family life, social customs, music, food, dancing, and picnics, Robinson's account abounds in exuberant simplicity, in that appetite for religion, family life, and simple pleasures which he believed was so characteristic of Hispanic California.

In one sequence Robinson describes taking a picnic with the Carrillos of Santa Barbara in two carts covered with leached cotton, the one for the children, watched over by Chumash retainers, the other filled with adults, together with an immense weight of roast turkeys, chickens, beef, mutton, tamales, and sweets. Riding behind were some twenty adults on horseback. "A large white table-cloth was spread on the grass," writes Robinson of an oak-dotted, flower-carpeted glade surrounding a pond, an hour's ride outside Santa Barbara, "upon which were tastefully arranged our different dishes of meats, pastry, fruits, and sweetmeats; and around these we accommodated ourselves, some reclining, others seated upon the ground. At the conclusion of the dinner the boys amused us with a 'toro' or bull, which they had brought from a neighboring farm; but he soon managed to escape, and made his way to the centre of the pond, where he remained quite secure from their torments."[2] The baiting of the bull adds an appropriately barbaric touch, softened by singing and guitar music.

Hispanic California possessed both the virtues and the vices of an undeveloped pastoral society, and Alfred Robinson knew each dimension. Despite Dana's spoofing of the Boston frock coat Robinson wore to his wedding feast, Robinson's contribution to the emergent Santa Barbara identity lay in his massive empathy for the Hispanic society into which he had married. Physically and imaginatively, Robinson grafted himself onto Hispanic roots in a place called Santa Barbara and in doing so in both life and writing he helped fashion an archetype. Like the stones gathered by Bishop García Diego, the suggestions of Life in California, together with the real life behind the book, lay in wait for the use of a later generation.

Meanwhile, Robinson's lesson of Yankee-Hispanic accommodation was proving of immediate value. When John Charles Frémont brought the California Battalion through Santa Barbara in early January 1847, he came under the influence of Señora Bernarda Ruiz, a respected matron who urged upon Frémont a pro-Hispanic policy. Frémont might very well have taken counsel of Don José De la Guerra himself, who for years, according to his son-in-law, had been saying that California's best future lies with the United States. In any event, Frémont left Santa Barbara, letting it be known that he favored a speedy conciliation between the Hispanic Californians and the United States. General Andrés Pico surrendered personally to Frémont on the Cahuenga Plain north of Los Angeles on 18 January 1847, in the belief (which turned out to be correct) that Frémont, a Frenchman with strong Catholic associations and a personal need for popular support, could be expected to set more lenient terms than those offered by the choleric Commodore Robert Field Stockton, the military governor.

Down through the 1860s, Santa Barbara sustained this ambience of Yankee-Hispanic cooperation. The cattle economy of the region, for one thing, held on, which helped stabilize the situation. The Spanish-surnamed Barbareños, they were now called, comprised 70 percent of the 2500 population of the city, which in turn comprised more than 60 percent of the population of the county.

Among others, Alfred Robinson's in-laws did well in the American order. In 1855 a majority of Americans joined together to elect Don José De la Guerra mayor of Santa Barbara over his Hispanic-baiting opponent C.R.V. Lee. Don José's sons, Pablo and Antonio María, each represented Santa Barbara County in the state senate, and Pablo also sat as District Judge for Santa Barbara and San Luis Obispo counties. One of Don José De la Guerra's daughters married Dr. James L. Ord, brother of Major General Edward Ord, a commander under Grant.

During the Civil War Don José De la Guerra opposed the Confederate sympathies of some Barbareños, keeping his people in the Union camp. Largely through Don José's efforts, Company C of the California Native Cavalry Battalion was raised in Santa Barbara, with Antonio María De la Guerra as captain, a nephew, Santiago De la Guerra, as first lieutenant, and another nephew, Juan De la Guerra, as first sergeant. The unit served as constabulary at Drum Barracks at Wilmington before being posted to border patrol in Arizona. When the ninety Barbareño cavalrymen returned by troop ship to Santa Barbara for discharge, minus two dead from tuberculosis and seven deserters, they were welcomed with a three-day festival that recalled the spontaneity of the pre-Conquest era.

Even the street names of Santa Barbara, formally adopted in 1851, seemed to constitute an acceptance of what history had wrought. A committee of three, American attorney Eugene Lies, Joaquín Carrillo, and Antonio María De la Guerra, supervised the naming process which incorporated successive levels of the Santa Barbara experience. There were the names of Chumash chiefs, first of all, followed by names from the Spanish and Mexican era. The leading families of the presidial era received memorialization (Carrillo, De la Guerra, Gutiérrez, Ortega, Cota), as well as figures from the recent American experience (military governor Richard Mason, the surveyor Salisbury Haley). Spanish topographical designations linked these names together, their liquid music suggesting that Santa Barbara, no matter what the future held, would always be recalling its origins: *Montecito*, a small grove or mountain; *Chapala*, a lake in Mexico; the saints *San Andrés* and *San Buenaventura*; *Los Olivos*, the olive trees, *Alisos*, the sycamores, *De la Viña*, of the vineyard.

Perhaps the most suggestive name of all was given to a central street: *Anacapa*, a Chumash word for a mirage or a pleasing delusion; for the Hispanic-Yankee accommodation, while poetic, had not the force of history or solid demographics behind it. Alfred Robinson, emblematically, suffered a decline of family that reflected a larger reversal. Robinson lost his beloved wife in 1855, his father-in-law in 1858, and his brother-in-law in 1874. Of his eight children, in whom ran the blood of New England and Hispanic California, seven died within his lifetime. Moving to San Francisco in his later years, where he worked as a real-estate agent, Robinson—the onetime Don Alfredo, baptized in Monterey fifty years earlier, a friend of the Franciscans, the loving husband who assured his father-in-law that New York City had not one but two bishops and a dozen churches—reverted to his Protestant faith.

When Don Alfredo died in San Francisco at age 88 in October 1895 after a brief bout of pneumonia, the Reverend Horatio Stebbins of the First Unitarian Church conducted services at the Laurel Hill Cemetery. So too did Santa Barbara run a parallel course of Americanization and Hispanic decline. The great drought of 1863–1864 weakened the cattle economy. Throughout the next decade Hispanic Californians began progressively to lose their lands to Anglo ranchers. The once flourishing Hispanic artisan class—carpenters, mechanics, irrigation workers, gardeners, skilled craftsmen of every sort—faced with a growing Anglo ownership and mechanic class, also began to migrate out of the area. A few upper-class families held on, picturesque Knickerbockers to be trotted out and fêted on ceremonial occasions, but they no longer played any important role in the import and merchandizing sector they had once dominated. By the mid-1870s Santa Barbara had become thoroughly Americanized. The surviving Hispanics, the mestizos especially, were now a racial minority, increasingly confined to the barrio.

3

Land constituted the basic wealth of Santa Barbara in the Spanish, Mexican, and American eras. Secure in their lands until secularization, the Franciscans directed their Native American charges in vast enterprises of cattle, grain, and fruit. When the founder of the royal presidio, José-Francisco de Ortega, retired from the army in 1795 with the brevet rank of captain, he petitioned and received from the Crown six square leagues of shoreline and Santa Ynez foot-hills twenty miles from the presidio, which he named El Rancho de Nuestra Señora del Refugio, Our Lady of Refuge. Here Ortega settled with his wife, María Antonia Carrillo, and their eight offspring, some of them grown and married with children of their own.

In 1826 the Captain's granddaughter Rafaela Ortega married a converted Yankee, Daniel Hill, and thereby established a blend of blood and land lines suggestive of the future. When Mission Santa Barbara was secularized, Hill and another gringo, Nicholas Den, secured the lease on its lands from Gover-nor Pío Pico. In 1846 Hill acquired over four thousand acres, Rancho Goleta, named for a shipwrecked schooner on the shoreline, which adjoined his part-ner Den's Dos Pueblos grant in the region to the west of the presidio settle-ment.

Meanwhile, in May 1843, another retired officer, Lieutenant Narcisco Fa-bregat, successfully petitioned Governor Manuel Micheltorena for over three thousand acres in the same area. In August 1845 Fabregat sold part of his grant to Thomas M. Robbins, an American who had settled in Santa Barbara around

1830, marrying a Carrillo. Robbins eventually managed to acquire the entire Fabregat grant, called La Calera, or the Lime Kiln, from a kiln operated there during the building of Mission Santa Barbara. Robbins added this extensive property to his own three-thousand-acre grant, Las Positas, Little Springs, granted him by Governor Pió Pico in July 1846. In 1861 Thomas Hope, a 41-year-old Irishman who had settled in Santa Barbara in 1850, acquired the conjoined Rancho Las Positas y La Calera from Robbins's widow Encarnación. Thus the Hope Ranch, as it now became—an amalgam of holdings from Narciso Fabregat, Thomas Robbins, his widow Encarnación Carrillo, and the Den family— recapitulated in its title line the land history of Santa Barbara and handed it on to purely American ownership. Between 1861 and 1868 six children were born to Thomas and Delia Hope, and their sheep ranch prospered in the wool boom brought on by the Civil War.

Hope died in January 1876. By that time Santa Barbara County, an area 2,630 square miles in extent, or two and a half times the size of Rhode Island, had become an Americanized sheep-raising and agricultural region, with only a quarter of the properties (as of 1870) remaining in Hispanic hands. Unlike the immigrants of the 1830s and 1840s, and even to a lesser extent the early 1850s, the new immigrants to the region remained American in culture, untouched by any Hispanic influence. Santa Barbara's leading citizen of this era, Colonel William Welles Hollister, tall, rangy, clear-eyed, and Lincolnesque in his chin whiskers, epitomized the American energies that were now transforming the region. Springing from the same Connecticut family that produced Gideon Welles, Lincoln's salty and uncorruptible Secretary of the Navy, the Ohio-born Hollister entered farming, stock-raising, and merchandising in his native Licking County after attending Kenyon College. In 1852 the 34-year-old entrepreneur brought 200 head of cattle across the plains to California, where he scouted development possibilities in the region between San José and Monterey. In 1854 Hollister made a second trip, this time with his brother, sister, fifty men, 5000 sheep, 200 cattle, and a herd of horses. This second trek, Boer-like in its scope and determination, took fifteen months—a year to cross the plains into Southern California via the Old Mormon trail, another three months to proceed up the coastal valleys to Monterey County. Settling in San Juan Bautista, Hollister busied himself in sheep-raising and land development. In association with Flint, Bixby and Company, he acquired and subdivided the Rancho San Justo and helped establish the town named in his honor. When Hollister married in 1862, it was to a quintessential Yankee girl, Annie James of San Francisco, the daughter of a prominent Unitarian family, the ceremony being performed by Thomas Starr King, the premier spokesman for the Yankee ethos on the Pacific Coast.

In 1869, having disposed of his San Justo holdings, Hollister moved south to Santa Barbara County and began a similar process of land acquisition and development, this time on the Rancho Lompoc in partnership with Thomas

Dibblee and Joseph Cooper, two Santa Barbarans possessing deep Hispanic connections. In 1874 the partners sold the Rancho Lompoc to the California Immigrant Union of San Francisco for subdivision into five- and ten-acre tracts surrounding the town of Lompoc, which Hollister himself laid out in spacious arrangements. He, meanwhile, maintained his interest with Dibblee in the 100,000-acre Rancho San Julian in western Santa Barbara County, where he raised cattle and merino sheep.

For his own residence Hollister acquired (or so he thought) the Rancho Dos Pueblos property in the Goleta Valley twelve miles west of Santa Barbara from the heirs of Nicholas Den, then still minors. Hollister renamed the property the Glen Annie Ranch in honor of his wife but was forced to spend the next twelve years of his life fighting off the eventually successful claim of the Den Estate, argued by San Francisco land attorney Thomas Bishop, that the sale was illegal. As the lawsuit dragged on, Hollister planted the Glen Annie property in wheat, olives, walnuts, almonds, oranges, lemons, limes, plums, nectarines, and peaches. Atop an elevated glen with a clear view of the channel he built a large home surrounded by a veranda and a large garden. Nearby, Ellwood Cooper was developing his two-thousand-acre Ellwood Ranch along similar lines. The largest olive and walnut ranch in California, Ellwood Ranch swept down from the Santa Ynez range to the sea, a utopian statement of fulfilled agricultural possibilities. Superbly sited on a foothill, the Cooper residence commanded a georgic vista of olive and walnut groves, drying ovens, oil presses, packing sheds, and subsidiary orchards of orange, lemon, peach, and pear trees.

Glen Annie, Ellwood, and the other Santa Barbara ranches—the Stowe Ranch, the Sturges Ranch, the venerable Dos Pueblos Ranch near Gaviota Pass, the farms and ranches of the four great valleys of the county, Santa Maria, Lompoc, Santa Ynéz, and Los Alamos—testified to the success of American agriculture in the 1870s and 1880s. Despite this success, the city of Santa Barbara did not select for itself a primary identity as an agricultural center or market town; for already in the 1870s another identity, that of a health resort, was being assembled on a preliminary basis. In the half-century to follow, the agricultural realities of Santa Barbara remained socio-economically relevant but conspicuously unpromoted, while another arc of identity—from sanitarium to hotel resort, from hotel resort to Newport on the Pacific to neo-Mediterranean Riviera to, finally, an idealized Spanish city, cream-white and carmine in the sunlight—asserted itself as a dream materialized.

4

In the winter of 1872 the New York journalist Charles Nordhoff, visiting Santa Barbara, stayed with friends in an oceanside cottage on the eastern edge of the city. Returning east, Nordhoff wrote a series of descriptive articles for *Harper's*

Magazine which were published in book form as *California: For Health, Wealth, and Residence, a Book for Travellers and Settlers* (1872). In a chapter headed "Southern California for Invalids" Nordhoff praised the healthfulness of Santa Barbara's climate. Because the California coast veered sharply in an east-west direction below Point Conception, Nordhoff observed, Santa Barbara faced south, not west, and was thus protected by mountains from the winds and fogs of the coast. Uniquely situated, Santa Barbara possessed a steadily sunny micro-climate perfect for recovering invalids. Santa Barbara was also blessed with a number of mineral springs in the city itself, at nearby Montecito and near the Arroyo Burro on former Mission property.

Nordhoff's best-selling guide brought an immediate influx of health-seekers to Santa Barbara despite the lack of a direct train connection. The very title of an 1878 promotional pamphlet, *All About Santa Barbara, California, the Sanitarium of the Pacific Coast*, a compilation of predictions regarding the future of Santa Barbara as a health resort, speaks to the willingness of the city to embrace this Nordhoff-inspired identity. By the late 1870s bottled Veronica Water from the Arroyo Burro springs, known for its gently laxative effects, was bringing the reputation of Santa Barbara as a health resort to the apothecary shops of the nation. Jesse D. Mason's *History of Santa Barbara County* (1883) abounded in climatological and statistical data, together with personal testimonials, on the healthfulness of Santa Barbara's Palestinian climate, as one writer describes it, for pulmonary diseases and nervous disorders. In Santa Barbara, one correspondent claimed, "nervous diseases . . . are shorn of half their terrors. All forms of mental disease find a specific in the soft but not enervating atmosphere that comes to the tired author like a sweet sleep."[3]

In order to accommodate health-seekers forced to crowd themselves into boarding houses and rented cottages, Santa Barbara evolved into the second phase of its identity, that of a hotel resort. In July 1874 a group of Santa Barbara investors, with Colonel Hollister as majority stockholder, formed the Seaside Hotel Company to build Southern California's first resort hotel. Heeding Nordhoff's advice to avoid the windy beaches, the investors acquired a site one mile inland on State Street between Victoria and Sola. There they built a three-story, ninety-room hotel surmounted by a seventy-five-foot tower. Each room had a fireplace, stocked with sweet-scented almond wood from the Glen Annie Ranch. Mrs. Hollister had journeyed north to San Francisco to purchase rugs, tapestries, and other furnishings. There was a separate dining room for children and governesses.

All in all, the Arlington, as the new hotel was named, cost an impressive $160,000. When the other investors could no longer carry their notes, Hollister became sole owner. He also acquired a second property, the bankrupt Santa Barbara College on State Street, which he converted into a second, less-luxuriant hostelry named the Ellwood in honor of his neighbor in the Goleta Valley. Putting the Arlington under the management of Dixie Thompson, a flamboyant Santa Barbaran of pre-Conquest lineage, Hollister assumed for himself the role of impresario and host. Personally greeting incoming passenger steamers at Stearns Wharf, Hollister would escort the obviously affluent to a horse-drawn omnibus heading for the Arlington. The others—salesmen, second-class passengers, the obviously modest—he directed to the Ellwood vehicle.

In the figure of the patriarchal Hollister, a bewhiskered city father, tall, frock-coated, separating the wealthy from the middle classes, one encounters without much interpretative strain a prophetic paradigm of the ensuing Santa Barbara experience: a sorting and consolidation, that is, of proper and improper social elements. In the Christmas week of 1882 no less than royalty itself, Princess Louise, the daughter of Queen Victoria, and the Princess's husband the Marquess of Lorne, Governor General of Canada, descended the gangplank at Stearns Wharf and were conveyed to the Arlington, where Hollister had refurbished the bridal suite for their visit. The Colonel himself died in the Arlington on 8 August 1886 at the age of 68 and was laid out in the lobby atop a draped catafalque. An entrepreneur who had crossed the plains with cattle and sheep, acquired land, founded two towns and helped orient a third, Santa Barbara, in a new direction, Hollister was buried with obsequies befitting a founding patriarch.

By the time of Hollister's death, Santa Barbara was making the transition from sanitarium to resort. Sick people continued to come to Santa Barbara to get well, but well people were also arriving to enjoy themselves. Santa Barbara might have tried to promote itself into a bustling business city, Edward Roberts observed in 1886, but the city has instead "accepted its alternative and laid siege, together with Nice, Mentone, and Newport, to the distinction of being a sanitarium and popular resort."[4] Such an identity, Roberts admitted, came at a cost. Santa Barbara offered few business opportunities, and "the quiet would be oppressive, at times, to one of an active temperament, were it not for the view of ocean, valley, and mountain, that is ever present. But with the sight of these gifts of Nature one forgets that Santa Barbara is listless, and is only cognizant of the fact that it is charming. Its beauty disarms energy and the power to criticise. The deep blue of the ocean, stretching far away to softly outlined islands; the clearness of the sky, which is only occasionally hid by clouds, and the long beach of sand, flecked with the white spray of ocean-waves, are sights that every town does not possess. Their attractiveness, with that of other scenes, is enticing. One comes for a week and remains a year, or for a lifetime. Seasons come and go, but no notice is taken of their arrival or departure. The fact is forgotten that life is ever real or earnest, and the happy dweller, satiated by delights he never before experienced, only dreams his time away."[5]

Climate and scenery, in other words, have become for Roberts, a quintessentially genteel observer from the East, both the causes and the symbols of delicious but subtly dangerous dream states in which languor and timelessness

The Los Angeles River was especially beautiful at sunrise, but the city would have to look elsewhere for its water. (UCLA Special Collections)

The irrigated township of Ontario forecast the civilized communities that water projects would materialize. (UCLA Special Collections)

The Bradbury Building foretold the modern metropolis that water and technology would bring to Los Angeles. (Security Pacific Historical Photograph Collection, Los Angeles Public Library)

[*Opposite above*] But first engineers (left to right) John Freeman, Joseph Schwyler, J.B. Lippincott, Fred Stearns, and William Mulholland had to take to the field and choose a route for the aqueduct. (Security Pacific Historical Photograph Collection, Los Angeles Public Library)

[*Opposite below*] An army of workers extended an aquatic lifeline to the newest imperial city of Anglo-America. (Security Pacific Historical Photograph Collection, Los Angeles Public Library)

[*Opposite above*] On Signal Hill oil was everywhere, and no place was exempt from the drilling. (Paul Weeks, UCLA Special Collection)

[*Opposite below*] Harry Culver (left) took the bankers and real estate men out to a vantage point on Baldwin Hill, and Culver City was a done deal. (Security Pacific Historical Photograph Collection, Los Angeles Public Library)

A great city needed first-class hotels, such as the Biltmore facing Pershing Square. (Security Pacific Historical Photograph Collection, Los Angeles Public Library)

Los Angeles envisioned itself as the Chicago of the Pacific, a big shoulders type of place. The tempo of Broadway at Sixth underscored the plausibility of the Chicago metaphor. (Security Pacific Historical Photograph Collection, Los Angeles Public Library)

[*Opposite above*] By the mid-1920s Los Angeles had a new headquarters for the Automobile Club of Southern California and the beginnings of a traffic problem. (Security Pacific Historical Photograph Collection, Los Angeles Public Library)

[*Opposite below*] Following the pathway created by the Native Americans of Yang-Na, Wilshire Boulevard pushed Los Angeles westward to the sea. (Security Pacific Historical Photograph Collection, Los Angeles Public Library)

An ambitious city required an equally ambitious Elks Club, *left* (Security Pacific Historical Photograph Collection, Los Angeles Public Library)—

and downtown office structures such as the Richfield Building, *below left* (UCLA Special Collections)—

and a new city hall, *below right* (Security Pacific Historical Photograph Collection, Los Angeles Public Library)—

and a monumental public library, *right* (Security Pacific Historical Photograph Collection, Los Angeles Public Library)—

and apartment buildings offering comfort and identity to newcomers, *below*. (Security Pacific Historical Photograph Collection, Los Angeles Public Library)

A developing sense of community necessitated outdoor places for people to gather, such as the Hollywood Bowl, where the Easter sunrise was greeted in 1924 (Security Pacific Historical Photograph Collection, Los Angeles Public Library)—

and the Greek Theater at Occidental College. (Security Pacific Historical Photograph
Collection, Los Angeles Public Library)

[*Opposite above*] A developing city also needed nightclubs, such as the Cocoanut Grove at the Ambassador Hotel on Wilshire Boulevard (Security Pacific Historical Photograph Collection, Los Angeles Public Library)—

and picture palaces such as the Pantages Theater on Hollywood Boulevard, *opposite below* (Security Pacific Historical Photograph Collection, Los Angeles Public Library)—

and resorts such as Avalon on Santa Catalina Island. (Security Pacific Historical Photograph Collection, Los Angeles Public Library)

[Opposite above] Flying at five thousand feet in November 1927, the pilot beheld a new kind of American city (The Warren School of Aeronautics, UCLA Special Collections)—

for which Simon Rodia created an enigmatic icon in Watts, *opposite below*. (Gordon William, UCLA Special Collections)

Gardens graced the region. (UCLA Special Collections)

At the Wattles residence in Hollywood, Mediterranean formalism asserted itself against the chaparal, evoking an interplay of wilderness and civilization. (Security Pacific Historical Photograph Collection, Los Angeles Public Library)

As in the case of architect John De Lario's 1926 design for the P.M. Longan estate in Hollywood, Spanish Revival embodied the poetry of Southern California living. (Security Pacific Historical Photograph Collection, Los Angeles Public Library)

Courtyard apartments such as Grauman Court in Hollywood offered instant community to a newly arriving population. (Security Pacific Historical Photograph Collection, Los Angeles Public Library)

Aspiring Paramount hopefuls Betty Compson and Ethel Sauds (left and center) preferred the more structured style of the Women's Studio Club. (Security Pacific Historical Photograph Collection, Los Angeles Public Library)

Posing for the camera in 1923, the executive board of the Los Angeles chapter of the NAACP presided over a small but prosperous black community which tended to vote Republican. (Security Pacific Historical Photograph Collection, Los Angeles Public Library)

Evangelist Aimee Semple McPherson preached a gospel of homes, health, and happiness in the Southland. (Security Pacific Historical Photograph Collection, Los Angeles Public Library)

Through the generosity of Edward and Estelle Doheny (right) and the grand ambitions of Archbishop John J. Cantwell, Catholic Los Angeles asserted itself alongside the dominant Protestantism. The group is shown welcoming to Los Angeles Patrick Joseph Cardinal Hayes, Archbishop of New York. (Security Pacific Historical Photograph Collection, Los Angeles Public Library)

[Opposite above] USC president Rufus Bernhard von KleinSmid (left) beams his approval as Douglas Fairbanks lectures to the newly established USC program in cinematography. (Security Pacific Historical Photograph Collection, Los Angeles Public Library)

[Opposite center] Football enabled USC to build buildings and make payroll. In 1930 the Trojans played the Fighting Irish of Notre Dame before a packed Coliseum. (Security Pacific Historical Photograph Collection, Los Angeles Public Library)

[Opposite below] On Sundays the Santa Monica beach was as crowded as the Coliseum on Saturdays during football season. (Security Pacific Historical Photograph Collection, Los Angeles Public Library)

Aviation provided Southern California a way of envisioning the future. (Security Pacific Historical Photograph Collection, Los Angeles Public Library)

On the morning of 26 August 1929 the *Graf Zepplin* touched down at Mines Field, having crossed the Pacific from Japan. In an instant, the future predicted by aviation was boldly materialized. (Security Pacific Historical Photograph Collection, Los Angeles Public Library)

In the early 1840s Bishop Francisco Garciá Diego y Moreno dreamed of Santa Barbara becoming the first cathedral city of California. (Security Pacific Historical Photograph Collection, Los Angeles Public Library)

For the newly emerging resort city, Mission Santa Barbara functioned as a tourist attraction and central metaphor. (Security Pacific Historical Photograph Collection, Los Angeles Public Library)

The Potter Hotel embodied the lush civility of Santa Barbara as a resort city. (Security Pacific Historical Photograph Collection, Los Angeles Public Library)

Major Max Fleischmann, on the white horse, had two passions, polo and Santa Barbara. (Security Pacific Historical Photograph Collection, Los Angeles Public Library)

Santa Barbarans considered themselves the direct heirs of the rancheros who once rode
the hills of *la tierra adorada*. (Security Pacific Historical Photograph Collection, Los
Angeles Public Library)

Their county courthouse was a castle in Spain, featuring the most beautiful jail in
America. (Security Pacific Historical Photograph Collection, Los Angeles Public Library)

have replaced history and action. Santa Barbara might confer health, but it could also become a land of narcotized lotus eaters, immobilized by the very beauty which nourished them. Fears to this effect are evident in the poetry of Santa Barbaran Mary Camilla Foster Hall-Wood, who published under the understandably shortened *nom de plume* Camilla K. von K. Issued locally in 1887, Hall-Wood's *Sea-Leaves* frequently strikes a note of opposition to the Santa Barbara situation. Suggesting in later verses that she is a widow, somehow exiled in Santa Barbara, the poet opens her volume on a note of rejection.

> I am sickened with sweets, I pine
> For the sound of a northern storm;
> The golden roses are too divine,
> The glimmering seas too warm.

The poems of *Sea-Leaves* abound in images of loneliness, exile, lost hopes, all in ironic contrast to the idyllic situation. Some of the poet's resentment proceeds from an angered feminism:

> A serious childhood; a religious youth;
> High aims, indefinite, checked with real tears;
> A womanhood of tedious household cares
> And petty wars with human savages.

Her anxiety, however, is also motivated by a failure to connect with her present circumstances, to have work to do and to be needed, either personally or as a poet, in the *dolce far niente* stillness of Santa Barbara.

Eleven years later another local poet, Marshall Isley, was feeling more optimistic. Isley's "An Ode to Santa Barbara," while expressing some of the same fears as Camilla K. von K. regarding the paralyzing languor of beauty-drenched isolation, nevertheless manages to make the genteel case for life in the Channel City. The peace, quiet, and beauty of Santa Barbara, Isley admits—

> This wide campania by tall gum-trees paced
> In long processionals toward sacred hills

has its dangers; yet it can also lead to a heightened consciousness of spiritual value impossible in a big city. Even at that, one must be on guard, lest the capacity for creative action be lost in a perpetually sunny afternoon:

> For northern races lose their northern will
> In lotus lands: as wax before the fire,
> Resolves flow down, and impulses expire,
> Tomorrow sits enthroned where sat Today.

Thus the genteel imagination struggled with the gains and losses of the resort metaphor for life in Santa Barbara. Remote edens, however soothing to the nerves, could also be experienced as regions of exile and ennui.

Nonsense! replied Kate Smith, later Kate Douglas Wiggin. Santa Barbara was fun, and that was that. Coming to Santa Barbara in 1876, the young Philadelphian quickly adjusted to the simple outdoor life, which she eulogized in A *Summer in a Canyon*, subtitled A *California Story* (1892), a novel for young readers. The story follows three male Berkeley undergraduates and three young women as they spend a summer camping in a Santa Barbara canyon under the supervision of Dr. Winship, a Berkeley professor. Established in tents at Camp Chaparall, the young people pass an idyllic summer hiking, horseback riding, reading, writing letters, preparing a production of the forest scenes from *As You Like It,* and touring the sites, including the Mission. What emerges from the novel is an enchanting sense of reinvigorating *pasear*, the country summer sojourns of Spanish California, transformed into an American version of the summer reading vacations conducted by dons for Oxford and Cambridge undergraduates. Hardly enervation here; good times, rather, in the interval between late adolescence and young adulthood.

And besides again: Santa Barbara was in its own way a busy, go-ahead kind of town anxious to end its isolation. In 1868 a wharf was built at the foot of Chapala Street, thereby making Santa Barbara a port of sorts. It was augmented in 1872 by an even grander wharf built by John P. Stearns which extended 1500 feet into the channel and was capable of accommodating coastal steamers of any size. The railroad arrived in August 1887, a spur line connecting Santa Barbara even further to the outside world. Five thousand visitors flocked by train to the city and were fêted at a huge outdoor barbecue picnic. The grading and paving of downtown streets began that year as well, together with the installation of electrical street-lighting. Some subdividing occurred, and Santa Barbarans talked of a boom hitting their city as in Los Angeles. Between 1886 and 1887 property assessments increased by an astonishing 75 percent. The boom of 1887, however, never materialized. It would take more than a railroad connection to transform Santa Barbara into a bustling city. Between 1890 and 1900 Santa Barbara gained a mere 723 new residents. With a turn-of-the-century population of 6587, Santa Barbara remained an American Nice, sunny gold and blue, languid and irrelevant.

5

An indigenous genteel tradition desirous of more than the resort metaphor, however, was managing to assert itself. It began with an attempt at secondary education, Santa Barbara College, a boarding school founded in 1869 as a joint stock operation by the ubiquitous Colonel Hollister, who had offspring of his own to educate, in a brand new brick veneer building (costing $40,000) at the corner of Anapamu and State streets. Wanting to create a Yankee Protestant version of the Colegio Franciscano at the Mission, Hollister sent Sarah Cooper, mistress of the neighboring Ellwood Ranch in the Goleta Valley, east to recruit a faculty. At Adelphi College in Brooklyn, Mrs. Cooper secured the services of impeccably Anglo-Saxon (seventeenth-century English colonial stock) Charles Albert Storke, age 25, as instructor in Latin and mathematics. Raised in frontier Wisconsin and self-supporting as a lumberman, printer, and proofreader since he was fourteen, Storke enlisted in the 36th Wisconsin Infantry as a youngster of sixteen. Only twelve of his regiment, including himself, survived the Wilderness Campaign and were taken prisoner. Eight of these surviving twelve died at Andersonville. Released from prison and discharged from the army, Storke spent three years at Kalamazoo College before transferring to the newly established Cornell University, where he graduated with honors in 1870 and accepted the Adelphi appointment. Eager, independent, a combat veteran who had been through two hells, the Wilderness and Andersonville, Storke accepted the Santa Barbara offer ("at the end of the world," he thought), not because he loved teaching, which he did not, but because it offered him a way out to California and a shot at the main chance.

Within a year of his arrival, Storke married the daughter of land baron rancher T. Wallace More, owner with his brothers of the Rancho Sespe, the Rancho Santa Paula y Saticoy, the Rancho Camulos, the offshore island Santa Rosa, and vast grazing tracts at Point Conception—all in all, an empire as large as the State of Delaware. With a $4500 grant from his father-in-law, Storke resigned his position at Santa Barbara College after a year (the college folded in 1878 for lack of enrollment) and moved to Los Angeles, where he founded the *Herald* in 1873, the newspaper which introduced the steam press to Southern California. The *Herald* lost money, although it did survive to be bought out by William Randolph Hearst, and so after six months Storke sold it and returned to Santa Barbara to study law in the chambers of Judge Charles Huse and become active in real estate. What William Welles Hollister was to frontier Santa Barbara, the orchestrator of a score of developmental projects, Charles Albert Storke was to the next era. Passing the bar, he used his legal fees to acquire a working ranch, together with property on the barren hillsides overlooking the northern end of the city which he later developed as the Riviera district. He organized an Immigration Bureau to promote population growth and, a committed Democrat, he served two terms in the state legislature. Locally, he served as district attorney from 1898 and mayor from 1900 to 1902. While mayor, Storke acquired the Santa Barbara *Daily News*, which he built into the most powerful newspaper in the county. Law, land, ranching, politics, real-estate development, newspapering—Storke seemed untouched by the resort metaphor. For him Santa Barbara had become, not an alternative, but the main chance: a for-real, go-ahead, get-rich city.

Storke prided himself on being a descendant of seventeenth-century English stock, a veteran of the Grand Army, a *summa cum laude* graduate of Cornell and a scholarly journalist who wrote seriously and well and was possessed of a sense of history. By the early 1900s, as he rounded and passed fifty, Storke, along with other contemporaries, became increasingly concerned with defining—with an eventual view towards controlling—the Santa Barbara heritage, which was now into its second hundred years. A sense of caste linked to a growing appropriation of the Hispanic metaphor had by then become essential to the Santa Barbara formula. Throughout the mid-nineteenth century Americans sustained a duality of attitude towards Hispanic Californians of the upper classes whom they perceived as aristocratic but ineffectual. Richard Henry Dana's portrayal of Don Juan Bandini in *Two Years Before the Mast* provides a perfect case in point. Dana describes the Peruvian-born *hidalgo* as a Gil Blas or Don Quixote figure, elegantly mannered, courteous, generous, but also helpless before the rising American tide. The fact is, Bandini played an active role in both the Mexican and American order, which he welcomed, marrying three of his daughters to Yankees and serving as the *alcalde* of San Diego in 1848 during the American military occupation. But Dana needed a symbol of the vanishing order, and Don Juan Bandini served the purpose.

Forty-five years later, this process of symbolic appropriation of Hispanic California reasserted itself as American California began to search about for a usable past. Helen Hunt Jackson provided the central formulation of the myth of Old California in her novel *Ramona* (1884), a haunting evocation of the mission era in its final twilight. As the only mission still in Franciscan hands, Mission Santa Barbara played a key role in helping Mrs. Jackson gather local color and formulate the myth that so energized *Ramona*. She visited Santa Barbara twice, once in January-February 1882 and again in May, gathering material for a series of articles in *Century* magazine. Unfortunately, the Arlington Hotel had no room for her in that busy winter month of her first visit, so she sojourned resentfully in a shabby boarding house, which affected her attitude towards the American city, which she dismissed as a stodgy, smug, boring New England town. Mission Santa Barbara, by contrast, left her enchanted. She saw it by morning, its limestone walls warmed by the sunlight, and at sunset when the last rays of light lingered on its western wall. Among the five priests and three brothers Mrs. Jackson met at the Mission was the saintly Padre Francisco de Jesús Sánchez, then seventy-one. In her *Century* article, Jackson added a decade to the Franciscan's age and made of him an even more pronounced twilight figure, easily translatable to myth. In *Ramona*, Padre Francisco de Jesús Sánchez appears as Padre Salvierderra, possessed of the same vanishing Franciscan characteristics, and thus Mission Santa Barbara as fact and fiction was placed at the very center of the Mission Myth in which the genteel tradition clothed itself in Hispanic garments.

The popularity of *Ramona* reinforced the growing power of Mission Santa Barbara as a tourist attraction. As early as 1872 a young Santa Barbaran, Louise Anderson, the mayor's niece and a good friend of Kate Douglas Wiggin, was reputed to have persuaded an equally young Franciscan novice enamored of Miss Anderson and not intending to persevere in the Order anyway to sneak her in by moonlight to the Mission cloister gardens, off-limits to females with the exception of wives of ruling heads of state. Father O'Keefe was alleged to have caught the culprits when Miss Anderson twisted her ankle and fainted, regarding the matter with forgiving humor. In any event, the young man left the Order and Miss Anderson went on to help establish Mills College in Northern California. Ten years later, Princess Louise was granted a daylight tour of the same cloister gardens, canonically permissible because she was not just a royal princess but also the wife of a governor general. Mrs. Benjamin Harrison received the same privilege in April 1891. By 1885 it had become necessary to assign a number of lay brothers as full-time tour guides. Photographs from the period show American visitors standing solemnly beneath the arched arcade of the Mission monastery, a Franciscan or two posing goodnaturedly with them before the camera. Voluntary contributions from visitors constituted an important source of support.

Between 4 and 8 December 1886 Santa Barbara celebrated the centennial of the Mission. Most of the activity originated with the Go-Ahead Club, an organization of Santa Barbara boosters. A full-sized replica of the Mission towers and arch, covered in evergreen and palms and surmounted by an arrangement of Spanish and American flags, spanned State and Figueroa streets. On Sunday, 4 December, solemn high mass was celebrated at the Mission, which was draped in ferns, boughs, palm leaves, pampas plumes, flowers, and more Spanish and American flags. An orchestra accompanied the rites with Lambillotte's Mass in D. Solemn vespers and a Te Deum followed in the afternoon. The following day a grand parade proceeded down State Street under the arch, then out to the Mission itself where the priests gave speeches in English and Spanish. On each of the following two days there were rodeos and athletic contests and grand balls in the evening. An antiquarian degree of historicism pervaded the celebration, in which boosterism wedded itself to scholarship in a way that pointed directly to the future Santa Barbara formula of coalesced history, boosterism, and politics. The parade, for example, featured marchers in Spanish uniforms of the mission era and horsemen in the elaborate saddlery and harness of *rancho* days. Bull-baiting was revived (for the last time) at the rodeo, despite its discomforting savagery, and at the evening balls descendants of old families wore their antique finery, spoke Spanish freely, and danced the dances of Old California. Even some Mission Indians were found, there being but a few survivors in the area, and were asked to sing and dance their ancient ceremonials.

The Santa Barbara establishment took these revived metaphors seriously as it began to re-envision itself as the direct heir of the era of Hispanic grandees. When Presidents of the United States passed through—Harrison in 1891, McKinley in 1901, Roosevelt in 1903—they each made pointed references to this connection. "Santa Barbara," said McKinley, "is an American tree grafted on a Spanish stalk." Mayor Charles Albert Storke beamed in approval. Both

McKinley and Roosevelt received personal tours of the Mission from its superior, Father Ludger Glauber. Roosevelt praised Santa Barbara for its Spanish
Californian atmosphere, for "perpetuating the memorials of an older civilization."[6]

TR also paid an unscheduled personal call on Annie Hollister, widow of the
Colonel. In 1898 the Hollisters' son Stanley had left the Harvard Law School
to enlist in the Rough Riders. Colonel Roosevelt said that he wanted two types
of young men in his regiment, college athletes and cowboys. Stanley Hollister
was both, having played for Harvard and grown up on horseback on the Glen
Annie Ranch. In 1890 Annie Hollister lost the Glen Annie Ranch to the heirs
of Nicholas Den after a fourteen-year lawsuit, and in 1898 she lost her son.
Felled by shrapnel at San Juan Hill, Stanley Hollister succumbed to his wounds
and typhoid at the Army hospital at Fort Monroe, Virginia. His body was
shipped back home for burial. Roosevelt called on Mrs. Hollister when another
Hollister son, Harry, serving in the mounted escort that accompanied the President's carriage, pointed out his mother, wearing a black silk dress and fanning
herself on the lawn of her adobe home at the corner of Chapala and Carrillo
streets. Bounding from his carriage, Roosevelt engaged Mrs. Hollister in private
conversation.

This scene, with its associations of caste—the bully aristocratic President,
the widow of a founder, so dignified in black, the respect paid to a Harvard
man from Santa Barbara who had fallen on San Juan Hill—entered local consciousness as an emblem of achieved identity. Santa Barbara was no longer just
a farming town or a sanitarium or even a resort. Santa Barbara had become a
distinctive city where elite values had taken hold. The Santa Barbara establishment possessed a new conception of itself. How best to express this sense of
achieved caste remained an open question.

Preservationism had emerged as a possibility. Properly regarded, the surviving adobes of Santa Barbara offered easily available emblems of caste. In 1896
Santa Barbaran Sarah Higgins published a scholarly description of the Aguirre
Adobe, together with interviews with those who had lived there decades earlier,
with a view to restoring the facility through some kind of public trust. Even
stronger attention began to focus on the De la Guerra Adobe, the grandest
survivor of old Santa Barbara. The De la Guerras had held on to their mansion, living there throughout the American era. An 1874 photograph shows the
two surviving sons of Don José De la Guerra, Don Francisco and Don Antonio, their sister-in-law Doña Josefa, widow of their deceased brother Pablo De
la Guerra, the judge and state senator, and her children, Carlos, Delfina, Her-
minia, and Francisca, wife of Thomas B. Dibblee (Colonel Hollister's partner),
serenely posing on the patio arcade, their bustled dresses, suits, and straw hats
in delightful contrast to the adobe itself.

On the lookout for local color from the Hispanic era, novelist Gertrude
Atherton visited the De la Guerra mansion in 1890, and Delfina, now grown

up, took her on a tour of its many rooms. Atherton was in the process of
formulating a body of fiction that would portray the Old Californians as an
embattled elite welcoming annexation by the United States and hence the direct ancestors of the upper classes of contemporary California: which is exactly
how Santa Barbarans of the Civic League regarded the De la Guerras in 1909
when the league met to launch the first major effort to restore the Casa De la
Guerra as a historical museum and arts center. Don José De la Guerra, orated
Judge Jarret Richards at a Civic League meeting, "was the autocrat of the community, and yet a mild-mannered autocrat. He was ruler, judge, counselor,
and everything." The De la Guerras, the judge continued, "willingly became
absorbed in our American civilization, and became devoted to our institutions."[7] The identification was obvious: an emerging elite had a ready-made
equation of itself to its counterparts in Old California and a useful tool, preservationism, with which to shore up that identification. The following year,
1910, Walter Hawley, an amateur archeologist, issued an ambitious inventory
of pre-Conquest Hispanic buildings in the city, praising Old Santa Barbara for
its ambience of aristocratic refinement.

Aristocratic refinement, however, did not characterize the realities of Santa
Barbara's surviving Spanishtown, a run-down collection of ancient adobes, many
of them little more than one-room hovels. Spanishtown provided housing to
Santa Barbara's embattled Mexican and Chinese communities and also served
as the city's saloon and red-light district. Visiting the area in the mid-1880s
travel writer Edward Roberts was almost offended that the residents of Spanishtown were not more picturesque. "The present dress of the Mexicans," Roberts
lamented, "has generally become sadly Americanized."[8] He also chided them
for expanding their adobes with wooden additions. The Hispanic residents of
Spanishtown, in other words, did not conform to the genteel myth of Old
California. They had mixed blood, expanded their adobes with wood, worked
precariously for a living, and dressed in what they could find. The Chinese
seemed equally mundane. Employed as laundry workers for the hotels, they
lived in Spanishtown because it was cheap. For a while the Carrillo Adobe
supported a Chinese wash house. In May 1899 the newly organized Santa
Barbara Chamber of Commerce, offended by "[unsightly] back yards, paddling
ducks and bare-legged Chinamen open to public view from the main artery
[State Street] of our business center," organized a campaign to move the Chinese
to the outskirts of the city. "An old adobe," agreed the Morning Press, "if the
surroundings are clean, is far from objectionable, as it recalls an early period
of our history. The main business blocks are creditable to the city, and the
merchants keep their stores in an attractive condition. The objectionable features of State Street are the open back yards in the vicinity of Chinatown.
Nowhere else in Santa Barbara are such nuisances permitted, and why should
they be allowed in the very heart of the city?"[9]

6

The workers of Spanishtown were allowed to live so shabbily in the very heart of the city because the labor-intensive hotels needed a conveniently located, inexpensive work force. By the early 1900s Santa Barbara had become one of the hotel capitals of the country. The city leadership deliberately encouraged this development. Galvanized by the arrival on 31 March 1901 of a direct railroad connection to San Francisco, Los Angeles, and points east, the Santa Barbara Chamber of Commerce approached Southern California hotelman Milo M. Potter with a proposal that Potter build at Santa Barbara a resort hotel comparable to the Coronado in San Diego and the Del Monte in Monterey. A thirty-six-acre tract was available on two shorefront blocks on West Boulevard directly adjacent to Southern Pacific property where private railroad cars could be accommodated. Never one to delay, Potter agreed and went to work. Forming a partnership which included United States Senator Thomas Bard, Potter acquired the property and retained architect John Austin of Pasadena, who designed a rambling five-story, 600-room Mission Revival caravansary capable of accommodating a thousand guests in world-class comfort. Construction began in January 1902 and by January 1903 the Potter Hotel was ready for its grand opening just as the direct-line railroad arrived.

Everything about the Potter was larger than life, including the gigantic Moreton Bay Fig Tree on one edge of the property. Planted in 1877, the tree had grown to a trunk circumference of 31 feet by the early 1900s. Its branches extended over half the size of a modern football field. As the largest fig tree in the world, the Moreton Bay Fig Tree stood as a perfect compliment to the Potter, one of the largest hotels in the country. Each room had its own direct access to sunlight and was furnished in sturdy Mission Revival furniture. Its thirty-six acres were luxuriously planted. Its roof gardens could accommodate hundreds. The hotel maintained its own ranching, poultry, dairy, and farming operations in the Goleta Valley and its own country club on the Hope Ranch, featuring a nine-hole golf course and a polo field. There was also an annex to house the hundreds of single employees. One Potter staffer, orchestra leader Paul Whiteman, began his career in the hotel's Palm Room. Part of the Potter Hotel stood on Burton Mound, whose sulphurous springs bothered the guests, so Potter sealed off the springs with poured concrete, thereby ending, practically and symbolically, Santa Barbara's sanitarium era. "Santa Barbara should not be a mecca for hypochondriacs anyway," Potter reasoned. "We have the finest year-round climate in the world here, so let's give the healthy a chance to enjoy it." [10]

When the original Arlington Hotel burned to the ground on 15 August 1909, it was replaced by a hotel of the same name, Santa Barbara's second sprawling Mission Revival hostelry, which opened in 1911 on upper State Street. The second Arlington catered to an affluent but more sedate clientele than the Potter in a comparable ambience of Mission Revival luxury.

The major effect of the Potter Hotel, and to a lesser extent the second Arlington, was to accelerate the transformation of Santa Barbara into a colony for the rich, a Newport on the Pacific. The Potter attracted the great names of American capitalism—Rockefeller, Vanderbilt, Astor, Carnegie, Du Pont, Studebaker, Harriman, Swift, Armour, Cudahy, Spreckels—and this in turn focused the attention of the wealthy on what the Santa Barbara area had to offer as a place for long-term residence. The Newport metaphor for Santa Barbara first emerged in 1878 in an article by Josephine Sanford published in the *New York Evening Mail*, but it took a full quarter of a century and more for Santa Barbara and its neighboring suburb of Montecito to emerge as a winter vacation resort and retirement colony for the rich. Francis T. Underhill, for instance, a scion of the Lorillard fortune of New York, arrived in the 1890s and married Carmelita De la Guerra Dibblee. Publisher Robert Cameron Rogers and Boston surgeon Richard J. Hall settled on property near the Mission. Retired Pittsburgh financier Thomas D. Wood and Edward Payson Ripley, president of the Atchison, Topeka & Santa Fe railroad, settled in Santa Barbara, as did J.R. Chapman, engineer of the London subway, Philander C. Knox, Attorney General under McKinley and Roosevelt and Secretary of State under Taft and Wilson, Dr. Henry Pritchett, former president of MIT, oilman Silsby Spalding, George Boldt, builder of the Waldorf-Astoria in New York, industrialist George J. Kaime, David E. Perkins of the Akron rubber fortune, San Francisco attorney E.S. Pillsbury, financiers John E. Beale and George Owen Knapp, and Max C. Fleischmann of Fleischmann's Yeast. They came for the scenery and the weather and for sport: polo, first of all, a Santa Barbara-Montecito speciality at the Santa Barbara County Polo Club, later the Santa Barbara Polo Association, a world force in this select sport; but also yachting based out of the Santa Barbara Yacht Club; golf and tennis at the Montecito Country Club; lacrosse (there was even a Santa Barbara La Crosse Club); horse and dog shows; and deepsea fishing in the channel.

The T. Stewart White family of Grand Rapids, Michigan, exemplified this process of Santa Barbarization and the muscular style. A wealthy lumberman, White began wintering in Santa Barbara in 1884, bringing along his wife and five boys. In 1905 White retired permanently to Santa Barbara. His son Stewart Edward, an aspiring writer, settled there permanently as well, living for a while with his young wife Betty at the Arlington Hotel before buying a home at the northeast corner of Santa Barbara and Los Olivos streets.

Stewart Edward White succeeded as a popular novelist, and the young couple soon found themselves at the center of the evolving smart set, cared for by their Chinese houseman Toy, who for $40 a month ran their household with swift efficiency. (Among his many accomplishments, Toy could handle spur-of-the-moment dinner parties without breaking stride.) White's reminiscences of this era, together with surviving family photographs, reveal the blend of athleticism and gentility that by then characterized the Santa Barbara style. When not in book-lined rooms, the couple are seen hiking, playing golf, surf bathing, or riding horseback. Everyone maintained horses and dogs, White later remembered, and it was not uncommon for Santa Barbarans to ride by horseback to formal luncheons or dinner parties. Riding attire was always acceptable at a social gathering. It was, in short, a horsey sort of life, not dissimilar, albeit less developed, than its counterparts on Long Island or further south in Chevy Chase. Being so new, it was at once well-bred and touched by a frontier that was only a horseback ride away in the backcountry.

Increasingly, the standard of taste for the men and women of the Whites' set, and the even wealthier denizens of Montecito, became most vigorously expressed through architecture as well as through yachting, riding, and polo. As in the case of their counterparts in the East, the American Renaissance plutocracy of Santa Barbara-Montecito turned increasingly to Mediterranean Revival to convey its sense of self. The Mediterranean metaphor had been vigorously developing in Southern California since the early 1880s and nowhere was it more plausible than in the Channel City. Throughout the 1880s and '90s comparisons of the Santa Barbara area to Italy (the Bay of Naples), Spain, Portugal, the south of France, and Greece become commonplace. Even as these Mediterranean metaphors multiplied, wealthy migrants to Montecito were in the process of creating their own Arcadia amidst the citrus groves.

Ever since the 1860s the valley of Montecito east of Santa Barbara had been attracting affluent genteel residents interested in garden villa living. The Montecito Hot Springs Hotel also brought temporary sojourners to the area, some of whom decided on Montecito as a place of second or retirement residence. By the late 1890s Montecito had developed into the Newport on the Pacific which had been so long predicted for the Santa Barbara area.

Each fall, as estates were reactivated for the winter season, large orders for fine food and drink were placed at the Diehl Grocery Company in Santa Barbara, purveyors to the carriage trade since its founding by three German-born brothers in 1891. Credit was encouraged at Diehl's, provided the customer's address proved suitable, a condition which bankrupted the store in the Great Depression when wealthy clients suddenly found themselves unable to pay. Aside from the brand names who maintained homes in Montecito—Armour, Billings, Fleischmann, McCormick, Du Pont—there was also a cadre of the quietly rich: residents such as Ernest Lawrence Thayer, a Harvard-educated scion of Lawrence, Massachusetts, woolen mills, whose one claim to fame, aside from being well-off, a Hasty Pudding man, and a friend of George Santayana, was writing "Casey at the Bat" while he was working for his classmate Will Hearst at the San Francisco *Examiner*. Favored by site and fortune, turn-of-the-century Montecitans covered the hillsides with Mediterranean villas which expressed their sense of themselves as landed gentry living in an aristocratic setting. Working with such empowered and aspiring clients, a host of local and regional architects—Francis Underhill, Francis Wilson, Bertram Goodhue, Carleton Winslow, and Reginald Johnson among them—transformed the hillsides and valleys of Montecito into a Tuscan idyll of gardens and villas.

In El Fureidis (the Little Paradise), a Roman villa which Bertram Goodhue designed for J. Waldron Gillespie of Montecito in 1906, every detail of architecture and landscaping orchestrated the Montecito as Mediterranean metaphor. Una Nixon Hopkins visited El Fureidis in 1915 on behalf of *Craftsman* magazine and discovered in the villa and its gardens a new type of American architecture and landscaping, at once Californian and Italian. She noted its palm trees and orange grove, its vine-covered pergolas, statuary, fountains, and pools. "Standing on the portico, at one side of the villa—under a silk awning, stretched like a bird's wing from the white columns across to pillars of pink marble," she noted, "you look out upon a maze of green tree tops waving in the sweet scented breeze, beyond to the iridescent sea in the distance lined against a cobalt sky, and marvel that the mirage does not fade." [11]

When a number of wealthy patrons—C.K. Billings, Frederick Forrest Peabody (Arrow shirts), and George Owen Knapp (Union Carbide)—needed an architect, they turned to one of their own, Francis Townsend Underhill, an Oyster Bay man, a friend of Theodore Roosevelt, whom he accompanied to Cuba as a captain of volunteer infantry, and a part-time Santa Barbara resident since the mid-1880s. A twotime participant in the America's Cup, a onetime congressman from New York, a former secretary and administrative assistant to E.H. Harriman, president of the Union Pacific, Underhill epitomized the Gibson man in the Arrow collar. He knew yachts, polo, horseflesh (he judged at Madison Square Garden in the 1890s), swine (he raised purebreds), and architecture, in which he functioned as a self-taught practitioner. Having first seen Santa Barbara as a lad of seventeen in 1880 while traveling for his health, Underhill returned in 1885 and began raising purebred horses, cattle, and swine on an increasingly full-time basis. After Cuba and the Union Pacific, Underhill retired completely to Santa Barbara and married Carmelita Dibblee, the granddaughter of Juan De la Guerra, in one of those Yankee-Hispanic alliances that even then were still surfacing.

For his wife Underhill designed La Chiquita on Channel Drive near the present-day site of the Hotel Biltmore, a home which *Country Life* in 1914 judged one of the dozen most beautiful in America. For his Montecito friends (*clients* would be too aggressive a term), Underhill rendered a series of Mediterranean Revival palaces that gave new splendor to this portion of the Southern California coast. Versatile, learned, eclectic, the Stanford White of Santa Barbara, Underhill understood perfectly the corroborating comfort which the imagery and idiom of Ancient Greece and Rome and the Italian Renaissance conferred on the new American plutocracy in its Montecito mode.

Occasionally, Underhill took daring departures within the framework of the Mediterranean idiom—as in the case of Solana, the villa he designed for Frederick Forrest Peabody in 1917. Basing his design on an ancient Greek villa, Underhill eschewed interior hallways in favor of an interior court on which all rooms opened. The façade of Solana possessed a severity at once classical and proto-Bauhausian, as if Underhill were struggling simultaneously with historical and futurist metaphors. Appropriately, Solana later housed the Center for the Study of Democratic Institutions. Underhill himself had the good taste to die two months before the crash of October 1929 decimated his fortune and ended the era whose preferences he so perfectly embodied.

Underhill's contemporary Francis Wilson showed the same American Renaissance characteristics. A Massachusetts Yankee, Wilson first saw California in 1887 at the same age as Underhill, seventeen. In Wilson's case, however, it was not the sunny coastal South but the forested Sierra Nevada of the North—Placerville specifically, where his sister was working as a school teacher—which formed the young man's first California connection. For three rugged years Wilson worked as a log-driver on the American River and a surveyor for the Southern Pacific before moving to San Francisco in the early 1890s where he found work as a draftsman in the architectural firm of Pissis and Moore. Nothing could have been more fortunate for the young man's developing talent. Trained at the Ecole des Beaux-Arts in Paris, Albert Pissis was even then in the process of creating for San Francisco a series of Classical Revival buildings—the Hibernia Bank, the Flood Building, and the Emporium department store—which would exercise major influence on the architectural vocabulary of that city for the next thirty years. From Pissis, whom he served as an articled draftsman, Wilson absorbed the grand neoclassical style of the Beaux Arts, which he supplemented with instruction at the San Francisco chapter of the American Institute of Architects and a period of travel and study in Europe.

Ready to strike out on his own at twenty-five, Wilson chose Santa Barbara in 1895 as the place to establish his practice. For the next quarter-century, he flourished there, a sportsman/socialite/architect busy with a succession of important commissions. If Francis Underhill was born to the upper class, Francis Wilson became its adopted son. Within a year of his arrival, he acquired two socially prominent clients, Dr. C.C. Park and General Henry J. Strong, for whom he designed homes in Montecito. Similar commissions followed, and an increasingly prosperous Wilson began to invest in local real estate and to design and build homes on speculation, which he sold at impressive profits. Athletic and well-mannered, Wilson was taken up by the younger social set revolving around Joel Remington Fithian (also a close friend of Stewart Edward White), the owner and director of the Santa Barbara Country Club in Montecito. Horses and polo soon became for Wilson a consuming passion. In July 1899 he played for the Santa Barbara Country Club polo team in its first public match and remained a force in polo throughout his Santa Barbara career. He also raced competitively as a gentleman jockey, winning a reputation as one of the top amateur racers in the state.

Out of these sporting and Santa Barbara Country Club connections—augmented by his marriage in April 1905 to the socially prominent Julia Redington, sister of his close friend fellow polo player and gentleman jockey, Lawrence Redington—flowed Wilson's practice. Joel Fithian, for instance, secured for Wilson commissions for the Santa Barbara Club (Fithian quashed an attempt to put the project to an outside bid) and the Central Savings Bank, where Fithian served as director and vice president. Wilson also designed the Santa Barbara railway station, post office, and public library, testimonies to his status as the pre-eminent local architect. Through his friendship with Edward P. Ripley, president of the Santa Fe and a member of the Santa Barbara Club, for whom he designed a winter home, Wilson received commissions for a series of hotels and Fred Harvey restaurants along the Santa Fe lines.

In the meanwhile, commissions for homes in Santa Barbara and Montecito continued. Beaux Arts in his architectural lineage through his connection with Albert Pissis, Francis Wilson preferred a Classical Revival or Italian Renaissance idiom although, with the insouciance of a talented semi-autodidact, he also performed successfully in American Colonial, Queen Anne, Gothic Revival, Mission Revival, and California Craftsman as well. In Montecito Wilson created late Renaissance Palladian villas for P.H. Murphy, a Pittsburgh financier, and for William Miller Graham, a mining and oil man.

In 1917, as the era of exuberant pre-income-tax spending approached its twilight, Wilson achieved the finest design of his career: Las Tejas, a Montecito villa modeled upon the Casino of the sixteenth-century Farnese Palace near Viterbo, Italy, which Wilson created for Mr. and Mrs. Oakleigh Thorne of Millbrook, New York. Aside from its superb architectural effects, so scholarly and so appropriate to the site, Las Tejas boasted the finest gardens in Montecito: a coordination of pools, fountains, plantings, terraces, lawns, and vistas in which princes and cardinals of Counter-Reformation Italy might have found themselves perfectly at ease.

Or perhaps even a simple missionary bishop by the name of Francisco García Diego y Moreno who seventy-five years earlier had once dreamed of similar structures, consecrated to God, rising splendidly on the hills facing the Santa Barbara Channel. However secular in intention and effect, Bishop García Diego's dream city was at last arising, and in the Romanesque Revival solidity of St. Anthony's Seminary (1901) near the restored Mission the dream city even had its ecclesiastical counterpart. Three-quarters of a century earlier Santa Barbara had offered Bishop García Diego a metaphor, a dream of Southern Europe on the channel, and now in the early 1900s architects such as Underhill, Wilson, Bertram Goodhue, and the others were responding to similar metaphors in secular terms.

That this dream city was a mirage, an *anacapa* for the privileged few, only

made it more Santa Barbaran. The Channel City had always remained a
Southern Californian alternative touched by privilege. In so many ways—their
seagoing canoes, their communal lodges, their sophisticated mythology, their
intricate basketry, their instinctive courtesy—the Chumash had been the most
aristocratic (to borrow a European term) of all of California's early people. In
Spanish times, the mission, architecturally the finest structure in California,
and the presidio, from which flew the royal pennant, established a metaphor
which Bishop García Diego enhanced and expanded: a conviction of caste and
cultural continuity with Spain which in later years the De la Guerras, the
Carrillos, and the other surviving Barbareños kept alive as an anchorage point
of identity. It was an *anacapa*, a pleasing illusion, of course: the Mission copied
from the plates of an old book of Roman architecture; the forgotten soldiers of
a forgotten garrison of Royalist Spain, on parade as if their remote presidio
were in Madrid itself; the retired lieutenants and captains who by default became the grandees of a land which soon slipped through their fingers; the
Americans who acquired it from them by Yankee cunning, then later reiden-
tified themselves with the Dons they had displaced; the health-seekers coughing
out their last days in crowded boarding houses, hoping beyond hope that climate might prove a cure.

Anacapa it was indeed, as unreal, all of it, as the Italian villas now shimmering in the opalescent haze of Montecito. For all the power of architecture,
Santa Barbara could never become Italy, and just beyond the valley, to the
south in the Los Angeles basin, Southern California was becoming a very different kind of American place. As this happened, as an urgent urban present
unfolded itself in Los Angeles, Santa Barbarans embraced the *anacapa* of architecture with even more conviction. *Anacapa*, the mirage, the pleasing illusion, increasingly became the dominant Santa Barbara alternative. In doing so,
in materializing genteel metaphors as architecture and giving dreams local habitation and a name, the pleasing illusion known as Santa Barbara soon assumed
the solidity of physical fact. During the 1920s *anacapa* was materialized as a
dream come true on the hillsides fronting the channel.

Castles in Spain

The Santa Barbara Alternative

The materialization of Santa Barbara as a Spanish dream city happened this way. In early 1909 the Civic League of Santa Barbara brought in planner Charles Mulford Robinson to create a masterplan for the city. On 27 February Robinson formally submitted his recommendations to the mayor and city council. Santa Barbara, Robinson reported, possessed a dramatic, topographically distinct site in a long valley running between the mountains and the sea. It also possessed obvious reference points in the Mission, the Plaza De la Guerra, the railroad station and hotel area, and the wharf which connected the line of downtown State Street with the channel. Santa Barbara, Robinson advised, needed roads, architecture, landscaping, and public spaces. Robinson proposed that the city integrate its east-west valley setting through an expanded series of landscaped roadways linking Montecito, the city itself, and the western districts later developed as Hope Ranch and Goleta. This road system should follow the natural contours of the hilly Riviera region rising so commandingly along the northern rim of the city. The oceanfront, meanwhile, should be improved through landscaping, especially where the wharf extended out from State Street. State Street itself required more appropriate architecture and zoning controls. Santa Barbara also needed a Civic Center grouping of its public buildings, which in Robinson's opinion were undistinguished and should be torn down, resited, redesigned, and rebuilt.

Most important for the future, Robinson suggested that the Mission and the Plaza De la Guerra be developed as the central symbols of the city. Lost from sight by haphazard stands of trees and obstructing vegetation, the Mission should be brought into visual contact with the city through the creation of a series of landscaped vistas that would make the Mission a constant reference point. The area adjacent to the Mission, Robinson recommended, should be developed as a public plaza, and so should the nearby Plaza De la Guerra. The Casa De la Guerra should be restored as a museum devoted to the Spanish era and the plaza should be surrounded by Spanish-style structures that would take their vocabulary from the surviving adobes in the vicinity.

Robinson's report was accepted, filed, and forgotten—except by the local elite which comprised the Civic League. Robinson's suggestion that Santa Barbara seize upon its Hispanic past as its controlling metaphor, together with his stated belief that Santa Barbara should avoid industrial development, spoke directly to a point of view that was only then emerging. Within the next fifteen years, this point of view would gain political control of the city, which it would proceed to remake into its own image.

Architecturally, the Santa Barbara which Robinson encountered in 1909 had emerged in the 1870–1890 period under the influence of two architects, Peter J. Barber and Thomas Nixon. Each of these designers practiced a high level of late Victorian eclecticism; and the buildings they created—among them Santa Barbara College (1871), the Santa Barbara County Courthouse (1872), the Arlington Hotel (1875), the Cook Clock Building (1875), and Hall of Records (1891), together with Nixon's Fithian Building on State Street (1896)—were presentable provincial buildings. Santa Barbara, however, did not have an overall appearence or controlling ambience beyond that of any other late Victorian city in California—or for that matter the entire Midwest, as some claimed. Nor did the domestic architecture of the area—with the exception of the modified Tuscan villa Barber designed for Thomas Dibblee in 1878—seek to say anything specifically Santa Barbaran beyond that assertion of picturesque prosperity that characterized upper-middle-class California throughout the nineteenth century. Lower State Street, meanwhile, as Robinson himself noted in his report, had become a disorderly array of sheds, awnings, portes cocheres, hitching posts, obstrusive signs, and overhead wires. With the exception of its spectacular site on the channel, Santa Barbara resembled Bakersfield, Fresno, Sacramento, Chico, or any number of agricultural towns in the interior.

Robinson also noted that Santa Barbara would not industrialize by deliberate choice. During these years, opportunities for diversification beyond agriculture, hotels, and a service economy keyed to the affluent did present themselves. Like San Diego or Long Beach, for example, Santa Barbara might have become a Navy town. The Great White Fleet, sixteen battleships and heavy cruisers sent around the world by Theodore Roosevelt as a display of American strength, called at Santa Barbara in April 1908, with the President himself on hand to review the ships and repeat his memorable speech about speaking softly while carrying a big stick. Two thousand sailors in white paraded through the city, many of them with bunches of flowers inserted into their rifles by cheering citizens. The public was welcomed aboard the USS *Philadelphia*; there was Spanish dancing under a great tent set up at oceanside (Ynez Dibblee, a De la Guerra, was among the performers); and a cotillion was held at the Arlington for the officers. Mabel Cooper Kroll, who had grown up on the Rancho Santa Rosa and in the Cooper house at Chapala and Sola streets in the city, attended the dance that evening, meeting a midshipman, Harris Laning, whom she later married. Their daughter Hester, later Mrs. Sargeant Pepper of Hartford, Connecticut, was long considered "the prettiest girl in the Navy." Decades later, Midshipman Laning retired from active duty as an admiral.

With an increased American naval presence in the Pacific, more homeports would be needed on the California coast, and Santa Barbara, had its leadership been so inclined, might have competed for a dreadnought or two. While parades and cotillions were great fun, a permanent naval presence, even one assigned to the offshore islands, would have involved such realities as harbor development, gunnery practice, and sailors on liberty, which meant saloons and worse, and so the fleet sailed off, leaving Santa Barbara behind until the Second World War. Unfortunately, the fleet also left behind its commander, Admiral Robert ("Fighting Bob") Evans, who took ill unexpectedly and was sent by his doctors to Paso Robles Hot Springs, where he died a few days later.

Santa Barbara might have become an aviation town like Los Angeles. Aviation was a light industry, a craft even, with few if any industrial side-effects, and thus it could take hold in Santa Barbara with minimal damage to the environment. During the war year 1918, the Loughead brothers were employing some 85 Santa Barbara residents, including Jack Northrop, in the manufacturing of the seaplane HS2L, designed by Glenn Curtiss for the Navy, a promising beginning for Santa Barbara as an aviation center. There were three Loughead brothers (in 1919 they changed their Scottish last name to its phonetic spelling Lockheed), Victor, the oldest, and his two half-brothers, Malcolm and Allen, sons of Flora Haines Apponyi Loughead, a journalist and novelist (including one Santa Barbara novel) associated with the *Daily Independent*. Ardent kite-flyers and bicycle mechanics, the Lougheads became enamored of flight as teenagers. They read, studied, tinkered: self-instructed, experimental, unintimidated. In 1909 Victor, coming it would seem out of nowhere (but then again the art of aviation was but five years old), wrote and had accepted for publication *Aeroplane Designing for Amateurs*, a pioneering treatise on aeronautics. It appeared a full two years before the French aeronaut Dedier Masson took off from the Hope Ranch and landed on the lawn of the Potter Hotel, thereby completing Santa Barbara's first heavier-than-air flight.

By March 1914 there was sufficient interest for an air show, held again on the Hope Ranch, where a crowd of thousands (it included Glenn Martin, Glenn Curtiss, Barney Oldfield, the brothers Loughead, and Jack Northrop) watched in horror as stunt-flyer Lincoln Beachey, age 27, went into an out-of-control corkscrew descent after flying upside down at 2000 feet and diving at 210 miles an hour. Some doctors had claimed that pilots would suffocate it they fell more than 500 feet, but Beachey disagreed and was out to prove his point. He also completed, incredibly, fourteen loops, perfect "O"s, the previous world record being less than ten. Fortunately, Beachey pulled into a glide at 500 feet, before smashing his thousand-plus pounds of bamboo, varnished linen, motor, piano wire, and bicycle gears into a Santa Barbara live oak. Beachey walked away from the debris with only a bloody nose, vowing never to fly again. A year later, doing loops and a dive of death before 50,000 spectators at the Panama-Pacific International Exposition, he met a tragic end in the chilly waters of San Francisco Bay.

Once again, the Loughead brothers, Allan and Malcolm, were in the crowd. Learning to fly in 1910 along with their fellow Californians Glenn Martin and Glenn Curtiss, the Lougheads designed and built a one-ton thirty-foot flying monster, the Model G, capable of sixty miles an hour and two passengers. Disassembling their pterodactyl, the brothers shipped it up to San Francisco for the 1915 Exposition. Charging $10 for a ten-minute ride, they accumulated $6000 in fifty days, which they used to found the Loughead Aircraft Manufacturing Company of Santa Barbara, bankrolled by Al Oviatt, a retired oilcloth manufacturer from Akron then living in Montecito. As design engineer, the Lougheads took on another local boy, John Northrop, then twenty-one and already showing signs of self-taught aeronautical genius.

From the Loughead shop in the rear of William Rust's Garage on State Street emerged nothing less than the most ambitious airplane thus far created in the short history of aviation, the F-1, a ten-passenger flying boat with triple tail fins and a 74-foot wingspread. Representing a quantum leap in airplane design and capacity, the F-1 was brought to Santa Barbara Beach for testing. To have seen this elegant flying vessel resting offshore in sight of the Potter Hotel, an oversized heron preparing for flight, led legitimately and without exaggeration to predictions that Santa Barbara had a future as an aviation center, a prediction made even more reasonable in 1918 when the Loughead factory got its Navy contract and put 85 men to work.

Aircraft manufacturing, alas, went into a slump when the war ended, the market being flooded with surplus aircraft. A surplus Curtiss JN-4, the famed Flying Jenny, sold for $400 or less, still disassembled and packed in its shipping crate. And so the Loughead brothers, with no orders to fill, closed their company and went back into the tourist passenger business. Reactivating the Model G from the 1915 fair, they used it and the F-1 to fly tourists around Santa Barbara and the channel at $5 per passenger. When Allan flew the King and Queen of Belgium out to the Channel Islands, he won for his brother and himself the Order of the Golden Crown. The brothers, however, were ambitious inventors and entrepreneurs psychologically unsuited to a tourist economy, and Santa Barbara soon became for them a very small place. Malcolm was already working on another invention, hydraulic brakes for automobiles, which he tested on his Paige roadster. Walter P. Chrysler, maker of the Maxwell, liked the idea and so in 1919 Malcolm broke off his association, temporarily, with his brother to join Chrysler in Detroit. Allan Lockheed, meanwhile, as the family name was now spelled, moved the company south to Los Angeles County, settling in Burbank. Malcolm rejoined him there in the mid-1920s as did Jack Northrop in 1927, and the reunited Santa Barbarans, operating as the Lockheed Aircraft Corporation, proceeded to transform Los Angeles, not Santa Barbara, into the aviation capital of America.

The swift evolution and de-evolution of aviation in Santa Barbara, from design innovation and manufacturing to tourist flights, had its own economic dynamics; yet it also can be seen as one more step on Santa Barbara's path away from the realities of industry (even light industry) and work. By the time the Lockheeds said goodbye, the resort metaphor, always so present in the Santa Barbara experience, was gaining further dominance.

Resortism developed another light industry, the cinema, which was also struggling to gain a foothold in the Channel City. Significantly enough, the first passenger to ride in the F-1 was film actress Mary Miles Minter. After the collapse of aircraft manufacturing the Lockheeds helped support themselves by taking camera teams aloft at the then formidable fee of $150 an hour. Actor/director William Anderson, more familiarly known as Bronco Billy, brought film to Santa Barbara as early as 1910. Anderson filmed a Western in Mission Canyon and San Marcos Pass, which he edited in a boxcar on a siding near the Potter Hotel. With the exception of the availability of a big city such as Los Angeles for urban scenes, Santa Barbara was in the year 1910 equally competitive, if not superior, to Hollywood as a possible film capital. Santa Barbara had diverse scenery, grand architecture, and gardens in Montecito for costume dramas, good hotels, and sunshine most days of the year. By 1911 some thirteen small companies were filming one-reel serials and comedies in the Channel City area.

The American Film Manufacturing Company of Chicago, meanwhile, was becoming increasingly discontented with its operation of La Mesa, a few miles from San Diego. The directors felt that they had exhausted the scenery of the region, and processing facilities were inadequate. Traveling throughout Southern California to scout new locations, company officials settled upon Santa Barbara, where they moved in July 1912, setting up a temporary studio on a former ostrich farm on upper State Street. American Film Manufacturing had solid resources, financial and filmic. Initially, films were shot in Santa Barbara at the rapid rate of two one-reelers a week, then sent to Chicago for development and editing, then sent back to Santa Barbara for secondary editing and retakes. After a year of this, the company decided to build a studio in Santa Barbara. Just as the Lockheed brothers launched Santa Barbara aviation with the largest, most up-to-date airplane ever built, American Film acquired a square block bounded by Mission, Chapala, Padre, and State streets and in 1913 constructed the largest, most up-to-date film studio in the world, complete with an imposing entrance surmounted by a Mission Revival tower. Built in steel, concrete, and glass (and hence called the Big Glass Studio) the Flying A facility (this from its oversized logo, an A with wings) allowed for indoor filming, either sun- or artifically lit, on a hitherto unprecedented scale. Concentrating mainly on Westerns and comedies, the Flying A maintained stables capable of handling up to 75 horses, and a permanently constructed frontier Western town.

Flying A was good for Santa Barbara. The studio, first of all, had a strong local payroll for carpenters, electricians, and other support personnel. Glenn Martin, Jack Northrop, and the Lockheed brothers received flying assignments. Models from the Magnin's boutique at the Potter found work as extras, pretty young girls being frequently in demand. Violinist James Campiglia and harpist Marjorie Greenwell got jobs playing mood music on the set. An excellent swimmer, Greenwell also doubled in swimming scenes for non-swimming actresses. She met and married Roy Overbaugh, the director of photography for Flying A. As his assistant cameraman Overbaugh hired a young local, Victor Fleming, an automobile mechanic, who later moved to Hollywood as cameraman for Douglas Fairbanks, Sr., before going into directing. At the peak of his career, Fleming directed *Gone With the Wind*.

Occasionally the film industry created hazards: a runaway car from a chase scene, for instance, careened down State Street, filled with dummies which were hurled to the sidewalk when the car crashed into a parked limousine from Montecito, terrifying bystanders who thought the mannequins were people. A stuntman with strong local connections jumped blindfolded from atop a stagecoach and smashed his skull on an overhanging rock, a fatality underscoring the often reckless search for realism in the early industry. Yet on the whole Santa Barbara took enthusiastically to this new industry, in so many ways the city's first gesture along with aviation in the direction of manufacturing and the larger world beyond the resort.

In the Los Angeles/Hollywood area, film people were shunned as disreputable. Santa Barbarans, by contrast, welcomed them as just another, if more exotic, species of tourist. Friendly crowds gathered around outdoor shootings. The Potter, the Arlington, and the other hotels welcomed the presence, among others, of Wallace Reid, Mabel Normand, Mary Miles Minter, the first lady of the air, Bronco Billy Anderson himself, the first celebrity, Richard Bennett and his two daughters, Constance and Joan, Lottie Pickford and her better known sister Mary, America's Sweetheart, Roscoe "Fatty" Arbuckle, and the pioneering directors D. W. Griffith, William Desmond Taylor, proving his talents in the serial *Diamond From the Sky*, and Thomas Ince. Their comings and goings lent excitement to otherwise staid establishments. Their weekly paychecks, furthermore, up to $1500 a week in that pre-income-tax era, stimulated the local economy at hotels and at the delicatessen restaurant attached to Diehl's Grocery Store, which became a hangout for movie people. On days off, Roy Overbaugh later reminisced, the movie people would, like everyone else, head for the beach.

Enroute to becoming by the 1930s a figment of its own imagination, Santa

Barbara responded enthusiastically to the ability of film to give the illusion of reality to dreams. There on the flickering screen, Santa Barbarans saw the Potter, the Arlington, the palm-lined Cabrillo Boulevard running parallel to the beach, and it all became so convincingly real: which is to say, Santa Barbara envisioned itself as a developed city by seeing itself on film. Illusion led to reality. Montecito, itself a stage set, became a favored locale for costume or society dramas, especially the Gillespie estate El Fureidis. Impressed by the success of Flying A, a group of Santa Barbarans and Monticitans formed their own Santa Barbara Motion Picture company in June 1914 and filmed a costume drama, *The Envoy Extraordinary*, at the El Mirasol estate. By 1914, with the world's largest studio in operation, its film colony happy and locally accepted, Santa Barbara had from a number of criteria the competitive edge on Hollywood as the center of this emergent Southern California industry, destined in a few short years to become the dominant industry of the Southland after agriculture. All in all, some 1200 productions would eventually bear the Santa Barbara Flying A imprint.

By the early 1920s it was over, finished, vanished like a dream. As in the case of aviation, Santa Barbara proved too small a place to sustain the industry it had so successfully but so briefly captured. As tastes in films grew more sophisticated, the Flying A found itself shipping actors, actresses, and film crews by train or bus to Los Angeles for urban backgrounds. The rushes were then returned to Santa Barbara for editing just as they had once been shipped from Santa Barbara to Chicago, and once again it became too troublesome and expensive. In 1918, realizing that Hollywood, not Santa Barbara, had become the film capital, the American Film Manufacturing Company moved its operation south to Hollywood, and with that the film economy collapsed as rapidly as it had arisen. Once again a resort city, Santa Barbara was left to pursue its dreams through architecture, not films. The Flying A studio was soon replaced by an entire city that was a stage set.

2

As the Navy, the airplanes, and the movie cameras came and went with symbolic transience, other identities were taking firmer hold. A floral metaphor, for example, proceeded easily from the fundamental agricultural realities—citrus, fruit, walnuts, vegetables, sheep, swine, cattle, and dairy—of Santa Barbara County, among the most prosperous and beautiful agricultural regions in the nation. The fabled garden of the West, sunny and fertile, Santa Barbara was also coming under visual interpretation from a growing community of painters, many of them in the *plein air* tradition, who began to settle and work in the area. John Marshall Gamble arrived in 1906, followed by Clarence Mattei in 1910, William Louis Otte in 1913, Dewitt Parshall in 1917, Lockwood De Forest in 1919, Colin Campbell Cooper in 1921, Thomas Moran in

1922, and Giovanni Troccoli in 1926. By the late 1920s, when Mary J. Coulter and Blossom Owen arrived, followed in the 1930s by William Bagdatopoulous, Clarence Hinkle, Edith Catlin Phelps, Ann Snider, Lyla Harcoff, Richmond Kelsey, and Standish Backus, Jr., Santa Barbara had emerged as a painting center paralleling Carmel and Laguna Beach.

What these painters had in common, aside from their impressive training (most were Paris-trained), overlapping lineages from common study with William Merritt Chase, and good prior reputations (Thomas Moran especially, but others as well) were the landscapes and seascapes of Santa Barbara which they celebrated on canvas. Their perception of *tierra adorada*, the Adored Land, as the Spanish termed the region, dovetailed with and further reinforced a pre-existing pastoralism that was now being further corroborated on canvas. Under the *plein air* influence, Santa Barbara came increasingly to define itself as a beautiful, undeveloped, and anti-developmental environment, a pastoral place that preferred to stay that way, thank you.

Then there were the flowers and gardens themselves. Since everything grew in Santa Barbara, gardening and landscape architecture became local obsessions. Seasonally, residences lost half their façades to banks of flowering chrysanthemums. Carpets of daisies and other wildflowers ran without intimidation along the edges of unpaved streets or joined adjacent backyards into harmonized landscapes of spontaneous color. Many Santa Barbara ranchers surrounded their residences with lavish horticulture. The Sawyer Ranch, Edwards Roberts reported in the mid-1880s, contained over twenty varieties of palm trees. "Among them are a graceful screw-palm, a sago from Ceylon, a group of Dracaenas palms, and one which bears dates. Of plants there is a large camellia japonica, twelve feet high, which bears fifteen hundred flowers and buds at one time. The flower is a bright red, and as large as a small saucer. Near it is a large tea-plant from China, and a rare specimen of the bamboo. With the commoner trees, the elm, oak, eucalyptus, pepper, orange, lemon, nectarine and cypress, are a large alligator-pear tree from Mexico, a valuable specimen of the silver tree, with bright silver leaves, from Cape of Good Hope, and camphor, Indian rubber, madrona, and magnolia trees."[1]

The famed Italian horticulturist Dr. Emanuele Francheschi lived and worked in Santa Barbara between 1893 to 1912, attracted there by the vigor and variety of native and introduced plants: 150 different species of palms, he noted joyously, the same number of conifers, 50 differing species of bamboo, 300 different kinds of vines and climbers, some 2000 or more species of trees, shrubs, and perennials. "They have convened here from the hottest and from the coldest regions of the globe," Francheschi noted, "as well as from the temperate zone, and they combine to make a display of vegetation that has no rival anywhere else."[2] Locating himself in a nursery on lower State Street, which he later moved to the Riviera, Francheschi—an angular, bearded, high-strung Tuscan savant, a Giuseppe Verde of plants—cultivated, observed, scientifically described, and promoted an array of flowers, trees, plants, fruits, and vegetables (he helped introduce the avocado and the zucchini to California) which he urged forward as the basis of the region's economy and its primary metaphor.

Equal to the Mission, the Casa De la Guerra, the Arlington, or the Potter as a local point of reference was the gigantic Moreton Bay Fig Tree, planted as a seed in 1874, replanted as a sprig in 1877 at the corner of Chapala and West Montecito streets, and later designated an official city landmark. Destined to reach a full growth of 68 feet in height, 151 feet in length on its north-south axis, its branches covering an amazing 21,150 square feet, its root system extending across an acre, the Moreton Bay Fig Tree in and of itself symbolized the floral exuberance of greater Santa Barbara. Its spontaneous strength found a cultivated counterpart in the park system of Santa Barbara and the villa gardens of Montecito. Under the guidance of park commission president A. Boyd Doremus, who held office from 1902 to 1920, Santa Barbara transformed its waterfront into a palm-lined promenade, landscaped its Plaza del Mar into a Mediterranean-style esplanade, planted its streets in shade trees, and otherwise improved its parks and public spaces. Montecito, meanwhile, was being transformed into the formal garden capital of the United States, its hedges, terraces, and fountains in stately contrast to the rambling natural growth of the Santa Ynez hillsides.

In April 1891, when President Benjamin Harrison visited, Santa Barbara organized its first floral festival. It combined pastoral and Hispanic motifs, with Dixie W. Thompson, general manager of the Arlington, his horse bedecked in silver ornaments, leading a parade of riders costumed in the style of Old California, followed by floral carts carrying female descendants of pioneer families. Between 1893 and 1896 Santa Barbara held four more flower festivals inspired by this extravaganza of April 1891, but the tradition collapsed for lack of support.

For the naturalist William Leon Dawson, the poetry of Santa Barbara was embodied in its rich and varied bird life. Ensconced in his home Los Colubris, the Hummingbirds, in Mission Canyon, Dawson made a specialty of birds and birds' eggs with a passion and encyclopedic knowledge paralleling Franceschi's devotion to plant life. A proper, precise man, peering at the world, its birds and birds' eggs, from behind a Van Dyke beard through round, lightly framed spectacles (if Franceschi were Verdi, Dawson was a Lenin lookalike and equally ambitious, albeit for birds not Bolshevism), Dawson announced in 1910 a multivolumed *The Birds of California*, which took thirteen long and very expensive years to appear.

To form a sponsoring institution for this project, among the most ambitious scientific undertakings of its sort ever to be attempted on the Pacific Coast, Dawson joined with a group of Santa Barbarans in January 1916 to found a museum of oology (the study of birds' eggs) based upon his private collection, the result of thirty-five years of acquisition. Housed initially at Los Colubris, the museum had the backing of such Santa Barbara stalwarts as banker-sports-man Joel Remington Fithian, its board president, railroad man Edward Payson Ripley, the vice president, and architect Francis T. Underhill, a member of the board. Caroline Hazard, past president of Wellesley College served as honorary curator. In 1919 the museum issued the first number of *The Journal of Comparative Oology*.

Dawson, meanwhile, continued the heroic task of identifying, describing, having painted or photographed the birds of California, and preparing the results for publication. His budget soon exceeded its initial $10,000 and as the years passed subscribers dating as far back as 1910 began to wonder whether or not they would ever receive their money's worth. They would, and they did. Four glorious volumes appeared in 1923, elegantly printed and bound, with more than 1400 illustrations and photographs of 580 species and subspecies, including 106 full-page color plates from paintings by the talented ornithological artist Allan Brooks. In every way possible—descriptions, illustrations, printing, binding—*The Birds of California*, especially the deluxe Santa Barbara Edition, bore special witness to Santa Barbara's love of the natural world and its reverence for natural beauty as a badge of local identity.

In this sentiment of aesthetic piety linked to the natural world, Dawson's ornithological scholarship dovetailed with Franceschi's botanizing, the floral festivals, the landscaping of the city, and the celebrations of the *plein air* painters. To this emergent Santa Barbara sensibility, privileged and genteel but compelling nevertheless as a California metaphor, was grafted the Hispanic metaphor as well; for the Spanish Southwest, symbolized so perfectly in Mission Santa Barbara, became increasingly to be held by artists and anti-boosters as an image of resistance to twentieth-century bustle and materialism. As Los Angeles grew into a metropolis, Santa Barbara came increasingly to be considered the last true outpost of the Hispanic Southwest in Southern California.

Side by side with the landscape/seascape *plein air* tradition, Santa Barbara attracted painters who celebrated Old California and the vanishing Southwest. Alexander Harmer led the parade, arriving in the early 1890s after two tours with the U.S. Cavalry in the Apache campaigns of the Southwest. An erect, athletic man who never lost his military bearing, the New Jersey-born Harmer enlisted in the Army in 1872 at the age of 16 precisely because he wanted to see the frontier before it vanished. Serving one tour as a hospital steward in Nevada and California, Harmer used his discharge pay of $85.35, augmented by subsequent work as a photographer's assistant, to enroll in the Philadelphia Academy of Fine Arts, where he studied for two years under the masters of realism Thomas Eakins and Thomas Anshutz. Tiring of civilian life and bored with civilian subjects, Harmer re-enlisted in 1881 on the condition that he be posted to cavalry duty in the Southwest. Two adventurous years followed as Harmer, stationed at Fort Apache, rode with the troops as a medic in the Apache wars of Arizona and northern Mexico. Soon after his second discharge in 1883, Harmer established himself as a leading illustrator of Apache life. A decade of work in the Southwest, Mexico, and the East followed before Harmer settled permanently in Santa Barbara in the early 1890s.

In 1893, nearing forty, Alexander Harmer married Felicidad Abadie, a Santa Barbaran of Hispanic and French descent. In the early 1900s the couple moved with their seven children into the Lugo-Abadie-Yorba adobe built in the late 1820s near the Casa De la Guerra. By this time, under the influence of his wife and *Land of Sunshine* editor Charles Fletcher Lummis, a close friend, Harmer had left off painting Apaches in favor of doing meticulously researched scenes of Old California. Felicidad's friends and relatives—Del Valles, De la Guerras, Don Antonio Coronel, whose *rancho* had helped inspire *Ramona*—assisted Harmer by emptying family trunks and modeling half-century or older costumes. Joyous, colorful, well-researched, action-packed, Harmer's canvases of Old California filled out in visual terms the Santa Barbara legend. *La Fiesta*, the most elaborate of these paintings, might very well serve as a prophetic gloss on the revival of *fiesta* pageantry through which the Santa Barbara oligarchy eventually expressed itself. Fortunately for someone with seven children to support, Harmer's work sold at good prices. He also did calendar, book, and magazine illustrations, and a special series of exquisite menus—some one hundred separate watercolor paintings on pasteboard to frame the daily bill of fare—for use in the dining room of the Arlington Hotel. To the Harmer adobe flocked like-minded artists—Frederic Remington, Maynard Dixon, Ed Borein, Carl Oscar Borg, Fernand Lungren, John Marshall Gamble, Charles Russell—who had also devoted their young manhood and later careers to experiencing and memorializing a Far West/Southwest frontier that Frederick Jackson Turner had announced as officially over in 1893.

Under his wife's influence, Harmer turned from Apaches to Hispanic Californians. Santa Barbaran Carl Oscar Borg, by contrast, Swedish-born, Paris- and Rome-trained (thanks to the sponsorship of Phoebe Apperson Hearst), had for some time been progressively engrossed by the Hopi and Navaho cultures of the Southwest. A poet and mystic as well as a painter, Borg pursued a lively interest in spiritualism and comparative religion, having gone so far as to study hieroglyphics and to make a pilgrimage to Egypt in an effort to penetrate the mysteries of the ancient cults. Finally, in the mystic midregions of the desert Southwest and in the Indian religions flourishing there, Borg discovered what he needed as a man and an artist: a world of supernal beauty, harmonized and kept whole through religion. Initiated by the Hopis into their kiva, Borg made a scholarly study of Hopi and Navaho culture under the guidance of various medicine men and his close friend Charles Fletcher Lummis of Los Angeles. Thus fortified, he embarked upon a number of rugged expeditions into the Southwest, sojourns which left him lean and bronzed by the discipline of the desert. A real-life counterpart of the desert-seeker Vanamee in Frank Norris's *The Octopus* (1901), an ascetic, a desert nomad, a mystic, Borg regarded life from behind drooping mustachios through piercing blue Swedish eyes long accustomed to both introspection and expansive vistas.

In early 1918, anticipating marriage to Madeline Carriel, a 17-year-old art student, the 18-year-old Borg began building (again, with the help of his patroness Phoebe Hearst) a permanent studio home in the upland La Mesa area of Santa Barbara modeled on an ancient Spanish church at Zuni, New Mexico. While another generation of Southwest artists were basing themselves inland at Taos and Santa Fe, Borg preferred to situate himself at the extreme edge of the western arc of the Spanish Southwest as it encountered the Pacific at Santa Barbara. Touched simultaneously by the Pacific, the desert Southwest and its Indian religions, and the Mission itself, Santa Barbara possessed a mystic intensity, Borg believed, that made it a force field of spiritual and aesthetic encounter conducive to creative life. Santa Barbara was also, he felt, the ideal garden, an *hortus conclusus* into which one might flee a world gone mad with war.

Into his Spanish/New Mexican chateau on La Mesa, Borg brought up from Los Angeles his impressive collection of coins, silver, rare books, armor, antiques, Chinese embroideries, etchings, engravings, photographs, textiles, Native American basketry and artifacts, together with one slightly awed teenaged wife whom he married in August 1918. Between 1918 and 1924 the Borgs lived in Santa Barbara at the center of a circle which radiated out from Alexander Harmer and the bearded patriarchal Thomas Moran, the good gray painter of Santa Barbara, and included other Santa Barbaran artists such as Fernand Lungren, a Thomas Eakins-trained painter of Southwest subjects, the cowboy artist Ed Borein, Borg's next-door neighbor Albert Falvy, a like-minded antique collector and Indian aficionado, and other assorted intelligentsia. From out of town regular visitors such as Lummis, impresario of all things Southwestern, writer Mary Austin, another Lummis protégé, cowboy artist Charles Russell, a winter resident, and, at least once, a delegation of Borg's Navaho friends who loved the colors emanating from the firelight to Falvy's crystal chandelier and later stood with Borg on a high place over the Pacific. Another onetime visitor was John Collier, the director of adult education for the State of California, who in the New Deal became such an empathic and effective Commissioner of Indian Affairs. Collier later said that he first absorbed the meaning of Native American culture and hence his own life's work from this early contact with Borg and his Santa Barbara circle.

Carl Oscar Borg returned to Los Angeles in 1924. Santa Barbara, alas, bored Madeline and with the ever-generous Mrs. Hearst gone (she died in 1919) Borg was now on his own and forced to keep close to the art markets, a difficult thing to do in such a remote and small city. Santa Barbara, after all, demanded an outside income for full enjoyment, an aspect of the resort metaphor, and Borg was now self-supporting. His presence there, however, even for six short years, as a painter of Native American subjects and an activist with the Indian Welfare League, as an instructor at the newly established Santa Barbara School of the Arts, and the center of an artistic circle helped attach to Santa Barbara a touch of Santa Fe and Taos. This Southwestern metaphor ran parallel to the hotel culture and the neo-Mediterranean Newport imagery of Montecito. It also dovetailed easily with the pre-existing Mission myth.

Architecturally, the Mission Revival arrived in Santa Barbara in 1894, brought there by San Francisco architect Arthur Page Brown in his designs for five adjacent residences on Garden Street commissioned by William H. Crocker, a winter resident, for family, friends, or sale or speculation. In 1905 Francis Wilson designed a Mission Revival railroad station near the Potter Hotel. With the exception of a few other buildings, however, Mission Revival never caught on in Santa Barbara despite—or because of—the powerful presence of the Mission which continued to assert itself as a local symbol.

A visit to the Mission by King Albert, Queen Elizabeth, and Prince Leopold of Belgium on Sunday morning, 12 October 1919, for a special mass offered ample opportunity for Mission-related royalist romanticism to reassert itself. Genuinely popular in the United States for its spirited resistance to Germany during the war, the royal family offered Santa Barbarans of Spanish royalist-era descent—and there were by now many of them, a good number bearing Yankee surnames—an opportunity to release and express their inner conviction of caste. At long last, Montecito, in the form of the appropriately palatial Bliss estate Casa Dorinda, designed by Carleton Winslow, Sr., where the royal family stayed, had its resident royalty, the real thing! The visitors were met at the Mission door by the brown-robed and sandaled Franciscan community. Albert and Leopold were in uniform; Elizabeth in a white silk coat with fur collar, pearls, and a golden brown paradise-feather fixed to her turban. Kneeling on purple-cushioned *prie-dieu* the royal family were blessed with holy water. They then followed the friars into the Mission for mass. A special section was reserved for descendants of the old Hispanic families. Kneeling in this section as the royal family became enveloped in fragrant incense from Father Julius Gliebe's swinging censer, Katherine Bell, an Ortega and a Den in descent, remembered the "four generations of my maternal forebearers [who] had mounted those old steps, entered those blessed doors, bent their knees and bowed their heads within. I looked up at saintly Barbara on her pedestal above the high altar, at the railing of the sanctuary, at everything around that was still as it had been in the long ago. A yearning came over me to get nearer to those inanimate things, to touch them, to rest my gray head on them, and to dream back through the bygone years."[3]

Which is exactly what the La Primavera Association had in mind when it incorporated itself eighteen days later: a dream back through bygone years in the form of a festival pageant planned for the coming spring. Comprised of Old California descendants and their frequently related allies in the oligarchy, La Primavera Association commissioned and produced a masque which was performed before a crowd estimated at eight thousand on 28 April 1920 in a sycamore- and cactus-shrouded natural amphitheater on Garden Street. Entitled "Primavera, the Masque of Santa Barbara," the pageant dealt with the history of the city from the prehistoric era through the raising of the American flag. Written by Wallace Rice, "Primavera" combined a verse narrator (El Barbareño, played by Irving Pichel, on loan as technical director from the Bohemian Club of San Francisco, whose specialty was similar pageants at the midsummer encampments in the Bohemian Grove) with spoken parts, including a villain—the Duende, or deceitful one. "Primavera" featured ambitious stage, lighting, and costume effects, Spanish dancing (with Geraldine Valde replacing Inez Dibblee as *premiere danseuse* when the latter took suddenly ill) and authentic songs from Old California as researched and recorded from oldtimers on cylindric discs by Charles Fletcher Lummis in the early 1900s. On the day following the pageant, a thousand school-children marched down State Street from the Arlington Hotel to the beach. Grouped around portable maypoles, the children waved Primavera flags—red, white, and yellow, Saint Barbara's tower in one corner, surmounted by three stars—which in 1925 became the official flag of the city.

Aside from authentic Spanish music, Lummis also provided Santa Barbara with the rationale for its growing preference for Hispanic nostalgia. Twenty-five years earlier, Lummis had promoted Hispanic imagery as the best development metaphor for Los Angeles. As Los Angeles exploded, however, it also outgrew Spanish nostalgia as an effective development vehicle. By the early 1920s Lummis, now entering his sixties, already seemed to most Los Angelenos a figure from the distant past. Every aspect of Lummis—his Spanish-cut green corduroy suit, his guitar and Spanish songs, his scholarly nostalgia for the Borderlands—seemed to go-ahead Los Angeles the imagery and preoccupations of a vanished era; and Lummis, progressively under-employed and perennially broke, had evidence enough of Los Angeles's opinion. In Santa Barbara, however, he saw another chance. Ignored in Los Angeles, Lummis found himself increasingly welcomed in Santa Barbara. In 1922 he and cowboy artist Ed Borein marched prominently in the Fourth of July parade. The next year Lummis issued an impassioned manifesto entitled *Stand Fast, Santa Barbara!* in the *Santa Barbara Morning Press*. Reprinted in pamphlet form and widely distributed, *Stand Fast Santa Barbara!* soon became the *Marseillaise* of the preservationist/Hispanic Revival movement.

Impassioned, at times even hysterical—the lion's last roar, the lion being Lummis's personal symbol and "The Lion's Den" the name of his magazine column—Lummis nevertheless foreshadowed the preservationist mentality that was even then seizing Santa Barbara and would fifty years later hold the allegiance of most California cities of any importance. Twinning Santa Barbara with Santa Fe, the two last small cities in the United States that had not yet succumbed to what Lummis termed the Vandal Age, Lummis advanced a simple argument. Not only was beauty good for the soul, it was good for the wallet. Citing his own work on behalf of the preservation of the missions, Lummis argued that Spanish Romance, as he termed it, had proven of greater economic benefit to Southern California than oil, oranges, or even the climate. The Ramona myth alone, Lummis argued, quoting an estimate provided him by Frank Miller, creator of the Mission Inn in Riverside, had brought some fifty million tourist dollars into the Southland. Now Santa Barbara, like Santa Fe, by capitalizing on its Hispanic heritage, had an opportunity to set up an alternative civic culture based on values of preservationism and controlled growth which would simultaneously promote aesthetic sentiment in the community and revitalize the local economy by creating a tourist destination point.

As if in response to Lummis's manifesto, the Southern Pacific, anxious to create traffic on its Santa Barbara line, retained the Mission myth publicist, poet, and dramatist John Steven McGroarty to write a promotional brochure echoing Lummis's themes. Santa Barbara, wrote the Poet of the Verdugo Hills, "soothes the heart and rests the soul to think that there once were times when the world was not crazy. Times when men did not hurry and scurry and rush feverishly to their graves, the victims of untimely and needless prostration, as they do now."[4] The paradox in Lummis's and McGroarty's position, which was the position of the Santa Barbara oligarchy for whom they spoke, was obvious. Wealth had captured Santa Barbara for its own, and now wealth envisioned its captive city as an escape from getting and spending, and this identity, paradoxically, was also good for the resort business.

Enter the Zorro myth which in the 1920s replaced the Mission myth of an earlier era. In 1919 Hollywood screenwriter and novelist Johnston McCulley created the Zorro character in a short story, "The Curse of Capistrano." The next year a novel, *The Mark of Zorro*, appeared, and an enduring popular hero, destined to survive sixty-plus years of pulp fiction, films, radio, comic books, and television, was launched. Douglas Fairbanks, Sr., made two very successful Zorro films in the mid-1920s, *The Mark of Zorro* (1924) and *Don Q, Son of Zorro* (1925), in which he played both father and son. To chide McCulley for the historical naïveté of the Zorro stories is to miss the power that both McCulley's hero and his setting possessed as popular myth. The masked swordsman Zorro, the Fox, defends the poor and fights corrupt officialdom in a Southern California more Spanish than Spain itself: an imaginary European dreamworld of aristocracy (Zorro is in reality Don Diego Vega, a wealthy aristocrat hiding behind a mask of languid, effete indifference), Spanish codes, civic institutions, and architecture. So Spanish was the Zorro myth, in fact, Fairbanks set *Don Q, Son of Zorro* in Spain itself.

The Zorro myth presented a Southern California that never existed, a material dream of chivalry, romance, swordplay, and roses rising up against a creamy white Andalusian wall. The myth arose in popular form just as Santa Barbara was making a similar determination, which the Zorro myth reinforced.

Not that Santa Barbara is to be equated directly to the shaping influence of the popular legend. The legend, rather, expressed in entertainment terms a parallel desire in Lummis, McGroarty, and so many others to fabricate a more completely romantic past than honest history would allow. Zorro the Fox represented the aristocratic impulse (and by extension the genteel tradition) battling Robin Hood-like the rapacity of the public order (an evil governor of California and his henchman Captain Ramón) on behalf of older, higher values. Zorro was Spain, or more correctly, Spanish romance coming to the rescue of an exploited, vulgarized Southern California. Thrust, parry, thrust—take that, Captain Ramón! Thrust, parry, thrust—take that, Captain Babbitt, as well!

3

By 1919, the year Zorro first donned his cape and mask, buckled on his sword, and rode off into the night, it had become clear to right-thinking Santa Barbarans that the time had come to establish more formally the identity of the Santa Barbara alternative. The city and its immediate environs, first of all, were beginning to experience a growth that would continue throughout the 1920s. In 1919 developer Maurice Heckscher acquired the Hope and Ontare ranches adjacent to the western edge of the city and began to subdivide. Purchased by the La Cumbre Estates Corporation in 1925, a company controlled by the aesthetically oriented Santa Barbaran Harold S. Chase, the two-thousand-acre Hope Ranch Park was developed along the lines of Montecito to the east, and Palos Verdes Estates, Brentwood, and Bel-Air in Los Angeles: as a landscaped residential suburb, two to fifty acres per site, crisscrossed by palm-lined avenues, each site skillfully oriented to the beach and the oak-dotted foothills. The Riviera rising to the north of the city, meanwhile, continued to be developed by Chase and others, including W. W. Catlin, representing the Warren H. Kerr Company of Los Angeles. In August 1923 Catlin opened the Los Alturas section of the Riviera, where newly arriving Santa Barbarans such as William Gibbs McAdoo, Douglas Fairbanks, Sr. (Zorro himself), and his wife Mary Pickford planned to build residences.

The Community Arts Association provided the vehicle whereby the alternative identity of Santa Barbara became fixed for more than half a century. The Association captured Santa Barbara politically, bringing the community under the control of a coherent group of affluent, genteel, preservationist-minded citizens who forced their will, quietly but effectively, on the community for the next two decades. It began innocently enough with another historical pageant and an arts program. Encouraged by the success of the Masque of La Primavera, the group calling itself the Community Arts Association then organized and produced "The Quest," a pageant depicting mankind's search for happiness and beauty, which was performed in a specially constructed shell at the seaside Plaza del Mar on 15 July 1920. Headquartered in a renovated adobe at the corner of Santa Barbara and Carrillo Streets, the Association formed three branches music, drama, and the arts. The arts section founded a School of the Arts and opened a small gallery for local painters.

Over the next two years the Community Arts Association increased its membership so that by 1922 it constituted, in effect, the who's who of the private sector. There were the magnates (Edward Payson Ripley of the Santa Fe, David E. Perkins, the Akron rubber baron, George Owen Knapp of Union Carbide), surviving Spanish (De la Guerras in abundance), and Yankee squires (Dwight Murphy the palomino breeder, John James Hollister, the Colonel's heir). A special interest was taken by the aesthetically inclined, Mrs. Christian Herter, for example, of the New York loom fortune, and Fanny Van de Grift Osbourne Stevenson, Robert Louis Stevenson's widow, who maintained a home in Santa Barbara after her husband's death. Major Max Fleischmann was interested, as was Frederick Forrest Peabody, the Arrow shirt heir, and his dynamic wife, the former Kathleen Burke, an experienced community activist. During the war Burke had helped raise $4 million in Red Cross relief funds (her striking Irish beauty and innate eloquence made her a star on the speakers' circuit) and her personal field supervision of Red Cross operations in Europe earned her a reputation as the Angel of France. The real power of the association, however, resided in an inner core of genteel Hispanicizing preservationists centered around activists Pearl Chase and Irene and Bernhard Hoffmann.

Thus motivated and positioned, the Chase-Hoffmann group (it included artist Fernand Lungren and had the backing of Max Fleischmann) formed a fourth section of the Community Arts Association in March 1922, the Plans and Planting Committee, headquartered in a restored adobe at 116 East De la Guerra Street. Through the efforts of Henry S. Pritchett, former president of MIT, head of the Carnegie Foundation, and current Santa Barbaran, the Plans and Planting Committee obtained a grant of $25,000 a year from the Carnegie Foundation beginning in 1922 to create a pilot project of civic improvement that would serve as a model to other cities. These annual grants continued to be made until 1930. All in all, nearly $1.3 million was to be spent over a ten-year period promoting beautification. With Bernhard Hoffmann serving as chair, the Plans and Planting Committee embarked upon a program of beautification and improvement that soon put the committee in virtual control of Santa Barbara as a shadow government of vigilante Hispanicizers. Santa Barbara thus became the first preservationist-controlled city in the nation.

At the urging of the committee, Santa Barbara established a City Planning Commission in 1923, hiring the well-known planner Charles H. Cheney as consultant. Cheney drafted a comprehensive building-zone ordinance, which the City Council adopted on 16 May 1924 as Ordinance No. 1203. This measure gave the program of the Plans and Planting Committee the power of the law; for Cheney and his associates reported to the committee as well as to elected and appointed officials, treating them both as co-equal authorities. The committee also commissioned Cheney to work with Olmsted and Olmsted of New York to prepare a seventy-page *Major Traffic Street Plan and Boulevard and Park System*, which the Planning and Park commissions, composed of genteel stalwarts, accepted in September and November 1924, but which the City Council, a less impressed demotic group of politicians who feared a complete loss of authority to the beautifiers, balked at accepting. The Plans and Planting Committee did succeed, however, in getting a comprehensive building code through the Council in May 1925 after three stormy readings. The committee, meanwhile went ahead with a Small Homes Program, launched in 1923 with Pearl Chase serving as chair. Chase organized a statewide architectural competition for small house designs appropriate to Santa Barbara and costing no more than $5000 to build. In 1924 the results of the competition were published by the Community Arts Association as a guide to new home builders. The Committee extended free advice and assistance to Santa Barbarans wishing to improve existing residences through landscaping and renovation. Under the auspices of the Better Homes in America campaign, Herbert Hoover, the honorary chairman, Pearl Chase, and her committee awarded prizes for successful improvements.

The Plans and Planting Committee of the Community Arts Association had as its goal nothing less than the materialization throughout the entire city of an identity some half a century in the making: a vision, that is, of Santa Barbara as a Spanish dream city, beyond the gritty realities of American life. In its architectural program, the committee had two existing points of reference, the surviving Hispanic adobes and an emerging Santa Barbara school of Spanish Revival architects. Serviceable, unpretentious, beautiful in their simplicity, the adobes offered physical corroboration of the surviving Spanish past. Within a few years, they ceased being what they had been throughout the entire American era, low-cost housing built unpretentiously of the very earth itself, and were transformed into icons of heritage. As early as 1917 Mrs. Gardiner G. Hammond, an early preservationist, purchased the Hill-Carrillo Adobe (1826), where Thomas Oliver Larkin, Jr., the first American child to be born in California, had made his debut in April 1834, and remodeled the building into artists' studios and a tea room. The Oreña Adobes (1849, 1858) were restored as a restaurant, art goods store, and antique shop, beginning in 1920. In 1922 Bernhard Hoffmann acquired the Lugo Adobe (c. 1830) and restored it as the headquarters of the Plans and Planting Committee. With the assistance of architect George Washington Smith, Hoffmann added two new wings to the Lugo Adobe, which he called the Meridian Studios, and rented them out to artists. That year as well, Mrs. A.L. Murphy Vhay, a power on the Plans and Planting Committee, purchased the Ramirez Adobe (1825) and rehabilitated it as a residence. The Santa Barbara Foundation moved into the Hill-Carrillo Adobe in 1930, a gift of Max Fleischmann to the organization he had also endowed, and in 1932 the newly organized Santa Barbara Historical Society occupied a cluster of adobes which architect Robert Ingle Hoyt had integrated into a unified structure.

4

Thus genteel Santa Barbara physically repossessed its Hispanic past, urging all the while that the adobes inspire a new civic architecture. Fortunately, the design talent was on hand to make such urgings realities. Within the decade, a Santa Barbara school of architecture asserted itself. It included permanent residents such as George Washington Smith, the dean of local practitioners; Winsor Soule; William Albert Edwards (born in Santa Barbara in 1888) and his partner Joseph Plunkett; a married couple, James and Mary Craig; and Lutah Maria Riggs. Santa Barbara also attracted the talents of important Los Angeles-area-based architects such as Carleton Monroe Winslow, Reginald Davis Johnson, and Wallace Neff.

Santa Barbara's resident maestro of the Spanish style, George Washington Smith, broke off his architectural studies at Harvard for lack of financial support and practiced as a construction supervisor before going into stocks and bonds in Philadelphia to make money, which he did with great success. Smith then studied painting at the Julian Academy of the Ecole des Beaux-Arts in Paris and traveled throughout Europe before returning to New York at the outbreak of the war. For the next two years, Smith, who maintained friendships in New York with George Bellows and Robert Henri, painted with the same success with which he had previously bought and sold stocks and bonds. He especially enjoyed painting the landscape of Southern California. His works were prominently exhibited at the Panama-California International Expositon. In 1916 Smith and his wife, the former Mary Catherine Greenough, moved from New York to Montecito, where Smith designed a home for themselves in the Spanish style. Traveled, educated, socially polished, wealthy, George Washington Smith fit easily into the Montecito-Santa Barbara mode.

He also possessed an architectural talent which Santa Barbara brought to light. A connoisseur and painter of Southern California landscapes, Smith devised an architectural vocabulary based on the picturesque simplicities, elegant and romantic, of rural Andalusia—red-tiled roofs, white massy geometric surfaces, shuttered fenestration, cool courtyards within—sited and landscaped with painterly care. In this he was assisted by his chief designer, the Berkeley-trained Lutah Maria Riggs, a young woman who joined his office in 1921 and remained his chief designer until Smith's death in his early fifties in 1930.

With the success of Smith's own Montecito home in 1916, in which he introduced the Andalusian vocabulary, a rapid succession of Montecito commissions followed with the building boom that began in 1919. By 1923, at first working alone and after 1921 working as the Smith Riggs team, Smith had completed some dozen Spanish Revival homes in Montecito. Smaller than the first generation of Montecito mansions, intimate and restrainedly picturesque, these Smith homes created a successor tradition to the Mediterranean ostentation of the prewar, pre-income-tax era. In 1921 Smith completed his first commission in Santa Barbara; three more Santa Barbara homes followed in 1922 and 1923, in addition to the commission for the Little Town Club on East Carrillo.

Born in Scotland, and largely self-educated as a designer (although it was claimed after his early death that he had studied at the Royal Academy in London), the young James Osborne Craig, a Santa Barbara resident since 1915, was following a similar course. In 1919 Craig designed a masterful Spanish home for Irene and Bernhard Hoffmann on Garden Street between the Mission and St. Anthony's Seminary, with Carleton Winslow, Sr., serving as supervising architect. Like Smith's home in Montecito, the Hoffmann House constituted a primary statement of the new Santa Barbara style. Its symmetries and rhythms, its poetic purity of design, demonstrated that historicism and modernity might find simultaneous expression in Spanish Revival as it was to emerge in this region. The Hoffmanns next retained Craig for a pilot project that would further the Hispanicization of Santa Barbara in a major way. Acquiring the De la Guerra Adobe for $50,000 from the family, with whom they had studied Spanish after arriving in Santa Barbara from Massachusetts, together with adjacent rear and Plaza properties, the Hoffmanns commissioned Craig to restore the one-hundred-year-old building as fully as possible and to design an El Paseo or Street in Spain complex to be constructed contiguous to the historic Casa. The entire complex—the De la Guerra Adobe, the Casa La Aguirre, also acquired, the El Paseo structure, and two studio wings for artists—was to be integrated architecturally and landscaped into one past/present statement of Santa Barbara as Spanish City.

Sadly, Craig succumbed to tuberculosis in 1922 after completing his first designs. Carleton Winslow, Sr., completed drawings for the El Paseo arcade, working with Mary Craig, who had studied architecture privately as her husband's assistant. Winslow and Craig also designed one studio wing, the Anacapa Annex, and Lutah Maria Riggs, then a 26-year-old recent graduate of the School of Architecture at Berkeley, devised a connecting courtyard. The El Paseo complex was thus variously designed by an extraordinarily talented team: James Osborne Craig, an instinctive designer, as his home for the Hoffmanns had already shown; Carleton Winslow, Sr., Bertram Goodhue's collaborator in San Diego and Los Angeles, and along with Goodhue one of the American masters of Spanish Revival and already (since 1905) a gold medalist of the Architectural League of New York; Mary Craig, like her husband an instinctive virtuoso in the Spanish idiom, going on from this sudden assumption of her husband's practice to a successful career on her own; and Lutah Maria Riggs, George Washington Smith's collaborator on more than thirty homes in Santa

Barbara and Montecito, a Fellow of the American Institute of Architects in later life, and for more than half a century the only woman registered as an architect in the city.

What this team designed and what the Hoffmanns built between 1922 and 1924 was nothing less than a recapitulative paradigm of the idealized Santa Barbara identity. Like Santa Barbara itself, the El Paseo began with history, the Casa De la Guerra, which it then elaborated outwards into an idealized orchestration of courts, courtyards, patios, arches, tiled arcades, balconies, loggias, red-tiled roofs, and sweeping surfaces: an Andalusian daydream, in short of a city that existed first and foremost in the mind and imagination of Santa Barbara. That the Street in Spain was also a commercial venture—a patio restaurant covered overhead by soaring colored swaths of Venetian sail cloth, cafes, specialty shops, art galleries, and studios, even apartments—served to return the economic and social center of Santa Barbara to the long-neglected Plaza De la Guerra area. By the 1930s it was said that if a person lingered sufficiently at El Paseo, he or she would encounter most of Santa Barbara. The El Paseo complex also represented a new way, perhaps the first, of recycling history and imaginatively extending a heritage into a tourist attraction. From this perspective, the Street in Spain anticipated by forty years a series of recyclings across America of historic districts and surviving facilities into themed destination points as a way of revitalizing declining urban areas.

It was now time to recycle Santa Barbara's theatrical heritage as well. The Community Arts Association, parent group of the Plans and Planting Committee, had begun its existence with the La Primavera masque of 1919 and the Quest pageant of 1920. Music and theater first came to Santa Barbara in 1864 in the person of José Lobero, a 41-year-old Genoa-born pianist and trombone player obsessed with the idea of bringing Italian grand opera to the Pacific Coast. Opening a saloon and billiard parlor at the corner of State and Canon Perdido streets, Lobero organized an orchestra which by 1870 numbered twenty-two players. Among other assignments, it marched in local funerals. Lobero also produced concerts, recitals, and homespun versions of grand opera. With the help of Colonel Hollister, ever eager to develop the attractions of Santa Barbara on behalf of the hotel business, Lobero adapted and expanded a former schoolhouse near the Plaza De la Guerra into an ambitious theater, 125 by 58 feet, with a 28-foot-high ceiling. Using an ingenious system of iron rods, Lobero suspended the balcony directly from the roof so as to avoid obstructing pillars. Hollister purchased a theatrical curtain in San Francisco depicting a clipper ship entering the Golden Gate and shipped it down to Santa Barbara by steamship.

The Lobero Theater opened on Washington's Birthday, 22 February 1873, with a performance of "La Culumala," an operetta written, composed, and choreographed by Lobero himself. Despite its location in the Chinese quarter and red-light district, the Lobero Theater, José Lobero impresario, flourished as Santa Barbara's window on the world of entertainment for the rest of the nineteenth century until it was supplanted by the theater in the Potter Hotel.

Lobero, unfortunately, lost ownership of both his saloon and the theater in the late 1880s. Growing progressively more broke and despondent, he shot himself to death in 1892, a sad but theatrical ending for this provincial impresario dreaming of grand opera in Santa Barbara and half-convincing others that they too were experiencing in a converted schoolhouse the grand music of Italy.

Even as José Lobero was going broke, the Reverend A.W. Jackson, an ordained local publicist, was predicting in 1888 the assured destiny of Santa Barbara as a center for the fine, practicing, and performing arts. Such predictions were commonplace in late Victorian California, but in Santa Barbara they took on their own intensity. A place so beautiful, it was argued, should nurture the production of beautiful things. Boston philanthropist Anna Sophia Cabot Blake believed this with great conviction, and having moved to Santa Barbara in 1891, she established in 1893 with her own funds an arts and crafts academy, or Sloyd School (*slojd* in Swedish means manual training and crafts), which she directed until her death in 1899.

Blake's successor, Ednah Rich, another arts and crafts activist from Boston with European training, succeeded in having the Sloyd School integrated into the state normal school system in 1913. Located on a choice Riviera property, the school became a state college in 1921 and in 1944 was incorporated into the University of California. The Arts and Crafts sensibility nurtured by the Sloyd School, a passionate concern for beauty in everyday objects, helped set the tone for the Community Arts movement of the 1920s, as did another local institution, the Santa Barbara School of the Arts, founded in 1920 by Fernand Lungren and since 1923 directed by the English woodblock printer Frank Morley Fletcher. The School of the Arts, in fact, was directly created by the Community Arts organization and continued through the 1920s as one of its divisions.

As a young man, Frank Morley Fletcher studied in Paris with two Americans, Fernand Lungren and Albert Herter, and the trio formed a lifelong friendship. Fletcher went on to become a skilled artist/craftsman (he helped introduce the Japanese woodblock to Europe) and art educator. While serving as director of the Edinburgh College of Art, Fletcher became active with the Design and Industries Association, an organization dedicated to promoting good design in every aspect of manufacture and daily life. In 1923 Fletcher's friends Lungren and Herter, by then well-established Santa Barbara artists, invited him to take over the direction of the Santa Barbara School of the Arts. Nearly sixty, looking for new challenges and tiring perhaps of the long Scottish winters, Fletcher agreed.

For the rest of the decade (the school closed during the Depression) the

Community Arts Association had the supportive presence of an artist/educator who was a well-known proponent of good design in daily life. Empowered by Carnegie funds, Fletcher could afford to hire an excellent staff—Edward Borein in etching, sculptors Amory Simmons and Archibald Dawson, Belmore Browne in painting, stained glass designer Charles Paine—as well as to bring local artists such as John Gamble, Colin Campbell Cooper, and Clarence Mattei into part-time teaching. Pursuing his own work, meanwhile, in his studio on Puesta del Sol (his woodblock prints found their way into the British Museum, the Victoria and Albert, the Boston Museum, the national museums of Dresden and Budapest, and the private collection of H.G. Wells, an early and avid enthusiast), Fletcher functioned as a direct channel of the British Arts and Crafts movement to Santa Barbara. His experience in broader questions of good design, moreover, in furniture, household objects, industrial manufacture, and the like made Fletcher a ready resource to the Plans and Planting Committee as it sought to transform Santa Barbara into the most beautiful small city in America.

Another interest of the Community Arts Association was the little theater movement as exported from Provincetown, Massachusetts. Bringing together assorted amateurs and aspiring professionals, the little theater movement sought at once to produce plays, develop talent, and build community. In acquiring the services of director Nina Moise, the Drama Committee of the Community Arts Association effected a direct connection with the Provincetown Players formed in 1915 and already performing the plays of Eugene O'Neill, Edna St. Vincent Millay, and Sherwood Anderson. Having directed a number of Provincetown performances, Moise had come west to Hollywood as an assistant director, one of the few such female directors in the industry. In 1922 the Drama Committee of the Community Arts Association invited Moise up to Santa Barbara to direct a production of Booth Tarkington's *The Country Cousin* at the Potter Theater on Lower State Street.

Moise found in Santa Barbara the beginnings of an energetic little theater movement, inaugurated in 1920 with the organization of the Community Arts Players by the Drama Committee of the Community Arts Association, with artist Albert Herter, dancer Ynez Dibblee, and civic activist Pearl Chase being especially active. Offered a salaried position as director, Moise accepted. Working with voice and drama coach Margaret Carrington of Montecito (she later coached John Barrymore for *Hamlet*), Moise developed a strong cast of local players. One of her tutees, a semi-retired vaudevillean and inveterate golfer by the name of Walter Huston, who was also Margaret Carrington's brother, became so adept under Moise's and Carrington's coaching that he left for New York and a second career as an actor on the legitimate stage. Huston's son John later followed his father on the stage before turning to directing. Margaret Carrington herself, Huston's sister and voice coach, began her career on the London concert stage and was one of many theatrically minded Montecitans who lent support to the Community Arts Players. A number of Montecito estates—Piranhurst, El Mirador, Bellosguardo, the Carrington's own Villa di Riposa—supported landscaped outdoor theaters seating up to as many as 250 guests for amateur performances and concerts.

Under Moise's guidance the Community Arts Players embarked upon an ambitious schedule of Potter Theater productions—among them Maurice Maeterlinck's *Pelléas and Mélisande,* George Bernard Shaw's *Pygmalion,* James M. Barrie's *Dear Brutus,* John Galsworthy's *Joy*—employing local actors, set and costume designers, and technicians. Funds were gathered to send Nina Moise to Europe, where she studied advanced production techniques in Berlin and Munich. It was also decided to acquire a theater larger than the Potter. For some years José Lobero's 1873 Opera House had been languishing in a state of disuse, its thousand seats filled only intermittently by an occasional political rally. For the past few years, in fact, the Opera House had stood condemned, its walls of adobe brick judged unsound. At a meeting in the Patio Restaurant of the recently completed El Paseo complex, the Community Arts Association agreed on 13 March 1922 to raise $100,000 to purchase the Opera House from the Hollister estate and to restore it as a theater for the Community Arts Players. Under the auspices of yet another organization, the Lobero Theatre Association, headed by Frederick Forrest Peabody, the money was raised, the property acquired, and George Washington Smith retained to do the restoration.

Upon investigation, however, Smith recommended against simple restoration in favor of the construction of a building that, while incorporating portions of the adobe walls of the original, would substitute a new edifice. Working with Lutah Maria Riggs, Smith designed yet another Spanish Revival masterpiece, this time Majorcan in inspiration: a cascade of geometric forms descending from an oversized backstage capable of flying elaborate scenery, the space continuing across a 655-seat auditorium to an arched lobby and tile-roofed entrance.

Dedicated in August 1924, the Lobero Theater opened with Nina Moise's production of the recently written *Beggar on Horseback* by George Kaufman and Marc Connelly, with music by Deems Taylor. In the lead Moise cast a young Anglo-American by the name of Arthur Bliss and a young Santa Barbaran named Gertrude Hoffmann. The son of Francis E. Bliss, a wealthy Mayflower descendant and naturalized British subject who had retired to Montecito in his later years and thus re-Americanized his family, Arthur Bliss had studied composition in England under Charles Stanford, Ralph Vaughan Williams, and Gustav Holst before joining his father in Southern California in 1923 at the age of 32. Personable and socially active, Arthur Bliss fit perfectly into the Monteciton mode, including its passion for theater. As the penniless composer Neil McRae in *Beggar on Horseback,* Bliss himself performed the piano sequences of Deems Taylor's difficult score which had to be pantomimed on stage and played from the pit in the Broadway production. Bliss was already at work on his own music, including the incidental music for a Community Players production of *The Queen of Sheba* by artist-activist Albert Herter, a chamber piece which he debuted in Montecito, playing in an ensemble he organized for the occasion; some piano pieces; a song cycle entitled "The Women of Yueh"; and a longer symphonic tone poem. Bliss also gave private recitals and lectures at various Montecito residences.

When he took his "Colour Symphony" to the Hollywood Bowl later in the year, however, personally conducting the orchestra, Bliss encountered the realities of continuing to pursue his career in a provincial setting, however congenial. The Bowl audience received Bliss's semi-avant-garde composition with cool restraint; and so it was back to London for Arthur, taking with him a new wife, Gertrude Hoffmann, his leading lady in the opening night production at the Lobero Theater. As Sir Arthur Bliss, Master of the Queen's Musick, which he became in 1950, it proved pleasant for the noted composer and conductor and Lady Gertrude to remember the inspired amateurism of their Santa Barbara beginnings. Community theater, Montecito recitals, even the Hollywood Bowl, had conspired to point Sir Arthur in the right direction.

5

In its efforts to beautify Santa Barbara, the Plans and Planting Committee of the Community Arts Association had the assistance of a massive urban renewal project. At 6:42 a.m. on Monday, 29 June 1925, a violent earthquake, 6.3 on the Richter scale, shook Santa Barbara. The shock began in the Mesa Fault beneath the Santa Barbara Channel, moved in a northwesterly direction, then triggered a major east-west reaction on the seaward side of the foothills when it reached the South Santa Ynez Fault. Since the earthquake struck early in the morning, the major downtown buildings, where most of the damage occurred, were relatively unoccupied and so casualties were light. A dentist working in his office at the San Marcos building was crushed when the corner section of the building collapsed. A sixty-thousand-gallon water tank crashed through the tower of the second Arlington Hotel, killing two guests, G. Allan Hancock of Los Angeles and his son Bertram. All in all, out of a population of 25,000, twelve died and over fifty were injured. New construction—the El Paseo complex, the Lobero Theater, the *Daily News* building on the Plaza De la Guerra (another Smith-Riggs masterpiece), the majority of the newer private homes—survived the temblor. Damage to older downtown buildings, however, and to the Mission itself was severe. Just about every major nineteenth- or early twentieth-century structure—the Fithian Building, the Mortimer Cook Building, St. Francis Hospital, the Californian Hotel, the Potter Theatre, the churches, the lighthouse, and the Dibblee mansion on the Mesa—suffered severe damage. Had the earthquake struck when the streets and sidewalks were busy, hundreds might have been killed or injured by falling debris. Outside the city, the Sheffield Reservoir, an earthfill dam, shuddered open. Miraculously, forty million gallons of water roared down Sycamore Canyon to the sea without loss of life. President Coolidge dispatched the USS *Arkansas*, a dreadnought, to steam up from San Diego and administer relief. Navy corpsmen helped with the medical chores, and detachments of sailors and marines patrolled the city against looters.

When it came time to rebuild, the Plans and Planting Committee was ready. Just prior to the earthquake, the committee had lobbied through the City Council an ordinance creating a Board of Architectural Review. Eleven days after the earthquake the ordinance was put into effect. Staunch Hispanicizers and Plans and Planting Committee activists such as Bernhard Hoffmann and architects George Washington Smith and Carleton Winslow, Sr., received seats on the board. Hoffmann also sat on the Architectural Advisory Committee, which reported directly to the Board of Public Safety and Reconstruction, and on the Relief Fund Committee as well. Hispanicizers, in short, seized control of the reconstruction apparatus. Thus situated, they got to work. For the first time in California and perhaps American history, preservationists, planners, and aestheticizers had gained control of a city and were refashioning it to their purposes. "Santa Barbara," urged Carleton Winslow, Sr., "now faces its opportunity. It can make of itself the most romantic, beautiful and best planned city in Western America."[5] Within the month, the Board of Architectural Review had approved 102 reconstruction permits, virtually every one in the Spanish style. All in all, the board processed some 2000 design proposals during the reconstruction period. In virtually every case, it urged a Spanish solution. Who, after all, could resist? The Southern Pacific went so far as to rebuild its waterfront roundhouse, for so long an eyesore, in the form of a Spanish bull ring. The Plans and Planting Committee also opened a Community Drafting Room, with architects on hand at no fee to assist in Spanish solutions for commercial and residential structures alike. Pearl Chase, meanwhile, stepped up her Better Homes campaign so that by 1926 the Better Homes in America jury judged Santa Barbara to be the most beautiful residential environment in the nation. Chase also came up with the bull ring idea for the SP roundhouse, fought billboards and garish signage, and prevented an oil company from chopping down the Moreton Bay Fig Tree to make room for a gas station.

In the Hispanicizing campaign, Hoffmann and Chase were joined, after some tension, by Thomas More Storke, the son of rancher/developer Charles Albert Storke who had come to Santa Barbara after the Civil War to teach at Santa Barbara College. Born in Santa Barbara in 1876, Thomas More Storke was the heir apparent to the Hispanic-Yankee tradition of the city. A direct descendant of Lieutenant José Francisco de Ortega, founder of the presidio, Storke also included in his blood lines the Massachusetts trader Daniel Hill, who married Ortega's granddaughter in 1826, and rancher T. Wallace More, who married Hill's daughter Susanna. The product of that union, Martha More, heir to lands, cattle, and lineage, married the ambitious newcomer Charles Albert Storke in 1873 and their union produced three Santa Barbara genealogies made flesh, Martha, Alice, and Master Thomas.

Graduating from the newly established Stanford University in 1898, young Thomas Storke, following in his father's footsteps, embarked upon a sixty-four-year career in politics and journalism that would gain him, eventually, a Pulitzer Prize, a brief stint in the United States Senate, and continuing regional and statewide influence. In so many ways, in fact, Storke—a wealthy, politically ambitious Democrat, adept at using newspaper power to further personal and civic ends—was a William Randolph Hearst who stayed home and achieved a localized but comparable mode of power and influence.

But Storke had to establish a newspaper and second he had to do battle for dominance within the oligarchy. In 1901, at age 24, Storke bought the *Independent*, a failing newspaper with a small circulation, and began its revival. He also entered Democratic party politics. Helping to deliver California and hence the presidency to Woodrow Wilson in 1912, Storke won appointment as the local postmaster. While he did not need the money, the patronage involved helped consolidate his position. Meanwhile, he sold the *Independent* in 1911 to Frederick W. Sherman, a Michigan publisher anxious to Santa Barbarize, and then, with more than a little ruthlessness, fought to void the agreement and regain control when Sherman fell behind in his payments. Sherman took Storke to court, charging that Storke had fraudulently inflated the value of the *Independent*, and prevailed. Despite Storke's promise to Sherman that he would stay out of newspapers for ten yers, Storke thereupon bought another newspaper, the *Daily News*, and drove Sherman to the ground. Destroyed by Stroke, Sherman sold him the *Independent* for a pittance, $25,000, having bought it from Storke a few years earlier for sixteen times that amount. Being born to wealth had not hampered Thomas Storke's ability to play hardball.

This left two newspapers, Storke's newly consolidated *Daily News and Independent* and Reginald Fernald's *Morning Press*, in contention for control of Santa Barbara. Forty years earlier, Reginald Fernald's father, Judge Charles Fernald, the unquestioned paladin of the local elite, formed an opinion of Charles Albert Storke that he was a crass, overly ambitious, even dangerous arriviste. (The Fernalds, after all, had been in Santa Barbara since the 1850s.) Charles Storke returned the contempt. Now the battle continued into the second generation as Storke's son Thomas and Judge Fernald's son Reginald, a bachelor bon vivant rarely seen in the office before lunch, fought for dominance. Invited to write for his son's newspaper, Charles Storke wrote a vitriolic series of anti-*Morning Press*, anti-Fernald editorials which he signed "The Old Man." The *Morning Press* replied in kind. The exchange grew uglier and uglier as old scores surfaced, demanding settlement. Finally, on 28 October 1922 *Morning Press* sub-editor E.P. Erwin, in the course of excoriating Charles Storke, invited readers to peruse the transcript of Storke's divorce in 1891 from his

second wife, Yda Addis Storke, herself a journalist. During the trial, which
abounded in semi-pornographic testimony, the second Mrs. Storke accused her
estranged husband of sexual perversion and other forms of immoral and illegal
behavior. Storke had been found innocent of these charges, such as they were,
and his second wife later went insane and died in an asylum; but the *Morning
Press* failed to mention these facts, preferring, rather, to suggest that Yda Addis
Storke's charges had been upheld. Charles Storke sued Reginald Fernald in
superior court and won a $6000 judgment.

More than this, however, the Storkes, father and son, also prevailed over the
Fernalds for leadership in Santa Barbara. The Judge was dead, after all, and
Reginald had gone too far in unnecessarily bringing up that unsavory mess of
1891. Defeated in court, rebuffed by his peer group for hitting below the belt,
his newspaper losing circulation and advertising to the Storke publication, Reginald Fernald ceded to Thomas Storke the leadership of his Santa Barbara
generation and spent increasingly more time, if that were possible, on social
pursuits. Around Montecito one could always find a party.

Having gained the mastery of the region, Thomas Storke celebrated with a
new building for the *Daily News* on the Plaza De la Guerra, designed by
George Washington Smith and Lutah Maria Riggs in an impeccable Spanish
idiom. Just as the Casa De la Guerra across the Plaza had functioned as the
hub of Santa Barbara life through the mid-nineteenth century, so too did its
Spanish Revival counterpart now become the hub of the rebuilt post-earth-
quake city. While Thomas Storke had reservations, which he expressed in the
paper, as to how far the odd individualist might be compelled to rebuild the
Spanish Revival if he or she preferred not to, he by and large supported the
movement. On his mother's side, after all, he was an Ortega.

Santa Barbara, Irving Morrow was reporting in the *Architect and Engineer*
for July 1926, was rebuilding itself even more rapidly and aesthetically than
had San Francisco after the earthquake and fire of April 1906. The Community Drafting Room was bringing the benefits of good design to even the least
expensive of the new houses. State Street, previously such an eyesore, was now
re-emerging as an arcaded *calle principal* worthy of the most lovely smaller
cities of the Mediterranean. The public fabric of Santa Barbara and Montecito—schools, churches, the city hall, police and fire stations, commercial
buildings—came under equally assertive Spanish controls, creating a built environment increasingly daydreamish as the ordinary procedures of American
life were channeled through an architectural filtration of Spanish romance.
Even gas stations rose like tiled and domed Moorish mosques or Churrigueresque mini-cathedrals dispensing petroleum sacraments.

Completed in 1929 from designs by William Mooser and Company of San
Francisco and the Architectural Advisory Committee, the third Santa Barbara
County Courthouse on an entire square block of Anacapa Street was in itself a
mirage worthy of that all-compelling Chumash word for a pleasing illusion.

Now at last Santa Barbara had the grand building, the castle in Spain, dreamt of by Bishop García Diego a hundred years earlier as he began to have stones gathered into one place. In preparation for his final design, architect William Mooser, Jr., traveled to Spain to make a detailed study of its architecture. After the narrow failure of a $980,000 bond issue in November 1925, a second bond issue for $700,000 passed. This first failure attested to the fact that on a countywide basis, as opposed to the Santa Barbara-Montecito area, the Spanish metaphor was not that all-persuasive. Certain county supervisors, in fact, opposed Mooser's design as too grandiloquent and too costly. They had a point. The courthouse would feature, among other expensive details, 140,000 square feet of floor tile, and even as the supervisors deliberated whether or not to go ahead with the design, contacts were being made with tile-makers in Algeria for North African tilework to line staircases, walls, and doorways. After some debate, the Spanish proposal passed the county Board of Supervisors, and by 1929 the most unusual public building in California, perhaps the United States, stood complete: a castle fortress surmounted by a grand clock tower, encompassing richly landscaped interior gardens.

Every detail of the courthouse—the arches and corridors, the wrought-iron grillwork, the ornamental lighting fixtures, the floor and wall tile, the Spanish Renaissance furnishings, the tapestries—bespoke a materialized Spanish metaphor in its most assertive statement to date. Doing their daily business in the Hall of Records, the Law Library, the Assessor's or Tax Collector's office, seated in Superior Court or in the council chambers of the county Board of Supervisors, Santa Barbarans were now bathed in an imagined Spanish identity. Even the sheriff's wing and adjoining jail, touted as the most beautiful jail in the United States, managed to subsume the business of arrest and incarceration in an architectural rhetoric of Spanish romance. As a final gloss on this idealized identity, the county retained artist Dan Sayre Groesbeck, a set designer and scenic painter for Cecil B. De Mille, to execute murals in the supervisors' chambers depicting a highly mythologized version of the Spanish settlement of Santa Barbara. To mention that Cabrillo never really raised the flag on Santa Barbara in 1542 as Groesbeck depicted is to miss the point. History had long since become romance.

As a distinguished public work in the Spanish style, the courthouse was one of many private and public projects which even as the Depression unfolded continued to be funded in the Santa Barbara area, thanks in great part to the rise of private philanthropy spearheaded by Major Max Fleischmann and the Santa Barbara Foundation which he organized and by the growing political influence of Thomas Storke with the Roosevelt administration. First, however, the Mission itself had to be restored. On the Monday morning of the earthquake, a sung high mass was in progress, attended by the Franciscan community and fifteen or so congregants. As the Mission shook, Brother Michael Lamm pushed the celebrant Father Raphael Vonder Haar aside just in time to save him from being crushed by a falling statue. Father Augustine Hobrecht, the superior of the Mission, sprang up and counseled the congregants to stay inside the shaking building. Had they run outside, they might have been crushed beneath the debris of the collapsing bell tower. John Shea, an aged workman at St. Anthony's Seminary, died from falling debris, and an elderly Franciscan in the infirmary, Brother Erasmus, died nine days later from the shock of having the ceiling and walls collapse on his bed.

The Alliance Engineers of Los Angeles estimated that the restoration plans drawn up by architect Ross Montgomery of Los Angeles would cost $394,000. The money was raised through a statewide subscription, chaired locally by rancher Dwight Murphy, who raised Santa Barbara's quota of $92,000 (Los Angeles sent $150,000; San Francisco, $100,000), which was augmented by another $75,000 contributed diversely by Murphy, Fleischmann, and Caroline Hazard of Santa Barbara, and by John Francis Nyland of San Francisco. Not only was Mission Santa Barbara rebuilt, reinforced concrete being brought to the aid of the original limestone to create a new level of seismic safety, it was also restored to something more closely approximating its 1820 condition through the efforts of local restoration specialists such as Andrew McDonough, Louis Mohr, and Theodore Probst.

On 7 August 1927, as part of the Old Spanish Days Fiesta, Father Augustine Hobrecht celebrated a solemn high mass of thanksgiving in the restored Mission church, with Jesuit Father Thomas Ewing Sherman, son of the Civil War general, preaching the sermon. The following December, Archbishop John J. Cantwell of Los Angeles reconsecrated the Mission church in the presence of a colorful gathering of Roman Catholic bishops from California and Mexico. Santa Barbarans loved the spectacle. It was like old times.

Major Max Fleischmann, meanwhile, the polo-playing, big-game-hunting yachtsman and yeast heir from Montecito who had so substantially assisted the Mission restoration project, was busy on another and long overdue project, the construction of a breakwater. The entire coast of California contains only three protected harbors of importance: San Diego, San Francisco, and Humboldt; the others, Long Beach and Wilmington-San Pedro most notably, are products of construction. When Richard Henry Dana, Jr., visited Santa Barbara in January 1836, the *Alert* was forced to anchor three miles offshore to avoid being washed up on the beach. While the Stearns Wharf allowed steamships to tie up one by one, it in no way created a harbor for commercial or recreational use. Ever since 1903 Santa Barbara had been discussing the construction of an offshore breakwater to create a protected harbor. Had Santa Barbara become a Navy town, the War Department would have seen to the proper dredging and construction. Had Santa Barbara been energized by any large-scale commercial ambitions, it might have developed its harbor on a smaller scale but parallel to that of Long Beach and Los Angeles. But Santa Barbara represented a non-commercial, non-institutionalized alternative, and so it took an avid yachtsman, Max Fleischmann, to drive to conclusion the breakwater project under discussion since 1903.

Interested in creating a world-class yacht harbor, Fleischmann made a simple offer in October 1925, shortly after the earthquake: he would give Santa Barbara $200,000 towards a breakwater if the city passed a bond issue for an equal amount. The bond issue passed in 1926 and plans were drawn up for an 1800-foot breakwater which went into construction in June 1927. A citizens' committee headed by Fleischmann and Dwight Murphy formed a non-profit syndicate to acquire all unsightly beach properties, including an especially offensive lumber mill, and raze them for open space. The syndicate also purchased the rickety Stearns Wharf and replaced it with a modern structure which housed an elegant headquarters for the Santa Barbara Yacht Club. Fleischmann then contributed another $250,000 for a 600-foot extension to the breakwater. Altogether, Fleischmann contributed a total of $630,000 to the harbor project by the completion of the breakwater in June 1930. Such was his commitment to the beautification of Santa Barbara—and to better yachting.

Major Fleischmann (his wartime rank) also established the Santa Barbara Foundation in 1929 with a $250,000 gift. One of the first civic foundations of its kind in the country, the Santa Barbara Foundation soon had a million dollars in endowment, thanks to Fleischmann, Henry S. Pritchett, the former president of MIT who obtained Carnegie funds for the foundation as he previously had for the Community Arts Association, George Owen Knapp, Dwight Murphy, Bernhard and Irene Hoffmann, and other members of a rapidly expanding Santa Barbara-oriented philanthropic community. For the Foundation's headquarters Fleischmann purchased the Carrillo Adobe, scheduled to be razed to make way for a movie theater, and had it restored and adapted for Foundation purposes. Collectively as a foundation, and individually as well, the Fleischmann circle continued the enhancement and embellishment of Santa Barbara and its quality of life. Fleischmann underwrote community concerts in Alameda Plaza, the Plaza del Mar, Oak Park, and the seaside Cabillo Pavilion. Over a period of years he poured a million dollars into the Cottage and St. Francis hospitals. George Knapp gave a pipe organ to St. Anthony's Seminary, to used for public recitals as well. Knapp also founded a college of nursing at Cottage Hospital. Mrs. William Clark gave $55,000 in memory of her daughter for the improvement of publicly owned marshlands.

The Andree Clark Bird Refuge offered further testimony to the continuing ornithological interests of the community that had just produced Leon Dawson's magisterial *Birds of California*. In 1934 Max Fleischmann assumed the presidency of the Santa Barbara Museum of Natural History, which Dawson founded in 1916. Since that time, the museum had continued to be improved as a scientific expression of the aesthetic naturalism that coexisted with Spanish romance at the core of the Santa Barbara metaphor. In 1922 Caroline Hazard, the retired president of Wellesley College, and her sister-in-law contributed the site and the funds for a new museum facility near the Mission in memory of Rowland Bigson Hazard, Miss Hazard's late brother. Designed by Floyd Brewster and expanded by Carleton Winslow, Sr., along lines suggestive of an intimate Spanish cloister, the museum took as its provenance natural Santa Barbara, including the culture of the Chumash. Fleischmann expanded its range to include general mammalogy and contributed a new wing for this purpose. He later donated a hall for the exhibition of mounted specimens. Mrs. Clinton Hale donated a Hale Hall of Botany in memory of her late husband. Similarly motivated, Mrs. Anna Blaksley Bliss purchased fifteen acres, later doubled to thirty, in Mission Canyon and developed it as a botanical museum of Southern California cacti and flora in memory of her late father.

Thus the private sector pursued a program that established Santa Barbara as an extraordinarily endowed, even privileged, smaller city: the model city, in fact, that the Carnegie grant of 1922 was intended to help create. Nor did the Depression seriously interrupt this continuing installation of cultural amenities and public works; indeed, for two major reasons, oil revenues and the political influence of Thomas Storke in Washington, the 1930s witnessed the addition of even more impressive additions to the Santa Barbara infrastructure. Oil constituted the exception to the anti-industrial Santa Barbara rule, but then again, oil was regulated on a county, state, and federal basis and was therefore beyond the City of Santa Barbara's immediate jurisdiction. Had oil been a purely civic matter, Santa Barbara might very well have tried to suppress its development. Activated in 1927, the Elwood field west of Goleta was by 1930 producing more than fourteen million barrels a year, making it the fourth largest oil field in the state. Tax revenues from Elwood helped pay for the $1.5 million new County Courthouse. Behind the Spanish romance of that building churned an oil rig. Throughout the Depression tax revenues from oil helped keep Santa Barbara County solvent while creating much-needed employment in the private sector.

Thomas Storke personally helped bring in more than $22 million in WPA and PWA construction projects. Storke accomplished this from a combination of consolidated editorial power and personal friendship with United States Senator William Gibbs McAdoo, a Santa Barbara resident. In 1932 Storke acquired the *Morning Press* from Reginald Fernald for $100,000. The *Morning Press* had never managed to recover from the libel suit of 1924, although, curiously enough, Reginald Fernald and Thomas Storke avoided the personal enmity felt for all Fernalds by Thomas Storke's father Charles, the Old Man. The two younger men were in fact, friends of a sort, despite the ancient grudge held by the Old Man, who died in 1936.

Bound together by class identity and a mutality of economic interests, Thomas Storke and Reginald Fernald were more than anxious to let bygones be bygones. Thus they were able to work out a joint operating agreement whereby Fernald remained on as vice president and copublisher of an editorially autonomous *Morning Press*, staunchly Republican in policy, while Storke directed the Democratic *News*. On Sundays a combined *News-Press* was issued. In 1938 a more complete merger was effected, leaving Thomas More Storke in control of the Santa Barbara *News-Press*. the sole surviving newspaper in the city and the most influential newspaper in Santa Barbara, Ventura, and San Luis Obispo counties.

In 1937 Storke also started a radio station, its call letters KTMS based on his initials. Its presence as the NBC affiliate in the region during the golden age of American broadcasting added further to Storke's local control. With much justification *Time* magazine would eventually refer to Storke as the benevolent dictator of Santa Barbara, a Don José De la Guerra in a double-breasted suit.

In 1918, while serving as Santa Barbara postmaster in the Wilson administration, Storke hosted Secretary of the Treasury William Gibbs McAdoo and his wife, Eleanor Wilson McAdoo, the president's daughter, on a visit to the area. A correspondence ensued which turned into a personal friendship when the McAdoos moved to Los Angeles in 1919. The following year at the Democratic Convention meeting in San Francisco, Storke played an active role in trying to win the presidential nomination for McAdoo, which eventually went to James Cox, with Franklin Delano Roosevelt as his running mate. Thus Storke had an opportunity to put McAdoo, a national figure but a recent Californian with few local attachments, into contact with the California Democratic party establishment. Over the next decade Storke and McAdoo became even closer personal friends and business associates. In 1924 McAdoo lost out to Ambassador John W. Davis of New York in his second bid for the Democratic presidential nomination, but his Los Angeles-based legal practice, centered in oil and film interests, continued to flourish.

Along with two of his clients, Douglas Fairbanks and Mary Pickford, McAdoo invested in Santa Barbara real estate and in the late 1920s he built a second home in Santa Barbara, which soon became his primary residence. McAdoo and Storke, meanwhile, promoted the presidential interest of Franklin Delano Roosevelt in California Democratic party circles. In 1932, when Roosevelt was elected President and McAdoo became the junior United States Senator from California, the stage was set for some assertive local patronage. "It may seem paradoxical for me to say that I personally questioned deficit spending on such a vast scale, " Storke later remarked of the New Deal WPA and PWA construction programs, "but I reasoned this way: the funds, having been appropriated, would be spent somewhere—so why not go after Santa Barbara's share?"[6]

The share Storke was referring to came to $22 million in public works projects, much more than Santa Barbara deserved, given its population and prosperity. The Sheffield Reservoir, destroyed by the 1925 earthquake, was reconstructed, its capacity increased to fifty million gallons. A water-softening and filtration plant was added the following year and another reservoir was later constructed at El Cielito. By the end of the decade Santa Barbara boasted one of the finest water storage and distribution systems in the United States. An outdoor amphitheater, the Santa Barbara County Bowl, was built with PWA funds off Milpas Street in Quail Canyon and a program of concerts inaugurated. As headquarters of the Old Spanish Days Fiesta, the Bowl also served the continuing local taste for historical festivals and pageants. In Santa Barbara the National Guard unit, the 143rd Field Artillery, had social cachet ever since Steward Edward White and Joel Remington Fithian first recruited it in 1917 for service in France. Thus it's not surprising that PWA funds were used to build an elegant Spanish Revival armory on De la Guerra Street, where Battery E was in 1938 ensconced in a splendor appropriate to a well-bred (and, incidentally, superbly drilled and trained) citizen militia.

As the Depression continued, other improvements—a sewage system, public tennis courts, a swimming pool and bath house, even new baseball bleachers for Laguna Park—found their way into the area, thanks to the lobbying efforts of Storke and the responsiveness of Senator McAdoo. Through the intercession of James Farley, FDR's Postmaster General, Storke the ever-involved former postmaster received authorization for the city, meaning Storke personally, to choose an architect for the proposed new Post Office and Federal Building which McAdoo had helped secure for Santa Barbara. Storke chose Reginald Johnson of Pasadena, architect of the eminently successful Santa Barbara Biltmore Hotel. The resulting structure, dedicated in May 1927, brilliantly combined Spanish Revival and Moderne and further enhanced the already impressive Santa Barbara cityscape. The federal government then sold the previous post office to the county for a fraction of its assessed valuation, and it became the site of the newly organized Santa Barbara Museum of Art. In 1938 McAdoo resigned from the Senate two months before his term ended. McAdoo's good friend Thomas Storke of Santa Barbara served out the remainder of his term, a fitting conclusion to a most remarkable partnership.

6

Storke's selection of Reginald Johnson for the post office assignment testified to Johnson's success with the Biltmore, which opened in 1927; and the Biltmore, in turn, testified to the final consolidation of the tourist economy in Santa Barbara. Intended to replace the Potter, renamed the Ambassador—which burned to the ground in April 1921—and the New Arlington, which was razed in the aftermath of the 1925 earthquake, the 175-room Biltmore occupied a commanding seaside site on Channel Drive in Montecito. Long experienced in Spanish Revival in Montecito and Santa Barbara, Reginald Johnson combined Spanish, Basque, Portuguese, and Moorish elements with scholarship and restrained sensitivity. Perceived offshore, the Santa Barbara Biltmore rose in white and carmine radiance against a backdrop of blue sky, forested green hills, white beachfront, and Capri-blue channel waters: a stunning materialization of the Santa Barbara dream. In the Santa Ynez foothills which formed the background of the Biltmore's dramatic setting was another famed hostelry, the San Ysidro Ranch of Montecito. Opened as a resort in 1893, the San Ysidro shared honors with the Biltmore as a destination point, the Arlington and Potter of the second hotel generation. Acquired in the late 1920s by screen star Ronald Colman and a local partner, the San Ysidro was a favorite with British visitors (Somerset Maugham, John Galsworthy, Winston Churchill) and film folk.

The Old Spanish Days Fiesta catered directly to this amalgam of Spanish Revival identity and affluent tourism. Again, the Community Arts Association came into play. To inaugurate the new Lobero Theater in mid-August 1924, Association director Hamilton McFadden suggested a festival based on Santa Barbara's Spanish heritage. Given local obsession with the Spanish identity, McFadden's suggestion had no trouble receiving a positive response. Not only would such a festival add one more element to the Hispanicization of Santa Barbara, it would also function as a tourist attraction in the dead month of August. Encouraged by the city manager Herbert Nunn, the Community Arts coalition began to create another instance—like the Lobero Theater itself and, later, the County Courthouse—of idealized history, Santa Barbara-style. Surviving Barbareños and their descendants were fêted, first of all, at a reception at the Casa De la Guerra by the committee in an effort to win their support and participation. As the De la Guerras, Carrillos, Ortegas, Ruíz's, de Aratas, Dibblees, and others sat politely, many of the women in dresses and mantillas from the pre-1850 era, Charles Fletcher Lummis gave one of his last public addresses on the legacy of the Spanish past. A program of music and dancing followed, with the 89-year-old Dōna María Antonia Jimeno de Arata singing songs she had learned eighty years earlier from Padre Narciso Durán. Festival president Dwight Murphy, meanwhile, had gone down to Hollywood to secure costumes from the Western Costume Company for the historical pageant that was being planned as part of the festival. Thus both Padre Durán, the last great Father President of the Missions, a skilled musician and voice coach who one hundred years earlier had trained the Native Americans choristers of San José and Santa Barbara to sing with an unearthly beauty still evident in the nonagenarian voice of Doña María Antonia, and Hollywood, even then releasing *The Mark of Zorro*, exercised their respective and symptomatic influences on the Old Spanish Days Fiesta.

By 1931 the Fiesta had grown to a three-day affair of costume parades, historical pageants, concerts, Spanish dancing, a rodeo, and special services at the Mission, which attracted thousands of visitors, including guest appearances by Will Rogers and Paul Whiteman who, remembering how he started at the Hotel Potter twenty years earlier, had brought in his orchestra during the 1929 Fiesta for a night of free public dancing on De la Guerra Plaza.

Prominent in these annual Old Spanish Days Fiesta parades was another revived legacy of the Hispanic era, the gold-colored, white-maned palomino horse, also then emerging as an important Santa Barbara symbol. The first president of the fiesta, rancher Dwight Murphy, singlehandedly recovered the palomino from its virtual disappearance as a type: the equestrian equivalent of George Washington Smith's revival of Andalusian architecture. Raised in Montecito by millionaire parents, Dwight Murphy regained his health in his early twenties by serving from 1905 to 1907 as a ranger in Los Padres National Forest. Marrying Santa Barbaran Grace Price, the daughter of a local judge, Murphy returned to Pittsburgh to run the family's railroad equipment company, which was eventually sold at a handsome profit. Shortly before the First World War, Murphy moved back to Santa Barbara, a gentleman of leisure, not yet forty and very interested in ranching and horse breeding.

In 1920 Dwight Murphy purchased property in the Santa Ynez Valley near San Marcos Ranch, which he named Los Prietos in honor of the 1845 Mexican land grant Rancho Los Prietos y Najalayegua which had held the earliest title to the property. At Los Prietos Murphy set about reviving the ancient golden palomino of Spain, Mexico, and Spanish California, a horse revered by the Spanish aristocracy since the days of Ferdinand and Isabella. With the assistance of Francis T. Underhill, architect and expert breeder, Murphy scoured the West from Texas to Washington in search of brood mares with the golden color and white mane of the nearly vanished equestrian type. Following Underhill's advice, Murphy bred and rebred his mares and their offspring from a stud he had located in Ventura County, an offspring of Elias "Lucky" Baldwin's great racing horse, Rey del Santa Anita. With Underhill's guidance, Murphy introduced a cross-breed of light sorrel Arabian into the re-emerging palomino strain to counter any ill effects from inbreeding. After five years of experimentation, one of Murphy's mares dropped a perfect palomino specimen, the stallion El Rey de los Reyes, the King of Kings, number one in the Palomino Registry which could now be established.

In Murphy's palominos, featured so prominently in the first and the following Old Spanish Days Fiesta, Santa Barbarans experienced yet another deliberately realized connection to the Spanish past. Here on the streets of a California city pranced the ceremonial royal horse of Spain, golden and triumphant.

Around Santa Barbara riding was a very pragmatic way of life on working ranches where the horse still earned its keep into the 1920s, and a more stylized response among sportsmen and recreational riders. Everyone rode, it seemed, dressed either in Western or Spanish attire. Even Senator McAdoo, Wall Street and Los Angeles lawyer turned Santa Barbaran, donned Western garb and rode a palomino across the hundreds of miles of bridle trails crisscrossing *tierra adorada*.

At the center of this riding cult stood artist John Edward Borein, himself a former cowboy in California and Montana and a protégé of Charles Fletcher Lummis. Borein initially maintained a studio near the adobe of Alexander

Harmer. Later, when the El Paseo complex opened, Borein moved there, where he produced well-regarded watercolors and etchings on Southwestern subjects, which he sold directly or through galleries across the country. Doing well, Borein built for himself and his wife a New Mexico-style adobe, La Barranca, on the mesa overlooking the Santa Barbara Channel. He chose a pueblo-style architecture for his home, importing two Hopi artisans up from the Southwest to help design and build it, because Borein believed that Spanish Revival as practiced in Santa Barbara was sentimental and unfaithful to the genuine traditions of the Southwest. Thus Borein belonged, like his friends Alex Harmer and Carl Oscar Borg, and to a certain extent Lummis himself, to those who envisioned Santa Barbara as Santa Fe on the Pacific—Spanish but linked to Native American traditions as well—in contrast to the to the Spanish romance that represented the preferences of the urban genteel. Even in affluence, Borein played the cowboy. Rolling his own cigarettes with Bull Durham, he featured modified ranch attire, even at El Paseo, and liked to tell long cowboy stories, most of them humorous, some of them true.

By the late 1920s Borein had positioned himself as a resident celebrity in Santa Barbara and the special spokesman for its ranching heritage. Deliberately theatrical in personality and style like his mentor Lummis, Borein easily made and kept friends with similar dispositions. Especially active in the Ed Borein circle were artist Charles Russell, another Westernizer; humorist Will Rogers, another cowboy performer, whom Borein converted into an avid Santa Barbaran (Max Fleischmann's polo matches in Montecito also helped); actor Leo Carrillo, the great-great-great grandson of founder José Raimundo Carrillo; writer Irvin S. Cobb, another country boy doing well in New York and Hollywood; and local notables such as Thomas Storke, Max Fleischmann, Dwight Murphy, longtime county supervisor Sam Stanwood, and others. Borein consolidated the Santa Barbara identity in its more virile, aggressively Southwestern orientation, all so perfectly expressed in the cult of riding and the palomino. He also linked up the local establishment to Hollywood, where he had excellent connections, and in this helped further embellish Santa Barbara as a resort for the film colony.

From these linked friendships and this common identity with the Spanish legacy and from riding itself, which served them both, emerged another ritual in the already stylized Santa Barbaran calendar, the yearly rides of the Rancheros Visitadores, the Visiting Ranchers, which, thanks in great part to Ed Borein, began in May 1930. Originally, some sixty-plus Santa Barbarans made the five-day ride, a stylized recreation of the visits of groups of *rancheros* and *vaqueros* from *rancho* to *rancho* in the Spanish era, to help one another with the spring roundup. Ed Borein initiated the idea and was joined on the first trek by the local oligarchy. Even on its first ride, Los Rancheros Visitadores recapitulated and ceremonially celebrated the synthesized, mythologized levels of the Santa Barbara alternative. From the Spanish era rode Adolfo Camarillo and Leo Carrillo. Representing the mixed Spanish-Yankee era rode Thomas Storke and T. Wilson Dibblee. From the American frontier period rode J.J. and Harry Hollister, Reginald Fernald, and Joel Fithian. Colonizing wealth was represented by Max Fleischmann and Dwight Murphy; political authority by Supervisor Sam Stanwood; and in Irvin S. Cobb, the upscale Hollywood resort Santa Barbara was also becoming. Within the decade Los Rancheros Visitadores, headquartered in the Covarrúbias Adobe, had grown to an organization of five hundred riders divided into eighteen different messes, or camps, each camp with its own chuckwagon and support staff. Assembling before Mission Santa Barbara each May for an early morning blessing, the riders moved out at the call "Ride Rancheros!" from the president, for a five-day procession along the Santa Ynéz River from ranch to ranch—San Marcos, Juan y Lolita, Alisal, San Fernando Rey, and the other *ranchos* of *tierra adorada*—ending the trek at Mission Santa Inés. Spectators into the thousands gathered each year to watch the annual departure from the Mission, with its colorful assembly of hundreds of horses and riders, many of them in charro suits or cowboy garb. Once again, Santa Barbara had evolved for itself another stylized connection to an idealized Spanish past, a time when *rancheros* and *vaqueros* rode the hills and canyons and stream beds of *tierra adorada*.

7

This men's-club version of the good life celebrated Santa Barbara as possessing some connection, however tenuous, with the authentic Spanish frontier. In its basic dynamics, Los Rancheros Visitadores was not a real roundup but a dude ranch in motion, a resort experience. By the late 1920s, the resort metaphor had prevailed over Santa Barbara in a manner suggestive of one important side of the California identity, as also evident in Carmel, Pebble Beach, Laguna Beach, and Palm Springs. One came to Santa Barbara (provided one had the means) in search of enjoyment, not work. Stylized in architecture and custom, pastoral and aesthetic, Santa Barbara—and by implication a segment of Southern California as well—lacked substance and reality. It was an *anacapa* illusion of mountains, seashore, and channel; of Andalusian architecture, polo fields, tennis courts, golf courses, hotels, costumed festivals, and ceremonial pageants such as the ride of Los Rancheros Visitadores in May; the Semana Náutica in July, when Navy ships anchored offshore were greeted by hundreds of yachts sailing forth from Max Fleischmann's breakwater; and the Old Spanish Days of August. In a subtle but very real way, Santa Barbara, a Southern California alternative (or, as many Santa Barbarans would insist, a South Central Californian alternative, they arguing that their region was not Southern California at all but the southern terminus of coastal Central California whose northern terminus was Santa Cruz), Santa Barbara stood in danger of having themed itself into irreality, into a permanent condition of *anacapa*. Was Santa Barbara, was coastal Southern California, real after all? One might legitimately ask this, and many did. And further more: was it in the American temperament to base a culture solely on beauty and the pleasure principle?

Literary journalist, aspiring novelist, and critic Edmund Wilson of New York was asking these questions during two Santa Barbara sojourns, the first in February 1924, the second from October to December 1928. Wilson warmly admired his host Edward Paramore, a retired businessman, and later wrote a long obituary for him for the *New Republic*. A Yale man, Paramore had read, traveled, inherited some money and made even more. In so many ways, Paramore epitomized the virile, assertive American businessman of the more successful sort—an entrepreneur, a yachtsman who had qualified on a wide variety of sailing ships, a skilled anecdotalist with a wealth of stories redolent of the varying textures and personalities of American life and a perfect ear for dialect. Yet Paramore seemed to have little to do in Santa Barbara, Wilson complained, to channel his considerable energies. What, after all, was there to do except go to the beach or to parties? As for himself: "I could not really accept a life that had no aim except drinking and laughing."[7] Wilson also feared the effect Santa Barbara might have on his friend Ted Paramore, his host's son and like his father an interactive mixture of Yale and Santa Barbara.

In his friend Ted's dilemma of choosing between an active life in New York versus the Santa Barbara alternative, Wilson envisioned and sketched into his notebook the possibilities of a novel about Santa Barbara and its temptation to escape: "The highballs they had on the beach—and the sun dropping into the Pacific—their underclothes blowing about them and gulls flapping overhead—so far from the war—so far from business—so far from the troubles of the world—with only the enormous sea and the spacious Pacific landscape—living and rejoicing in life among the primordial magnificence of the world. What had he really cared then, what could he ever really care, for politics or society or learning—so long as he had that happy life to go back to, that life of eternal sun—the Pacific at night, not violent against the shore, but insistent and wild like the high sun."[8]

Four years later, Edmund Wilson was back, in pursuit this time of Ted Paramore's former girlfriend Margaret Canby, a Santa Barbaran whom Wilson would soon marry. Staying at a beach house in the nearby seaside suburb of Carpinteria near Margaret Canby's home, Wilson worked on *I Thought of Daisy* (1929), a novel of Greenwich Village, and pursued Margaret Canby amidst the distractions of the beach and the social season. "I have a little house here on the beach," Wilson wrote his editor Maxwell Perkins at Scribner's, "and have done nothing but read, write and swim. The weather is beautiful and all the days are exactly alike. The calm Pacific spaces are excellent for work—I always feel cramped in New York. But if you stayed out here very long, you would probably cease to write anything, because you would cease to think—it isn't necessary out here and the natives regard it as morbid."[9]

While in Santa Barbara Wilson looked up his old Hill School classmate Albert Isham, a wealthy bachelor with a neo-Pompeian mansion in Montecito and a Moorish-style beach house in Carpinteria, complete with minaret, designed by George Washington Smith. Wilson found the Moorish beach house an eccentric film set. The thought of Isham working out in the gymnasium of his pseudo-mosque on the shores of the Pacific, rich, struggling to stay thin, lingered in his mind as a visual parable worthy of recording in his notebook. Even the beauty of the area impressed Wilson as strangely insubstantial and unnourishing. "Dawn at Carpinteria," he noted, "with the answering pink and blue of sea and sky (the pink against the blue sky a little cheap and ugly—too pretty) with the mountain in the middle. Swimming at sunset—how soft the islands lie—Santa Cruz and Santa Rosa—on the dreamy misted horizon. The sun makes the water pink against its own blue, and the islands are blue against the sun's pink, against the western sky. An earthly paradise—a little soft and cloying—the seascapes are bonbons for the eye."[10] It was soon time for Edmund Wilson to return to New York.

For those remaining, such as the characters in Hugo Ballin's novel *Dolce Far Niente* (1933), Santa Barbara could become a formula for idle days. Inspired by Norman Douglas's novel of decadence on Capri, *South Wind* (1917), Ballin depicts Montecito-Santa Barbara as a Southern Californian Côte d'Azur of enervating *dolce far niente*. Ensconced in their sun-splashed mansions, Ballin's characters pursue an easy agenda of dilettantism, sunbathing, dinner parties, drinking, and sexual intrigue while somewhere out there in the rest of America a Depression rages. Mention Santa Barbara, travel writer Charles Stephen Brooks observed in 1935, and "it is likely that the excited eye of your fancy, instructed by the talkies and other gossip, will alight on marble pools and stairways (Hollywood's commonest symbols of our nation's bloated grandeur), on Spanish houses that out-castle the palaces of Europe, on satin apartments larger than a city railway station where a whole company at dinner could be swallowed by lofty walls without the slightest wiggle of their gilded Adam's apples."[11]

Brooks struggles to counter this image with proofs that Santa Barbara was also an everyday working city filled with everyday working Americans; but he seems himself only half-convinced. The image of Santa Barbara that most lingers in his mind is that of a leisurely late morning in the restaurant of the El Paseo as polo players, a retired senator from an eastern state with a young lady on his arm, a Hollywood actor, an affluent cattle rancher, a handful of artists, and tanned and beautiful women of all ages drift in for cocktails and luncheon. "To find another group so smart," Brooks admits, "one would need to visit a best resort of Europe."[12]

IV

LIFE AND LETTERS
IN THE SOUTHLAND

But I had other and better reasons for being pleased that I had come to live in Los Angeles. I soon came to know an interesting group of intellectuals: painters, writers, bookmen, designers, architects, and journalists, most of whom had arrived in Southern California at about the same time I did. In sober fact, we became the first "bohemians" of modern Los Angeles.

The Education of Carey McWilliams (1979)

11

Opinion and the Aristocracy of Art

The Search for Common Ground in Emergent Los Angeles

On the evening of Wednesday, 5 February 1930, a group of intellectuals met for dinner at the Taix Restaurant in Los Angeles to discuss the progress of *Opinion*, the journal they had founded together the previous October. As business manager and recording secretary, the bookseller Jacob Israel Zeitlin took notes and, three days later, distributed a memorandum of the meeting. Zeitlin's memo dealt with the problems—circulation, costs, article selection, deadlines, proofreading—normally expected from a fledgling journal in a fledgling city. What was unusual, however, was the decision to increase the board of contributing editors from twenty to thirty in an effort to win a wider acceptance. *Opinion* was not so much an embattled journal (destined to fold within the year, to everyone's embarrassment) as it was a groping on the part of a loosely affiliated group in the direction of its own identity and a forecast of the intellectual coming of age of Los Angeles. *Opinion* collapsed, Jake Zeitlin later remarked, because its editors had too many opinions. It took more than good will to launch a magazine, much less a movement.

The men and women to whom Zeitlin distributed his memo had little in common except Los Angeles. Politically, the *Opinion* circle included the left (Carey McWilliams, Herbert Klein), the liberal center (Judge Leon Yankwich, Zeitlin himself), and the far right (Phil Townsend Hanna, José Rodríguez). There were even a crypto-anarchist (Louis Adamic) and an aesthetic falangist (Merle Armitage) on hand to round out the perimeters of received opinion. Occupations ranged from impresario (Armitage), to architect (Lloyd Wright), to journalist (Salvatore Baguez, Paul Jordan-Smith, Hanna, McWilliams, Rodríguez), to lawyer (Yankwich), to graphic artist (Grace Marion Brown), to bookseller in Zeitlin's case. "*Opinion* has no particular axe to grind," ran an early editorial. "It seeks rather to grind all axes." By August 1930 everyone's axe had become no one's axe, and with articles and funds in short supply *Opinion*, after trying to regroup itself as a quarterly, folded. (Fifty-five years later Zeitlin was still lamenting the fact that Los Angeles had still not developed a first-rate journal of criticism and opinion.)

The creativity expressed by *Opinion*, however, did not disappear. Like a river blocked from one channel, it flowed into a dozen or more other outlets. *Opinion* might fold, but the painting, the poetry, the architecture, the literary journalism, the bookmanship—all of it so attuned to a mood, a belief, a hope that Los Angeles's time was about to arrive—this continued, and by the late 1930s an impressive creative presence had been achieved in and on behalf of the City of the Angels.

As diffuse as the *Opinion* circle was, as diffuse and indeterminate as Los Angeles itself, it did enjoy an informal headquarters downtown on Sixth Street at the bookstore "At the Sign of the Grasshopper," designed for Zeitlin by Lloyd Wright. In Zeitlin himself, a craggily handsome 28-year-old poet and bookseller (had satyrs been permitted in ancient Israel they would have resembled this small, dark, curly-haired, hawk-nosed sensualist hierophant), the *Opinion* circle found more than the business manager for the short-lived journal or the proprietor of its headquarers. Creative Los Angeles found in Zeitlin an emblem, a principle of aspiration and continuity, a listener, a patron, a friend. By the late 1930s Zeitlin had become the center of what he later described as a small Renaissance, Southern California-style. From this perspective, the *Opinion* circle was really the Zeitlin circle and as such it did not fold in 1930 with the magazine but lasted for another fifty-plus years, as long as Zeitlin himself, as the energized center of artistic Los Angeles exclusive of the film industry, where Zeitlin also had strong connections.

Born in 1902 in Racine, Wisconsin, Zeitlin grew up in Fort Worth, Texas, where his father owned a vinegar business. An orthodox Jew, Zeitlin Senior intended his son for the rabbinate, or at least for Acme Vinegar, the family company, but young Jacob had come under the spell of the Chicago Literary Renaissance, the poetry of Carl Sandburg especially, and had determined to leave Fort Worth for either Chicago or the emergent Chicago on the Pacific, Los Angeles. By 1925, when he was twenty-three, a high-school dropout writing literary reviews for the Fort Worth *Star-Telegram* and secretly married as well (his pregnant wife was still living with her parents, not daring to inform them of her situation), he chose in favor of the City of the Angels, flipping a coin, he later tells us, to make the final choice of destination. Announcing their marriage to Edith Motheral's parents, Zeitlin shipped his pregnant bride by train out to friends in Los Angeles in April 1925 and followed along the next month as an hitchhiker, with only his tenuous connection to the *Star-Telegram* as an introduction to the city. "I was stunned," he later recalled of his first entry into the City of the Angels. "I had never been in a city where there were such crowds. I was completely dazzled by the enormous numbers of different kinds of people and how they streamed down the sidewalks and across the streets. And I remember the first time I went downtown, Edith had to take me by the hand and lead me across the street."[1]

Capitalizing on his short-lived assignment to send to Fort Worth a series of Los Angeles profiles, Zeitlin secured an interview with Marco Newmark, the son of Harris Newmark, author of the classic *Sixty Years in Southern California* (1916), the Pepys' Diary of Los Angeles, and an active local historian in his own right. Newmark introduced Zeitlin to Charles Fletcher Lummis, then nearing the end of his life, and in the meeting of the two—the 66-year-old Hispanicizer, quintessentially Harvard, WASP, and Republican behind his sombrero and charro suit of green corduroy; the 23-year-old Russian Jew from Fort Worth, a Democrat, a Sandburgian populist—two Los Angeleses, the day-dream capital of Ramona Land and the jazzy Jazz Age capital of what would soon be known as the Coast, faced each other and, as it turned out, passed the torch.

Lummis, however, arrived in Los Angeles in 1885 with a fully secured job as city editor of the *Los Angeles Times* and was greeted at Mission San Gabriel by no one less than the boss himself, Harrison Gray Otis. Zeitlin, by contrast, had a terrible time getting started, although the details of his Horatio Alger struggle do in retrospect seem allegorically Southern Californian. Broke upon arrival, he took a job as a bus boy in a Boos Brothers Cafeteria, from which he was fired for eating an orange. He then went to work as a gardener at the Doheny estate at Number Eight Chester Place, with his pregnant wife slaving away all day as a caretaker at the St. Catherine Apartments in Hollywood—sweeping, dusting, vacuuming, even doing the laundry—in exchange for rent. Smelling of the fertilizer he had spent the day spreading, Zeitlin was asked by the landlady to enter the St. Catherine by the rear door. His child, a daughter, was born in the indigents' ward of the county hospital, and the horror of this experience remained present in his consciousness throughout his life as the symbol of the desperation of those first days in Los Angeles. Evicted from the Hollywood apartment by a landlady who did not want a crying baby on the premises, the Zeitlins moved to a small apartment near USC. It burned down. The couple found a third domicile on Landa Street at the north end of Echo Park in a redwood bungalow with a view of the Los Angeles River, the railroad yards, Forest Lawn, and the San Gabriel Mountains to the northeast.

Zeitlin, meanwhile, turned to peddling books at the Holmes Book Store on West Sixth Street. He was fired for incompetence. After an equally brief career with the book department of May Company, he found his niche as a retail clerk in the book department of Bullock's department store, working under the supervision of June Cleveland, a kind-hearted bear of a lady who drilled Zeitlin in the fundamentals of the trade. At Bullock's, Zeitlin earned $27 a week and made his first contacts with the literati of the city, who in turn became the nucleus of the *Opinion* circle. As a fledgling impresario connected to the one retail trade which is respected by all authors, the selling of books, Zeitlin also arranged Los Angeles appearances for visiting celebrities such as Vachel Lindsay, Edgar Lee Masters, and Carl Sandburg.

Within a year of his arrival, the aspiring poet/bookseller had established himself as a sympathetic presence in reading and writing Los Angeles. It was a minor presence, to be sure, in a minor town, literarily speaking; but both Zeitlin and Los Angeles were young, and everything seemed possible. Zeitlin eventually lost his Bullock's job when he developed a spot on his lung and had to enter the Barlow Sanitarium, his fees there paid by Jewish charity. When he emerged, he had no recourse but to take to the road as a consignment salesman for Dawson's Book Store, peddling books from a satchel to the book collectors of the city.

However déclassé, this itinerant Willy Loman life proved a blessing in disguise, for it got Zeitlin out of the retail trade and into the fine printing, antiquarian, and special-edition market and introduced him to the book-collecting elite of Los Angeles, which meant the elite, period; for book collecting had already by the 1920s achieved a special intensity in Los Angeles as a ritual of cultural identity. The very thinness of cultural institutions, the absence, that is, of competing forms and institutions, conferred on books a special valence as material embodiments of traditional culture. The boom of the 1880s brought to the city its first generation of educated booksellers—Frederick Jones, a Haverford-educated "evolutionary socialist," as he described himself; J.W. Fowler, an astute businessman; C.C. Parker, resplendent in wing collar (he also taught elocution); James Wallen Smith, the first to specialize in Californiana and rare imprints; Henry W. Collins, who had apprenticed in rare books at Edwin Parsons and Sons in London—and these sellers in turn took the book culture of provincial Los Angeles into its second phase after its first era of frontier simplicity.

The third stage was represented by the creation of establishments such as Vroman's in Pasadena and Dawson's in downtown Los Angeles, two enterprises as sophisticated and encompassing as any bookstores in the United States. Adam Clark Vroman and Ernest Dawson were in their differing ways each intellectuals possessed of the ambition to found bookstores that would also become cultural institutions. Having moved to Pasadena in the health rush of the late 1880s on behalf of his tubercular wife (a sweet Quaker woman who did not long survive the transplantation), Vroman became a convinced Pasadenan of the outdoorsy Arroyan mode. An ardent photographer of the desert Southwest, Vroman also ran a Kodak agency out of the bookstore he established in 1894 after his wife's death. Serving the bookish population of Pasadena and environs, Vroman's became in the 1920s the largest bookstore in the West. While Vroman's did handle a small stock of rare or unusual books, its primary business was in current trade imprints.

Dawson's, by contrast, was founded in 1905 as the first antiquarian bookstore in the Southland. A native Californian born in San Luis Obispo and raised in Los Angeles, Ernest Dawson first learned the book trade as a teenaged clerk in the store of the Dickensian Henry Ward, where the ardent Los Angeles High School student read as many books as he sold. By 1905 Dawson was in business for himself at 713 Broadway, stocking his store with his personal collection. Through his partner, Henry Collins, an Englishman, Dawson absorbed the spirit and lore of antiquarian books as Collins himself had absorbed them in the seventeen years he had spent with Edwin Parsons and Sons in London. From the learned ex-Londoner, Dawson soaked up the equivalent of a first-rate university education: the books themselves, first of all, which Dawson read and mastered with rapidity, but also the mood of London, as Collins remembered it from the 1860s and 1870s. Regaled by Collins with descriptions of visits to Parsons by such eminent Victorians as Carlyle, Dickens, Dobson, Thackeray, Gladstone, Millais, Morris, Hunt, Burne-Jones, and Whistler, Dawson read their books and studied their lives. The material fact of the surviving books in his hands, transformed by the alchemy of Collins's reminiscences, engendered in Dawson a sense of civilization coming to Los Angeles via antiquarian books and other distinguished imprints in which the texture of civilization itself, its intellect and imagination, was preserved for the enjoyment of the citizens of this emergent English-speaking city on the Pacific.

In December 1907 Dawson published the first rare-book catalogue ever to orginate in the City of the Angels. In 1911 he traveled to the city of his imagination, London, where he augmented his stock from the more than two hundred antiquarian booksellers in the city. He was especially thrilled to haunt Edwin Parsons and Sons, whose ambience, remotely absorbed, had been such a strong influence on his young life. At Parsons and elsewhere, Dawson bought for his own establishment Fox's *Book of Martyrs*, an elephant folio of Irving's *Alhambra* illustrated by Owen Jones, and first editions of eighteenth- and nineteenth-century literary and historical classics. Case after case of notable books were packed by Dawson for shipment by steamer around the Horn through the Straits of Magellan to Los Angeles, the vanguard of a hegira of imprints that would by 1940 transform the region into a library and book-collecting center of international importance.

In the spring of 1922 Ernest Dawson, by now the grand man of antiquarian books in Southern California (Father Dawson he was beginning to be called, not just for his deanship in the business, but because of the Methodist-inspired utopian streak that ran so deeply in his nature) moved his store to 627 South Grand Avenue, at the corner of Wilshire Boulevard. Although tea was served every afternoon at three, Dawson eschewed a snobby pseudo-Anglophilic ambience as being inappropriate to Los Angeles. In the genuinely haphazard manner of Continental booksellers, Dawson was constantly uprooting and marking down his stock to insure turnover. Many a fine bargain found its way into Dawson's sale bins, which he kept constantly replenished as a means of attracting repeat visits by browsers. Bred to the dynamics of retail as a teenager, Dawson grew nervous if a book, no matter how distinguished, remained on his shelves for more than six months. Few did.

The dynamic retail culture of Dawson's, its availability to foot traffic, was repeated in other bookstores in the downtown area, conferring on the central portion of Los Angeles a bookish atmosphere quite unexpected in such a new city. Sixth Street functioned as the axis for this retail book trade, with its scores of stores and estimated half-million books for sale through the 1930s, and the nearby Public Library served as its architectural rallying point. Booksellers' Row began with Fowler Brothers just off Pershing Square and meandered through establishments such as the Jones Book Store, C.C. Parker's, Ralph Howie's (snug, like Toad Hall, with a cozy leather armchair taking up a significant portion of the floor space), the Argonaut, the Abbey, Warren Rodgers' place (during the Depression, Rodgers tried door-to-door selling before seeking refuge as a clerk in the post office), Lofland & Russell, the Holmes Book Company (a blockbuster store founded in 1900, with endless shelves containing thousands of secondhand books), and finally, at the northwest edge of the sector, Dawson's itself, favored haunt of the carriage trade.

This, then, was the world Jacob Israel Zeitlin entered in 1927 after a number of months in the satchel-retail end of the book trade: an almost eighteenth-century world of grouped bookstores functioning as retail outlets, publishers, clubs, and coffee houses. Zeitlin's first store was a small cubbyhole at 567 Hope Street, near the Public Library and the Bible Institute. It rented for $35 a month. Jake's friend Lloyd Wright designed the shelving. Father Dawson provided much of his start-up book stock at 10 percent above cost. Visiting Los Angeles in 1928, the London dealer Ernest Maggs left a Shakespeare folio for Zeitlin to sell on commission. Two years later, when Zeitlin moved to larger quarters at 705½ West Sixth Street next door to the Dover Hotel, Wright designed a second exquisitely arranged bookstore and mini exhibition gallery (Edward Weston photographs would soon be selling there for $2 apiece) long remembered for its taste.

With Wright's help, Zeitlin created an harmonized environment in which each effect—from the grasshopper logo (chosen from the protagonist of Aesop's fable who fiddled and sang in the summer and therefore froze and starved in the winter) down to the orange and black wrapping paper and the fragrance of Zeitlin's Turkish cigarettes—was calculated to bespeak literary culture in a Los Angeles setting. With each move westward, following Los Angeles in its expansion to the sea—to 614 West Sixth Street in 1935, to a converted carriage house at 624 South Carondelet in 1939, to a converted red barn at 815 North La Cienega Boulevard in 1948—Zeitlin took care to recreate the atmospheric setting of these first two establishments; for Zeitlin knew that he was not just in the business of selling books. Like Sylvia Beach in Paris, albeit without her rich array of civic and literary resources, Zeitlin was selling place, identity, the possibilities of bohemia and the literary life in the City of the Angels, newly arrived just as he had arrived a few years earlier, hitchhiking in from Texas.

The magic worked. The spell was cast. One by one, then two by two, the Zeitlin circle formed. It was not a movement or an ideology in the formal sense of the term, as the failure of *Opinion* made perfectly clear. It was, rather, a sense of moment and place, of things happening or about to happen in literature, architecture, the fine and performing arts, and scholarship. It was a bohemia with a left wing and a right, with dissident and established elements intersecting within the Zeitlin radius with an eclectic catholicity of power, wealth, taste, preference, and opinion highly unusual in groupings of this sort.

The inner twenty of the circle, those supporting contributors who each put up fifty dollars to launch *Opinion* in late 1929, constituted a most fascinating grouping. José Rodríguez and Carl Haverlin were in radio, then entering its golden era. Leon Yankwich was a Superior Court judge, later promoted to the federal bench; Will Connell, a photographer and literary critic; Joseph Pijoan, a professor of art history at Pomona College. Kem Weber designed furniture. Lloyd Wright was following in his father's footsteps. Henry Mayers was a printer; Herbert Klein, a print journalist; Lawrence Tibbett, an aspiring opera singer from Riverside, where his family had pioneered in citrus. Louis Samuel, a quondam bookseller and Hollywood agent, entered the circle thanks to his girlfriend Grace Marion Brown, a graphic artist with a beautiful face, pharonic in its reserve, who occasionally let down her impassivity and surprised everyone with her salty speech.

Another supporting contributor, Walter Arensberg, had begun life as an aspiring poet but soon used his wife's considerable wealth to collect post-Impressionist art (Klees, Duchamps, Picassos, Renoirs, Kandinskis crowded the Arensberg home in Hollywood, even the closets) and to establish a foundation intended to prove that Francis Bacon wrote the works of Shakespeare, an idée fixe to which Arensberg had been converted while serving as an English instructor at Harvard.

While the Arensbergs represented major wealth, a supporting contributor such as Louis Adamic kept body and soul together working as a watchman in the pilots' station office on the breakwater at the entrance to San Pedro harbor. Adamic liked such work (he previously served as a fire-watcher in the San Gabriel forests above the Los Angeles plain) because it left him plenty of time to read and write and talk to visitors such as Carey McWilliams, who frequently came over to San Pedro from Los Angeles, the two aspiring writers talking about books and other things late into the night as firefly-ships skimmed serenely in and out of the harbor and a distant foghorn intoned its melancholy and mysterious music.

Born in 1899 in present-day Yugoslavia, Adamic fled the Austro-Hungarian Empire just before the war. During the war Adamic served in the American Army and had settled in San Pedro after his discharge because of the Dalmatian fishing colony in the vicinity. A massively read freelance intellectual, with both right- and left-wing dimensions to his thought, Adamic wrote for Mencken occasionally while working on short stories, a novel set in Byzantium, a history of theology, a life of Christ, and reports from the local scene, most of them excoriating.

In the 1930s, along with McWilliams, Adamic would emerge as a skilled non-fiction writer, debuting in 1931 with *Dynamite, the Story of Class Violence in America*. Like McWilliams, Adamic was spending his twenties in the 1920s reading, thinking, experiencing, beginning to write, gathering energies for an extraordinarily creative outburst of writing during the Depression. Adamic had been sent to see McWilliams by the San Francisco poet George Sterling, a good friend of the late Ambrose Bierce, whose biography McWilliams was writing. Typically, Adamic had presented himself without introduction to Sterling at the poet's inner sanctum, the Bohemian Club in San Francisco, and they had gotten on famously. When you return to Los Angeles, Sterling had suggested, look up Carey McWilliams, a USC law student who was up here recently asking questions about Bierce. McWilliams and Adamic became close friends, each of them given to long well-read literary conversations and rambling junkets through the esoteric realms of Southern California cults whose gurus, swamis, prophets, and mystics they observed and catalogued with a mixture of ironic detachment and fascination.

Raised on a prosperous cattle ranch near Steamboat Springs, Colorado, McWilliams matriculated at the University of Denver at age 16 determined to act out a scenario from Fitzgerald's *This Side of Paradise*. Despite his tender years, he succeeded. In the spring of his freshman year he was expelled for throwing a rowdy St. Patrick's Day party. When the cattle ranch collapsed in the deflation of the beef market following the end of the war, McWilliams's father, a self-made capitalist of pre-Revolutionary Scotch-Irish Presbyterian stock, rigorous and exacting, died of the stress and shame of bankruptcy. Mrs. McWilliams thereupon sought the protection of her brother in Los Angeles, moving there with her truant son. Both Los Angeles and reduced circumstances helped young McWilliams focus his considerable talents and energies. No longer a spoiled rich kid, he went to work for the credit department of the *Times*, writing dunning typewritten letters to overdue advertisers at lightning speed. Throughout his life, McWilliams could type almost as fast as he could think. Like many journalists, in fact, he did his thinking primarily at the typewriter, the machine becoming an extension of his cranial self. This ability to produce high-quality first-draft copy at a rapid rate, together with the habit of thinking things through at the typewriter, made McWilliams a ferocious machine for the production of prose. How else could such a ceaseless activist edit the *Nation* for so many years while writing so many fine articles and important books?

In any event, all that was in the future. For the time being, McWilliams put himself through two degrees at USC while working a full schedule at the *Times* and writing for the *Daily Trojan* student newspaper, *The Wooden Horse* campus literary review, and the *Wampus* humor magazine. He also wrote literary profiles, at ten dollars apiece, for Samuel Clover's *Saturday Night*, and these essays of the mid- to late 1920s—profiles of his pal Adamic, of Jake Zeitlin as poet, of poet Hildegarde Flanner (another member of the Zeitlin circle, whose sister Janet would eventually cover Paris for the *New Yorker*), of Mary Austin, and Berkeley novelist Clarkson Crane—almost singlehandedly revived serious literary journalism in California, dormant since the fin de siècle.

Two contradictory strains ran parallel in McWilliams, law and literary journalism, and only when the Depression finally caught up with California and thus with him would McWilliams be able to synthesize the conflict. In the meanwhile, he advanced himself on both fronts. Literarily, he hung out with the Zeitlin gang, wrote for *Saturday Night*, the *Overland Monthly*, the *American Mercury*, the *Bookman*, the *Saturday Review of Literature*, and worked on his biography of Ambrose Bierce, which appeared in 1929. Through his mentor H.L. Mencken, McWilliams learned to respect regional American civilization, and no one mastered his region more completely than this young journalist, social historian, and literary critic. Meanwhile, the displaced one-time rich boy, anxious not to pass his life in the credit department of the *Times* or writing for peanuts for minor literary magazines, kept his eye on the main chance. Securing his law degree and passing the bar, McWilliams joined the heavily Princetonian law firm of Black, Hammack and Black headquartered in the American Bank Building at Second and Spring in the downtown, a blue-chip partnership specializing in oil and real estate with a clientele drawn mainly from Pasadena and San Marino. He also married Dorothy Hedrick in 1930, the proper daughter of a UCLA professor. For the time being, bohemia remained the dream of youth.

The calling which McWilliams was temporarily leaving behind, literary journalism, was also represented in the Zeitlin circle by the Tory men of letters Phil Townsend Hanna and Paul Jordan-Smith. In Hanna's case, the choice of literary journalism had not come easy. Born and raised in Los Angeles, Hanna had been forced by his parents into the pre-medical course at USC totally against his will. At the start of his second year of pre-medical studies, Hanna walked out of class one day and headed into the mountains. There he contracted a violent form of mountain fever which left him near death in a remote cabin. Carried down to safety, Hanna hovered in a hospital between life and death, and when he recovered it was at the price of a curved spine which bent his tall gaunt body forward like a question mark. No matter: his parents no longer demanded that he become a physician.

Joining the *Tribune* in 1915, Hanna moved on to the *Express*, the *Herald*, and then the *Times*, where he became night city editor at the age of 21. In

1919 he moved on to the position of general manager of the Associated Press for greater Los Angeles. Not for Phil Townsend Hanna, however, was there to be the sort of hell-raising, burn-out-early career common to newspaper life in the *Front Page* era.

In 1925, at the age of 30, Hanna became editor of *Touring Topics*, the magazine of the Automobile Club of Southern California. This meant that Hanna became the resident spokesman and arbiter of establishment Southern California, for in Southern California the automobile and its club stood as the very center of organizational life. Hanna soon made *Touring Topics* (*Westways* after 1934) an important literary and life-style magazine, remaining today in its files a mine of information and suggestion regarding the emergent culture of the Southland. For thirty-one years Hanna did for Southern California what Charles Fletcher Lummis did for a previous era in the *Land of Sunshine:* publish and promote its aspiring writers (M.F.K. Fisher, Carey McWilliams, Lawrence Clark Powell) and photographers (Will Connell, Edward Weston, Ansel Adams), explore its hinterlands, and, most important, help its life-style define itself through intelligent articles on gardening, architecture, wine and food, tennis, surfing, patios, barbecues, books, films, and automobile touring which still emanate from their bound pages the promise of American life, Southern California-style, in that era.

Of simple origins (his father, so anxious for him to go to medical school, held a minor position with Wells Fargo), Hanna delighted in his thirties to refashion himself as the archetypal clubman and political conservative. Taken into the California Club, the Sunset Club, the Zamorano Club, Hanna assumed an establishment identity. His brother had by then become a top corporation attorney, which eased Hanna's way in the making of social connections. When it came time to defeat Upton Sinclair's bid for the governorship of California in 1934, Hanna helped prepare the strategy that kept California Republican throughout the Depression. A man of many interests—photography, Gregorian chant, Mayan archeology, California history (he claimed to be the only man alive who had ever read through Bancroft's *History of California* in its seven-volume entirety), philosophy, psychiatry, medicine, desert flora and fauna—Hanna emerged as one of the accomplished conversationalists of his era, the Monckton Milnes of the Southland, the grand talker at the center of a thousand evenings. Not surprisingly, Hanna collected books, western Americana, and cookery (now in the library of Scripps College), which is how he first came into contact with Jake Zeitlin, who later distanced himself from Hanna because of their divergent political opinions. A streak of the dandy and the Don Juan surfaced in Hanna as well. Despite his calcified spine, he dressed with Adolph Menjou flair: the exquisite tailoring of his suit, the correctness of his collar and cuff links, the dazzling perfection of his tie and pocket handkerchief, diverting attention from his bent body and transforming him into Richard III at the bier of Henry VI, a paradoxically attractive troll, electric with underlying magnetism.

Publicly, Hanna's schooled sensuality surfaced in an erudite epicureanism that made him the high priest of the wine and food culture of Southern California that was soon to produce M.F.K. Fisher, the Virginia Woolf of cuisine. Writing under the name Savarin St. Sure, the assured chevalier of kitchen, cellar, and dining table, Hanna covered the wine and food scene of Southern California in a manner totally suggestive of a later age of refection journalism. He also edited *Bohemian Life*, a monthly devoted to fine food and drink. Hanna's knowledge in these matters was extensive and impeccable, and for years he ran the Los Angeles chapter of the London-based Wine and Food Society as a personal fiefdom, presiding over its dinners like a cardinal-protector celebrating founders' day with his order.

Hanna found a companion and conservative counterpart in the Zeitlin/*Opinion* circle in Paul Jordan-Smith, literary editor of the *Los Angeles Times*. An aspiringly aristocratic Southerner born in Virginia to pre-Revolutionary stock and raised in Chattanooga, Jordan-Smith studied for the Unitarian-Universalist ministry, taking his bachelor of divinity degree in 1908 from the Ryder Divinity School in Galesburg, Illinois. A succession of Midwest pulpits—Galesburg, Kansas City, Chicago—followed. Like so many creative citizens of Los Angeles, Jordan-Smith arrived in the City of the Angels already possessed of a strong Chicago experience, in his case, an intense involvement as a Chicago pastor and settlement house administrator, a part-time graduate student at the University of Chicago, and an aspiring novelist on the periphery of the Chicago Literary Renaissance. Trouble with women plagued Jordan-Smith into his fifties. A secret marriage drove him from Tennessee, and a messy and very public divorce cost him his pulpit in Chicago. He then moved to Berkeley, where he enrolled as a Ph.D. candidate in English while holding a temporary appointment in the local Congregational church. (Jordan-Smith's theology was flexible enough to accommodate the Trinity.)

While in the Bay Area, Jordan-Smith wrote *The Soul of Woman, an Interpretation of the Philosophy of Feminism*, published in 1916 by the San Francisco bookseller Paul Elder. In this manifesto the Universalist litterateur rhapsodized on the emergent higher feminism, vibrant, ethereal, pulsating with spiritual power.

Such idealism did not preclude more immediate attachments on Jordan-Smith's part, and once again he found himself involved in a scandal, in this case, an involvement with the jilted wife of the permanent pastor of the church where he was serving as *locum tenens*. The lady's name was Sarah Bixby Smith, and she happened to come from the most prominent family in Southern California. Some years earlier in Southern California, Sarah Bixby had married Arthur Maxson Smith, a Congregationalist minister whom she accompanied to

Honolulu when he was appointed president of Punahou College, a missionary institution. Amorous inclinations on the part of Reverend Smith towards certain Punahou coeds necessitated a hasty transfer back to Pomona College in Claremont, where he joined the faculty. When Reverend Smith later grew overly attentive to an au pair in the household, Sara Bixby Smith maneuvered her loving spouse north to First Congregational in Berkeley. From thence the indefatigable Reverend Smith decamped with a young lady parishioner, leaving Mrs. Smith to solace herself with Paul Smith (not yet Jordan-Smith), the curate with a taste for literature.

Learning of all this, the San Francisco newspapers spread the story of the two Reverend Smiths and the one Mrs. Smith across the front pages, prompting the embattled *locum tenens* to hyphenate his middle and surname to Jordan-Smith since, to make matters even worse, a second Reverend Paul Smith was occupying the pulpit of First Methodist in San Francisco. The combination of the feminist manifesto and the newspaper scandal made Paul Jordan-Smith persona non grata in the English department at Berkeley, presided over by Professor Charles Mills Gayley, who had already earned the scorn of both Frank Norris and Jack London for his priggishness. Paul Jordan-Smith found his fellowship lifted and his hoped-for second career as an academic in ruins.

No matter: Sarah Bixby Smith (no need to change her name when she remarried) owned a fourteen-room stone mansion in Claremont in eastern Los Angeles County, to which the couple repaired, bringing along Paul Jordan-Smith's already impressive personal library and, eventually, the eight children they had between them from their former marriages. With one stroke, this union, begun so scandalously, put the quondam Unitarian/Congregationalist minister at the core of the Southern California establishment; for the Bixbys were positively baronial in their land holdings, including the oil-rich Signal Hill. Paul Jordan-Smith was thus able to devote himself to a country squire's life of studious leisure and book collecting, which he had begun to pursue in earnest during his time in Chicago. Book collecting brought Jordan-Smith into the Zeitlin circle and, as in the case of Phil Townsend Hanna, the relationship remained cordial until strained by Jordan-Smith's increasingly ultramontane political opinions.

In the meanwhile, the Claremont squire, who lectured regularly in town at the UC extension, became a regular At the Sign of the Grasshopper. In 1934 Oxford University Press published Jordan-Smith's *For the Love of Books, the Adventures of an Impecunious Collector*, a delightful autobiography of bibliographical adventures revealing the non-pedantic erudition of this independent scholar. That same year Jordan-Smith also published *A Key to the Ulysses of James Joyce*, among the first such guides to appear in the United States dealing with this difficult work by an author whose miscellaneous learning, together with his temperament and sense of exile, spoke to something very deep in Jordan-Smith's own psyche. Jordan-Smith's real obsession, however, was not

Joyce but Robert Burton (1577–1640), the English country vicar who poured his titanic learning into *The Anatomy of Melancholy* (1621), a treatise on medicine and psychology which constitutes a storehouse of late Renaissance literary culture. Jordan-Smith made two lengthly trips to England, in 1920 and 1923, pursuing at the British Museum and the Bodleian and Christ Church libraries manuscripts and printed materials in support of the edition of *The Anatomy* which he was jointly editing with Floyd Dell. It appeared in 1927, bearing the title "Sometime Fellow in the University of California" beneath his name on the title page, a poignant suggestion of his blasted hopes for an academic career. In 1931 the Oxford and Stanford university presses jointly issued Jordan-Smith's *Bibliographia Burtoniana*, a scholarly key to the printed sources of Burton's treatise.

As satisfactory as this scholarship might be, it did not answer the question of career—What to do? What to be?—even when one has a rich wife. Fortunately, the literary editorship of the *Los Angeles Times* became available, and Paul Jordan-Smith, like Phil Townsend Hanna at *Touring Topics*, found an outlet and role beyond the limits of private scholarship. Along with Carey McWilliams, who had temporarily buried himself in the law, Paul Jordan-Smith became through the *Times* an important spokesman for the literary and intellectual life as it was asserting itself throughout greater Los Angeles and the Southland. The fact that he went through life more than half convinced that he was a failure, a failed novelist, a failed academic, was beside the point from the perspective of literate Los Angeles, which profited immeasurably from his wide knowledge of books and his concise reviews. He, in turn, had great faith in the future of the city which had granted him refuge and status. "If the place exhibits all the vices of the middle plains," he once noted, "it is also alive with the same eagerness in pursuit of an illusory progress and a conventionally idealized culture. I am convinced that there is much more familiarity with 'high brow' books in this too frequently berated city than in any other considerable center of population west of Chicago."[2]

Paul Jordan-Smith blossomed as literary curator to Los Angeles. In certain cases, Julian Hawthorne and Hamlin Garland, for example, he exercised a species of curatorial receivership for writers now past their prime, Garland feeling so lonely and forgotten in the sunshine, and Hawthorne knowing full well that his final claim to fame, after so much striving, remained the fact that he was Nathaniel's son. To read Jordan-Smith's autobiography *The Road I Came* (1960) is to re-experience the expatriate density of the Los Angeles literary life he reported upon and partially presided over. Locally represented by many of the writers in the Zeitlin circle, and by Upton Sinclair, himself a circle of one, this free-floating literary community included English writers attracted to the Hollywood market—Hugh Walpole, for example, working on the script for *David Copperfield* starring Freddie Bartholomew; visiting English authors, scouting out the possibilities of such employment—Rebecca West and John

Cowper Powys, among others; American writers having their books being made into films—Sinclair Lewis, Theodore Dreiser; writers working on scripts—F. Scott Fitzgerald, William Faulkner; and lastly, as the war approached, refugees such as Thomas Mann and Emil Ludwig, who became Jordan-Smith's friends. At a dinner party given by Upton Sinclair in honor of Rebecca West, Jordan-Smith got tight on bootleg cocktails and called Miss West's sometime love H.G. Wells "the Harold Bell Wright of England." At the same party, and fueled by the same cocktails, he provided an obviously infatuated Mary Miles Minter with an orchidaceously affectionate inscription to his novel *Cables of Cobweb*. When Miss Minter became involved in the William Desmond Taylor murder case, Jordan-Smith rued the indiscretion, fearing that the police might do a spot check of Miss Minter's library and discover in him a possible suspect.

Sarah Bixby Smith and Paul Jordan-Smith eventually moved from bucolic Claremont to a mansion on Los Feliz Boulevard. As generous as ever, Sarah built her husband a detached library and writing studio to the rear of the property. She also entertained with equal generosity, bringing under her social wing the various bohemias represented in the Zeitlin group, unifying them through her parties and authenticating their status via her own First Family approval. This interconnection of social strata was characteristic of bohemian Los Angeles partly because the oligarchy was itself so protean and assimilative. Few other cities of the period might show a doyenne such as Sarah Bixby Smith moving so sincerely and so unceremoniously in bohemian circles. This inclusiveness cut across political lines as well; for while Sarah was apolitical, her husband, a pacifist liberal in his pulpit days, active with David Starr Jordan of Stanford in the effort to keep America out of the European war, moved progressively to the right under the twin influences of his prosperity by marriage and the upheavals of the Depression.

As in the case of Phil Townsend Hanna, politics eventually put a distance between Zeitlin and Jordan-Smith, but for the time being such differences seemed entirely surmountable of an evening on Los Feliz Boulevard over pasta and red wine, with everyone, including the plumpish Sarah, dancing Nijinsky-like at the end of the evening, Jake Zeitlin leading the dance like an Hebraic satyr cavorting on a Samarian hillside to the cymbals and lyre of a passing caravan.

Unfortunately, Paul Jordan-Smith danced out of the house one day for good, leaving his comfortable life with Sarah for a less certain existence with his cousin Dorothy, Sarah now having lost two husbands named Smith to younger women. Characteristically, she refused to be bitter over this abandonment by the man whose children she had supported and whom she had kept in such comfortable circumstances for these many years. Ironically, she, not he, was to write the better-known book, *Adobe Days* (1925), which Jake Zeitlin's Primavera Press reissued in 1933. Two years later Sarah Bixby Smith succumbed after hideous pain to trichinosis brought on by a serving of steak tartare contaminated at the butcher's by pork left in the meat grinder.

2

In the late 1920s a Los Angeles group calling itself the California Art Club used to meet for a monthly Open Forum in the Hollyhock House designed by Frank Lloyd Wright for Aline Barnsdall in 1917 as a conference center for the arts. Spearheaded by Arthur Millier, art critic for the *Times*, the club was concerned with the theoretical and critical side of art and aesthetics. On the evening of 4 March 1929, a key member of the Zeitlin circle, impresario Merle Armitage, gave an electrifying address entitled "The Aristocracy of Art." Shortly thereafter Zeitlin published Armitage's speech as a bound pamphlet designed and decorated by Grace Marion Brown with assistance from typographer Grant Dahlstrom. Like so many good speeches energized by time, place, and occasion, *The Aristocracy of Art* is less impressive sixty years later in the cold light of print. Still, Armitage struck a chord, which was why Zeitlin published the speech, although he was later embarrassed by the elitism of Armitage's point of view, which contrasted so dramatically with Zeitlin's own Chicago School theory of the arts as an expression of democratic populism. Art, argued Armitage, is essentially aristocratic, which is to say, it is highly selective in its strategies and audiences. It is also its own autonomous frame of reference and need not justify itself through corroboration from politics, sociology, economics, or any other criteria, even ethics. In an effort to place his hyper-aesthetic modernism into an acceptably American perspective, Armitage argued that people insensitive to art come in all social classes and that people sensitive to art can likewise be found up and down the social scale. The aristocracy of art was not a matter of social position. It was a matter of sensitivity and perception. Despite these protestations, there is in *The Aristocracy of Art* more than a little of that crypto-falangist sense of art as an elite, ontologically autonomous defiance of the commonplace that pervaded so much of the modernist movement.

Even granting Armitage's distinction that common and uncommon people are found in all social conditions, one senses in the thought of the dynamic impresario a tendency dramatically at odds with a Los Angeles in which the Folks reigned triumphant. Los Angeles itself represented a triumph of the commonplace—which was precisely the point. Armitage's talk struck a chord in aspiring artists and aestheticians of many persuasions, even poet Jake Zeitlin, who was trying to bring the spirit of Carl Sandburg and Vachel Lindsay to the West Coast. The *Opinion* circle was pursuing its calling amidst what art collector Walter Arensberg described in *Time* magazine as "the most perfect vacuum America can produce"—by which he meant Los Angeles.[3] This vacuum had positive and negative effects and it both baffled and energized its protagonists. On the one hand, the vacuum of Los Angeles allowed people such as Arthur Millier of the *Times* and Merle Armitage to invent themselves in the first place, in a way that would perhaps be more difficult in Chicago, Boston, or New York.

Millier, for example, an English-born adventurer of a type common to Southern California, charming, versatile, self-actualizing, parleyed a job as a salesman with the Schmidt Lithograph Company, designers and printers of orange-crate labels, into the art editorship of the *Times*. Was this appointment proof positive of the arriviste nature of Los Angeles, or did it testify to the upward mobility and creative self-invention so dynamically possible in the Southland? Millier, it must be acknowledged, was himself a watercolorist and etcher of recognizable if minor talent and he did write well. In any event, the question of credentials and identity came to plague Millier in the long run. He abandoned his half-Native American wife and their three children, with whom he lived in picturesque circumstances in Santa Monica Canyon, and took to compulsive womanizing and drink. By the time it was over, Millier had lost everything, wife, children, job, and was living in a skid-row hotel room before he joined Alcoholics Anonymous and straightened himself out.

For all his ultra-high-brow posturing regarding the aristocracy of art, Merle Armitage was likewise an intermittently insecure product of self-invention: a glib Professor Harold Hill sort of fellow, ever promising to bring seventy-six trombones to River City but, unlike the hero of Meredith Willson's *The Music Man*, most often delivering what he said he would. Born in Waterloo, Iowa, in 1893 (everyone in Los Angeles seemed to come from the Midwest) Armitage enjoyed little formal education. He read and read at the local public library, however, helped in his book choices by Marian the Librarian (to continue the *Music Man* comparison) and dreamed of music and art, bright lights and the big city. After high school Armitage changed his name from Elmer to the more *recherche* anagram Merle and headed east to New York where, after Army service during the war (as a soldier Armitage excelled at shooting craps) he joined impresario Charles Wagner in arranging tours and appearances for figures such as John McCormack, Mary Garden, Rosa Ponselle, Arnold Schoenberg, and Igor Stravinsky. "Armitage," recalled his good friend Ward Ritchie, "was accused of occasionally using unethical schemes to get newspaper publicity for his clients in the cities in which they were scheduled to appear. He admitted to planting occasional fictitious gossip to keep his clients' names in the news, but denied responsibility for an episode that salvaged a tour which he was handling for a Russian Opera Company. The tour had begun on the West Coast with lagging success and was in deep red by the time it arrived in Chicago. Armitage had had to borrow from several friends just to pay the railroad fare to get the troupe there from a disastrous engagement in the South. On the opening night of the opera *The Tsar's Bride*, there was a wild Cossack ballet with eight girls doing dizzy dervish whirls. During this frenzy one of the girls lost her panties and unaware continued the dance quite bare bottomed. The publicity that followed salvaged the tour."[4]

Quite something else, indeed, from the aristocracy of art! Merle Armitage represented a fascinating combination of con man and talented impresario, *poseur* and producer, which perhaps only the Los Angeles of the interwar era could fully assimilate. He arrived there in 1920 in his early twenties, fresh-faced behind his Harold Lloyd tortoiseshell glasses, with just a suggestion of later weight in his cherubic features, looking for new horizons and aware that self-invention might occur more easily in the Southland than in New York. Among the first things Armitage did was to angle himself into a position of influence in the Los Angeles Philharmonic, displacing L.E. Behymer as music advisor to patron William Andrews Clark and maestro Walter Henry Rothwell. "His ineptness," Armitage later claimed of Behymer, the man who first brought serious music to Southern California, "plus his greed to acquire some of the Clark cash, soon led the discerning Walter Henry Rothwell to protest the appointment. In desperation, Clark fired Behymer and turned to the woman who had for years been his secretary at the Clark's hotel, a public stenographer named Caroline E. Smith. Her husband, 'Chummie,' later to be known as George Leslie Smith, hauled sand for a contractor. He quickly advanced to wearing kid gloves, carrying a stick, and assisting his wife in *running* the orchestra." Wisely, the Smiths deferred to the young impresario from the East, or so Armitage later claimed in his autobiography: "Soon I was being literally courted by them, and overnight, sans salary or authority, I became Godfather of the Orchestra. Busy as I was launching a new business in an unknown community, the actual orchestral management fell on my shoulders. The Smiths made no single move without consulting me."[5]

The business Armitage was referring to was the association he formed with Los Angeles music company owner J.T. Fitzgerald (sheet music and score-books, musical instruments, Victrolas, and records) to bring name performers to the City of the Angels, splitting the profits fifty-fifty. Armitage later helped organize the Los Angeles Grand Opera Association in conjunction with the San Francisco Opera being founded by Gaetano Merola. To everyone's astonishment Armitage frequently filled the ochre-colored, neo-Moorish, six-thousand-seat Shrine Civic Auditorium on West Jefferson Boulevard for grand opera performances.

Between 1920 and 1941 when he left to become a procurement officer for the Army Air Corps, Armitage brought scores of operatic figures to the City of the Angels. He also successfully promoted modern dance (Ruth St. Denis, Martha Graham), concert appearances by composers (Igor Stravinsky, George Gershwin), and a lecture tour by Eleanor Roosevelt. Personable when he chose to be, amazingly energetic, Armitage won the friendship of most of his clients. George Gershwin sent him an autographed comic self-portrait, the only such sketch known to exist. In order to get Maria Jeritza to agree to go to Los An-

geles against the wishes of her husband, Armitage pursued her aboard the
Twentieth Century Limited leaving New York for Chicago on the evening of
23 March 1928. Charmed, Jeritza signed an obliquely worded but legally binding agreement which Armitage hastily dictated to a train stenographer to appear
in Los Angeles in productions of *Fedora*, *Tosca*, *Turandot*, and *Carmen*.

Throughout his career as Los Angeles impresario, Armitage acted with a
sense of mission mingled with the profit motive and fueled by his monstrous
egomania, all this enlivened by the love/hate relationship he bore towards his
adopted city. "For many years," he later recalled of these Los Angeles years,
"I had a ringside seat from which to watch the incredible performances of the
most case-hardened climbers, opportunists, social gate-crashers, and assorted
lunatics that have ever existed outside the asylum. Today, we would call many
of these 'Members of the Establishment,' for actually they comprised the banking, business, professional solid citizens, they and their more or less frantic
wives, mistresses, and girl friends."[6] No one to Armitage's way of thinking
epitomized the nouveau and arriviste quality of the City of the Angels, its
bumptuous Babbittry, better than *Express* publisher and University of California regent Edward Dickson, who as a board member of the Opera Association
protested to Armitage that *Così fan tutte* was too long to sit through. Armitage
blamed Dickson for losing the Arensberg Collection to the Philadelphia Museum by refusing to build a museum for it at UCLA, as he and the regents
had initially promised. In calling for an aristocracy of art, Merle Armitage was
not only authenticating an idea, or even his own sense of personal superiority.
He was making a valid challenge to Los Angeles to pursue the arts on their
own terms, which were the terms of knowledge and a commitment to excellence devoid of boosterism. Do it right, Armitage was saying, with a very strong
sense of the potentiality of Los Angeles as a capital city of the arts. Pursue the
arts on their own terms and not as a species of regional development.

In the interim, as he waited for Los Angeles to heed his message, Armitage
enjoyed himself with Rabelaisian gusto. A lover of Packard automobiles (he
owned seven throughout his life), Armitage took Jake Zeitlin and Arthur Millier on a motor tour of California in October 1927 partly financed by Lawrence
Tibbett, the Riverside baritone. Motoring up the eastern side of the Sierra in
Armitage's Packard roadster, the trio ate their way up through the Basque and
lumberjack restaurants of the region, visited Reno, then kept themselves warm
with cognac as they crossed the Sierra Nevada and descended into Sacramento.
There they visited Maynard Dixon, busy at work on the murals at the State
Library. In San Francisco they dined at Coppa's, headquarters of that city's
bohemia, with Albert Bender, a Dublin-born insurance man and arts patron,
and Hugo Friedhofer, soon to win fame and fortune as a composer for the
movies but then barely getting by as a picture-palace organist. Zeitlin, Armitage, and Millier later partied with Bender, the photographer Edward Weston,
and scores of others in their rooms at the Chancellor Hotel. Returning to Ne-

vada via the Mother Lode country, they retraced the trail of Mark Twain's *Roughing It* (1872). At Gold Hill, Nevada, they visited an abandoned bank, its floor strewn with certificates and papers, which Zeitlin, ever the collector, scooped into a cardboard box. In the years to come, this collection of financial and mining memorabilia brought Zeitlin hundreds of dollars in retail trade.

Returning to the Bay Area, the trio visited Charles Erskine Scott Wood, the former Indian fighter turned writer and left-wing activist, whom Jake Zeitlin took as his *beau ideal*, seeing in Wood and his consort the poet Sara Bard Field the embodiment of affluent literary bohemianism mixed with left-liberal politics that would soon become the model for his own life. From Los Gatos they motored south to Carmel to call upon Robinson Jeffers at Tor House: an evocation of another identity as well, for Zeitlin still had high hopes, as he later put it, of drawing the long bow of poetry for himself. As a clerk at Bullock's, Zeitlin had persuaded his boss June Cleveland to order generous quantities of *Roan Stallion* from Liveright, which he personally recommended to customers as the work of a major American poet. He had also written Jeffers in Carmel to state his high opinion of Jeffers's talent and to tell him how the book was moving at Bullock's. Remote, olympian, capable of being as impassive as the stones of the Carmel/Big Sur seacoast, Jeffers also recognized the importance of the retail trade, not to mention the *Los Angeles Times* as represented by Millier. The poet received Zeitlin, Armitage, and Millier warmly, even garrulously—especially when Una Jeffers was not around to oversee the legend.

The trio ate and drank commodiously on this pilgrimage through literary and artistic California thanks to Tibbett's money and Armitage's insistence. Like Phil Townsend Hanna, Armitage prided himself on his knowledge of food and drink. In 1939 he published two food-related books, *Post Caviar*, a memoir of food and Russian opera, and *Fit for a King*, a collection of recipes by Alfred Lunt, Lewis Mumford, Edward Weston, Raymond Loewy, Rockwell Kent, Jean Hersholt, and James M. Cain, among others (Armitage loved celebrities), together with essays by, among others, himself, Louis Untermeyer, and the Abbé Ernest Dimnet, a scholarly French priest whose acquaintance reflected Armitage's lifelong fascination with Roman Catholic theology, culture, and liturgy. Teilhard de Chardin later became an acquaintance.

Observant Catholicism, however, would have proved impossible for someone of Armitage's sultanic inclinations. Armitage might possibly have had one wife prior to coming to Los Angeles. His first visible consort on the Coast was the dancer Fanchon, a leggy beauty responsible for the lavish Fanchon and Marco dance review which played movie palaces such as Grauman's, Loew's, and the Paramount in conjunction with the featured film performance. All in all, Armitage had six wives, possibly seven if one accepts Zeitlin's story that, swimming off the Santa Monica pier one afternoon, Armitage proposed to a girl he had just met in the water, the two of them swimming ashore, looking each other over before getting dressed, then driving down to Tijuana in Armitage's Packard for the ceremony with José Rodríguez in tow as a witness. Another possible union had no legal status, being self-performed by Armitage and the lady in question atop a mountain overlooking Prescott, Arizona. In between his own second and third marriages, Zeitlin roomed with Armitage and found himself amazed at the eclectic procession of starlets, society matrons, and demimondaines with whom Armitage maintained active relationships. Visiting Armitage in another lair, a bungalow on Orange Street, Ward Ritchie was intrigued by the impresario's super-king-sized bed, a rare event in the early 1930s. It was covered, he remembered, with a purple spread. Armitage told Ritchie that he needed the oversized bed because he was living at the time with two women, simultaneously. Armitage's most constant wife in the 1930s was the comedienne turned painter and illustrator Elise Cavanna, who played a comic foil opposite W.C. Fields, another close friend, in the Ziegfeld Follies and in many early Fields films. Elise adored Armitage, which he appreciated, and the couple built a small home overlooking Silver Lake in Los Angeles, which then became the party headquarters of choice for the Zeitlin circle.

By this time, Armitage had become an impresario and designer of books, with an emphasis on art books, as well as a promoter of music and dance. As testimony to the soon fatal conflict of views in the *Opinion* circle, it must be noted that Paul Jordan-Smith loathed non-representational art. For a number of years in the late 1920s, in fact, Jordan-Smith submitted hoax abstract paintings under the pseudonym Pavel Jerdanovitch, beginning with "Yes We Have No Bananas," made by swirling tubes of yellow paint across an empty canvas. When Pavel Jerdanovitch began to get serious attention, including the January 1926 cover of *Art World* published in Chicago and an entry in a French guide to contemporary art ("among the best artists of the avant-garde"), Jordan-Smith, believing that he had proved his point, broke the story in the Los Angeles *Times*.

Merle Armitage, by contrast, worshipped Klee, Picasso, Kandinsky, Miró, and the other modernists. His own collection of prints and drawings numbered more than six hundred. When the performing arts business slowed down in 1932 due to the Depression, Armitage, not overly burdened by his duties as manager of the Philharmonic Auditorium, began to package and design a series of studio books, most of them subsidized by the artists, dealing with the avant-garde painters of Southern California. Doing this, Armitage discovered that among other things he was an extraordinarily gifted graphic designer: a pioneering figure, in point of fact, in the graphics revolution which was breaking out in the 1930s and which Armitage would accelerate after the war when he became design director for *Look* magazine. Interestingly enough, it was Grace Marion Brown's innovative designs for *The Aristocracy of Art* which first got Armitage interested in book design. Conservative typographer Grant Dahlstrom later disassociated himself from the design of this imprint, believing it to be too self-consciously experimental.

Once Armitage became active in the field, however, he soon outstripped most of his Southern California contemporaries, achieving a national reputation as a book designer in the avant-garde. As an impresario Armitage viewed the printed page as a species of theater, the *mise-en-scène* through which a book communicates. Theatrically, Armitage played off dark print against bold white spaces in a balletic flow of emptiness and imagery. Abstract, kinetic, quintessentially modern, Armitage's designs made fundamental departures from formats that had been in effect through four and a half centuries of printing. Thus at age 40, beginning with his studio art books (Edward Weston, Rockwell Kent, Eugene Maier-Krieg, and others) and continuing through a hundred-plus other books and magazines, Merle Armitage found his own personal art form in graphic design. He became, in effect, the Raymond Loewy of the printed page, one of the important figures in the evolution of graphic design as a language coequal to type in the communication of symbols and messages—and recognized as such by his peers, who elected him president of the American Institute of Graphic Arts.

But that was after the war. Ahead of Armitage lay a whole new life, his own, in his own art form, with more books to design, more eclectic celebrities to collect (Teilhard de Chardin, Lucius Beebe, Joan Crawford, the Duke of Windsor), a few more wives to marry—and all this after distinguished wartime service with the Materiel Command of the Army Air Corps, impresarioing the flow of airplanes from factories to the theaters of operations, and, later, as the chief of the Army Air Corps rehabilitation program for fliers suffering from combat fatigue. The versatility of the man continued to be astonishing. Having invented himself in Los Angeles, Major Merle Armitage, USAAF, was ready for vigorous service in the second world war of his career. Improbably, he flourished in the military.

3

Jake Zeitlin, meanwhile, had given up the struggle to find in poetry the métier Armitage was to find in design. For Zeitlin poetry represented the promise of regional vernacular America. Growing up in Texas, he mastered the guitar and innumerable cowboy songs, so much so that Carl Sandburg, then in the process of gathering material for *The American Songbag* (1927), stayed up late one night in February 1922 at the Adolphus Hotel in Dallas, recording with his own system of manual notation cowboy songs which Zeitlin played and sang until four o'clock in the morning. Zeitlin himself, then only twenty, had aspirations to becoming a poet in the Sandburgian manner: purely American, that is, without recourse to European or English themes, forms, allusions, or idioms. Zeitlin brought this urge with him to Los Angeles, and throughout the 1920s he thought of himself primarily as a poet. Zeitlin's poem "Gypsy Nights," first published in *The Southwest Review*, was included in the anthology *Best Poems of 1926*. In 1927 the Lantern Press, operated by San Francisco bookseller-publishers Theodore Lilienthal and Leon Gelber, issued a collection of Zeitlin's verse under the title *For Whispers and Chants*. Impressively designed by the Grabhorn brothers, Edwin and Robert, and illustrated by Valenti Angelo, *For Whispers and Chants* was greeted in Los Angeles as the harbinger of a poetic career about to skyrocket. Paul Jordan-Smith reviewed it enthusiastically in the *Times*. Reading this review, Carey McWilliams sought out Zeitlin for an interview in *Saturday Night*, which appeared on 19 November 1927. McWilliams found in Zeitlin a poet from central casting, living dramatically on a hilltop near Elysian Park. All the poetry America needs can be found in simple people and ordinary things, Zeitlin told McWilliams. He was writing in the tradition of Sandburg, Robert Frost, and George Ade, vernacular poet of the Indiana countryside.

Retrospectively, one can delineate the apparent contours of conflict that most likely terminated Zeitlin's poetic career. Throughout his long life, Zeitlin had little to say about his withdrawal from poetry. "I could not draw long bow," he might remark, a sadness coming into his eyes, followed by a hardening of his face and: "I prefer not to talk about it." First of all, there was the matter of the poetry itself. It was good but not great. Even Carl Sandburg, who wrote the foreword, felt the necessity of suggesting that Zeitlin might want to revise some of his lines as the years went on. On the other hand, while Zeitlin's poetry was good but not great, it was as Sandburg suggested good enough, sometimes even better than that, and if he worked on it, it would invariably get better.

Or would it? Did Zeitlin already realize that pulling the long bow would elude him? And what about the birth of his first child in the indigents' ward of the county hospital? He would later make allusions to this traumatic experience in his elliptical remarks as to why he left poetry. Or was it the hard times of the Depression, as Carey McWilliams suggested, which forced Zeitlin to spend less time courting the muse and more time minding the store? Was bohemia itself the problem, especially in that Zeitlin as the center of the circle functioned almost rabbinically as counselor, consoler, and confidante, each generous contact dissipating something of his own concentration and force? Or was there a cultural problem as well?

Zeitlin might very well dedicate *For Whispers and Chants* "to Texas, great treasure-cache of poems and legends," but he was now living in Los Angeles and hearing a much different music. The poems of this solitary publication show a transition: from the "Train Portrait of an East Texas Farm Woman" with its we-the-people minimalism, to the "Fragment of an Elemental Symphony" with its more luxuriant subject matter and imagery. For better or worse Texas and Sandburg did not translate to Los Angeles, which was Art Deco and

Hollywood and sunshine warming the villas of Beverly Hills and Bel-Air, not the flat plains and windmilled ranch houses and tumbleweeds of West Texas. Zeitlin might play his guitar and sing cowboy songs for Sandburg back in Dallas; but the music of Los Angeles was George Gershwin performing *Rhapsody in Blue* at the piano on a starry night at the Hollywood Bowl or Duke Ellington jamming for the dancers at the Cocoanut Grove. The ordinary people of Los Angeles, the Folks, had left behind much of their American Gothic dignity when they sold out the farm and drove to the Southland. Elements of eccentricity, held in place in traditional settings and cultures, now surfaced, creating a new type whose suburbanized folksiness eluded, for the time being at least, Sandburgian celebration. Soon after publishing it, Zeitlin grew hostile to Merle Armitage's *The Aristocracy of Art*. No wonder: Armitage was arguing a case diametrically opposed to the Sandburgian ideal which had itself collapsed for Zeitlin amidst the exotic eclecticism of Los Angeles.

This conflict between Zeitlin as bardic poet and the non-bardic aspects of Southern California pervades a novel which caused great stress in the Zeitlin circle, *The Flutter of an Eyelid* by Myron Brinig, published in 1933. Later described by Zeitlin as "a sulky baby elephant," Brinig was a minor novelist from Montana and a sometime writer for *The New Yorker* in his early thirties. Zeitlin introduced Brinig to the circle, most extensively in its beach-going mode at a swimming club at Palos Verdes. Grant Leenhouts, the manager of the club, wrote short stories for the *American Mercury*. Another member of the swimming circle, Tone Price, was a beautiful lesbian who had followed Zeitlin out from Texas. Others included Merle Armitage, the photographer Edward Weston, and Lee Jarvis, a former Olympic swimmer. Hanging out with the group, Brinig was soon accepted by them as another aspiring Southern Californian. Not so: Brinig loathed the place and the Zeitlin circle, and in *The Flutter of an Eyelid* he savaged Southern California and the Zeitlin group in its beach-party phases.

Looking to do a *South Wind* set on the beaches of Southern California, Brinig centered his *roman à clef* on Caslon Roanoke, a New England novelist who has fallen in with a group of seaside bohemians in a town very much resembling Palos Verdes or Laguna Beach. At times *The Flutter of an Eyelid* becomes surreal, even hallucinatory; through it all, however, one recognizes in the cavorting, drinking, nude-swimming, fornicating cast of characters caricatures of the individual members of the Zeitlin circle, including, most obnoxiously, Jake Zeitlin himself in the figure of Sol Mosier, a Jewish antique dealer obsessed by Walt Whitman's and Carl Sandburg's America.

Even by the most forgiving of standards Brinig's caricature of Zeitlin edges into anti-Semitism. At best it was an insulting betrayal of the man who had introduced Brinig into the circle. Securing a set of advance galleys, Zeitlin got a lawyer, Homer Crotty, a prominent Los Angeles book man, who contacted a lawyer friend of his in New York, John J. McCloy, later the High Commissioner to Germany after the Second World War; and the most offensive portions of Brinig's savaging of Zeitlin were removed under threat of a lawsuit. Left in, however, were the sequences in which Sol Mosier, tiring of his Hebraic conscience, takes to the open road in search of the beauty and meaning of America. The sequence constitutes a mean-spirited parody of Zeitlin's hitchhiking hegira to Los Angeles from Fort Worth, which Brinig learned of from Zeitlin himself. It also presents Mosier, and by implication Zeitlin, as psychologically and imaginatively displaced: a serious-minded seeker amidst eccentrics and lunatics, on the golden country-club shores of frivolous WASP Southern California, forced finally to walk back the way he came.

4

Mixing apocalyptic and environmental modes, Myron Brinig ends his novel with an earthquake collapsing California into the sea: not the first or the last time this fate would be dealt by fictionists to the Pacific Coast. Less spectacular but more relevant were the collapse of *Opinion* and Zeitlin's poetic hopes. Neither failure left its protagonists without hope. For Zeitlin, there remained the calling of books and the patronage of literature. For the *Opinion* circle there remained the memory of the good French dinners at Renee and Jean's on West Sixth Street (dinners seventy-five cents, a bottle of wine for half a dollar) where the talk was all of the next issue and the promise of Los Angeles. "What we had in common was the love of fun and argumentation," Zeitlin later remembered of the *Opinion* circle. "We were gregarious. We were all ambitious and had the desire to excell and to be recognized."[7]

For Zeitlin, recognition would now come for his skills as a bookseller and his central importance as patron and sponsor of the cultural and intellectual life of Los Angeles in the 1930s and beyond. The poet became the cultural godfather, which yielded its own form of creativity. There remained as well the question of private life, for as Samuel Johnson wisely observes, the object of all public striving is that one might be happy at home. Zeitlin's first marriage ended sadly in 1929 when his wife, diagnosed as an advanced manic depressive, demanded a divorce. His second wife, a judge's daughter of French Jewish background, demoralized by the devastating effects of the Depression on the couple's financial and personal life, asked for a divorce in 1937. In October 1939 Zeitlin married Josephine Ver Brugge, a native Kansan of Dutch descent, very beautiful, very serene, who loved the business side of bookselling. Both the marriage and the business partnership, incorporated in 1942 as Zeitlin & Ver Brugge Books, flourished until Zeitlin's death in September 1987. From 1938 to 1948 the Zeitlins occupied a remodeled red brick carriage house on the Earl estate at Carondelet and Wilshire (Aldous Huxley made the dedicatory speech) with spacious quarters upstairs for Jake, Josephine, and their three children. In 1948 Zeitlin & Ver Brugge moved to an oversized Pennsylvania Dutch red barn on La Cienega Boulevard which in turn became an ambient mecca for locals and visitors alike.

In addition to rare books and a growing international subspeciality in the history of science, Zeitlin used his adjunct galleries to promote the visual arts. He was among the first to sponsor exhibitions for photographer Edward Weston, then a resident of Glendale. Rockwell Kent became a friend of Zeitlin's after doing the engravings for the Primavera Press edition of Lawrence Clark Powell's pioneering study of Robinson Jeffers, and was in turn regularly exhibited at Zeitlin's bookstores. Merle Armitage had introduced Kent to Zeitlin and the three palled around together until Kent's leftism and Armitage's rightism broke out into personal bitterness in the late 1930s and Zeitlin, instinctively siding with Kent, also became estranged from Armitage.

Zeitlin also encouraged the work of sculptor Gordon Newell, who had trained under Bay Area sculptor Ralph Stackpole in the late 1920s. Married to screen actress Gloria Stuart, who together with film director Delmer Daves linked the Zeitlin set to Hollywood, Newell belonged with Zeitlin to an artists' circle that met for talk, instruction, live-model painting, and late-night parties at the hillside ranch house of printer and book designer Ward Ritchie. Near the Disney studios, a few hills away from the still pastoral Silver Lake district, the neighborhood where Ritchie lived was the closest thing Los Angeles had at the time to an artists' quarter. Developed as the Semi-Tropic Spiritualists' Tract (perhaps the most exotic subdivision of them all!), this montane wedge at the northern edge of the Echo Park district, called the Hill by its residents, had survived as a semi-rural pocket of modest hillside homes a brief distance from the center of the city. The night-time diorama of light from central Los Angeles proved one of the major attractions of living in this urban woodland where small wildlife—raccoons, possums, birds—abounded in the thickets and chaparral. It is not surprising that the Hill became the bohemian quarter of the 1920s and 1930s, a pastoral alternative to Bunker Hill in the downtown.

Other members of the artists' circle on the Hill included painters Fletcher Martin and Alexander Brooks; woodcut artist Paul Landacre; sculptors Gordon Newell, Archibald Garner, and George Stanley; muralist Barse Miller; watercolorist Theodore Criley; the versatile painter, illustrator, printmaker, and muralist Thomas Craig; Merle Armitage; writer/librarian Lawrence Clark Powell; Hollywood director Delmer Daves; Disney studio composer Leigh Harline ("When You Wish Upon a Star"); Disney animator Tee Hee (his very name bespeaking a Disney character); and Jake Zeitlin. Many in this informal circle of amateurs and professionals had or would soon have notable careers. George Stanley, for example, went on to create the moderne statuette Oscar for the Academy of Motion Pictures Arts and Sciences, one of America's best-known icons.

Of all these artists, the association between Zeitlin and wood engraver Paul Landacre was professionally, and perhaps even personally, the closest. Landacre's wife Margaret became Zeitlin's secretary in 1928. Because her husband had been crippled by disease while an undergraduate at Ohio State, Margaret Landacre, a Quaker woman radiant with goodness, served as Paul Landacre's total other self. She even helped him pull the lever on his handpress. Landacre patiently taught himself wood engraving in the mid-1920s after taking courses at the Otis Art Institute. He worked initially in linoleum before mastering the difficult but subtle medium of wood. Within the decade Landacre was in the front ranks of this revived artform, which encompasses the skills of engraving, printing, and the art of the book. A genius in a minor medium (his contemporary and counterpart in England was Eric Gill), Landacre created engravings of primal, titanic power, as if to catch in the drama of landscape or the movements of female nudes or powerful animals the physical elasticity which disease had denied him. He presented these woodcuts through books or printed them directly with a nineteenth-century hand press on soft, fibrous Japanese paper, selling them as signed limited editions.

In February 1930 Zeitlin gave Paul Landacre his first one-man show. Zeitlin introduced Landacre to Edward Weston, with whom Landacre's work had much in common despite the two artists' differing media. Through Zeitlin, Landacre also met New York art critic Carl Zigrosser, who got Landacre's work carried by the Wyeth Gallery and later reviewed him enthusiastically in *The Artist in America* (1942). Zeitlin also introduced Landacre to Merle Armitage, a connection that would prove very valuable when Armitage was put in charge of recommending artists for WPA employment, and to screenwriter-director Delmer Daves, who would also prove an important patron.

In 1931 another Zeitlin connection, printer/publisher Bruce McCallister, issued Landacre's *California Hills and Other Wood Engravings*, printed directly from the artist's woodblocks by McCallister's skilled pressman Harold Young. A masterpiece in its genre, *California Hills* complimented and counterpointed the scenic photographs of Edward Weston and the poetic evocations of Robinson Jeffers and remains today an outstanding artistic achievement of the Depression era. Forced by his medium to capture essentials, Landacre depicted the hills of the California coast in their intrinsic structural power as the architecture of the planet itself. In 1933 Zeitlin commissioned Landacre to engrave the illustrations for the Primavera Press edition of Marguerite Eyer Wilbur's translation of Alexandre Dumas's Gold Rush novel *A Gil Blas in California*. The result: another masterpiece, one of the most beautiful books of the decade.

When the Depression caught up with the Landacres, Zeitlin and Delmer Daves organized a subscription society through which subscribers received a monthly print in return for regular fees. A timely advance from McCallister allowed the Landacres to purchase a one-bedroom redwood ranch house on the Hill which clung to its steep incline like an eagle's aerie and gave them a spectacular view of the city. They enjoyed their home together, a couple of truly symbiotic attachment on every level, until her death from cancer in 1963 and his botched suicide a short time later. The pilot light ignited a houseful of gas, and so instead of dying quietly and painlessly of asphyxiation as he had intended, Landacre lingered for a fortnight in the burn ward.

All this patronage of Landacre and other visual artists, including Eric Gill, whose work Zeitlin prominently featured, takes on an increased significance when considered in the context of the Los Angeles of this era. Museum and gallery culture came slowly to greater Los Angeles, especially if one counts the Huntington collection as, initially at least, a New York City-based enterprise. The Los Angeles County Museum functioned under a mixed mandate of science and art that hobbled distinction in either area in spite of the continuing efforts of William Preston Harrison, the wealthy son of the five-time mayor of Chicago who had been spectacularly assassinated on the last day of the Chicago World's Fair. As a former Chicagoan, Harrison struggled as patron, director, and honorary curator to point the Los Angeles museum towards an art-oriented program analogous to that of the Art Institute of Chicago. Meanwhile, he collected American painters—Robert Henri, George Luks, George Bellows, John Sloan, Charles Demuth—together with French impressionist, post-impressionist, and contemporary painters, while doing everything in his power to raise the level of art consciousness in greater Los Angeles.

Fortunately, the bulk of Harrison's collection remained intact and under local jurisdiction. Unfortunately, the also impressive collection of Aline Barnsdall (it included works by Cezanne, Gaugin, Matisse, Renoir, Utrillo, Braque, Dufy, Picasso, and Grandma Moses) was distributed for sale by her heirs in 1949 after her death and was thus lost to the city. Even while the Barnsdall collection had been on loan to the county museum, it had been casually treated and remained uninsured by the host institution. Not until the arrival of Dr. Wilhelm Valentiner in 1946 would the Los Angeles County Museum enjoy a level of direction sophisticated enough to attract and keep major bequests. Louise and Walter Arensberg, meanwhile, angered by the failure of UCLA to house their world-class collection of European and American moderns in a campus museum as initially promised, were beginning negotiations with the Philadelphia Museum of Art which were formalized in 1950.

Los Angeles, in other words, remained comparatively undeveloped as an interactive, supportive art community through the 1940s. While distinguished collections were continuing to be, or were beginning to be, assembled in the 1930s—the collections of Edward G. Robinson, Charles Laughton, Josef von Sternberg, Billy Wilder, Fanny Brice, and Vincent Price come to mind—the museum world of Los Angeles was provincial and sluggish and the gallery scene in its infancy. Thus Zeitlin's advocacy of the visual arts, together with his willingness to show and sell the work of so many local artists, helped pioneer the role of the gallery and gallery owner in Los Angeles.

Science, however, not art, paid the bills. In contrast to art, science was flourishing in the Southern California of this era. At Cal Tech in Pasadena

Albert Einstein was lecturing and might have not been lost to Princeton had Cal Tech come forward with an attractive offer. Over in the Cal Tech astronomy department in the Mount Wilson Observatory, Edwin Hubble and his colleagues were inching towards the theory of the expanding universe. Atop Mount Palomar astronomer George Ellery Hale was building the most ambitious telescope yet known to mankind in order to be able to verify, qualify, or disqualify the theories of Hubble and others. For a number of interactive reasons, California and the sciences were made for each other. Jake Zeitlin caught the fever in its bibliophilic dimensions, becoming in the postwar years an international figure in this sector of the rare-book trade. Between 1934 and 1967 he assisted Professor Herbert M. Evans of Berkeley in assembling seven great collections in the history of science, totaling 20,000 volumes. Zeitlin also helped Robert B. Honeyman of La Jolla assemble a history of science collection which Zeitlin in turn sold through Sotheby's between 1978 and 1981 for $4 million in cash: a warm-up, as it were, for Zeitlin's sale in 1983 of 144 illuminated manuscripts to the Getty Museum in Malibu for $30 million—the largest single sale by a rare-book dealer anywhere up to that time.

Working with physician collector Elmer Belt provided Zeitlin the added satisfaction of helping assemble collections that remained in Los Angeles. Raised and educated in Los Angeles, Belt developed into a bibliophile so ardent that he employed his own librarian to assist in the collections he housed in a separate wing of his medical offices at 1893 Wilshire. Belt maintained parallel interests in the general history of science, Florence Nightingale, the noted American neurologist and novelist Silas Weir Mitchell, and Leonardo da Vinci. Each of these collections eventually went to UCLA, the renowned da Vinci collection being received into specially created rooms in the Edward Dickson Art Center. Eventually, Zeitlin's own archives, 27 large boxes containing 81,000 separate items, went to UCLA as well.

These archives document Zeitlin's many involvements and remain a treasure trove for future historians. Zeitlin's career as a bookseller and cultural catalyst constituted his highest art form and the archives constitute its material expression. But did his busy life yield its intended result? Yes and no. Yes, he helped Los Angeles emerge as a national book and library center. Yes, he helped innumerable artists and writers and other creative aspirants toward fulfillment. And yes, because of his marriage, his fatherhood, his many friendships, his professional success and associations, the persistence of his health and the vigor of his appetites, he lived as fully as possible in his personal life. But did the Los Angeles he envisioned in the 1920s and 1930s come about? Did his dream materialize?

As late as the mid-1970s Zeitlin was still regretting that Los Angeles as of yet possessed no nationally ranked magazine or review. "This was, and still is," Zeitlin remarked, "one of our greatest deficiencies. We will continue to rank as a less than first-rate cosmopolitan cultural center until we develop a medium through which our creative writers, scholars, and critics may communicate with the larger world."[8] The collapse of *Opinion* still rankled. It was perhaps some lingering peevishness over the failure of *Opinion* that led Zeitlin to erase from consciousness John Entenza's Los Angeles-based magazine *Arts & Architecture* which, beginning in the 1940s, functioned on the cutting edge of international design.

When it came time to evaluate the totality of energies and crosscurrents unleashed in Los Angeles in the late 1920s and 1930s among locals as opposed to the American or European expatriates, Zeitlin was very, very cautious. At most, he noted, it had been a small Renaissance, Southern California-style— this gathering of books and building of libraries, this nurturing of literature and the art of fine print. "Whether this small renaissance is truly a prelude to cultural greatness," Zeitlin admitted, "I cannot predict. . . . Between the mere indulgence of vanity, the accumulation of treasures as a child hoards bright colored stones and sea shells, the display of affluence in order that others might be made humble or envious, and the proper use of such riches, there is a wide gulf. If our libraries, our book clubs, our printers and our collectors can have the vision properly to use what the vagaries of geography and history had given us towards the greater glory of the free human mind, then we may hope for a renaissance, albeit small and Southern California-style. If they do not, then all that I have boasted shall be as the sand-covered ruin of Shelley's *Ozymandias*."[9]

The Book Triumphant

Bibliophilia and Bohemia
in Greater Los Angeles

The Los Angeles into which Jacob Israel Zeitlin immersed himself as a cultural force nurtured a broad community of people who cared passionately about books and literature. Their ambition did not represent the literary and intellectual regionalism of an earlier generation. It was not, that is, an effort to define the world in terms of Southern California. It was, rather, an effort to bring the world into Southern California, to seek out the symbols and artifacts of older civilizations so as to possess and re-express them locally. The movement began with grand collectors and it encompassed the bohemias of downtown and Hollywood and went on to embrace a generation of aspiring fine printers, writers, and poets. A number of important institutions were established in the process, and when it was over Los Angeles was an even more complete place.

The story begins with the collecting activities of Henry Edwards Huntington and the founding of the Huntington Library, although even with this beginning there was a previous context. Historian Hubert Howe Bancroft was not the only late nineteenth-century Californian to collect on a grand scale. Even more impressive, San Francisco mining engineer and real-estate developer Adolph Sutro assembled what was at the time of his death in 1898 the largest private library in the world—350,000 volumes. Born in Prussia in 1830, Sutro left for California in 1850 and became fabulously wealthy as a result of his involvement in the successful effort to tunnel through to the Comstock Lode in Nevada. He next involved himself in San Francisco real estate and at one point owned fully a twelfth of the city limits. Dreaming of establishing an Athenaeum research library in San Francisco, Sutro began to travel and collect in the early 1880s. Entire libraries were soon finding their way back to San Francisco from England, the Continent, Palestine, the Levant, Mexico, and South America. Stored in two warehouses on Battery Street and the Montgomery

Block the collection languished in litigation and neglect after Sutro's death in 1898, and in April 1906 earthquake and fire destroyed the bulk of it. Of 350,000 volumes, only 70,000 survived, thanks to the fireproofing of the Montgomery Block facility.

Determining not to allow this to happen to his books, Henry Edwards Huntington took steps to institutionalize and safely house his collection within his lifetime. If, as has been suggested, Los Angeles considered itself the last imperial Anglo-American city to emerge in the twentieth century, then Huntington's collection, devoted as it was so heroically to British and American literary culture and art, reinforced this identity. Point for point, the genesis of the Huntington recapitulated the successive sequences and layers of meaning inherent in the Southern California experience. A frontier California fortune in railroads goes east and triples itself through investment in real estate. The fortune returns to California in the next generation and through the creation of an interurban electric streetcar system helps create sub/urban Los Angeles. It then appropriates unto itself the material culture of Anglo-American civilization in the form of books, manuscripts, and art, scouted and purchased for Huntington by Sir Joseph Duveen of London, George D. Smith of New York, and Dr. A.S.W. Rosenbach of Philadelphia, cities themselves part of the Anglo-American metaphor. From this perspective, the Huntington Collection, with Sir Joseph, Mr. Smith, and Dr. Rosenbach as de facto cofounders, stands as a type for the emergent Los Angeles itself: vigorous, plutocratic, imperially ambitious, importing books and paintings with the same rapacious audacity that it blasted a deep-water port and appropriated the water of the Owens River.

Arabella Huntington never adjusted to Southern California. She would have preferred to divide her time between London and New York. In many ways the book and art collection constituted her husband's attempt to bring the mountain to Mohammed, to create a replication of British civilization in the Southland such as the Anglo-Canadians were creating at Riverside. Given the pervasiveness of the Anglo-American metaphor, however, the British nature of the Huntington Collection seems not so much escapist as a deliberate translation of household gods from Great Britain to Southern California: from London, the first imperial English-speaking city, to Los Angeles, the most recent English-speaking arrival.

Beginning in 1916, Huntington began to sink taproots into the soil of Southern California with the purchase *en bloc* through Robert Ernest Cowan of the 3500-volume Augustin S. Macdonald collection of Californiana. Huntington always bought *en bloc*. Within a few short years, more than twenty great libraries poured into his house on Fifty-seventh Street in New York for eventual shipment to San Marino. Between 1911 and 1917 he spent some $6 million on book purchases, a dazzling feat of American Renaissance acquisitiveness. With the development of this third area of collecting—Western Americana, Californiana, the archives and manuscripts of nineteenth-century Southern

California—the Huntington Library and Art Gallery now stood as a materialization through books, manuscripts, and paintings of the forces that had brought English-speaking civilization to the Southland.

By 1919, the take-off year of Southern California development, it had become time to institutionalize this accumulation of literary and artistic treasures. Having materialized his collection with the concentration and energy of a corporation president, Huntington now saw to the forms and procedures of succession. On 30 August 1919 Huntington signed an instrument which stated his intention to devote his San Marino estate with its exquisite gardens, its collection of priceless paintings, its library of 600,000 books and 2.5 million manuscripts, to the advancement of learning and the enjoyment of the public "by founding, endowing and having maintained a library, art gallery, museum and park within this state." Huntington spent the remaining eight years of his life overseeing the transformation of his collection into an organized library while dickering with his trustees about the size of the endowment necessary to keep the institution functioning on the ambitious level they all envisioned. Before he died on 23 May 1927 he agreed to double his initial grant.

Huntington continued to collect to the end of his life, pending the further organization of the library as an institution devoted to "the origin and progress of the civilization of the English-speaking peoples with special reference to their intellectual development."[1] To that end, librarian Leslie Bliss and rare-book curator Robert O. Schad spent the 1920s transforming a warehouse of great libraries into a functional research collection. Under the guidance of historian Max Farrand, a polished Princetonian connected by marriage to prominent New York circles (Edith Wharton was his wife's aunt), the Huntington emerged as an important research institution in history and humanities, the All Souls of Southern California, to which were attached on a permanent basis senior scholars such as Frederick Jackson Turner, Louis B. Wright, Allan Nevins, and, later, Robert Glass Cleland. Other researchers came for shorter fellowships. As the first center of humanistic study to emerge in Southern California, the Huntington both prefigured and helped bring about the eventual emergence of this region as an international center of humanities research.

UCLA and USC, meanwhile, were finding their patron/collectors and library builders as well in William Andrews Clark, Jr., and Estelle Doheny. Like Huntington, Clark collected primarily in the area of British culture, with an emphasis upon John Dryden and Oscar Wilde. This affinity for British civilization provides only one of many parallels between the two collectors. As in the case of the Huntington enterprise, the Clark fortune was a western one, Montana copper, which had gone east and tripled itself on Wall Street before returning in the second generation to Southern California.

When it came time to convert his collection into a library in 1926, Clark used the very wording of Huntington's 1919 instrument to express his own intention to establish a research collection that would, after his death, pass on to UCLA. Just as Huntington relied on Dr. A.S.W. Rosenbach, Clark relied on Robert Ernest Cowan, the San Francisco bookseller and bibliographer. In 1919 Clark offered Cowan a full-time position as librarian, and Cowan moved south to Los Angeles. Clark paid Cowan a thousand dollars a month, an extraordinary salary in that era, and provided him with a home near his own. Cowan dined almost nightly in the Clark household. It was one thing for Rosenbach to make his annual visits from Philadelphia. Los Angeles now had its own accomplished bibliographer in residence, the erudite Sir Robert (even this sobriquet expressed the Anglophilia of establishment culture), who promptly began to organize the Clark collection into a library and to issue a series of important bibliographies printed by master printer John Henry Nash. Enshrined in a French Renaissance palazzo in the West Adams district designed in 1923 by Robert Farquhar, the Clark Library was formally presented to UCLA in 1934 after the death of its founder: a second bastion of Anglo-American self-awareness along with the Huntington.

The third major collector and library patron of this era, Estelle Doheny, was neither old-boy nor Anglo-American in her collecting interests. As a collector, Mrs. Doheny devoted major attention to items expressive of continental Europe and the Roman Catholic Church, the flip-side of the Anglo-American Protestant preoccupations of Huntington and Clark. Here again, however, another ingredient of the Southern California formula found expression; for Catholic Spain had founded Los Angeles long before the in-migration of Protestant mid-America, and even amidst the WASP ascendancy of the new Los Angeles, a strong Catholic population continued to assert itself. While the Huntington and the Clark represented second-generation Protestant money recycled through the East, the first-generation Doheny oil fortune, Irish and German Catholic, had gushed from the soil of Los Angeles itself.

Under the influence of her husband's lawyer Frank J. Hogan, himself a noted collector in the fields of Elizabethan and Romantic literature, Estelle Doheny became interested in the collecting of rare books during the long ordeal of Teapot Dome. Under stress from her husband's two trials, the murder of her stepson, and her husband's rapid decline following the tragedy, Mrs. Doheny welcomed the distraction offered by this new pursuit. A methodical woman, loving detail and administration, she had for years acted as her husband's private secretary, learning shorthand for this purpose. She now pursued rare books with the same methodical efficiency with which she administered her husband's private affairs and personally ran the huge staff at Chester Place. (One of her garden laborers in the mid-1920s was Jake Zeitlin, just in from Texas and flat broke. Within the decade he was dining at her table, discussing rare books.) Using Merle Johnson's bibliography *High Spots of American Literature* (1929) as her guide, she compiled two complete collections of first editions of American classics, doing much of her business through Dawson's. She and Frank Hogan had a friendly competition to see who could first assemble Johnson's list. She won. By 1931 Estelle Doheny was busy acquiring the titles listed in Robert Ernest Cowan's pioneering *Bibliography of California*. She gathered a thousand items or more from this list, including the 1835 broadside announcing the elevation of *Pueblo de Nuestra Señora la Reina de los Angeles* to full city status under Mexican law and designating it the capital of Alta California.

These American and Californian collecting interests dovetailed perfectly with the memorial the Dohenys had chosen to commemorate their slain son, a new main library at his alma mater USC. To design the library, the Dohenys turned to Ralph Adams Cram of Cram & Ferguson, who created a splendid Italian Romanesque structure, the Edward Laurence Doheny, Jr., Memorial Library at USC, dedicated on 12 September 1932. In honor of the dedication, Mrs. Doheny displayed her collection of American first editions and the beginnings of a major collection of European books and manuscripts. Numbering 234 items, the exhibition signaled to the book world that an important new American collector had arrived on the scene.

Estelle Doheny also donated to USC the Los Angeles collection of J. Gregg Layne which she had purchased, thereby conferring on USC in one fell swoop a distinguished building and the start of an important regional collection. Unfortunately, the Layne collection was later removed from its special building and integrated into the main collection so as to make way for even more impressive offices for USC President Rufus B. von KleinSmid. Discovering this, Estelle Doheny was furious, and USC ceased to be the primary object of her largess. Rarely has a blundering president, ambitious for better office space, cost an institution more in probable future dollars than von KleinSmid cost USC by his highhanded treatment of the Doheny bequest.

Or was this fully the case? Von KleinSmid's affront, as undiplomatic as it was, might have simply provided the excuse for Estelle Doheny to detach herself from the Methodist-sponsored USC and proceed even more deeply into the materialization of her European Catholic daydream through the acquisition of bibliographical treasures evocative of high European civilization and the grandeur of the Roman Church. Having collected the Cowan list and purchased the Layne library, she left California behind (it was, after all, so strongly an Anglo-American Protestant enterprise, despite its Spanish foundations) in favor of a collecting policy that reinforced her growing involvement in Catholic charities and anticipated her eventual identity as a papal countess.

Felled by grief and a series of strokes, E.L. Doheny died in 1935, leaving Estelle even more dependent upon her charities, her collecting, and the administration of her various estates as an outlet for her energies. Since 1931, she had been employing a full-time librarian, Lucille Miller, to manage her bibliographical activities. With the death of her husband and the growing intensity of her collecting, the relationship between Estelle Doheny and Lucille Miller became even closer. Miller approached becoming a cocreator of the

Doheny collection in the sense that she scouted for treasures, handled correspondence with booksellers, and recommended regarding purchases. The other
influential figure in the creation of this great library, four thousand important
volumes assembled between 1930 and 1940, so much of it Roman ecclesiastical in orientation, was a third woman, Alice Millard of Pasadena, the single
most influential antiquarian bookseller in Southern California in the 1920s and
early 1930s.

It was a working relationship, not a close personal friendship, between the
German Catholic doyenne of vast wealth and the Christian Scientist of approximately the same age, a widow as well, embattled in her rare-book practice by
the Depression but still careful to make her calls to Chester Place in a hired
chauffeur-driven limousine. Alice Millard embodied the spirit of Pasadena,
which was a far different thing from the more tumultuous life of the oil-rich
Dohenys with their nouveau ambitions, indictments, and scandalous tragedies.
As a Chicago school teacher in her late twenties, Alice fell in love with and
married George Millard, a rare-book seller twenty-seven years her senior because he, bearded, distinguished in demeanor, manager of the rare-book department of McClurg's Department Store in Chicago, knew so much about the
things she was ever dreaming of: London, Oxford, and the pre-Raphaelites. At
the time, Alice herself enjoyed a rich halo of dark reddish hair, wavy and
unruly like the tresses of Elizabeth Siddal, the Blessed Damozel, mistress, model,
and wife to Dante Gabriel Rossetti.

Walking into McClurg's one day in the late 1890s, Alice asked George Millard for a biography of William Morris, for she was also enamored of the Arts
and Crafts movement. Millard told her that he knew Morris, which was true,
and that he was also a close friend of the book designer and binder T.J. Cobden-
Sanderson, which was also true. Alice fell in love (of such fragile suggestions
and hopes is love made!) and the couple went off to London to be married at
St. Bride's Church. They returned to Chicago to live in Highland Park in a
Prairie-style house designed by Frank Lloyd Wright, where they devoted themselves to books and beauty and to their daughter, born retarded, the tragic flaw
in the idealized world they had created for themselves. The shock of their
child's retardation converted Alice Millard to Christian Science as a means of
transcending the error inherent in flesh: the beautiful baby girl, so innocent,
so needlessly flawed.

Moving to Pasadena in 1914, George now sixty-eight, Alice just turning
forty, the couple entered into the genteel rhythms of that community during
George's years of semi-retirement. George Millard promoted local business with
lectures at the Friday Morning Club and at the soirées put on by Mrs. Robert
Burdette at her home on South Orange Grove Avenue. Tastefully, discreetly,
Millard sold from his home, Casa de las Flores, a bungalow enclosing a garden
court. Alice sat quietly in the background pouring tea as George chatted with
clients, a figure from Rosetti or Burne-Jones, still very much the dutiful hand-

maiden to the father-figure whom she addressed as Daddy or, in more intensely pre-Raphaelite moments, as My Liege Lord.

When his lordship passed on in November 1918 at the age of 72, Alice Millard revealed her true colors. It was one thing to be an admiring disciple when one was twenty-eight and in love. But she was now a widow nearing fifty and had a handicapped child to support. And besides: she was tired of the teacups and the timidity of her husband's business. She envisioned something more ambitious: collecting on a grand scale, competing in the international markets, developing an important clientele in Southern California—not just Huntington or Clark, but all the other prosperous people as well who were waiting to be coaxed (and coached) beyond the limits of the merely genteel. All this money in Southern California, Alice Millard correctly reasoned, begged for instruction in the matter of taste. Selling off her late husband's pleasing but uneventful stock, she obtained a line of credit from a Pasadena bank and went to London and the continent and began buying on an ambitious scale.

It has been claimed that she was the first woman to bid at Sotheby's. How wonderful to have been there that day in the summer of 1920 to hear her female voice ring out in its deliberately fashioned Anglo-American accent, bidding, rebidding, and the stares of discomfort of the Sotheby regulars. Who was this American woman? Not only did she buy books and manuscripts, she bought paintings, tapestries, sculpture, porcelains, and antique furniture as well, for it was her ambition to assist the taste of her emergent Southern California clientele in as many directions as possible.

Returning to Pasadena, she began selling with great success. When Frank Lloyd Wright returned to Southern California in 1922 from his work on the Imperial Hotel in Tokyo, she commissioned from him La Miniatura, a charmingly romantic home and exhibition gallery situated amidst the sycamores in a Pasadena Arroyo ravine. Here she lived and received clients and organized elegant exhibitions of books and *objets d'art*—illuminated manuscripts, rubricated incunables, Gothic tapestries, Renaissance sculptures, watercolors by William Blake, a *Das Kapital* bound by Cobden-Sanderson, a Kelmscott Chaucer, and other books by William Morris, Doves, and Ashendene imprints—which she also displayed in various formats downtown at the Biltmore, the Zamorano Club, and other places where a potential clientele was gathering. Alice Millard became tutor to 1920s Los Angeles, a direct conduit of Edwardian culture and civility to the Southland. Her Burne-Jones tresses now coiffed and rinsed a surreal blue as a mark of election, Alice Millard functioned as a priestess of taste for an affluent era struggling to shake off its Babbittry. By the Depression, she was dealing in half-million-dollar lines of credit from her bank and had earned a reputation as the A.S.W. Rosenbach of Southern California.

The Depression devastated Alice Millard's business, which was why her connection with Estelle Doheny became such an important lifeline in her struggle

to stay afloat and keep up the payments for her daughter's care. It was Millard
who initiated the relationship by letter on 2 January 1931, deftly suggesting
books in her inventory, one of them an important work on orchids, which
might be of interest to Mrs. Doheny. Would Mrs. Doheny perhaps like to
come to La Miniatura or would Mrs. Millard be permitted to call at Chester
Place? Neither alternative was acceptable, librarian-secretary Lucille Miller replied. Mrs. Doheny enjoyed a limited amount of collecting but did not envision the creation of a great library. More letters from Mrs. Millard. More
rebuffs. From the beginning, this relationship between wealth and self-supporting
gentility, Catholic Chester Place and Christian Science Pasadena, would not
be easy. Finally, after a number of letters, Mrs. Millard was allowed to call.
She arrived with her treasures in a rented limosine, just as she continued to
arrive at the symphony and the opera despite her Depression-straitened circumstances. It took another two years and many more letters and a lesser number
of limousine calls for Mrs. Millard to pierce Estelle Doheny's reserve and make
an energizing imaginative connection—however qualified the relationship remained psychologically. Only when Mrs. Millard touched Mrs. Doheny's affinity for European Catholic civilization did the proper forces coalesce to transform a collector into a library-builder, although even then Alice Millard worked
hard for each sale.

Unlike Henry Huntington, Estelle Doheny, the onetime telephone operator
from South Alvarado Street, did not buy libraries by the lot. She and her
librarian Lucille Miller required negotiation item by item. With the metaphor
of medieval and Renaissance Roman Catholic Europe in place, however, the
negotiations increasingly came out in Alice Millard's favor. In 1933 alone, at
the very depth of the Depression, a 1488/89 edition of Homer, Breydenbach's
Peregrinationes in Terram Sanctam (1486), the *Hypnerotomachia Poliphili* (1499)
of Francesco Colonna, considered by many the most beautiful book ever printed,
a twelfth-century manuscript of Zacharias Chrysopolitanus, a thirteenth-century
Flemish *Speculum*, and a sixteenth-century missal from the library of Cardinal
Pompeo Colonna, viceroy of Naples, flowed into the library at Chester Place
thanks to the saleswomanship of Alice Millard and the receptivity of Estelle
Doheny. Protestant Pasadena was helping Catholic Los Angeles materialize its
dream. Before Alice Millard's death in 1938, Estelle Doheny allowed some
mitigation in the aloofness with which she learned to protect herself from the
strain and disgrace of her husband's trials and her stepson's murder. "I love my
gorgeous books and manuscripts more all the time," she wrote Alice Millard,
"and the more I love them the more I appreciate all you have done for my
library."[2]

What to do with this library now became a challenge. Had President von
KleinSmid not been so greedy for space, it might have gone to USC. But even
had there not been a breech, would so aggressively a Catholic collection, assembled by a papal countess, have sat well in such a persistently Methodist

institution? The alternative chosen by Estelle Doheny, a library in honor of her husband at St. John's Seminary in Camarillo north of Los Angeles in Ventura County, answered the question perfectly. Approached on the question by Archbishop John Cantwell in 1939, the year of her papal ennoblement, Mrs. Doheny responded enthusiastically to the prospect of creating a library devoted to scholarship and the education of young men for the diocesan priesthood. Architect Wallace Neff, who had pleased the Dohenys so much with his design for their house at Ferndale Ranch near Santa Paula and had helped remodel Chester Place in 1934, was retained to draw up the design. Neff created for Estelle Doheny a shimmering Spanish-Italian daydream of Catholic Europe translated to a sunny hilltop rising from orange and walnut groves. Into the second floor of this exquisite building, completed in September 1940, Mrs. Doheny removed the manuscripts, books, tapestries, and *objets d'art* gathered across a heroic decade of collecting: the manuscript riches of a thousand years of European monasticism, Bibles and liturgical books of beauty and distinction, culled from the libraries of cardinals and bishops. She also established a special Western Room to house her husband's paintings and books and to honor his rough-and-ready prospecting career. (Not his papers, however, which Mrs. Doheny had destroyed.)

Here in the Edward L. Doheny Memorial Library of St. John's Seminary of the Archdiocese of Los Angeles, and not in the memory of the indictment, was how Estelle Doheny hoped her husband would be remembered. Here was the proper legacy for the consort of a papal countess. On dedication day, 14 October 1940, the Apostolic Delegate to the United States, the Archbishop of Los Angeles, and assorted bishops and *monsignori* swept in procession through Neff's arched and columned loggias, past sunsplashed walls and Churrigueresque portals, in a triumphalist swirl of magenta choir capes and cassocks that operatically confirmed, had there been any doubt, the strong presence of the Roman Catholic Church in Protestant Los Angeles.

Forty-six years later, another Archibishop authorized the sale of Mrs. Doheny's library through Christie's. However grand, the Edward L. Doheny Memorial Library was too remote for convenient use by scholars, and the Roman Catholic community of the 1980s showed little if any interest in Mrs. Doheny's books.

2

In the Los Angeles of the 1920s and 1930s, collectors were everywhere, even in Hollywood, which was why Jake Zeitlin and the others felt such confidence in opening their shops. Ernest Dawson and Alice Millard and the others managed to create a book culture that had become a regional badge of identity. It was not so surprising that physicians, lawyers, prosperous businessmen, or wealthy women collected; but W.O. Schneider, general manager of the Los Angeles Country Club, also collected, as did a number of Hollywood actors. The collections thus formed, most of them, passed into local libraries, and greater Los Angeles continued its evolution towards world-class stature as a library and research center.

Art collector Walter Arensberg's twelve-thousand-volume collection centered on Sir Francis Bacon, for example, found a home at Pomona College. The Denison Library of Scripps College in Claremont received into its exquisite Renaissance chapel interior the five-thousand-volume collection of English literature, fine printing, and book arts assembled by Los Angeles investor John I. Perkins, a collector so respected by local booksellers that Ernest Dawson broke a cardinal rule and allowed the tall, elegant gentleman (Perkins wore flannels and a straw boater and resembled throughout his life a Rudy Vallee boy of the 1920s) to remain browsing after five o'clock.

The Los Angeles book world had its proper and its raffishly bohemian polarities: its Zamorano Club downtown at the University Club on Hope Street and its more democratically eclectic counterpart at Musso & Frank's bar and restaurant and Stanley Rose's bookstore in Hollywood.

Modeled on the Grolier Club of New York, the Club of Odd Volumes of Boston, the Rowfant Club of Cleveland, the Caxton Club of Chicago (each of these, in turn, was modeled on the Roxburghe Club of London), the Zamorano Club of Los Angeles showed in its origins the usual Chicago/Los Angeles connection. It was a former Chicagoan, bookman Washington Irving Way, who provided the initial stimulus to found the organization. Before arriving in Los Angeles in 1904 at the age of 51, Way, a railroad man with the Santa Fe in his earlier days, had been a bookseller and publisher in Chicago. Although his firm Way & Williams collapsed after a brief existence in the 1890s, it did manage to publish William Morris's edition of Dante Gabriel Rossetti's *Hand and Soul*, Morris's only American imprint. A literate essayist and bibliophile, Way joined the Grolier Club of New York in 1884, the very year it was founded. In 1895 Way helped found the Caxton Club of Chicago along similar lines of clubbable bibliophilia and was a regular in the circle gathered around George Millard, whom Way preceded to Los Angeles, in the Saints and Sinners corner of the book department of McClurg's, which functioned as an important center of literary gossip and comings and goings in Chicago during that era.

In Los Angeles, Way pursued a career as a peripatetic bookseller, catalogue writer, and occasional literary journalist in association with another former Chicagoan, Samuel T. Clover, publisher of *Saturday Night*. In 1922, sponsored by the book department of Bullock's, Way pioneered the broadcasting of book reviews on the new medium of radio. By 1927 Way, then in his early seventies and embattled in his financial circumstances, had developed into a central figure, half grand old man, half mascot, in book-collecting circles. A widower since 1920, Way had long since been reduced to supporting himself by selling off his own books, one by one, passing from friend to friend to make his sales. Ernest Dawson allowed Way to use his store to collect his mail and make telephone calls.

Motivated by a desire to do something for Irving Way and by their mutual love of good books, fine dining, and good conversation, two Los Angeles law-yer/bibliophiles, Arthur M. Ellis and William Webb Clary, began discussions in late 1927 regarding the formation of a bibliophilic association on the lines of the Roxburghe, the Grolier, the Odd Volumes, the Rowfant, and the Caxton. As a member of the Grolier and a founder of the Caxton, Washington Irving Way brought a quality of apostolic succession to these intentions. Formally organized at a dinner meeting at the University Club on 25 January 1928, with Arthur M. Ellis elected president, the Zamorano Club, named in honor of California's first printer, secured a lease on room 446 of the Bradbury Building, where a small library was installed with Way as librarian, available weekdays from two to five in the afternoon at a stipend of $50 a month. A year later the club moved to a two-room suite on the fourth floor of the Alexandria Hotel, which architect member Gordon Kaufmann transformed into oak-paneled clubbiness.

In April 1934, the Alexandria, once the favored downtown haunt of Holly-woods agents and producers, succumbed to the Depression, and the Zamorano Club was forced to seek new quarters in the University Club on Hope Street, where it remained for the next thirty-three years. Organized around dinner discussions and the usual sherry, port, and cigar white male camaraderie of club life in that less challenged era, the Zamorano testified in its restrictive way to the presence of an active intelligentsia among the bourgeoisie: men such as the insurance man A. Gaylord Beaman, the Number One Clubman of Los Angeles, the unofficial chief of protocol, the leading greeter and social gadfly and, if need be, an available walker in the current sense of that term (available, that it, to grace a social occasion), a man who made the rounds, table by table, at every event, whom one could easily imagine making the rounds at even his own dinner party, smiling and shaking hands and saying glad to see you. Bea-man, in fact, can in one sense be considered a founding figure, for it was he who organized the lunch with Will Clary and Arthur Ellis at which the idea of founding a club of bibliophiles and incidentally helping out Irving Way first came up.

With so many bibliophiles of the Southern California of this era elected to the Zamorano, a consolidation was achieved that went beyond the merely cer-emonial and celebratory aspects of the dinners on the first Wednesdays of the month, sherry at six, and the weekly Wednesday luncheon roundtables. For all its elitism, to use the current term, the Zamorano Club represented a clustering of the like-minded that helped further focus the level of civic self-awareness in Los Angeles. Historian Henry Wagner, for whom a three-tier silver cigar box was kept replenished at club headquarters, warned his colleagues early on that it was a danger inherent in all such organizations to devolve into mere knife and fork societies, which is one reason why the Zamorano launched such an ambitious publication program so soon after its foundation. In publishing member George Harding's first-rate biography of Don Augustín Zamorano in 1934, the club made an important contribution to the historiography of California. Its 1945 publication *The Zamorano 80, a Selection of Distinguished California Books* remains to this day the starting point for any serious program of reading in California history.

Where in all this, however, was Jake Zeitlin? Present at so much else, Zeitlin is absent from the rosters of the Zamorano Club until his belated admission in 1971. Zeitlin, for one thing, was a bookseller, and the Zamorano, following its interpretaion of the Grolier, banished booksellers from its midst so as not to cloud the proceedings with commercialism. This was despite the fact that A.S.W. Rosenbach was a member of the Grolier; Irving Way, the initiating raison d'être of Zamorano, was a bookseller; and another bookseller, the eminently clubbable C.C. Parker, was also a member. Jake Zeitlin was Jewish, but then again, so was architect Gordon Kaufmann. Kaufmann, however, had left his Jewishness behind as a matter of acknowledged identity while Zeitlin remained Hebraic and rabbinical, with developing left-liberal political opinions that kept him distanced from an organization dominated by arch-conservatives such as Phil Townsend Hanna, Paul Jordan-Smith, and attorney Homer D. Crotty, who once tried to get a bill passed through the state legislature disbarring attorneys who defended communists. And so while the intermittently unruly albeit politically conservative Merle Armitage was taken into the fold, Jake Zeitlin remained uninvited to membership until 1971. By then it did not mean what it might have meant in the late 1920s when he craved such recognition.

Out in Hollywood, the non-Zamoranans could not care less. They had their own circles. In most of these, admission requirements consisted of an active mind and the ability to hang out. Through the 1920s Hollywood was developing its own version of bohemia. As Marshall McLuhan points out, the book supports film as a source of story and idea—and hence as a source of authentication. The printed book became the screenplay (only recently has this process shown movement in the other direction); indeed, the screenplay depended upon the book for its validity. By the 1930s a significant percentage of the major screenplays were scenario versions of literary classics. Thus books and writers were essential to the film industry in the deepest possible, if frequently troubled, symbiosis; and so a literary intelligentsia sometimes (but not always) ambivalent to its current situation emerged around the studios. Some of these writers—Hugh Walpole, William Faulkner, John Dos Passos—were there for a brief time for the money. Others—F. Scott Fitzgerald, Nathaniel West— were also there for the money, but they stayed longer and sustained for Hollywood a kind of love/hate fascination that engendered much good writing. Still others—Aldous Huxley, Christopher Isherwood, Budd Schulberg—found in their new circumstances the place and theme for a renewed career. The Hollywood intelligentsia even included a number of figures—Upton Sinclair, Rupert Hughes, Irvin S. Cobb, Myron Brinig—who were Southern Californians by a previous and more encompassing definition.

An urban bohemian intelligentsia such as that found in Hollywood required places to hang out. Two restaurants—the Brown Derby on Vine and, more important, Musso & Frank at 6667 Hollywood Boulevard—were especially favored. William Faulkner, for example, was a Musso & Frank regular, as were Nathaniel West, F. Scott Fitzgerald, Budd Schulberg, S.N. Behrman, Dashiell Hammett, Max Brand, Lillian Hellman, Horace McCoy, John Fante, Joel Sayre, and A.I. Bezzerides. Hanging out at such haunts were not only these writers associated with the studios but also indigenous artists such as sculptor Gordon Newell, illustrator Paul Landacre, photographer Will Connell, architect Lloyd Wright, short-story writer Gordon Raye Young, Arthur Millier of the *Times*—but not Upton Sinclair, who loathed drinking and saloons. When visiting literary firemen—Sherwood Anderson, Somerset Maugham, Christopher Morley—came to town, Gaylord Beaman of Zamorano fame would meet them at the station and whisk them around town before an evening at the Authors Club of Hollywood, presided over by Rupert Hughes and Irwin S. Cobb, two stalwarts of the local screenwriting community.

The Hollywood intelligentsia also included actors and directors, many of them book collectors in their own right. Edward Everett Horton, Cecil B. De Mille, Frank Capra, Edward G. Robinson, Charles Boyer, Robert Montgomery, John and Lionel Barrymore, Joseph Schildkraut, and Delmer Daves bought, read, and collected books while most of their colleagues relegated bibliography to the care of their interior decorators. Actor Jean Hersholt, a serious collector of English and American literary first editions, of Sinclair Lewis, Sir Hugh Walpole, and, most impressive, Hans Christian Andersen, including 600 different editions of Andersen's work translated into English, bridged the informal bohemian book worlds of Hollywood and the formal downtown rituals of the Zamorano to which he also belonged.

The studios themselves assembled major research collections. Many younger booksellers, such as Jake Zeitlin, got themselves started in part through supplying the studio libraries with appropriate books for reference. One such dealer, Jean French, became a wealthy woman buying and selling expensive art books for the studios. Zeitlin estimated that MGM spent close to a million dollars over a twenty-year period building up its reference library. Gladys Percy, librarian for Paramount, was another important buyer: an edition of Diderot's *Encyclopedia*, for example; full sets of the *London Illustrated News* and *Harper's Weekly*, to be used for images of period architecture and costume; and a complete set of the volumes produced by the scholars attached to Napoleon's expedition to Egypt, as a source for the costume and sets for De Mille's production of *Cleopatra* starring Claudette Colbert.

Two very different booksellers—Louis Epstein, businessman, and Stanley Rose, bohemian—provided Hollywood with books to buy and places to browse and hang out. Opened in 1938, Epstein's Pickwick Bookshop soon became a Hollywood landmark and social institution alongside Musso & Frank and Grauman's Chinese Theatre. Born in Russia and raised in Cleveland, where his father worked in the garment industry, Epstein migrated to Southern California with his family in 1923 seeking a better climate for his tubercular brother and sister. Abandoning his legal studies, Epstein went into the book business in Long Beach, then moved in 1926 to Eighth Street near the booksellers' row developing on Sixth Street near the Los Angeles Public Library.

An instinctive businessman, Epstein replenished his inventory in a way that testified to the extraordinary mobility of Southern California in that era. Epstein bought books by the lot from unclaimed storage deposits at Belsin's and Lyon's—books and furniture and personal effects shipped west by people once seeking a new start who now seemed to have vanished into the anonymity around them, no longer needing or able to afford the items which just a short time ago had reinforced their identities. Epstein admired the merchandizing skills of the Los Angeles department stores—Bullock's, Broadway, the May Company, Robinson's—especially the panache with which they mass-merchandized books, and he determined to follow suit. While Jake Zeitlin pursued a model of the bookseller as bibliophile, patron of the arts, tutor to taste, Louis Epstein—who provided Zeitlin with much of the stock for his first store—pursued a goal of informed merchandizing to as many people as possible.

Strategically located on Hollywood Boulevard, the Pickwick maintained a huge stock, including remainders, then an innovation, and it stayed open long into the night. The mystique which the Pickwick soon acquired came from the people who browsed through its counters and shelves. F. Scott Fitzgerald, then living at the Garden of Allah, came by, sad and subdued and polite. Fitzgerald loved to browse in the upstairs floor where the older books were, some of them written by himself at a better time. Raymond Chandler likewise came and went stealthily, like Philip Marlowe on a case. William Faulkner was another quiet and solitary patron. Faulkner lived nearby on Highland Avenue and ate frequently at Musso & Frank. Faulkner knew his books, Epstein later remembered, and was a good customer, as was the young English writer Aldous Huxley, so weak in his sight that his thick glasses required a third lens mounted like a jeweler's lens to one side of the eyeglass frame. Sometimes Huxley would tire of this contraption altogether and hold the book against his face, peering at it from an angle, his head cocked, like an expectant secretary bird. Unlike the silent Fitzgerald and the laconic Faulkner, Huxley talked: evaluations of books he was perusing, anecdotes regarding the writers, so many of whom he knew, all expressed in felicitous phrasing which itself seemed to be rising from a printed page in clear English-accented tones. One day a customer, mistaking Marlene Dietrich for a clerk, asked her for advice. Good humoredly, Dietrich played out the part until she could pass the customer on to a member of the Pickwick staff.

For all its celebrity customers, the Pickwick primarily embodied effective merchandizing. Stanley Rose's two Hollywood stores—the first on Vine near Hollywood Boulevard, the second on Hollywood Boulevard itself next door to Musso & Frank's—represented the bookstore as bohemian hangout. Born in Matador, Texas, Rose took to books while recovering from wounds and psychiatric damage (feigned, it was later claimed) incurred in France during the First World War. The clinic was in Palo Alto near Stanford University and Rose absorbed the atmosphere of books as if by osmosis. Essentially uneducated and never himself an energetic reader, Rose learned his way around the trade by intuition, like trading horses back in Texas. Rose's first Hollywood venture, a partnership appropriately named the Satyr Bookshop, dissolved after Rose took the rap for his partners when they issued some pornography. Released early from a sixty-day jail sentence through the efforts of his lawyer Carey McWilliams, Rose peddled books on consignment before opening the Stanley Rose Bookshop on Vine across the street from the Satyr. "After a few drinks," McWilliams later remembered, "Stanley would now and then emerge from the store and, to the amusement of his customers, swagger to the curb, shake his fist at his two former associates across the street, and hurl eloquent Texas curses at them."[3]

A master humorist and anecdotalist, Stanley Rose maintained an ongoing party at his establishment which frequently spilled next door to the lively bar at Musso & Frank and continued into the early hours. Rose usually held court in the late afternoon, McWilliams later remembered, fueling himself up for the long evening with a few drinks. The next-door establishment also served as Rose's informal banker. The bookshop and the bar restaurant operated together with superb synergy, creating a welcomed sense of community for screenwriters suffering from an understandable sense of displacement. The Stanley Rose Bookshop/Musso & Frank's circle was, as are all such entities, a non-organized movable feast, peopled by whoever happened to be in town at the time. Rose had film clients—John Barrymore, Red Skelton, Edward G. Robinson, Marion Davies, who took him up to San Simeon for a weekend—as well as writing clients. He personally preferred writers from the minimalist hardboiled school, the Boys in the Back Room, as Edmund Wilson described them—James M. Cain, Erskine Caldwell, John Fante, A.I. Bezzerides, Frank Fenton, Jo Pagano, Raymond Chandler—who became, literally, boys in Stanley Rose's back room, enjoying his talk and whiskey. Louis Adamic, Budd Schulberg, William Saroyan, William Faulkner, and Nathaniel West were also regulars at both Rose's and Musso & Frank. Like many hard-drinking people, Stanley Rose eventually came to grief, dying broke and long before his time in the mid-1950s, his wife and son poorly provided for.

Other Los Angeles literary circles (bohemians would be too strong a designation) revolved around regional history, regional publishing, and printing as a fine art. The history circles naturally centered upon the Historical Society of Southern California headquartered at El Alisal, the stone pueblo built earlier in the century by Charles Fletcher Lummis, who also founded the nearby Southwest Museum. With its first-rate collection of some one hundred thousand items building on the Spanish Southwest library of Lummis himself and the Arizona collection of Los Angeles physician Joseph Amasa Munk, the Southwest Museum attracted a steady flow of resident regional researchers who also frequented the Historical Society of Southern California, the Huntington Library, and the impressive Southern California collections of the Los Angeles Public Library, USC, and UCLA. As director of the Southwest Museum, the Indian expert Frederick Webb Hodge, as range-lean and leather-tanned as a New Mexico cowboy, functioned as titular head of this circle of archeologists, anthropologists, ethno-historians, and Hispanicists for whom Southern California would always remain, not downtown Los Angeles or cultivated Pasadena, but Spanish Southwest border country.

Overlapping this muscular group were the Californianists proper, an informal circle that included at its core attorney Carl Wheat, insurance man W.W. Robinson, salesman J. Gregg Layne, later the historian for the Department of Water and Power, Huntington librarian Lindley Bynum, printer Ward Ritchie, and real-estate man Robert Woods. Also part of the Californianist scene, but with varying degrees of involvement in its bohemia, were *Touring Topics/Westways* editor Phil Townsend Hanna, a California Club man very much on the right, and lawyer/journalist Carey McWilliams, who the Depression was drawing increasingly into radical politics. Professors Robert Glass Cleland of Occidental and John Caughey of UCLA, displaying that social isolation that would become increasingly characteristic of the academy in the postwar era, tended to do their hanging out at the faculty club. Social center for the Californianists was the Mexican restaurant La Golondrina on Olvera Street in old-town Los Angeles, which was at the time introducing the margarita to a grateful United States, and the patio of Robert Woods's hillside home on Briarcliffe Road, where the full California circle, including Henry Raup Wagner, Frederick Webb Hodge, Phil Townsend Hanna, and visiting celebrities such as Texas historian J. Frank Dobie, would gather for drinks, dinner, and conversation. The Californianist circle intersected with Zamorano (Hanna, Wagner, Hodge, Ritchie, Bynum, Layne, and Robinson were each Zamoranans) and with the Los Angeles chapter of the Wine and Food Society presided over by Phil Townsend Hanna. Lindley Bynum, for example, an erudite oenophile with a preternatural nose, played a significant role in creating an awareness of the wines of the Napa Valley alongside their French counterparts.

3

With so many productive regionalists at work, book publishing came to Los Angeles as well. It began with Jake Zeitlin's Primavera Press, which in 1929 published a translation of Archduke Ludwig Louis Salvator's account of his 1876 visit to Los Angeles, first published in Prague in 1878. Between 1929 and 1933 Zeitlin operated the Primavera Press as a sole proprietorship. It was then incorporated with Zeitlin, Hanna, and Ritchie serving as directors. Carey McWilliams and Lawrence Clark Powell also held shares. The Primavera Press specialized in California classics. The Arthur H. Clark Company, meanwhile, founded in Cleveland in 1902 by the English-born bookseller whose name the company bore, relocated its 100,000-title book stock and publishing operation to Glendale in 1930. Overnight, Los Angeles acquired the pre-eminent publisher of frontier-related books in the United States: the company which had issued *The Jesuit Relations* in fifty-four volumes and the thirty-volume *Early Western Travels, 1748–1846* series edited by Reuben Gold Thwaites, together with hundreds of other significant monographs and annotated translations and reprints. In Glendale, the Arthur H. Clark Company continued its ambitious publishing program under the direction of its founder, then in his vigorous early sixties.

The presence of the Arthur H. Clark Company further strengthened and consolidated the book culture of greater Los Angeles, as did the quality publishing programs being carried on by Jack Zeitlin at Primavera and Thomas E. Williams at the Fine Arts Press of Santa Ana in Orange County. Operated as an adjunct to the printing program run by Williams for high school and junior college students, the Fine Arts Press surpassed even the Primavera in the ambition and historical importance of its list. The last of these regional presses, the San Pasqual, was founded in Pasadena by the Security Title and Trust Company in 1938 under the direction of Val Trefz and Ned Stirling, who had studied printing under Porter Garnett at Carnegie Tech in Pittsburgh.

These Primavera, Arthur H. Clark, Fine Arts, and San Pasqual books were all exquisitely designed and printed. Typographers Bruce McCallister, Grant Dahlstrom, Saul Marks, and Ward Ritchie designed the Primavera books with taste and unmannered elegance. With their heavyweight, ivory laid, deckle-edged, uncut pages, their gold-leaf spine lettering, their generously proportioned Caslon type, the books published by Arthur H. Clark Company set national standards for the publishing industry. At San Pasqual, Ned Stirling showed himself a master of Janson Linotype and Bodoni. The bibliographically distinguished titles issued by the Fine Arts Press became collectors' items upon publication.

The first book published in Los Angeles, Horace Bell's *Reminiscences of a Ranger* (1881), while lacking the distinction of Edward Bosqui's work in the north (Bosqui's *Grapes and Grape Vines of California* captivated the judges at the Paris Exposition of 1878), was nevertheless a solid example of bookmaking. Fifteen years later, a circle of Pasadena Arroyoans gathered around writer book-binder Ida Meacham Strobridge organized the Arroyo Press, which issued a number of books in a regional variation of Arts and Crafts. The most flamboy-ant proponent of Arts and Crafts printing and life-style, Clyde Browne, a news-paperman turned printer, began construction in 1915 on a monastery-style res-idence and workshop in Highland Park near Occidental College, the Abbey San Encino, which lushly expressed his Morrisite conception of himself as a medieval craftsman living in the twentieth century. As a young printer and reporter on the staff of the *Marin County Tocsin* in the early 1890s, Browne fell under the spell of the Arts and Crafts movement and the nearby Missions San Rafael and San Francisco Solano and dreamed of building a mission-like cloister in the hills of Sonoma County where he could gather a community of craftsmen and artists under his leadership. Twenty years later, having moved to Southern California to work in the pressroom of Hearst's *Los Angeles Ex-aminer*, the dream still held. Leaving the *Examiner* in a labor dispute, Browne launched into a printing partnership in Highland Park, a suburb on the banks of the Arroyo Seco near Pasadena. For the rest of his life, until his death in 1942, Clyde Browne supported himself as a job printer—with a difference.

In 1915 Browne began construction on the stone and brick cloister residence and workshop he had first envisioned for Sonoma County twenty-one years earlier. The Abbey combined elements of the Carmel mission and the Holy-rood chapel of Mary, Queen of Scots, and eventually rambled out to encom-pass an adjacent set of hillside apartments intended for artists and artisans. Working diligently as an antique hunter, a scavenger even, Browne painstak-ingly developed the Abbey as a dream-fantasy of ecclesiastical culture. He bought and installed the stained-glass windows from the bar of the Van Nuys Hotel in Los Angeles, put out of business by prohibition, and decorated the Abbey with church stones and statuary from Europe, tapestries, banners, manuscript mis-sals, church-related *objets d'art* of varying quality, ranging from passable to junk, and in the large music room he installed a grand pipe organ which Browne himself, an accomplished organist, constructed and played.

The Abbey San Encino was, obviously, just another instance of fantasy ac-tualizing itself in the hothouse climate of the Southern California of that era, but it had a practical purpose as well—printing, which Browne pursued through nearly thirty years of programs, handbills, announcements, pamphlets, menus, the *Journal of the Cactus and Succulent Society of America*, on two platen presses, one with an automatic feeder, in a large pressroom dominated by an oval stained-glass window depicting a Franciscan padre supervising a Native American printer at a hand press, something that never actually happened in the mission era.

Although he never formed the community of artists called for by the Arts and Crafts movement and the adjacent apartments at Abbey San Encino, Clyde

Browne did achieve a symbiotic relationship to nearby Occidental College. He did the college's printing and he also provided an off-campus haven for undergraduates. Students and faculty rented apartments in the artists' quarters. Occidental fraternities met in the lower rooms—the dungeons, they were called—of the Abbey. Alumni returned to be married in the music room, which evolved into a semi-official Occidental wedding chapel, with a benevolent Browne presiding at the organ. As a fine arts printer—in works such as *Cloisters of California* (1918), *San Encino* (1921), *The Abbey Fantasy* (1929), *Olden Abbey of San Encino* (1932)—Browne's style has been criticized for its lush fussiness. But no matter: he supported his wife and children with his job printing, not his fine art. Mostly importantly, Clyde Browne introduced the entrepreneurial master printer as cultural protagonist into Southern California.

And so even more effectively did Bruce McCallister, a South Dakota-born ex-printer's devil, a semi-professional ice hockey player, and traveling salesman of job printing who arrived in Los Angeles in 1906 and went to work for Senegram Printers. In 1915 McCallister and his partner Fred Young purchased the Senegram plant and went into business as Young & McCallister. When the real-estate boom exploded after 1919, Young & McCallister aggressively dominated the printing of promotional books, pamphlets, and brochures. To this day, more than half a century after the boom, these Young & McCallister productions still delight us with their color typography, technical excellence of line drawing, and photographic reproduction. Nearly every major research library in Southern California keeps an extensive file of this promotional material, for it embodies the subliminal appeal of the hope for a better life in a home of one's own in a landscaped suburb, which functioned as such a powerful metaphor in the Southern California of this and a later era.

In 1927 McCallister, a salesman and fine print aficionado but not himself a typographer, hired a 25-year-old typographer and book designer by the name of Grant Dahlstrom and embarked upon an ambitious program of book design and publishing. A Mormon from Idaho and Utah, Dahlstrom had worked as a journeyman printer in Ogden between 1921 and 1926, educating himself through an assiduous reading of current and back issues of *The Inland Printer*, the dominant American journal of printing as a trade, business, and fine art. In 1926 Dahlstom spent a year at the school of printing at the Carnegie Institute of Technology in Pittsburgh, studying under Porter Garnett, whose message of revitalized traditionalism he brought to Los Angeles in 1927. The importance of the presence this talented young designer in Los Angeles became immediately apparent. The first book Bruce McCallister put Grant Dahlstrom to work on, *The History of Warner's Ranch and Its Environs* by Joseph J. Hill (1927), was chosen by the American Institute of Graphic Arts as one of the fifty best-designed books to appear that year. It was the first time this award had come to Southern California. Teamed with Jake Zeitlin, Young & McCallister and Grant Dahlstrom produced many of the books of the Primavera Press. In 1931 the team won a second award from the American Institute of Graphic Arts for *California Hills and Other Wood Engravings* by Paul Landacre.

So many of the important books to emerge from Southern California through the late 1920s and the 1930s—*The Aristocracy of Art, Adobe Days,* the scholarly books of the newly established Huntington Library Press—were materialized through Bruce McCallister and Grant Dahlstrom. In 1943, two years before McCallister's death, Dahlstom established his own business and printing plant through the acquisition of the Castle Press in Pasadena, where he continued in close association with his wife Helen as dean of typography and fine printing in Southern California.

The Dahlstroms were joined in 1930 by another young printing couple, Saul and Lillian Marks. Born Yisroel Chaim Miodownik in Warsaw in 1905, Saul Marks was apprenticed to printing at the age of 12. When his two proprietors were arrested during World War I for counterfeiting German marks, Saul and another apprentice operated the shop for the duration of the war. Migrating to the United States in 1921, Yisroel Chaim Miodownik changed his name to Saul Marks and joined the Army to learn English and become Americanized. While serving in Panama, he continued his study of printing and typefaces. After working in Detroit as a printer in the late 1920s and marrying Lillian Simon there in 1928, Marks and his wife moved to Los Angeles in 1930, motivated in part by his Army service in a warm climate, which had made him increasingly resentful of the Detroit winters. In Los Angeles, Bruce McCallister helped Marks find work, and Grant Dahlstrom provided some hasty instruction in typography.

In 1931 Jake Zeitlin gave Marks and his partner Paul Rising their first major commission, a deluxe catalogue of rare books for sale by Zeitlin At the Sign of the Grasshopper, researched and written by Paul Jordan-Smith. Painstakingly setting the type by hand, Marks went through his partnership and the sale of most of Zeitlin's books before the catalogue was completed at Marks's newly established Plantin Press, named in honor of the great sixteenth-century printer of Antwerp; but the result was worth it, even for Zeitlin; for *The King's Treasury of Pleasant Books and Precious Manuscripts,* as Jordan-Smith's catalogue was titled, set important new standards for the rare-book business across the country and for Los Angeles typography and book design. The catalogue represented a bold debut for the Plantin Press of Saul and Lillian Marks, founded in partnership with banker Kenneth McKay in November 1931 at the Printing Center Building at 1220 Maple Avenue near Pico in Los Angeles, and it was soon followed by an equally impressive production, also for Zeitlin's Primavera Press, an edition of Alexandre Dumas's *A Gil Blas in California.* This stunning book, which also made the Institute of Graphic Arts list of fifty for 1933, testified to the convergence of book production talent in the City of the Angels. Zeitlin published it; Ward Ritchie designed it; Paul Landacre engraved the illustrations; and Saul Marks set the type and did the printing.

A *Gil Blas in California* also represented Ward Ritchie's coming of age as a typographer/designer following his return from France, where he had studied for a year as a resident in the household of Parisian book designer François-Louis Schmied. A native Southern Californian, born in Los Angeles in 1905, Harry Ward Ritchie graduated from Occidental and desultorily entered the USC law school with an unfocused desire to do something literary with his life. He began to write poetry and within the decade developed an exquisite minor talent, but like his friend and sometime employer Jake Zeitlin, Ritchie in no way saw poetry as a career, especially after the crash of October 1929. The death from congenital heart trouble of his girlfriend Marion Carr, to whom he had become pinned at Occidental, left Ritchie even further discombobulated. Browsing one day in August 1928 in the book department of Robinson's department store in Los Angeles, Ritchie happened upon *The Journals of Thomas Cobden-Sanderson* in two volumes, marked down from $25 to $6.25. The searching law student bought the *Journals* and in the weeks that followed he absorbed with a shock of recognition the first-hand story of how Cobden-Sanderson, a well-connected English lawyer with literary inclinations ("Great God, souse me in literature!"), left the law at age 40 to join the William Morris circle as a bookbinder and later founded the Doves Press. Intrigued by the prospect of following in Cobden-Sanderson's footsteps, Ritchie turned to a number of local resources for guidance.

At the Huntington Library, his first stop, Ritchie was told that while bookbinding remained virtually untaught in the United States, San Francisco was an important center of fine printing, particularly in the establishments of John Henry Nash and the Grabhorn brothers. Traveling north to San Francisco in mid-November 1928, Ritchie called upon Robert and Edward Grabhorn, who half-promised Ritchie a job. An apron-clad John Henry Nash, setting type in his shop when Ritchie called, was equally receptive. Nash, however, suggested that since it took about forty years to make a great printer, Ritchie should return to Southern California and learn the fundamentals. Nash recommended that Ritchie call upon Bruce McCallister, then at the height of his boom-era busyness.

Back in Los Angeles, Ritchie found McCallister at the gleaming new Young & McCallister plant at the corner of Pico and Santee, where a large staff of artists and printers was kept busy on real-estate brochures, Sunkist labels, restaurant menus, and the thousand and one printed items a burgeoning urban society was devouring on a daily basis. Using his influence as a member of the advisory board, McCallister got Ritchie admitted at mid-semester into the Frank Wiggins Trade School, the vocational arm of the Los Angeles public school system, where alongside teenagers six to seven years his junior the former law student learned the fundamentals of his newly chosen calling.

Ritchie's instructors at Frank Wiggins allowed him to proceed at his own pace in his mastery of types, typesetting, typographic composition, and print technology. Ritchie also read deeply in the history and art of printing and sought further informal instruction from Alice Millard out in Pasadena. There, at La Miniatura, Ritchie had the opportunity to examine under the white-haired but still beautiful Mrs. Millard (the image of First Lady Barbara Bush comes to mind) examples of great printing from the continent and from the Kelmscott, Doves, and Ashendene presses of England. Having expanded upon her late husband's contacts through buying trips to Europe and England, Alice Millard sketched out for Ritchie, rapidly, anecdotally, the present situation in fine printing and graphic arts in these faraway magical places. She also dispatched him to the Huntington and the Clark libraries to examine specific books on deposit in these institutions. Between the hardheaded instruction at the Frank Wiggins Trade School and the sensitive tutelege of Mrs. Millard, Harry Ward Ritchie rapidly assimilated the rudiments and subtleties of his art within the greater Los Angeles confines of the Huntington, the Clark, La Miniatura, and the Frank Wiggins Trade School.

Next up in this bibliographic batting order was the instructive friendship of another young aspiring printer, Ward Ritchie's eventual partner Gregg Anderson. Because he died young in World War II, an infantry first lieutenant leading his men on patrol in Normandy a month into the invasion, a mood of elegaic regret has always clung to the memory of Gregg Anderson, the fallen prince of fine printing in Southern California. Remembered as a young man without guile, an *anima naturaliter christiana*, Anderson had already by late 1928, when he first met Ritchie made precocious progress in his chosen field. He had begun printing at age 15 while still in high school. Impressed by his printing and his knowledge of the field, Robert Schad, curator of rare books and fine printing at the Huntington Library, offered Anderson a position helping sort and arrange the fine print collection so swiftly assembled by the founder, George D. Smith and A.S.W. Rosenbach. Sorting out the Huntington collection, while pursuing an ambitious program of reading, Anderson became even more precociously informed. While at the Huntington, Anderson also took the equivalent of a correspondence course from Porter Garnett at Carnegie Tech, who generously answered his inquiries by letter and sent him guidelines and assignments. Working with another Huntington employee, Roland Baughman, Anderson established the Grey Bow Press at the Huntington, where the two aspiring printers put Garnett's instruction into practice and pursued their own creative experiments.

Thus when Ward Ritchie met Gregg Anderson in South Pasadena in November or December 1928, he was meeting the crown prince of fine print in the Southland, a man who had been elected to the Zamorano Club when barely twenty-one. The friendship between the two future partners was immediate. Generously, Anderson guided Ritchie through a course of secondary reading which supplemented and professionalized his instruction from Alice Millard. Anderson also shared his letters from Porter Garnett, which Ritchie read and absorbed, and provided him with the names and addresses of the finest book-sellers in France, England, and the United States, encouraging Ritchie to write away for catalogues.

By early 1930, having finished his courses at the Frank Wiggins Trade School, Ritchie was ready for creative contact with a remaining cast of local worthies. Supporting himself as an employee of Vroman's in Pasadena, in itself a rite of passage for those aspiring after books and literature, Ritchie rented press time on weekends from Clyde Browne at Abbey San Encino (Browne charged him a dollar a day) and began printing a series of poetry booklets—Carl Sandburg, Archibald MacLeish, Leonie Adams, Robinson Jeffers, and Ritchie's Occiden-tal professor Carlyle MacIntyre—for sale by Jake Zeitlin At the Sign of the Grasshopper. Gregg Anderson, who had introduced Ritchie to both Zeitlin and Browne, had in the meanwhile entered Pomona, rooming with John Cage, a student of music and an aspiring composer. By this time both Anderson and Ritchie had exhausted the resources of Southern California.

Withdrawing from Pomona, Anderson moved to San Francisco to intern with the Grabhorns, while Ritchie left for Paris to present himself to the pre-eminent printer and book designer François-Louis Schmied. Alice Millard had first introduced Ritchie to the work of this Swiss-born Parisian, showing Ritchie a copy of Schmied's *Le Cantique des Cantiques* (1925), a sumptuously colored and illustrated version of Ernest Renan's translation of the *Song of Songs* and one of the great books of the twentieth century, which Millard was about to sell to Estelle Doheny. Holding this bold but exquisite book in his hands, Ritchie discovered the style, the school, the tradition he would work in: inter-actions of print and space and color at once bold and subtle. Schmied's hand-engraved, hand-painted color blocks especially enchanted the aspiring typogra-pher. Schmied would combine up to forty of them to create one illustration. In these adornments Schmied was bridging the book with the other visual arts, creating a pattern of cross-reference which prompted *The Fleuron* to claim (thanks to Gregg Anderson, Ritchie read this as well) that François-Louis Schmied was developing the book of the future: the book, that is, restored to its rightful place as a high art form synergistically related to the other visual arts.

Joining his mother and aunt on a tour of the continent, Ritchie made ar-rangements to stop off in Paris for a year while retaining the right to return to Los Angeles on the original tour ticket. He had previously contacted Schmied by letter to his Paris bookseller Seligmann and Son enquiring as to instruction. Schmied did not take students, Seligmann wrote back, but if he did it would cost Ritchie six thousand francs a month, which for Ritchie was financially beyond the question. With the impudence of youth, Ritchie boldly presented himself to Schmied at the master's atelier at 74 bis rue Halle near the Porte d'Orleans and asked for a non-paying apprenticeship. Frustrated by Ritchie's pigeon French, Schmied called for an interpreter. Where exactly was Southern California, asked the master, a bearded bear of a man well over six feet in height. Near Hollywood, Ritchie replied. A gleam of recognition sparkled in Schmied's eyes. Ah, Hollywood . . . the young man has indeed come a long way. "We had some [more] conversation back and forth," Ritchie later remembered, "and I noticed Mr. Schmied was looking at me very carefully. All of a sudden he threw up his hands in a typical French gesture, said something to the young man and walked out. He then turned to me and said, 'Well, Mr. Schmied doesn't know what to do. He said that since you'd come all the way from California to work for him, he can't send you back. Come to work on Monday.' "[4]

Despite his initial difficulties with spoken French and with printed French accents and the French type case, which is differently arranged from the English, Ritchie spent a transforming year in Paris as an intern in the atelier of the world's greatest book designer. Ritchie's duties included English lessons for Schmied's daughter and assistance in bottling wine from casks for the family's private cellar: Indeed, as his French improved, Ritchie was taken more closely into the Schmied family circle and was a frequent guest at their well-set table. Ensconced *au grenier* in a small hotel on rue Bonaparte across from the church of St. Germain des Près, Ritchie spent his off-hours browsing in the bookstores and outdoor bookstalls along the Seine before the cold drove him into the Deux Magots for a warming brandy and coffee. Armed with introductions from Alice Millard, he crossed the channel to call upon Richard Cobden-Sanderson, the son of the man whose *Journal* had so transformed his life, and Sir Sydney Cockerell, William Morris's associate, and May Morris, the poet/printer's surviving daughter. When one is young and making one's start, such contacts, however superficial, possess a power of identification that lasts for a lifetime.

Returning to Southern California in 1931, Ward Ritchie (he had dropped the Harry as too cumbersome) worked for a short time selling books for Jake Zeitlin, who quickly fired him and told him to get on with his proper work, which was printing. Scratching together the first month's rent, Ritchie established a press in a converted barn in South Pasadena, using old type he bought from the Grabhorns in San Francisco for twenty-five cents a pound. A year and a half later, armed with a new type fount and a Colt's Armory press, Ritchie moved to an old ranch house in a valley between Hollywood and Los Angeles just over the hill from the Silver Lake district.

The contracts began to come in. In the summer of 1932, thanks to the recommendation of Alice Millard, Ritchie received the commission for the catalogue for the inaugural exhibition of Mrs. Doheny's books at the new library at USC. Ritchie designed it with appropriate sumptuousness, using for the preface an unusual English typeface, Poliphilus, which he borrowed from

Clyde Browne. Two more commissions from Mrs. Doheny, *The Book as a Work of Art* and a description of the Morris-Burne Jones *Aeneid*, followed. Alice Millard commissioned a catalogue of Doves books. Jake Zeitlin sent Primavera Press work along, including *A Gil Blas in California*. Occidental commissioned a new handbook; the Getty family required an *In Memoriam* for the recently departed George Franklin Getty. The Historical Society of Southern California retained Ritchie to design its *Quarterly*. The Zamorano Club ordered an auction catalogue and elected Ritchie to membership. When a group of Hollywood stars of British and Commonwealth descent wished to congratulate His Britannic Majesty King George V upon the occasion of the twenty-fifth anniversary of his accession to the throne, Ritchie prepared a sumptuous folio in one copy which they all signed and sent with due ceremony to Buckingham Palace.

In the summer of 1935 Gregg Anderson joined his former tutee as an employee. A few years later, Ritchie and Anderson became partners. The next year, Joseph Simon, Lillian Marks's younger brother, joined the firm as a compositor, becoming a partner in 1951. The commercial firm of Anderson & Ritchie held together through the 1940s, with the Ward Ritchie Press maintained as its book publishing imprint. Despite the Depression, Southern California had work for Anderson & Ritchie and the Ward Ritchie Press. The cultural and literary life of the region, in fact, can be significantly reassembled from a selective survey of their imprints. The Ward Ritchie Press did design work for books by Merle Armitage (a study of the U.S. Navy for Longmans, an edition of Bellamy's *Looking Backward* for the Limited Editions Club) and for books by Aldous Huxley and Rockwell Kent on consignment from eastern publishers. Robinson Jeffers-related material was extensively published, including a pioneering study by Lawrence Clark Powell, while the younger poets William Everson and Alfred Young Fisher were also introduced. Powell wrote an important study of the manuscripts of D.H. Lawrence, for which Huxley wrote the preface. The Ward Ritchie Press continued to produce catalogues for Estelle Doheny, Alice Millard, Zamorano, and the Huntington and Clark libraries. In the field of regional history, it issued Cleland's *The History of Occidental College* (1937) and his classic *The Cattle on a Thousand Hills* (1941), the latter for the Huntington Library Press. The emergent wine and food culture of Southern California, even then in the process of nurturing the important talent of M.F.K. Fisher, was evident in many excellent food and wine books issued by the Ward Ritchie Press during this period.

In Northern California the earlier tradition of formality, simplicity, and heritage, pioneered by San Francisco printer Edward Bosqui, was counterposed by the early twentieth-century Nash tradition of decorative medievalism and the Art Nouveau. Edwin and Robert Grabhorn, who moved their studio from Indianapolis to San Francisco in 1919, began in this vein of luxuriance as influenced by William Morris and the Arts and Crafts movement but soon simplified their style under the influence of another English master, St. John Hornby of the Ashendene Press. While eclectic in their approach, the Grabhorns were consistent in their clarity and simplicity, thus reviving the Edward Bosqui side of the design dialectic. The Grabhorns also used color in their designs, which was their link to Schmied in Paris and to Ward Ritchie. Like Schmied, the Grabhorns considered the book an art form in dialogue with other genres in the visual arts. A book was a design solution for specific materials. It was also an aesthetic presentation akin to painting. From 1926 to 1933 the artist Valenti Angelo was an essential member of the Grabhorn team.

In Southern California this Bosqui/Grabhorn tradition of disciplined simplicity divided into two streams, Grant Dahlstrom and Saul Marks dominating one fork, Thomas Williams and Ward Ritchie dominating the other. Merle Armitage and his disciple Alvin Lustig comprised an avant-garde stream that gushed forth from independent sources. Temperamentally, aesthetically, Grant Dahlstrom was a traditionalist. Influenced by the book designs of Sir Francis Meynell for the Nonesuch Press, Grant Dahlstrom favored an assuredly elegant style based upon a clean and direct presentation of traditional typefaces—Caslon, Granjon, Bembo, Linotype Aldus, Trajanus, Times Roman—whose matrices for casting he imported into Los Angeles, in many instances for the first time. Dahlstrom also followed Meynell in the sparing use of printer's flowers, many of them from the sixteenth century, as decorative devices. While Dahlstrom admired the typefaces created by Nicolas Jenson in 1470, Saul Marks admired the sixteenth-century printer Christopher Plantin. Marks favored a light, graceful style, suggestive of Plantin's work itself. Whatever their differences, Dahlstrom and Marks were essentially historicists, with Marks being a de facto antiquarian in his adherence to a fixed, traditional format.

Thomas Williams and Ward Ritchie, by contrast, while prizing tradition and restraint, saw in the book—as did Schmied and the Grabhorns—an opportunity for other art forms, engravings and woodcuts especially, and for color. Into his Fine Arts Press books Williams introduced as rubricated lettering and other decorative devices the earth and sky colors of Southern California and the Southwest. Ward Ritchie understood this synesthetic technique perfectly, having absorbed it from the master himself in Paris. Over the years, in his designs for the Ward Ritchie Press, but also in his work for Knopf and the University of California Press, Ritchie's books would glow with color like Southern California itself. A student of Schmied, Ritchie loved woodcuts. In 1932 he gained his first national attention with a design he did for an eight-page insert for *Colophon* to accompany a short essay by Robinson Jeffers discussing the publication of the poet's first book. Ritchie's design featured a druidic woodcut by Paul Landacre of Hawk Tower floating atop five lines of type like an ancient Celtic citadel glimpsed through an Irish fog. One could almost feel the winds of the Carmel coast. The composite strength of Ritchie's blending of typography, color, decoration, and illustration emerged most vividly in his Southern

California, Southwest, and Mexico books, including those published by Knopf, the University of California, and the Huntington Library; his many books dealing with Native American culture; his cookbooks; and his many books on wine and food, beginning with Robert Balzer's pioneering *California's Best Wines* (1947).

Thus the fine print community of greater Los Angeles found itself, a bohemia of sorts, dovetailing with the book communities of downtown and Hollywood, the history circles of Pasadena/San Marino and the downtown, and the writers' movable feast flowing through Stanley Rose's bookstore, the Brown Derby, and Musso & Frank's. By October 1931 the fine print community had reached such a point of self-awareness that yet another organization was formed, the Thistle Club, modeled on the Double Crown Club of London. Meeting at Jake Zeitlin's hillside house at 1559 Altivo Way in the Echo Park district of Los Angeles on the evening of 19 November 1931, the group changed its name to the Rounce & Coffin, the names for two components of a hand press, and elected Grant Dahlstrom president. Begun lightheartedly as a circle of like-minded fine print aficionados meeting informally in one another's homes, the Rounce & Coffin evolved in the late 1930s into a more coherent organization meeting monthly at the Constance Hotel in Pasadena. Beginning in 1938, the Rounce & Coffin sponsored an annual exhibition of books designed and printed in the West, with a published catalogue denoting excellence in various categories.

Gregg Anderson functioned as the informally chosen paragon and leader of the fine print wing of the greater Los Angles book community. Left a widower when his young wife succumbed to tuberculosis, Anderson threw himself wholeheartedly into his work at Anderson & Ritchie. Under Anderson's influence the L-shaped ranch house between Hollywood and downtown Los Angeles, set near a grove of sixty eucalyptus trees, developed into a studio workshop worthy of William Morris himself. For the entrance, sculptor Gordon Newell cut a tavern signboard depicting the anchor and bull imprint of Antonio Espinosa, the first printer in the New World. One wing of the studio held the two main presses, a Galley Universal and a Colt's Armory. In the long gallery, polished type cabinets banked the whitewashed pine walls, frequently hung with page proofs. A high brick fireplace dominated one end of the gallery, and there was also a grandfather's clock and a grand piano. Off this central space was a separate library room, with a collection of three thousand volumes devoted to bibliography and fine print. It is not surprising that this place became a resort, a point of reference, for the fine print and bibliophilic community— Ritchie's Road House, as Lawrence Clark Powell described it. In the Ritchie ranch house was materialized the dream of printing as a fine art and the concept of the printer's role as central to intellectual and literary life as it had been in the Renaissance.

Jake Zeitlin's designation of this period as a small Renaissance, Southern

California-style, held much validity; for through bibliophilia and its attendant activities—reading, collecting, printing, and, most important, gathering together for talk at the University Club with the Zamoranans, in the back room at Stanley Rose's bookstore or over the bar at Musso & Frank, at meetings of the Authors' club at the Brown Derby or the Rounce & Coffin at the Constance Hotel in Pasadena, or with Jake Zeitlin At the Sign of the Grasshopper or near the fireplace at the Ward Ritchie Press—an urban intelligentsia formed itself. Like any first-rate city Los Angeles would need this urban intelligentsia in the years ahead: this one, oriented towards books and writing, the design-oriented circle gathering during the same period around John Entenza and *Arts and Architecture* magazine, and the musical and performing arts circles spinning off from the film studios. Coming of age, Los Angeles needed more than its Automobile Club or its Board of Realtors. The book provided the City of the Angels with an available and relatively inexpensive way for its intelligentsia to galvanize itself into interconnected communities. The book and its related arts served as a vehicle of enjoyment and self-identification for intellectuals who were finding themselves in a relatively unprecedented city: oligarchs in search of something to identify with beyond business, Hollywood writers holding out for better days beyond the hack assignments of the studios, locals aspiring towards the larger world of art and literature beyond Los Angeles, printers desirous of restoring their craft. The book materialized these individual dreams and also helped in the process to solidify the identity of Los Angeles. The book helped Los Angeles come of age and identify itself to itself and to others as a city ready for the next stage of cultural evolution.

13

On the Blue Train Through Dijon

Pasadena Begins Its Literary Career

By the late 1930s, literary Southern California, like Caesar's Gaul, was divided into three parts: Hollywood, *Europa*, and locals. The Hollywood and European communities were by and large the product of exile, although many of them evolved into ardent Southern Californians. The locals, in turn, tended to divide into two camps: the hardboiled minimalists epitomized by Raymond Chandler but also including lyrical minimalists such as John Fante of Los Angeles and Judy van der Veer of backcountry San Diego; and the literary Pasadenans. This last group represented a noticeably indigenous camp. The Hollywood and European exiles, many of them at least—William Faulkner, Thomas Mann, F. Scott Fitzgerald, Franz Werfel, Theodore Dreiser, Emil Ludwig—are today considered from the perspective of world literature; and many of the hardboiled minimalists, Edmund Wilson's Boys in the Back Room, are not lagging far behind in reputation, favored as they are by ordinary readers and by deconstructivist critics alike. The Pasadenans, by contrast, constitute the most regional, and occasionally provincial, grouping, which for the cultural historian confers upon them their own special value as protagonists in a social setting.

Like similar places across the United States—Cambridge, Massachusetts; Charleston, South Carolina; Oak Park, Illinois; Palo Alto and Berkeley in Northern California—Pasadena and its attendant communities of South Pasadena, San Marino, Altadena, and Highland Park once upon a time constituted a state of mind. Here the genteel tradition grafted itself onto Southern California circumstances. Pasadena embodied the certainties and pursuits of the white Protestant upper middle classes: education, refinement, a cautiously progressive point of view on social and political issues, all of it modified but not enervated by the sunshine of Southern California. Thus Pasadenans played tennis and golf and spent time at country clubs but they also read books and cared intensely about literature and serious theater, a concern that led to the founding of the Pasadena Community Playhouse in 1916, which soon became one of the important little theater companies in the United States. The Altadena poet Hildegarde Flanner lectured at the Pasadena Community Playhouse in the late 1920s on contemporary poetry, her presence on the platform being perhaps the most important aspect of her communication; for Hildegarde Flanner—intense, ethereal, as fine-tuned in her perceptions as her sister Janet, who wrote letters from Paris under the name Genêt for *The New Yorker*—reigned as poet laureate of Pasadena during this period.

Like so many in that town, Hildegarde Flanner was originally a Midwesterner, born in Indianapolis. First visiting Southern California in 1915 as a girl of fifteen, Flanner met the renowned Miss Olive Percival, whom she would eventually join as a presiding divinity of place. Then in her mid-forties, Olive Percival lived with her mother in a two-story stone and timbered Elizabethan country seat set in a grove of eucalyptus, sycamores, and oaks in the Garvanza district on the Arroyo Seco near Pasadena. Choosing to remain single after the loss of an early admirer ("I believe I am the only virgin in Los Angeles County," she once remarked), Percival read and collected books, ten thousand of them, and Japanese *objets d'art*. She was also an inveterate gardener and made flowers the subject matter of many of her poems. Lunching with her mother and Miss Percival at Robinson's department store that day in 1915, Hildegarde Flanner might have glimpsed in the way that young people sometimes experience such prophetic intuitions the role that was waiting for her some fifteen years hence as co-avatar along with Percival of the Pasadena sensibility, acted out and poetically expressed.

In 1919 Flanner returned to Berkeley as an undergraduate. Her poetry won the approval of Witter Bynner, a poet teaching in the English department, and in 1920 *Young Girl*, a book of her verse, was elaborately printed by Porter Garnett in San Francisco. In 1923, after being burned out by the great Berkeley fire, Hildegarde and her mother moved to Southern California where in 1926 she married Frederick Monhoff, an artist and architect, and moved with him to Altadena, a rustic suburb north of Pasadena. Over the course of the next decade Hildegarde Flanner produced another four volumes of poetry by 1942. She also resumed her acquaintanceship with Olive Percival, by now in her fifties and growing stout beneath her great flowered hats—such as the particularly grand creation Percival wore at a garden party for Harold Nicholson and Vita Sackville-West: "a hat extraordinary," Flanner later remembered, "in its crowded tumult of velvet pansies, a stampede of pansies. It was a beautiful, even a terrifying hat. It completed Miss Percival's dignity on top of Miss Percival, in a way that left the rest of us breathing hard with pride of Los Angeles County."[1]

Like her friend and mentor Olive Percival, Hildegarde Flanner sustained a

note of something remote, disengaged, virginal even in both her personal demeanor and her poetic voice. She was, as Jake Zeitlin observed, the Emily
Dickinson of Pasadena, as in her very Dickinsonian poem "Dianthus":

> They say that my grandmother often
> picked you
> And placed your quaint perfume
> At her tight girdle.
>
> My grandmother
> Did Vergil into French
> And then had seven children.
> I shall not pick you,
> Dianthus.

Or the equally Dickinsonian "Mood":

> My shadow going on before
> Flutters like a leaf,
> But it can never reach the door
> Before my grief.
> My grief goes first and takes the key
> To open the door and welcome me.
> He offers me a lonely cup
> Full of lily wine
> And says, "Come sister, share this drink,
> Yours and mine."

Flanner played a perfect role for Pasadena, the Edwardian girl, seriously interested in faith, doubt, mysticism, gardens, and flowers. In the 1930s she evolved
into an academic minimalist with no embarrassing interval of flapper rebellion
in between. There was something fundamentally traditional, safe, Pasadenan,
to everything Hildegarde Flanner wrote. The strength in her poetry emerged
from its surge of romantic feeling disciplined by highly classical forms. As a
poet, she evolved over the years. The vague persona of *Young Girl* became
more localized, more willing to submit herself to realities of time and place.
By the publication of *If There Is Time* (1942) she was filling her poetry with
images of Mount Wilson Observatory, Spanish Revival stucco suburbs, the
Arroyo Seco Parkway, the hawks, owls, rattlesnakes, and deer of the chaparral,
the sound of a Santa Fe freight train passing through Pasadena in the lonely
night.

   If Hildegarde Flanner epitomized the literary spirit of Pasadena, its academic
expression could be found in the nearby Occidental College. While the California Institute of Technology was located in Pasadena itself, it belonged to the
national and international world of science in terms of both its faculty and its

students. Occidental, by contrast, a Presbyterian-related institution, derived its students and spirit from greater Pasadena as a center of upper-middle-class Protestant culture. Located since 1914 in the community of Eagle Rock five miles from downtown Pasadena, Occidental flourished under the leadership of president Remsen Bird, an ordained church historian with a genius for public relations and development, and trustees chairman Alphonzo Bell, a multimillionaire developer responsible for Bel-Air and many other successful suburban districts. Himself an Occidental alumnus, Bell studied briefly for the ministry after graduation, before devoting himself to tennis (men's singles champion for Southern California in 1900, 1901, and 1904), real estate, and, after a huge field of crude was discovered beneath his Santa Fe Springs Ranch in 1921, the oil business.

While Bell lined up support from Protestant oligarchs who preferred a more refined alternative to rah-rah USC, Remsen Bird, an instinctive socializer, established himself as a leading Los Angeles celebrity intellectual, including an active membership in the Jake Zeitlin circle, where he amused one and all with his gifts as a quick-sketch caricaturist. It was Bird, in fact, who first suggested organizing the artists' sketch club which met at various places on the Hill. Adoring celebrities, especially in the arts, Remsen Bird had Occidental alumnus Robinson Jeffers honored with a doctorate and brought figures such as Thomas Mann, Frieda Lawrence, and Aldous Huxley into the Occidental circle. Huxley later repaid Bird by satirizing him in *After Many a Summer Dies the Swan* (1939), a blow from which, so Jake Zeitlin believed, Bird never recovered. With Alphonzo Bell and Remsen Bird working in tandem, Occidental attracted support whose material expression was the opulent Mediterranean Revival campus masterplanned and designed by Myron Hunt and landscaped by the Harvard-trained landscape architect Beatrix Farrand (her husband Max directed the nearby Huntington Library and Art Gallery), who had performed similar landscaping services for Princeton, Yale, Chicago, and Cal Tech. By the late 1930s the Occidental campus glistened elegantly in the sunshine, a perfect expression of Protestant high-mindedness having achieved its sunny Mediterranean material dream.

To Occidental College came local boys such as Lawrence Clark Powell and Ward Ritchie of South Pasadena. Each later wrote extensively of the special texture of Pasadena life in the teens and twenties, with its mingled associations of Craftsman bungalows amidst the orange groves and the genteel rhythms of daily life in their citrus-banked community. Their recollections, scattered across some two dozen imprints, constitute a lyrical, elegaic preservation through memory and prose of what it meant to come of age in the greater Pasadena of that era. Considered cumulatively, Lawrence Clark Powell's recollections, the more extensive of the two, constitute an achieved *Bildungsroman* of great value for anyone wishing to re-experience Southern California in its early twentieth-century upper-middle-class Protestant ascendancy. The Powell family constituted a case study in Pasadena style and value. Both parents were of Hudson River Valley Quaker descent and were graduates of Cornell, where they had met. A student of the Cornell horticulturist Liberty Hyde Bailey, G. Harold Powell joined the Bureau of Plant Industry of the Department of Agriculture in Washington, D.C., as a pomologist and won a national reputation as an expert in the cooperative packing, shipping, and marketing of fresh fruit. Powell's specialty, the orange, took him frequently to Southern California, where he made many friends in the citrus industry. In 1911 Powell accepted the post of general manager of the California Fruit Growers Exchange, better known by its packaging label Sunkist, and moved his wife and three sons to South Pasadena.

The orange was Powell's passion. He wrote on it as a plant scientist. He managed its marketing and distribution for Sunkist. He amused his sons by his ability to strip a giant navel with a continuous encirclement of his pocket knife without allowing the growing ribbon of peel to break. The orange was also the primary fact and symbol of South Pasadena. Orange groves ran right into and partially through the town itself, skirmishing flanks of an orange front that ran from Riverside and Redlands along the base of the San Gabriels before cascading westward as an advancing army of fruit and flowers which at its greatest strength held the valleys of the southern shore from Santa Barbara to San Diego. Located on the southern side of Pasadena's Raymond Hill and adjacent to San Marino, South Pasadena had grown up as an exurban township connected to Pasadena and downtown Los Angeles by the big red cars of the Pacific Electric. Surrounded by orange groves which also hosted a rich wildlife of rabbits, doves, quails, and an occasional coyote loping in from the hills, South Pasadena simultaneously provided a pastoral and a developed civic environment, the deliberate creation of the middle and upper middle classes who dominated the greater Pasadena region northeast of Los Angeles.

A Phi Beta Kappa graduate of Cornell in classics and mathematics, Gertrude Clark Powell fit easily into the Pasadenan mold. She read constantly. She kept a private journal and grew roses. She was active in the PTA and sang in the Pasadena Women's Glee Club. There was some suggestion—not a reproach, merely a suggestion—that she found her energetic husband's physical demands a trifle excessive. Meanwhile, there were Red Seal records of Schubert and Brahms to play on the manually wound Victrola and poems from A Child's Garden of Verses which she recited by heart to her children. She collected books by and about the English diarist Samuel Pepys and maintained an ongoing interest in spiritualism and the New Thought. On intermittent Saturdays Gertrude Powell took the Pacific Electric in to Los Angeles to shop at Robinson's department store.

The Powell household in South Pasadena (there were two temporary places before a permanent home was acquired on Marengo Avenue) was filled with pictures, books, fine furniture, and Oriental rugs, all of it blending perfectly into the warm redwood interior of the U-shaped fourteen-room Craftsman structure built in 1900 in a grove of oak and eucalyptus. With a salary of $20,000 a year, G. Harold Powell could afford to keep himself and his family in affluence. He dressed in great style: tailored suits, celluloid collars, a luxuriant necktie held in place by a diamond stickpin. After dinner he smoked a fine Havana cigar which his youngest son Larry, snuggled in his father's lap, was allowed to light. Since the membership of his cooperative extended throughout much of Southern California, Powell maintained an air-cooled 1914 Franklin automobile, replaced in 1916 with a maroon-colored Marmon with cream-colored wire wheels, the initials GHP scripted in gold leaf on the doors. All three Powell boys had piano lessons. A Lithuanian woman cooked dinner each evening, and a Japanese couple came in two days a week to do house-cleaning and gardening. The Powells belonged to the local tennis club (Upton Sinclair came over from Altadena to play in tournaments) and maintained a beach cottage at East Newport on the Orange County shore and a mountain cabin in the Big Santa Anita Canyon from which hiking and fishing trips into the San Gabriels were organized.

Big enough and small enough, town and country, South Pasadena afforded its boys and girls a mixed Tom Sawyer/Huck Finn, Becky Thatcher/tom-girl sort of life, which both Lawrence Clark Powell and Ward Ritchie later remembered and set down with pointillist detail. The boys of South Pasadena were allowed to roam the orange groves in wild democratic packs which mixed the classes to the advantage of everyone. Supplementing these experiences of rabbit hunts and green orange fights between competing gangs and the smoking of purloined cigarettes in irrigation ditches were dancing lessons on Wednesday evenings at the Women's Clubhouse and the rigors of the Marengo Grammar School, where starched pinafores for girls and knee breeches for boys were mandatory through the eighth grade. To Marengo Grammar came the offspring of South Pasadena bourgeoisie, local merchants, railroad and orange grove workers, and the scions of San Marino, which had no public school, driven over in chauffeured limosines. What Josiah Royce described as the democracy of the schoolyard frequently asserted itself, especially among the boys, for certain abilities (to be able to piss across a road, for example, hitting a distant tin can) pre-empted social class, however temporarily.

By 1922 G. Harold Powell, increasingly well known since his association with Herbert Hoover in the Food Administration in Washington from 1917 to 1919, was being mentioned as a Republican candidate for the U.S. Senate. The very night of 18 February 1922 when his name formally surfaced as a pro-Hoover, anti-Hiram Johnson candidate, Powell succumbed to a heart attack at a Republican banquet held at the Hotel Maryland in Pasadena. Overwork during the war as Hoover's manager for perishable foods had helped shorten his life. Had he lived, Powell might have gone on to the Senate or, more likely, joined his friend Herbert Hoover as Secretary of Agriculture when Hoover went to the White House in 1928. Secretary of Commerce Hoover spoke at Powell's memorial services. As it was, the Powells were left with sufficient income to maintain their position amidst the urban gentry of greater Pasadena. After high school, the three Powell boys went on, variously, to Stanford, Berkeley, and, in Lawrence Clark's case, Occidental. While at South Pasadena High School, Powell served as yell leader, played the male lead Willie Baxter in a production of Booth Tarkington's *Seventeen*, mastered the saxophone and formed a jazz band, wrote for the school paper, and perfected his stenography and typing skills, of great use to him later in his research and writing career. Ward Ritchie excelled at track, field, and football. When Ritchie broke his arm on the grid-iron, Powell did the honors behind the wheel of Ritchie's red Buick roadster. High-school high-jinks in the Jazz Age could take their toll. With the exception of the courses he liked, Powell had mediocre grades. It took the personal intervention of Gertrude Powell, conspicuously wearing her Phi Beta Kappa key, to persuade the principal of South Pasadena High School to recommend Lawrence Clark to Occidental.

Powell's portrayal of Willie Baxter, hero of *Seventeen*, on the stage of South Pasadena High serves as a fitting gloss to the fact that life in greater Pasadena, and much of Southern California for that matter, possessed in these early decades of the twentieth century, continuing through the 1950s, a Midwestern, mid-American texture worthy of Booth Tarkington in his most Indianaizing mode. The Powells and thousands of other affluent, educated, bookish, energetic, Midwestern (or upstate New York) Protestant families played out their roles as the magnificent Ambersons of greater Pasadena; but then again, it is not surprising that Midwesterners—such as the Indianans who founded Pasadena in the first place—should translate the values of their home region to Southern California or that these values should in turn help create a society quintessentially mid-American or upper-middle-American Protestant in texture. The definition of Southern California via its eccentricities and exceptions (and there were plenty of these) must be balanced by the broader realities of greater Pasadena.

Founded to express and preserve these values, Occidental College welcomed its class of 1928. While the lyrics of Occidental remained formally Presbyterian (daily chapel was compulsory), the music to which the undergraduates sang and danced in the year of Our Lord 1924 was becoming, increasingly, the synchopations of the Jazz Age: as in "Jazz Me, Baby," which Lawrence Clark Powell was playing one night on the parlor piano at Phi Gamma Delta when Dean Robert Glass Cleland entered, ministerial behind his rimless glasses (the same style of spectacles favored by Dr. Remsen Bird) and, finding the room in an uproar around Powell's music, realized that new currents were pulsating through the college of choice of Presbyterian Pasadena. More intensely than any prewar generation, collegians of the 1920s were defining themselves through their music which, as Louis "Satchmo" Armstrong joyously gravel-crooned, was jazz, jazz, jazz! Adept at piano and tenor saxophone, Powell played his way, musically and otherwise, through a five-year Joe College career, riveted to the piano in his fraternity house parlor or playing piano or sax with the Varsity Vagabonds, which he organized, or other college bands out of Pomona or UCLA.

Withdrawing from Occidental at the end of his freshman year, Powell spent a semester seeing the world as a musician on the *President Harrison* of the Dollar Line in its leisurely cruise of the major ports of Europe and the Far East. He spent the summer of 1926 playing the resorts around Big Bear Lake in the San Bernardino Mountains; the summer of 1927 playing a Hollywood nightclub; the summer of 1928 serving as a ship's musician on the S.S. *Yale*, which plied the coast in tandem with the S.S. *Harvard* between San Diego, San Pedro, and San Francisco. Back at Occidental during the regular semester it was jazz, jazz, jazz as well: late hours at the fraternity or at weekend college dances, jam sessions at local clubs, little sleep, bootleg booze and cigarettes, and constant rebellion against the pieties of Dean Cleland, who suspended Powell for a week in his senior year when one late-night party at Phi Gamma Delta where Powell was president got out of hand.

It was, after all, the Jazz Age, even in Pasadena, and with it came an expanded sense of personal possibilities as well as the rhythmns of "Jazz Me, Baby" pounded out on the fraternity piano. As a ship's musician on the *President Harrison*, Powell visited twenty-six ports of call, playing the hotels of Honolulu, Shanghai, Hong Kong, Manila, and Singapore while the ship was in port. But it was the port cities of France and Italy—Naples, Genoa, Marseilles—which most captivated Powell's imagination, awakening in him another 1920s dream, the lure of Europe, meaning France, Spain, and Italy, Goethe's lands of sunlight and oranges, the Southern California of Europe.

To articulate these dreams of art and life and Europe in literary and personal terms to the young Pasadenans, in whom the hungers of imagination were so splendidly quickening, fate sent to Occidental College a most idiosyncratic and ultimately unassimilable presence, the academic poet Carlyle Ferren MacIntyre. Fresh from Europe, where he had taken his doctorate at the University of Marburg with a dissertation on the employment of color in the poetry of Dante Gabriel Rossetti, the 34-year-old instructor in comparative literature— tall, skinny, pugnacious, a rangeland cowboy Europeanized—was pursuing at full throttle a life of teaching, poetry, Jazz Age dissipation, and something more elusive: a sense of culture, meaning Europe, which was simultaneously conservative and anarchic, formal and unruly and, as in the case of Ezra Pound, whom MacIntyre resembled in minor fashion, highly judgmental of the bourgeoisie and tending towards a conservatism energized by affronted taste.

In the classroom MacIntyre mesmerized the Pasadenans with dramatic presentations of great books, great ideas, and triumphant personalities. Preternaturally erudite, he drew upon world culture for his frame of reference, but his deepest passion was reserved for Europe which, like Ezra Pound, he envisioned as a continuity of culture: passionate, hierarchical (with artists heading the hierarchy), energetically Mediterranean, extending from classical times down through the present in linked expressions of ardor and imagination. While at Marburg, MacIntyre was not an academic approaching the art past as a series of discrete tidepools to be explored and charted. Art and the human experiences distilled into art constituted for him, rather, a massive present, a compelling here and now as well as something preserved in an art form.

Outside the classroom, MacIntyre suggested by his flamboyant life-style, at once *fin de siècle* bohemian and Jazz Age playboy, that Pasadena did not hold a monopoly on the possibilities for human behavior. In the Fitzgeraldian side of his life, MacIntyre said smart things and wore smart clothes and buzzed about Pasadena and Los Angeles in a speeding Pierce Arrow roadster, the top inevitably down. As an Europeanized bohemian, with just a touch of the Arroyo Pasadenan thrown in for grafting stock, MacIntyre lived in the nearby village of La Crescenta at the end of a road near a vineyard and winery in a home which he personally constructed from boulders, field stones, and cement. He filled it with books and paintings and *objets d'art* purchased in Europe, and he brought selected undergraduates there—among them, Lawrence Clark Powell, Ward Ritchie, and Gordon Newell, a Southern Californian bent on becoming a sculptor—for sessions of Prohibition-defying wine drinking (MacIntyre made his own wine from grapes from the nearby vineyard), poetry reading, listening to records (MacIntyre possessed a major collection of classical music and European folk songs), and talk. To Remsen Bird and Robert Glass Cleland's distress, MacIntyre was rumored to bring Occidental coeds there as well for purposes of seduction: "bedding down the missionaries' daughters," MacIntyre described these activities with contemptuous acknowledgement that part of the fun came from debauching the Presbyterian pieties of Pasadena through its female offspring. Finding MacIntyre unassimilable to Occidental, Remsen Bird traded him to UCLA in 1928, where he lasted for a decade, openly contemptuous of his colleagues for the academic leisure they fretted away in talk and committees, until UCLA traded him to Berkeley, where he lasted for a short while, as sarcastic and unassimilable as ever, before being required to take early retirement.

Whatever the contents of his flooded verse diary might have been, the poetry MacIntyre published in the *Atlantic Monthly*, *Harper's*, the *Virginia Quarterly*, the *Yale Review*, and elsewhere during these years, later gathered into the books *Poems* (1936), *Cafés and Cathedrals* (1939), and *The Black Bull* (1942), reveal an appropriately Pasadenan correctness of metrics, verse form, and subject matter. MacIntyre's poetry deals with the immemorial themes of desire and time, permanence and mutability, played out against the time-soaked landscape and litanic place names of Western Europe. Restrained, precise, academically correct, MacIntyre's poetry constitutes an antitype to his defiant, unconventional life-style, save for the fact that its very classicism indicated MacIntyre's major point of contention with his colleagues: their avoidance of hard work within the context of the classical tradition of Western culture. Like Ezra Pound, MacIntyre was in revolt from the right in favor of a more formally correct, more intense, more learned art (among others, MacIntyre revered Ben Jonson) which, paradoxically enough, fit him perfectly into the Pasadenan tradition of which he was so mockingly dismissive. Savagely genteel, MacIntyre was genteel nonetheless, a Peck's Bad Boy in love with culture with a capital C, who felt the necessity to disparage Walt Whitman, which he did continually, in favor of classical-aristocratic alternative voices from Europe. MacIntyre's rebellion was, like all such stances, part statement, part sham, part defensiveness.

It is not surprising that MacIntyre found his true métier as a translator of Goethe, Georg, Rilke, Baudelaire, Verlaine, Corbière, and others for the University of California Press, then directed by his patron and protector the distinguished scholar/publisher August Fruge. Royalties from these translations, together with his small pension from Berkeley, which he reluctantly accepted only after his third and final termination, supported him in Paris in his last years, the most famous American expatriate (so *Time* magazine profiled him) to hang out in ceaseless drink and talk at Le Café des Deux Magots and Café Le Flore before a stroke confined him to his bedroom. There he continued to talk, caustically, and to recall his amorous conquests of the 1920s to visiting Pasadenans until death took him in 1967. "You really couldn't stand to be with him for too long a time," remarked former student Ward Ritchie after returning from Paris, where he had visited his bedridden, paralyzed, but evertalkative former teacher. "There was so much talk going on and a man can never be that witty and brilliant for a long stretch without repeating himself."[2]

Counterbalancing and complementing the Europeanizing influence of Carlyle MacIntyre was the pervasive presence among the Pasadenans of another Occidental poet, Robinson Jeffers. By the 1920s a subtle but discernible cult had attached itself to the former Pasadenan turned Carmelite. In terms of class and cultural background Jeffers was the complete Pasadenan. His father, a Presbyterian professor of Old Testament studies, accomplished in Hebrew, Arabic, Greek, and Latin, Calvinist in persuasion, widely traveled in the Middle East, moved to Pasadena from Pittsburgh in 1903 for his health. The Jefferses were of English, Irish, and Scots descent, hence proper Pasadenans in terms of ethnicity. They were obviously more than a little bookish. Robinson Jeffers commenced Greek at age five under his father's tutelage and grew up being regularly read to from the Bible and classical authors. Acolytes of the genteel, the Jefferses revered Europe. Before he was fifteen, Robinson had traveled extensively throughout Great Britain and the continent and had spent three years in boarding schools in Switzerland and Germany, where he became proficient in German and French. At Occidental, where Jeffers matriculated in 1903 at age 16 with third-year standing, he distinguished himself in Scripture, classics, and literature, much of which he could handle in the original language. He also wrote poetry for and edited *The Aurora*, the undergraduate literary magazine. His first poem, "The Measure," published in *The Aurora* in December 1903, predicted in its imagery of vast nebulae and galactic voids a later poetry based upon a sense of man's accidental place in an infinite and indifferent universe. In this early poem God makes a cameo appearance in the finale as a pious assertion, but empty infinities dominate the debate.

The ethos of the Jeffers household was muscular as well as religious and literary. As a teenager in Switzerland, Robinson achieved distinction as an alpinist, an activity which he transferred easily to the mountains of Southern California. An Occidental classmate, with whom Jeffers climbed Mount San Gorgonio near San Bernardino, later remembered him as someone who "could travel all day with a heavy pack on his back without showing any sign of fatigue. The most vivid picture I have of him is of a tall, loose-jointed individual wearing a very dirty khaki outfit with a blue shirt, swinging along over the mountain trails with a stride that made it difficult for the rest of us to stretch our legs to equal, a pack on his back and on this pack a gunny-sack with two or three frying-pans and a coffee-pot that banged and clattered with every step he took, hatless, and bursting every now and then into a long quotation of poetry from Tennyson or Homer or some other of the great poets."[3] Graduating from Occidental in 1905 at age 18, Jeffers undertook a pre-medical and medical course at USC largely out of fascination with the biological sciences, which he pursued with the same passion he had previously pursued theology, philosophy, and literature during his first undergraduate course. He also ran long distance, swam competitively for USC, and wrestled his way to the intramural heavyweight championship.

Reserved and reclusive despite these athletic accomplishments, Jeffers was also pursuing while at USC a clandestine love affair with a married philosophy student, Una Call Kuster, which added the proper note of *Sturm und Drang* to his developing abilities as a poet. Moody, he spent summer vacations hanging out at Hermosa Beach, beachcombing, writing poetry, and drinking more than was good for him in waterfront saloons. Withdrawing from medical school, he entered the School of Forestry of the University of Washington in Seattle, then returned to his beach-bum life at Hermosa, supported by a small legacy from his maternal grandmother's side of the family. Una's long-suffering lawyer husband eventually discovered the relationship, and sent her to Europe to think it over. But while Una was away, her husband found someone else as well and was glad to grant his wife a friendly divorce in late July 1913.

A few days later Una and Jeffers were married in Tacoma, at long last, after six years of anxiety and frustration. The couple planned to live an expatriate life in Europe, settling quietly and remotely, in the west of Ireland perhaps, but the war intervened, and so they moved to Carmel by the Sea instead, living frugally in a log cabin on Jeffers's legacy. For the next two decades Jeffers averaged a book of poetry a year. Twin boys, Donnan and Garth, were born in 1916. Their father spent his free time constructing from nearby boulders and stones an Arroyo Craftsman-inspired family home, Tor House, named from Celtic myth, on a bluff overlooking the surf-whitened Carmel Coast. Next to this he built the Hawk Tower, a citadel resembling the medieval watchtower Yeats was living in at the time in the west of Ireland.

It was all so very Pasadenan in its mixture of art, scholarly reference, exclusivity, and Arroyo stone, and the Pasadenans, including their friends from Los Angeles, always recognized Jeffers as one of their own. A pilgrimage to Tor House became a rite of passage for young Southern Californians en route, so they hoped, to literary creativity. Paul Jordan-Smith and his wife Sarah Bixby Smith visited Tor House in the autumn of 1927, close to the visit of Jake Zeitlin, Arthur Millier, and Merle Armitage, motoring south in Armitage's Packard from San Francisco. Carey McWilliams and Louis Adamic drove up from Los Angeles in the summer of 1928, armed by a previous letter of introduction from the San Francisco poet George Sterling. The following summer, Lawrence Clark Powell, recently graduated from Occidental, came up to Carmel, although the Jefferses were in Ireland at the time, just to soak up the atmosphere. Powell and his friend sculptor Gordon Newell paid a moonlight visit to Tor House as to a sacred shrine and later sat up all night in their cabin in the Carmel pinewood taking turns reading Jeffers's *Cawdor* aloud by firelight as Bach and Cesar Franck played on the gramophone.

Intoxicated by Jeffers's descriptions of the Big Sur coast, Newell moved south to Carmel after graduating from Berkeley and completing an apprenticeship with Ralph Stackpole, who was doing the sculpture for Timothy Pflueger's masterful Pacific Stock Exchange Building in San Francisco. Newell brought with him his beautiful young wife Gloria Stuart, whom he had met and married at Berkeley. At Carmel Newell sculpted large pieces in redwood and stone and taught sculpturing to the Jeffers twins, while Gloria wrote for *The Carmelite*, the gossipy newspaper of this burgeoning art colony, and continued an interest in acting and the theater which would soon win her fame in Hollywood, followed by the inevitable divorce. In January 1932 Newell brought Ward Ritchie, back from his Paris apprenticeship, over to meet the great man himself, whose poetry Ritchie had already been printing in authorized limited editions.

In their similarities of descriptive detail and response, the accounts of these visits testify to Jeffers's status as a cult figure among the aspiring. First of all, there was the feeling of regard, of awe even, for Jeffers in his physical presence: his tall sinewy physique, kept spare by four hours of daily labor on the construction of Hawk Tower, dragging boulders up from the shore with a simple winching system as ancient as Egypt; his classically handsome Anglo-American face and adamantine blue-gray eyes; his costume of a leather jacket, an open-necked shirt, Army pants, puttees, and boots, as if poetry were a military campaign and Jeffers the charismatic commander. (Cecil B. De Mille made this outfit standard attire for film directors.) Louis Adamic said that Jeffers reminded him of Lawrence of Arabia in his aura of separateness and his reluctance to be touched. While accounts from the late 1930s stress Jeffers's friendly voluability, especially when relaxed by drink, accounts from the late 1920s stress his reserve, his silences amidst company, as if the poet were meditating truths too deep for conversation. Jeffers pushed the Pasadenan propensity for reserve to its utmost—out of shyness, his defenders claimed—yet there remains something a little morbid in the early acceptances of what in others might be considered arrogance or at the least bad manners.

Then there was Una, keeper of the flame: Una with her looped braids and flowing robes, a druidic figure amidst her researches into the symbology of the unicorn. Of Irish descent, Una fostered an atmosphere of West Ireland Celticness at Tor House: a composite of mythologies studied and discussed, the names given the twins, Donnan and Garth (as if they were a Gaelic chieftain's sons), the clothes she wore, her braids, the homemade bread she baked, and the tea she served in heavy red-brown cups. Una was interested in legends and unicorns and never fully renounced the dream of her and Robin and the boys living in some wild place facing the Irish Sea, although Big Sur to the south of Carmel, where her husband set his long narrative poems, came in due course to offer a more than adequate substitute. Una did bring Jeffers to Ireland a few times, however, and she wrote of her experiences in diaries which reveal her to be capable of prose as fresh and clear as an Irish spring morning.

Reports from the late 1920s accord Una Jeffers a regard in kind, if not degree, to the respect accorded her spouse. While Jeffers wrote in the mornings and worked with stone in the afternoons, Una presided over the rustic, wood-warm, book-lined interior of Tor House, with its long horizontal window looking to where the Carmel River flows into the Pacific, its Old English and Celtic sayings carved onto lintels and doors, its Craftsman furniture and lighting fixtures. The Jefferses lived a simple but comfortable life characteristic of Carmel. Jeffers smoked a pipe and enjoyed his wife's homemade wine and fermented brew of oranges, rice water, and raisins. There was a Ford in the garage and horseback rides for the boys at the Tevis stables between Carmel and Monterey, and for them also, Haig, a white English bulldog.

Guarding the flame had its risks as well as its rewards, as Una discovered in the late 1930s when Robin became infatuated with another woman during a visit to Taos and persisted in seeing her, saying that "he needed more than one woman in his life, that if they should dissect him, they would find nothing but Una in him, just Una, Una, Una, and he was tired of it."[4] She fled into the bathroom and shot herself with a pistol, not fatally, but seriously enough to endanger her life and damage the legend based on their perfect marriage.

2

In the fall of 1930 three young Southern Californians, students in the Faculty of Letters at the local university, were living at a pension at 14 rue du Petit-Potet in the city of Dijon, 150 miles southeast of Paris. Two of the students, a recently married couple, Alfred Young Fisher and Mary Frances Kennedy Fisher, lived in a two-room apartment to the rear of the townhouse; the third, Lawrence Clark Powell, lived in a room in the attic. On holidays the trio was frequently visited by another Southern Californian, Ward Ritchie, an intern in the Paris atelier of book designer François-Louis Schmied. In their varying way (and with varying results) all four Southern Californians, then in their twenties, were on a Pasadenan pilgrimage to Europe, although Mary Frances Kennedy Fisher had grown up in Whittier and her husband was from Los Angeles. By Pasadenan is meant that they were each privileged, Protestant, and serious-minded in their interests. Powell and Alfred Fisher were doing doctorates in literature; M.F.K. Fisher (as she later signed herself) was rounding out her undergraduate education; Ritchie was an intern with the great Schmied. While the four can easily be considered generic young Americans of a certain back-ground, with an agenda of ambitions characteristic of their social class and time of life—the magic and sudden pain of love, the involvement in studies, the dreams of future career, the pleasures of Dijon and the Burgundian country-side—they were also, three of them at least, Southern Californians destined to return from Europe and flourish across five decades of creativity, no easy task. Because the three who found themselves so completely as artists in France were each Southern Californians of a discernible sort, Pasadenans, where they came from, what they discovered in France, and what they did with it later on in life is of importance to the story of Southern California.

First on the scene, the Fishers arrived in the autumn of 1929 shortly after their marriage. Boyishly handsome, with brown wavy hair and piercing blue eyes, Alfred Fisher grew up in Los Angeles where his father served as pastor of the Third Presbyterian Church on Adams Boulevard. Like Robinson Jeffers, Fisher was nurtured in an environment of theological learning, prayers, and Bible readings, and classical music played by his mother, a talented pianist. After an unhappy year at UCLA, where he loathed the compulsory ROTC, Fisher followed in his father's footsteps to Princeton. There he read vora-ciously, worked on the *Princetonian*, played excellent handball, wrote poetry, and came under the spell of Professor Archibald Bowman, a philosopher and poet interested in the anthropology of religion. Graduating as class poet in 1927, Fisher had already embarked upon his intended career as a literary scholar and poet. A Hobey Baker of undergraduate literary studies, Fisher was reputed to have written a brilliant seventy-thousand-word essay on the function of lit-erary criticism, only to burn it when it came under criticism from a friend: a prophetic gesture in view of the later course of his career. While teaching English at the Valley Ranch College Preparatory School in Wyoming, Fisher wooed Mary Frances Kennedy of Whittier, whom he had met at UCLA, through sonnet sequences sent through the mail.

Tall, dark-haired, reserved in demeanor, with a tendency towards snobbishness, strikingly beautiful (the contemporary actress Sigourney Weaver comes to mind), Mary Frances Kennedy, just turning twenty-one, had come to maturity in a family of transplanted Iowans. For five generations on both sides of the family, her forebears had been journalists of the bookish sort. Her mother had lived long in Europe as a young woman. Her father owned and published the *Whittier News*. The Kennedys were a vigorous, intelligent, stylish family: upper-middle-class Episcopalians amidst the larger Quaker realities of Whittier, an eastern suburb of Los Angeles. Every small American town in this period had at least one such family: scaled-down magnificent Ambersons who set a certain tone, who were aware of a wider world and lived in a house filled with books, the offspring headed for college like their parents and grandparents before them. The Powells were such a family in South Pasadena, the Kennedys in Whittier, the Fishers in Los Angeles. Mary Frances attended the exclusive Bishop's School for Girls in La Jolla, arriving there with an already formidable scholarship she had acquired reading in her father's large library. A certain restlessness born of strong prior preparation and other factors as well, which she would soon be writing about with exquisite insight, kept her on the move as an undergraduate from Illinois College to Occidental in 1927 with her sister Anne, where she met Powell and Ritchie, to UCLA where she met Fisher. Thus the University of Dijon, where she enrolled as a candidate for the licentiate, was offering Mary Frances Kennedy Fisher an opportunity to consolidate her already formidable intellectual and imaginative powers through systematic study in the exacting manner of French higher education.

Her husband, meanwhile, was writing a dissertation on Shakespearean comedy under the supervision of professor Georges Connes, a blond blacksmith of a figure from the region of Rouergue, affirmatively Burgundian in his love of life, literature, and (fortunately) Americans. Connes presided over English literary studies at Dijon. Alfred Fisher also conceived the idea of writing an epic poem, which he called *The Ghost in the Underblows*, based upon the books of the Bible, in much the same way that Joyce had based *Ulysses* on Homer. Every noon when the university library closed for two hours, Fisher would repair to the Café de Paris on the Place de Theatre and there, seated outdoors in sight of the Church of Saint Michel and the former ducal palace, now the Hôtel de Ville or City Hall, or indoors during the cold weather behind the great glass window of the cafe, he would fill notebook after notebook with spidery handwriting before returning to his afternoon stint at the library. By the spring of 1931 Fisher had completed six hundred pages of manuscript covering twelve books of his projected sixty-book epic. When Ward Ritchie, returning to Paris from Majorca via the Barcelona train, stopped off at Dijon to sit up late with Mary Frances and Larry Powell and hear Fisher read from his work in progress, he believed that he was present at a privileged moment in American literary history.

The previous year when Ritchie had arrrived in Paris, his path had been smoothed by a letter of introduction to another Southern Californian in France, William van Wyck, a friend of Carlyle MacIntyre. Independently wealthy, van Wyck maintained a smart apartment in Montparnasse. A graduate of USC, to which he had returned in 1917 after a number of years in Europe, taking an A.B. and an M.A. in record time by challenging courses through oral examination, van Wyck was enjoying the life of an affluent Parisian *homme des lettres*. Like MacIntyre, van Wyck's métier was translation—Chaucer, Fracastoro, Ronsard—but he also read and collected Robinson Jeffers as well, about whom he wrote a pioneering critical study, published by Ritchie in 1938. Learned, worldly, a lover of language, wine, and food, van Wyck invited Ritchie to lunch at his apartment on Montparnasse or to one or another of his posh clubs. Van Wyck also oriented Ritchie to the districts, cafés, theaters, nightclubs, and bookstores of Paris, which gave Ritchie an aura of seasoning in the great city by the time Larry Powell arrived in Le Havre on the MS *Oregon* of the Compagnie Generale Transatlantique in mid-August 1930.

Anxious to write a doctoral dissertation on Robinson Jeffers, something no English department in the United States would allow, Powell had come to France at the suggestion of Mary Frances Kennedy Fisher, his girlfriend Fay Shoemaker's sorority sister at Occidental. M.F.K. Fisher had alerted Powell by letter to the encouraging presence at Dijon of Georges Connes, Charles Lambert, and other faculty members favorable to American literary studies, including the contemporary period. Powell spent the remainder of August and most of September with Ritchie in Paris, ensconced in the Hotel Crystal on the Left Bank near the Café La Flore and the Café des Deux Magots. Powell began a jazz novel, working at it each morning in the Luxembourg Gardens. Nights were spent with Ritchie and two California girls, Margery Schwartzel, a fashion model, and Ruth Henderson, an art student, dining inexpensively in small restaurants in St.-Germain-des-Prés, followed by a night in the cafés that ended with watching dawn break over the city from the steps of Sacre-Coeur and sitting later within the great church to hear the chanting of the early morning divine office. One night at the Brasserie Lipp, an Alsatian restaurant near their hotel, Powell and Ritchie beheld the great Hemingway himself drinking with a crowd of American journalists, and dreams of the literary life, thus corroborated, grew even more incandescent.

In late September 1930 Powell left for Dijon, where he presented himself to Connes, who accepted him as a doctoral candidate in the Faculty of Letters. Ensconced in the attic room of the Fishers' pension (room and board for the equivalent of $1.20 a day), Powell grew a beard and bought an appropriately bohemian corduroy suit. He worked on his spoken French by attending the cinema. When he completed requisite lectures and seminars in English and European literature, he was authorized by the Faculty of Letters to begin his thesis on Robinson Jeffers, orienting himself to California through the aid of a series of topographic survey maps of the Big Sur coast, which he pinned across the walls of his room.

The academic year 1930–31 proved close and enriching for the Fishers, Powell, and Ritchie, who came down from Paris for special events such as the Foire Gastronomique, during which Dijon celebrated itself as the wine and food capital of Burgundy. As usual, the Southern Californians would fore-gather at the Café du Paris for drinks and talk. For a splurge, the four would set off for Les Trois Faisans, arguably one of the three or four finest restaurants in France, for a sumptuous meal graced by Romanée-Conti or Chambertin, followed by visits to more cafes and a late-night reading from Alfred Fisher's poem in progress.

In the summer of 1931 Mary Frances returned to Southern California for a visit, and Powell and Alfred Fisher relished their status as the only two American students at Dijon. Stumbling into a local bordello one evening after an evening of drinking, Powell played the parlor piano until dawn while Fisher danced with the girls. For a Presbyterian minister's son, it was quite an evening. Impressed by Powell's music, the madam offered him regular employment, which Powell declined. Powell's initial $400 in living money, raised back home through the sale of his Chevrolet, was augmented by a like amount sent him by his uncle, and so another year in Dijon was possible.

When Mary Frances returned from Southern California, the Fishers moved to their own apartment above a pastry shop at 26 rue Monge and Powell took over their chambers on rue du Petit-Potet. For his third year, Powell lived in Dijon with his mother, who was spending the years 1931–1934 in Europe, supported by a small family legacy. By then Alfred Fisher had been appointed Lecturer in English in the Faculty of Letters. In the spring he took his doctorate *mention très honorable* (as did Powell the following year) and the Fishers moved on to Strasbourg for further study and research. Powell joined them on the French Riviera in the spring of 1932 for a brief vacation in a fishing village near Nice before the couple departed for Southern California. He also wrote a long letter to the editor of *Le Jazz Hot*, a magazine out of Brussels, which put him in contact with a number of French jazz aficionados and musicians.

In late October Powell defended his thesis before a panel of Dijon faculty augmented by Charles Cestre of the Sorbonne. Sitting in the audience as Powell defended his explication of Robinson Jeffers together with two ancillary topics, the theme of incest in Byron and Shelley, and the Pacific Coast in the poetry of Walt Whitman, were students, professors, his mother, the Rigoulot family, who ran the pension where he and the Fishers had lived, two waiters from the Café du Paris, "and—so help me God—the Madame, if not the girls, of the whorehouse where I had played the piano till dawn. The local paper had announced the time and place of my public examination. When I saw her in the farthest back row and caught a kiss blown to me, I knew it was going to be all right."[5]

The literary results of these Dijon years for the Pasadenans and for the Southern California to which they had all returned by 1933 ranged from dazzling, to significant, to bitterly disappointing, to a mixture of the three. Ward Ritchie began writing poetry in Paris and continued to do so intermittently through the 1930s, publishing two small books under the pseudonym Peter Lum Quince. Ritchie was a good poet, precise and elegaic, might have gotten even better had he not turned his major energies to printing and book design, his more promising calling. Alfred Fisher's *The Ghost in the Underblows* fizzled when a long fragment of it was published in 1940. Fisher tinkered with his epic throughout the 1930s. Stimulated to action by the success of his by then ex-wife M.F.K. Fisher, he allowed Ward Ritchie to publish a 300-page fragment which Powell edited and introduced and Ritchie produced with a subsidy from Dr. Elmer Belt. The most notable thing about *The Ghost in the Underblows* was Alvin Lustig's innovative design, which has since earned the book an enduring place in the history of American graphics. Despite advance testimonials from Robinson Jeffers and William Everson and a lengthy, somewhat over-wrought introduction by Powell, who discoursed energetically about Dante, *The Golden Bough*, T.S. Eliot, and Fisher's Biblical structures and analogies, *The Ghost in the Underblows* earned one regional review, then receded from sight. Whatever Fisher's original ambitions, linked to his theological and anthropological studies at Princeton, his poem rumbled and roared sonorously—but with an obscurity that even academic commentators found impassable.

His former wife, by contrast, went on to become one of the most respected essayists of her generation, the most important writer on wine and food since the French lawyer Jean Anthelme Brillat-Savarin (1755–1826), whose classic treatise *La Physiologie du goût* (1825) she edited and translated. The Fisher marriage had come under strain as early as the spring of 1931 when Mary Frances returned to Southern California to visit her parents. Alfred Fisher told Powell he was convinced she would not return. He ceased writing his poem, which he never resumed except for minor revisions. Returning to the United States, the Fishers moved into a cottage at Laguna Beach owned by Mary Frances's parents. When Alfred received an appointment to Occidental College, the couple moved to Highland Park, and for two years Mary Frances struggled with the role of faculty wife. When Alfred's father died, their relationship became a marriage in name only. Fisher's father had never approved of Mary Frances, and his son somehow blamed his wife for his death.

The Fishers, meanwhile, had become friendly with artist Dillwyn Parrish and his wife Gigi, a film actress with the Wampus starlets troupe. The brother of novelist Anne Parrish and the cousin of the artist Maxfield Parrish, Dillwyn

Parrish was charming, outgoing, companionable, a friend from Harvard days of e.e. cummings and Conrad Aiken—and an accomplished generation older than Alfred Fisher. Dillwyn and Gigi Parrish eventually divorced and he and Mary Frances drew closer. In 1935, with her husband's approval, Mary Frances accompanied Dillwyn Parrish (or Chexbres as she referred to him in print) and his mother on a voyage to Europe aboard the German ship *Hansa*. "The whole thing," she later wrote, "seems so remote now that I cannot say what was sea change and what had already happened on land. I know that I had been in love with Chexbres for three years or so."[6] In Parrish's company she revisited Dijon and enjoyed a meal at the restaurant she and Alfred used to frequent on special occasions.

M.F.K. Fisher had already begun to close the loop between gastronomy and civilization. The years in Dijon, the wine and food capital of France, had strengthened insights into this truth based upon memories of meals at home, at the Bishop's School, at college, in Dijon, and on dining expeditions throughout Burgundy which she and Alfred had enjoyed as part of a gourmet excursion society which they belonged to as students. During her two years as a faculty wife she supplemented these insights with extensive reading in the Los Angeles Public Library. Phil Townsend Hanna, governing archpriest of gastronomy in Southern California and a family friend, was ever ready to discuss wine, food, and civilization.

In 1934 Hanna commissioned for *Touring Topics* from M.F.K. Fisher her first published piece, an account of life at Laguna Beach. A year later, during the ambiguous journey to old haunts with the man she loved but did not yet plan to leave her husband for, eating with him in places where she and Alfred had eaten together as hopeful newlyweds, re-experiencing with him the places and foods and wines of Burgundy, M.F.K. Fisher began to close an even more powerful linkage in her mind and personal life. In intuitive association, she melded eating and drinking, time and place, the hungers of heart and body with sex, love, security, strength, exhilaration, and identity. Food and drink were not merely the emblems of these terrible hungers; they were the natural sacraments and memories of them as well. Gastronomy sunk taproots into the landscape of personal memory as well as into the soil of civilization. Eating and drinking provided materials for literary art as compelling as any other human themes or events, provided that deeper perspectives were sustained as one experienced, perceived, remembered, and wrote.

When M.F.K. returned to Southern California from this second and very crucial European sojourn, she apprised her husband of her developing relationship with Dillwyn Parrish. Resigning his position at Occidental, Fisher followed his wife to Switzerland, where Parrish had rented a chateau. This arrangement lasted only a short time before Fisher returned to the United States to take a teaching job at Smith College, where he remained for the rest of his career. The Fishers were divorced in 1938, the year after M.F.K. Fisher's first book, *Serve It Forth*, appeared to oven-warm reviews.

Serve It Forth marked Fisher at once as a new kind of food writer, the fulfillment in a most promising way of diverse strains so pertinent to the composite culture of the Southern California from which she came. Dedicated to her parents, *Serve It Forth* exuded the learned literacy characteristic of the Kennedy household, with its generations of well-read journalists and writers on either side of the family. It also suggested a European connection which was reflective, simultaneously, of her mother's long sojourn there, her student days in Dijon, and the immemorial yearnings of the genteel tradition for the storied homeland which was such a vital side of the Pasadenan mentality.

In her next book, *Consider the Oyster* (1941), which she dedicated to her gravely ill second husband, M.F.K. began to tap deeper realms of association and memory. Her first eating of oysters, for example, at a Christmas party at the Bishop's School in 1924, constituted an intensely personal event in her passage to adult identity. Deep personal tragedy drove Fisher to even further intensity and power as a writer. She adored her second husband and they lived happily together for a number of years in Vevey, Switzerland, growing grapes and produce, painting, collaborating on a comic novel, entertaining friends, until the war drove them back to Southern California, where they settled in Hemet, a small town in the San Jacinto Basin of Riverside County.

Dillwyn Parrish had already contracted Buerger's disease, a form of gangrene which necessitated the amputation of a leg. Feverishly, he fought for life, painting an explosive series of canvases dominated by angels of death. At M.F.K.'s request, Larry Powell, then on the library staff at UCLA, helped organize a final exhibition there of Parrish's paintings. The once gay, light-hearted Chexbres, the champagne essence of good-humored sophistication, had been reduced to a one-legged invalid ("a small wracked man with snowy hair and eyes large with suffering"), helped by Powell and Mary Frances painfully, step by step, up the staircase to the gallery. Shortly thereafter, Parrish, in great pain and faced with the necessity of further amputations, mercifully passed away. M.F.K. Fisher also lost a beloved younger brother shortly after her husband's death, a second and equally devastating bereavement.

Forged in the pain of catastrophic personal loss, *The Gastronomical Me* (1943) constitutes M.F.K. Fisher's debut as a writer moving into new depths of memory and imaginative expression via the vehicles of wine and food criticism. As autobiography, it joins a rich array of such statements to be produced in the years to come by Pasadenans Powell and Ritchie. It is, from this perspective, a vivid account of Whittier, the Bishop's School, college life, and Dijon by a remarkable observer; but it is also a book, occasionally desperate, about love and loss and the deepest hungers possible. "I tell about myself," she wrote, "and how I ate bread on a lasting hillside, or drank red wine in a room now blown to bits, and it happens without my willing it that I am telling too about the people with me then, and their other deeper needs for love and happiness. There is food in the bowl, and more often than not, because of what honesty I have, there is nourishment in the heart, to feed the wilder, more insistent hungers."[7]

The Gastronomical Me is dominated by the people and places of Dijon and the underlying drama of the breakup of her first marriage and the tragic death of her second husband. As writers, she and Lawrence Clark Powell had each internalized the ancient ducal city as a permanent component of their inner identities. Dijon taught Fisher how food, drink, culture, place, and personal life all intersect, and how one leads invariably to the others. Her family life in Southern California had first suggested such relationships, but this American region lacked the consolidated depth of Dijon and Burgundy, where men and women had been eating and drinking and sustaining cultural continuities by their appetites since the Romans. In later writings, she would return at length to her family life, to Whittier, Hollywood, Los Angeles, and Laguna Beach; but that was after Dijon first taught her how all things—food, family, love, and death—fit together.

3

In a parallel manner, Dijon taught Lawrence Clark Powell how books as well as food and drink emerge from and fit into a multilayered, multidimensional landscape. In Dijon and the surrounding Burgundian countryside, Powell observed the elements of history and literature—past and present experience, memory and myth—in a rich localized setting. At Morvan in western Burgundy Powell visited the Benedictine monastery of La Pierre-Qui-Vire, the Stone That Tilts. In pre-Roman times the site had been a Celtic shrine. It was then absorbed into the Roman cult, then Christianized, then augmented by a Benedictine monastery during the Romanesque era. The woodcutters from the region who prayed at the monastery shrine sustained a continuity of response that incorporated levels of meaning from the Celtic, Roman pagan, Roman Christian, Romanesque, and later eras, all brought forward into the present. Returning to Dijon, Powell meditated on the maps of Big Sur spread around his walls and upon the long narrative poems of Robinson Jeffers set in these wild seashore canyons and hills half a world away from Burgundy. It was, he later remembered, like looking at Big Sur through the wrong end of a telescope.

The mythic structure of Burgundy as well as a sympathetic Dijon faculty helped Powell see how the poet Jeffers was detecting and expressing myth—classical, Biblical, and the myths behind even these fundamental mythologies—in the context of Big Sur and its backcountry ranchers. From this perspective Jeffers's poetry, especially the narratives, was totally comprehensible to a Burgundian such as Georges Connes, who approved a thesis on a living poet in his mid-forties, working obscurely in far-off California. There was in Jeffers's work a readily identifiable infrastructure of myth, of repeated patterns of experience, totally congenial to the Burgundian point of view. Peeling away the historical layers of La Pierre-Qui-Vire, Powell encountered the dawn world of Celtic, perhaps even pre-Celtic, consciousness. In Jeffers's stories of Tamar, Cawdor, Judas, the roan stallion, and the women at Point Sur, the old myths were working in a parallel manner, half-remembered and even less understood, yet compulsive, remorseless, in their power to shape and express human action. Jeffers approached poetry with enormous, albeit controlled reserves of learning and reference. Behind the highly localized nature of his stories, there was at work an almost academic employment of Greek and Hebrew analogues. Robinson Jeffers, after all, was a Pasadenan.

A France which had so recently exhausted itself in war might very well be expected to respond through literary academics such as Connes and the others at Dijon to Jeffers's vision of violent suffering and destruction, self-induced or inflicted, as constituting a terrible but necessary stage of experience before reintegration or, even more precisely, as a plateau prior to holiness. As a stretcher-bearer in the trenches of the western front, the Jesuit Pierre Teilhard de Chardin had come to a similar insight. Matter, Teilhard de Chardin discovered, must be destroyed before energy is released. So too must humanity be broken before it could grow. Only broken humanity, Jeffers believed (or he at least believed this as a poet), truly understood and could therefore accept the vast, terrible, indifferent nature of creation and mankind's accidental place in the scheme of things. (Teilhard de Chardin came to a less accidental conclusion.) Only people in whom the mold of humanity and its delusions had been cracked, who accepted the indifferent otherness of creation beyond distortions of ego and hope, could find the courage to continue. Science, Jeffers believed, repeatedly demonstrated that it took catastrophes to create new forms. It is not surprising that such a bleak proto-existentialist vision of things, articulated through violent stories in a primal setting, struck a chord in Frenchmen who vividly remembered the machine-gun fire across the trenches of Verdun.

Powell returned to Southern California in 1933 with his doctorate and a printed edition of his thesis, which Jake Zeitlin published in 1934 at the Primavera Press as *Robinson Jeffers, the Man and His Work*, with a foreward by Jeffers and decorations by Rockwell Kent. Powell was by no means the first critic to take Jeffers seriously as a poet. Mark Van Doren, Babette Deutsch, Lincoln Steffens, Louis Untermeyer, Edgar Lee Masters, Dwight Macdonald, Loren Eiseley, Havelock Ellis, and Charles Cestre had already praised Jeffers's poetry in print. Nor did Powell initiate the Jeffers cult. San Francisco poet George Sterling, critic Benjamin de Casseres, and a host of other Californians, including Una Jeffers, had long since been fanning that particular flame. Powell, however, brought it all together for the first time—the life, the poetry, the themes, the philosophical and literary influences—into a study that firmly rooted Jeffers in time and place while at the same time explicating the universal themes of his work. Powell confirmed Jeffers to be profoundly Californian in his choice of material, his life-style, his scientifically reinforced mysticism of transcendence through nature. Powell even managed to make Jeffers's ultimately tedious pessimism regarding the decline of the West, including the United States, seem arguably Californian in its imagery of the Pacific as the symbol of the void and the end of things as they are. (So too was Edmund Wilson finding the Pacific at the very same time.) On what grounds and by what authority, one is tempted to ask after a steady multivolumed dose of Jeffers's pessimism, does a Pasadenan living on a legacy in Carmel dismiss his fellow Americans as so futilely striving?

As the Jeffers study announced, Powell was discovering the processes of creating imaginative literature just as M.F.K. Fisher was discovering the processes behind food and drink. Powell's eventual profession, the librarianship of UCLA as that library was boosted into national stature in the postwar era, allowed him the widest possible aquaintanceship with books and authors. As a bookish Pasadenan, Powell moved naturally into librarianship after his return from Dijon. He trained in library science at Berkeley after a stint as an assistant in Jake Zeitlin's bookshop and became University Librarian and Director of the William Andrews Clark Memorial Library at UCLA in 1944. In 1960 Powell became founding professor and dean of the UCLA school of librarianship. He also managed to write during these busy years hundreds of literary essays and reviews which appeared at regular intervals in book form. Taken cumulatively, these essays established Powell as an important literary journalist and practical critic. At once inside and outside of the academy, Powell wrote on an extraordinarily wide range of topics—books, librarianship, history, music, travel, sports cars, personal reminiscence—for a wide range of popular, middlebrow, and specialized publications.

Like M.F.K. Fisher, Powell approached each writer, each book, each travel encounter as he experienced it most fully in its physical and imaginative landscape: the lesson of Burgundy and Dijon. In his bookscapes, as he called them, Powell sought to evoke the alchemical energy surging electrically through setting, personal experience, art forms, and shared historical culture: a process moving from place, to experience, to art, to history, then back again through the circuit as what was fashioned in imagination returns to its place of origin and intensifies that originating landscape through the prism of art. Thus is achieved the Wessex of Thomas Hardy, the Shropshire of A.H. Houseman, the Border Country of Sir Walter Scott, the Florence of the Brownings, the Dublin of Joyce.

Encouraged by Phil Townsend Hanna, Powell embarked in the late 1930s upon a literary map of California for *Westways* which he continued across twenty-three years of installments. While the landscapes and cityscapes Powell thus evoked lacked the time-span and density of Burgundy and Dijon, they were nevertheless keyed to an earlier stage of the same process in which history is transmuted into literature as myth and symbol condition facts. Despite its newness, Powell suggested, California had already been soaked in literature; and the music and echoes and special places of this heritage—the Palm Springs and the southern coast trails of J. Smeaton Chase, the San Diego backcountry of Judy van der Veer, Mary Austin's land of little rain, the San Pedro waterfront of Raymond Chandler, the south central coast of Richard Henry Dana, Robinson Jeffers's Big Sur, William Saroyan's Fresno, the Salinas Valley of John Steinbeck, the Sierra Nevada of John Muir, the Napa Valley of Robert Louis Stevenson and Idwal Jones, the Mother Lode of Bret Harte and Mark Twain—all these places and scores of others besides were each energized by the presence there of voices which might be heard in much the same way that Gilbert Highet heard the echoing murmurs of classical poetry in the landscapes of Italy, Greece, and Asia Minor and Larry Powell heard the music of Robinson Jeffers seeping from the other side of the planet into his map-plastered attic room on the rue du Petit-Potet in Dijon.

Powell's personal landscape encompassed the arc of cities, suburbs, and still wild places that swept from Riverside and Hemet up along the Sierra Madre, veered through Pasadena into Los Angeles, then continued westward to the Santa Monica Mountains and Malibu. But this region, so new, so rapidly developing, could never be assimilated straightaway by the Pasadenans. Shaped as they were by the genteel tradition, Powell and M.F.K. Fisher alike needed the alternative of Europe, the charmed and transformed landscapes of France especially, as a prism and frame of reference for their activities as cultural critics. Thus M.F.K. Fisher returned to France for long periods of residence after the Second World War, encountering and writing about its people, places, wines, and food for *The New Yorker* before returning to settle permanently in the Napa Valley, the most Europeanized landscape in America. And thus Lawrence Clark Powell returned via *The Blue Train*, a novel based on his Dijon years which he wrote in 1941.

Evocative and erotic within the confines of its minimalist style, *The Blue Train* represented Powell's hail and farewell to his European years. D.H. Lawrence encouraged its eroticism, and Beethoven's last quartets, Opus 135 especially, inspired its sparse economy. One day in 1936, Galka Scheyer, a Hungarian émigrée who supported herself as the West Coast agent of the Blue Four—Kandinsky, Klee, Feininger, and Jawlensky—brought Frieda Lawrence into Jake Zeitlin's shop, where Powell was working. Lawrence's widow wanted to discuss the cache of manscript drafts of virtually every novel, novelette, short story, poem, play, essay, travel sketch, and translation in the Lawrentian canon which she was keeping in a trunk on her ranch in San Cristobal, New Mexico. Long before his death in 1930, Lawrence had recognized in his manuscripts an eventual source of income and had preserved them scrupulously.

In the summer of 1937 Zeitlin drove to San Cristobal, where Frieda was ensconced with her Italian boyfriend, Angelino Ravagalli, and an English couple, Aldous and Maria Huxley. Zeitlin examined the manuscripts, virtually uncorrected first drafts in bound exercise books, before going on to Santa Fe with Frieda, Ravagalli, the Huxleys, and the poet Witter Bynner to enjoy the annual Pueblo Indian rain dances. Zeitlin persuaded Frieda to send the trunk of manuscripts to him in Los Angeles where a descriptive catalogue could be prepared and printed prior to sale. Fresh from his bibliographical training at Berkeley, Powell inventoried and described the contents of the trunk. Dr. Elmer Belt and Susannah Bryant Dakin subsidized the publication of Powell's catalogue by Ward Ritchie, and Aldous Huxley contributed the foreword.

Re-experiencing the Lawrentian canon in manuscript was a powerful experience for an aspiring writer such as Powell, for whom Lawrence's writings had been both a source of literary inspiration and even, dangerous at times, a guide to life. It was akin to reading a long letter, direct and personal, from Lorenzo himself. Powell especially admired Lawrence in his minimalist mode, as in the novelette *St. Mawr*, just as he admired the economy of Beethoven's final quartets. Hearing the Opus 135 performed by the Pro Arte quartet one Sunday afternoon in the fall of 1941 at Occidental's Thorne Hall, Powell resolved to try a minimalist-Lawrentian novel based upon his Dijon years, as tight and spare as the jazz novel, with which he was still struggling, was talky and discursive.

Knopf rejected *Quintet*, as the novel was then called. Minimalism had its dangers, especially for a first-time novelist in the blockbuster Book of the Month Club era. In contrast to Knopf editor Emily Morison (the daughter of the Harvard historian), who had rejected *Quintet*, Powell's friend Henry Miller wrote him a long letter of praise. As might be expected, Miller was totally sympathetic to Powell's Lawrentian evocation of love, Europe, and youth as seen from an American perspective. Putting *Quintet* aside, Powell threw himself into his library career, the aspiring novelist becoming lost in the busyness of administration and a prolific non-fiction career. Also put aside were the jazz novel begun in Paris in 1930 and an Occidental college novel written in 1943 during hours stolen from war work.

Not until 1977, when Powell was seventy, was *The Blue Train* (renamed at the suggestion of Paul Horgan) published by the Capra Press of Santa Barbara with Henry Miller's letter of 29 May 1943 as an afterword. Along with M.F.K. Fisher's *The Gastronomical Me* and certain other of her reminiscences, *The Blue Train* remains the second important literary recovery from the Pasadenans' youthful time in France.

Like Fisher, Powell put on record all that Europe, France especially, promised the Pasadenans in their search for identity and metaphor. Jack Burgoyne (the name suggests Burgundy) is a San Diegan pursuing a doctorate in biochemistry at Dijon. Of Franco-American descent, Burgoyne has broken off his medical studies to pursue a degree in pure science and also to attend lectures in the Symbolists, given by the dean of the Faculty of Letters. Aside from his biochemistry, Burgoyne is also researching a book on the relationship between tuberculosis and art, ending with a long account of D.H. Lawrence's last days in Italy and France. Burgoyne goes on pilgrimage to Lawrence's grave at Vence near Nice, where he interviews Lawrence's physician.

The story line of *The Blue Train* is equally Lawrentian. Over the course of his studies, Burgoyne has encounters with five women: an American music student in Switzerland, a Swedish student of literature at Dijon, a hard-drinking English widow returning from Saigon to take possession of an inherited villa at Antibes, a middle-aged Parisian journalist vacationing in the fishing village of Cros de Cagnes outside Nice on the Côte d'Azur, and a young Californian from Calistoga in the Napa Valley studying art in London. Each woman offers Burgoyne, along with herself, successive lessons in his *l'education sentimentale*. Significantly, the education begins and ends with Californians, the first, a wealthy, self-absorbed music student, driving him further into European expatriation by her difficult American princess manner, and the last (Burgoyne's only unconsummated relationship) reminding him that real life and responsibilities awaited them both back in California. In the intervals between, the Swedish student Erda Lindstrom, the English expatriate Joyce Davies, and the Parisian journalist Madeleine Montrechet each make a gift of themselves and their states of cultural consciousness.

Physically powerful and athletic, Erda is engaged to an older Stockholm banker, to whom she returns in the belief that her highly structured bourgeois life is inevitable. Seduced by a Catholic prelate when she was fifteen, Joyce Davies, the Gallicized English widow, brings with her the sandalwood scent and heavy cigarette smoke of Saigon. She is the European as wandering colonial—damaged, restless, drinking too much, driven to expatriation by an early hurt. The Parisian journalist Madeleine Montrechet, by contrast, is everything passionate and wise in the French character. Based upon a very real woman Powell had met, a former mistress of the novelist and poet François Mauriac, Madeleine Montrechet is thirty-six, a decade older than Burgoyne, and has come to terms with her life as a single professional woman in Paris. Eager and passionate within the limits of her class (she refuses Burgoyne's request to make love outdoors in the Lawrentian manner of Lady Chatterley and her lover), Montrechet is ever aware of time and its passing. As a girl, she spent time in the Morvan in western Burgundy where her father, a professor of history at the Sorbonne, conducted researches into the Celtic culture of pre-Roman Gaul, and a sense of history—repetitious, ever-renewing, long for itself, short for its participants—pervades her brief affair with Burgoyne. He protests that they must eventually part. "That is our fate," she answers. "I would have you think of this coast and those who have loved here before us. Phoenicians, Greeks and Romans, the barbarians, Italians, French."[8] On their last night together, Montrechet reminds Burgoyne that she will soon be growing old and that he will not be long in following along that road. She leaves him early the next morning before he awakes and returns to Paris on the Blue Train, and soon after her departure Burgoyne leaves France.

The Blue Train is an elegaic hail and farewell to five women, to youth, and to France. Hail and farewell to the food and wine of France, which Powell evokes in the manner of M.F.K. Fisher as a material metaphor for other hungers: the white fish of Lake Neuchâtel, sauteed and served beside watercress along with a chilled and sparkling white wine, eaten at a corner table of a restaurant with a view of the star-speckled lake; the gruyere, ham, rye bread, and grapes hastily flung into a haversack for an afternoon hike and picnic; the marvelous station buffet meals—roast lamb, white beans, and chicory salad—eaten in the course of greetings and departures; the simple but special dinners at one of the many fine restaurants in Dijon, washed down with Beaujolais *en carafe*. And the music of Europe as well, coming in by night on the wireless from London to Warsaw, alive with the magic of the night and the storied cities from which the concerts begin their swift flight by airwaves across the continent to Dijon.

Alone in his pension, headset in place, Burgoyne feels that all Europe is pouring forth its music into his room, that he is listening to the collective symphony of an entire culture. Hail and farewell to Paris, glimpsed on a winter night from a hotel window, the air smelling of snow, coal smoke, and Chanel; the buildings blue-gray in the moonlight. Farewell to Cros de Cagnes on the Côte d'Azur, where Powell had stayed with the Fishers and where Jack Burgoyne drinks chilled white wine and nibbles olives in an outdoor cafe as shawled women on the beach repair their men's fishing nets, and where the flora—bougainvillea and oleander, orange, lemon, olive, pepper, and eucalyptus trees, mimosa and persimmon—recalls the Southern California to which he must now return.

Hail and farewell, above all else, to Dijon, the ducal university city where Powell, the Fishers, and Burgoyne experienced the *gaudeamus igitur* of prolonged university days in a *moritorium* before reality and struggle. On his last night there, Burgoyne tours the city on foot: the park on the edge of the River Ouche where he had strolled with Erda arm in arm on a wintry afternoon; the Place Emile Zola where he had sat with Joyce at the Café du Midi on a sunny Sunday drinking warm beer from green bottles as the Dijonnais promenaded and a concert band of uniformed railway workers oompa-pahed on their instruments; the statues of the composer Rameau and the eloquent prelate Bossuet, two Dijonnais who had done well at court; the library and lecture halls of the university; the cafés, each with their venerable waiters and distinct but similar ambiences of provincial reserve, yet coziness as well, once one was accepted as the Southern Californians had been accepted by the café waiters of Dijon.

All this, for Burgoyne at least, has now passed—like the high-speed Blue

Train running north-south to and from Paris. Streaking through the night, the Blue Train symbolizes the romance of Europe as Burgoyne was experiencing it in the early 1930s. The Blue Train bespoke past and present departures: the passing of time and the coalescence of individual lives into a *rapide* called history. Love, time, and trains arrive and depart with an inevitability that must be accepted. France becomes a leave-taking. Southern California becomes a return. Romantic journeys on the Blue Train yield to workaday commutes on the big red car. The rails through Dijon lead back to Pasadena.

Epilogue

Material Dreams

By 1930 Southern California stood materialized as a metropolitan and suburban region, and Los Angeles, its population standing at 1.2 million, had become the dominant American city west of Chicago and a maritime center on the Pacific Rim. This society depended upon the water projects through which it had been first envisioned in the nineteenth century. Water dominates the surface of the planet and nurtures life. The human body is itself largely water, and the human social body materialized as city, suburb, or farm requires water for the same functions of cleansing and nurture. Thus the water prophets of the nineteenth and early twentieth century operated on the deepest levels of matter and metaphor when they envisioned and made California happen through water. Life itself, water constituted the material premise and absorptive symbol for the Southern California which Americans had so rapidly materialized.

The creation of the Imperial Valley offers an extreme, hence dramatic paradigm of the process whereby Southern California as a materialized society was wrestled from semi- or outright aridity. The name chosen for the region, Imperial, underscored the factors of vision and will involved in the creation of this place. Neither the Imperial Valley nor Los Angeles merely happened naturally, nor would either place have developed without a conscious and sustained rearrangement of the environment. There was no environmental or socioeconomic inevitability, in other words, to either place: no ports, no rivers, no railroad crossings—not even a sense of strategic necessity, for the Navy had already learned to operate effectively out of other coastal locations.

Both places, the Imperial and Los Angeles, furthermore, were materialized by private elites who controlled public resources, land, and water, and the mechanisms of government at the municipal, county, state, and federal levels. From this perspective, government as well as private enterprise called Southern

California into being. The federal government created the port of Los Angeles in 1900 and a few years later gave both San Francisco and Los Angeles its water. Federal intervention finally rationalized, if not harmonized, the confused situation in the Imperial. Yet these very same governmentally empowered elites were also acting as private developers in a mixture of public and private motivation and behavior that recalled the great franchised trading companies, British, Dutch, French, and Portuguese, so active in the colonization of North America, India, and Southeast Asia.

In the matter of water, in fact, Los Angeles and, to a lesser extent, San Francisco, functioned more like entrepreneurial corporations or actively investing Swiss cantons than passive municipalities concerned narrowly with public safety and the delivery of local governmental services. Los Angeles, moreover, exercised its own expansionist foreign policy as it used its water to coerce adjacent townships and unincorporated communities to join it in exchange for water concessions. In annexing the San Fernando Valley in 1915, Los Angeles made its Louisiana Purchase. Because the oligarchy controlled or decisively influenced the governmental bodies which controlled the water, it grew rich and powerful beyond measure. It also helped that the most active land speculator owned the dominant newspaper. Thus one might make reference, almost, to a Southern California Raj—an orchestration of business, financial, political, and governmental power, all of it controlled by one oligarchy—proceeding directly from the fact and symbol of the Imperial metaphor.

Water required land and people to attain its full power, and vice versa. In the Imperial Valley this triadic relationship of water, land, and people occurred as agriculture, with some town building. In coastal sub/urbia it occurred as real-estate development. The story of Southern California through the 1920s constitutes an epic of real-estate development of significance to the American national experience. The desire for land of one's own constituted a powerful force as fact and myth among Americans. The Imperial Valley experience showed no new developments in this trait. The Imperial settlers wanted farms, as did their seventeenth- and eighteenth-century predecessors. But what about the desire for single-family home ownership so evident in greater Los Angeles and the sub/urban Southern California coast? Had the home-owning instinct ever previously emerged with such materializing force in our national experience as it did in Southern California in the early twentieth century? Was real estate and housing development ever such a cutting edge of a regional economy? Did real-estate developers ever play such an important role in shaping a region in terms of its value system and identity as well as its physical fabric? Along with their architects, the developers of this era were embarked upon a complex, compelling work of physical and imaginative interpretation through the construction and sales of cities, suburbs, and individual properties. They were the Wizards of Oz, the middlemen of symbols and dreams.

Had Henry Adams been alive in 1930 to ponder on Los Angeles as he had meditated on Chicago in 1893, he might have wondered, first, as he did then, how such an astonishing city came to be in the first place. (Sydney engenders similar wonderment in our own era.) Further reflection would have led Adams to see Los Angeles as the Chicago of the Southwest: the energetic, solid, powerfully materialized capital of an American region sweeping inland to Texas. He might also have envisioned the City of the Angels as the Chicago of the Pacific Basin, this in its futurity if not in its 1930 present: a matrix city for the United States in the twenty-first Asia Pacific century, orchestrating that region as Chicago orchestrated the heartland through the previous era. Like Chicago from which so many of its creators came, Los Angeles exuded elemental power from its impressive physical presence, especially in its downtown which contrary to cliché was solid, central, and assertive. Los Angeles had only to wait until the 1932 Olympics for its counterpart to the Chicago World's Fair of 1893: a festival, that is, celebrating a consolidated civic identity put proudly before the world. In a very real way, the 1932 Olympics represented a culmination of a quarter-century of self-definition and self-assertion which had both its bright and dark, serious and comic dimensions. And while Henry Adams could not be there for the occasion, a phalanx of lesser commentators were on hand to note the impressive material presence of the City of the Angels in the year 1932 of the Common Era.

History, historical myths and imagery, architecture and design had played key roles in this process of materialization. Relatively unimportant in comparison to Los Angeles, Santa Barbara attains importance as a defiantly postmodernist city almost before modernism arrived in the Southland. Decoded as a statement of value, Santa Barbara's architectural program is at once an alternative, a rejection of Los Angelization, and a genteel gloss on the magical, transforming Oz-aspects of Southern California. The Santa Barbara formula of upper-middle-class Anglo-American in search of safety, health, prosperity, and subliminal release through romantic myth materialized as architecture was of relevance to most affluent communities in the Southland, from San Diego to Santa Barbara, inland to San Bernardino, Redlands, and Riverside. Southern California attained a special valence because its dreams and metaphors stood so close to the surface of its material texture, like the schematized components of a successful stage set.

It was one thing to materialize metaphors in the physical fabric of a civilization. It was another to reflect on what was being done and why. The collapse of the magazine *Opinion* underscored that the materialization of Southern California was running out ahead of its capacity to generate a unifying body of articulated ideas or assumptions. While Southern California possessed design ideas aplenty in this era, it did not produce until the late 1930s the roll-call of print-media intellectuals and artists one might expect. What came so glibly to architects and landscapists—a sense, that is, of meaning as well as physical presence—took more time to consolidate among the print-oriented. Thus an almost Alexandrian passion for the printed text in its antiquarian book form or as fine printing or as the occasion for club and associational life emerged to shore up an as-of-yet non-verbalized, non-verbalizing culture. The culture of France helped the Pasadenans perceive the possibilities of their own time and place, which might have seemed disconcertingly unsubstantial without such a magnifying prism. By helping them expand their imaginative apprehension of history, culture, and art, France taught the Pasadenans better, deeper ways of becoming productive Southern Californians.

The differing textures of the 1920s and the 1930s in California, together with the amplitude of each story, necessitated the division of the 1920s into a separate narrative. In California and elsewhere, the 1920s represented the exuberant takeover of urban America by corporate business structures and materialistic values. Suddenly, the world became filled with manufactured objects, consumer goods, as they later came to be called. A solid comfortable conservativism characterized political life. It began with a postwar Red Scare which in California took the form of the Criminal Syndicalism Act of 1919, the jawbone of an ass with which to smite the Industrial Workers of the World and its successors. There was some very real ugliness, in the San Pedro waterfront strike of 1923, for example, but, as this narrative has perhaps suggested, the major social and political energies of the 1920s, in Southern California especially, focused upon material construction and the pursuit of the good life.

In the 1930s this Babbittry came under grave stress, and nowhere more so than in California, where the left and the right cannonaded each other in a regional mimesis of the fascist/communist struggles that culminated in the Spanish Civil War in Europe. Even as this story is divided off, however, into an ensuing volume, the point must be made that the dreams and metaphors that brought about the materialized built environment of California in the 1920s did not evaporate in the anxieties and social conflicts of the Depression. Indeed, as the next volume will show, they became more intense than ever. By the end of the 1920s an agenda had been set and metaphors had been materialized which endured as shaping social forces through the troubled Depression era. Even as California was being wracked by a series of unprecedented strikes and was driven to entertain seriously the election of a Socialist governor advocating a radical program, other Californians were designing better patios and backyard swimming pools, were introducing the outdoor barbecue to America and experimenting with surfboards from Hawaii. The resort metaphor which had taken hold of Santa Barbara was translated to Palm Springs. Hollywood grew more powerful than ever.

In the 1930s a golden age of California as a regional American civilization would soon be asserting itself in architecture, landscaping, interior design, film, fiction, painting, photography, public works, the research and writing of history, sport, competitive athletics, and the good life—all of it coexisting with and running parallel to scenes of unprecedented wretchedness in the fields where the grapes of wrath would soon be harvested. Juxtaposed to the 1930s, the 1920s seem a prosaic Babbitt time of country clubs and golf courses. Yet it was the building time as well when the California Dream was materialized as solid interactions of people, developed places, and constructed identities. In the 1920s nearly two million people chose to become Californians, Southern Californians especially, and citizens of Los Angeles most noticeably. The society they materialized established a sub/urban identity which became the matrix of the California Dream for the rest of the century.

Notes

Frequently used citations

Agh	Agricultural History
AC	American City
AW	The American West
AEC	Architect and Engineer of California (later Western Architect and Engineer)
CHS	California Historical Society
CHSQ	California Historical Society Quarterly
CH	California History
HLQ	Huntington Library Quarterly
LAR	Los Angeles Realtor
NR	New Republic
NAR	North American Review
OM	Overland Monthly
PHR	Pacific Historical Review
QNBCC	Quarterly Newsletter of the Book Club of California
SEP	Saturday Evening Post
SCB	Southern California Business
SCQ	Southern California Quarterly
WAE	Western Architect and Engineer

Chapter Two. Dreams and Realities of Irrigation

1. "Our Great Pacific Commonwealth," *Century*, 53 (1896), 302.
2. Remi Nadeau, *The Water Seekers* (1974), 147.
3. Collis Huntington Steere, *Imperial and Colorado Valleys* (1952), 35; Henry Thomas Cory, *The Imperial Valley and Salton Sink* (1915), 80.
4. *The Winning of Barbara Worth* (1911), 95ff.

Chapter Three. Aqueduct Cities

1. *The Water Seekers*, 28–29.
2. *Ibid.*, 51.

Chapter Four. Oz to Oildorado

1. *The Annotated Wizard of Oz* (1973), 100.
2. "Money from Elsewhere," *The Saturday Evening Post*, 195 (12 May 1923), 140.
3. Bruce Bliven, "Los Angeles: The City That Is Bacchanalian—In a Nice Way," *NR*, 51 (13 July 1927), 197.
4. "Selling Sub-divisions," *LAR*, 3 (July 1924), 7.
5. "The Essentials of Selling Real Estate," *LAR*, 4 (June 1925), 40.
6. "Selling Sub-divisions," 29.
7. *Tarzan and the Golden Lion* [1923], (second edition 1924), 242.
8. "Los Angeles", 197.
9. *Oil!* (1927), 161.
10. "Los Angeles," 200.

Chapter Five. Boosting Babylon

1. "Why Chicago Came to Los Angeles," *SCB*, 2 (August 1923), 21.
2. "Here Is a $1,000,000,000 Banking City," SCB, 5 (December 1926), 38.
3. "Fortune and Friendship," *LAR*, 3 (December 1923), 30.
4. Jo Neely, "A Dream Come True," *AEC*, 53 (May 1918), 80–86.
5. "Reflections on the Grauman Metropolitan Theater, Los Angeles," *AEC*, 73 (June 1923), 101.
6. E. Bingham, "Grauman Theater, a Work of Art," *AEC*, 73 (May 1923), 76.
7. Burton Smith, "In Defense of Babbitt's 'How's Business?' " *LAR*, 7 (April 1928), 22; Hamlin Garland, *Diaries*, edited by Donald Pizer (1968), 40.
8. "The Bright Side Of Los Angeles," in *Facts You Should Know About California* (ca. 1927), 6.
9. *The Boosters* (1924), 8–10.
10. *Ibid.*, 352.
11. "Los Angeles—Dreamer and Doer," *SCB*, 1 (October 1922), 9.
12. "The Los Angeles of Tomorrow," *SCB*, 3 (September 1924), 34.
13. "Relieve Traffic Congestion—How?" *SCB*, 3 (September 1924), 9, 42–43.
14. "The Future of Aviation," *LAR*, 8 (August 1929), 12.
15. Quoted in Paul Ditzel, "The Day Los Angeles Had Zeppelin Fever," *Westways*, 61 (April 1969), 24.

Chapter 6. Oligarchs, Babbitts, and Folks

1. Joseph Lilly, "Metropolis of the West," *North American Review*, 232 (September 1931), 243.

2. *Leaves from a Marlborough Diary, 1888–1915* (1987), 16.

3. "Los Angeles: The City That Is Bacchanalian," 199.

4. *Ibid.*

5. "The Bright Side of Los Angeles," *Facts You Should Know About California*, 10–11.

6. Entry for 5 January 1929, *Diaries*, 41–42.

7. "Los Angeles: The City That is Bacchanalian," 17.

8. Entry for 27 December 1930, *Diaries*, 42.

9. "The Bright Side of Los Angeles," 9–10.

10. "Los Angeles: The City That Is Bacchanalian," 17.

11. Victor E. Walkers, "A Look at California," in *Facts You Should Know About California*, 59.

12. Paul Jordan-Smith, "Los Angeles: Ballyhooers in Heaven," *The Taming of the Frontier*, edited by Duncan Aikman (1925), 279.

13. "Los Angeles, the Chemically Pure," *The Smart Set*, 39 (March 1913), 109.

14. *Ibid.*, 108.

15. Charles Queenan, *Long Beach and Los Angeles, a Tale of Two Ports* (1986), 86–87.

16. Jordan-Smith, "Los Angeles: Ballyhooers in Heaven," 281.

17. "Los Angeles, the Chemically Pure," 111.

18. "Los Angeles: Ballyhooers in Heaven," 285.

19. *Bob Shuler's Magazine* (June 1922), p. 100.

20. *Ibid.*, (March 1922), p. 17.

21. *Ibid.*, (March 1925), p. 2.

22. "Sample of Monday Night Radio Hour," 3 October 1927, *ibid.*, (November 1927), 228–231.

23. *The American Jitters, a Year of the Slump* (1932), 231.

24. "Westward Ho," *In the Service of the King, the Story of My Life* (1927), 214–215.

25. *This Is That, Personal Experiences, Sermons and Writings* (ca. 1923), 157.

26. Max Vorspan and Lloyd Gartner, *History of the Jews of Los Angeles* (1970), 136.

27. J. Max Bond, *The Negro in Los Angeles* (1936), 39.

28. "Across the Generation Gap," *Los Angeles, Biography of a City*, edited by John and Laree Caughey (1976), 286–287.

Chapter Seven. Emergence of Institutional Los Angeles

1. "A Look at California," *Facts You Should Know About California*, 64.

2. *Saturday Night*, 14 April 1928, 9.

3. "The Bright Side of Los Angeles," 6–7.

4. Robert William Matson, *William Mulholland, a Forgotten Forefather* (1976), 47.

5. Quoted in, Abraham Hoffman, *Vision or Villainy: Origins of the Owens Valley-Los Angeles Water Controversy* (1981), 205.

6. E. Avery McCarthy, "Symphonic Music as a Civic Force Affecting Realty Values," *LAR*, 6 (December 1926), 19–20.

7. Joseph Lilly, "Metropolis of the West," *NAR*, 232 (September 1931), 245.

8. Walter Watrous, "Behind the Scenes in Los Angeles," *Facts You Should Know About California*, 38–40.

9. Bruce Henstell, *Sunshine and Wealth: Los Angeles in the Twenties and Thirties* (1984), 50.

10. *Ibid.*, 50.

11. *Angel's Flight*, 14.

12. "Los Angeles in Fact and Dream," *SEP*, 203 (18 October 1930), 138, 144.

13. "Los Angeles," 136.

14. *Ibid.*, 135.

15. "Metropolis of the West," 242.

16. "Los Angeles in Fact and Dream," 144.

17. Walkers, "Behind the Scenes in Los Angeles," 48.

18. "Our Stake in the Pacific," *SCB*, 8 (August 1929), 14–15.

19. *Collected Letters*, edited by Harry T. Moore (2 vols., 1962), II, 752–753.

20. "The Bright Side of Los Angeles," 19.

21. "Los Angeles," *Out West*, ns, 85 (May 1927), 136.

22. Jordan-Smith, "Los Angeles: Ballyhooers in Heaven," 290.

23. "Los Angeles," 197.

Chapter Eight. Designs for Living

1. *Looking Backward* (Riverside Library edition, 1926), 38ff.

2. Esther McCoy, "A Vast Hall Full of Light, the Bradbury Building," *Arts & Architecture*, 70 (April 1953), 21.

3. Anne Galli, "What We Accomplished in Three Years in Our Garden in Southern California," *House Beautiful*, 69 (March 1931), 270.

4. Elizabeth C. White, "California Winter Garden," *The Garden Magazine*, 29 (December 1915), 142.

5. Grace Tabor, "Garden Influence in the Film Drama," *The Garden Magazine*, 32 (December 1920), 210.

6. "House With a Garden Room, *The Craftsman*, 27 (February 1915), 565.

7. Quoted in Jay Belloli and others, *Myron Hunt, 1868–1952, the Search for a Regional Architecture* (1984), 25.

8. "A Look at California," *Facts You Should Know About California*, 55.

9. "The City of Our Lady the Queen of the Angeles," *The American Jitters* (1932), 226.

10. "The Bright Side of Los Angeles," 9.

11. "Los Angeles," 200.

12. "Architecture in Los Angeles," *OM*, ns, 85 (May 1927), 138.

13. *The Garden of Allah* (1970), 27.

14. "Home of the Future: The New Architecture of the West," *The Craftsman*, 30 (May 1916), 141–142.

15. Jules Langsner, "Fantasy in Steel, Concrete and Broken Bottles," *Arts & Architecture*, 76 (September 1959), 27.

16. Robert S. Bryan, "Sam Rodia and the Children of Watts," *Westways*, 59 (August 1967), 30.

Chapter Nine. The Santa Barbara Heritage

1. *Two Years Before the Mast*, edited by John Haskell Kemble (1964), 236–239.

2. *Life in California*, edited by Joseph Sullivan (1947), 127.

3. Jesse D. Mason, *History of Santa Barbara and Ventura Counties of California* (1883), 456.

4. *Santa Barbara and Around There* (1886), 17–18.

5. *Ibid.*, 21–22.

6. Maynard Geiger, *Mission Santa Barbara, 1782–1965* (1965), 236.

7. Stella Rouse, *Santa Barbara's Spanish Renaissance* (1974), 28–30.

8. *Santa Barbara and Around There,* 73.

9. Rouse, *Santa Barbara's Spanish Renaissance,* 27–30.

10. Walker A. Tompkins, *Santa Barbara Yesterdays* (1962), 50.

11. "El Fureidis, the Little Paradise," *The Craftsman,* 29 (October 1915), 34.

Chapter Ten. The Santa Barbara Alternative

1. *Santa Barbara and Around There,* 34–35.

2. Frank Selover, *Santa Barbara County* (1915), 29.

3. *Swinging the Censer, Reminiscences of Old Santa Barbara* (1931), 274.

4. *Santa Barbara, California* (1925), unpaged brochure.

5. Allied Architects Association of Los Angeles, "A Prophetic Resume," *Bulletin, Santa Barbara Earthquake Number, Second Edition* (1925), unpaged brochure.

6. *California Editor* (1958), 346.

7. *The Twenties,* edited by Leon Edel (1975), 173.

8. *Ibid.,* 178.

9. *Ibid.,* 459.

10. *Ibid.,* 466–467.

11. *A Western Wind* (1935), 81–83.

12. *Ibid.,* 104.

Chapter Eleven. Opinion and the Aristocracy of Art

1. Jacob Israel Zeitlin, "Books and the Imagination: Fifty Years of Rare Books," edited by Joel Gardner for the UCLA Oral History Program (2 vols., typescript, 1980), 551.

2. "Los Angeles: Ballyhooers in Heaven," 280.

3. *Time,* 34 (11 September 1939), 60.

4. *Armitage, His Loves and His Many Lives* (1982), 10–11.

5. *Accent on Life* (1964), 259–260.

6. *Ibid.,* 255–256.

7. "The Cultural Flowering of Los Angeles in the 30s and 40s," typescript of a talk given at California State University at Long Beach, 2 April 1979, Zeitlin Archives, UCLA, p. 8.

8. *Ibid.,* 9–10.

9. "Small Renaissance: Southern California Style," *Papers of the Bibliographical Society of America,* 50 (1956), 16.

Chapter Twelve. Books and Bohemia in Los Angeles

1. John E. Pomfret, *The Henry E. Huntington Library and Art Gallery From Its Beginnings to 1969* (1969), 54.

2. Robert Rosenthal, "Los Angeles & Chicago: Two Cities, Two Bibliophiles," *A Bibliophile's Los Angeles* (1985), 25.

3. *The Education of Carey McWilliams,* 49.

4. Ward Ritchie, "Printing and Publishing in Southern California," edited by Elizabeth I. Dixon for the UCLA Oral History Program (1969), p. 128; hereafter cited as Ritchie Oral History.

Chapter Thirteen. Pasadena Begins Its Literary Career

1. *Different Images* (1987), 76.

2. Ritchie Oral History, 42.

3. Quoted in Lawrence Clark Powell, *Robinson Jeffers, the Man and His Work* (1940 edition), 10.

4. Ritchie Oral History, 556–557, reporting a diary account of a conversation with Edith Greenan, author of *Of Una Jeffers* (1939), on the late afternoon of 9 January 1939.

5. *Fortune & Friendship* (1968), 39.

6. *The Gastronomical Me* [1943] in *The Art of Eating* (1954), 463.

7. *Ibid.*, 353.

8. *The Blue Train* (1977), 102.

Bibliographical Essay

Chapter One

William L. Kahrl and others, *The California Water Atlas* (1979), Chapters One through Six especially, provides the most comprehensive introduction to water in California. For general histories, see: Remi A. Nadeau, *The Water Seekers* (rev. ed. 1974); Erwin Cooper, *Aqueduct Empire* (1968); and the authoritative Donald J. Pisani, *From the Family Farm to Agribusiness: The Irrigation Crusade in California and the West* (1984). Revisionist histories begin with John Graves, T.H. Watkins, and Robert H. Boyle, *The Water Hustlers* (1971), and continue through Donald Worster's influential *Rivers of Empire: Water, Aridity, and the Growth of the American West* (1985). See also Marc Reisner, *Cadillac Desert, The American West and Its Disappearing Water* (1986). Regarding early irrigation efforts in San Bernardino, see: Edward Otho Cresap Ord, *The City of the Angeles and the City of the Saints; or, a Trip to Los Angeles and San Bernardino in 1856*, edited by Neal Harlow (1978); L.M. Holt, *The Great Interior Fruit Belt and Sanitarium* (1885); Edson D. Hale, *The County of San Bernardino* (1888); *Ingersoll's Century Annals of San Bernardino County, 1769 to 1904* (1906); Hallock Floy Raup, *San Bernardino* (1940); and Pauliena B. La Fuze, *Saga of the San Bernardinos* (2 vols., 1971).

Dr. Oliver Meredith Wozencraft recounted his first crossing of the Colorado Desert in "Through Northern Mexico in '49," *Californian*, 6 (1882), 421–428. See also Wozencraft, "The Wilds of the Darien," *Californian*, 4 (1881), 80–86, 163–171, 250–256. For Wozencraft as a railroad advocate, see his *Address Delivered Before the Mechanics' Institute on the Subject of the Atlantic and Pacific Rail-road* (1856). Regarding Wozencraft, see also: George Wharton James, *Heroes of California* (1910); George Lyman, "The Scalpel Under Three Flags in California," *CHSQ*, 4 (1925), 142–206; Chester Lee White, "Surmounting the Sierras," *CHSQ*, 7 (1928), 3–19; and Annie R. Mitchell, "Major James D. Savage and the Tuareños," *CHSQ*, 28 (1949); 323–341. Regarding flood conditions in the North, see Kenneth Thompson, "Historic Flooding in the Sacramento Valley," *PHR*, 29 (1960), 349–360. Robert Kelley's masterful *Battling the Inland Sea: American Political Culture, Public Policy, and the Sacramento Valley 1850–1986* (1989) appeared too late for my use. It now commands the subject.

William Hammond Hall made his first bold proposals in *Memorandum Concerning the Improvement of the Sacramento River Addressed to James B. Eads* (1880). He announced even bolder plans in *Report of the State Engineer to the Legislature* (1881) and *Outline of Matter and Advance Sheets of the Report on Irrigation* (1884). Of Hall's announced volumes, three appeared: *Physical Data and Statistics of California* (1886); *Irrigation Development: History, Customs, Laws, and Administrative Systems Relating to Irrigation, Water-Courses, and Waters in France, Italy and Spain* (1886); and *Irrigation in California (Southern): The Field, Water-Supply, and Works, Organization and Operation in San Diego, San Bernardino, and Los Angeles Counties* (1888). In the terrible year of 1886, Hall defended himself in *The Irrigation Question, a Memorandum to the Legislature of California* (1886) and *The Irrigation Question, Memorandum No. 2* (1886). See also *Irrigation in California, a Lecture Delivered Before the National Geographic Society at Washington* (1889) for a summary statement of Hall's position.

In 1891 Hall, then a consulting engineer in private practice, issued surveys for the Central Irrigation District, the Butte Water Supply and Land Project, the Alessandro Irrigation District, and the Perris Irrigation District. For Hall's later involvements, see *A Study of Panama Canal Plans and Arguments* (1905). Hall's *Personal Papers, 1887–1916* are in the Library of the California Historical Society in San Francisco. The Bancroft Library in Berkeley has the unpublished ms. "The Romance of a Woodland Park," Hall's memoir of his Golden Gate Park career, together with other reminiscences and an outline of this park theory. The best overall assessment of Hall's career as state engineer is in Pisani, *From the Family Farm to Agribusiness*, pp. 154–190. See also Charles P. Karr, "William Hammond Hall: The Failure of Attempts at State Water Planning in California, 1878–1888," *SCQ*, 45 (1963), 305–322, and Raymond H. Clary, *The Making of Golden Gate Park, the Early Years, 1865–1906* (1980), pp. 7–27. J.A. Alexander's *The Life of George Chaffey* (1928) is annoyingly hagiographical but informative. See also Frederick D. Kershner, Jr., "George Chaffey and the Irrigation Frontier," *AH*, 27 (1953), 155–122.

Chapter Two

For a general description of the Colorado River, see Frank Waters, *The Colorado* (1946). Regarding the Salton Sink/Sea, see: Daniel Trembly MacDougal, *The Salton Sea, a Study of the Geography, the Geology, the Floristics, and the Ecology of a Desert Basin* (1914); George Kennan, *The Salton Sea* (1917); Collis Huntington Steere, *Imperial and Coachella Valleys* (1952); and Mildred de Stanley, *The Salton Sea, Yesterday and Today* (1966). William P. Blake reported on the Salton Sink in "Geological Reconnaissance California," *Report for Railroad Survey*, Sen. Ex. Doc. No. 78, 33rd Cong., 2d. Sess., Vol. V, Part II. Regarding Wozencraft's plans for the Colorado Desert, see *Report of Public Lands Commission on Wozencraft Bill*, 37th Cong., 2d. Sess, H. Doc. (1862). Robert G. Schonfeld's "The Early Development of California's Imperial Valley," *SCQ*, 50 (1968), 279–307, 395–426, is the most complete, balanced, and documented account of the valley's early years. I have drawn upon its facts and conclusions extensively. *The Story of the First Decade in Imperial Valley* (1910) by Edgar F. Howe and Wilbur Jay Hall is anecdotal *Magnalia*, rich with first-hand observatons, as is Otis Burgess Tout's *The First Thirty Years* (1931). Helen Hosmer's "Imperial Valley," *AW*, 3 (1966), 34–79, is a compelling revisionist essay which has qualified my temperamental affinity for the drama of large-scale public works. Also of value are: Finis C. Farr, ed., *The History of Imperial County, California* (1918), and Margaret A. Romer, "A History of Calexico, California," *SCQ*, 12 (1922), 26–66. Charles Robinson Rockwood wrote his autobiography "Born of the Desert" in 1909 for the annual magazine of the Calexico

Chronicle. It has been extensively republished. See also Margaret Darsie Morrison, "Charles Robinson Rockwood: Developer of the Imperial Valley," *SCQ*, 44 (1962), 307–330. Other interesting memoirs include W.T. Heffernan's *Personal Recollections of the Early History of Imperial Valley* (1930) and Frederick William Peterson, *Desert Pioneer Doctor* (1947).

For the context of William Ellsworth Smythe's thought, see John Wesley Powell, *Report on the Lands of the Arid Region of the United States,* edited by Wallace Stegner (1962), and Wallace Stegner, *Beyond the Hundredth Meridian, John Wesley Powell and the Second Opening of the West* (1954), especially pp. 301–368. Smythe expounded his theories in *The Conquest of Arid America* (1900, rev. ed. 1905) and *Constructive Democracy: The Economics of a Square Deal* (1905). For Smythe's specific views on California, see his *The Greatest Irrigated Farm in the World* (1893); "Our Great Pacific Commonwealth," *Century*, 53 (1896), 300–307; and "Empire State on the Pacific," in *Conquest*, pp. 149–160. Smythe began his "The Twentieth Century West" department in *The Land of Sunshine/Out West* in June 1901. See also "After Private Enterprise—What?," *Out West*, 19 (1903), 437–441, and "Significance of Southern California," *Out West*, 32 (1910), 286–303. On Smythe himself, see, Edwin R. Bingham, *Charles F. Lummis, Editor of the Southwest* (1955), pp. 144–151.

To promote sales, the Imperial Land Company issued *From Desert to Garden* (1902), *An Album of the Imperial Settlements* (1902), and *Imperial Catechism, Questions and Answers Regarding the Imperial Valley* 1904). Also of interest is Allen Kelly and Edgar F. Howe, *Calexico, King Cotton's Capital* (1914). Two opposing opinions regarding the Reclamation Service are in L.M. Holt, *The Unfriendly Attitude of the United States Government Towards the Imperial Valley* (1907), and George Wharton James, *Reclaiming the Arid West, the Story of the United States Reclamation Service* (1917). Harry Thomas Cory recounted the complex story of containing the Colorado River flood in *The Imperial Valley and Salton Sink* (1915), which also contains an introductory monograph on the Sink by the pioneer explorer William P. Blake. See also George Kennan, *The Salton Sea, An Account of Harriman's Fight With the Colorado River* (1917).

For background and critical commentary on Harold Bell Wright's *The Winning of Barbara Worth* (1911), see: James D. Hart, *The Popular Book* (1950), Franklin Walker, *A Literary History of Southern California* (1950), and Lawrence Clark Powell, *California Classics, the Creative Literature of the Golden State* (1971). For other irrigation novels, see: Frank Lewis Nason, *The Vision of Elijah Berl* (1905); Ednah Aiken, *The River* (1914); and Belle Willey Gue, *The Last Ditch* (1923). J. Smeaton Chase recounted his visit to the Imperial in *California Desert Trails* (1919).

Chapter Three

The story of Los Angeles's acquisition of water from the Owens Valley has inspired two masterworks of California history: Abraham Hoffman, *Vision or Villainy: Origins of the Owens Valley-Los Angeles Water Controversy* (1981), and William L. Kahrl, *Water and Power: The Conflict Over Los Angeles' Water Supply in the Owens Valley* (1982). I have guided myself by these authoritative studies. Also of importance are: Oscar O. Winther, "Los Angeles: Its Aquatic Life Lines," *The Journal of Geography*, 49 (1950), 45–46; Vincent Ostrom, *Water & Politics: A Study of Water Policies and Administration in the Development of Los Angeles* (1953); and Remi Nadeau, "Water + Land = People," *Westways*, 57 (1965), 22–25. See also Carey McWilliams, *Southern California Country* (1946), pp. 183–204. Contemporary accounts which I have found valuable include Los Angeles City, Department of Public Service, *Complete Report on Construction of the Los Angeles Aqueduct with Introductory Historical Sketch* (1916), and Allen Kelly, *His-*

torical Sketch of the Los Angeles Aqueduct (1913). For an idea of Owens Valley before its destruction as an agricultural settlement, see the Owens Valley Chamber of Commerce, *Inyo County* (1909); the Inyo Register, *Inyo County, California, Anno Domini 1912, Beautiful Owens Valley* (1912); and Inyo County Board of Supervisors, *Inyo, 1866–1966* (1966). A complete description of the valley is available in Genny Schumacher Smith, *Deepest Valley, a Guide to Owens Valley, Its Roadsides and Mountain Trails* (rev. ed., 1978). See also William E. Smythe, "The Social Significance of the Owens River Project," *Out West*, 23 (1905), 443–453, and "Big Water Scheme for Los Angeles," *Pacific Municipalities*, 13 (1905), 15.

Burt A. Heinly, Mulholland's private secretary and publicist during the planning and construction of the aqueduct, turned out a series of laudatory articles that, when considered as promotional writing, amply reveal the attitudes of Los Angeles toward the aqueduct as well as provide much interesting technical information. Heinly's articles appeared in *Outlook* (25 September 1909), *Sunset* (December 1909), *Architect and Engineer* (January 1910), *National Geographic* (July 1910), *American City* (April 1912), and *Engineering News* (6 November 1913). Of special interest is his "Los Angeles—A City in Business," *National Municipal Review*, 3 (1914), 97–102. Also of value are: E.W. Bannister, "Construction Work on the Los Angeles Aqueduct," *Engineering Record* 59 (1909), 393–397; William W. Hurlburt, "Completion of the Los Angeles Aqueduct," *Engineering Record*, 68 (1913), 482–486; and Henry Z. Osborne, "The Completion of the Los Angeles Aqueduct," *Scientific American*, 109 (1913), 364 ff. See also Frank Bush Davison, *Commemorative of the Official Opening, the Los Angeles Aqueduct and Exposition Park* (1913). For a hostile evaluation of the aqueduct, see "Municipal Water Works," *Sunset*, 34 (1915), 1081–1083. Doyce B. Nunis, Jr., has edited and extensively annotated Dr. Raymond G. Taylor's *Men, Medicine & Water: The Building of the Los Angeles Aqueduct, 1908–1913: A Physician's Recollections* (1982), a source of much information and lively detail. For examples of the virtual canonization of Mulholland, see two sketches by close associates: Burt A. Heinly, "The Aladdin of the Aqueduct," *Sunset*, 28 (1912), 465–467, and Joseph B. Lippincott, "William Mulholland," *Civil Engineering*, 2 (1941), 105–107, 161–164. For a fine overall consideration of Mulholland's career, see Robert William Matson, *William Mulholland, A Forgotten Forefather* (1976).

Chapter Four

The study of Los Angeles begins with the comprehensive bibliography *Los Angeles and Its Environs in the Twentieth Century*, edited by Doyce B. Nunis, Jr. (1973). See also Joseph Gregg Layne, *Books of the Los Angeles District* (1950). General histories consulted and drawn upon include: Remi Nadeau, *Los Angeles, From Mission to Modern City* (1960); W.W. Robinson, *A Profile* (1968); Lynn Bowman, *Los Angeles, Epic of the City* (1974); David Lavender, *Los Angeles Two Hundred* (1980); John D. Weaver, *Los Angeles: The Enormous Village 1781–1981* (1980); and David L. Clark, *Los Angeles, a City Apart* (1981). See also John Steven McGroarty, *Los Angeles From the Mountains to the Sea* (3 vols., 1921), and Stephen Longstreet, *All Star Cast, an Anecdotal History of Los Angeles* (1977). Of special importance to this study as sources of fact and interpretation are Bruce Henstell's *Los Angeles, an Illustrated History* (1980) and *Sunshine and Wealth: Los Angeles in the Twenties and Thirties* (1984). For background material on the personalities of the period, I have drawn upon: *Constructive Californians*, foreword by S.T. Clover (1926); William A. Spalding, *History of Los Angeles City and County* (3 vols., 1931); and Carol Dunlap, *California People* (1982). See also Max Binheim, *Women of the West* (ca. 1928). Spalding's *History* also possesses a valuable year-by-year chronology of events through 1929. See also Spalding's earlier version *History and Reminiscences, Los Angeles City and County, California* (3 vols., 1930). In *Los Angeles, Biography of a City* (1976) John and LaRee Caughey have assembled a very useful anthology of personal and scholarly statements.

Regarding the places and buildings of the city, the *Rand McNally Guide to Los Angeles and Environs* (ca. 1925) and *Los Angeles, a Guide to the City and Its Environs* (1941), produced by the WPA, are each invaluable. For architectural facts and interpretations, I have drawn upon: David Gebhard, Robert Winter, Julius Shulman, and Marc Treib, *A Guide to Architecture in Los Angeles & Southern California* (1977); Charles Moore, Peter Becker, and Regula Campbell, *The City Observed: Los Angeles, a Guide to Its Architecture and Landscapes* (1984); and Sam Hall Kaplan, *LA Lost and Found, an Architectural History of Los Angeles* (1987). Of special interest are Arnold Hylen, *Los Angeles Before the Freeways, 1850–1950: Images of an Era* (1981), and *Commercial Los Angeles 1925–1947, Photographs From the "Dick" Whittington Studio,* compiled by Bill Bradley (1981).

Facts You Should Know About California, Number 752 in the Little Blue Book series edited by Emanual Haldeman-Julius (ca. 1927), contains four important essays: "The Bright Side of Los Angeles" and "Paganism in Los Angeles," by Louis Adamic, "Behind the Scenes in Los Angeles," by Walter Watrous, and "A Look at California," by Victor E. Walkers. See also Adamic's *The Truth About Los Angeles,* Little Blue Book Number 647 (ca. 1927) and "Los Angeles! There She Blows!," *Outlook and Independent,* 155 (13 August 1930), 563–565. Other pivotal observations include: Albert W. Atwood, "Money From Everywhere," *SEP,* 195 (12 May 1923), 10–11, 136ff; Paul Jordan-Smith, "Los Angeles: Ballyhooers in Heaven," in Duncan Aikman, ed., *The Taming of the Frontier* (1925), pp. 271–290; Bruce Bliven, "Los Angeles: The City That Is Bacchanalian—In a Nice Way," *NR,* 51 (13 July 1927), 197–200; Garet Garrett, "Los Angeles in Fact and Dream," *SEP,* 203 (18 October 1930), 6–7, 135ff; and Joseph Lilly, "Metropolis of the West," *NAR,* 232 (September 1931), 239–245. See also Marie Giles Saltus, *Edgar Saltus, the Man* (1925), and *Hamlin Garland's Diaries,* edited by Donald Pizer (1968).

L. Frank Baum's son Frank Joslyn Baum joined Russell P. MacFall to write *To Please a Child, a Biography of L. Frank Baum, Royal Historian of Oz* (1961). *The Annotated Wizard of Oz,* with an Introduction, Notes, and Bibliography by Michael Patrick Hearn (1973), is magisterial. See also Hearn's anthology of critical commentary, *The Wizard of Oz* (1983). The following articles from *The Baum Bugle, a Journal of Oz* also proved important: Ben P. Indick, "Utopia, Allegory, and Nightmare," 18 (Spring 1974), 14–19; Scott Olsen, "The Coronado Fairyland," 20 (Winter 1976), 2–5; and Maud Baum, "Correspondence With Jack Snow," 27 (Spring 1983), 2–8.

Study of the growth of Los Angeles during this period begins with the authoritative *The Fragmented Metropolis, Los Angeles 1850–1930* by Robert M. Fogelson (1967), especially Chapter Seven, "The Urban Landscape." See also Henstell, *Sunshine and Wealth,* pp. 13–17. The growth of the city can be tracked in: "Los Angeles Becomes the Largest City in Area in the United States," *AC,* 15 (July 1916), 65–66; "Los Angeles Climbs to Fifth Place," *SCB* 2 (February 1923), 9–10; "The World's Greatest City—In Prospect," *World's Work,* 47 (December 1923), 140–142; "Los Angeles, Fifth City in the United States," *LAR,* 6 (August 1927), 20–21; and B. C. Forbes, "Cities in the Making," *OM,* ns 88 (October 1930), 305, 318. Regarding real estate, see W.W. Robinson, "The Southern California Real Estate Boom of the Twenties," *SCQ,* 24 (1942), 25–30. For contemporary accounts, see: Tom Ingersoll, "Los Angeles Is Truly the Nation's Home," *LAR,* 1 (September 1922), 7, 16; Arnold T. Anderson, "Subdivision Activity in Los Angeles," *LAR,* 7 (April 1928), 15; and Phil Norton, "Real Estate

Trusts, What They Are and Why," *SCB*, 8 (April 1929), 16, 47, 50. Regarding specific districts, see: Edward Lewis, *Palos Verdes, Los Angeles* (ca. 1922); the J.B. Ransom Organization, *Montebello Park* (ca. 1925); "Los Angeles' Other Half, the San Fernando Valley," *LAR*, 7 (November 1927), 35–39, 73–74; R. Strosnider, "Forward—Burbank," *LAR*, 8 (November 1928), 32; Gerald B. Burnett, "A Profitless Subdivision," *LAR*, 8 (December 1928), 14; and F.L. Meline, Inc., *Los Angeles, the Metropolis of the West* (ca. 1929). Of special interest is Frank M. Keefer, *History of the San Fernando Valley* (1934). Regarding Harry Culver see *Constructive Californians*, pp. 211–214; "Harry H. Culver, 1927 President," *LAR*, 6 (January 1927), 11, 37; and the obituary in the *Los Angeles Times* for 17 August 1946. See also W.W. Robinson, *Culver City, a Calendar of Events* (1939). Culver expressed his philosophy in "Selling Sub-divisions," *LAR*, 3 (July 1924), 7, 28–29, and "The Essentials of Selling Real Estate," *LAR*, 4 (June 1925), 19, 38–40.

Regarding Edgar Rice Burroughs, see the comprehensive illustrated biography by Irwin Porges, *Edgar Rice Burroughs, the Man Who Created Tarzan* (1975), especially Chapter 16, "Tarzana—Family, Business, Creativity," pp. 333–379. For an assessment of Burroughs as a writer, see Erling B. Holtsmark, *Edgar Rice Burroughs* (1986). Burroughs's *The Efficiency Expert* appeared in 1921. See also Roger Dionne, "Tarzan's Valley," *Westways*, 69 (August 1977), 48–51, and, Leo Rosenhouse, "Edgar Rice Burroughs: The Californian Who Created Tarzan," *California Highway Patrolman*, 41 (February 1978), 16–20.

Spencer Crump's *Ride the Big Red Cars: How Trolleys Helped Build Southern California* (1962) is at once nostalgic and authoritative. For contemporary views, see Rufus Steele, "The Red Car of Empire," *Sunset*, 31 (October 1913), 710–717, and J.G. Jeffery, "The Street Railway as a City Builder," *LAR* 5 (January 1926), 17, 35. For the system in decline, see Fogelson, *Fragmented Metropolis*, pp. 164–185. Regarding the traffic problems that brought on the streetcars' demise, see: Ernest McGaffey, "Living in the Age of Motorization," *SCB*, 7 (March 1928), 20–21, 34–35; William C. Garner, "Cities Shift With the Motor Car," *LAR*, 6 (January 1927), 15, 33–36; Miller McClintock, "Relieve Traffic Congestion—How?," *SCB*, 3 (September 1924), 9, 42–43; and Edwin Berstrom, "Relief of Traffic Congestion Seen in Acceptance of Civic Center Plan," *LAR*, 4 (February 1925), 12–13. Regarding the development of Wilshire Boulevard, see: W.W. Robinson, *History of the Miracle Mile* (1965); Esther McCoy, "Wilshire Boulevard," *WAE*, 222 (September 1961), 25–51; and Moore, *The City Observed*, pp. 143–163. Scott Bottles's *Los Angeles and the Automobile, the Making of the Modern City* (1987) commands the subject.

Early California Oil: A Photographic History, 1865–1940, by Kenny Franks and Paul Lambert (1985), contains an exhaustively researched text as well as photographs. See pp. 101–130 for the oil boom of the 1920s. For contemporary assessments, consult: "Where Flow Rivers of Liquid Wealth," *SCB*, 2 (February 1923), 7–8; E.C. Noel, "Oil Industry Offers Surprises," *SCB*, 2 (January 1924), 9, 38; and Joseph Jensen, "Oil, the Magic World of Southern California," *SCB*, 5 (August 1926), 9–11. See also Charles Lockwood, "Oil Boom Fueled Growth of L.A.," *Los Angeles Times*, 18 August 1985, Part 8, pp. 17–18. Regarding the Julian scandal, see Henstell, *Sunshine and Wealth*, pp. 31–43. For details of Julian's suicide, see "Julian's Spectacular Exit," *Saturday Night*, 14 (31 March 1934), 3. Regarding the Getty dynasty, see J. Paul Getty's *My Life and Fortunes* (1963) and *As I See It*, with B. von Block (1976), and Robert Lenzner, *The Great Getty* (1985).

Chapter Five

Regarding port development, see Charles F. Queenan's *The Port of Los Angeles: From Wilderness to World Port* (1983), pp. 69–78, and his *Long Beach and Los Angeles, a Tale of Two Ports* (1986), pp. 85–96. For contemporary views, see "Los Angeles Harbor Second in U.S.," *SCB*, 2 (April 1923), 9, 50, and F.J. Buckley, "Marvelous Growth of Los Angeles Harbor," *LAR*, 3 (June 1924), 14–19, 54–58. For the rise of manufacturing, see: James Scherer, "What Kind of a Pittsburgh Is Los Angeles?" *World's Work*, 41 (February 1921), 382–392; H.E. Poronto, "Why Chicago Came to Los Angeles," *SCB*, 2 (August 1923), 21, 45; Orra Monnette, "Industrial Southern California," *SCB*, 5 (July 1926), 9–11, 51; John Austin, "Pioneering the World's Second Tire Center," *SCB*, 8 (February 1929), 9–10, 47, 50; and Shannon Crandall, "Industrial Los Angeles County," *SCB*, 8 June (1929), 9–11, 32. For the agricultural economy, see B.R. Holloway, "Southwest Agriculture Centers in Los Angeles," *SCB*, 8 (March 1929), 12–13, 46. The story of banking and finance from this era is told in Ira Brown Cross, *Financing an Empire, History of Banking in California* (4 vols., 1927), III, 462–474, and the files of *Southern California Banker*. See also J.F. Sartori, "Here Is a $1,000,000,000 Banking City," *SCB*, 5 (December 1926), 28, 38–39.

Details regarding Hollywood as an employer can be gleaned from: Rufus Steele, "In the Sun Spot," *Sunset*, 34 (April 1915), 690–699; Charles Christie, "California—Home of World's Movie Capitol," *LAR*, 1 (May 1922), 21, 58–59, 60; James Bowen, "Bright Future Ahead of Photoplays," *SCB*, 1 (September 1922), 46, 66; Joseph M. Schenck, "A Business View of Motion Pictures," *SCB*, 1 (June 1922), 9, 44; Jerome Sengel, "Hollywood," *LAR*, 5 (October 1925), 13–14; Harry H. Beall, "The Capitalization of Sunshine and Shadows," *LAR*, 4 (December 1925), 21, 27; Harry Brown, "Why Movies Will Stay in Hollywood," *SCB*, 4 (January 1926), 18–19, 50; Harry Barratt, "Hollywood—Motion Picture Capitol [sic] of the World," *LAR*, 5 (June 1926), 16, 22–23, and "This Is Hollywood," *LAR*, 6 (November 1926), 15–16, 52–53; Carl Bush, "Hollywood Still Center of Picture Industry," *LAR*, 6 (November 1926), 18, 32; and Willis Owen, "Motion Pictures Build a Bigger Hollywood," *LAR*, 7 (November 1927), 40. For Cecil B. DeMille as bridge between Los Angeles and Hollywood, see his statements "Fortune and Fellowship," *LAR*, 3 (December 1923), 5, 30; "Los Angeles and the Film Industry," *LAR* 3 (August 1924), 6; and "The Spotlight of Los Angeles," *SCB*, 5 (July 1926), 20–21. See also Edwin Obadiah Palmer, *History of Hollywood* (2 vols, 1937).

For details regarding the rise of tourism, see: "New Peak-Load of Tourists Coming," *SCB*, 2 (November 1923), 26, 34; "Over 600,000 Motorists Will Come," *SCB*, 3 (April 1924), 14–15; "Tourists Pouring into Southland," *SCB*, 6 (November 1927), 30, 36; and "Sixty Conventions Scheduled for Los Angeles," *SCB*, 6 (December 1927), 16–17, 30. For Los Angeles as a place to visit, see Katherine Ames Taylor, *The Los Angeles Tripbook* (ca. 1928). The hotel industry can be understood from Francis Shanley, "Over $250,000,000 Invested in Guest Rooms," *SCB*, 5 (February 1926), 9–11. Regarding the Ambassador Hotel, see Margaret Tante Burk, *Are the Stars Out Tonight? The Story of the Famous Ambassador Hotel* (1980). Regarding the Biltmore, see Matlack Price, "The Los Angeles Biltmore," *Arts and Decoration*, 21 (June 1924), 25–28, and Frederick W. Jennings, "Recent Hotel Architecture in California," *AEC*, 80 (January 1925), 49–69, esp. 54–57. Details relating to theaters are available in: "A California Theater of Reinforced Concrete," *AEC* 17 (May 1909), 67–73; "The Majestic Theatre Building at Los Angeles," *Engineering Record*, 59 (30 January 1909), 128; William H. Cline, "The New Orpheum Theater Building, Los Angeles," *AEC*, 26 (September 1911), 34–50; Jo Neely, "A Dream Come True," *AEC*, 53 (May 1918), 80–86; Frederick Jennings, "A Theater Designed in the Egyptian Style," *AEC*, 72 (March 1923), 77–84; E.

Bingham, "Grauman Theater a Work of Art," AEC, 73 (May 1923), 76–77; G. Albert Lansburgh, "The El Capitan Theatre and Department Store Building, Hollywood," AEC, 88 (February 1927), 35–43; and "Southland's Finest Theater Completed" (United Artists), Saturday Night, 8 (10 December 1927), 2. Of special interest is Bernard Maybeck, "Reflections on the Grauman Metropolitan Theater, Los Angeles," AEC, 73 (June 1923), 99–102. See also Carrie Yoshimura, "A Celebration of LA's Movie Palaces," Los Angeles Times, 15 July 1987, Part Six, p. 3.

The envisioning of Los Angeles's future can be chronicled through: Irving Hellman, "Los Angeles in 1950, a Prophecy," LAR, 1 (March 1922), 9, 20; "Where Future Empire Will Center," SCB, 2 (March 1923), 13–14; "The World's Greatest City—In Prospect," World's Work, 47 (December 1923), 140–142; Clarence Matson, "The Los Angeles of Tomorrow," SCB, 3 (September 1924), 18, 32–35; and Stanley McMichael, "The Future of Los Angeles as Seen by an Easterner," LAR, 4 (January 1925), 9, 41. Regarding boosterism, see Tom Zimmerman, "Paradise Promoted: Boosterism and the Los Angeles Chamber of Commerce," CH, 64 (Winter 1985), 23–33. See also The Chamber of Commerce, Los Angeles County, Some Facts and Figures (1925) and the files of the Chamber magazine Southern California Business. Typical boostering statements include: Ernest McGaffeey, "Los Angeles—Dreamer and Doer," SCB, 1 (October 1922), 9–10; Sherley Hunter, Why Los Angeles Will Become the World's Greatest City (1923); and "What Is the Strength of Los Angeles?" LAR, 3 (March 1924), 13, 26. For an outside assessment, see Edgar L. Hampton, "Los Angeles, a Miracle City," Current History, 24 (April 1926), 35–42. Of special interest are "Ole Hanson Tells Why He Adopted Los Angeles," LAR, 1 (November 1921), 5, and Burton Smith, "In Defense of Babbitt's 'How's Business?' " LAR, 7 (April 1928), 22–23, 37. Regarding the city's leading booster, see Frank J. Taylor, "It Costs $1000 to Have Lunch with Harry Chandler," SEP, 212 (16 December 1939), 8–9ff.

Regarding city planning in this era, see Fogelson, Fragmented Metropolis, pp. 248–272, and Mellier Goodin Scott, Cities Are for People (1942) and Metropolitan Los Angeles, One Community (1949). Important statements include: Charles Mulford Robinson, "The City Beautiful," in the Los Angeles Municipal Art Commission, Report to the Mayor, the City Council and Board of Public Works (1909); G. Gordon Whitnall, "Importance of Broad City Planning," SCB, 1 (February 1922), 8, 45; and Lawrence McNeil, "Should Los Angeles Maintain Its Limit Height on Office Buildings?" LAR, 6 (January 1927), 15, 26. The Property Republic by John Caspar Avakian (1925) is an occasionally eccentric but informative call for regional planning. Regarding parks, see Griffith J. Griffith, Parks, Boulevards and Playgrounds (1910), and Citizens' Committee on Parks, Playgrounds and Beaches, Parks, Playgrounds and Beaches for the Los Angeles and Region (1930). Regarding the City Hall, see George P. Hales, Los Angeles City Hall (ca. 1928). Regarding the Central Library, see: Forty-Eighth Annual Report of the Board of Library Commissioners of the Los Angeles Public Library for the Year Ending June 30, 1936 and Brief History of the Los Angeles Public Library (1936); Hand Book of the Central Building, Los Angeles Public Library (1927); and Laura Cooley, "The Los Angeles Public Library," SCQ, 23 (1941), 5–27. Faith Holmes Hyers introduced the new Central Library in AEC (November 1926); Libraries, 31 (February 1926), 74–77; Library Journal, 51 (August 1926), 77–82; Sunset, 57 (December 1926), 17ff; and SCB, 8 (July 1929), 16–17, 38. See also Alan Franklin, "Industry Finds Profit in Public Library," SCB, 6 (February 1927) 16–17, 38, 50. Regarding the Union Station controversy, see Bill Bradley, The Last of the Great Stations (1979).

The story of the importance of aviation to Los Angeles and Southern California is fully treated in William A. Schoneberger with Paul Sonnenburg, California Wings, a History of Aviation in the Golden State (1984), pp. 30–50. Southern California Business did a special aviation issue in August 1928. See also: C.C. Moseley, "Thirty Hours Nearer New York," *SCB*, 5 (March 1926), 9–11; H.R. Brashear, "Shall Los Angeles Have a Municipal Airport for Commerce?," *SCB*, 6 (September 1927), 14–15, 39; A.W. Poole, "Where the Aviation Industry Centers," *SCB*, 8 (May 1929), 9–10, 26–27, 43, 50; Arnold T. Anderson, "Commercial Aviation in Southern California," *LAR*, 8 (June 1929), 7–8, 24–27, 33–35; W.D. Longyear, "Take Airplanes for Instance," *SCB*, 8 (August 1929), 9–11, 27, 49; and Robert L. Smith, "The Future of Aviation Rests on the Ground," *LAR*, 8 (October 1929), 7–8. Of special interest is Harry H. Culver, "The Future of Aviation," *LAR*, 8 (August 1929), 12, 21–22. Regarding the visit of the *Graf Zeppelin*, see Paul Ditzel, "The Day Los Angeles Had *Zeppelin* Fever," *Westways* 61, (March 1969), 2–5; (April 1969), 24–26ff.

Chapter Six

Regarding the sporting preferences of the Oligarchs and the Babbitts, see the regular golfing column by Jane Frederickson, "On Southland's Golf Links," in the *Saturday Night* of the early to mid-1920s. See also "Summer Polo at Uplifters Club Field," *Saturday Night*, 12 May 1928, p. 2. Regarding Samuel Travers Clover, editor of *Saturday Night*, see *Who's Who in California 1928–1929* (1929), p. 194. Marco Newmark chronicled the history of club life in "Pioneer Clubs of Los Angeles," *SCQ*, 31 (1949), 299–317. See also: *Annals of the Sunset Club of Los Angeles* (5 vols., 1905–1970); the California Club of Los Angeles, *Officers, Members, Articles of Incorporation, By-laws and House Rules* (1926); and "California Club's Picturesque New Home on Flower Street," *Saturday Night*, 23 March 1929, p. 1. The *Marlborough* alumnae magazine for Winter 1986 and Spring 1987 contains a number of articles dealing with the history of the school. See also *Leaves From a Marlborough Diary, 1888–1915* (1987) and *Leaves From a Marlborough Diary, 1916–1938*. Bishop Robert B. Gooden wrote "Harvard School—A Southland School for Boys" in the *Saturday Night* of 18 August 1928.

Frank Gruber wrote the biography *Zane Grey* (1970). Also of importance are Lawrence Clark Powell, "Southwest Classics Reread: *Riders of the Purple Sage*," *Westways*, 64 (August 1972), 50–55, and Leo Rosenhouse, "Zane Grey, King of the Western Novels," *California Highway Patrolman*, 39 (May 1975), 31–34. See also T. K. Whipple, *Study Out the Land* (1943). For Grey the Southern Californian, see Rockwell D. Hunt, *California and the Californians* (3 vols., 1932), III, 575, and Sarah Noble Ives, *Altadena, Compiled for the Altadena Historical and Beautification Society* (1938), p. 314.

For the social habits of the Folks, see Joseph Boskin, "Associations and Picnics as Stabilizing Forces in Southern California," *CHSQ*, 44 (1965), 17–26, and Henstell, *Sunshine and Wealth*, pp. 109–115. For the religious celebrations of the city, see: Paul H. Dowling, "The Masque of the Nativity: A Triumph in Municipal Pageantry," *AC*, 15 (December 1916), 655–657; Harriett Day, "Back Stage of the Pilgrimage Play," *Saturday Night*, 25 August 1923; "Sixth Season of America's Passion Play," *Saturday Night*, 27 June 1925; and Katherine Doyle, "A Real Home for the Pilgrimage Play," *SCB*, 10 (June 1931), 16. The classic description of puritanical Los Angeles is Willard Huntington Wright's "Los Angeles, the Chemically Pure," *The Smart Set*, 39 (March 1913), 107–114, republished in *The Smart Set Anthology*, edited by Rascoe Burton and Groff Conklin (1934), pp. 90–102. See also Conrad Seiler, "Los Angeles Must Be Kept Pure," *Nation*, 122 (19 May 1926), 548–549. Edmund Wilson profiled Robert Pierce Shuler in *The American Jitters, a Year of the Slump* (1932), pp. 225–243. See also Henstell, *Sunshine and Wealth*, pp. 50–53. *Bob Shuler's Magazine* ran from March 1922 to July 1933. Of special relevance to this chapter are Shuler's articles "The Way of the West Leads East," 1 (March 1922), 17; "Hail 'Fatty,' Thy Fame Is Final," 1 (May 1922), 45; "The Other Side," 1 (September 1922), 100; and "Thou City of the Angels," 4 (March 1925), 2. See also Shuler's pamphlet *Jailed* (1931).

The standard biography of Aimee Semple McPherson is Lately Thomas's *Storming Heaven* (1970), which supersedes his earlier *The Vanishing Evangelist* (1959). McPherson told her own story in *This Is That, Personal Experiences, Sermons and Writings* (ca. 1923), *In the Service of the King, the Story of My Life* (1927), and the posthumously published *The Story of My Life* (1951). Her theology and some idea of her power as a preacher can be experienced in *Divine Healing Sermons* (1921), *The Second Coming of Christ* (ca. 1921), and *Tabernacle Revivalist* (1923). Two hymnals from this period, *Foursquare Melodies* and *Foursquare Favorites*, suggest the temper and tone of worship at the Echo Park Tabernacle. *Give Me My Own God* (1936) is a collection of travel sketches by McPherson. In *"McPhersonism": A Study of Healing Cults and Modern Day "Tongues" Movements, Containing Summary of Facts as to Disappearance and Re-appearance of Aimee Semple McPherson* (ca. 1924), Bob Shuler outlined his disagreements with the competition.

Observations regarding the declining Chinese population come from J.M. Sanland, "Chinatown's Fading Local Color," *Saturday Night*, 14 July 1923, pp. 20, 26, and Henstell, *Sunshine and Wealth*, pp. 89–93. For Jewish life in this period, see Max Vorspan and Lloyd P. Gartner, *History of the Jews of Los Angeles* (1970), pp. 124–145. See also: Harriet and Fred Rochlin, *Pioneer Jews: A New Life in the Far West* (1984); Neil Sandberg, *Jewish Life in Los Angeles: A Window to Tomorrow* (1986); and Neal Gabler, *An Empire of Their Own: How the Jews Invented Hollywood* (1988). Regarding the Japanese of Los Angeles, see Ichiro Mike Murase, *Little Tokyo: One Hundred Years in Pictures* (1983). Regarding the Mexican-American population of the city, see Antonio Rios-Bustamante and Pedro Castillo, *An Illustrated History of Mexican Los Angeles, 1781–1985* (1986), pp. 122–141, and Richard Griswold del Castillo, *The Los Angeles Barrio, 1850–1890: A Social History* (1983). J. Max Bond published his USC study *The Negro in Los Angeles* in 1936. It was reprinted in 1972. Of special relevance are pp. 32–53. See also Ralph Bunche's speech "Across the Generation Gap," in Caughey and Caughey, editors, *Los Angeles*, pp. 282–287.

Chapter Seven

The standard history of USC is *Southern California and Its University* by Manuel P. Servin and Iris Higbie Wilson, with a Foreword by Carey McWilliams (1969). An earlier history is Rockwell D. Hunt, *The First Half Century* (1930). See also *The Semi-centennial Celebration of the Founding of the University of Southern California, 1880–1930*, edited by Herbert Wynford Hill (1930). On USC as a football power, see also Henstell, *Sunshine and Wealth*, pp. 117–129. Regarding the mission of USC during the 1920s, see Rockwell D. Hunt, "Higher Education for Bigger Business," *SCB*, 1 (March 1922), 7, 34–35, and Rufus B. von KleinSmid, "Training College Men for Business," *SCB*, 2 (May 1923), 15, 50.

The saga of water and power is told by Vincent Ostrom in *Water & Politics, a Study of Water Policies and Administration in the Development of Los Angeles* (1953). For further insight, see Fogelson, *Fragmented Metropolis*, pp. 229–246. For contemporary assessments, see Edgar Lloyd Hampton, "Cheap Power as a City Developer," *SCB*, 2 (May 1923), 12–13, 42, and Don J. Kinsey, *The Romance of Water and Power* (1928). Regarding the quest for the Colorado, see Remi Nadeau, *The Water Seekers* (1950), pp. 167–218, and Robert William Matson, *William Mulholland, a Forgotten Forefather* (1976), pp. 43–49. See also Revel Leslie Olson, *The Colorado River Compact* (1926), and Norris Hundley, *Water in the West: The Colorado River Compact and the Politics of Water* (1975). Remi Nadeau gives a balanced account of the resistance and the buyout of the Owens Valley settlers in "The Water War," *American Heritage*, 13, (1961), 30–35ff. John Walton, "Picnic at Alabama Gates: The Owens Valley Rebellion, 1904–1927," *CH*, 65 (1986), 192–207, is rich in sociological insight. For accounts hostile to Los Angeles, see "California's Little Civil War," *Literary Digest*, 83 (6 December 1924), 15, and the vitriolic Marrow Mayo's "The Rape of Owens Valley," in his uniformly hostile *Los Angeles* (1933), pp. 220–246. For an assessment of Los Angeles's expansionist policies, see Winston W. Crouch and Beatrice Dinerman, *Southern California Metropolis, a Study in Development of Government for a Metropolitan Area* (1964), pp. 56–63. Regarding the collapse of the St. Francis Dam, see Charles F. Outland, *Man Made Disaster, The Story of St. Francis Dam, Its Place in Southern California's Water System, Its Failure and Tragedy of March 12 and 13, 1928 in the Santa Clara River Valley* (1963). See also "A Moral Responsibility Accepted," *AC*, 38 (April 1928), 11; 'Seeking a Scapegoat for the Santa Clara Flood," *Literary Digest*, 97 (14 April 1928), 34; "Defective Foundations Generally Accepted as the Cause of Failure," *Engineering News-Record*, 100 (10 May 1928), 639; and D.C. Henry, "Important Lessons of Construction Taught by Failure of St. Francis Dam," *Hydraulic Engineering*, 4 (December 1928), 731–735, for contemporary evaluations of the disaster.

Based in part upon the L.E. Behymer Papers in the Huntington Library, Howard Swan's *Music in the Southwest, 1825–1950* (1952) is the standard guide to its subject. Caroline Estes Smith, secretary to the Philharmonic Association, produced *The Philharmonic Orchestra of Los Angeles, the First Decade, 1919–1929* (1930). For contemporary opinions, see E. Avery McCarthy, "Symphonic Music as a Civic Force Affecting Realty Values," *LAR*, 6 (December 1926), 19, 33, and William May Garland, "The Philharmonic Orchestra of Los Angeles," *LAR*, 7 (November 1927), 41, 77. See also Merle Armitage, "Los Angeles, the Home of Grand Opera," *SCB*, 7 (October 1928), 18–19, 45. Regarding the Hollywood Bowl, see John Orlando Northcutt, *Magic Valley, the Story of the Hollywood Bowl* (1967), which amplifies his earlier *The Hollywood Bowl Story* (1961), and Naima Prevots-Wallen, *A Vision for Music* (1984). See also Allan C. Balch, "Hollywood Bowl, Its Place in the Community," *LAR*, 7 (November 1927), 31, 63, and C.J. Williamson, "Los Angeles Dedicates New $200,000 Greek Theatre," *Western City*, 6 (November 1930), 12–14.

For the underworld, see Wendell E. Harmon, "The Bootlegger Era in Southern California," *SCQ*, 37 (1955), 335–346. See also: Walter Watrous, "Behind the Scenes in Los Angeles," in *Facts You Should Know About California*, pp. 27–41; Nathan Douthit, "August Vollmer and the Emergence of Police Professionalism," *CHSQ*, 54 (1975), 101–124, esp. 108–109; and Henstell, *Sunshine and Wealth*, pp. 45–71. See also Florence G. Rogers, "Los Angeles' Street Types," *Saturday Night*, 16 June 1923, pp. 19, 31. The meager roll-call of Los Angeles novels of the 1920s includes: Gene Stratton Porter, *Her Father's Daughter* (1921); Elizabeth Dejeans, *The Double House* (1924) and *Winning Game* (1925); Nell Martin, *Constant Simp* (1927); Octavius Roy Cohen, *The Valley of Olympus* (1929); and John B. Campbell, *Rose of Los Angeles* (1929). Aside from *Angel's Flight* (1927), Don Ryan also wrote *A Roman Holiday* (1930), set partially in Hollywood. Carey McWilliams profiled Louis Adamic in the *Saturday Night* of 22 October 1927. In 1938–1939 McWilliams conducted a column "Tides West" in *Westways*, filled with details of literary Los Angeles. His "Los Angeles" essay appeared in the combined *Overland Monthly and Out West Magazine*, ns 85 (May 1927), 135–136. See also Chester Rowell, "Our Stake in the Pacific," *SCB*, 8 (August 1929), 14–15, 42–43, 47, and *The Collected Letters of D. H. Lawrence*, edited with an Introduction by Harry T. Moore (2 vols., 1962), II, 752–753.

Chapter Eight

Regarding the nineteenth-century backgrounds of architecture in California, see Harold Kirker, *California's Architectural Frontier, Style and Tradition in the Nineteenth Century* (1960), reprinted in 1986 with an introduction by Karen Weitze. Also central is Richard Longstreth, *On the Edge of the World, Four Architects in San Francisco at the Turn of the Century* (1983). For pertinent images, see also Oscar Lewis, *Here Lived the Californians* (ca. 1957), and Edward Geoffrey Bangs, *Portals West, a Folio of Late Nineteenth-Century Architecture in California*, preface by Robert Gordon Sproul (1960). Contemporary assessments and presentations include: Samuel and Joseph Newsom, *Picturesque California Homes* (1886) and *Picturesque and Artistic Homes and Buildings of California* (ca. 1890); Frank Calvert, ed., *Homes and Gardens of the Pacific Coast* (ca. 1905); Francis Gates, ed., *Modern Homes of California* (1913); and Porter Garnett, *Stately Homes of California* (1914). See also David Gebhard et al., *A Guide to Architecture in San Francisco & Northern California* (1973).

Regarding the general background of design and architecture in late nineteenth- and early twentieth-century Southern California, see Timothy J. Andersen, Eudora M. Moore, and Robert Winter, *California Design 1910*, photographs by Morley Baer (1974). See also David Gebhard and Robert Winter, *A Guide to Architecture in Southern California* (1965). Earlier assessments include: P.R. Hunter and Walter L. Reichardt, *Residential Architecture in Southern California* (1939); Frank Harris and Weston Bonenberger, *A Guide to Contemporary Architecture in Southern California* (1951); and Douglas Honnold, *Southern California Architecture, 1769–1956* (1956). Basic to all study of the architecture of this region is the work of Esther McCoy. Of special relevance is *Five California Architects* (1960), studies of Bernard Maybeck, the Greene brothers, Irving Gill, and Rudolph Schindler. See also McCoy's "Roots of California Contemporary Architecture," *Arts and Architecture*, 73 (October 1956), 14–17ff., an earlier study for the book, and her *Modern California Houses* (1962). Two crucial interpretations of architecture in Los Angeles include Reyner Banham, *Los Angeles: The Architecture of Four Ecologies* (1971), and Thomas Hines, "Los Angeles Architecture: The Issue of Tradition in a Twentieth-Century City," in David G. De Long, Helen Searing, and Robert A.M. Stern, eds., *American Architecture: Innovation and Tradition* (1986), pp. 112–129.

For the historical background, see the ambitious USC master's thesis by John Connolly, "A Survey of Nineteenth Century Building in Los Angeles" (1962), filled with glossy, enlarged illustrations. See also David Gebhard and Robert Winter, *A Guide to Architecture in Los Angeles and Southern California* (1977), enlarged in 1985 as *Architecture in Los Angeles, A Compleat Guide*. See also Charles Moore, Peter Becker, and Regula Campbell, *The City Observed: Los Angeles* (1984), and Sam Hall Kaplan, *LA Lost and Found, an Architectural History of Los Angeles* (1987). Contemporary assessments of Southern California and Los Angeles architecture which proved useful to this study include: Harrie T. Lindeberg, "Some Observations on Domestic Architecture," *AEC*, 33 (June 1913), 46–72; Louis Christian Mullgardt, "Country House Architecture on the Pacific Coast," *The Architectural Record*, 38 (October 1915), 422–451; George D. Hall, "An Eastern Architect's Impression of Los Angeles," *AEC*, 61 (May 1920), 90–91; T. Boyd, Jr., "Jury of Artists Appraises the Architecture of Los Angeles," *The Architectural Record*, 48 (November 1920), 461–462; Frederick W. Jones, "Some Notable Architecture in Southern California," *AEC*, 72 (March 1923), 47–74; "Southern California Architecture Given Recognition," *AEC*, 78 (September 1924), 53–74; and Harris Allen, "Architecture in Los Angeles," *OM*, ns, 85 (May 1927), 138. William I. Garren, "Architecture and the Motion Picture," *AEC*, 63 (October 1920), 66–70, is an early recognition of an important relationship. See also "Cathedral Built for a Motion Picture," *AEC*, 61 (June 1920), 76–77, and "Beautiful Churchs House Hollywood's Congregations," *LAR*, 6 (November 1926), 25–29. The booster spirit of the 1920s is evident in Marc N. Goodnow, "Distinction and Dollars in New Southern California Architecture," *SCB*, 6 (November 1927), 20, 36, and Mark Lee Luther's *The Boosters* (1920). In *The American Jitters, a Year of the Slump* (1932), Edmund Wilson satirically describes the excesses of Los Angeles, architectural and otherwise.

Victoria Padilla's *Southern California Gardens, an Illustrated History* (1961) is the most comprehensive introduction to its subject. Of nearly equal importance is the UCLA master's thesis in geography by Charles Henry Rowan, "Ornamental Plants as a Factor in the Cultural Development of Southern California" (1957). See also Winifred Starr Dobyns, *California Gardens* (1931), and Leonid Enari, *Ornamental Shrubs of California* (1962). Of direct relevance to this chapter are Viola Lockhart Warren, "The Eucalyptus Crusade," *SCQ*, 44 (March 1962), 31–42, and Waldron Gillespie, "Why Palms Belong in Southern California," *The Garden Magazine*, 36 (December 1922), 187–190. For impressions of the interaction between gardens and architecture, see: "House With a Garden Room," *The Craftsman*, 27 (February 1915), 564–566; E. Urquhart, "A Garden House in California," *House Beautiful*, 50 (July 1921), 17–19; and "A Group of California Houses and Gardens," *House Beautiful*, 51 (January 1922), 37–43. For the importance of the patio in both architecture and gardening, see Bertha H. Smith, "The Heart of the House Is the Patio," *Sunset*, 39 (September 1917), 47–48, and Marion Brownfield, "Spanish Influence in the Gardens of Southern California," *The Garden Magazine*, 32 (December 1920), 185–188. See also Elizabeth Urquhart, "The Garden House in California, a Dream Garden for All to Enjoy," *House Beautiful*, 50 (July 1921), 17–19. Other significant statements include: Chapin Hall, "California, Our Lady of Flowers," *National Geographic*, 55 (June 1929), 703–750; Charles Francis Saunders, "Awakening Self-Consciousness in the California Garden," *The Garden Magazine*, 36 (December 1922), 191–194; Albert R. Gould, "Cultural Briefs for the California Garden," *The Garden Magazine*, 36 (December 1922), 185–186; Anne Galli, "What We Accomplished in Three Years in Our Garden in Southern California," *House Beautiful*, 69 (March 1931), 270–272; and Elizabeth C. White, "California Winter Garden," *The Garden Magazine*, 29 (December 1915), 141–144.

The garden culture of Northern California in this period can be glimpsed in: Mary Goodrich, *Piedmont Gardens* (1928); Lillian Burger Slater, *Rose Carnivals of Santa Rosa, 1894–1932* (1932); Florence Atherton Eyere and Bell Mhoon Magee, *Reminiscences of Peninsula Gardens From 1860 to 1890 With Reminiscences of East Bay Gardens From 1860 to 1890* (1933); Margaret Kittle Boyd, *Reminiscences of Early Marin County Gardens* (1934); the Garden Club of America, *Annual Meeting, April 23 to 26, 1935, Including Short Histories and Descriptions of Residences and Gardens in Hillsborough, Woodside, Atherton, and Piedmont* (1935); and Helen Weber Kennedy, *Vignettes of the Gardens of San Jose de Guadalupe* (1938). For impressions of the gardens of Santa Barbara, see Ervanna Bowen Bissell, *Glimpses of Santa Barbara and Montecito Gardens* (ca. 1926).

Regarding the garden culture of Los Angeles and Southern California, see: Philip Alexander Monz, *A Short History of Rancho Santa Ana Botanic Garden* (1947); William Hertrich, *The Huntington Botanical Gardens, 1905–1949, Personal Recollections* (1949); and Douglas G. Thompson, *Descanso Gardens, Its History and Camellias* (1962). Of special interest is Charles F. Saunders, "A City of Wild-flower Park," *Sunset*, 38 (May 1917), 34, dealing with Exposition Park. Regarding the California Botanic Garden subdivision in Los Angeles, see three articles by publicist Gerald Burtnett: "A Profitless Subdivision," *LAR*, 8 (December 1928), 14; "Brilliant Future of Botanic Garden Assured," *Saturday Night*, 8 (4 February 1928), 2; and "Eden in Los Angeles," *Touring Topics*, 21 (March 1929), 44. For the Hollywood perspective, see Grace Tabor, "Garden Influence in the Film Drama," *The Garden Magazine*, 32 (December 1920), 209–211. Regarding the Japanese influence, Dorothea Demeritte Dunlea's "Japanese Gardens on the California Coast," *The Garden Magazine*, 39 (July 1924), 341–343, is of special importance. See also A.W. Alley, "A Southern California House in Japanese Style," *AEC*, 21 (July 1919), 62–63, and George V. O'Dodd, "The Castle on the Hill (Yama Shiro)" *AEC*, 73 (June 1923), 87–94.

David Gebhard's "The Spanish Colonial Revival in Southern California (1895–1930)," *Journal of the Society of Architectural Historians*, 26 (May 1967), 131–147, is the best analytical and bibliographical introduction to the subject. Important sources of scholarship and imagery for the architects of the period include: Bertram Grosvenor Goodhue, *The Architecture and the Gardens of the San Diego Exposition* (1916); Austin Whittlesey, *The Minor Ecclesiastical, Domestic, and Garden Architecture of Southern Spain*, preface by Bertram Grosvenor Goodhue (1923); W. Sexton, *Spanish Influence on American Architecture and Decoration* (1926); and Rexford Newcomb, *Mediterranean Domestic Architecture in the United States* (1927). Regarding the indigenous roots of Spanish Revival, see: Arthur B. Benton, "The California Mission and Its Influence Upon Pacific Coast Architecture," *AEC*, 24 (February 1911), 35–75; Irving F. Morrow, "A Restored Spanish Adobe," *AEC*, 65 (April 1921), 47–55; Charles Ray Glass, "The Return of the Spanish Hacienda," *Arts and Decoration*, 26 (January 1927), 40–42, 77; and Donald R. Hannaford, *Spanish Colonial or Adobe Architecture of California, 1800–1850* (1931). See also Richard Garrison and George Rustay, *Mexican Houses* (1930). Regarding the Southwest Museum and its influence, see W.W. Robinson, *The Story of the Southwest Museum* (1960), and Richard F. Bach, "The Southwest Museum," *Architectural Record*, 42 (July 1917), 18–26. For impressions of San Clemente, see Tod Bates, "City of Spain Reproduced in Southern California," *Saturday Night*, (30 June 1928), 2, and E. Avery McCarthy, "San Clemente's Third Anniversary," *Saturday Night* (29 December 1928), 15. See also Eloise Roorbach, "Some Modern California Architecture: From the Wealth of Its Spanish and Indian Legacies Architecture on the Coast Is Evolving Significant Types," *House and Garden*, 40 (November 1921), 21–25. For the look of the region after the Spanish Revival, see Paul Robinson Hunter and Walter Reichardt, *Residential Architecture in Southern California* (1939). Regarding the bungalow tradition, see Robert Winter, *The California Bungalow*, foreword by David Gebhard (1980). See also "True Craftsman," *California*, 13 (March 1988), 108–115. For the rise of apartment-house culture, see Frederick W. Jennings, "Los Angeles the Home of Many High Class Apartment Houses," *AEC*, 34 (September 1913), 65–75. *Courtyard Housing in Los Angeles, a Typological Analysis*, by Stefanos Polyzoides, Roger Sherwood, and James Tice, with photography by Julius Shulman (1982), is a model of architectural scholarship. Far less scholarly yet of importance to understanding the bungalow-court phenomenon is Sheilah Graham's *The Garden of Allah* (1970).

For studies of individual architects discussed in this chapter, the following sources have proven useful. Regarding George Herbert Wyman: Esther McCoy, "A Vast Hall Full of Light, the Bradbury Building," *Arts & Architecture*, 70 (April 1953), 20–21ff. Regarding Bertram Grosvenor Goodhue: "El Fureidas, Montecito," *Sunset*, 32 (May 1914), 1060–1063. Regarding Greene & Greene: Rendell L. Makinson, *Greene & Greene, Architecture as Fine Art*, photographs by Marvin Rand, introduction by Reyner Banham (1977), and *Greene & Greene, Furniture and Related Designs* (1979); and Jean Murray Bangs, "Greene & Greene," *Architectural Forum*, 89 (October 1948), 80–89. Regarding Elmer Grey: Elmer Grey, "What a Home in California Should Mean," *AEC*, 47 (December 1916), 38–61; A. Marple, "Home Which Embraces Studio and Domestic

Features," *The Craftsman*, 28 (September 1915), 608–609; "Adaptation of Old Cloisters, the Home of Mrs. M.C. Russell at Hollywood," *House Beautiful*, 38 (September 1915), 124–126; and Helen Lukens Gant, "Individuality in Western Architecture," *American Homes and Gardens*, 12 (June 1915), 196–200. Regarding Myron Hunt: *Myron Hunt, 1868–1952, the Search for a Regional Architecture, 3 October - 9 December 1984, Baxter Art Gallery, California Institute of Technology*, with essays by Jay Belloli, Jean Block, Alson Clark, Jan Furey Muntz, Robert Winter, Robert Judson Clark, Stefanos Polyzoides, and Peter de Bretteville (1984), and David C. Allison, "The Work of Mr. Myron Hunt, FAIA," *AEC*, 53 (April 1918), 38–68. See also Hunt's own brochure *Palos Verdes—Where Bad Architecture Is Eliminated* (1927), reprinted from *Pacific Coast Architect* for April 1927. Regarding Wallace Neff: Wallace Neff, Jr., editor and compiler, *Wallace Neff, Architect of California's Golden Age*, text by Alson Clark, foreword by David Gebhard (1986). Regarding Allison & Allison: "History and Organization of Allison & Allison Architects," typewritten ms. (1940) in the possession of Dr. Richard Allison of Los Angeles, and William Andrew Spalding, *History and Reminiscences, Los Angeles City and County* (2 vols., 1931), II, 174–177. Regarding Walker & Eisen: Donald J. Schippers, "Walker & Eisen: Twenty Years of Los Angeles Architecture, 1920–1940," *SCQ*, 46 (December 1964), 371–391. Regarding Irving Gill: Irving Gill, "Home of the Future: The New Architecture of the West," *The Craftsman*, 30 (May 1916), 140–151; Esther McCoy, "Irving Gill," *Five California Architects*, pp. 59–101; Bertha H. Smith, "California's First Cubist House," *Sunset*, 35 (August 1915), 368–370, 372, 374, 376; "Concrete Cottages in California," *AEC*, 31 (January 1913), 67–72; "Garden Apartment-Houses of the West," *AEC*, 57 (June 1919), 72–78; George D. Hall, "The Estate of Mr. W.L. Dodge, Hollywood," *AEC*, 61 (April 1920), 87–90; Eloise Roorbach, "California House of Distinguished Simplicity," *House Beautiful*, 49 (February 1921), 94–95; and "More Is Less," *Arts & Architecture*, 80 (October 1963), 10, 35. Regarding Frank Lloyd and Lloyd Wright: Brendan Gill, *Many Masks, a Life of Frank Lloyd Wright* (1987), esp. pp. 265–284, and Esther McCoy, "Lloyd Wright," *Arts & Architecture*, 83 (October 1966), 22–26. Regarding Simon Rodia: "Sam of Watts," *Arts & Architecture*, 68 (July 1951), 23–25; Jules Langsner, "Fantasy in Steel, Concrete and Broken Bottles," *Arts & Architecture*, 76 (September 1959), 27–28; Los Angeles County Museum, *Simon Rodia's Towers in Watts*, photography by Seymour Rosen, text by Paul La Porte (1962); Robert S. Bryan, "Sam Rodia and the Children of Watts," *Westways*, 59 (August 1967), 3–6; Jon Madian, *Beautiful Junk, a Story of the Watts Tower* (1968); Jack Smith, "A Day in the City, Miracle on 107th Street," *Westways*, 62 (August 1970), 6–8; and Andrew F. Rolle, *The Immigrant Upraised* (1968), pp. 285–287.

Chapter Nine

Santa Barbara has inspired a significant number of local histories, each useful as a source of social patterns and telling anecdotes. Pertinent to this study are: Jesse D. Mason, *History of Santa Barbara and Ventura Counties of California* (1883), reprinted in 1961 with an introduction by Walker A. Tompkins; Yda Addis Storke, *A Memorial and Biographical History of the Counties of Santa Barbara, San Luis Obispo and Ventura, California* (1891); Charles Montville Gidney, *History of Santa Barbara, San Luis Obispo and Ventura Counties, California* (2 vols., 1917); Michael James Phillips, *History of Santa Barbara County* (2 vols., 1927); and Owen Hugh O'Neill, James Clement Reid, and Marion Parks, *History of Santa Barbara County, State of California* (1939). See also David B. Rogers, *Prehistoric Man of the Santa Barbara Coast* (1929). Descriptive guidebooks are an equally fruitful source of information and developing interpretations. As usual, one begins with the WPA series, in this case, *Santa Barbara, a Guide to the Channel City and Its Environs*, compiled and written by the Southern California Writers' Project of the Work Projects Administration (1941). Also for relevance, decade by decade, are: Abraham Willard Jackson, *Barbariana, or, Scenery, Climate, Soils and Social Conditions of Santa Barbara City and County* (1888); E. McD. Johnstone, *By Semi-Tropic Seas, Santa Barbara and Surroundings* (ca. 1888); Frank Sands, *Santa Barbara at a Glance* (1895); M.B. Levick, Santa Barbara County, California (ca. 1911); Frank M. Selover, *Santa Barbara County* (1915); and Leila Weekes Wilson, *Santa Barbara, California* (1919). The Santa Barbara Chamber of Commerce issued *Resources of Santa Barbara County* (1901), *The City and County of Santa Barbara* (1902), and *The City and Valley of Santa Barbara* (1904), each a valuable source of detail and establishment self-evaluation.

As the author of 46 books of local history, newsman and broadcaster Walker A. Tompkins is the undisputed Nestor of the Santa Barbara region. Of special importance to this and the following chapters are Tompkins's *Santa Barbara Yesterdays* (1962), *Historical High Lights of Santa Barbara*, with Russell A. Ruiz (1970), and *Santa Barbara Past and Present, an Illustrated History* (1975). Also of value are Laurance Landreth Hilla and Marion Parks, *Santa Barbara, Tierra Adorada, a Community History* (1930), and Edward Seldon Spaulding, *Adobe Days Along the Channel* (1957). On Sunday, 25 April 1954, the *Santa Barbara News Press* issued its information-laden Centennial Edition. In 1988 Jarrell C. Jackman, executive director of the Santa Barbara Trust for Historic Preservation, issued *Santa Barbara, Historical Themes & Images*. David F. Myrick has embarked upon a multivolumed history of the region. *Montecito and Santa Barbara, Volume I* appeared in 1987.

Franciscan scholar Maynard J. Geiger, archivist of Mission Santa Barbara, has produced the invaluable A *Pictorial History of the Physical Development of Mission Santa Barbara, 1786–1963* (1963), and *Mission Santa Barbara, 1782–1965* (1965). For earlier descriptions by Franciscans, see J.J. O'Keefe, *The Buildings and Churches of the Mission of Santa Barbara* (1886), and Zephyrin Engelhardt, *Santa Barbara Mission* (1923). See also James A. Colligan, *Some Facts About Santa Barbara Mission* (1923), and Kurt Baer, *Painting and Sculpture at Santa Barbara Mission* (1955). Regarding the life and times of Garcia Diego y Moreno, the First Bishop of California, and other Franciscans of the period, see Engelhardt's *Franciscans in California* (1897); Geiger's *Franciscan Missionaries in Hispanic California, 1769–1848* (1969); and Francis J. Weber, A *Biographical Sketch of Right Reverend Francisco Garcia Diego y Moreno, First Bishop of the Californias, 1785–1846* (1961). The *History of California* produced by Henry Lebbus Oak for the History Company of Hubert Howe Bancroft (7 vols., 1886) contains much information of relevance to Santa Barbara. For romantic yet relevant sources of background, see also Nellie Van de Grift Sanchez, *Spanish Arcadia* (1922), and Myrtle Garrison, *Romance and History of California Ranchos* (1935).

Regarding the De la Guerra era, see Joseph Thompson and Maynard Geiger, "Casa De la Guerra, Santa Barbara," *Noticias* (The Journals of the Santa Barbara Historical Society), 18 (1972), 1–7. The most scholarly edition of Richard Henry Dana, Jr.'s *Two Years Before the Mast* (1840) was issued in 1964 by the Ward Ritchie Press of Los Angeles, edited by John Haskell Kemble. For a revisionist view of Dana's California experience, see Tony Stanley Cook, "Historical Mythmaking: Richard Henry Dana and American Emigration to California, 1840–1850," *SCQ*, 70, 97–113. Alfred Robinson's *Life in California* (1846) was edited by Joseph Sullivan in 1947 and Andrew Rolle in 1970. Maynard Geiger edited *The Letters of Alfred Robinson to the De la Guerra Family of Santa Barbara, 1824–1873* for the Zamorano Club of Los Angeles (1972). For a biography of Robinson, see "Alfred Robinson, New England Merchant in Mexican

California," *CHSQ*, 23 (1944), 193–218. Regarding the Spanish street names of Santa Barbara, see Rosario Andrea Curletti, *Pathways to Pavements* (1950). The experience of Hispanic Californians in the American era is analyzed by Albert Camarillo in *Chicanos in a Changing Society: From Mexican Pueblos to American Barrios in Santa Barbara and Southern California, 1848–1930* (1979). For the American side of the story, see Walter C. McKain, Jr., and Sara Miles, "Santa Barbara County Between Two Social Orders," *CHSQ*, 25 (1946), 311–318. Regarding Colonel Hollister, see Yda Addis Storke, A *Memorial Biographical History*, pp. 649–653. For further details of the period, see Walter A. Tompkins, A *Centennial History of Stearns Wharf* (1972). Also of interest is the Santa Barbara County ranching novel *The Black Curtain* by Flora Haines Loughead, mother of the Lockheed brothers (1898).

Charles Nordhoff's important discussion of Santa Barbara as a health resort was found in *California for Health, Pleasure, and Residence, a Book for Travellers and Settlers* (1872), pp. 110–113. For further enhancements of the resort metaphor, see *All About Santa Barbara, California, the Sanitarium of the Pacific Coast* (1878) and Newton H. Chittenden's *The Watering Places, Health and Pleasure Resorts of the Pacific Coast* (1881) and his *Health Seekers', Tourists', and Sportsman's Guides to the Sea-side, Lakeside, Foothill, Mountain and Mineral Spring Health and Pleasure Resorts of the Pacific Coast* (1884). See also: *Santa Barbara, the Ideal Summer Resort* (1895); *Santa Barbara, a Midsummer Paradise, the Newport of the Pacific*, issued by the Chamber of Commerce in the early 1900s; and Prentice Marsh Brown, *Taking Life Easy* (1911), reprinted from the May 1911 issue of *Sunset* magazine. For a novel set in the health-resort era of the 1880s, see Margaret Cameron's *Johnover* (1923).

The genteel tradition in Santa Barbara can be traced through its poetry. In this regard, see: Camilla K. von K. [Mary Camilla (Foster) Hall-Wood], *Sea Leaves* (1887); Henry Lathrop Turner, *In the Lovely Land of Sunset, a Souvenir of Santa Barbara* (1887); Marshall Ilsley, *By the Western Sea* (1898); and Edwin Arthur Hunt, *Santa Barbara Days and Other Poems* (1920). Helen Hunt Jackson described Santa Barbara in *Glimpses of Three Coasts* (1886). See also Katheryn E. Marriott, "Helen Hunt Jackson in Santa Barbara," *Noticias*, 28 (1982), 85–89. For another important visit, see Edward Roberts's *Santa Barbara and Around There*, illustrations by H.C. Ford (1886), and "A Santa Barbara Holiday," *Harper's New Monthly Magazine*, 75 (November 1887), 813–835. Other significant responses are in: Kate Douglas Wiggin, A *Summer in a Canyon* (1892); L. Studdiford McChesney, *Under Shadow of the Mission, a Memory of Santa Barbara* (1897); and Ernest Peixotto, *Romantic California* (1910). Regarding Stewart Edward White's Santa Barbara, see the article by Stella Haverland Rouse in *Noticias*, 19 (1983), 21–37, and Edna Rosemary Butte's 1960 USC Ph.D. thesis, "Stewart Edward White, His Life and Literary Career." For further details of outdoor life, see Charles Frederick Holder's *The Channel Islands of California* (1910).

Chapter Ten

Written in great part by Walter A. Tompkins, Thomas More Storke's *California Editor*, foreword by Earl Warren (1958), has value as a general history as well. Regarding early aviation in Santa Barbara, for example, see "Our Aviation Pioneers," pp. 228–235. For Santa Barbara's brief fling with the movies, see Mr. and Mrs. Roy Overbaugh, "In the Days of the Flying A," *Noticias*, 22 (1976), 1–18. William Leon Dawson's *The Birds of California* (4 vols., 1923) should be consulted in the Deluxe Santa Barbara Edition. For Dawson's background, see: June W. Hopkins, "The First Twenty Five Years of the Santa Barbara Museum of Natural History," *Noticias*, 11 (1965), 1–24. Regarding the artists of Santa Barbara, see Hector Alliot, *Art in California* (1916) and, Edan Hughes,

Artists in California, 1786–1940 (1986). See also *A Portfolio of Reproductions of Oil Paintings and Etchings by Famous Artists of Santa Barbara* (1967). For specific studies, see: John A. Berger, *Fernand Lundgren* (1930); Arthur Woodward, *A Biographical Sketch of Alexander Harmer* (ca. 1962); Harold G. Davidson, *Edward Borein, Cowboy Artist* (1974), pp. 101–135; and Helen Laird, *Carl Oscar Borg and the Mystic Region* (1986), pp. 87–95. See also Frank Morley Fletcher, *Woodblock Printing* (1916).

Charles Fletcher Lummis's *Stand Fast, Santa Barbara!* first appeared in 1923 in the *Morning Press* and was reprinted in pamphlet form by the Plans and Planting Committee of the Community Arts Association in 1927. *The Mark of Zorro* by Johnston McCulley appeared in 1920. Regarding the Zorro legend, see Abraham Hoffman, "Zorro: Generic Swashbuckler," *The Californians*, 3 (1985), 23–25, and Edward Connor, "The Genealogy of Zorro," *Films in Review*, 8 (August/September 1957), 330–333. The increasingly preservationist mindset of Santa Barbara can be traced through: Sarah Higgins, *La Casa de Aguirre of Santa Barbara, 1841–1884* (1896); Walter Augustus Hawley, *The Early Days of Santa Barbara* (1910); John Reginald Southworth, *Santa Barbara and Montecito, Past and Present* (1920) and *Los Adobes Antiquos de Santa Barbara* (ca. 1921); John Steven McGroarty, *Santa Barbara, California*, photographs by Samuel Adelstein (1925); and Katherine M. (Den) Bell, *Swinging the Censer, Reminiscences of Old Santa Barbara* (1931). Regarding growth in the area, see: Farnsworth Crowder, "Ojai, Little Santa Barbara," *Westways*, 29 (July 1937), 10–14; Marjorie Hayes, "History of Hope Ranch," *Noticias*, 18 (1972), 10–16; and Stella Haverland Rouse, "Development of the Riviera," *Noticias*, 30 (1984), 68–74.

The theatrical origins of the Community Arts Association can be traced through: Litti Paulding, "Primavera, the Masque of Santa Barbara," *Noticias*, 6 (1960), 17–21; Irving Wills, "Some Vagrant Musings on Community Theatre in Santa Barbara," *Noticias*, 11 (1965), 18–27; and Patricia Gardner Cleek, "Private Outdoor Theatres in Montecito," *Noticias*, 19 (1983), 71–78. Regarding the Lobero Theater, see: Hewett Reynolds, "Jose Lobero," *Noticias*, 11 (1965), 6–8; Ernestine Koefod, "The Story of the Lobero Theatre," *Noticias*, 11 (1965), 8–16; and Florentino Bonilla as told to Michael J. Phillips, "I Knew Jose Lobero," *Noticias*, 20 (1974), 1–15. Regarding the opening of the new Lobero Theatre, see Reginald Faletti, "Beggar on Horseback," *Noticias*, 11 (1965), 1–5, and Patrick Mahony, "Sir Arthur Bliss in Santa Barbara," *Noticias*, 17 (1971), 2–6. See also Sir Arthur Bliss's *As I Remember* (1970). Regarding the Old Spanish Days celebration launched at the Lobero Theatre August 1924 opening, see Paul G. Sweetser, ed., "History of Santa Barbara's Fiesta, 'Old Spanish Days in Santa Barbara,'" *Noticias*, 12 (1966), 1–26, and the especially detailed *Official Program* for 27–29 August 1931 in the Bancroft Library. See also Dorothy G. Spicer, *The Book of Festivals* (1937), and Stella Haverland Rouse, *Santa Barbara's Spanish Renaissance and Old Spanish Days Fiesta* (1974).

For the gardens of Santa Barbara and vicinity, see Ervanna Bowen Bissel, *Glimpses of Santa Barbara and Montecito Gardens* (1926), and the Garden Club of America, "Arcady," *Montecito, Santa Barbara, California* (1926). The single most authoritative work on the architecture of the area is Herb Andree and Noel Young, *Santa Barbara Architecture, From Spanish Colonial to Modern*, photography by Wayne McCall, introduction by David Gebhard (second edition, 1980). For an earlier assessment, see Henry Philip Staats, *Californian Architecture in Santa Barbara* (1929). See also Mary Louise Days, *A Visit to Santa Barbara's Historical Architectural Highlights* (1984). Regarding individual architects, see: Herbert W. Andree, "The Santa Barbara of P.J. Barber," *Noticias*, 21 (1975), issues Number 2 and Number 3 throughout; Patricia Gardner Cleek, "Francis W. Wilson, Architect," *Noticias*, 31 (1985), 40–53; and Scott L. Boyd, "George Washington Smith," *Noticias*, 11 (1965), 16–18. See also David Gebhard, *George*

Washington Smith: The Spanish Colonial Revival in California (1964). Regarding specific important buildings, see: Una Nixson Hopkins, "El Fureidis, the Little Paradise," *The Craftsman*, 29 (October 1915), 33–39; the Santa Barbara County Board of Supervisors, *The Santa Barbara County Court House* (1929); Elane Griscom, "Casa del Sueño, a Visit With Dorothy and Burl Ives," *Montecito*, 5 (1985), 10–17; and Norman Neuerburg, *Eighteenth Century Santa Barbara Presidio Chapel* (1985). Charles Mulford Robinson's *Report to the Honorable Mayor and City Council of Santa Barbara* appeared on 27 February 1909. See also Eric P. Hvolboll, "The Santa Barbara County Planning Commission," *Noticias*, 31 (1985), 21–39. Regarding the reconstruction program of the Plans and Planting Committee, see its *New Santa Barbara* (1926), especially Pearl Chase's "Better Small Homes in Santa Barbara," pp. 48–56. See also Vern D. Hedden, *Santa Barbara Builders Handbook*, issued by the Architectural Advisory Committee (1926). Regarding Bernhard Hoffmann, see Pearl Chase's essay in *Noticias*, 5 (1959), 15–23. For the effects of the earthquake of 29 June 1925, see Bailey Willis, *The Santa Barbara Earthquake* (1925), and Arthur Carl Alvarez, *The Santa Barbara Earthquake, Effects on Buildings of Various Sizes* (1925). Regarding the rebuilding of the city, see Allied Architects Association of Los Angeles, *Bulletin, Santa Barbara Earthquake Number, Second Edition* (1925), and Irving Foster Morrow, *New Santa Barbara*, reprinted from *The Architect and Engineer* for July 1926 by the Plans and Planting Committee (1926). Regarding the very influential Pearl Chase, see Vivian Obern's article in *La Campaña*, the magazine of the Santa Barbara Trust of Historic Preservation, for Fall 1988.

Charles A. Storke expressed his pride of ancestry in *The English Storkes in America* (1935). The Old Man also wrote the preface to Bell's *Swinging the Censer*. Regarding Thomas More Storke, see Walker A. Tompkins's "Santa Barbara Journalists, 1855–1973," *Noticias*, 19 (1973), 1–19, esp. 8–17. For an example of Storke's Depression-era influence, see Wallace C. Penfield, "The Santa Barbara County Bowl," *Noticias*, 19 (1973), 1–9. Regarding the Fernald family, see Charles Fernald, *A County Judge in Arcady*, introduction and notes by Cameron Rogers (1954). The equestrian aspects of the Santa Barbara style are detailed in: E.M. Heath, *A Guide to the Rides and Drives in Santa Barbara and Its Vicinity* (ca. 1894); Dwight Murphy, "The Palomino Horse," *Noticias*, 8 (1962), 23–27; Leo Carrillo, *The California I Love* (1961), esp. p. 240–246; and William K. Baxter, "Ride Rancheros!," *Noticias*, 9 (1963), 1–9. Further suggestions of the good life are evident in: John Reginald Southworth, *Santa Barbara and Montecito, Past and Present* (1920); Patrick Mahony, "Ernest Lawrence Thayer at the Bat," *Noticias*, 24 (1978), 71–75; Frances Cooper Droll, *Memories of Rancho Santa Rosa and Santa Barbara* (1964); Hugo Ballin, *Dolce Far Niente* (1933); and Charles Stephen Brooks, *A Western Wind*, with pen and ink pictures by Mary Seymour Brooks (1935). For Edmund Wilson's Santa Barbara, see *The Twenties*, edited by Leon Edel (1975), pp. 153–184, 459–490.

Chapter Eleven

The Zeitlin & Ver Brugge Archives are at UCLA. Of special pertinence to this chapter are two anthologies: J.M. Edelstein, ed., *A Garland for Jake Zeitlin* (1967), containing sixteen essays, and the Autumn 1982 issue of *The Book Collector*, with biographical studies by Ward Ritchie, Lawrence Clark Powell, John Dreyfus, and Douglas Cleverdon. See also Ward Ritchie, *Jake Zeitlin* (1978); Bernard Rosenthal, *Remarks on the Occasion of the Celebration of Jake Zeitlin's 80th Birthday* (1984); the obituary in the *Los Angeles Times*, 31 August 1987; and Ward Ritchie, "Los Angeles' Man About Fine Letters," *Los Angeles Times*, 6 September 1987. Throughout 1985 and 1986 Mr. Zeitlin kindly responded to many of my inquiries in person and by telephone. He also lent me his personal files and correspondence relating to *Opinion*. Regarding the atmosphere of Mr. Zeitlin's early establishments, see Lawrence Clark Powell, *Recollections of an Ex-Bookseller* (1950).

Jake Zeitlin was himself a forceful writer. See especially his "Small Renaissance: Southern California Style," *The Papers of the Bibliographical Society of America*, 50 (1956), 17–27, reprinted as a pamphlet in 1972, which provides an overall glimpse into the 1920s and 1930s. Of relevance as well to this chapter are Zeitlin's pamphlet *What Kind of Business Is This? Reminiscences of the Book Trade and Book Collectors* (1959); "The Bookseller and the Librarian," *California Librarian*, 23 (April 1962), 91–94; "Some Rambling Recollections of a Rambling Bookseller," a pamphlet (1970); "Herbert M. Evans, Pioneer Collector of Books in the History of Science," *Isis*, 62 (1971), 507–509; and "The Cultural Flowering of Los Angeles in the 30s and 40s," typescript of a talk given at California State University at Long Beach, 2 April 1979, Zeitlin Archives. Joel Gardner interviewed Zeitlin at various times throughout 1977–78 for the UCLA Oral History Program. The resulting "Books and the Imagination: Fifty Years of Rare Books" with an introduction by Ward Ritchie (2 vols., typescript, 1980) is a major source of information for literary life in greater Los Angeles in the prewar period. Carey McWilliams previewed Zeitlin as a poet in *Saturday Night*, 19 November 1927; and later that year Zeitlin's *For Whispers and Chants*, foreword by Carl Sandburg, appeared from the Lantern Press of San Francisco. Regarding Dawson's Book Shop, see: Fern Dawson Shochat, *The Fiftieth Anniversary of Dawson's Book Shop, 1905–1955* (1955); Russell Arthur Roberts, "Dawson's Book Shop: Publishers of Western Americana and Patron of the Book Arts," *California Librarian*, 25 (April 1964), 97–101; and Mary Patricia Dixon, *Ernest Dawson* (1967). See also *Publications of Dawson's Book Shop, 1905–1972* (1972); Ernest Dawson's *Los Angeles Booksellers of 1897* (1947); and Warren S. Rogers, *My Own Los Angeles, 1894–1982* (1982). Regarding Vroman's, see Lawrence Clark Powell, *Vroman's of Pasadena* (1953).

Carey McWilliams wrote his "Tides West" column for *Westways* from January 1937 to August 1939. Joel Gardner interviewed McWilliams in 1978 for the Oral History Program at UCLA. The resulting "Honorable in All Things" (typescript, 1982) supplements McWilliams's sometimes sketchy *The Education of Carey McWilliams* (1978). See also McWilliams's *The New Regionalism in American Literature* (1930). Also of relevance to this chapter are: Aubrey Burns, "Regional Culture in California," *Southwest Review*, 17 (July 1932), 373–394; Winifred H. Higgins, "Art Collecting in the Los Angeles Area, 1910–1960," a UCLA doctoral dissertation in art history (1963); and Edwin Wolf and John F. Fleming, *Rosenbach* (1950). Paul Jordan-Smith's autobiography is *The Road I Came* (1960). See also his *The Soul of Woman, an Interpretation of the Philosophy of Feminism* (1916), *For the Love of Books, the Adventures of an Impecunious Collector* (1934), and *A Key to the Ulysses of James Joyce* (1934). In 1927 Jordan-Smith coedited with Floyd Dell Robert Burton's *The Anatomy of Melancholy*. See also Jordan-Smith's *Bibliographia Burtoniana, a Study of Robert Burton's The Anatomy of Melancholy* (1931).

Merle Armitage's autobiography is *Accent on Life*, with a foreword by John Carles Thomas (1964). Its bibliography updates Robert Marks's *Merle Armitage Bibliography* (1956), which lists the many books and magazines designed and/or written by Armitage through the mid-1950s. Of immediate relevance to his chapter are Armitage's *The Aristocracy of Art* (1929); his series of art books from the 1930s; and the food and wine books *Fit for a King* (1939) and *Post Caviar* (1939). See also Ward Ritchie's *Armitage, His Loves and His Many Lives* (1982) and *A Tale of Two Books* (1985). Regarding Phil Townsend Hanna, see "Phil Townsend Hanna, 1896–1957," *Westways*, 49 (July 1957), 32, and *Farewells to Phil Townsend Hanna by Members of the Sunset Club, the Wine and Food Society, and the Zamorano Club of Los Angeles* (1957). Regarding Hanna as a food and wine writer, see the files of *Bohemian Life* for the period and Hanna's *Let's Dine Out in Southern California* (1940). Also consulted: *The Menu, Annual Members' Dinner of the Wine & Food Society of Los Angeles at the Bel-Air Country Club, 15 December 1937* and Wine and Food Society of Los Angeles, *Fifty Distinguished California Wines*, foreword by Maynard McFie (1941). Of overall importance to this chapter is Richard Burton, "Culture in California," *Bookman*, 51 (May 1925), 297–301.

Chapter Twelve

There are two important anthologies dealing with Los Angeles as a book center. The first, *A Bookman's View of Los Angeles* (1961), was published by the Zamorano Club of Los Angeles for the Grolier Club of New York. The second, *A Bibliophile's Los Angeles* (1985), was prepared for the Fourteenth Congress of the International Association of Bibliophiles, held in Los Angeles from 30 September to 11 October 1985. The essays in these two collections will be cited separately. See also: Ward Ritchie, *Bookmen and Their Brothels: Recollections of Los Angeles in the 1930s*; Kenneth Klein, "The Book Community of Los Angeles, 1920–1940," *QNBCC*, 49 (1984), 59–76; Tyrus G. Harmsen, *Forty Years of Book Collecting* (1985) and "Early Book Collectors of Southern California," *A Bibliophile's Los Angeles*, pp. 29–42; and the chapter on Los Angeles booksellers in Madeline B. Stern's *Antiquarian Bookselling in the United States* (1985). The library background of California has been explored by J.N. Bowman in "Libraries in Provincial California," *SCQ*, 43 (December 1961), 426–439, and by Maynard J. Geiger, OFM, in "The Story of California's First Libraries," *SCQ*, 46 (June 1964), 109–124. Also of interest are Dora Smith, "History of the University of California Library to 1900," a UC Berkeley MA thesis (1930), and *One Hundred Years of the Mechanics' Institute of San Francisco, 1855 - 1955* (1955). Regarding the Sutro Library, see Helen M. Bruner, "Possibilities for Research in the Sutro Collection," *Library Journal*, 60 (15 October 1935), 787–789, and Richard Dillon, "Sutro Library, San Francisco's Hidden Huntington," *Library Journal*, 82 (15 April 1957), 1024–1026. Regarding the great libraries of Southern California, see John Bidwell, "Four Founders of Rare Book Libraries," *A Bibliophile's Los Angeles*, pp. 135–156. See also: Carl Schaefer Dentzel, "The Southwest Museum Library," *Bookman's Los Angeles*, pp. 33–38; Donald W. Davies, "The Honnold Library," *ibid.*, pp. 23–27; Richard D. Johnson, *Special Collections at the Claremont Colleges and Affiliated Institutions*; John H. Kemble, *Western Americana in the Libraries of the Claremont Colleges* (1977); and Roger H. Woelfel, *The Story of the Los Angeles County Public Library* (1987).

John E. Pomfret's *The Henry E. Huntington Library and Art Gallery From Its Beginnings to 1969* (1969) commands the subject. See also: Ray A. Billington, "The Genesis of the Research Institution," *HLQ*, 32 (1968–69), 351–372; Robert O. Schad, "Henry E. Huntington, the Founder and the Library," *HLQ*, 1 (May 1931), 3–32, and "Henry E. Huntington Library and Art Gallery," *Bookman's Los Angeles*, pp. 27–33; and the special issue of the *HLQ*, 32 (1969), 291–373, relating to the library. Regarding Max Farrand, see Harold D. Carew, "Don of the Archives," *Touring Topics*, 21 (December 1929), 28–30. Regarding George Watson Cole, see Carew's "Toiler in the Vineyard of Books," *Touring Topics*, 21 (February 1929), 32–34ff. Regarding the William Andrews Clark Memorial Library, see *Report of the First Decade, 1934–1944* (1946); Lawrence Clark Powell, "From Private Collection to Public Institution," *The Library Quarterly*, 20 (April 1950), 101–108, and Powell's essay in *A Bookman's Los Angeles*, pp. 19–23; and Edna C. Davis and Betty Rosenberg, "UCLA's Laboratory for Humanists," *Library Journal*, 84 (1 January 1959), 46–49. Clark's librarian Robert Ernest Cowan produced a series of elegant bibliographies describing the collections of the Clark Library which were published by John Henry Nash between 1920 and 1931.

Ward Ritchie's *The Dohenys of Los Angeles*, with a bibliography by Francis J. Weber (1974), is a complete introduction to its subject. See also: Robert O. Schad, "The Estelle Doheny Collection," in *Addresses at a Meeting of the Zamorano Club, May 6, 1950* (1950); Carey Bliss, "The Estelle Doheny Collection in the Edward Laurence Doheny Memorial Library," *QNBCC*, 22 (Spring 1957), 35–43; and two articles by close associates of Mrs. Doheny, Lucille V. Miller, "Edward and Estelle Doheny," *The Ventura County Historical Society Quarterly*, 6 (1960), 3–20, and Ellen Shaffer, "Reminiscences of a California Collector," *The Book Collector*, 14 (1965), 49–59. The relationship between Estelle Doheny and Alice Millard is set forth by Robert Rosenthal in "Los Angeles & Chicago: Two Cities, Two Bibliophiles," *A Bibliophile's Los Angeles*, pp. 3–28, from which I have liberally drawn. See also Alexander Inglis, *Among Quiet Friends* (1926) and *The Alice and George Millard Collection Illustrating the Evolution of the Book* (1939). The interests of Mrs. Doheny as a collector can be seen in the catalogues designed and printed for her by Ward Ritchie: *A Selection of Books and Manuscripts From the Private Library of Mrs. Edward Laurence Doheny* (1932), *The Book as a Work of Art* (1935), and *Catalogue of Books and Manuscripts in the Estelle Doheny Collection* (3 vols., 1940–1946). See also Richard H. Rouse, "Medieval Manuscripts & Early Printed books in Los Angeles," *A Bibliophile's Los Angeles*, pp. 43–80, and the auction catalogue *The Estelle Doheny Collection From the Edward Laurence Doheny Memorial Library, St. John's Seminary, Camarillo, California* issued by Christie's of London in 1986. Regarding the library building itself, see *Wallace Neff, Architect of California's Golden Age*, pp. 170–173.

Regarding the Zamorano Club, see George Fullerton, Carey Bliss, Tyrus Harmsen, and Edwin Carpenter, *The Zamorano Club, the First Half Century* (1978). See also Harmsen's "The Zamorano Club, 1927–1961" in *A Bookman's Los Angeles*, pp. 91–100, and Charles Heiskell, "Book Collectors' Clubs of Southern California," *ibid.*, pp. 81–91. Regarding the Grolier Club, see John T. Winterich, *The Grolier Club, an Informal History* (1950). Irving Way's *Migratory Books, Their Haunts and Habits* was printed by John Henry Nash for Dawson's Book Shop in 1924. See also William Webb Clary, *Fifty Years of Book Collecting* (1962), and the chapters on Cowan and Wagner in Powell's *Bibliographers of the Golden State*. *Hoja Volante* is the publication of the Zamorano Club. See *Zamorano's Choice, Selections From the Zamorano Club's Hoja Volante 1934–1966*, compiled with a foreword by W.W. Robinson (1966). Since its founding, the Zamorano Club has published many significant books, the most influential being *The Zamorano 80, a Selection of Distinguished California Books* (1945). Regarding Jake Zeitlin and Zamorano, see Zeitlin's oral history "Books and Imagination," pp. 255–262. The best source on the Hollywood book scene is the UCLA Oral History Program interviews of Louis Epstein conducted by Joel Gardner between May and August 1974 and issued as "The Way It Was: Fifty Years in the Southern California Book Trade" (2 vols., 1977). Regarding Stanley Rose, see also *The Education of Carey McWilliams*, pp. 48–49. For the atmosphere at Musso & Frank's, see Meta Carpenter Wilde and Orin Borsten, *A Loving Gentleman, the Love Story of William Faulkner and Meta Carpenter* (1976), pp. 56, 60–61.

For the background of the arrival of fine printing in Southern California, see Theodore Gould's "The History of Printing and Publishing in California, 1833–1900," *California Librarian*, 27 (April 1966), 97–106, and Edwin Carpenter, *Printers and Publishers in Southern California, 1850–1876, a Directory* (1964). *Fine Printing in California* (1960) by James D. Hart is the best overall assessment. Regarding the Southland, see:

Ward Ritchie's "Fine Printing in Southern California," in *A Bookman's View of Los Angeles*, pp. 39–87; "Tradition and the Printers of Southern California," in *Modern Fine Printing* (1968); and "A Rush of Memories of Printers Past," in *A Bibliophile's Los Angeles*, pp. 91–101. See also the Occidental M.A. thesis by Jane Frampton, "Fine Printing in Southern California" (1940). Theodore Grivas, "The Arthur H. Clark Company, Publisher of the West," *Arizona and the West*, 5 (Spring 1963), 63–78, tells an important story. See also Russell A. Roberts, "The Arthur H. Clark Company and Its Contributions," *California Librarian*, 22 (January 1961), 35–38. The Clark Company issued its *The United States, a Catalogue of Books* in 1928. For a contemporary response, see "The First Book Publisher Comes to Southern California," *SCB*, 9 (October 1930), 32. Regarding the Primavera Press, see Ward Ritchie's article in *Influences on California Printing* (1970), pp. 37–64. Regarding the Fine Arts Press, see Richard D. Curtiss, *Thomas E. Williams and the Fine Arts Press* (1973). Regarding Edward Bosqui, see my introduction to the edition of *Grapes and Grape Vines of California* [1877], published in 1981. Regarding Clyde Browne, see Edwin Carpenter, "Clyde Browne— 'Master Printer,' " *QNBCC*, 13 (Summer 1948), 56–60. Philip Brown, John Dreyfus, Ward Ritchie, Roby Wentz, Hermann Zapf, and Jake Zeitlin contributed to *Grant Dahlstrom, Master Printer, a Tribute on His 75th Birthday* (1977). Richard F. Doctor interviewed Dahlstrom for the UCLA Oral History Program in May 1975. The result is "Impressions From the Castle Press" (1982). Dahlstrom's designs for the period can be studied in *Typography, Books, and Printing, an Exhibition Beginning March 25, 1946, Library Rotunda, UCLA* (1946). Lillian Marks wrote the biography of her husband *Saul Marks and the Plantin Press, the Life and Work of a Singular Man* (1980). Glen Dawson compiled and arranged *The Plantin Press, Los Angeles, Catalogue of an Exhibition of the Work of Saul & Lillian Marks* (1955). Robert Schad, Keith Anderson, Roland Baughman, Oscar Lewis, Harold Hugo, and Ward Ritchie contributed essays to *To Remember Gregg Anderson* (1949), for which Lawrence Clark Powell did the bibliography. Powell also wrote *Ten Years (Almost) of Rounce & Coffinism* (1941). Regarding Paul Landacre, see Anthony Lehman, *Paul Landacre, a Life and a Legacy* (1983), and Ward Ritchie, *Some Books with Illustrations by Paul Landacre* (1978). See also the catalogue *Paul Landacre, Wood Engravings* issued by Zeitlin & Ver Brugge in 1986.

Along with Lawrence Clark Powell, Ward Ritchie has become an important memoirist of the era in which he played such an important role. This chapter, the previous chapter, and the following chapter have drawn extensively upon Ritchie's writings, augmented by personal interviews, for numerous details and interpretations. In 1961 Ritchie produced the extensive memoir and bibliography *The Ward Ritchie Press and Anderson, Ritchie & Simon*. Between 1964 and 1966 Elizabeth I. Dixon interviewed Ritchie for the UCLA Oral History Program. The resulting volume, "Printing and Publishing in Southern California" (1969), is a gold mine of researched and cross-checked information which Ritchie himself has drawn upon for subsequent essays and addresses. In this regard, see Ritchie's Engelhard Lecture for the Library of Congress, "Fine Printing: The Los Angeles Tradition," given first at the Library of Congress and repeated at the Clark Library in Los Angeles on 13 October 1987. Regarding Ritchie and Schmied, see Ritchie's *Art Deco, the Books of François-Louis Schmied, Artist/Engraver/Printer, With Recollections and Descriptive Commentaries on the Books*, preface by Lawrence Clark Powell (1987). Tyrus Harmsen, Lawrence Clark Powell, John Dreyfus, Adrian Wilson, Jake Zeitlin, and Ritchie himself contributed to *Ward Ritchie Printer, a Seventy-Fifth Birthday Salute on June 15, 1980* (1980). Also of importance are: Paul A. Bennett, "Ward Ritchie—Designer, Printer, Publisher, Man of Books," *Publishers' Weekly*, 186

(October 1964), 85–90; J.E. Reynolds, *Southern California Printing from the Personal Library of Ward Ritchie* (1974); and David W. Davies, *A Concise Account of Ward Ritchie, His Printing & His Books* (1984).

Chapter Thirteen

Hildegarde Flanner remembered Olive Percival in *Different Images* (1987), pp. 73–94. Flanner's own career as a poet can be traced through *Young Girl* (1920), *That Endeth Never* (1921), *This Morning* (1921), *A Tree in Bloom* (1924), *Time's Profile* (1929), *Valley Quail* (1929), *Morning on the Desert. (1929)*, *In Galilee* (1932), and *If There Is Time* (1942). See also her *At the Mercy of Plants, Essays and Poems* (1986). Regarding Flanner, see: Carey McWilliams, "Southern California Begins to Write: Hildegarde Flanner," *Saturday Night*, 19 January 1929; Peter Hanff, "A Gift to California," *Bancroftiana*, No. 93 (January 1987), 1–3; and Betty Hughes's review of *Different Images* in the Los Angeles *Times* for 26 August 1987.

Robert Glass Cleland wrote *The History of Occidental College, 1887–1937* (1937), which was augmented and updated by Andrew Rolle in *Occidental College, the First Seventy Five Years, 1887–1962* (1962). Regarding Robinson Jeffers, Occidental's best-known poet, there has been written a library of biography and criticism. Crucial to the emergence of the Jeffers cult in the late 1920s and 1930s are: George Sterling, *Robinson Jeffers, the Man and the Artist* (1926), and the pamphlet by Louis Adamic, *Robinson Jeffers, a Portrait* (1929). See also Adamic's *My America* (1938), pp. 463–476. Following in rapid succession in the 1930s are: S.S. Alberts, *A Bibliography of the Works of Robinson Jeffers* (1933); Lawrence Clark Powell, *Robinson Jeffers, the Man and His Work* (1934); Rudolph Gilbert, *Shine, Perishing Republic: Robinson Jeffers and the Tragic Sense in Modern Poetry* (1936); Melba Berry Bennett, *Robinson Jeffers and the Sea* (1936); and William Van Wyck, *Robinson Jeffers* (1938). See also Edith Greenan, *Of Una Jeffers* (1939), and the posthumously published *Visits to Ireland, Travel Diaries of Una Jeffers* (1954). Regarding Big Sur, see Emil White, ed., *Big Sur Guide to the Circle of Enchantment* (1964), and David Brower, *Not Man Apart, Lines from Robinson Jeffers, Photographs of the Big Sur Coast* (1965). See also Robert Flagg, "Jeffers at Tor House: Poet of the Pacific," *The Californians* 4 (1986), 40–45. For the longstanding relationship between Jeffers and Occidental College, see: Lawrence Clark Powell, *Robinson Jeffers, 1905–1935, an Exhibition Commemorating the Thirtieth Anniversary of His Graduation From Occidental College* (1935); *Robinson Jeffers at Occidental College, a Checklist of the Jeffers Collection in the Mary Norton Clapp Library Published on the Fiftieth Anniversary of His Graduation* (1955); and the immensely valuable *Robinson Jeffers, Poet, 1887–1987, a Centennial Exhibition*, with contributions by Tyrus Harmsen, Linda Lyke, and Robert J. Brophy (1987). For the poetic career of the Peck's Bad Boy of Occidental, Carlyle Ferren MacIntyre, see his *Poems* (1936), *Cafes and Cathedrals, Poems* (1939), and *The Black Bull, Poems* (1942). Regarding Ward Ritchie as a poet, see Peter Lum Quince, *XV Poems for the Heath Broom* (1934) and *The Years at the Spring* (1938). See also Ritchie's *A Bowl of Quince* (1977), *Adventures with Authors* (1978), and *The Poet and the Printers* (1980). Five of M.F.K. Fisher's early books—*Serve It Forth* (1937), *Consider the Oyster* (1941), *How to Cook a Wolf* (1942), *The Gastronomical Me* (1943), and *An Alphabet for Gourmets* (1949)—were gathered in 1954 as *The Art of Eating*, with an introduction by Clifton Fadiman and an appreciation by James M. Beard, reprinted in paperback in 1976. *The Gastronomical Me* is especially relevant to the Dijon years. Regarding Fisher's early life in Whittier, see *Among Friends* (1970). In 1949 Fisher translated and extensively annotated Jean Anthelme Brillat-Savarin's *The Physiology of Taste* for the Limited Editions Club, reprinted in 1971. The sketch of Fisher in *Current Biography Yearbook 1983*, edited by Charles Moritz, pp. 133–136, serves as a rudimentary account. I have also drawn upon Ward Ritchie's UCLA oral history and Lawrence Clark Powell's autobiography *Fortune & Friendship* (1968) for details of the Dijon years. See also Jerry Carrol, "At Home with MFK Fisher," *San Francisco Chronicle*, 27 September 1988, Section B, p. 5, for a portrait of the writer at age 80.

Lawrence Clark Powell has joined with Ward Ritchie to create a virtual sub-genre of Southern California reminiscences. In addition to *Fortune & Friendship*, I have drawn upon the following works by Powell for details of Pasadena and Dijon: *H. Clark Powell, 1900–1938, Memoirs of His Life and a Bibliography of His Writings* (1939), *Recollections of an Ex-Bookseller* (1950), *Portrait of My Father* (1986), and *An Orange Grove Boyhood, Growing Up in Southern California 1910–1928* (1988). Powell also appended reminiscences to two works by his mother Gertrude Eliza Clark Powell: *The Quiet Side of Europe* (1959) and *Looking Back and Remembering* (1987). See also Powell's 1986 Engelhard Lecture at the Library of Congress, *Next to Mother's Milk* (1987), and Ward Ritchie's 1986 Coulter Lecture for the UC Berkeley Library School Alumni Association, *Growing Up With Lawrence Clark Powell* (1987). Betty Rosenberg documented Powell's lengthy and diverse output in her *Checklist of the Published Writings of Lawrence Clark Powell* (1966), which was updated to September 1976 by Robert Mitchell in *Voices From the Southwest, a Gathering in Honor of Lawrence Clark Powell* (1976), pp. 146–159. A third and even more complete bibliography by Robert Mitchell and Betty Rosenberg is in Powell's *Life Goes On, Twenty More Years of Fortune and Friendship* (1986), pp. 134–164. Of special relevance to this chapter are Powell's printed Dijon dissertation *An Introduction to Robinson Jeffers* (1932), published in book form in 1934 and 1940; his descriptive catalogue *The Manuscripts of D.H. Lawrence* (1937); and his edition of Alfred Young Fisher's *The Ghost in the Underblows* (1940). Regarding Powell's approach as a regional literary critic, see "Bookscapes of California," in *Islands of Books* (1951), pp. 169–179. Powell maps his inner geography in "Personal Landscape," *ibid.*, pp. 105–111. For the circumstances and intent behind *The Blue Train*, I have relied on a number of personal interviews with Powell and upon his manuscript introduction to his collected novels, "The Evening Redness," scheduled for publication in 1990. In 1969–1970 James V. Mink interviewed Powell for the UCLA oral history program. The result was "Looking Back at Sixty: Recollections of Lawrence Clark Powell, Librarian, Teacher, and Writer" (2 vols., 1973).

Acknowledgments

For specific points of guidance, I wish to thank the following: Eliot Brownlee, Francis Carney, Charles Fracchia, Gladys Hansen, James D. Hart, Jarrell Jackman, Andrew George Jameson, Gary Kurutz, William Monihan, S.J., and Neil Morgan. Lawrence Clark Powell, Ward Ritchie, and the late Jacob Israel Zeitlin generously made themselves available for interviews. For helping me better understand Los Angeles, I am grateful to James Miscoll and Jane Pisano of the Los Angeles 2000 Committee and to Peter Gordon, Alan Kreditor, Martin Krieger, and James Moore of the School of Urban and Regional Planning of the University of Southern California. For special support, I must also thank Donald Andrew Casper, Dorothy Colla Casper, Andrew George Jameson, and John Lo Schiavo, S.J.

The staffs of the California State Library in Sacramento, the Bancroft Library in Berkeley, the California Historical Society Library, the San Francisco Public Library, the Mechanics' Institute, and the Gleeson Library of the University of San Francisco, where this book was researched, were especially helpful. Joyce Albers of the Los Angeles Public Library played an important role in researching and selecting photographs. Mary Lou LeVan provided typing and fact-checking services in the early stages of the project. Sarah Ereira of London prepared the index.

As ever, I am grateful to Sheldon Meyer of the Oxford University Press for guiding and shaping this volume as he has its predecessor. As I work on the fourth installment, I realize more than ever how much the *Americans and the California Dream* series owes to this remarkable editor. Richard Allison of Los Angeles, J.S. Holliday of Carmel, Frank Norris of the University of Washington in Seattle, and Peter Pierson of Santa Clara University gave this book an exhaustive review in its final stages. I am profoundly grateful to these friends and colleagues for their generous assistance.

My family—Sheila Starr, Jessica and David Brunicardi, Marian Starr and Arthur Imperatore, Jr.—remains my continuing source of identity, pleasure, and encouragement.

Index